77
TRUTHS

Bret L. Corbridge

TruthWorks Publishing
P.O. Box 3292
Montrose, CO 81402
77 Truths.com

PRINTED IN THE UNITED STATES OF AMERICA

ISBN-13:978-1500825461

Prophecy For Our Day:

"Our sons and daughters must live pure lives so as to be prepared for what is coming. After a while the gentiles will gather by the thousands to this place, and Salt Lake City will be classed among the wicked cities of the world. A spirit of speculation and extravagance will take possession of the Saints, and the results will be financial bondage. Persecution comes next and all true Latter-day Saints will be tested to the limit. Many will apostatize and others will be still not knowing what to do."

Apostle Heber C. Kimball [1]

Introduction

For almost 200 years, Latter-day Saints have been invited to come unto Jesus Christ, receive the fullness of the gospel, and become a Zion people. (D&C 101:22). We have struggled to fulfill this commission and now find ourselves on the cusp of political oppression and religious cleansing.

With great upheaval approaching America and the LDS Church, now is the time to deepen our spiritual consecration to Jesus Christ, that by receiving the mysteries of godliness (D&C 8:11), we might yet contribute to Latter Day Zion.

Each chapter within the *77 Truths* has been specifically ordered in a way that blends the majesty of God's gospel into one great symphony. Scripture provided within the text reveals a doctrinal story that is abundantly delicious to those who hunger to build Millennial Zion and receive Celestial Glory.

If you are one who desires to receive *all* that God offered through the Prophet Joseph Smith, and if you are like Moroni of old and *"will not deny the Christ,"* (Moroni 1:3), then this text may be of use to you as you fulfill your specific errand from the Lord.

Within God's *"one eternal round,"* planets are organized into existence, nations rise and fall, and even true religion cycles during times of restoration and apostasy.

Through it all, Jesus Christ remains the sure Rock. The Mighty Redeemer...our Savior...even *"Messiah."* As the Anointed One who came as a meek and lowly Lamb, He will return as a roaring and powerful Lion. Oh how great is the majesty of our King! Indeed, He is the Lord of Lords. The Alpha and Omega. The Great I Am!

In Him, we have nothing to fear. In Him, all victory is assured. Now and forever.

Bret L. Corbridge
June 27, 2014

77 TRUTHS

CHAPTER ONE: FATHER'S ETERNAL LIFE

TRUTH #1 "ETERNAL LIFE" IS TO KNOW GOD PERSONALLY AND LIVE AS HE LIVES. ENTERING INTO CELESTIAL ONENESS WITH FATHER AND MOTHER REQUIRES COMPLETE KNOWLEDGE, POWER, AND LOVE.

TRUTH #2 TO DWELL WITH OUR HEAVENLY PARENTS REQUIRES SPIRITUAL TRANSFORMATION THROUGH THE ATONEMENT OF JESUS CHRIST. BECAUSE OF THE SAVIOR'S DIVINE SACRIFICE, WE CAN BE CLEANSED FROM SIN AND REDEEMED FROM THE FALL.

TRUTH #3 THOSE SEEKING SALVATION IN THIS LIFE AND EXALTATION IN THE WORLDS TO COME MUST HAVE AN EYE SINGLE TO THE GLORY OF GOD. CENTERING OUR FAITH ON A "LESSER GOD" IS NOT SPIRITUALLY SUFFICIENT.

CHAPTER TWO: THE GLORIOUS GOSPEL OF JESUS CHRIST

TRUTH #4 AS CHILDREN OF GOD LIVING WITHIN A VEIL, WE CANNOT BE SAVED IN IGNORANCE. WE MUST LEARN AND LIVE THE FULLNESS OF THE GOSPEL.

TRUTH #5 SINCE 1832 THE MEMBERSHIP OF THE CHURCH HAS BEEN UNDER CONDEMNATION FOR VANITY AND UNBELIEF. THIS SPIRITUAL LIMITATION REMAINS TODAY.

TRUTH #6 THE BOOK OF MORMON IS THE PRIMARY TOOL FOR REMOVING CONDEMNATION AND BRINGING US CLOSER TO JESUS CHRIST.

TRUTH #7 THE BOOK OF MORMON WAS WRITTEN TO BOTH JEW AND GENTILE. UNTIL MEMBERS OF THE CHURCH ACHIEVE A MIGHTY CHANGE OF HEART AND ARE SPIRITUALLY ADOPTED INTO THE HOUSE OF ISRAEL, WE REMAIN GENTILES.

TRUTH #8 JOSEPH SMITH WAS EMPOWERED WITH THE PRIESTHOOD AND THEN CHOSEN TO RESTORE THE CHURCH OF JESUS CHRIST. JOSEPH REMAINS THE LORD'S PROPHET FOR THIS FINAL DISPENSATION.

TRUTH #9 THE PURPOSE OF THE LDS CHURCH IS TO ASSIST SOULS IN COMING UNTO JESUS CHRIST. THOSE WHO ARE OBEDIENT TO THE LAWS AND ORDINANCES OF THE GOSPEL ARE ELIGIBLE TO BE SAVED BY GRACE.

TRUTH #10 THE ORDINANCES OF THE TEMPLE ARE ESSENTIAL FOR TAKING UPON US THE NAME OF CHRIST. A FUNDAMENTAL SHIFT OCCURS WHEN WE GROW FROM BEING CHURCH CENTERED TO TEMPLE FOCUSED.

TRUTH #11 SALVATION IS AN INDIVIDUAL WORK REQUIRING AN EVER-DEEPENING REPENTANCE. LIVING IN THE LIGHT OF THE CHURCH OR ITS LEADERS IS NOT SUFFICIENT FOR REDEMPTION IN CHRIST.

TRUTH #12 ONLY THOSE LATTER-DAY SAINTS WHO REPENT AND COME UNTO JESUS CHRIST ARE REALLY IN "HIS CHURCH."

TRUTH #13 A LACK OF DOCTRINAL UNDERSTANDING HAS RESULTED IN THE ONGOING REVIEW OF GOSPEL BASICS AND A PROMINENT ATTITUDE THAT "ALL IS WELL IN ZION."

TRUTH #14 FOR MANY YEARS INSTRUCTION AT CHURCH AND IN GENERAL CONFERENCE HAS PRIMARILY INVOLVED A REVIEW OF GOSPEL BASICS. THIS LEVEL OF LIGHT IS NOT SUFFICIENT TO REDEEM ZION OR RECEIVE CELESTIAL GLORY.

TRUTH #15 THE ZION STANDARD WILL NOT BE MINIMIZED TO ACCOMMODATE THE MAINSTREAM OF THE CHURCH. THROUGH PERSONAL SACRIFICE AND COMPLETE CONSECRATION, ALL MEMBERS ARE INVITED TO FORSAKE BABYLON AND RISE TO THE CHALLENGE OF CELESTIAL LAW!

TRUTH #16 THE ABSENCE OF ADDITIONAL PROPHECY AND REVELATION IS ONE CONSEQUENCE OF OUR CONTINUING CONDEMNATION. THOSE WHO FAITHFULLY OBEY THE PREPARATORY GOSPEL RECEIVE FURTHER LIGHT AND KNOWLEDGE.

TRUTH #17 PROPHECY HAS NOT BEEN REVEALED TO THE CHURCH FOR MANY YEARS. DURING THIS TIME OF "SILENCE" MEMBERS ARE REQUIRED TO TURN TO THE LORD AND HIS HOLY SPIRIT FOR ADDITIONAL REVELATION.

TRUTH #18 GOD IS WILLING TO REVEAL MANY GREAT AND GLORIOUS TRUTHS. ADVANCED TEACHINGS SHOULD ONLY BE TAUGHT TO OTHERS WHEN DIRECTED BY THE HOLY SPIRIT.

TRUTH #19 THERE IS NO LIMIT TO WHAT CAN BE LEARNED AND ACCOMPLISHED. GOD IS NOT A RESPECTER OF PERSONS AND ALL WHO ACHIEVE THE REQUIRED REPENTANCE ARE BLESSED WITH THE GIFT OF PROPHECY.

TRUTH #20 JOSEPH SMITH ENCOURAGED ALL TO HAVE THEIR CALLING AND ELECTION MADE SURE. ALTHOUGH RARELY SPOKEN OF IN THE CHURCH TODAY, THE CHALLENGE TO ACHIEVE THIS SPIRITUAL BENCHMARK REMAINS.

TRUTH #21 THOSE WHO DILIGENTLY SEEK TO OVERCOME ALL SIN BECOME ELIGIBLE TO RECEIVE THE SECOND COMFORTER IN THIS LIFE.

TRUTH #22 WITH PERSEVERANCE AND COMPLETE CONSECRATION, EVERY SOUL CAN PART THE VEIL, RECEIVE THEIR FULL ENDOWMENT, AND SUCCESSFULLY COMPLETE THEIR TELESTIAL PROBATION.

TRUTH: #23 LATTER-DAY SAINTS SEEKING MEMBERSHIP IN THE CHURCH OF THE FIRSTBORN SHOULD CONTINUE TO SERVE IN THE LDS CHURCH WITH MEEKNESS AND LOVE.

CHAPTER THREE: APOSTASY BY OMISSION

TRUTH #24 THE CHURCH OF JESUS CHRIST OF LATTER DAY-SAINTS IS THE LORD'S TRUE CHURCH.

TRUTH #25 UNIVERSAL LAW IS IRREVOCABLE AND APPLICABLE TO ALL. THE DEGREE TO WHICH WE RECEIVE THE GOSPEL OF JESUS CHRIST IS AN INDIVIDUAL AND COLLECTIVE CHOICE.

TRUTH #26 WE AS A PEOPLE CAN RECEIVE A MUCH GREATER MESSSAGE FROM THE BOOK OF MORMON IF WE APPLY THE PROPHECIES AND WARNINGS DIRECTLY TO OURSELVES.

TRUTH #27 PRIOR TO THE FALL OF THE NEPHITE NATION, THE CULTURE DIGRESSED INTO PRIDE, WEALTH, AND SPIRITUAL IGNORANCE. TODAY MANY OF GOD'S CHILDREN APPEAR TO BE REPEATING THE SAME PATTERN.

TRUTH #28 THE WORLD IS FULL OF DARKNESS AND SUBTLE DECEPTION. EVEN AT CHURCH WE MUST BE ABLE TO DISCERN TRUTH FROM ERROR. GOD'S HOLY SPIRIT IS OUR SURE GUIDE.

TRUTH #29 RELIGIOUS TRADITION AND LIMITED DOCTRINAL UNDERSTANDING HAS RESULTED IN THE PHILOSOPHIES OF MEN BEING MINGLED WITH SCRIPTURE.

TRUTH #30 THE BOOK OF MORMON WARNS THAT IN RELATION TO PURE DOCTRINE, THE HOLY WORD OF GOD WILL BE TRANSFIGURED.

TRUTH #31 THE PROPHET MORONI EXPLICITLY WARNS THAT IN THE LAST DAYS, THE LORD'S CHURCH WILL BE POLLUTED.

TRUTH #32 ENDOWED MEMBERS HAVE COVENANTED NOT TO SPEAK EVIL OF THE LORD'S ANOINTED. IT IS WISE TO LOVE ALL PEOPLE AS WE SEEK THE UNITY AND PURITY OF ZION.

TRUTH #33 SINCE THE DEATH OF THE PROPHET JOSEPH SMITH, A SIGNIFICANT LOSS OF LIGHT HAS OCCURRED BY OMISSION AND NEGLIGENCE. OVER THE PAST 185 YEARS, ESSENTIAL ELEMENTS OF THE RESTORATION HAVE BEEN MIS-INTERPRETED, DISTORTED, OR ABANDONED. THE DEGREE TO WHICH THIS HAS OCCURRED COULD BE CONSIDERED AN APOSTASY BY OMISSION.

TRUTH #34 THE MORMON MASSES WILL NOT ACKNOWLEDGE OR UNDERSTAND THE SIGNS OF OUR LATTER-DAY APOSTASY.

TRUTH #35 THE DECREASE OF TRUE SPIRITUAL POWER HAS CONTRIBUTED TO TRADITION, POLICY, LEGALISM, DOGMA, AND BUREAUCRACY BECOMING DOMINANT IN THE CHURCH.

TRUTH: #36 WORSHIPPING THE BRETHREN THROUGH FOCUS AND ADORATION MINIMIZES THE SAVIOR AND HIS ATONEMENT. THIS MORMON TREND OFTEN DELAYS A SPIRITUAL REDEMPTION THAT CAN BE FOUND ONLY IN AND THROUGH THE LORD JESUS CHRIST.

TRUTH: #37 BEFORE ZION IS FULLY ESTABLISHED, THE GOSPEL WILL BE TAKEN FROM THE GENTILES AND RETURNED TO THE HOUSE OF ISRAEL.

TRUTH #38 DURING THE CLEANSING, THE TARES WILL CONTINUE TO CHOKE THE WHEAT. TRUE PROPHETS HAVE ALWAYS BEEN PERSECUTED AND REJECTED BY THE MAJORITY.

TRUTH #39 ABANDONING THE CHURCH AND ITS MEMBERS IS USUALLY NOT THE ANSWER. THE WHEAT MUST HOLD FAST TO THE PROPHECIES AND TEACHINGS RECORDED IN SCRIPTURE. THIS INCLUDES SERVING OTHERS WITH WISDOM, PATIENCE, AND LOVE.

TRUTH #40 THE LDS CHURCH CONTINUES TO PROVIDE SACRED ORDINANCES, ANCIENT SCRIPTURE, AND INSPIRED DOCTRINE.

TRUTH #41 THROUGHOUT HISTORY EVERY APOSTASY HAS RESULTED IN ANOTHER RESTORATION. DURING THIS FINAL DISPENSATION, THOSE CALLED OF GOD WILL RECLAIM ALL THAT HAS BEEN LOST OR GONE DORMANT SINCE THE DEATH OF THE PROPHET JOSEPH SMITH.

CHAPTER FOUR: CLEANSING AMERICA AND THE CHURCH

TRUTH #42 AMERICA IS A PROMISED LAND WITH A SACRED COVENANT AND OBLIGATION.

TRUTH: #43 MANY MEMBERS AND NON-MEMBERS ARE POLITICALLY DECEIVED. SOME ARE TEACHABLE, BUT KNOW NOT WHERE TO FIND THE TRUTH.

TRUTH #44 IN AMERICA AND THROUGHOUT THE WORLD, SECRET COMBINATIONS ARE BEING ENACTED TO ELIMINATE FREEDOM AND ENSLAVE GOD'S CHILDREN.

TRUTH #45 NUMEROUS EVENTS ARE NOW OCCURRING WHICH WILL EVENTUALLY RESULT IN THE DESTRUCTION OF ALL NATIONS. CORRUPTION AND SUFFERING ARE BEING IMPLEMENTED BY SATAN TO PROMOTE HIS ONE-WORLD ORDER, BUT THESE SAME EVENTS WILL BE UTILIZED BY THE LORD TO CLEANSE THE EARTH AND INVITE HIS SAINTS TO A GREATER REPENTANCE.

TRUTH #46 TO SURVIVE THE FUTURE WILL REQUIRE HEARING THE VOICE OF GOD PERSONALLY. BEING DEPENDENT ON CHURCH LEADERS WILL NOT BE SUFFICIENT IN THE DAYS TO COME.

TRUTH #47 POLITICAL INFLUENCE, ECONOMIC CORRUPTION, AND MORAL RELATIVITY WILL COMBINE AGAINST ALL TRUE BELIEVERS OF JESUS CHRIST. THE FULFILLMENT OF PROPHECY WILL INCLUDE THE LORD'S HOUSE BEING CLEANSED AND A SEPARATION OF THE WHEAT FROM THE TARES.

TRUTH #48 DESTRUCTION IN AMERICA WILL BEGIN UPON THE LORD'S HOUSE, SPREAD ALONG THE EAST AND WEST COASTS, AND EVENTUALLY AFFLICT EVERY LARGE METROPOLITAN AREA.

TRUTH: #49 A PORTION OF GOD'S PEOPLE WILL ENDURE THE PERSECUTION AND SURVIVE THE DESTRUCTION. A RIGHTEOUS REMNANT WILL GATHER TO FULFILL LATTER-DAY PROPHECY.

TRUTH #50 GOD WILL REMOVE THE RIGHTEOUS PRIOR TO TOTAL DESTRUCTION. HE IS NOW PREPARING AND PLACING HIS TRUE FOLLOWERS.

CHAPTER FIVE: THE FALL OF BABYLON

TRUTH #51 THE FATE OF THE GADIANTONS WILL BE TO FALL INTO THE PIT THEY DUG FOR THE SAINTS. THE GREAT AND ABOMINABLE CHURCH WILL FAIL, AND SATAN'S ONE-WORLD ORDER WILL NOT STAND.

TRUTH #52 SURVIVING THE FUTURE WILL REQUIRE ACCESSING SPIRITUAL POWERS INTRODUCED IN THE LORD'S HOLY HOUSE. WHEN ACCESS TO LDS TEMPLES IS NO LONGER AVAILABLE, INDIVIDUALS WILL CONTINUE TO UTILIZE DIVINE KNOWLEDGE TO COMMUNE WITH HEAVEN.

TRUTH #53 DESPITE INTENSE PERSECUTION AND HARSH DESTRUCTION THE RIGHTEOUS WILL ENDURE. REGARDLESS OF WHAT THE FUTURE HOLDS, GOD'S TRUE SAINTS WILL TRANSCEND THIS LONE AND DREARY WORLD.

TRUTH #54 THE SUFFERING ENDURED WILL ONLY BE A SMALL MOMENT COMPARED TO THE JOY OF ZION IN THIS LIFE AND THE GLORY OF EXALTATION IN THE ETERNITIES TO COME!

TRUTH #55 DURING THE CLEANSING, THOSE WHO HAVE TASTED THE GRACE AND MERCY OF JESUS CHRIST WILL DEMONSTRATE LOVE AMONGST A LOST AND RAGING WORLD.

TRUTH: #56 THE LORD JESUS CHRIST IS OUR MESSIAH AND HERO. DURING THE LAST DAYS HE WILL FIGHT OUR BATTLES.

CHAPTER SIX: GATHERING THE REMNANT

TRUTH #57 THE PRIMARY CHARACTERISTIC OF THE LDS REMNANT IS AN INTENSE REFUSAL TO MINIMIZE, BETRAY, OR DENY THE LORD JESUS CHRIST.

TRUTH #58 THOSE WHO PERSONALLY "KNOW GOD" HAVE A BROKEN HEART AND CONTRITE SPIRIT. THESE SAINTS ARE THE RIGHTEOUS "FEW" WHO WILL BE GATHERED HOME TO ZION.

TRUTH #59 EACH PERSON HAS BEEN GIVEN A UNIQUE ERRAND FROM THE LORD. WITH FAITH AND PERSEVERANCE EVERY SOUL CAN COMPLETE THEIR LIFE'S MISSION AND RETURN HOME WITH HONOR.

TRUTH #60 TO FULFILL THE MEASURE OF OUR CREATION REQUIRES SURRENDERING OUR PERSONAL AGENDA INTO GOD'S WILL. DAILY CONSECRATION RESULTS IN A DEEPENING FRIENDSHIP WITH JESUS CHRIST.

TRUTH #61 ALL OF GOD'S CHILDREN HAVE THE INNATE ABILITY TO DEVELOP SPIRITUAL GIFTS. SURVIVING THE APOCALYPSE WILL REQUIRE ACCESSING GIFTS OF THE SPIRIT.

TRUTH #62 EVERY SON AND DAUGHTER OF GOD IS OF DIVINE WORTH. TO APPRECIATE THE INFINITE AND ETERNAL NATURE OF THE SOUL REQUIRES AN UNDERSTANDING OF "THE INTELLIGENCE" OR "HIGHER SELF." EACH AWAKENS TO THEIR PERSONAL POTENTIAL AND IDENTITY AT VARIOUS TIMES AND IN DIFFERENT WAYS.

TRUTH #63 THE FUTURE WILL INVOLVE MANY GREAT AND GLORIOUS EVENTS. TO EXPERIENCE THE FULFILLMENT OF PROPHECY IN THE FLESH IS WORTH THE SACRIFICE REQUIRED.

TRUTH #64 PRIOR TO THE WORLD BEING AFFLICTED WITH SEVERE DESTRUCTION, HEAVENLY FATHER WILL GATHER AND PROTECT HIS CHILDREN.

TRUTH #65 FLEEING TO THE MOUNTAINS WILL BE AN INTIAL STEP FOR ESCAPING THE DESTRUCTION. DURING THIS TIME OF CLEANSING, THE SURVIVING SAINTS WILL BEGIN TO ESTABLISH ZION.

TRUTH #66 OBTAINING A MORE ACCURATE VIEW OF "ZION" REQUIRES UNDERSTANDING THE ROLE OF LAMANITE ISRAEL. WITH STUDY AND GUIDANCE FROM THE HOLY SPIRIT, GREATER PERSPECTIVE CONCERNING THE GENTILES AND LATTER-DAY ZION CAN BE RECEIVED.

TRUTH #67 ESTABLISHING AN ETERNAL FAMILY KINGDOM WAS THE PASSION OF JOSEPH SMITH AND AN ESSENTIAL ASPECT OF THE ORIGINAL CHURCH. AS WE ACCEPT AND LIVE THE FULLNESS OF THE GOSPEL, WE CAN BECOME THE KINGS AND QUEENS GOD INTENDS US TO BE.

TRUTH #68 THE ZION INVITATION REMAINS TODAY.

TRUTH #69 THE PURITY OF ZION MUST BE ACCOMPLISHED BY A SIGNIFICANT NUMBER OF SOULS INTERNALLY BEFORE AN EXTERNAL CITY CAN BE SUCCESSFULLY MANIFESTED.

TRUTH #70 THE LORD JESUS CHRIST WILL RETURN IN FIRE AND GLORY TO DWELL AMONG HIS PEOPLE. WITHOUT A RIGHTEOUS REMNANT PREPARED TO RECEIVE THE SAVIOR, THE WHOLE EARTH WOULD BE UTTERLY WASTED AT HIS COMING.

TRUTH #71 UNDERSTANDING WHY THE FIRST ATTEMPT TO BUILD ZION FAILED CAN ASSIST US IN SUCCEEDING NOW.

TRUTH #72 DRIFTING ALONG WITH THE MEDIOCRITY OF THE MAINSTREAM WILL NOT RESULT IN THE ESTABLISHMENT OF ZION.

TRUTH #73 THE WHEAT OF THE CHURCH YEARN FOR THE POWER AND HOLINESS OF ZION. SIMILAR TO ENOCH AND HIS PEOPLE, THEY ARE WILLING TO SACRIFICE THE COMFORTS OF BABYLON TO SUCCEED AT BUILDING THE NEW JERUSALEM.

TRUTH: #74 ZION IS NOT AN "LDS-ONLY" EVENT. TRUE SAINTS FROM VARIOUS SPIRITUAL BACKGROUNDS WILL DWELL WITHIN THE HOLY CITY.

TRUTH # 75 THE LORD HAS CHOSEN JOSEPH SMITH TO BE THE PROPHET FOR THIS FINAL DISPENSATION. JOSEPH HAS NOT FINISHED HIS WORK AND WILL BE PERSONALLY INVOLVED IN ESTABLISHING MILLENNIAL ZION.

TRUTH #76 THE KINGDOM OF GOD WILL BE FULLY ESTABLISHED UPON THE EARTH. JESUS CHRIST WILL REIGN AS KING OF KINGS AND LORD OF LORDS. THROUGHOUT THE EARTH, EVERY KNEE SHALL BOW AND EVERY TONGUE CONFESS THAT "JESUS IS THE CHRIST!"

TRUTH #77 THE LORD JESUS CHRIST WILL RETURN IN VICTORY AND THE EARTH WILL RECEIVE HER PARADISIACAL GLORY. THE RIGHTEOUS WILL ENJOY A THOUSAND YEARS OF MILLENNIAL PEACE AND REST.

CHAPTER ONE: FATHER'S ETERNAL LIFE

Hearken ye to these words.
Behold, I am Jesus Christ, the Savior of the world.
Treasure these things up in your hearts,
and let the solemnities of eternity rest upon your minds.
Doctrine and Covenants 43:34

To Know God

"… This is eternal life to know the only wise God and Jesus Christ whom He has sent—that is eternal life. If any man inquire, what kind of a being is God…he will realize that unless he knows God, he has not eternal life for there can be eternal life on no other principle."
Joseph Smith, *The King Follett Discourse* [2]

In 1919, Apostle Melvin J. Ballard related the following: *"I received a wonderful manifestation and impression which has never left me…I was led into a room where I saw, seated on a raised platform, the most glorious being I have ever conceived of, and was taken forward to be introduced to Him. As I approached He smiled, called my name, and stretched out His hands toward me. If I live to be a million years old I shall never forget that smile. He put His arms around me and kissed me, as He took me into His bosom, and He blessed me until my whole being was thrilled. As He finished I fell at His feet, and there saw the marks of the nails; and as I kissed them, with deep joy swelling through my whole being, I felt that I was in heaven indeed. The feeling that came to my heart then was: Oh if I could live worthy, though it would require four-score years, so that in the end when I have finished I could go into His presence and receive the feeling that I then had in His presence, I would give everything that I am and ever hope to be."*[3]

To enter into the presence of Jesus requires understanding and then obeying all that Father defines as "the fullness of the gospel."(D&C 20:9). Those who receive *all truth,* and become *all loving,* inherit *all things.*

"It (eternal life) is the greatest of all the gifts of God (D&C 14:7), for it is the kind, status, type and quality of life that God himself enjoys. Thus those who gain eternal life receive exaltation; they are sons of God, joint-heirs with Christ, members of the Church of the Firstborn; they overcome all things, have all power, and receive the fullness of the Father. They are gods."
Bruce R. McConkie, *Mormon Doctrine* [4]

To repent individually that we might personally *know* God is the divine opportunity of our mortal lives. Those who seek the oneness of celestial fire, find the journey toward exaltation to be the great invitation, the amazing secret, and the unfathomable mystery.

"God is giving away the spiritual secrets of the universe, but are we listening?"
Neal A. Maxwell, *Moving in His Majesty and Power* [5]

To assist us on this journey Father has provided The Church of Jesus Christ of Latter-Day Saints. To the degree the church supports us in "knowing God" the institution represents a great blessing. When the church or its leaders become the focus of our adoration, we have not yet received a salvation that can be found only in knowing *"The Christ."*

A monumental shift occurs when we grow from being "active in the church" to also being converted unto the Lord Jesus Christ. For it is He, and He alone who can redeem us into a state of sufficient sanctification. *If salvation is to occur, it will not be because "the church is true," but because we have personally aligned ourselves with the truth.* Being in the church does not save us and church programs do not redeem us. The priesthood, scriptures, and ordinances provided are meant to be utilized as a means to an end. Elder McConkie clarified, *"The fullness of the gospel cannot be preserved in the written word. The scriptures bear record of the gospel, but the gospel itself consists in the power of the priesthood and the possession of the gift of the Holy Ghost."* [6]

In today's religious "wheat and tare" culture, it is essential to differentiate between the purity of the gospel and the institution God uses to deliver that gospel. Obtaining this essential mindset was reinforced during the April 2012 General Conference.

A Proper Emphasis

"Some have come to think of activity in the Church as the ultimate goal. Therein lies a danger.
It is possible to be active in the Church and less active in the gospel. Let me stress: activity in the Church is a highly desirable goal; however, it is insufficient. Activity in the Church is an outward indication of our spiritual desire. If we attend our meetings, hold and fulfill Church responsibilities, and serve others, it is publicly observed. By contrast, the things of the gospel are usually less visible and more difficult to measure, but they are of greater eternal importance. For example, how much faith do we really have? How repentant are we? How meaningful are the ordinances in our lives? How focused are we on our covenants? I repeat: we need the gospel and the Church. In fact, the purpose of the Church is to help us live the gospel."
Donald L. Hallstrom, *Converted to His Gospel through His Church* [7]

Those who insist on conceptualizing "God," "church," and "truth" as being synonymous are setting themselves up for spiritual disaster. When reading church history, truth seekers quickly realize the eternal gospel of Jesus Christ is indeed perfect, but the church as an institution has a long history of making spiritual and temporal errors. (see Truths #28 and #33).

"Some struggle with unanswered questions about things that have been done or said in the past.
We openly acknowledge that in nearly 200 years of Church history—along with an uninterrupted line of inspired, honorable, and divine events—there have been some things said and done that could cause people to question. Sometimes questions arise because we simply don't have all the information and we just need a bit more patience. When the entire truth is eventually known, things that didn't make sense to us before will be resolved to our satisfaction. Sometimes there is a difference of opinion as to what the 'facts' really mean. A question that creates doubt in some can, after careful investigation, build faith in others...And, to be perfectly frank, there have been times when members or leaders in the Church have simply made mistakes. There may have been things said or done that were not in harmony with our values, principles, or doctrine."
Dieter F. Uchdorf, *Come Join Us* [8]

Despite the weaknesses of others, it is our divine opportunity to grow from "knowing the church is true," to truly *knowing God*. This process is accelerated when we grow from trusting in the arm of flesh to trusting in the Holy One of Israel. For only in knowing the voice of the Master can the power of godliness be manifest within our souls. In relation to Father's eternal life, surely nothing less than a personal friendship with Deity will suffice.

"For their sakes I sanctify myself, that they also might be sanctified through the truth…That they all may be one; as thou, Father, art in me, and I in thee, that they also may be one in us…"
John 17:19,21

Those who serve in the church and are repeatedly sanctified by the Holy Ghost come to understand that **salvation is not something we earn, but something we become.** As we surrender our hearts unto Christ we begin to sense that **"fulfilling the measure of our creation"** is the **"reward in heaven."** (Matthew 5:12).

"Here then is eternal life—to know the only wise and true God. **You have got to learn how to make yourselves Gods** *in order to save yourselves and be kings and priests to God, the same as all Gods have done—by going from a small capacity to a great capacity, from a small degree to another, from grace to grace, until the resurrection of the dead, from exaltation to exaltation till you are able to sit in everlasting burnings and everlasting power and glory as those who have gone before."*
Joseph Smith, King Follett Discourse [9]

As godliness increases within the soul, we cease to create separation from God through sin. The veil of forgetfulness fades and we grow closer to the oneness of Father's light. Those who desire communion with Deity yearn to be as Christ, not as a Savior or Redeemer, but as a son or daughter of God who has *"become…one in the Father, as the Father is one in me…"* (D&C 35:2).

In truth, the "oneness of God" is *metaphorical and literal*. By opening our mind and spirit to the divine mysteries of the universe, we sense that it is our personal choice whether we will be *individually sanctified* that we might be ***collectively glorified!***

All Are Invited
"Listen to the voice of the Lord your God, even Alpha and Omega, the beginning and the end, whose course is one eternal round, the same today as yesterday, and forever. I am Jesus Christ, the Son of God, who was crucified for the sins of the world, even as many as will believe on my name, **that they may become the sons of God, even one in me as I am one in the Father, as the Father is one in me, that we may be one."**
D&C 35:1-2

If we believe this level of union impossible while still in mortality, we should remember the example of Enoch, who, although a mortal man, accessed at least momentarily the oneness, glory, and eternity of God!

And it came to pass that the Lord spake unto Enoch, and told Enoch all the doings of the children of men;
wherefore Enoch knew, and looked upon their wickedness, and their misery, and wept
*and **stretched forth his arms, and his heart swelled wide as eternity;***
and his bowels yearned; and all eternity shook.
Moses 7:41

Enoch Principle: To be of one heart and one mind in *"The Christ"*

Those who desire redemption in this life and godhood in the eternities to come utilize mortality to *walk the way of The Christ*. Once committed to this progression, all of life becomes a sacred quest to *"know God."* These are they who dream… someday…somehow…Oh, Father, could it be? Is there a way that through the grace of thy most Holy Son, I too might someday state:

"I and my Father are one!"

TRUTH #2 TO DWELL WITH OUR HEAVENLY PARENTS REQUIRES SPIRITUAL TRANSFORMATION THROUGH THE ATONEMENT OF JESUS CHRIST. BECAUSE OF THE SAVIOR'S DIVINE SACRIFICE, WE CAN BE CLEANSED FROM SIN AND REDEEMED FROM THE FALL.

And they stripped him, and put on him a scarlet robe. And when they had planted a crown of thorns, they put it upon his head, and a reed in his right hand: and they bowed the knee before him, and mocked him, saying, Hail, King of the Jews! And they spit upon him, and took the reed, and smote him on the head. And after that they had mocked him, they took the robe off from him, and put his own rainment on him, and led him away to crucify him.
Matthew 27: 28-31

The Lord's victory on the cross and at the tomb completed His mortal mission as Redeemer and King. His blood offering in Gethsemane is the crowning moment of all love, oneness, and truth. He is now and forever the Messiah, and our only hope for personal redemption.

Surely he hath borne our griefs, and carried our sorrows: yet we did esteem him stricken, smitten of God, and afflicted. But he was wounded for our transgressions, he was bruised for our iniquities: the chastisement of our peace was upon him; and with his stripes we are healed. All we like sheep have gone astray; we have turned every one to his own way; and the LORD hath laid on him the iniquity of us all.
Isaiah 54: 4-6

As we mature spiritually, we begin to realize that our supposed "good works" and self-declared "righteousness" will not suffice. Those who make a serious attempt to live *all* of Fathers commandments inevitably fall short until they become like Nephi, who, sensing his true spiritual standing, cried out in anguish:

"O wretched man that I am! Yea, my heart sorroweth because of my flesh; my soul grieveth because of mine iniquities. I am encompassed about, because of the temptations and the sins which do so easily beset me. And when I desire to rejoice, my heart groaneth because of my sins; nevertheless, I know in whom I have trusted. My God hath been my support..."
2 Nephi 4:17-20

Jesus Christ is the way, the truth, and the life, and the only valid escape from our own lone and dreary world of sin. To receive a full and complete salvation may require more than we initially conceptualized. Scripture reveals a pattern where receiving a full and complete salvation includes overcoming the Fall, parting the veil, and being received of the Master in this life. (see Truth #21).

19

Overcoming the Fall
"When we choose such a lifestyle of obedience we enter into a process of ever-increasing light
and truth and understanding. Every opportunity to sin, or to be selfish, or to yield to temptation,
is met with faith, and the choice is made again and again to yield to truth.
Such a life is a life of repentance. Such a life is a life of faith. Such a life is a life of Joy.
Repentance is not limited to refusing to choose evil. It is also choosing to embrace godliness
and to act Christ-like in dispensing grace to others.
It is, quite literally, to repent of the human condition."
John Pontius, *The Triumph of Zion: Our Personal Quest for the New Jerusalem* [10]

Through the blessed anesthesia of the Atonement, we are molded ever closer toward receiving our own personal *"baptism of fire."* (2 Nephi 31:13). This sacred process, referred to as being *"born of God"* or *"born again"* (Mosiah 27:25), involves allowing the grace of Jesus Christ to change, heal, and transform us into the purity of a *"new creature."* (2 Corinthians 5:17).

Have I Been Born of God?
"And now behold, I ask of you, my brethren of the church,
have ye spiritually been born of God? Have ye received his image in your countenances?
Have ye experienced this mighty change in your hearts?"
Alma 5:14

For us to be redeemed fully, and thus received of Christ in the flesh, requires that we not only ***"endure to the end,"*** but that we **endure to the end of our repentance.** Those who become holy to this degree come to a place internally where they desire to obey all of Father's commandments, not because they "have to," but because they "want to."

"The real act of personal sacrifice is not now nor ever has been placing an animal on the altar.
Instead, it is a willingness to put the animal that is in us upon the altar-
then willingly watching it be consumed! Such is the sacrifice unto the Lord
of a broken heart and a contrite spirit.' (3 Nephi 9:20)."
Neal A. Maxwell, *Meek and Lowly* [11]

Continual repentance will eventually result in a full and complete recovery from the Fall. Those who are willing to give away *all* of their sins experience the *"mighty change of heart"* and sing the *"song of redeeming love."* (Alma 5:26). This sacred transformation is the fundamental difference between a "Mormon" and a "Saint."

"I have frequently said, and say again, that there are and always have been a great many in this Church
that are not Saints. **There are more "Mormons" than Saints;** *and* **there are different degrees and**
grades of "Mormons" and of Saints. *There are many that are "Mormons" that are not Saints;*
and so it will be until Jesus comes to separate the sheep from the goats;
This must be; this we all believe and understand."
Brigham Young, *Journal of Discourses* [12]

Those members who desire to become **partakers of the divine nature** (2 Peter 1:4) realize *"the redemption of the soul is through him that quickeneth all things…Therefore, it must needs be sanctified from all unrighteousness, that it may be prepared for the celestial glory; For after it hath **filled the measure of its creation**, it shall be crowned with glory, even with the presence of God the Father."* (D&C 88:17-19). Because of Him and the sacred blood He offers, we are healed, not only from sin, but from all weakness and imperfection.

*"The Savior's victory can compensate not only for our sins, but also for our inadequacies; not only for our deliberate mistakes, but also for sins committed in ignorance, our errors of judgment, and our unavoidable imperfections. Our ultimate aspiration is more than being forgiven of sin — we seek to become holy, endowed with Christlike attributes, at one with him, like him. Divine grace is the only source that can finally fulfill that aspiration, after all we can do. **The Atonement of Jesus Christ applies not just to our sins, but to all of life."***
Bruce C. Hafen, *The Broken Heart: Applying the Atonement to Life's Experiences* [13]

To access our divine potential requires not only the absence of sin, but the presence of godliness.

All Things
"The highest achievement of spirituality comes as we conquer the flesh… As givers gain control of their desires and properly see other needs in light of their own wants, then the powers of the gospel are released in their lives. They learn that by living the great law of consecration they insure not only temporal salvation, but also spiritual sanctification."
Spencer W. Kimball, *Conference Report* [14]

Consecrating our lives, as well as every sin, onto the altar of Jesus Christ allows Father to finalize our salvation through the blood of the Lamb. This is the glory. Jesus is the victory.

"Behold, I have graven thee upon the palms of my hands."
1 Nephi 21:16

> **TRUTH #3** THOSE SEEKING SALVATION IN THIS LIFE AND EXALTATION IN THE WORLDS TO COME MUST HAVE AN EYE SINGLE TO THE GLORY OF GOD. CENTERING OUR FAITH ON A "LESSER GOD" IS NOT SPIRITUALLY SUFFICIENT.

Note to Reader: The purpose of this section is not to criticize the brethren or speak evil of the Lord's anointed. There is a difference between being intentionally negative about the church versus providing the light needed to obtain a proper hierarchy of focus and worship.

> *"If you have not chosen the Kingdom of God first,*
> *it will in the end make no difference what you have chosen instead."*
> Neal A. Maxwell, *Smallest Part* [15]

The gospel of Jesus Christ invites us to have an *"eye single to the Glory of God."* (D&C 4:5). Nowhere in scripture are we instructed to worship the prophet, church, or family, and yet much of today's Mormon conversation repeatedly focuses on these secondary aspects of the gospel.

> *"Therefore, in all ages when men have fallen under the power of Satan and lost the faith,*
> ***they have put in its place a hope in the arm of flesh***, *and in gods of silver and gold…*
> ***whatever thing a man sets his heart and his trust in most is his god;***
> *and if his god doesn't also happen to be the true and living God of Israel,*
> *that man is laboring in idolatry."*
> Spencer W. Kimball, *The Teachings of Spencer W. Kimball* [16]

It is an individual and collective choice whether "our god" will be the telestial toys of Babylon, the terrestrial treats of the church, or the Celestial Gods of this Universe.

Growing believers may initially place their faith in the church and its prophet. This trend is observed during fast and testimony meetings where what is frequently repeated can best be summarized as *emotional stories* and *vain repetitions*. Heartfelt proclamations such as *"I know the church is true,"* *"We are led by a living prophet,"* and *"I love my family"* are commendable beliefs. Unfortunately, when these supportive elements become the core of our testimony, we may have *looked beyond the mark* of Christ. (Jacob 4:14).

> *"The fundamental principles of our religion are the testimony*
> *of the Apostles and Prophets,* ***concerning Jesus Christ,***
> ***that He died, was buried, and rose again the third day, and ascended into heaven;***
> ***and all other things which pertain to our religion are only appendages to it."***
> Joseph Smith, *Discourses of the Prophet Joseph Smith* [17]

In Mormonism today, emphasis on prophet, church, and family frequently overshadows focus on the Lord Jesus Christ. When the Savior is mentioned, it is often implied that He is supportive of "the church" instead of the other way around!

A Jealous God

Thou shalt have no other gods before me. Thou shalt not make unto thee any graven image, or any likeness of any thing that is in heaven above, or that is in the earth beneath, or that is in the water under the earth: Thou shalt not bow down thyself to them, nor serve them:
for I the LORD thy God am a jealous God...
Exodus 20:3-5

Being a "jealous God" means that the Almighty wants our problems, praise, devotion, focus, worship, affection, and sins. Thus, a significant difference exists between *knowing* Jesus Christ as Savior, Redeemer, and friend and having a testimony based on *"following the prophet."*

Who is Your God?

"If our faith is in Jesus Christ and not in the arm of flesh, then we will know that we are members of the Church of Jesus Christ and not the church of men."
Ezra Taft Benson, *Jesus Christ-Gifts and Expectations* [18]

The Prophet Joseph Smith taught that remaining dependent on other human beings-even if they are true prophets, correlates with telestial glory. (D&C 76:99-101). Those who place their trust primarily in church leaders and fail to demonstrate a valiant testimony for Jesus Christ, do not qualify for celestial glory.

The Glory of Men

*And the **glory of the telestial** is one...For these are they who are of Paul, and of Apollos, and of Cephas. These are they who say they are **some of one and some of another**—some of Christ and some of John, and some of Moses, and some of Elias, and some of Esaias, and some of Isaiah, and some of Enoch; But **received not the gospel**, neither the testimony **of Jesus**, neither the prophets, **neither the everlasting covenant.** Last of all, these all are they who will not be gathered with the saints, to be caught up unto the **church of the Firstborn**, and received into the cloud.*
D&C 76:98-102

Under Father's tutoring hand disciples grow from emphasizing other men to worshipping God the Father personally without apology. This essential shift occurs through sacrifice and adversity, for it is when our hearts have been shredded and torn asunder that we finally stop making excuses and reach out to the only being who can truly save us.

In the Mirror

"The blame for the condition we each find our selves in this world today falls squarely in one place only— upon me—this natural man enemy to God. I have chosen it. It is not about "the church", or "the Brethren" or the failings and weaknesses of others. It is about whether I choose to be stripped completely of my vanity and pride and ego and self, and "see" that there is only one way out of this self-created Hell, to turn back to Him, repent and receive His fullness."
Jeff Ostler, *My Choice* [19]

To assist us in surrendering our entire souls unto Christ, endowed members are invited to consecrate *themselves, time, talents, and all that they possess* to the building up of the kingdom of God on earth. To fulfill this covenant requires that we honor the true Bridegroom and end our "affair" with any of the "lesser gods."

Father First

As a young college student, I was told that a general authority would be speaking at the stake center. Although I was not officially invited, I was anxious to prepare for my mission and decided to sneak into the chapel. At the end of his inspiring message, he agreed to take questions from the audience on *any gospel subject*. My eyes were opened as I witnessed incredible questions and amazing answers concerning things that I had never even thought about before.

A few months later, I was in the missionary training center listening to his biological brother give an inspirational message. After the meeting, I walked up to the general authority, shook his hand, and excitedly told him, "I know your brother." He kindly looked at me and said, "That's good, but do you know my Father?" I shook my head that I did not. He just smiled, pointed skyward, and said, "Well, you should get to know Him."

Gratefully, our Father did not send His Son into the world to condemn the world, but *"that the world through Him might be saved."* (John 3:17). Because of His divine patience and endless love Father stays with His children until they are ready to grow beyond mortal distraction and worship Him as *the only living and true God!* (D&C 20:19). The result of this process is **a proper hierarchy of worship.**

Ye shall be my people, and I will be your God.
Jeremiah 30:22

Another type of "false-god" involves trusting in our own "arm of flesh." With so much focus on goals, personal performance, and "hastening the work," is it possible our obsession with doing good works actually represents a subtle form of self-worship? Does being active in the program of the church and answering a few temple recommend questions really make us worthy?

"We foolish virgins, who have been "called" to be the bride of Christ, are so busy making our selves
beautiful and creating a mansion for our selves in heaven, that we don't even "see"
that our Bridegroom-to-be has already built a mansion for us, and that He does not seek a bride
who focuses on her self and dotes on her self and complains when she does not get what she "wants,"
and who is so "self-righteous" and self-absorbed that she cannot even "see" Him.
This is the reason Israel (we LDS) have never found "righteousness" because we sought it
in the works of the law—and never by faith in Him, and therefore we have stumbled
at that stumbling stone—for we have never realized that "righteousness" is one of His names
and is only found in Him. We will never find His righteousness if we keep looking
for it in ourselves. We are only "made righteous" by "His righteousness"
when we choose to come unto Him and be one with Him."
Jeff Ostler, *His Righteousness* [20]

Under the chastening hand of our Father, a mighty and disturbing day arrives wherein you realize that what "you want," your passions, desires, and vain ambitions, and all that you have sought to do with "your life," is a form of idolatry. During this disturbing and freeing moment, the growing disciple realizes that he or she has been worshiping self over God. This awakening can result in a needed "coup," which involves our personal spirit again becoming dominant over the natural man. It is then that individual enters into God's sacred errand.

In relation to this process, consider Joseph Smith's observation..."*all the religious world is boasting of righteousness; it is the doctrine of the devil to hinder our progress, by filling us with self-righteousness.*"[21] His warning requires us to ask, have we too become prideful about being active in the Lord's church?

Saving Ourselves?

"Like the Jews of old, we are prone to imagine the law sufficient. We delude ourselves into thinking if we can just keep every commandment, then we will be worthy of His Holy presence. These mental assumptions contradict scripture which clearly state our good works and supposed "righteousness" is nothing but "filthy rags" (Isaiah 64:6), and that even if we serve him with our whole soul, we are still "unprofitable servants." (Mosiah 2:21). "Yes we as Latter Day Saints have a serious spiritual illness. We seem to be suffering from the chronic illusion that we can save ourselves. We talk and act in ways that suggest if we are just obedient enough that somehow our own works will "qualify" us. Occasionally a token offering is made to 2 Nephi 25: 23, wherein the Lord assures us that it is by grace we are saved, after all we can do. Then we go back to worshipping our good works, instead of truly surrendering the focus on "I" and the importance of my great big "self."
Jeff Ostler, *Saving Ourselves?* [22]

To imagine ourselves independently "worthy" is an illusion of the ego. The shadow within loves to focus on self and proclaim, "*Now is the day of my power!*" When this occurs, our imagined "righteousness" delays us from receiving the only one who can really save us.

Author M. Catherine Thomas provides an excellent example of growing from a "self-salvation" mindset to a place where we can be transformed in Christ.

Just Come

"I remember a liberating experience I had during our mission in the Canary Islands. We were staying in the old mission home up toward the top of a mountain. We had just returned from some diligent teaching. I was feeling that I hadn't done a good enough job. When I was alone, I knelt down and told the Lord how sorry I was, how I had let Him down, and so on--all my self-doubt surfacing. In the middle of praying, a voice suddenly said to me, "Stop it! Stop evaluating yourself and just come to Me." My whole neurotic life passed before me, and I saw how much time I had wasted feeling apologetic about my own performance. How often anxiety replaces the comfort of the Gospel!... Let me say that finding greater spiritual comfort is not so much, in my experience, a matter of trying harder, but of shifting our thinking. My experience is that the Voice is still speaking saying, "Stop creating obstacles and just come to Me; the transformation is in Me." And once we take the Lord seriously and stop treating lightly the things we have received (see D&C 84:54), then all the petty aberrations in our soul that loomed so large in our inner vision seem to thin and fade into nothingness, leaving us clean and content to be who we are as we humble ourselves and grow better in the warm bosom of the Lord Jesus Christ."
M. Catherine Thomas, *Shifting Our Thinking and Bridging the Gap* [23]

In choosing God and His gospel above all else, much of the world becomes superficial and meaningless. The previous glitter of Babylon fades and we discover *"it is better to trust in the Lord than to put confidence in man."* (Psalms 118:8).

With consistent effort, every believer can come to that glorious day when he or she makes an irrefutable stand for Christ, and with broken heart and bleeding knees, proclaims:

"THE KINGDOM OF GOD OR NOTHING!"

John Taylor, *Conference Report* [24]

CHAPTER TWO: THE GLORIOUS GOSPEL OF JESUS CHRIST!

*Hearken and listen to the voice of him who is from
all eternity to all eternity, the Great I AM, even Jesus Christ—
The light and the life of the world; a light which shineth in darkness
and the darkness comprehendeth it not...And verily, verily,
I say unto you, he that receiveth my gospel receiveth me;
and he that receiveth not my gospel receiveth not me.*

Doctrine and Covenants 39:1-5

> **TRUTH #4** AS CHILDREN OF GOD LIVING WITHIN A VEIL, WE CANNOT BE SAVED IN IGNORANCE. WE MUST LEARN AND LIVE THE FULLNESS OF THE GOSPEL.

Whatever principle of intelligence we attain unto in this life, it will rise with us in the resurrection.
And if a person gains more knowledge and intelligence in this life through his diligence
and obedience than another, he will have so much the advantage in the world to come.
Doctrine and Covenants 130:18-19

The gospel of Jesus Christ is our invitation to receive the Truth of All Things. Brigham Young taught, *"Mormonism includes all truth. There is no truth but what belongs to the Gospel. It is life, eternal life; it is bliss; it is the fullness of all things in the gods and in the eternities of the gods."*[25]

It can be uncomfortable to acknowledge how very little we actually know. And yet the mysteries of the kingdom await! Yea even the very glory of God is available, if we will only stretch beyond our current assumptions, and by study, faith, and personal revelation receive the greater light!

<u>Cultural Assumption</u>
We should *not* seek the mysteries of God.
They are too dangerous and not important for our salvation.

Those who consider gospel basics to be sufficient should remember that the portion of the Book of Mormon we currently study is considered the *"lesser portion of the word."* (Alma 12:10). God has not released the sealed portion of the plates, and the church does not teach the *"greater things"* referred to in 3 Nephi 26:9-10. Although it sounds drastic (compared to our "chosen people" mindset), the prophet Alma considered those who have not yet received the mysteries of God to be living in the *"chains of hell."* (Alma 12:11).

And now Alma began to expound these things unto him, saying: It is given unto many to know
the mysteries of God... therefore, he that will harden his heart, the same receiveth the lesser portion
*of the word; and **he that will not harden his heart, to him is given the greater portion of the word,***
until it is given unto him to know the mysteries of God until he know them in full.
And they that will harden their hearts, to them is given the lesser portion of the word until they
***know nothing concerning his mysteries;** and then they are taken captive by the devil,*
*and led by his will down to destruction. **Now this is what is meant by the chains of hell.***
Alma 12: 9-11

Few members consider themselves shackled in "hell," but we as a people have struggled to receive and live the greater principles of the Restoration. (see Truth #14). After the death of the Prophet Joseph Smith doctrinal errors began to increase and circulate within the church. Each new generation was able to embrace some of what Joseph originally taught, but then mistakenly passed on that same reduced portion to the next generation, as if it were a "true fullness."

An objective study of church history reveals that over time gospel light has been diminished. What is now considered "sufficient" is really only a "doctrinal diet." (See Truth #33). Due to religious apathy and other factors which will be discussed in this text, much of the "fullness" God offered the Saints has gone dormant or been omitted.

In general, this dire circumstance has occurred unbeknownst to the general membership of the church. (see Truths #5 and #33). The result appears to be a religious people who promote a form of godliness, but often lack the power thereof. (2 Timothy 3:5).

> *"Latter-day Saints, give their young and old awards for zeal alone…for sitting in endless meetings,*
> *for dedicated conformity and unlimited capacity for suffering boredom. We think it more commendable*
> *to get up at five a.m. to write a bad book than to get up at nine o'clock to write a good one;*
> *that is pure zeal that tends to breed a race of insufferable, self-righteous prigs, and barren minds.*
> *One has only to consider the present outpouring of "inspirational" books in the Church that bring little*
> *new in the way of knowledge: truisms and platitudes, kitsch and clichés have become our everyday diet.*
> *The Prophet would never settle for that."*
> Hugh Nibley, *Zeal Without Knowledge* [26]

This spiritual trend was fully expected and planned for by the Lord. He knew that regardless of what the Mormon mainstream settled for, a meek and powerful minority would insist on receiving all that God once offered through Joseph Smith.

The preparing wheat is content to review the preparatory gospel and lesser portion of the word. (D&C 84:26-27).
The wheat of God are engaged in seeking and receiving the mysteries of godliness and the greater portion of the word. (D&C 19:10).

In truth, salvation requires living gospel basics as well as understanding the so-called "mysteries of the kingdom." With intense commitment and study, any who hunger for a true fullness can still receive the *greater gospel* and be freed from the chains of hell.

> *"The Nephites in the land of Nephi experienced several different kinds of bondage.*
> *I would categorize their bondage into four types: mental, financial, spiritual, and physical.*
> ***Mental bondage comes as the result of ignorance of spiritual things.*** *When one does not understand*
> *the purpose of life and **man's ultimate potential**, he is in bondage to ignorance*
> *and **man cannot 'be saved in ignorance'** (D&C 131:6)."*
> Ezra Taft Benson, *LDS Church News* [27]

Those choosing to seek out and learn the mysteries are offered access to pure knowledge through scripture and the writings of the early prophets. With perseverance, anyone can transcend cultural limitation and accept God's original invitation to grow into *"all that the Father hath."* (D&C 84:38).

1832: A Personal Journey

*Great and marvelous are the mysteries of His kingdom which he commanded us NOT to write,
and are not lawful for man to utter; neither is man capable to make them known, for* **they are
only to be seen and understood by the power of the Holy Spirit, which God bestows on
those who love Him***; to whom He grants this privilege of seeing and knowing for themselves,
through the power and manifestation of the Spirit, while in the flesh,
that they may be able to bear His presence in the world of Glory.*
D&C 76:114-119

1844: Joseph's Approach

*"I advise all to go on to perfection, and search deeper and deeper into the mysteries of Godliness.
A man can do nothing for himself unless God directs him in the right way."*
Joseph Smith, *Teachings of Prophet Joseph Smith* [28]

1859: What Are We Waiting For?

*"…there is much which appears mysterious in the plan of salvation, and there is an eternity
of mystery to be unfolded to us; and when we have lived millions of years in the presence of God
and angels, and have associated with heavenly beings, shall we then cease learning?
No, or eternity ceases. There is no end. We go from grace to grace,
from light to light, from truth to truth."*
Brigham Young, *Journal of Discourses* [29]

1924: A Transition in Attitude that Delays Salvation

*"Teach and live the first principles of the gospel,
and let the mysteries of heaven wait until you get to heaven."*
Heber J. Grant, *Learning and Teaching the Gospel* [30]

1981: Becoming Cautious and Afraid

*"Leave the mysteries alone and avoid gospel hobbies. We do not and in our present state
of spiritual progression cannot comprehend all things. We are obligated to understand
the basic doctrines which lead to eternal life; beyond this, how much we know
about the mysteries depends upon the degree of our spiritual enlightenment.
It is unwise to swim too far in water over our heads."(Mosiah 4:27; D&C 10:4).*
Bruce R. Mckonkie, *The Parable of the Unwise Builder* [31]

2010: Preaching the Mysteries

"We proclaim we "have the truth" but we do not preach it. We claim to have authority, but we have no power to redeem and exalt. We pretend it is unlawful to preach mysteries, yet Alma is preaching the deepest doctrines to the non-converted. If we preach the truth, it will attract those whose lives are empty. Why would they join us if what we offer is as trite and superficial as the false religions they already believe?... It does raise some troubling concerns as we claim to be the "true church" but do not act the part as shown in these scriptures. How are we justified in masking the fullness, hiding the mysteries, putting away deep doctrine that will save, and still proclaim that we are the "only true and living church upon the earth?"

Does "living" require us to create sons and daughters of God who are "come to an innumerable company of angels, to the general assembly and church of Enoch, and of the Firstborn?" If so, why do we hear so little about it in our day? *I suppose our audacity springs from our history? If we have lost something vital that conflicts with our current understanding of the history that GUARANTEES us that we are perfect, and that we cannot be misled, then we wouldn't want to acknowledge that. Thank goodness for these guarantees. It does let us relax a bit, doesn't it? Broad and wide are the guarantees we have inherited. We don't need to worry about that narrow and strait fringe who rummage about in the mysteries."*

Denver Snuffer, *Removing Condemnation* [32]

> **TRUTH #5** SINCE 1832 THE MEMBERSHIP OF THE CHURCH
> HAS BEEN UNDER CONDEMNATION FOR VANITY AND UNBELIEF.
> THIS SPIRITUAL LIMITATION REMAINS TODAY.

And every man whose spirit receiveth not the light is under condemnation.
D&C 93:32

In two short years the *"only true church…with whom the Lord was well pleased,"* (D&C 1:30) became the only true church *"under condemnation."* (D&C 84:55). Like the children of Israel, early church members struggled with *"vanity and unbelief"* and were unable to live the greater laws of Zion. Even though this *"condemnation"* is rarely spoken of today, for almost two centuries the Lord has pled with His people to listen, learn, and live the fullness of the gospel.

Cultural Assumption
Because the church is growing in membership and building temples,
our spiritual standing as a church is acceptable to the Lord.

For those who think the status of "condemnation" no longer applies, President Ezra Taft Benson reiterated that the church as a whole continues to suffer under the scourge and judgment of condemnation.

"Now, in the authority of the sacred priesthood in me vested, I invoke my blessing upon the Latter-day Saints and upon good people everywhere. I bless you with increased discernment to judge between Christ and anti-Christ. I bless you with increased power to do good and to resist evil.
I bless you with increased understanding of the Book of Mormon. I promise you that from this moment forward, if we will daily sup from its pages and abide by its precepts, God will pour out upon each child of Zion and the Church a blessing hitherto unknown—and we will plead to the Lord that He will begin to lift the condemnation—the scourge and judgment.
Of this I bear solemn witness."
Ezra Taft Benson, *The Teachings of Ezra Taft Benson* [33]

Ignoring our spiritual status only reinforces low expectations and doctrinal ignorance. For those "truth-seekers" who are willing to be honest and desire to grow beyond the *preparatory gospel*, a *"more excellent way"* is available. (D&C 84:26-27, 1 Corinthians 12:31).

> My name is on the records of the Church…
> Is my soul written in the Lamb's book of Life?
> Revelations 21:27

To receive all that God offers requires a hungry heart, an open mind, and a willingness to give away false traditions. Those who repent of their inherited *"vanity and unbelief"* are released from the curse of condemnation and become candidates for Zion. To accomplish this spiritual freedom requires understanding correct doctrine.

> *"No people can rise above their beliefs, and in the present dispensation*
> *we have under-whelmed ourselves by taking our commission to build Zion lightly."*
> John Pontius, *The Call To Zion* [34]

The process of differentiating between celestial truth and human error can be accelerated by making a distinction between the following terms: faith, belief, unbelief, and knowledge.

Faith: Exists only in relation to that which is eternally true. (Alma 32:21). To increase in faith requires that we identify and eradicate incomplete or inaccurate beliefs. The essence of faith does not naturally reside within the natural man or woman, but is a gift literally placed within the soul by God and His Holy Spirit. The *"substance"* of faith referred to in Hebrews 11:1 is literal. When we "believe" and then "act" in harmony with that which is eternally correct, godliness is magnified within the soul. The more faith we possess, the more commandments Father reveals. When we choose to be obedient to the knowledge He has given us, *the Holy Spirit* increases within us, and the process repeats until our faith becomes *"unshaken."* (Jacob 4:6). With time and experience, we develop confidence in Him *"unto the perfect day."* (Proverbs 4:18).

Unbelief: To believe in error or to accept incorrect doctrine as being true and accurate. In scripture, *"unbelief"* correlates with forsaking doctrine and losing light. Thus, a people can *"dwindle in unbelief"* even while digressing further into ignorance. (4 Nephi 1:34). This spiritual decline includes believing in a principle or teaching that is doctrinally erroneous, incomplete, or exists as a partial or full deception. Failing to believe that which is eternally true might be termed "disbelief," while the meaning of "unbelief" more accurately relates to accidentally promoting the false traditions of a society. Unbelief in any form is a hindrance to the magnification of faith. Within Mormonism our collective condemnation relates in part to doctrinal misunderstanding. There are many instances where false precepts and cherished traditions have been accidentally mingled with true scripture. This gradual corruption of pure doctrine has been going on for so many generations that the dominant masses unknowingly accept doctrinal error as if it were the truth.

Belief: To put confidence, trust, and mental support toward a principle or teaching that may or may not be eternally accurate. When we understand and accept what is actually "correct," a "true belief" is established and faith is increased. In comparison many beliefs stem from human bias, ignorance, tradition, false assumption, or individual experience. Much of what mankind believes is only the philosophies of men laden with falsehood and error. Church members can fully believe something *"with every fiber of their being,"* but that doesn't necessarily make it eternally accurate or binding. Within life's veiled reality, it is us who determine what degree of light and truth we are willing to receive. We are free to "believe" what is eternally true, partially accurate, or simply false. This choice then directly influences what we experience. In other words, belief directly effects and shapes what occurs. Because all things are created spiritually before they manifest physically, even a partially accurate view of God, life, and self is reinforcing. Through the gift of the Holy Ghost, we are invited to grow *"line upon line"* (2 Nephi 28:30) until we have fully eradicated error from our belief system and become "faithful" to the Truth of All Things.

Believing in Unbelief

"How vital, therefore, for us to know the realities: There is a plan of salvation; there was an apostasy; and now there has been a restoration. God has given man moral agency, leaving him free to believe or disbelieve, or to disregard the divine and spiritual evidence. Thus an incredible irony emerges: As people become less believing there are fewer spiritual experiences, and this is twisted by the disbeliever into confirmation of his premises."
Neal A. Maxwell, *Men and Women of Christ* [35]

Knowledge: Possessing intelligence which has been, is now, and always will be true. To "have knowledge" is to be individually and internally aligned with that which simply "IS." To possess pure knowledge is to "know that you know," independent of any external source.

"One does not have faith in propositions, creeds, or institutions, to which one is merely loyal. One has faith in God alone—all else is subject to change without notice. Faith does not seek security by boxing itself in with definite and binding creeds, as did the Doctors of the Church in a time of desperate uncertainty and insecurity…Professor Gaylord Simpson likes to cite the case of Santa Claus as providing the futility of all faith. But has belief in Santa Claus ever closed the door to knowledge as loyalty to a scientific credo so often has? Is it better for a child to believe in Santa Claus with the understanding that someday he is going to revise his views than for him to be taught what is scientifically correct . . . from infancy, so that he will never, never have to revise his views on anything and thus go through life always right about everything? Which course is more liable to lead to disaster, the open-ended Santa Claus, or the ingrained illusion of infallibility?"
Hugh Nibley,*Sophic and Mantic* [36]

Receiving greater perspective requires a willingness to question that which was once believed to be true *"without a shadow of a doubt."* Contrary to cultural fears, participating in this process does not have to result in a "loss of faith," **since believing in something that is incorrect can never be real faith anyway**. Sincere study and heartfelt prayer can result in correct doctrine being learned, believed, and acted upon. Whenever truth is sincerely pondered, the Holy Ghost descends upon the individual and religious assumptions are then replaced with corrected clarification.

It is true that many feel betrayed or misled when they discover that the traditional narrative they have been taught is incomplete and/or inaccurate. Although eradicating "unbelief" from our testimonies is disturbing and sometimes painful, the spiritual benefit is to own a pure knowledge that is "bullet-proof" from the philosophies of men which have been mingled with scripture. During this transformation, religious errors which have been passed down for generations and integrated into the mind are enlarged and corrected. (see Truths #28–#31).

In Christ, the doubts of the natural man are dispelled, and the soul waxes strong in the confidence of the Lord. (D&C 121:45).

Asleep in the Light

But behold, verily I say unto you, that there are many who have been ordained among you,
whom I have called but few of them are chosen. They who are not chosen have sinned
a very grievous sin, in that they are walking in darkness at noon-day.
D&C 95:5-6

Every soul is free to awake, arise, and overcome their own personal condemnation. The life of Joseph Smith demonstrates a pattern where those who possess a righteous desire, commit to intense study, and overcome subtle and explicit opposition are blessed to receive revelation and cultivate a personal companionship with Almighty God! (James 1:5).

How amazing that we too can fulfill the same spiritual pattern in our own lives. For when we choose to receive the light and come out of condemnation, *"true religion"* is no longer about Nephi, Alma, or the current LDS prophet, but rather, an individual journey of fire and light beyond the veil.

Bye-Bye Binkies

"The reason we have difficulty believing these blessings apply to us is because,
spiritually speaking, we are yet little children, and we struggle with small obediences
and lesser commandments. We content ourselves with warm feelings and spiritual testimonies
of true things without catching the vision of what all those baby steps are toddling us toward.
Nevertheless, the Lord has promised to lead us as a child, and bestow these blessings upon us.
And though his tender mercies are all around us, He has been leading us as children now
for 175 years. The time must shortly come when we abandon our spiritual binkies
and actually build Zion."
John Pontius, *Call to Zion*[37]

"Now, in our day, the Lord has revealed the need to re-emphasize the Book of Mormon to get the Church and all the children of Zion out from under condemnation- the scourge and judgment. This message must be carried to the members of the Church throughout the world."
Ezra Taft Benson, *Ensign* [38]

The Book of Mormon is true, correct, and persuasive unto the convincing of men that Jesus is the Christ! Delving into the teachings and patterns of the text increases spiritual connection with the Master. Initially the reader may study the message to gain knowledge, but those who analyze and ponder every word discover the Book of Mormon to be a sacred medium for *experiencing God.*

"I have noted within the Church a difference in discernment, insight, conviction, and spirit between those who know and love the Book of Mormon and those who do not. That book is a great sifter."
Ezra Taft Benson, *News of the Church* [39]

With sincere study, the darkness of condemnation is overcome by the light of truth. As principles are applied and practiced, scripture becomes the pathway for accepting a sacred and personal covenant between the reader and the Lord.

"We have made some wonderful strides in the past. We will be lengthening our stride in the future. To do so, we must first cleanse the inner vessel by awaking and arising, being morally clean, **using the Book of Mormon in a manner so that God will lift the condemnation,** *and finally* **conquering pride by humbling ourselves."**
Ezra Taft Benson, *Cleansing the Inner Vessel* [40]

The Book of Mormon also provides a pattern for leaving the external suffering of the world. The examples of Lehi, Nephi, Alma, and others who left the world to serve the Lord describe both a metaphorical and literal escape from Babylon. (see Truths #49 and #58).

"The Book of Mormon is the instrument that God has designed to 'sweep the earth as with a flood,' to gather out His elect unto the New Jerusalem."
Ezra Taft Benson, *The Teachings of Ezra Taft Benson* [41]

Those who love Christ love the Book of Mormon. To receive its primary message includes coming unto Jesus Christ with full purpose of heart and being redeemed though His blood. Those who partake of His majesty become pure in heart and are gathered into the peace of His Zion.

*"Take away the **Book of Mormon** and the revelations, and where is our religion? We have none; for without **Zion, and a place of deliverance, we must fall;** because the time is near when the sun will be darkened, and the moon turn to blood, and the stars fall from heaven, and the earth reel to and fro. Then, if this is the case, and if we are not sanctified and gathered to the places God has appointed, with all our former professions and our great love for the Bible, we must fall; we cannot stand; we cannot be saved; for **God will gather out his Saints from the Gentiles**, and then comes desolation and destruction, and none can escape **except the pure in heart who are gathered.**"*

Joseph Smith, *Discourses of the Prophet Joseph Smith* [42]

TRUTH #7 THE BOOK OF MORMON WAS WRITTEN TO BOTH JEW AND GENTILE. UNTIL MEMBERS OF THE CHURCH ACHIEVE A MIGHTY CHANGE OF HEART AND ARE SPIRITUALLY ADOPTED INTO THE HOUSE OF ISRAEL, WE REMAIN GENTILES.

"The Book of Mormon was not written for ancient peoples. **It was written for us** *(Mormon 8:35; Ether 12:23). From the standpoint of its prophets,* **we constitute the latter-day gentile church of Christ** *(1 Nephi 22:8; 3 Nephi 21:5-6).* **Nevertheless, the blood of Abraham, Isaac, and Jacob flows in our veins** *(D&C 86:8-10; 113:8; Abraham 2:9-11). We are bound by lineage, by faith, and by covenant to the Israelites of the Book of Mormon. They knew of us, prophesied of us, prayed for us, and wrote to us. It is for us to learn—both as individuals and as a church— from their achievements and mistakes, and to receive their counsel, admonitions, warnings."*
Paul R. Cheesman, *The Book of Mormon: The Keystone Scripture* [43]

In scripture, the word "Gentile" has several different meanings. In some instances the word is used to categorically describe those who do not belong to the House of Israel (1 Nephi 10: 12-14), while in other verses, "Gentile" refers to both non-members and members of the Church. (3 Nephi 16).

Who Are the Gentiles?

"Question: In our class we are studying the Acts of the Apostles, and the question arose, who are the Gentiles? There was a difference of opinion. Are the Gentiles of the blood of Israel? Will you kindly inform us?" The definition in the Standard Dictionary of a Gentile is as follows: "
(1) Among the Jews, a person of a non-Jewish race or faith; one who is not a Jew.
(2) Among Christians, one who is neither Jew or Christian; a pagan; heathen. (3) Among the Mormons, one not a Mormon… This definition does not enlighten us in relation to the original meaning, nor does it accurately fit the doctrine of the Church of Jesus Christ of Latter-day Saints. There are many races on the earth not members of the Church whom the Mormons do not class as Gentiles. The Polynesians, the American Indians, Jews, Arabs, and other races of Semitic origin who trace their lineage back to Abraham are not Gentiles in the strict sense of the word. The African Negroes, according to Mormon teachings, are not Gentiles."
Joseph Fielding Smith, *Answers to Gospel Questions* [44]

Members usually assume that once they have been baptized into the LDS Church, they have become part of the House of Israel. This belief is reinforced when patriarchal blessings identify potential lineage. But is it possible that a greater holiness is required to be fully accepted into God's eternal family? And if so, what message do we as growing Gentiles need to receive?

"Christ also used the name "Gentile" to identify those through whom the gospel would go to the Lamanites. (3 Nephi 21:2-4) If Church members from Gentile nations will bear in mind that the term "Gentile" when used in the Book of Mormon includes them, the prophecies therein will have much greater meaning and be more disturbing."
H. Verlan Andersen, *Apostasy of the Latter Days* [45]

Despite our cultural assumptions about belonging to the House of Israel, Book of Mormon prophets clearly referred to members of the church as "*Gentiles.*" (3 Nephi 16:7).

"While the non-Jewish, non-Lamanite members of Christ's Church
may not call themselves Gentiles, the Book of Mormon prophets did."
Verlan H. Anderson, *The Apostasy of the Latter Days* [46]

The Prophet Joseph Smith was pure Ephraimite, yet the Book of Mormon declares that the text is "*to come forth in due time by way of the Gentiles.*"[47]

Sealed by the hand of Moroni, and hid up unto the Lord,
to come forth in due time by way of the Gentile.
Book of Mormon Title Page

In truth, most members of the church are Gentiles who have been offered the fullness of the gospel that they might be redeemed and eventually adopted into the House of Israel. Even if we have the literal "blood of Israel" in our veins, accepting our initial status as "Gentile" is essential so we do not rationalize away the message Book of Mormon prophets wanted *us* to receive.

"Now, it should take no amount of brilliant insight to realize that the restoration involved Joseph Smith,
a man of English descent. (He) may have some Israelite blood in him from the earlier disaporia of the
Lost Ten Tribes, but he is nevertheless the one through whom the restoration was brought.
He is necessarily identified as a "Gentile" in this prophecy by Christ, given by the Father.
If Joseph Smith is NOT a Gentile, then the whole promise of the Father and word of the Son is defeated.
Therefore, you may know for a surety that the Gentiles are not those nasty non-members.
It is US. WE are the Gentiles who receive the first offer in the last offering."
Denver Snuffer, *Removing Condemnation* [48]

Jews: Those who are descendents from the ancient kingdom of Judah. A person who traces his or her lineage from the Hebrews. The Jews referenced to in the Book of Mormon refer to the people in Jerusalem from which Lehi and his family fled. (1 Nephi 2:13; 4 Nephi 1:31).

Gentiles: Pertaining to any people who are not Jewish. Those described in 1 Nephi 13 are generally of European descent. Most Caucasians fall into this category, including LDS members. (2 Nephi 10:10-11; 26:20, 3 Nephi 16:4-13; 29:1; 30:1-2; Mormon 5:15; 5:19-22; 7:8; Ether 8:23).

Why Has God Provided His Children With the Book of Mormon?

Book of Mormon prophets envisioned our day and recorded the principles and covenants necessary for salvation. The divine purpose of the text is to assist *both* Jew and Gentile, that all might know *Jesus is the Christ!* As Gentiles, we now have the opportunity to repent and be spiritually adopted into the House of Israel.

Primary Purpose
To show unto the remnant of the House of Israel what great things the Lord hath done
for their fathers; and that they may know the covenants of the Lord, that they are not cast off forever —
And also to the convincing of the Jew and Gentile that Jesus is the Christ...
Book of Mormon Title Page

What is Required for a Gentile to Be Adopted into the House of Israel?

Repent and Return
I will remember my covenant unto you, O house of Israel, and ye shall come unto the knowledge
of the fullness of my gospel. But if the Gentiles will repent and return unto me, saith the Father,
behold they shall be numbered among my people, O house of Israel.
3 Nephi 16:12-13

Almost anyone can make a few initial changes and be baptized into the LDS church. But to be worthy of dwelling with God as part of His eternal family requires that a "child of God" take upon them the name of Christ, not just on a preparatory baptismal level, but with real power and meaning. In taking upon us the sacred name and nature of *"The Christ,"* the soul becomes a "son" or "daughter" of God.

Entering into the Family
"Now how are we going to become the sons of God and, of course, daughters as well?
How is it done? Can we become the sons and heirs of our Eternal Father simply by being
baptized for the remission of our sins after we have repented and have had faith,
and have had hands laid upon us for the gift of the Holy Ghost, and have come into the Church?
No, it takes more than that...*we must suffer with him, that we may be glorified with him.*
*In other words, we must receive in our hearts, accept in our hearts, **every principle of the gospel***
which has been revealed; and insofar as it is in our power to do so,
*we must live in accordance with these principles and keep the **commandments of God in full**."*
Joseph Fielding Smith, *Doctrines of Salvation* [49]

It is important to understand that belonging to the tribe of Ephraim is a worthy beginning, but until we repent, receive the mighty change of heart, and are spiritually adopted into the House of Israel, we remain Gentiles. Let all understand: It is not blood, genetics, or church membership that matters, but internal conversion to Jesus Christ that determines our true spiritual standing with Father and His family.

"After true conversion; after baptism of water and of the Spirit; after dross and iniquity have been burned out of the human soul as though by fire; and thus after one is adopted into the house of Israel- when these things have happened there is no distinction between Israelite and Gentile, no separation of spiritual states, no difference in ultimate rewards. "For as many of you as have been baptized into Christ have put on Christ," Paul wrote. "There is neither Jew nor Greek, there is neither bond nor free, there is neither male nor female: for ye are all one in Christ Jesus. And if ye be Christ's, then are ye Abraham's seed, and heirs according to the promise. (Galatians 3:27-29)."
Joseph Fielding McConkie, Robert L. Millet, *Doctrinal Commentary on the Book of Mormon* [50]

Whether Jew or Gentile, literal blood or seeking adoption, inclusion within the House of Israel centers on ever-deepening repentance, keeping temple covenants, and personally knowing the Lord Jesus Christ. *"For behold, I say unto you that **as many of the Gentiles as will repent are the covenant people of the Lord**...for the Lord covenanteth with none save it be with them that repent and believe in his Son, who is the Holy One of Israel."*(2 Nephi 30:2).

Why Does Being Adopted into the House of Israel Matter?

In today's church, many Caucasian non-House of Israel members assume the Mormons will lead the way to Zion. However, careful study of scripture reveals that only those Gentiles who *"repent and return,"* (thus having a chance to survive the destructions), will enjoy the privilege of "assisting" the blood of Israel as *they* establish Zion. Hugh Nibley affirms,

"And so we get to the ultimate prophecies, which we also share with the Indians. And I command you that ye shall write these sayings after I am gone...But wo...unto the unbelieving of the Gentiles... [who] have scattered my people... and have...trodden [them underfoot...At that day when the Gentiles shall sin against my gospel, and shall reject the fulness of my gospel, and shall be lifted up in the pride of their hearts above all nations, and above all the people of the whole earth, and shall be filled with all manner of lyings, and of deceits, and of mischiefs, and...hypocrisy, and murders, and priestcrafts, and whoredoms, and of secret abominations [again consult your TV Guide]. (3 Nephi 16:4, 8—10) Note that lying comes first in the list, a judgment that few will dispute today. "If they shall do all those things, and shall reject the fulness of my gospel,...I will bring the fulness of my gospel from among them. And then will I remember my covenant which I have made unto my people...and I will bring my gospel unto them...The Gentiles shall not have power over you;...and ye shall come unto the knowledge of the fulness of my gospel. But if the Gentiles will repent and return unto me,...behold, they shall be numbered among my people, O house of Israel. And I will not suffer my people...[to] tread them down" (3 Nephi 16:10—14). *There is an ominous note here which we cannot pursue. The promise is repeated in the last speech to the Nephites: "Verily, verily, I say unto you, thus hath the Father commanded me— that I should give unto this people this land for their inheritance (3 Nephi 16:16). And it shall come to pass that all lyings, and deceivings, and envyings, and strifes, and priestcrafts, and whoredoms shall be done away...**But if they will repent...I will establish my church among them, and they shall come in unto the covenant and be numbered among this the remnant of Jacob, unto whom I have given this land for an inheritance; And they shall assist my people, the remnant of Jacob, and also***

41

as many of the house of Israel as shall come, that they may build a city, which shall be called the New Jerusalem" (3 Nephi 21:19, 22—24). Throughout these explicit prophecies it is the Gentiles who join: "the Lamanites and those who have become Lamanites," not the other way around. If we are to be saved we must move in their direction."
Hugh Nibley, *Promised Lands* [51]

Valiant Saints who intend to contribute to Latter Day Zion need to understand their true spiritual status or they might not pursue the level of righteousness required to be adopted into the House of Israel. Perhaps the Lord in His patience allows us to apply the "Gentile scriptures" to those poor lost "non-members" until we are finally willing to accept what God truly requires of us.

Privileged to Assist

*"There are four major events to take place in the Last Days with regards to these people. First, a remnant will be converted; second, Zion will be redeemed and **all among the Gentiles who believe will assist this remnant of Jacob in building the New Jerusalem;** third, missionaries will be sent…to gather all…His people unto the New Jerusalem; fourth, the power of heaven will be made manifest in the midst of this people, and the Lord also will be in their midst."*
Orson Pratt, *Journal of Discourses* [52]

In truth, every soul is received of God based on their faithfulness, purity, and relationship with the Fathers. (See Truth #67). Adoption into the family of God is a personal matter which includes knowing Father, Mother, and their son Jesus Christ. Those who are invited to the "family reunion" will be privileged to *sing the song of redeeming love* within the House of Israel. (Alma 5:9).

"If a man gets a fullness of the Priesthood of God, he has to get it in the same way
that Jesus Christ obtained it, and that was by keeping all the commandments
and obeying all the ordinances of the house of the Lord."
Joseph Smith, *History of the Church* [53]

In May of 1829, John the Baptist ordained Joseph Smith and Oliver Cowdery to the Aaronic Priesthood. The following year, Joseph Smith established The Church of Jesus Christ. This sequence of events reminds us that priesthood can be held independent of a church. A righteous soul may be given power from God without being in an organization, but a true church cannot exist without holy priesthood.

No Real Priesthood = No Real Church

"Where the Melchizedek Priesthood is, there is the Church and kingdom of God on earth;
there is the gospel of salvation; and where there is no Melchizedek Priesthood,
there is no true Church, and no power that will save men in the kingdom of God."
Bruce R. McConkie, *The Ten Blessings of the Priesthood* [54]

In the 2010 General Conference, Elder Boyd K. Packer made a key distinction between having *authority* and possessing genuine *power*. During his message, he lamented the current lack of real power manifested within the church today.

"We have done very well at distributing the authority of the priesthood. We have priesthood authority
planted nearly everywhere. We have quorums of elders and high priests worldwide. But distributing
the authority of the priesthood has raced, I think, ahead of distributing the power of the priesthood.
*The priesthood does not have the strength that it should have and will not have **until the power of the***
priesthood is firmly fixed in the families as it should be...*The authority of the priesthood is with us.*
*After all that we have correlated and organized, **it is now our responsibility to activate the power***
***of the priesthood** in the Church. Authority in the priesthood comes by way of ordination;*
power in the priesthood comes through faithful and obedient living in honoring covenants.
It is increased by exercising and using the priesthood in righteousness." [55]

When the power of the Melchizedek Priesthood is in full force, spiritual manifestations include:

- The gift of healing (Moroni 10:11)
- Visitation of angels (1 Nephi 11:30)
- The ministering of spirits (Moroni 10:14)
- Ongoing prophecy (1 Corinthians 11:4)
- Continuing revelation (Article of Faith #7)
- Ordinances which are sealed by the Holy Spirit of Promise (D&C 132:19)

Real Power in Christ

And it came to pass that Nephi—having been visited by angels and also the voice of the Lord, therefore having seen angels, and being eye-witness, and having had power given unto him that he might know concerning the ministry of Christ…went forth among them in that same year, and began to testify, boldly, repentance and remission of sins through faith on the Lord Jesus Christ…And Nephi did minister with power and with great authority. And it came to pass that they were angry with him, even because he had greater power than they, for it were not possible that they could disbelieve his words, for so great was his faith on the Lord Jesus Christ that angels did minister unto him daily. And in the name of Jesus did he cast out devils and unclean spirits; and even his brother did he raise from the dead, after he had been stoned and suffered death by the people. And the people saw it, and did witness of it, and were angry with him because of his power; and he did also do many more miracles, in the sight of the people, in the name of Jesus.
3 Nephi 7:15-20

If we as a religious people are not observing and participating in this degree of spirituality, it becomes appropriate to question how much true priesthood power remains.

Are You Possessed?

"Ok, let's really get down to the nitty-gritty here. What is the power of the priest-hood? I am sorry to say we LDS folks have a really funny idea of what the "priesthood" is, and we actually think that some man can give us the "power of God." What actually happens when hands are laid on our heads is that we are commissioned or encouraged or charged to go ahead and "receive" from God the enumerated blessing or gift. This process is similar to "receive ye the Holy Ghost," but that gift does not ever really become "received" until the Holy Spirit of Promise seals it within us (D&C 132:7). There is only one thing that is priest-hood, there is no alternate priesthood—there is only supposition of "authority." That is the part that we do—we "suppose" we have "authority." What indeed is the only creative power in the universe, by which all things are created and organized and held in place by? Everything else is only illusion. Everything else will FAIL! What do you have to "receive" before you can "receive" the fullness of the priesthood? It's about time we stopped continuing on in the illusions we were taught by the traditions of the fathers and started asking the hard questions. Within the LDS Church, there are a lot of things we think we know, but we actually only know the things we have been taught… You see, "the priest-hood" is a function of relationship with the Holy Spirit of Promise, not some man's hands or supposed "authority". It is time we go to the Spirit and are taught pure doctrine, and when we do we will know we cannot "possess" the priesthood, but we can allow the priesthood to possess us."
Jeff Ostler, *Power In the Priesthood*[56]

When Moses was leading the children of Israel, he attempted to establish the Melchizedek Priesthood among the people. His desire was that each follower might become sanctified to the degree that they could individually behold the face of God. (D&C 84:23). The people refused, and instead worshipped false idols. This rejection of God and the greater priesthood required the Israelites to continue practicing obedience to the *preparatory gospel and law of carnal commandments.* (D&C 84:26-27). To function at this level of spirituality correlates with Aaronic Priesthood.

And this greater priesthood administereth the gospel and holdeth the key of the mysteries of the kingdom, even the key of the knowledge of God. Therefore, in the ordinances thereof, the power of godliness is manifest. And without the ordinances thereof, and the authority of the priesthood, the power of godliness is not manifest unto men in the flesh; For without this no man can see the face of God, even the Father, and live. Now this Moses plainly taught to the children of Israel in the wilderness, and sought diligently to sanctify his people that they might behold the face of God; But they hardened their hearts and could not endure his presence; therefore, the Lord in his wrath, for his anger was kindled against them, swore that they should not enter into his rest while in the wilderness, which rest is the fulness of his glory. Therefore, he took Moses out of their midst, and the Holy Priesthood also; And the lesser priesthood continued, which priesthood holdeth the key of the ministering of angels and the preparatory gospel;
D&C 84:19-26

Is it possible that in our struggle to receive a true fullness, we too have become like the children of Israel? Have we become "Latter Day Jews," who, due to apathy and disobedience, have also forfeited the greater priesthood and are now required to practice strict rules centered in the lesser law?

"The day will come when man's priesthood and authority will be called to question, and you will find that there will be hundreds who have no priesthood, but who believe they hold it, they are holding only an office in the church."
George Q. Cannon, *Truth* [57]

Obviously many men in the church have been technically commissioned to receive the Melchizedek Priesthood. The vital question is, how many souls can avoid forfeiting God's power as a result of seeking praise and aspiring to the honors of men? (D&C 121:34-37).

"When we see the time that we can willingly strike hands and have full fellowship with those who despise the Kingdom of God, know ye then that the Priesthood of the Son of God is out of your possession."
Brigham Young, *Journal of Discourses* [58]

The Church's current obsession with maintaining good public relations, as well as the frequent reminders of "who has the keys," suggests that our current religious structure is becoming very similar to the Jewish culture at the time of Christ.

Power and Tradition
"They [scribes, Pharisees, etc.] learned to practice fanaticism. They resented any challenge to their rights and authority. They learned to defend their claims of righteousness... Too many historic indignities had made them resent any trespass onto their remaining turf. So they resorted to claiming they had "authority" and that was enough. God "told them" to do what they did. Their "traditions" were handed down from holy sources and were beyond being subject to any questioning. However, when a religious leader is one of God's true messengers, his message will never rely upon a claim of authority as reason to follow him. Indeed, true messengers always understand that no power or influence can or ought to be asserted because of their authority.

45

The words of truth alone are sufficient (see D&C 121:41-42). Their testimony has authority which transcends any institutional trappings. When there is no Spirit which animates the messenger, then he knows his voice is weak. Because of an internal recognition of this weakness, these religious leaders always buttress their words with claims to priestly authority. This claim of priestly authority empowers them to impose their will upon others. This is one of the reasons it is so abhorrent to "take the name of the Lord, thy God, in vain," which was included as one of the Ten Commandments. Whenever someone proclaims their own agenda in the name of the Lord they take His name in vain. It is not swearing, but rather when one claims to speak from the Lord when they do not, that violates the command against vainly using the Lord's name... Christ's message is his authority. His words are what distinguish His true ministers from false ones He never sent. Anyone teaching His truth should be recognized as His messenger. He taught this to Moroni. Those who will receive Christ in any generation do so because they hear and recognize His words (see Ether 4:12). Anyone who will not believe in His words, no matter who He sends to speak them, will not believe in Christ or His Father. Those who trust only institutional sources of truth, whether they are Catholic, Baptist, Lutheran, or Latter-day Saint, believe in an institution, and do not believe in Christ. The ability to individually recognize His words distinguishes those who are saved from those who are lost."
Denver Snuffer, *Come Let Us Adore Him* [59]

Those who see and accept our limited spiritual position can have hope that all is not lost. Regardless of what the Mormon masses continue to assume is ratified by God, the fullness of the priesthood is still available directly from the Lord Jesus Christ! Through Him, and in Him, individual sanctification does bring real power and authority.

"We do not have the fullness of the priesthood as of yet. The priesthood that Enoch and Melchizedek held included being in the Holy Order. It does not come by man or lineage. It only comes when God Himself lays His hands upon your head and ordains you to that Holy Order. Unless we have experienced that then it would seem that all we are doing now is "practicing" for the real thing. But until we are filled with His love and are received of Him personally, then we remain in the "practice priesthood."
Mark Hudson, *Fullness of the Priesthood* [60]

While those stuck in the "traditional mindset" obsess about inherited "keys" and "authority," the hungry and meek search the depths of their soul—repenting of all that is offensive to God. Those who finally qualify for a true fullness of the priesthood know that this level of power is not derived from institutional protocol (D&C 124:28), but can only be received directly from the Lord Jesus Christ. (Matthew 10:1-3).

46

Who Really Has the Priesthood?

"Who can deny such a power to another? No man. Who can bestow it on another? No man.
We like to think that the Church is divided into those who have it and those who don't have it;
but it is the purest folly to assume that we can tell who has it and who does not. God alone knows who is
righteous and how righteous. ... If there is anyone who really holds the priesthood, no one is in a position
to say who it is – only by the power to command the spirits and the elements is such a gift apparent.
But as far as commanding or directing other people, there every man must decide for himself...
[Of] all those who "hold" the priesthood almost none really possess it... [There are only] a few humble,
unpretentious, and unworldly people as the sole holders of a valid priesthood. ... Priesthood is strictly
an arrangement between the individual priesthood holder and his brethren in the eternal worlds,
as personal and private as anything can be. ... Is not the priesthood everything? Not on this earth.
On this earth it is nothing. ... One cannot give orders to another by the priesthood...Over whom does it
exercise dominion? Over the spirits and over the elements – but not over one's fellow-men,
who cannot under any circumstances be deprived of their complete free agency...
Very few men on earth, including those in the Church are really qualified. In terms of prestige, status,
power, influence, pleasure, privilege...the priesthood has absolutely nothing to offer...
[Those] who take it seriously do so in "fear and trembling."
Hugh Nibley, *Sunstone Magazine* [61]

Those who truly receive the priesthood understand that Joseph Smith remains the head of this final dispensation. He has retained all of the keys/knowledge necessary to gather Israel, and is even now actively engaged in establishing Latter Day Zion! (see Truth #75).

Joseph Maintains the Keys

*Therefore, thou art blessed from henceforth that **bear the keys of the kingdom given unto you;***
*which kingdom is coming forth for the last time. Verily I say unto you, the keys of this kingdom **shall***
never be taken from you, while thou art in the world, neither in the world to come;
D&C 90:2-3

In the future, the prophet Joseph Smith will lead the righteous into the great and dreadful day of the Lord. (D&C 110:11-16.). Scripture exhorts, *rebel not against my servant Joseph; for verily I say unto you, I am with him, and my hand shall be over him; and the keys which I have given unto him, ...**shall not be taken from him till I come**.* (D&C 112:15).

In truth, the Lord has ordained Joseph Smith with power and knowledge that he might re-enact the work of this final dispensation. What we frequently conceptualize as "the fullness" was only the beginning portion of Father's great latter day work. Although much of what God offered His people has been discarded by the Mormon culture, Joseph will yet be involved in completing the restoration and re-instituting all that has gone dormant since his death. (see Truths #33 and #75).

...the redemption of Zion must needs come by power; Therefore, I will raise up unto my people
a man, who shall lead them like as Moses led the children of Israel. For ye are the children
of Israel, and of the seed of Abraham, and ye must needs be led out of bondage by power,
and with a stretched-out arm. And as your fathers were led at the first,
even so shall the redemption of Zion.
D&C 103:15-18

Until that man arrives, we are invited to deepen our own discipleship under the hand of the Lord Jesus Christ. If we know the voice of God, and possess real power in Him, we will be prepared to enact the work of Latter Day Zion. (see Truth #21 and Truth #75). Then when the times of the Gentiles is fulfilled, we can assist Jesus and Joseph in establishing the Kingdom of God upon the earth. (see Truth #76).

"God gives us the cross, and then the cross gives us God"
Jeanne Guyon, *Experiencing the Depths of Jesus Christ* [62]

As mortal children we unavoidably sin and fall short. The life choices we make require constant tutoring and forgiveness from the Almighty. At the precise moment we become honest about our frail and flawed state, we can choose to turn directly to the Lord Jesus Christ and receive His transforming grace.

For all have sinned, and come short of the glory of God;
Being justified only by his grace through the redemption that is in Christ Jesus:
Romans 3:23-24

For "true repentance" to occur our Lord and Savior must be involved beyond a casual prayer for forgiveness. But "repentance" is one of those words that has been used so frequently that it has lost almost all meaning. Instead of making a list of things we can and can't do, we could simply *turn to Jesus, receive His grace, and experience the mighty change of heart.* In this, "repentance" becomes a sacred relationship of love. In Him, we are made whole.

If the Savior is overshadowed by religious procedures, technicalities, and the arm of flesh, a cycle is created which could be termed a "church atonement." This type of "religious repentance" occurs when both the believer and ecclesiastical leader accidentally look past the mark of Christ. When this occurs the participant may feel the relief of confession, but be delayed in tasting the condescension of Christ's pure love. The cycle then continues when the un-purged Saint again repeats the same sin or shortcoming. Without a fundamental change of heart, only a portion of the growth and sanctification available through the Savior is experienced. The result is a member may believe the *"the church is true,"* but not yet know *Jesus Christ.*

Is it really about "The Church?"
"Salvation is not "corporate"…Whatever the church does or doesn't do, salvation is an individual
process to work out person by person. If you say: "The church is perfect!" Then I wonder how
that saves me. Am I not imperfect? Does the church's perfection aid me in any respect unless
I will repent and return? Also, if you say: "The church is a corrupt mess!" Then I wonder how
that damns me. Am I not still required to follow the Master? Was Peter perfect? Was Paul?
Did their quirks and imperfections damn those who came forward and accepted baptism,
received the Holy Ghost, and lived the Lord's commandments?"
Denver Snuffer, *A Bit of a Detour* [63]

Regardless of how wonderful the bishop is, or how many organizational polices are created, there is no substitute for Him who redeems the broken heart. Now and forever, it is in and through the blood of Jesus Christ that we can be saved. Literally.

49

*And in the fourth watch of the night Jesus went unto them, walking on the sea. And when the disciples
saw him walking on the sea, they were troubled, saying, It is a spirit; and they cried out for fear.
But straightway Jesus spake unto them, saying, Be of good cheer; it is I; be not afraid.
And Peter answered him and said, Lord, if it be thou, bid me come unto thee on the water.
And he said, Come. And when Peter was come down out of the ship, he walked on the water,
to go to Jesus. But when he saw the wind boisterous, he was afraid; and beginning to sink,
he cried, saying, Lord, save me. And immediately Jesus stretched forth his hand, and caught him,
and said unto him, O thou of little faith, wherefore didst thou doubt?*
Matthew 14:25-31

For many years the church has been reviewing gospel basics such as faith, repentance, baptism, and the gift of the Holy Ghost (D&C 84:26). To assist the Saints, various programs such as Boy Scouts, home teaching, youth activities, ward socials, seminary, etc. have been promoted. These programs, and the principles they advance, provide concrete guidance concerning what we should "do." Eventually, life experiences takes us to a desperation for Christ until we are finally ready to focus on what we need to "become."

*"The Final Judgment is not just an evaluation of a sum total of good and evil acts-what we have done.
It is an acknowledgement of the final effect of our acts and thoughts-what we have become.
It is not enough for anyone just to go through the motions. The gospel of Jesus Christ is a plan
that shows us how to become what our Heavenly Father desires us to become."*
Dallin H. Oaks, *The Challenge to Become* [64]

If we want to imagine that salvation is an "obedience contest" where he who serves best in the church wins, the Lord will allow us to do so. However, this religious attitude does not change what is required for true redemption.

*And men are instructed sufficiently that they know good from evil. And the law is given unto men.
And by the law no flesh is justified; or, by the law men are cut off. Yea, by the temporal law
they were cut off; and also, by the spiritual law they perish from that which is good,
and become miserable forever. Wherefore, redemption cometh in and through the Holy Messiah;
for he is full of grace and truth.*
2 Nephi 2: 5-6

Surely obedience to the commandments of the Lord is essential, and yet *the great secret* concerning the commandments is that they are provided to act as a *"schoolmaster"* upon our souls. (Galatians 3:24-25). Like the children of Israel who were laden down with heavy and demanding laws, we too in the LDS Church are continually bombarded with "have-to's, should-do's, and do-more's." This is intended and effective, for in personally attempting to *comply with every commandment, every moment, and in every way,* we unavoidably fail and fall short.

It is during this beautiful moment of surrender that the real miracle happens. In our dark and dreary waste, we reach out for the grace of His redemptive mercy to save us. As we plead for help, Jesus patiently touches us, wipes away our tears, and encourages us upward and onward toward the Father.

He will swallow up death in victory; and the Lord God will wipe away tears from off all faces…
And it shall be said in that day, Lo, this is our God; we have waited for him, and he will save us:
this is the Lord; we have waited for him, we will be glad and rejoice in his salvation.
Isaiah 25: 8-9

Those who taste this unmerited compassion are never the same. It becomes obvious that we really are *"less than the dust of the earth."* (Helaman 12:7). With sincere humility, the disciple begins to obey *"all of Fathers commandments,"* not because they "have to," but because they "want to." The nature of "being obedient" changes from something that is required to a simple demonstration of love for Him. It is then understood that compliance with eternal law is merely a "pre-requisite," and that it is Jesus Christ who is the ultimate *author and finisher of our faith.* (Hebrews 12:2).

"Indeed, he that loses his self for the Savior, will find eternal life with Him. Our concept,
generally speaking of "obedience" is really very much "self" focused and reflects an employer/employee
or master/slave perspective. We think that "obedience" we "have to" do,
even though we really don't want to. True obedience is only out of love, and without any desire
for our self, nor any "gain." Let me paint a picture: God is your loving Father/Mother.
He is walking beside you every step of the way during this life. With love He puts His hand on your back
and says, "Come my son, walk this way with me." You have two choices. You can resist
His gentle hand upon your back and say, "No, I would rather do it myself." At that point,
you have rejected the gift of His direction. You have communicated to Him that you do not really
appreciate Him or trust His way. You have hardened your heart against Him, and stiffened your neck—
as Israel has always done. This is "dis-obedience" or "non-compliance." The other choice,
if love is in your heart, and you have a softened heart, is to "RECEIVE" His love and you flow
with Him. With complete surrender to Him, you willingly, lovingly, and with all your heart are open
to Him and His direction. You would gladly and gratefully walk a mile, ten, or even a million
just to be with Him. You count your own desires as "dung," as Paul said. (Philippians 3:8).
You care nothing of yourself and would do anything for Him with all of your heart.
Your eye is single to His glory, never your own. You are completely and utterly stripped of all self,
and can see only Him. He is everything and you are nothing in your own eyes. This is "obedience."
Jeff Ostler, *True Obedience* [65]

Those born of the Spirit know that man is *not justified* by the works of the *law,* but by faith in the Redeemer.(Galatians 2:16). The purpose of the law is not to save us, but that through obedience to the law, we might be raised to a spiritual place where we can finally be saved.

I'll take the Grace…

"Behold, I have graven thee upon the palms of my hands,"
1 Nephi 21:16

As a young missionary I quickly came to understand why they call South Carolina "the buckle" of the "Bible Belt." My first area was full of revival excitement and salvation drama. On every corner there was a church full of religious zealots anxiously awaiting their chance to tell the Mormon missionaries they were going straight to hell. On one particularly humid day, we began teaching a Baptist man who was extremely interested in the message of the Restoration. During one of our conversations, he asked, "Elder Corbridge, when you get to heaven, are you going to want God's justice or God's grace?" Feeling pleased with my missionary efforts and anticipating my "reward in heaven," I responded that I would take the justice. He smiled and kindly said, "Well Elder, you can have your justice, I'll take the grace…"It would be many years before I understood the great tutoring this Baptist man had given me. With the unfolding of life and all its complexities, I came to understand that justice and mercy were two aspects of the same love. And although justice would undoubtedly be served, I too "would take the grace."

Until we come to the day of full redemption, the law provides the structure we need to advance within the *strait and narrow path*. The frame is not the artwork itself, but with time and sacred experience, all come to understand that *"he that loveth another hath fulfilled the law."*(Romans 13:8).

"Faith without works is dead, but works without love are also dead."
James Custer, *The Unspoken Gift* [66]

Jesus Christ offers us a holiness that can only be found in Him. In our zeal to achieve "righteousness," we often look at religion as if it were an "obedience contest" rather than a pathway to holiness. The good news is that we can change our perspective and be personally embraced by The Christ. This requires improving our emphasis from "coming to church" to a personal quest to "come unto Christ."

When we choose the Lord to be our Savior and friend, He begins to direct our life in each holy moment. Once on His errand, His guiding voice becomes "THE LAW."

Behold, I am the law, and the light.
Look unto me, and endure to the end, and ye shall live…"
3 Nephi 15:9

Life's complexities invite us to understand that *God is the law,* and that whatsoever He speaks in any given moment, and in any given circumstance, is "THE TRUTH."

The Alpha and Omega

Brethren, my heart's desire and prayer to God for Israel is, that they might be saved.
*For I bear them record that **they have a zeal of God**, but not according to knowledge.*
*For they being **ignorant of God's righteousness**, and **going about to establish their own***
righteousness, have not submitted themselves unto the righteousness of God.
For Christ is the end of the law *for righteousness to every one that believeth.*
Romans 10:1-4

Those who actually listen for His whisper find the Lord's voice to be pure…sweet…light. Inevitably, obeying the Lord's directives will result in being rejected of men, but loyalty to a lesser god will never suffice.

And they who are not sanctified through the law which I have given unto you,
even the law of Christ, must inherit another kingdom…
D&C 88: 21

Obeying God's momentary message is often uncomfortable, especially when the direction from above challenges religious norms. Examples of "doctrinal dissonance" include God instructing Nephi to cut off Laban's head, (1 Nephi 4:8-19), Abraham being commanded to lie and say that Sarai was his sister, (Genesis 12:11-20), and Joseph Smith living plural marriage quietly for many years. These and many other surprising commands stretch the faithful and remind us that God's will is not always an "Ensign story." In relation to any moral or doctrinal dilemma involving "the law," Joseph summed up the entire issue when he stated:

"I made this my rule: When the Lord commands, Do it."
Joseph Smith, *History of The Church of Jesus Christ of Latter-day Saints* [67]

"There is a difference between church-attending, tithe-paying members who occasionally rush into the temple to go through a session and those members who faithfully and consistently worship in the temple."
David A. Bednar, *Honorably Hold a Name and Standing* [68]

A significant difference exists between the level of doctrine taught at church and the depth of knowledge available in the house of the Lord. One important distinction involves the invitation to take upon us the name of Christ. (D&C 109:22).

*"Elder Dallin H. Oaks has explained that in renewing our baptismal covenants by partaking of the emblems of the sacrament, "we do not witness that we take upon us the name of Jesus Christ. [Rather], we witness that we are willing to do so. (See D&C 20:77.) The fact that we only witness to our willingness suggests that **something else must happen before we actually take that sacred name upon us** in the [ultimate and] most important sense" ("Taking upon Us the Name of Jesus Christ," Ensign, May 1985, 81). The baptismal covenant clearly contemplates a future event or events and looks **forward to the temple**. In modern revelations the Lord refers to temples as houses **"built unto my name"** (D&C 105:33; see also D&C 109:2–5; 124:39). In the dedicatory prayer of the Kirtland Temple, the Prophet Joseph Smith petitioned the Father "that thy servants may go forth from this house armed with thy power, and that **thy name may be upon them**" (D&C 109:22). He also asked for a blessing " over thy people upon whom **thy name** shall be put in this house" (v. 26). And as the Lord appeared in and accepted the Kirtland Temple as His house, He declared, **"For behold, I have accepted this house, and my name shall be here; and I will manifest myself to my people in mercy in this house"** (D&C 110:7). These scriptures help us understand that the process of taking upon ourselves the name of Jesus Christ that is **commenced in the waters of baptism is continued and enlarged in the house of the Lord.** As we stand in the waters of baptism, we look to the temple. As we partake of the sacrament, we look to the temple. We pledge to always remember the Savior and to keep His commandments as preparation to participate in the sacred ordinances of the temple and receive the highest blessings available through the name and by the authority of the Lord Jesus Christ. Thus, **in the ordinances of the holy temple we more completely and fully take upon us the name of Jesus Christ."***
David A. Bednar, *Honorably Hold a Name and Standing* [69]

Jesus Christ is the Savior of this world, and yet as part of our individual journey to exaltation, we too are invited to come and participate in the same "Christ pattern" Jesus fulfilled. This includes taking upon us the name, nature, and title of "The *Christ.*"

"The name Christ is derived from the Greek work "chrio" which means "anoint." So Christ means "anointed one" and is actually a title. That title is applicable to all who attain Christhood or Godhood. It is a title applicable not only to Jesus the Christ but also to His Father and all of us who attain to the stature and fullness that Jesus attained."
James A. Custer, *The Unspeakable Gift* [70]

Members are required at baptism to *"take upon them the name of Christ."* If commitment is demonstrated, the member can then be washed and anointed in the temple, with the promise that if they are true and faithful, they might become *"kings and queens unto the most high God."* To assist the soul in becoming worthy of these titles, the endowment provides sacred symbols, ordinances, keys, and covenants.

All that is provided on both a church and temple level requires participants to increase their unification with the omnipotent, omnipresent, and omniscient Truth of All Things.

"Paul said…there is none other God but one. For though there be [others] that are called gods, whether in heaven or in earth, (as there be gods many, and lords many,) but to us there is but one God, the Father, of whom are all things…'(1 Corinthians 8:4-6). Thus Paul is saying that the Father is the one God who is supreme that he is thus the God even of the Lord Jesus Christ, who himself also is God; that many others bear the name of Deity, including all exalted beings."
Bruce R. McConkie, *A New Witness for the Articles of Faith* [71]

Just as Michael entered mortality and began to know himself as "Adam," we too live in a veil of incomplete perceptions. Until we awaken and remember the "Holy of Holies" deep within our soul, we are like Adam, and having forgotten all, do not remember our true and eternal nature.

In and through Jesus Christ, the veil begins to thin. It is then that we understand why Joseph stated, *"If men do not comprehend the character of God, they do not comprehend themselves."*[72]

His Exalted Name
*"This reference to taking upon us the name of Christ and being "saved at the last day" is a clear reference to **exaltation**, which means **attaining the essence of Christ**. Thus, in the concluding lecture on faith, the prophet taught that "salvation (exaltation) consists in the glory, authority, majesty, power, and dominion which Jehovah possesses and in nothing else; and no being can possess it but himself or one like him. (Lectures on Faith, 7:9)."*
Dallin H. Oaks, *His Holy Name* [73]

The new name received in the temple has a variety of meanings and applications. One purpose for receiving the new name is to create "doctrinal space" in our testimonies concerning who we *really* are. Scripture records that when personal transformation occurs, a change in name often follows. Saul became Paul, Abram increased to Abraham, and Jesus of Nazareth became *Jesus the Christ*. Thus, the new name in the temple relates to who we once were and who we may yet become! The name is considered sacred because who we truly are is sacred. (see Truth #62).

HOLINESS

And now, **because of the covenant** *which ye have made ye shall be called* **the children of Christ,** *his sons, and his daughters; for behold, this day* **he hath spiritually begotten you;** *for ye say that your* **hearts are changed** *through faith on his name; therefore, ye are* **born of him and have become his sons and his daughters.** *And under this head ye are made free, and there is no other head whereby ye can be made free.* **There is no other name given whereby salvation cometh;** *therefore, I would that ye should* **take upon you the name of Christ,** *all you that have entered into the covenant with God that ye should be obedient unto the end of your lives. And it shall come to pass that whosoever doeth this shall be found at the right hand of God,* **for he shall know the name by which he is called;**
for he shall be called by the name of Christ.
Mosiah 5:7-9

TRUTH #11 SALVATION IS AN INDIVIDUAL WORK REQUIRING EVER-DEEPENING REPENTANCE. LIVING IN THE LIGHT OF THE CHURCH OR ITS LEADERS IS NOT SUFFICIENT FOR REDEMPTION IN CHRIST.

Messiah!

"It is to the Lord Jesus that you abandon yourself. It is also the Lord whom you will follow as the Way; it is this Lord that you will hear as the Truth, and it is from this Lord that you will receive Life. (John 14:6). If you follow Him as the Way, you will hear Him as the Truth., and He will bring life to you as the Life."
Jeanne Guyon, *Experiencing the Depths of Jesus Christ* [74]

Authentic spirituality is a personal journey. Every soul is responsible for their own individual repentance and salvation. To be born again through the blood of Jesus Christ is a mortal process with everlasting effect.

"If Brother Brigham shall take a wrong track, and be shut out of the kingdom of heaven, no person will be to blame but Brother Brigham. I am the only being in heaven, earth, or hell, that can be blamed. This will equally apply to every Latter-day Saint. Salvation is an individual operation. I am the only person that can possibly save myself. When salvation is sent to me, I can reject or receive it."
Brigham Young, *Discourses of Brigham Young* [75]

We have been commanded to individually work out our *own salvation with fear and trembling.* (Philippians 2:12). There is no collective church salvation. To become Zion in this life, and dwell in eternal glory in the worlds to come, requires a "stand alone testimony."

Saved by Brother Somebody?

"Though our interest is one as a people, yet remember, salvation is an individual work; it is every person for himself. I mean more by this than I have time to tell you in full, but I will give you a hint. There are those in this Church who calculate to be saved by the righteousness of others. They will miss their mark. They are those who will arrive just as the gate is shut, so in that case you may be shut out; then you will call upon some one, who, by their own faithfulness, through the mercy of Jesus Christ, have entered in through the celestial gate, to come and open it for you; but to do this is not their province. Such will be the fate of those persons who vainly hope to be saved upon the righteousness and through the influence of Brother Somebody. I forewarn you therefore to cultivate righteousness and faithfulness in yourselves, which is the only passport into celestial happiness."
Brigham Young, *Discourses of Brigham Young* [76]

Nephi gives a prime example of the process available to all. Even though his father Lehi was a prophet, Nephi hungered to visit the *"exceedingly high mountain"* for himself. (1 Nephi 11:1). He was not content to live in the light of another, but instead chose to grow from believer to disciple to prophet.

*For it came to pass after I had **desired to know** the things that my father had seen,*
*and **believing that the Lord was able** to make them known unto me, as **I sat pondering** in mine heart*
I was caught away in the Spirit of the Lord, yea, into an exceedingly high mountain,
which I never had before seen, and upon which I never had before set my foot.
And the Spirit said unto me: Behold, what desirest thou?
1 Nephi 11:1-2

Nephi's experience teaches us that if we will desire, believe, ponder, and act, we too can enter into the prophetic path. Any who believe and obey are eligible to receive Christ and His angels, that they might take us to our own personal mountaintop!

"The genius of the kingdom with which we are associated is to disseminate knowledge through
all the ranks of the people, and to make every man a prophet and every woman a prophetess,
that they may understand the plans and purposes of God."
George Q. Cannon, *Journal of Discourses* [77]

Although we are blessed to learn from institutional apostles and prophets, the degree of discipleship required to become Zion is not something the brethren can do for us. Our common mantra to *"just follow the prophet"* may be helpful initially, but this belief can also become limiting if our testimony never grows beyond trusting in other men.

"There are those among this people who are influenced, controlled, and biased in their thoughts,
actions, and feelings by some other individual or family, on whom they place their dependence for spiritual
and temporal instruction, and for salvation in the end. These persons do not depend upon themselves
for salvation, but upon another of their poor, weak, fellow mortals."
Brigham Young, *Discourses of Brigham Young* [78]

Human tendency is to trust others for spiritual guidance. This trend has resulted in many members imposing a heavy and unrealistic burden on the brethren. Even the scriptures don't make the Lord's chosen servants omniscient, but the Mormon masses often do. Is it possible the prophet is not the problem, but rather, our spiritual dependence on him?

A Cycle of Dependence
"I am fearful that some of the Latter-day Saints simply come to the leaders and listen to the servants
of God, and they never study; they never go to the written word, and compare it with
the servants of God in their doctrines and teachings, and consequently they are unable
to judge righteously, and they are losing confidence. "Their confidence is being shaken,
because they are unable to judge, because they have not first studied it out in their minds…
because, as a people, we are mentally lazy. I will say that because
I do not expect to preach here again for a long time."
J. Golden Kimball, *The Story of a Unique Personality* [79]

"I am more afraid that this people have so much confidence in their leaders that they will not inquire for themselves of God whether they are led by Him. I am fearful they settle down in a state of blind self-security, trusting their eternal destiny in the hands of their leaders with a reckless confidence that in itself would thwart the purposes of God in their salvation, and weaken that influence they could give to their leaders, did they know for themselves, by the revelations of Jesus, that they are led in the right way. Let every man and woman know, by the whispering of the Spirit of God to themselves, whether their leaders are walking in the path the Lord dictates, or not."
Brigham Young, *Discourses of Brigham Young* [80]

During the early stages of conversion, it may be helpful to just "ask the bishop." Because the Church is full of gifted leaders who model righteous lives, this introductory approach initially works well. Unfortunately, after becoming acquainted with the basic program of the church, many remain dependent on others for spiritual direction. President Ezra Taft Benson addressed this problem when he stated,

"Less spiritually advanced people, such as those in the days of Moses, had to be commanded in many things. Today those spiritually alert look at the objectives, check the guidelines laid down by the Lord and his prophets, and then prayerfully act—without having to be commanded in all things. This attitude prepares men for godhood." [81]

Sunday worship often implies, "You lead, I will follow, and we'll all get to the celestial kingdom just fine." In contrast to this attitude, Joseph Smith warned members about being dependent on church leadership.

Darkened in Our Minds

*"President Joseph Smith read the 14th chapter of Ezekiel—said the Lord had declared by the Prophet, that **the people should each one stand for himself, and depend on no man or men** in that state of corruption of the Jewish church—that righteous persons could only deliver their own souls— applied it to the present state of the Church of Jesus Christ of Latter-day Saints— said if the people departed from the Lord, they must fall—**that they were depending on the Prophet, hence were darkened in their minds**, in consequence of neglecting the duties devolving upon themselves, envious towards the innocent, while they afflict the virtuous with their shafts of envy."*
Joseph Smith, *Teachings of the Prophet Joseph Smith* [82]

God's true prophets do not enable dependence upon themselves. They teach correct principles and let the Saints learn to govern themselves. Instead of allowing young believers to think they have the "keys" to save them, they point to the one true Source.

*"The message of The Church of Jesus Christ of Latter-day Saints is that there is but **one guiding hand in the universe, only one truly infallible light**, one unfailing beacon to the world. That light is Jesus Christ, the light and life of the world, the light which one Book of Mormon prophet described as "a light that is endless, that can never be darkened" (Mosiah 16:9).*

As we search for the shore of safety and peace, whether we be individual women and men,
*families, communities, or nations, **Christ is the only beacon on which we can ultimately rely.**"*
Howard W. Hunter, *The Teachings of Howard W. Hunter* [83]

Some might argue that they believe the prophet walks and talks with the Lord on a daily basis. But even if he does, how is this relevant to our own personal redemption? Are *we* walking and talking with Him each day?

Eventually it becomes essential to ask: Where have I placed my faith? Have I been expecting the righteousness of the brethren to save me? If not, then why is my focus and trust so overwhelmingly placed on the church and its leaders?

Avoiding Spiritual Socialism

"The growth required by the gospel plan only occurs in a culture of individual effort and responsibility.
It cannot occur in a culture of dependency. Whatever causes us to be dependent on someone else
for decisions or resources we could provide for ourselves weakens us spiritually and retards our growth
toward what the gospel plan intends us to be."
Dallin H. Oaks, *Repentance and Change* [84]

In truth, no other human being, not even a prophet, can save us spiritually or temporally. All faithful Saints should support those who are real prophets and apostles without becoming dependent on them for salvation, protection, and personal revelation. If we want to obey the Lord's admonition to be *"led of the spirit,"* (Galatians 5:18), we must outgrow human dependency and become passionately acquainted with the still small voice of truth.

Growing from dependence on leaders to a passionate trust in the Holy Spirit usually involves being broken and tested to capacity. When this occurs, instead of imagining our lives tragic and unfair, wisdom can be found in understanding that sanctification is, and always has been, required for the prophetic path.

Can You Hear the Voice?

*But he (Elijah) himself went a day's journey into the wilderness, and came and sat down under a juniper tree: and **he requested for himself that he might die**; and said, It is enough; now, O LORD, **take away my life**; for I am not better than my fathers…And he came thither unto a cave, and lodged there; and, behold, **the word of the LORD came to him,** and he said unto him, What doest thou here, Elijah? And he said, I have been very jealous for the LORD God of hosts: for the children of Israel have forsaken thy covenant, thrown down thine altars, and slain thy prophets with the sword; and I, even I only, am left; and they seek my life, to take it away. And he said, Go forth, and stand upon the mount before the LORD. And, behold, the LORD passed by, and a great and strong wind rent the mountains, and brake in pieces the rocks before the LORD; **but the LORD was not in the wind: and after the wind an earthquake; but the LORD was not in the earthquake: And after the earthquake a fire; but the LORD was not in the fire: and after the fire a still small voice.***
1 Kings 19:4, 9-12

Therefore, I will unfold unto them this great mystery; Yea, if they will come, they may, and partake of the waters of life freely. Behold, this is my doctrine-whosoever repenteth and cometh unto me, the same is my church. And now, behold, whosoever is of my church, and endureth of my church to the end, him will I establish upon my rock, and the gates of hell shall not prevail against them.
Doctrine and Covenants 10:64, 66-67,69

Almost anyone can make a few initial changes and be baptized onto the records of the LDS church. A much greater consecration is required of those who desire to be part of the Lord's eternal kingdom.

"In the usual sense of the term, Church membership means that a person has his or her name officially recorded on the membership records of the Church. By that definition, we have more than six million members of the Church. (1989) But the Lord defines a member of His kingdom in quite a different way. In 1828, through the Prophet Joseph Smith, He said, 'Behold, this is my doctrine –whosoever repenteth and cometh unto me, the same is my Church' (D&C 10:67). To Him whose Church this is, membership involves far more than simply being a member of record."
Ezra Taft Benson, *Ensign* [85]

In truth, there is no collective Mormon salvation-only a universal invitation. According to scripture and prophecy, only those who actually repent and come unto Jesus Christ are eligible for salvation.

"Not only did Jesus come as a universal gift, He came as an individual offering with a personal message to each one of us. For each one of us He died on Calvary and His blood will conditionally save us. Not as nations, communities or groups, but as individuals."
Heber J Grant, *A Marvelous Growth* [86]

Only when we come unto Christ with a broken heart and contrite spirit is the Lord able to receive us as a little child into His family. (see Truth #67).

Mouth of Babes

My three-year-old daughter: "I hope Jesus will come and visit me today. I want to give Him a picture of me."

Daddy: "Well, how are you going to do that? He lives in the sky."

Three-year-old: "Yeah, but you don't know Daddy. He is really big, and you are very small. You don't really know him."

Daddy: "Well, that is the problem isn't it.

Many in the Mormon culture have been conditioned to relate to the church as if it were a vehicle taking them to the celestial kingdom. They believe, talk, and act, as if "being active" in the church is sufficient for salvation.

In truth, only those who are cleansed from their own sins, as well as from the blood and sins of this generation, are acceptable before God. The LDS church can assist in the process, but in the end, The Lord Jesus Christ is the only Way.

The Church is not a Vehicle
By James Custer

"We should not be distressed when things run counter to what it would seem they should. We have been baptized, we've had the laying on of hands for the gift of the Holy Ghost, and we have received the preparatory ordinances. With those essential performances we should access the Holy Spirit and move forward. The church is not a vehicle to take us anywhere. It's a gate and a respite designed to help us find the Holy Spirit, which shall then lead us to Zion and the now invisible church of the firstborn. The LDS church is not a place of residence, it is a halfway house through which we must pass. The keepers of the halfway house are supposed to receive members, nourish and strengthen them and point the way to that higher place of residence, to Zion and to the Church of the Firstborn (D&C 76:50-70). For their own reasons some of the keepers wish to regard the halfway house as the place of residence and have therefore failed to point beyond the visible church.

The Gentile church will never bring anyone to Christ nor to Zion, because we had rejected and lost that power prior to 1844. After that it became a halfway house to receive us, prepare us and point the way to higher things. From there on it is all between us and the Holy Spirit until we arrive home to be received by Christ, baptized in the fire of the Spirit, given his name (Christ, Mosiah 5:7-15) and the truth of all things.

Since President Benson presented his agenda, (inviting all to come out from condemnation) there has been but few pointers along the way and many falter, but so what? The valiant will find their own way unless they allow anger, pride and frustration to derail them. That is Ephraim's test: the pride, the utter frustration, and the appearance that all has failed while actually everything is right on course and right on time as prophesied and provided for.

Satan wishes to drive a wedge into the hearts of the remnant. He sparks their pride by attempting to persuade them that since everything is wrong, and since they are the only ones who see it, they have to take things into their own hands. That concept has consumed too many otherwise valiant people. Every valiant son or daughter of Ephraim must pass or fail that test. And whether they pass or fail is entirely dependent upon their ability to conquer their pride and surrender to Christ—total, absolute, unqualified surrender ('...*for this cause I know that man is nothing which thing I never had supposed*,' Moses 1:10). Pride is such an illusive thing. In a monumental address (spring conference 1989) President Benson called it the universal sin and indeed it is. Pride prefers Babylon's nourishment, but when denied that preferred diet it will feed and fatten on our righteousness, our wisdom, our good works and even our humility. If pride is not conquered it will inevitably destroy, it will never yield to Christ. It wants to reject his grace and conquer heaven by the "arm of flesh", proclaiming its worthiness. It will do that or perish in the attempt."

"Says one:

    You can't tell me I'm not worthy! Look what I've done! I've attended my meetings, I've, paid my tithing, I've labored in high office in the church, My statistics were always high, I've even neglected my family for the church, but I always provided well for them. What else could I have done?"

"Another responds:

    Did you study the scriptures?
    Well, I read them. I didn't have time to study a lot, I was always too busy with church work, and I had to maintain my profession. There simply wasn't time for everything.

    Did you find Christ? I found the church, I was baptized and gave myself to the work.
    It's His church. What else is there?" (James Custer, *The Church is not a Vehicle*).[87]

Being "active" in the Church and making covenants in the temple is a worthy beginning. Growing into a deeper discipleship involves progressing from "church," to "temple," to "eternity." During our time here on earth, the soul is privileged to serve within the *The Church of Jesus Christ of Latter Day Saints* until after many years of experience, sacrifice, and sanctification, the soul is finally able to move beyond the veil and enter into the *Church of the Lamb*. (1 Nephi 14:10). This beautiful and holy transition occurs when we transcend the Fall and the Lord is inclined to speak, *"Let him enter."* (see Truths #20 and #23).

Verily, verily, I say unto thee, Except a man be born of water and of the spirit,
he cannot enter into the kingdom of God.
John 3:5

TRUTH #13 A LACK OF DOCTRINAL UNDERSTANDING HAS RESULTED IN THE ONGOING REVIEW OF GOSPEL BASICS AND A PROMINENT ATTITUDE THAT "ALL IS WELL IN ZION."

<u>Cultural Assumption</u>
Since the fullness of the gospel has been restored,
we are actually hearing and learning what is required for celestial glory.

We have been taught the Book of Mormon contains the *"fullness of the gospel."* It would therefore be wise to ask what exactly does that phrase mean. (D&C 20:9, D&C 27:5, D&C 42:12). Are there different levels of "fullness" as we progress toward knowing the *"truth of all things?"* (Moroni 10:5). And is the "fullness" we claim to possess refering to doctrinal knowledge, spiritual power, or both?

"Those who have the gospel fulness do not necessarily enjoy the fulness of gospel knowledge or understand all of the doctrines of the plan of salvation. But they do have the fulness of the priesthood and sealing power by which men can be sealed up unto eternal life."
Bruce R. McConkie, *Mormon Doctrine* [88]

Many assume that because the *"fullness of the gospel"* has been restored, they are actually hearing it at church. In reality, what has been taught for decades on Sunday and in general conference constitutes only a simple review of gospel basics. Compared to the level of light Joseph Smith taught new members and even non-members, the message being promoted today is more like the "half-ness of the gospel."

It is assumed this constant review of "the milk" has occurred in anticipation of a day when the people are finally prepared to receive what is required for Zion and Celestial Glory.

Starving to Death
"As we water down even further the true principles of what our faith contains by requiring Relief Society and High Priests to labor over a Gospel Essentials Manual as the sole fodder for our spiritual fare, we strain every particle of solid food out of the diet. The remaining gruel is so thin, lacking in substance, that we become universally malnourished. Yet in that emaciated state, as our bellies distend from the bloating of starvation, we all proclaim how well fed we are. Our bellies are swollen! We have enough of the word of God! We need no more of the word of God! All is well! Better than well, we prosper in the land of promise!"
Denver Snuffer, *Weep for Zion, for Zion has fled* [89]

Since the deaths of Joseph and Brigham, the church seems to have consistently tailored the message to the weakest of the Saints. Even though prophets in scripture did not hesitate to boldly teach young believers the difficult truths, many today shun the "mysteries" as if they were ashamed. Those who think gospel basics are adequate for salvation do not understand scripture.

A Fullness Required

*And there are **none doeth good except those who are ready to receive the fulness of my gospel,** which I have sent forth unto this generation. Therefore, **I call upon the weak things of the world,** those who are unlearned and despised, to thrash the nations by the power of my Spirit;*
D&C 35:12-13

In truth, what a majority of members incorrectly imagine to be a "fullness" is actually termed by God as the *"preparatory gospel."*

The Preparatory Gospel: Obedience to the Law of Carnal Commandments

*And the lesser priesthood continued, which priesthood holdeth the key of the ministering of angels and the **preparatory gospel;** Which gospel is **the gospel of repentance and of baptism, and the remission of sins, and the law of carnal commandments,** which the Lord in his wrath caused to continue with the house of Aaron among the children of Israel…*
D&C 84: 26-27

Bruce R. Mckonkie identifies several distinctions between the preparatory gospel we teach at church and the everlasting gospel required for celestial inheritance.

*"Two true gospels are spoken of in the revelations and have been revealed to men as occasions have warranted; one is the fullness of the everlasting gospel (Rev. 14:6; D. & C. 14: 10), the other is the preparatory gospel (D&C 84:26-27). The fullness of the gospel consists in those laws, doctrines, ordinances, powers, and authorities needed to enable men to gain the fullness of salvation. Those who have the gospel fullness do not necessarily enjoy the fullness of gospel knowledge or understand all of the doctrines of the plan of salvation. But they do have the Fullness of the priesthood and sealing power by which men can be sealed up unto eternal life. The fullness of the gospel grows out of the fullness of the sealing power and not out of the fullness of gospel knowledge. On the other hand, **the preparatory gospel is a lesser portion of the Lord's saving truths, a portion which prepares and schools men for a future day when the fullness of the gospel may be received, a portion which of itself is not sufficient to seal men up unto eternal life or assure them an inheritance in the celestial world.** The preparatory gospel is the gospel of repentance and of baptism, and the remission of sins, and the law of carnal commandments. (D&C 84:27)."*
Bruce R. McConkie, *Mormon Doctrine* [90]

Honest observation of our collective performance reveals the need for the preparatory "milk" to be preached. Contributing to our doctrinal stagnation are those who, after hearing the first principles of the gospel year after year, mistakenly believe that what is being taught is spiritually sufficient. ***This lack of understanding is demonstrated almost every Sunday when true disciples try to teach a gospel which members incorrectly think they have already found.***

"Some have reached provincial conclusions and do not really want to restructure their understandings of things. Some wish to be neither shaken nor expanded by new spiritual data...
most are quite content with a superficial understanding or a general awareness of spiritual things. This condition may reflect either laziness or the busyness incident to the pressing cares of the world."
Neal A. Maxwell, *Meek and Lowly* [91]

Doctrinal apathy and religious contentment delays many from partaking of the full gospel buffet. When Jesus appeared to the Nephites, the prophet Nephi wanted to record the *"greater things"* taught by the Lord, but as Nephi began to write he was forbidden from recording the deeper truths until the people first proved their faithfulness. (3 Nephi 26:9). As a result, the portion available today is considered the *"lesser part."* (3 Nephi 26:8). For those wanting to receive additional revelation, including the truths recorded in the sealed portion of the plates, the opportunity to demonstrate faith remains.

Facing The Mormon Test
And now there cannot be written in this book even a hundredth part of the things which Jesus did truly teach unto the people; *But behold the plates of Nephi do contain the more part of the things which he taught the people. And these things have I written,* ***which are a lesser part*** *of the things which he taught the people...* ***And when they shall have received this, which is expedient that they should have first, to try their faith, and if it shall so be that they shall believe these things then shall the greater things be made manifest unto them.***
And if it so be that they will not believe these things, then shall the greater things be withheld from them, unto their condemnation. Behold, I was about to write them, all which were engraven upon the plates of Nephi, ***but the Lord forbade it, saying: I will try the faith of my people.***
3 Nephi 26:6-11

Study and careful pondering reveal that without those *"greater things,"* what we may have previously considered to a sufficient fullness was only a spiritual introduction.

"Much of My Gospel"
And it came to pass that the angel of the Lord spake unto me, saying...I will be merciful unto the Gentiles in that day, insomuch that I will bring forth unto them, in mine own power, ***much of my gospel***, *which shall be plain and precious, saith the Lamb.*
1 Nephi 13: 33-34

Perspective increases when we question: If a man or woman cannot be saved in ignorance, what keys of knowledge are required to successfully complete our telestial probation and progress into a terrestial sphere? Is there a monumental difference between being "active in the church" and having been personally sealed unto the Lord Jesus Christ?

> *"The fulness of the everlasting gospel, on the other hand, is the higher program of salvation*
> *which is concerned with developing in man the divine truths, powers, gifts, and blessings*
> *of the Holy Spirit until he is able to partake of the divine nature, or glory, of God and make*
> *his calling and election sure to a fulness of glory in the resurrection. . . .*
> *The earthly program of this higher phase of the plan of life and salvation is consummated*
> *when man receives the fulness of the sealing power of the priesthood."*
> Hyrum L. Andrus, *Principles of Perfection* [92]

One prophet of God, who seeks no personal acknowledgment and desires only to magnify God, defines "having a fullness" as simply possessing the ability to ask God a question and receive an answer. For those who hunger after the plan of salvation *and* the path to exaltation, there is an eternity of knowledge and light available.

A True Fullness?

> *"We may, from all these various principles quoted above, draw this tentative portrait of what constitutes*
> *the "fullness of the gospel." It is that man may seek and obtain every promised blessing that any mortal*
> *has ever received by obedience to law, partaking of the full glory and power of the Priesthood,*
> *enjoying the fulfillment of every covenant, and thus "partake of the divine nature"*
> *and seek and obtain the supernal promise of having their calling and election made sure,*
> *and thereafter obtain a personal audience with their Savior, which is the gateway into Zion.*
> *Thus, rejecting the fullness of the gospel consists of failing, for any reason, to claim the full glory*
> *and power available to us. This failure could constitute a willful rejection, but much more profoundly,*
> *it would more likely constitute a simple failure to take seriously what is being offered by the priesthood,*
> *and then by ignorance, rather than willfulness, failing to partake of these supernal blessings,*
> *including having one's calling and election made sure and much more.*
> *In this light, the condemnation of D&C 84:54-56 makes frightening sense."*
> John Pontius, *The Fullness of the Gospel* [93]

Elder David A. Bednar has taught that when we keep the commandments, God blesses us by giving us more commandments.[94] (D&C 59:4).

In Christ, we are to journey step by step, law by law, and grace upon grace until eventually we become one with the Truth of All Things!

LINE UPON LINE

From social Mormonism
To discipleship in the Lord Jesus Christ.

From a testimony of the Church
To a friendship with Father, Mother, and their Holy Son Jesus Christ.

From being "active in the Church"
To being washed and cleansed from the blood and sins of this generation.

From the fullness of the lesser gospel
To a fullness of the greater gospel.

From technical "authority"
To true power within the fullness of the priesthood.

From the seduction of Babylon
To the holiness of Zion.

From feeling the Holy Spirit
To being sealed by the Holy Spirit of Promise.

From baptism into the LDS Church
To membership in the Church of the Firstborn.

From having a calling in the Church
To having your calling and election made sure.

From being sealed in the temple
To possessing sealing power.

From being endowed in the temple
To being a king and queen unto the most High God!

Exchanging Pleasantries

Woe to the rebellious children, saith the LORD, that take counsel, but not of me; and that cover with a covering, but not of my spirit, that they may add sin to sin…Now go, write it before them in a table…
That this is a rebellious people, lying children, children that will not hear the law of the LORD:
*Which say to the seers, See not; and to the prophets, **Prophesy not unto us right things, speak unto us smooth things, prophesy deceits:** Get you out of the way, turn aside out of the path, **cause the Holy One of Israel to cease from before us.***
Isaiah 30:1, 8-11

Human nature desires compliments, comfort, and consistency. To actually change and increase requires work, sacrifice, and a willingness to correct error. Few want their cultural beliefs enlarged- even by God or His true prophets. Thus, many are content to simply maintain the status quo.

*"Who are they? (Meaning the "unvaliant.") All who refuse to receive the fullness of the truth, or abide by the principles and ordinances of the everlasting gospel. They may have **received a testimony;** they may be able to testify that they know that Jesus is the Christ; but in their lives they have refused to accept ordinances which are essential to entrance into the celestial kingdom. They have refused to live the gospel, when they knew it to be true; or **have been blinded by tradition;** or for other cause have not been willing to walk in the light. "In this class we could properly place those who **refuse to take upon them the name of Christ, even though they belong to the Church**; and those who are not willing when called to go forth and preach to a perverse world …"*
*They may live clean lives; they may be **honest, industrious, good citizens, and all that;** but they are not willing to assume any portion of the labor which devolves upon members of the Church, in carrying on the great work of redemption of mankind."*
Joseph Fielding Smith, *Doctrines of Salvation* [95]

When we choose to remain comfortable in our current understanding, we usually insist that additional teaching fit neatly into our religious norms. The result is many read scripture *"line across line,"* reinforcing **the same assumptions** present since their initial conversion. Some behave like religious sixth graders who refuse to learn spiritual algebra because 2+2=4, and the truth never changes.

If you have most of the answers,
You are not asking the right questions.

*"The Things of God are of deep import; and time, and experience and careful and ponderous and solemn thoughts can only find them out. Thy mind, O man! If thou wilt lead a soul unto salvation, **must stretch as high as the utmost heavens, and search into and contemplate the darkest abyss,** and the broad expanse of eternity-thou must commune with God."*
Joseph Smith, *Discourses of the Prophet Joseph Smith* [96]

Surely there are some among the current apostleship who could stand and prophecy with great power—if only the people were willing and able to "hear the message." It appears our ongoing struggle to internalize scripture requires the leadership to continuously delay teaching the higher laws. Thus, the general membership is subjected to a ongoing review of the *"lesser portion of the word."* (Alma 12:10).

"This was the promise the Lord made through Mormon. He said he would try the faith of the people and if they were willing to accept the lesser things (i.e. the Book of Mormon) then he would make known to them the greater things. That we have failed in this is very apparent, we have not accepted the revelations in the Book of Mormon neither in the Doctrine and Covenants with that faith and willingness to know the will of the Lord which would entitle us to receive this greater information."
Joseph Fielding Smith, *Church History and Modern Revelation* [97]

Some argue that reviewing gospel basics is necessary for the systematic conversion of new members. Others point out a large portion of the church is unconverted and inactive. With more Saints now living outside of the U.S. than within, it is also extremely difficult for a single church curriculum to meet the diverse needs of a multi-cultural membership. Even within the boundaries of any chosen ward, the spiritual diversity present represents a significant doctrinal dilemma for anyone teaching the gospel. Church leaders are faced with the challenge of nourishing new converts without losing the wheat to doctrinal boredom and contagious apathy. Elder Dallin H. Oaks alluded to this challenge when giving a talk on repentance.

"Most of what I have said here has been addressed to persons who think that repentance is too easy. At the opposite extreme are those who think that repentance is too hard. That group of souls are so tender-hearted and conscientious that they see sin everywhere in their own lives, and they despair of ever being able to be clean. The shot of doctrine that is necessary to penetrate the hard shell of the easygoing group is a massive overdose for the conscientious. What is necessary to encourage reformation for the lax can produce paralyzing discouragement for the conscientious. This is a common problem. We address a diverse audience each time we speak, and we are never free from the reality that a doctrinal underdose for some is an overdose for others."
Dallin H. Oaks, *Morality* [98]

Observing that the church is choosing to cater to young believers requires anyone wanting additional light to learn directly from God and His Holy Spirit. Those who follow the admonition of Joseph study scripture and then go directly to Father for spiritual tutoring. When the light comes, these souls experience a key personal shift from being "church dependent" to "Spirit led." This important growth step often occurs because what the church *is* teaching (and isn't teaching) requires the hungry Saint to transcend religion and go deeper privately into the gospel paradigm.

To be taught of the Spirit is absolutely key, for it is through spiritual enlightenment that God is able to correct our misunderstandings and enlarge our doctrinal perspective. A fundamental growth step occurs when we **stop** reading the scriptures to confirm what we think we already know, and **start** reading God's word to understand all truth. Thus, the ongoing review of gospel basics, as well as relative silence of the brethren, may be part of Lord's universal strategy for bringing souls unto a greater salvation. Oh how wise is our God!

Are We Teachable?

"There are a great many wise men and women too in our midst who are too wise to be taught; therefore they must die in their ignorance, and in the resurrection they will find their mistake. Many seal up the door of heaven by saying, so far God may reveal and I will believe."
Joseph Smith, *Discourses of the Prophet Joseph Smith* [99]

Regardless of what the Mormon culture chooses to ignore or reject, every soul who desires to become "Zion" must receive the higher laws. This first requires a willingness to perceive the massive incompleteness of our common gospel understanding. Acknowledging that the teachings reviewed at church, in the *Ensign*, and during general conference are useful, but introductory, creates space within our testimonies so we can receive a greater fullness.

And there are none that doeth good
except those who are ready to receive the fullness of my gospel.
D&C 35:12

When we become teachable God is pleased to reveal the everlasting gospel of Jesus Christ. The teachings of real prophets come alive and the power of the original Restoration is received. Learning accelerates, and the light required for Zion and celestial glory pours down from heaven into the soul.

Give ear, O ye heavens, and I will speak; And hear, O earth, the words of my mouth.
My doctrine shall drop as the rain…and as the showers upon the grass.
Deuteronomy 32:1-2

Those who begin to *"see things as they really are"* find it difficult to pretend *"all is well in Zion."*(2 Nephi 28:21). These are they who grow from reviewing the preparatory gospel to seeking a complete fullness, that they might eventually become one with the Truth of All Things.

Every soul chooses when their day of awakening will begin. Until then, God's incredible universe of light, love, and truth remains waiting.

Have I received the "Fullness of the Gospel?"

Spiritual Rebirth

Born of God

Calling and Election

Receiving the Second Comforter

Celestial Marriage

Sealed by the Holy Spirit of Promise

144,000 Born Again High Priests

The Apocalypse

The Literal Gathering of Zion

The Plan of Salvation

The Plan of Exaltation

The Eternal Nature of Godhood

Second Anointing

Fullness of the Priesthood

Miracles and Spiritual Gifts

Speaking in Tongues

Seership and Seer Stones

Law of Consecration

Gift of Translation in Zion

Keys of the Kingdom

Adam-ondi-Ahman

Sealing Power

Church of the Firstborn

Adoption to the Fathers

Zion

We might ask, what would happen if these important gospel elements were taught to the general public? How would the majority respond? Who could receive the increase? Would we as a church be able to endure the unavoidable persecution that would follow?

Even if the general membership is not willing and/or prepared at this time, all are invited to ponder: Am I personally working to receive all that God offers through the restoration of His gospel? Am I willing to sacrifice my comfortable religious assumptions that I might receive and experience all that Father offers His sons and daughters?

VISION OF FATHER

"Brother Zebedee Coltrin said: I believe I am the only living man now in the church who was connected with the School of the Prophets when it was organized in 1833, the year before we went up in Zion's Camp. Every time we were called together to attend to any business, we came together in the morning about sunrise, fasting, and partook of the Sacrament each time, and before going to school we washed ourselves and put on clean linen. At one of these meetings after the organization of the school, [the school being organized] on the 23rd of January, 1833, when we were all together, Joseph having given instructions, and while engaged in silent prayer, kneeling, with our hands uplifted each one praying in silence, no one whispered above his breath, a personage walked through the room from East to west ,and Joseph asked if we saw him.
I saw him and supposed the others did, and Joseph answered that is Jesus, the Son of God, our elder brother. Afterward Joseph told us to resume our former position in prayer, which we did. Another person came through; He was surrounded as with a flame of fire.
I experienced a sensation that it might destroy the tabernacle as it was of consuming fire of great brightness. The Prophet Joseph said this was the Father of our Lord Jesus Christ. I saw Him. When asked about the kind of clothing the Father had on, Bro. Coltrin said: I did not discover His clothing for He was surrounded as with a flame of fire, which was so brilliant that I could not discover anything else but His person. I saw His hands, His legs, His feet, His eyes, nose, mouth, head and body in the shape and form of a perfect man. He sat in a chair as a man would sit in a chair, but this appearance was so grand and overwhelming that it seemed I should melt down in His presence, and the sensation was so powerful that it thrilled through my whole system and I felt it in the marrow of my bones. The Prophet Joseph said: Brethren, now you are prepared to be the apostles of Jesus Christ,for you have seen both the Father and the Son, and know that They exist and that They are two separate Personages. This appearance occurred about two or three weeks after the opening of the school."
Zebedee Coltrin, *Mormonism* [100]

Today, the wheat of the church seek the Truth of All Things. They are not content to review the milk year after year, but instead desire to receive all that Father offers. These are they who will succeed at joining the entire Eloheim in the oneness of celestial fire!

*"Zion is Zion because of **the character, attributes, and faithfulness of her citizens**. Remember, "the Lord called his people Zion, because they were of one heart and one mind, and dwelt in righteousness; and there was no poor among them." (Moses 7:18). If we would establish Zion in our homes, branches, wards and stakes**, we must rise to the standard**. It will be necessary (1) to become unified in one heart and one mind; (2) to become, individually and collectively a holy people; and (3) to care for the poor and the needy with such effectiveness that we eliminate poverty among us. We cannot wait until Zion comes for these things to happen-*
Zion will come only as they happen."
D. Todd Christofferson, *Come to Zion* [101]

Eternal law governs the establishment of Zion. All Saints who yearn for the holiness, joy, and safety of Zion must personally rise to the challenge of becoming aligned with celestial law.

*"Jesus will never receive the Zion of God unless **its people are united according to celestial law**, for all who go into the presence of God have to go there by this law. Enoch had to practice this law, and we shall have to do the same if we are ever accepted of God as he was. It has been promised that the New Jerusalem will be built up in our day and generation, and it will **have to be done by the United Order of Zion and according to celestial law**."*
Wilford Woodruff, *Journal of Discourses* [102]

Zion is complete purity, power, and holiness. It is a principle, a place, and a microcosm of heaven. Brigham Young stated, *"no person can be exalted in the kingdom of heaven without first submitting himself to the rules, regulations, laws and ordinances of that kingdom, and being perfectly subject to them in every respect."* [103] To be worthy to live in God's Holy City requires knowing God, being healed through the grace of His Son, and possessing a loving desire to serve and unify with all of God's children. In truth, the people of Enoch achieved it, and so can we.

"We must attain the same spiritual stature enjoyed by those who built the original Zion. Then and then only will we build our latter-day City of Holiness."
Bruce R. McConkie, *A New Witness for the Articles of Faith* [104]

As fallen children living in a corrupt world, attempting to live the Zion standard can be a daunting challenge. One strategy is to live life ten minutes at a time. By pre-determining that we will live each new moment as directed by the Holy Spirit, segments of time are more likely to accumulate into a "perfect day."

The Apostle Paul taught that by casting down *"imaginations"* and *"every high thing that exalteth itself against the knowledge of God,"* we can bring *"into captivity every thought to the obedience of Christ."* (2 Corinthians 10:5).

When we avoidably err and are overtaken by emotional wounds and selfishness, the process is rectified by simply returning to God and our soul center.

Thankfully, the Lord sees our small and simple efforts. With love, He utilizes daily life to break us down and help us to be more teachable. Whenever our faith allows, the mercy of Jesus Christ is administered to our bleeding souls until eventually we become the essence of unconditional love. This is the miracle of transformation that all who want to become Zion must experience and successfully complete.

> *"Our spiritual purpose is to overcome both sin and the desire to sin,*
> *both the taint and tyranny of sin...To have our hearts changed by the Holy Spirit*
> *such that we have no more disposition to do evil, but to do good continually."*
> David A. Bednar, *Clean Hands and a Pure Heart* [105]

Before the external city of Zion can be built, a great cleansing must occur on at least three levels. First within the soul. (Mosiah 27:25). Second, among the Lord's church. (D&C 112:24-26). Finally, throughout the entire world. (Matthew 24:6-7). This process of purification will include personal calamities, religious destruction, and global war. During the cleansing the gospel will be taken from the Gentiles and given to the house of Israel. (3 Nephi 16 and Truth #37).

When this spiritual transition occurs we may be surprised at the degree of righteousness required to participate in Zion. The Lord's surviving remnant will include those who may not be well known for their religious position (Matthew 7:21-24), but are meek, deep, powerful, and compassionate. The Holy City will shelter those who, in the quietest and most obscure moments, choose to be a hero for Christ.

> *"Have you ever imagined that, when it came to the test, you would perform some act of bravery?*
> *I know I did, as a boy. I imagined that someone was in peril and that, at the risk of my own life,*
> *I saved him. Or in some dangerous confrontation with a fearsome opponent, I had the courage*
> *to overcome...But the opportunities to stand for that which is right-when the pressures are subtle*
> *and when even our friends are encouraging us to give in to the idolatry of the times-those come along*
> *far more frequently. No photographer is there to record the heroism, no journalist will*
> *splash it across the newspaper's front page. Just in the quiet contemplation of our conscience,*
> *we will know that we faced the test of courage: Zion or Babylon?"*
> David R. Stone, *Zion in the Midst of Babylon* [106]

Becoming Zion at heart requires a willingness to sacrifice all things. Even while living in the temporary comforts of Babylon, those who become Zion will lay all that God requires on the altar of sacrifice.

> *"A religion that does not require the **sacrifice of all things** never has power sufficient to produce*
> *the faith necessary unto life and salvation; for, from the first existence of man, the faith necessary unto*
> *the enjoyment of life and salvation never could be **obtained without the sacrifice of all earthly***
> ***things. . . . It is through the medium of the sacrifice of all earthly things that men do actually***
> ***know that they are doing the things that are well pleasing in the sight of God.***
> *When a man has offered in sacrifice all that he has for the truth's sake, not even withholding his life,*
> *and believing before God that he has been called to make this sacrifice because he seeks to do his will,*

75

he does know, most assuredly, that God does and will accept his sacrifice and offering,
and that he has not, nor will not, seek his face in vain...*"*
Joseph Smith, *Lectures on Faith* [107]

Those who yearn to be in the Lord's presence are willing, and even eager, to leave the glitter, temptations, and filthy lucre of this world behind. These Saints do not try to serve two masters, but rather look forward to escaping the economy of the beast that they might live to contribute to the United Order.

<u>Cultural Assumption</u>
The law of consecration was something tried in the early days of the Church.
We are no longer required to live this law.

"The law of consecration is a law for an inheritance in the celestial kingdom. God, the Eternal Father, His Son Jesus Christ, and all holy beings abide by this law. It is an eternal law.
It is a revelation by God to His Church in this dispensation. Though not in full operation today, it will be mandatory for all Saints to live the law in its fullness to receive celestial inheritance."
Ezra Taft Benson, *The Teachings of Ezra Taft Benson* [108]

Celestial glory requires living celestial law. In today's church, there are many aspects of the greater paradigm which have been minimized by the whole but are still available for individual acceptance and application.

"We covenant to live the law of consecration. This law is that we consecrate our time, talents, strength, property, and money for the up building of the kingdom of God on this earth and the establishment of Zion. Until one abides by the laws of obedience, sacrifice, the gospel, and chastity, he cannot abide the law of consecration, which is the law pertaining to the celestial kingdom.
'For if you will that I give you place in the celestial world, you must prepare yourselves by doing the things which I have commanded you and required of you.' (D&C 78:7)."
Ezra Taft Benson, *Temple Blessings and Covenants* [109]

After the early Saints migrated to the Salt Lake Valley, the United Order was again attempted. These additional attempts failed because of greed, selfishness, and a lust for the things of this world.

...Zion cannot be built up unless it is by the principles of the law of the celestial kingdom; otherwise I cannot receive her unto myself. And my people must needs be chastened until they learn obedience, if it must needs be, **by the things which they suffer***...there are many who will say:* **where is their God?** *Behold, he will deliver them in times of trouble, otherwise* **we will not go up to Zion, and will keep our moneys.**
D&C 105: 5-8

Scripture explains, *"it is not given that one man should possess that which is above another, wherefore the world lieth in sin."*(D&C 49:20). In America the LDS church has flourished financially for so long that many now interpret financial success to be a sign of God's approval.
In relation to correlating spirituality with financial abundance, Hugh Nibley warned;

*"In every dispensation of the gospel, the Lord has insisted on **segregating his covenant people from the rest of the world**: if they were not ready to "come out of her, [O] my people"*
*(Revelation 18:4) willingly, he saw to it that **the world was more than willing to persecute and expel them**. Two ways were placed before Adam, to see which one he would follow. Cain followed the one; Abel, and after him, Seth, the other. But soon Seth's posterity drifted over to the camp of Cain. Things being very bad, Enoch, the super-missionary, was sent out and was able "in [the] process of time" (Moses 7:21) to draw many after him into his city of **Zion, which was then totally segregated from the rest of the world, pending the world's destruction**. After the Flood, things went bad again, so that the call to Abraham was lech lecha—get out of here! And he kept moving all his days, forming his own society as he went, initiating all his followers into a special covenant with God. The law of Moses insists before all else that the Chosen **People preserve their aloofness from the world by constant purification and instruction**: the people must be qadosh, "**sanctified**," both words having the basic meaning of "cut off," "separated." **God has always given his people the same choice of either living up to the covenants made with him or being in Satan's power; there is no middle ground** (Moses 4:4). True, we spend this time of probation in a no-man's-land between the two camps of salvation and damnation, but at every moment of the day and night we must be moving toward the one or the other. Progressive testing takes place along the way in either direction; the same tests in every dispensation and generation mark the progress of the people of God.*

(1) Do you, first of all, agree to do things his way rather than your way—to follow the law of God? (2) If so, will you be obedient to him, no matter what he asks of you?
(3) Will you, specifically, be willing to sacrifice anything he asks you for?
(4) Will you at all times behave morally and soberly?
(5) Finally, if God asks you to part with your worldly possessions by consecrating them all to his work, will you give his own back to him to be distributed as he sees fit, not as you think wise?

*That last test has been by far the hardest of all, and few indeed have chosen that strait and narrow way. The rich young man was careful and correct in observing every point of the law— up to that one; but that was too much for him, and the Savior, who refused to compromise or make a deal, could only send him off sorrowing, observing to the apostles that passing that test was so difficult to those possessing the things of the world that only a special dispensation from God could get them by. Like the people of Lehi and the primitive Christians, **the Latter-day Saints were asked and forced to make a clean break with the world— "the world" meaning explicitly the world's economy**. The first commandment given to the Saints in this last dispensation, delivered at Harmony, Pennsylvania, in April of 1829, before the formal incorporation of the Church, was an ominous warning: "**Seek not for riches but for wisdom**" (D&C 6:7)—all in one brief mandate that does not allow compromise. Why start out on such a negative note? The Lord knew well that the great obstacle to the work would be what it always had been in the past. The warning is repeated throughout the Doctrine and Covenants and the Book of Mormon again and again. The positive and negative are here side by side and back to back, making it clear, as the scriptures often do, that the two quests are mutually exclusive— **you cannot go after both, you cannot serve both God and Mammon**, even if you should be foolish enough to try."*

Hugh Nibley, *Approaching Zion* [110]

77

Those who have tasted the miracle of Christ know that the attractive enticements of the world are meaningless. These are they who see *"things as they really are"*(Jacob 4:13) and are willing to sacrifice all that is necessary to become Zion.

"Reputation, social standing, popularity and success must be **burnt on the alter** *as a sacrifice before any person can learn they have eternal life. Since our lives are going to be lost anyway- and all the world has to offer will be meaningless-the trade is illusory. We are asked to give up what has never been ours to keep.* **This life presents the opportunity to be heroic in the cause of Christ***. But life is brief, the opportunity fleeting.* **Viewed in the proper light, the sacrifice of all things is nothing.** *You gain everything by giving up what is truly nothing. Only a fool would make the calculation otherwise."*
Denver Snuffer, *Beloved Enos* [111]

Today we casually mention *"being in the world, but not of the world,"* but the day will come when a complete separation from the beast is the only safe path. Similar to how Laman and Lemuel were required to exit Jerusalem, many who are now comfortable will be tested to see if they will leave the false security of Babylon in favor of accomplishing the will of the Lord. Those who have become like Lehi and Nephi and have prepared themselves emotionally, mentally, and spiritually will go forward into the wilderness of deliverance.

Am I Ready?
"The time must come when there will be a separation between this kingdom and the kingdoms of the world, even in every point of view (D&C 63:53-54). The time must come when this kingdom must be free and independent from all other kingdoms. Are you prepared to have the thread cut to-day?"
Brigham Young, *Journal of Discourses* [112]

To be "Zion" requires growing from "paying tithing" to offering a "complete consecration" of the soul and all that we possess. To increase from a daily life based on selfish wants to a daily ministry based on God's will. Love for neighbor must overwhelm comfort for self. Similar to how Joseph Smith, John the Baptist, and the prophet Isaiah each forsook Babylon and died for the cause, God's Saints must be willing to stand for truth at any cost.

True to the Faith
"We contemplate a people who have embraced a system of religion, unpopular, and the adherence to which has brought upon them repeated persecutions. A people who for their love of God, and attachment to His cause, have suffered hunger, nakedness, perils, and almost every privation. A people who, for the sake of their religion have had to mourn the premature death of parents, husbands, wives and children. A people, who have preferred death to slavery and hypocrisy, and have honorably maintained their characters, and stood firm and immovable, in times that have tried men's souls.... Your names will be handed down to posterity as Saints of God and virtuous men."
Joseph Smith, *Teachings of the Prophet Joseph Smith* [113]

The wheat look toward Eternal life while the tares are more concerned with success in this world. Both will eventually receive what they truly desire. Today the choice is ours: Babylon or Zion?

"Every step in the direction of increasing one's personal holdings is a step away from Zion...
one cannot serve two masters...so it is with God and business, for mammon is simply the standard
Hebrew word for any kind of financial dealing."
Hugh Nibley, *Approaching Zion* [114]

In truth, the Zion standard will not be minimized. The price of true discipleship is set. For those who choose Christ and His Zion there is no other way.

"Evil is coming toward us...we have to create Zion in the midst of Babylon.
People in every culture move within a cocoon of self-satisfied self-deception,
fully convinced that the way they see things is the way things really are...
All too often, we are like puppets on a string, as our culture determines what is "cool."
Seduced by our culture, we often hardly recognize our idolatry, as our strings are pulled
by that which is popular in the Babylon world. Indeed, as the poet Wordsworth said:
'The world is too much with us.'"
David R. Stone, *Zion in the Midst of Babylon* [115]

"Wo be unto him that shall say We have received the word of God,
and we need no more word of God, for we have enough."
2 Nephi 28:24

Receiving global revelation through the church is granted or withheld in direct relation to the spiritual status of the people and their leaders. True prophets provide that which is appropriate based on what the people are willing to receive. The prophet Mormon explains:

I, being fifteen years of age and being somewhat of a sober mind, therefore I was visited
of the Lord, and tasted and knew of the goodness of Jesus. And I did endeavor to preach
unto this people, but my mouth was shut, and I was forbidden that I should preach unto them;
for behold they had wilfully rebelled against their God; and the beloved disciples
were taken away out of the land, because of their iniquity. But I did remain among them,
but I was forbidden to preach unto them, because of the hardness of their hearts;
and because of the hardness of their hearts the land was cursed for their sake.
Mormon 1:15-17

Our wise and benevolent God does not reveal additional light that will only be misunderstood and rejected by the religious majority. Thus, **a key distinction exists between the optimal "will of the Lord" and what the people require the "will of the Lord" to be. Let all understand: what may be doctrinally <u>appropriate</u> today will not be spiritually <u>adequate</u>** in the future.

"I could explain a hundred fold more than I ever have of the glories of the kingdoms manifested
to me in the vision, were I permitted, and were the people prepared to receive them. The Lord deals
with this people as a tender parent with a child, communicating light and intelligence
and the knowledge of his ways as they can bear it."
Joseph Smith, *Teachings of the Prophet Joseph Smith* [116]

For those who want to learn the glories of the kingdom, it is essential to understand that administrative decisions implemented by the church are not prophecies. New policies based on opinion polling and survey data is not revelation, and touching stories published in the *Ensign* do not represent new scripture.

Blaming church leadership for this problem is not helpful, for how quickly we forget that we are responsible to work our own salvation with fear and trembling. (Philippians 2:12).

"Looking for deeper meaning does not get satisfied through criticism of the Lord's servants.
That seems to be an easy outlet, because men are always going to be flawed. What of that? Do we reject
Peter of the New Testament Church because of Peter's failings? He denied Christ three times the night
of Christ's trial. What of it? He fought with Paul over the Gentile question...What of that?

If both strength and weakness coincide in Peter, are not the Lord's current leaders entitled
to at least as much patience and tolerance for their strengths and weaknesses? You may think you could
do a better job than your Bishop or Stake President. You might be right. But they were called, not you.
When they were called you were asked to sustain them…The seriousness of this issue is reflected
in the Temple covenants. Refraining from 'evil speaking of the Lords anointed'
should be given it's broadest possible application."
Denver Snuffer, *The Second Comforter-Conversing with the Lord Through the Veil* [117]

Instead of blaming the brethren, is it possible that our loving God withholds new revelation because the information would only add to the condemnation already upon our heads? Perhaps Father is simply waiting for a righteous remnant capable of embracing the increase.

Until that day of light arrives, it is the wheat of the church who seek personal revelation that they might individually come out of condemnation and receive true messengers sent from Father.

Give ear, O ye heavens, and I will speak; And hear, O earth, the words of my mouth.
My doctrine shall drop as the rain…and as the showers upon the grass.
Deuteronomy 32:1-2

Behold, the days come, saith the Lord GOD, that I will send a famine in the land,
not a famine of bread, nor a thirst for water, but of hearing the words of the LORD.
Amos 8:11

Although this scripture is usually applied to the initial Apostasy, several decades have passed since doctrinal revelation was received by leadership and disseminated as scripture to the church.

The reality that the church is not providing additional prophecy and scripture is self-evident. Contrary to popular belief, reviewing teachings offered by previous prophets in general conference is not "new revelation." This requires us to ask, of what great use is believing in "continuing revelation" if we as an organization aren't receiving any? What are the ramifications of today's *famine in the land,* and does it have any effect on my personal salvation?

"And be it known that whenever a people believe the canon of scripture is complete;
whenever they try to feed themselves spiritually upon the prophetic word of the past alone;
whenever they are without prophets and apostles to give them the living word;
whenever they cease to receive new revelations—then they are no longer capable
of interpreting and understanding past revelations."
Bruce R. McConkie, *The Mortal Messiah: From Bethlehem to Calvary* [118]

It is essential to understand the difference between "prophecy" and "policy," new revelation vs. ongoing bureaucracy. For those who understand correct doctrine, perceiving today's *famine in the land* is easy to see, but difficult to accept.

"The truth will set you free, but first it will make you miserable."
James A. Garfield

In truth, the doctrinal drought has lasted for decades. The result is a general membership that no longer expects new prophecy or additional revelation. There are numerous causes for this trend, but despite the reasons and/or rationalizations, this lack of *"hearing the word of the Lord"* has resulted in the *"traditions of men"* dominating the religious discussion.

This spiritual tragedy *"causeth silence to reign and all eternity is pained, and the angels are waiting the great command to reap down the earth, to gather the tares that they may be burned..."*(D&C 38:12). Until the dreaded day of reaping and cleansing arrives, teaching gospel basics will likely remain necessary for the mainstream culture. Simultaneously, what the church continues to review with the general membership, will remain thoroughly insufficient for the awakening wheat.

Why Are the Brethren So Quiet?

"When a people becomes rich and prosperous, they often forget God and become prideful.
The Lord's anointed respond by warning of impending calamities and destruction if the people
don't turn and repent from their evil ways. From scripture we observe just before complete destruction,
the Lord's prophets stop warning and start teaching about the three things that will get the righteous
through the difficulties and tribulations ... 1) Faith in Jesus Christ, 2) Hope in the Atonement, and
3) Charity to our fellowmen. The greater the focus on faith, hope, and charity;
the closer we are to the destruction of the wicked and the saints being humbled. Examples include
the Apostle Paul to the Corinthians, Ether to the Jaredites, and Moroni to the Lamanities."
David Christenson, *Faith, Hope, and Charity* [119]

Those who love the gospel hope the day will come when God will again provide additional revelation through the leaders of His church. Until that time, the wheat of the church are to seek learning, *"even by study and also by faith."* (D&C 88:118).

Behold, you have not understood; you have supposed that I would give it unto you,
when you took no thought save it was to ask me. But, behold, I say unto you, that you must study it out
in your mind; then you must ask me if it be right, and if it is right I will cause that your bosom
shall burn within you; therefore, you shall feel that it is right.
D&C 9:7-8

Due to the relative silence of the Brethren,
are we not required to obtain further light and knowledge for ourselves?

Those seeking personal revelation and the gift of prophecy can still give deference to the organizational prophet and acknowledge his singular role in leading the church. Personal testimony can include support for the guidance leadership does provide while simultaneously choosing to be dependent on Father and His Holy Spirit as the final authority.

Nevertheless I tell you the truth; It is expedient for you that I go away: **for if I go not away,**
the Comforter will not come unto you; *but if I depart, I will send him unto you...I have yet many*
things to say unto you, but **ye cannot bear them now.** *Howbeit when he, the Spirit of truth, is come,*
he will guide you into all truth: *for he shall not speak of himself; but whatsoever he shall hear,*
that shall he speak: and he will shew you things to come.
John 16:7,12-13

TRUTH #18 GOD IS WILLING TO REVEAL MANY GREAT AND GLORIOUS TRUTHS.
ADVANCED TEACHINGS SHOULD ONLY BE TAUGHT TO OTHERS
WHEN DIRECTED BY THE HOLY SPIRIT.

*"That man **who cannot know things without telling any other living being** upon the earth,
**who cannot keep his secrets and those that God reveals to him, never can receive the voice
of his Lord** to dictate to him and the people on this earth. It was asked me by a gentleman how
I guided the people by revelation. I teach them to live so that the Spirit of revelation may make plain
to them their duty **day by day that they are able to guide themselves**. To get this revelation
it is necessary that the people live so that their spirits are as pure and clean as a piece of
blank paper that lies on the desk before the inditer, ready to receive any mark the writer may
make upon it. Yes, my brethren and sisters here, **both men and women, have revelation**,
and I can say with Moses of old —
"Would God that all the Lord's people were prophets."*
Brigham Young, *Discourses of Brigham Young* [120]

Those who personally receive the gift of prophecy can also develop the gift of seership. These visionaries literally "see" past, present, and future, and are capable of peering into specific aspects of *"all that is." **Seers "remember" events that haven't yet happened in linear time.***

A prophet or prophetess who is blessed with the gift of seership may possess a seer stone or an interpreter—sometimes referred to as a "Urim and Thummim." In other cases, such as with Enoch and Joseph Smith, the seer grows in ability until no external instrument is required. The seer advances to the point where **the individual soul becomes the Urim and Thummim.** (Moses 6:35-36). Elder John A. Widtsoe explained, *"The Prophet did not always receive his revelations by the assistance of the Urim and Thummim. As he grew in experience and understanding, he learned to bring **his spirit** into such an attitude that it became a Urim and Thummim to him, and God's will was revealed without the intervention of external means."*[121]

Whether utilizing an external aid or not, the gift of seership is available to all willing to abide by the laws associated with this gift. Because certain individuals were deceived in the early days of the church, and because of a common mis-trust among members concerning spiritual gifts, many appear hesitant to seek out and receive meaningful visions from God. Nevertheless, all spiritual gifts remain available to those who seek and receive His power. With life on earth becoming so complex and demanding, the gift of seership is a spiritual skill desperately needed today.

*"It is not enough to accept the testimony of deceased seers. The Restoration of the Gospel
was intended to bring such visionaries to life again, and reintroduce people willing to accept
testimony from these witnesses about "things which are not visible to the natural eye."
We need living seers or we are cut off from one of the gifts intended to guide us."*
Denver Snuffer, *Eighteen Verses* [122]

84

It is common for seers to be shown the history of the earth from beginning to end. During rare occasions, when the seer is instructed to reveal what they have witnessed, observations offered represent the hidden glories of the kingdom coming to light. (Mosiah 8:17). Because of general unbelief among the people, seers are usually required to remain silent concerning the details of their sacred visions. (Alma 12:9).

Can I Be Trusted?

"The vision of this earths history, from beginning to end, is a common experience
for many seers…More often than not, however "they are laid under a strict command that they
*shall not impart" (Alma 12:9)…The **censorship of the seers visions is purposeful**. Most importantly,*
***censorship serves to limit the disruption of history**. It prevents self-fulfilling prophecies by avoiding*
the conspiracies of men to achieve a result either in harmony with or in opposition to prophecy in ways
which would distort the authority of God over the affairs of men. It is best to keep some information away
*from men…**Some things can be learned but cannot be taught**. Seers are people who can be trusted*
to keep information to themselves which they have been forbidden to reveal."
Denver Snuffer, *Eighteen Verses* [123]

To be trusted of the Lord requires cultivating the ability to speak only when directed. Just because something is "true" doesn't mean it has to be spoken. Many truths have been edited out of this text—not because they are false, but because the Holy Spirit warned it was not God's will to discuss certain content. Today's religious context requires constant evaluation of when to speak and when to remain silent.

And the high priest stood up in the midst, and asked Jesus, saying, Answerest thou nothing?
What is it which these witness against thee? But he held his peace, and answered nothing.
Again the high priest asked him, and said unto him, Art thou the Christ, the Son of the Blessed?
And Jesus said, I am: and ye shall see the Son of man sitting on the right hand of power,
and coming in the clouds of heaven.
Mark 14:55-64

During His ministry, the Lord Jesus demonstrated that there is a time to speak and a time to remain quiet. The prophet Joseph Smith explained, *"It is not always wise to relate all the truth. Even Jesus, the Son of God, had to refrain from doing so, and had to restrain His feelings many times for the safety of Himself and His followers, and had to conceal the righteous purposes of His heart in relation to many things pertaining to His Father's kingdom."* [124]

When "young prophets" or "baby seers" are in training, it is essential to walk a verbal tightrope. When new revelations or sacred visions are received, it is natural to want to share with others, but the desire to teach the mysteries must be handled with wisdom. Boyd K. Packer, a seasoned Apostle, referred to this dilemma when he stated, *"To see clearly what is ahead and yet find members slow to respond or resistant to counsel or even rejecting the witness of the apostles and prophets brings deep sorrow…there are limits to what the Spirit permits us to say."* [125] If we are not directed to speak sacred truth and then still choose to declare greater light anyway, we are being selfish and disobedient. Casting treasured pearls before those who are not yet prepared only adds to their spiritual condemnation. The Lord would have us assist others, not contribute to their spiritual struggles. Unless we have His will and wise timing at the center of our actions, He cannot trust us with greater light.

> *"The real key is to have purity of purpose. To appropriately communicate to the proper people,*
> *the proper information, in the proper spirit, patiently waiting for the Lord to turn the lights on,*
> *rather than assuming it is our responsibility or right to immediately bathe them in light.*
> *The temptation is to defend our point of view, to think less of those who will not see,*
> *and to distance ourselves emotionally and spiritually from those we should love."*
> Anonymous Saint

It must be acknowledged that the church is full of new converts as well as lifetime members still working on gospel basics. In a culture where eighth-generation scriptorians mingle with those who have never finished reading the Book of Mormon, teaching the greater mysteries from the pulpit is rarely the answer.

Sometimes at church there is so much to say, nothing can be.

This spiritual reality often results in the wheat sitting quietly at church *"observing things generally."* These souls acknowledge the current absence of real revelation but wait for the Holy Spirit to instruct them concerning what to say. Successful navigation through this spiritual dilemma requires wisdom and exact obedience.

> *"You see, there are two kinds of people who keep silent. The first one is one who has nothing to say,*
> *and the other is one who has too much to say…Silence is produced from excess, not from lack…*
> *To die of thirst is one thing; to be drowned is quite another. Yet water causes both.*
> *In one it is a lack of water, and in the other too much water causes death."*
> Jeanne Guyon, *Experiencing the Depths of Jesus Christ* [126]

Those who have tasted the living waters of salvation may find it difficult to remain quiet with family, friends, and those whom they love. Jesus anticipated this religious dilemma when He stated, *"Give not that which is holy unto the dogs, neither cast ye your pearls before swine, lest they trample them under their feet, and turn again and rend you."*(Matthew 7:6). This reference to "dogs and swine" was obviously not meant to create pride in the growing disciple, but rather to act as a protection for those who have not yet awakened to greater spiritual realities. To truly make a difference the disciple must speak in a spirit of love with those whose testimonies are capable of accommodating the increase. The Holy Ghost, not personal agenda, must lead the conversation.

When members are pre-maturely taught greater truths, which they are not yet prepared to assimilate into their belief systems, they are likely to feel confused and reject the new principles being shared. Even when what is being taught is doctrinally correct, if the member is to have any chance of growing *"line upon line, precept upon precept,"* (2 Nephi 28:30), the higher perspective must be provided in the right way and at the right time.

In relation to receiving all truth, especially the difficult principles, each of us must also be careful and wise in how we interpret that which initially seems inaccurate or false. Determining that greater light is a deception of the devil, because it makes us feel uncomfortable, only reinforces our condemnation and ignorance. This is why questioning our religious traditions is so essential, for only when we are truly teachable and have *"become as little children,"* (Matthew 18:2-3), can the Lord enlarge our understanding and teach us of the *"mysteries of God."* (D&C 6:7).

Constantly reviewing at church how "right we are about everything" only keeps us *walking in darkness at noon day.* (D&C 95:6). Therefore, it is wise to seek deeply, believe boldly, and refrain from condemning that which we do not yet understand.

In today's world, ***there is admittedly a deluge of deception***. Since the time of Restoration, some of the corruption and false philosophy has even filtered into the Lord's church. Thus, our "mortal test" is a least three-fold. First, we must be willing and able to reject the false teachings of men. Second, we must be hungry and able to grow beyond our initial perspectives, into the ever-deepening glory of God and His universe! And finally, through the blood of Jesus Christ, we must have the laws of God integrated into our hearts. Thus those intend to "pass the test," must be willing to reject error, receive His continual increase, and become one with Celestial law.

Misinterpreting Greater Light

Do you think the Jews, who were buying and selling in the temple, felt "a dark spirit," when Jesus cleansed the temple and rebuked the money changers?
Matthew 21:13

Is it possible that thousands of awakening Saints "got a sick feeling"
when they re-read the prophecies of Isaiah, and for the first time realized
that the prophet was talking about us as a Mormon culture?
Isaiah 24:1-6

Did the people of God feel all "warm and fuzzy" when the prophet Nephi predicted who had murdered their chief judge, and then warned them, *"...O ye fools, ye uncircumcised of heart, ye blind, and ye stiffnecked people, do ye know how long the Lord your God will suffer you that ye shall go on in this your way of sin? O ye ought to begin to howl and mourn, because of the great destruction which at this time doth await you, except ye shall repent."*
Helaman 9: 21-22

Do you think King Noah and his priests felt confused and angry when Abinadi rebuked them for failing to understand prophecy and perverting the ways of the Lord? (Mosiah 12:26).
Didn't He invite them to receive a greater truth, only to have them misinterpret him
and say that he was *"mad?"*
Mosiah 13:1

> What does it mean, that instead of hearing and believing the greater law Jesus taught,
> the Pharisees were willing for one man to die, that the whole nation perish not?
> Is this pattern, in smaller degree, now occurring within the church today?
> John 11:50

By reviewing the life of Amulek, we can find hope that all will eventually awaken. Amulek was similar to many in that he had not yet seen an angel, but knew that he had been *"called many times (and) would not hear."*(Alma 10:6). Eventually the Lord sent the prophet Alma, as well as His angelic messenger, to minister to the slumbering saint. Amulek responded by awaking, arising, and becoming a powerful prophet for Jesus Christ. (Alma 14:28).

In summary, those who ask spiritual questions are taught an abundance of amazing and spectacular answers by God. Once the journey starts, we need to be open and teachable to new ideas, while also accepting that if God wants something sacred revealed to another, He will usually do the teaching Himself . When He does require us frail humans to deliver the message, wisdom suggests we speak the truth *in His way and in His time*. Such revelations may include:

What does it mean to personally take upon us the name of Christ?

Why did Joseph Smith, many years after the First Vision, encourage the Saints
to lift their minds to a more lofty sphere and then inquire: What kind of being is God?[127]

What is the lesser and greater portion of the Word?

When will we receive the sealed portion of the plates?

What is required to have our calling and election made sure?

What is the difference between The Church of Jesus Christ of Latter Day Saints and
the Church of the Firstborn?

What is required to successfully complete our telestial probation?

Is it possible to receive the Second Comforter in this life?

Is it possible for a member to receive the sealing power directly from Jesus Christ?

What is the greater meaning of "eternal lives?"

Is it important that our method of blessing and administering the sacrament
is not consistent with scripture?

What does it mean that the temple ordinances have been changed?

Why do the scriptures and some of the brethren warn about
apostasy in the latter days?

When the gospel is taken from the Gentiles and given to the house of Israel,
how will this process occur and what will it involve?

Who is the one mighty and strong spoken of in scripture,
and when will he return to set the house of God in order?

Who is the servant, ordained by the hand of the Lord,
who will gather a righteous remnant from the four corners of the earth?

What was the council of fifty, and when will the political arm of the kingdom be re-established?

Who and what are the beast, the dragon, and the church of the devil?

What destructions, plagues, and secret combinations
will combine against the Saints during the Apocalypse?

How will the parable of the ten virgins
and parable of the wheat and the tares be fulfilled?

How might using the true order of prayer assist us in parting the veil
and becoming a holy people?

When will the Holy City of Zion be organized upon the earth?
What gospel will be taught within the City of God?

Why are so many called,
but only a few choose to be chosen?

*"The genius of the kingdom with which we are associated is to disseminate knowledge through
all the ranks of the people, and to make every man a prophet and every woman a prophetess,
that they may understand the plans and purposes of God."*
George Q. Cannon, *Journal of Discourses* [128]

In the early days of the church members were encouraged to receive personal revelation and then prophecy unto each other. The President of the Church was always the one who was sustained by common consent to lead the organization as a whole, but initially every member was allowed the freedom to prophesy and share revelation.

*"Well, you say, the President of the Church should give revelation. Yes, it is true, the President holds
the keys of revelation to the Latter-day Saints. But is he alone to give revelation? No, verily, no!
There is not an Apostle in this Church, there is not an Elder in this Church that stands up in this
congregation to teach this people, but should be full of revelation. There is where your revelation should
come - from those who teach you day to day. . . . But we want revelation every day.
And I want these Apostles and these Saints to go before the Lord in your secret places and ask Him
to pour out revelations upon this people, that we may give you the word of the Lord while we are with you,
and that these Apostles, when they speak, may speak by the power of God, by the Holy Ghost.
Then that will be the word of the Lord, it will be scripture, it will be the power of God unto salvation
unto every one that believes. God bless you. Amen."*
Wilford Woodruff, *General Conference* [129]

Over time, attitudes and expectations in the church changed concerning prophecy. Assumptions about keys, leadership, and prophecy were regulated into the faith. Eventually, "being a prophet" was correlated with a position in the church. This spiritual limitation was not what God intended for the people in His church.

Glory Days

*"If the Lord requires anything of this people, and speaks through me, I will tell them of it;
but if he does not, still we all live by the principle of revelation. Who reveals? Everybody around us;
we learn of each other. I have something which you have not, and you have something which
I have not; I reveal what I have to you, and you reveal what you have to me.
I believe that we are revelators to each other."*
Brigham Young, *Discourses of Brigham Young* [130]

Some believe the President of the Church is the only one who can be a prophet, seer, and revelator. This cultural attitude is doctrinally incorrect.

A Kingdom of Equals

*"There are in this greater priesthood five offices or callings—elder, seventy, high priest, patriarch, and apostle—yet the priesthood is the same; and the priesthood is greater than any of its offices. We are a kingdom of brethren, a congregation of equals, all of whom are entitled to receive all of the blessings of the priesthood. **There are no blessings reserved for apostles that are not freely available to all the elders of the kingdom; blessings come because of obedience and personal righteousness, not because of administrative positions.**"*
Bruce R. McConkie, *The Ten Blessings of the Priesthood* [131]

Most members are proficient at repeating the words of institutional prophets, but they may not have yet accessed the *"gift of prophecy"* for themselves. (1 Corinthians 13:2). Devout Mormons, who are currently dependent on church leadership, may hesitate to access their own spiritual gifts, but within the soul, the power to prophesy awaits!

Choosing Prophecy

"The gift of prophecy is an extension and an enlargement of the gift of testimony. The testimony of Jesus is the spirit of prophecy" (Revelation 19:10). A person who gains personal revelation from the Holy Spirit that Jesus is Lord of all, being thus attuned to the Infinite, 'may prophesy concerning all things' (Moroni 10:13. See also Doctrine and Covenants 46:22; 1 Corinthians 12:10)....Prophecy came not in old time by the will of man: but holy men of God spake as they were moved by the Holy Ghost' (2 Peter 1:21). And even as men seek for a testimony so should they desire the gift of prophecy. Thus it is that Paul says: "Let the prophets speak. . . . For ye may all prophesy one by one. . . . Wherefore, brethren, covet to prophesy. (1 Corinthians 14:29, 31, 39)."
Bruce R. McConkie, *A New Witness for the Articles of Faith,* [132]

It was mighty Moses who told the children of Israel, *"would (to) God that all the Lord's people were prophets, and that the Lord would put his spirit upon them!"* (Numbers 11:29). In scripture we are each encouraged to seek out and receive the gift of prophecy. (1 Corinthians 12:10). Those who obey and *"covet to prophecy"* (1 Corinthians 14:39) obtain a personal witness of Jesus Christ and are then privileged to proclaim truth in His name. (Revelations 19:10).

"Is Joseph Smith a prophet? Yes, and every other man who has the Testimony of Jesus. For the testimony of Jesus is the spirit of Prophecy. If I be a true teacher and witness, I must possess the Testimony (personal witness) of Jesus, and thus the spirit of Prophecy, and that constitutes a prophet, and any man who says he is a teacher of righteousness, who denies the spirit of prophecy, is a liar and the truth is not in him. By this key false teachers and impostors may be detected."
Joseph Smith, *Teachings of the Prophet Joseph Smith* [133]

It is the position of the church that only the president has the keys necessary to receive revelation *for* the church. This, however, does not stop anyone in tune with the Spirit from receiving revelation *about* the church.

Who is a True Prophet?

"It has been remarked sometimes, by certain individuals, that President Young has said in public that he was not a prophet nor the son of a prophet. I have traveled with him since 1833, or the spring of 1834; I have traveled a good many thousand miles with him and have heard him preach a great many thousand sermons; but I have never heard him make that remark in my life. He is a prophet, I am a prophet, you are, and anybody is a prophet who has the testimony of Jesus Christ, for that is the spirit of prophecy. The elders of Israel are prophets…"

Wilford Woodruff, *Journal of Discourses* [134]

One of the great ironies of life is that some men who claim to be true prophets are actually false, while those who are real prophets are often ignored and dismissed as being irrelevant. The Prophet Joseph Smith observed, *"The world always mistook false prophets for true ones, and those that were sent of God, they considered to be false prophets, and hence they killed, stoned, punished and imprisoned the true prophets and these had to hide themselves 'in deserts and dens, and caves of the earth,' and though the most honorable men of the earth, they banished them from their society as vagabonds, whilst they cherished, honored and supported knaves, vagabonds, hypocrites, imposters, and the basest of men."*[135]

This spiritual phenomenon leaves each believer to determine for themselves who is a true prophet and who is simply a pretender. Scripture recommends observing the fruits of any given ministry (Matthew 7:16) and then making a determination as led by the Holy Spirit. (D&C 45:57). To make an accurate determination concerning this matter is part of "our test" here in mortality.

Beware of false prophets, which come to you in sheep's clothing,
but inwardly they are ravening wolves. Ye shall know them by their fruits.
Matthew 7:15-16

Glory unto Father

True prophets are always pointing to Jesus Christ as the only source of salvation. (Mosiah 3). False prophets allow themselves to be held up as a light by others, subtly enabling the magnification of themselves. (Mosiah 11).

"Several times a year, we sustain fifteen Apostles as prophets, seers, and revelators. So we know to whom to look, even though a few seek not the welfare of Zion and set themselves up for a light."
Neal A. Maxwell, *General Conference* [136]

Honoring Choice

True prophets teach correct principles and let the people govern themselves. (Joseph Smith).
False prophets use power, control, and unrighteous dominion to enforce compliance.
(Politicians).

"A true prophet is not a corporate CEO, ordained of God to force compliance to God's commandments, tell everyone what to believe and how life must be lived. Instead of using unrighteous dominion and thereby forfeiting his priesthood power, a true prophet continually points to the true source of salvation, always refusing the priestcraft of being held up as a light."
Jeff Ostler, *True Prophets* [137]

Tough Love

True prophets rebuke believers with a call to repentance. Those who are humble appreciate the correction and determine to change. (D&C 95:1).
False prophets offer popular "feel-good stories" and minimize the consequences of sin. (Helaman 13). The masses love the message and rejoice that all is well. (Mosiah 7).

"I realize that the bearer of bad news is always unpopular. As a people we love sweetness and light—especially sweetness…Those who will learn nothing from history are condemned to repeat it. This we are doing in the Americas today."
Ezra Taft Benson, *Human Liberty is the Mainspring of Human Progress* [138]

Persecution and Popularity

True prophets are persecuted by the world, and sometimes by his own people. (Alma 31).
False prophets are accepted by the world, and loved by those who are worldly. (Alma 1).

*"Many are prone to garnish the sepulchers of yesterday's prophets
and mentally stone the living ones."*
Spencer W. Kimball, *Instructor* [139]

Truth vs. Tradition

True prophets do not rely on their "position of authority" for recognition.
They are supported and followed because of the spiritual power they demonstrate. (Enoch).
False prophets rely on authority, religious assumption,
and historical tradition for support. (King Noah).

"The duty of a High Priest is to hold communion with God and to be better qualified to teach principles and doctrines, but not to exercise monarchial government. It is a great thing to inquire at the hands of God and to come into His Presence."
Joseph Smith, *Teachings of the Prophet Joseph Smith* [140]

Voice of Warning

True prophets provide warnings about the world and make correct predictions concerning the future. (Helaman 14).
False prophets do not offer a voice of warning or make accurate predictions, but instead speak pleasantries. (2 Nephi 28).

"But behold, if a man shall come among you and say: Do this and there is no iniquity: do that and ye shall not suffer: Yea, he will say: Walk after the pride of your hearts: Yea, walk after the pride of you eyes, and do whatever your heart desireth and if a man come among you and say this,
ye will receive him and say he is a prophet."
Helaman: 13:27

Condemning Evil

True prophets warn of deception and secret combinations throughout the world. (D&C 38).
False prophets are silent concerning deceptive corruption, and thus enable secret combinations. (Helaman 6).

"What are we to understand by a Prophet?
It is his character to predict things that are in the future."
Joseph Smith, *Words of Joseph Smith* [141]

Spiritual Gifts

True prophets have dreams, visions, and visitations, sharing them as directed. (Numbers 12:6).
False prophets do not manifest spiritual gifts which are from God. (Exodus 7).

Hear now my words: If there be a prophet among you, I the LORD will make myself known unto him in a vision, and will speak unto him in a dream.
Numbers 12:6

The Greater Good

True prophets teach others to become prophets within their own stewardship.
They are not threatened by additional revelation and rejoice in all truth. (Joseph Smith).
False prophets are restrictive and require all revelation to be received through themselves.
(Pharaoh's).

"Now if any man has the testimony of Jesus, has he not the spirit of prophecy?
And if he has the spirit of prophecy, I ask, is he not a prophet?
And if a prophet, will he not receive revelation?"
Joseph Smith, *Teachings of Presidents of the Church* [142]

Differentiating between a true prophet from a false one is not always easy to discern. Beyond our religious assumptions, the temple teaches that true messengers provide further light and knowledge and that they administer the truths of salvation to mankind. In comparison, false prophets teach the people want they want to hear. (Alma 30).

Sleeping Shepherds and Wandering Sheep

Son of man, prophesy against the shepherds of Israel, prophesy, and say unto them,
Thus saith the Lord God unto the shepherds; Woe be to the shepherds of Israel that do feed themselves!
should not the shepherds feed the flocks? Ye eat the fat and ye clothe you with the wool, ye kill them that
are fed: but ye feed not the flock…My sheep wandered through all the mountains, and upon every high
hill: yea, my flock was scattered upon all the face of the earth, and none did search or seek after them.
Therefore, ye shepherds, hear the word of the Lord; As I live, saith the Lord God, surely because my flock
became a prey, and my flock became meat to every beast of the field, because there was no shepherd,
neither did my shepherds search for my flock, but the shepherds fed themselves, and fed not my flock;
Therefore, O ye shepherds, hear the word of the Lord; Thus saith the Lord God; Behold, I am against
the shepherds; and I will require my flock at their hand, and cause them to cease from feeding the flock;
neither shall the shepherds feed themselves any more; for I will deliver my flock from their mouth,
that they may not be meat for them. For thus saith the Lord God; Behold, I, even I,
will both search my sheep, and seek them out. As a shepherd seeketh out his flock in the day that he
is among his sheep that are scattered; so will I seek out my sheep and will deliver them out of all places
where they have been scattered in the cloudy and dark day.
Ezekiel 34: 2-3, 6-13

This matter of discerning who is a true shepherd is further complicated due to a spiritual-historical reality best summarized by Denver Snuffer. He explains, *"Throughout the Dispensation of Moses, there were two traditions that operated independent of one another. The one was official and priestly. The other was unofficial and prophetic. The priestly tradition held recognized office, and could be easily identified. The other was "ordained of God himself" and those who possessed it had His word to them as their only credential."*[143]

In addition to the men who are well known and lead the church, every son and daughter of God is invited to become a prophet or prophetess within the stewardship of their own family kingdom.

*"**Personal revelation is not limited** to gaining a testimony and knowing thereby that Jesus,*
through whom the gospel came, is Lord of all, nor is it limited to receiving guidance in our personal
and family affairs—although these are the most common examples of revelation among the Lord's people.
*In truth and in verity, **there is no limit to the revelations each member of the Church may receive.***
It is within the power of every person who has received the gift of the Holy Ghost to see visions,
entertain angels, learn the deep and hidden mysteries of the kingdom, and even see the face of God…
If all things operate by law, and they do; if God is no respecter of persons, and certainly he is perfectly
impartial; if his course is one eternal round, never varying from age to age, and such truly is the case—
then all of the gifts and graces and revelations ever given to any prophet, seer, or revelator
in any age will be given again to any soul who obeys the law entitling him so to receive."
Bruce R. McConkie, *A New Witness for the Articles of Faith* [144]

Imagine what would happen today if a brave man or woman stood up in sacrament meeting and prophesied. Would not most of the Mormon congregation be uncomfortable and consider it inappropriate? And yet this type of spiritual outpouring is desperately needed if we are to become a Zion people!

Also I heard the voice of the Lord, saying, Whom shall I send, and who will go for us?
Then said I, Here am I; send me.
Isaiah 6:8

The challenge of prophesying among the Mormons is heightened when the message from God comes from a woman. Despite the historical contributions of Eliza R. Snow and others, as well as the righteous example of women in scripture, gender limitations continue to influence the culture. Many erroneously believe prophecy is a priesthood function limited strictly to males.

And the next day we that were of Paul's company departed, and came unto Caesarea:
and we entered into the house of Philip the evangelist, which was one of the seven;
and abode with him. And the same man had four daughters, virgins, which did prophesy.
Acts 21:8-9

In truth, Zion will be abundant with both prophets and prophetesses who lead with power, healing, and vision. In that day the current social limitations we labor within will be enlarged and both holy men and women will bless those who dwell in Zion.

Women Prophets?
*"To get this revelation it is necessary that the people live so that their spirits are as pure and clean as a piece of blank paper that lies on the desk before the inditer, ready to receive any mark the writer may make upon it. Yes, my brethren and sisters here, **both men and women, have revelation**, and I can say with Moses of old-"**Would God that all the Lord's people were prophets.**"*
Brigham Young, *Discourses of Brigham Young* [145]

Those who possess the spirit of Jesus Christ are qualified to receive revelation and prophesy. Information received can related to self, family, church, nation, world, and even the entire universe and all eternity. Nothing that the soul is capable of receiving is off limits, for if we are willing to listen and learn, God Almighty is willing to teach us how to prophesy.

Joseph's Encouragement
"God hath not revealed anything to Joseph, but what He will make known unto the Twelve, and even the least Saint may know all things as fast as he is able to bear them."
Joseph Smith, *Teachings of the Prophet Joseph Smith* [146]

In truth, Adam is the Father of the human family. Jesus Christ is the Savior and King, and Joseph Smith is the head Prophet of this last dispensation. For those "prophets in training" who want to contribute to the Lord's harvest, now is the time to develop fully into prophets, seers, and revelators.

*"No man is a minister of Jesus Christ
without being a Prophet.
No man can be a minister of Jesus
except he has the Testimony of Jesus,
and this is the Spirit of Prophecy."*
Joseph Smith, *Teachings of the Prophet Joseph Smith* [147]

"I would exhort you to go on and continue to call upon God until you make your calling and election sure for yourselves, by obtaining this more sure word of prophecy..."
Joseph Smith, *History of the Church* [148]

To receive "calling and election" means that a man or woman has been judged in the flesh and found worthy of celestial glory. This spiritual benchmark occurs on an individual basis and may coincide with a personal visit from the Lord Jesus Christ.

"To have one's calling and election made sure is to be sealed up unto eternal life; it is to have the unconditional guarantee of exaltation in the highest heaven of the celestial world; it is to receive the assurance of godhood; it is, in effect, to have the day of judgment advanced, so that an inheritance of all the glory and honor of the Father's kingdom is assured prior to the day when the faithful actually enter into the divine presence to sit with Christ in his throne, even as he is "set down" with his "Father in his throne."
Bruce R. McConkie, *Doctrinal New Testament Commentary* [149]

Although very few who receive their calling and election will discuss the details, it appears that the recipient is told their salvation has been *"made sure."* Some report hearing an audible voice declare it unto them, while others receive this spiritual assurance during a visit with the Lord Jesus Christ. (see Truth #21).

Personal Salvation

*"It is one thing to be on the mount and hear the excellent voice, etc...
and another to hear the voice declare to you, you have a part and lot in that kingdom."*
Joseph Smith, *Discourses of the Prophet Joseph Smith* [150]

Receiving what is referred to as the *"more sure word of prophecy"* may occur privately or in connection with receiving the fullness of the priesthood during the Second Anointing. (see glossary at 77truths.com). Some consider hearing the voice of the Lord adequate, while others look to the religious ordinance as the official declaration. Regardless of order and emphasis, something beautiful happens when the quest to receive calling and election grows beyond a theoretical study into a personal journey.

Anchor to the Soul

"Speaking on Sunday, the 14ᵗʰ of May, 1843, the Prophet Joseph Smith took this statement of Peter for his text. From the Prophet's sermon I quote: 'Though they might hear the voice of God and know that Jesus was the Son of God, this would be no evidence that their election and calling was made sure, that they had part with Christ, and were joint heirs with Him. They then would want that more sure word of prophecy, that they were sealed in the heavens and had the promise of eternal life in the kingdom of God. Then, having this promise sealed unto them,

it was an anchor to the soul, sure and steadfast. Though the thunders might roll and lightning's flash,
and earthquakes bellow, and war gather thick around, yet this hope and knowledge
would support the soul in every hour of trial, trouble and tribulation.'"
Marion G. Romney, *Conference Report* [151]

To assist faithful Saints in their progression, God provides unique and difficult life experiences. The final stages of growth usually involve a personal "Abrahamic trial" requiring great faith and perseverance. D&C 101:4 states, *"...they must needs be chastened and tried, even as Abraham, who was commanded to offer up his only son."* This does not mean every disciple will be required to sacrifice a child, but that God will tailor the appropriate offering to match our life path journey. In reverencing Father's will above our own, the natural man is overcome, and ***our confidence in the Lord becomes invincible.***

Ye Shall Never Fall
Brethren, give diligence to make your calling and election sure;
for if ye do these things, ye shall never fall;
2 Peter 1:10

To come to this holy place and be fully approved of God requires fulfilling the same selfless pattern demonstrated by Jesus, Abraham, and all of the holy prophets.

Hero for Christ
"Sergeant Rafael Peralta built a reputation as a man who always put his Marines' interests
ahead of his own. He showed that again, when he made the ultimate sacrifice of his life Tuesday,
by shielding his fellow Marines from a grenade blast. Peralta, 25, as platoon scout, wasn't even assigned
to the assault team that entered the insurgent safe house in northern Fallujah, Marines said.
Despite an assignment that would have allowed him to avoid such dangerous duty, he regularly asked
squad leaders if he could join their assault teams, they said. One of the first Marines to enter the house,
Peralta was wounded in the face by rifle fire from a room near the entry door...
Moments later, an insurgent rolled a fragmentation grenade into the area where a wounded Peralta
and the other Marines were seeking cover. As Morrison and another Marine scrambled to escape the blast,
pounding against a locked door, Peralta grabbed the grenade and cradled it into his body, Morrison said.
While one Marine was badly wounded by shrapnel from the blast, the Marines said they believe more lives
would have been lost if not forPeralta's selfless act. "He saved half my fire team," said Captain Brannon
Dyer, 27, of Blairsville, Ga. The Marines said such a sacrifice would be perfectly in character for Peralta,
a Mexico native who lived in San Diego and gained U.S. citizenship after joining the Marines."
Daily Kos, *Marine jumps on grenade, saves squad* [152]

During mortality every soul is tested and broken to capacity. Monumental decisions appear and flicker in time as the choice between selfishness and God's will is made in an instant. Adversity provides the context we need so God can mold and re-shape the soul. It is during the fire of affliction, when sorrow overcomes the weak and feeble heart, that we discover the true essence of our faith.

Whosoever will save his life shall lose it:
And whosoever will lose his life for my sake shall find it.
Matthew 16:25

When a person repeatedly ministers to others without even a thought for self, that particular soul has reached a personal benchmark. He or she has begun to walk the way of The Christ.

"Joseph Smith said that some people entirely denounce the principle of self-aggrandizement as wrong. 'It is a correct principle,' he said, and may be indulged upon only one rule or plan—and that is to elevate, benefit and bless others first. If you will elevate others, the very work itself will exalt you.
Upon no other plan can a man justly and permanently aggrandize himself."
Hyrum L. Andrus, Helen Mae Andrus, *They Knew the Prophet* [153]

Every member has covenanted to "*stand as witnesses of God, at all times and in all things, and in all places that ye may be in, even until the death,*" with the promise that he or she will..."*be redeemed of God, and...have eternal life.*"(Mosiah 18:9). Those who honor this agreement daily, receive His glory eternally.

*"After a person has faith in Christ, repents of his sins, and is baptized for the remission of his sins and receives the Holy Ghost, (by the laying on of hands), which is the first Comforter, then let him continue to humble himself before God, **hungering and thirsting after righteousness**, and living by every word of God, and the **Lord will soon say unto him, Son thou shalt be exalted**.*
*When the Lord has **thoroughly proved him**, and finds that **the man is determined to serve Him at all hazards, then the man will find his calling and his election made sure...**"*
Joseph Smith, *Discourses of the Prophet Joseph Smith* [154]

For one to receive calling and election requires overcoming the world and being found true and faithful in *all things*. In addition to being clean from the blood and sins of this generation, scripture specifically states that he or she must demonstrate unyielding commitment to live by "*every word that proceedeth forth from the mouth of God.*" (D&C 84:44). Those able to hear and obey Father with exactness look forward to the day when "*the Lord will soon say unto him, Son thou shalt be exalted.*"[155]

The Quest for Exaltation
*"**The Lord said to the Prophet Joseph Smith** on one occasion, For I am the lord thy God, and will be with thee even unto the end of the world, and through all eternity; for verily **I seal upon you your exaltation, and prepare a throne for you in the kingdom of my Father, with Abraham your father** (D&C 132:49)....Behold, **I have seen your sacrifices**, and will forgive all your sins;*
*I have **seen your sacrifices in obedience** to that which I have told you. (D&C 132:50)....*
*He had been urging the people of his day to **make their calling and their election sure.***
He himself had made his calling and election sure. He gave that same witness to Heber C. Kimball.
*I suppose that a man who had that witness would be enjoying **the more sure word of prophecy, which the Prophet defines as...a man's knowing that he is sealed up unto eternal life, by revelation and the spirit of prophecy,** through the power of the Holy Priesthood."*
Marion G. Romney, *Conference Report* [156]

Today the church rarely discusses calling and election over the pulpit. It has been several decades since any type of encouragement to pursue that level of righteousness has been mentioned in general conference. Doctrine that Joseph Smith once taught as being essential has now become obscure and misunderstood.

"Oh! I beseech you go forward, go forward and make your calling and election sure;
and if any man preach any other gospel than that which I have preached, He shall be cursed.
Joseph Smith, *Teachings of the Prophet Joseph Smith* [157]

Cultural Assumption
Calling and election is *not* something we need to concern ourselves with in this life.

Before this current attitude became dominant, Elder Joseph Mcmurrin of the Seventy spoke in the 1904 General Conference and promised, *"Through keeping these commandments we can also depend upon the fullness of the promises made pertaining to the future…We must live in the present and attend to our duties as they are made known to us, if we are to have the approval of our Father in Heaven, and if we desire to make our calling and election sure. God has pointed out the way whereby we can make our calling and election sure."*[158]

Regardless of what the institution is currently choosing to omit, the Lord Himself eagerly awaits the time when He can lovingly proclaim, *"well done thou good and faithful servant."* (Matthew 25:21). To this end, calling and election has always been an individual journey and it remains so today. The Mormon masses may not be seeking the *"more sure word of prophecy"* (2 Peter 1:19), but a small and growing "few" know that the invitation to be sealed unto eternal life is literal, real, and essential.

A Personal Choice
"So far as I understand salvation, it is to be in harmony with the eternal principles of
the everlasting Gospel, to endeavor to be kind to ourselves, and to make our calling and election sure,
regardless of what others do."
George Teasdale, *Conference Report* [159]

From scripture and the words of early church leaders, all have been invited to come unto Jesus Christ and receive their calling and election. To arrive at this spiritual benchmark requires great knowledge, personal purity, and a willingness to serve Christ in all things. Those who meet these qualifications are blessed to receive this most sweet and glorious assurance:

"Thou shalt be exalted in the kingdom of thy Father!"

Who Will Believe?

*Verily, thus saith the Lord: It shall come to pass that every soul who forsaketh his sins and cometh
unto me, and calleth on my name, and obeyeth my voice, and keepeth my commandments,*
shall see my face and know that I am...
D&C 93:1

Those who adore the Lord Jesus Christ yearn for the day when they can return to His presence. Due to the "homesickness for heaven" they feel, they can't help but dream of a time when they will again be in His sacred embrace. These are they who wonder, if the scriptures are literal, is it really possible for me to be with Jesus in this life? And if so, what is required to grow from believing...to knowing...to touching?

*"The Prophet Joseph Smith informs us that the first Comforter or Holy Ghost has no other effect
than pure intelligence, and the Prophet continues by saying "The other Comforter spoken of is a subject
of great interest and perhaps understood by few of this generation. After receiving the first Comforter then
let him continue to humble himself before God, hungering and thirsting after righteousness, and living
by every word of God, and the Lord will say unto him, Son, thou shalt be exalted, etc.
When the Lord has thoroughly proven him and finds that the man will serve Him at all hazards then the
man will find his calling and election made sure. Then it will be his privilege to receive the other Comforter
which the Lord has promised the Saints as recorded in the testimony of St. John, 14: 12, 27. "Now what is
this other Comforter?" says Joseph: "It is no more nor less than the Lord Jesus Christ, and this is the sum
and substance of the matter, that when any man obtains this last Comforter he will have the personage
of Jesus Christ to attend him, or appear unto him from time to time
and even He will manifest the Father unto him."*
J. Golden Kimball, *Conference Report* [160]

If miracles and visitations of this magnitude continue to happen on the earth, what is required to have these type of holy experiences while still in the flesh? Must a person hold the position of prophet or apostle in the church?

All Are Eligible

*"If **all things operate by law**, and they do; if **God is no respecter of persons**, and certainly he is
perfectly impartial; if his course is one eternal round, never varying from age to age, and such truly is the
case—then **all of the gifts and graces and revelations ever given to any prophet, seer, or revelator
in any age will be given again to any soul who obeys the law entitling him so to receive.**
While discoursing about the Second Comforter and in setting forth that those whose callings and elections
have been made sure have the privilege of seeing the face of the Lord while they yet dwell **in the flesh**,
the Prophet Joseph Smith said: 'God hath not revealed anything to Joseph, but what He will make known
unto the Twelve, and **even the least Saint may know all things** as fast as he is able to bear them.'"*
Bruce R. McConkie, A New Witness for the Articles of Faith [161]

102

Is it possible that we have minimized certain scriptures, which were intended to be applied to this lifetime, by projecting their message out into the "next life?" Perhaps if we had taken the text literally and believed more deeply, miracles would have occurred. How we interpret scripture influences what we believe, and thus what we experience. Therefore receiving the Second Comforter may seem impossible to most-or even sacrilegious to some, but for those who deeply believe, "now" is the day of salvation!

His Promise

I will not leave you comfortless: I will come to you. Yet a little while, and the world seeth
me no more; *but ye see me: because I live,* ye shall live also. At that day ye shall know that
I am in my Father, and ye in me, and I in you. He that **hath my commandments,**
and keepeth them, he it is that loveth me: and he that loveth me shall be loved of my Father,
and I will love him, and will **manifest myself to him.** Judas saith unto him, not Iscariot,
Lord, how is it that thou wilt manifest thyself unto us, and not unto the world?
Jesus answered and said unto him, If a man love me, he will keep my words:
and my Father will love him, **and we will come unto him, and make our abode with him.**
John 14:18-23

If we insist on waiting until physical death to be embraced by the Lord, He will patiently wait. Those who choose to regain His holy presence in this life are required to keep His commandments, follow His voice with exactness, and be proven faithful in all things. It may seem impossible, but it can be done.

Whenever a soul comes to a place where they are ready to "get serious" about salvation and being redeemed from the Fall, it is wise to begin the process by making a conscious spiritual announcement.

This personal proclamation usually begins by finding a place within the soul where he or she can make a total surrender to God. In other words, you must "give permission" to Father to enact, inflict, and facilitate *all that is necessary,* that you might be able to endure kneeling in the Lord's presence. Making this conscious decision and then announcing it unto Father should be undertaken with serious contemplation and sacred intent, for the Lord will accept this choice, and thus unleash the necessary experiences to cleanse the soul from the blood and sins of this generation. (Warning: when this permission is sincerely given to God, the phrases *"to work out your salvation with fear and trembling,"* and a *"broken heart and contrite spirit,"* become literal.)

After making this sacred and private announcement, researching the content provided in the temple becomes paramount. For it is in the house of the Lord that we are introduced to the pattern required to part the veil and come into the Lord's presence. (see Truths #10 and #52).

"To those of understanding we say: The purpose of the endowment in the house of the Lord
*is to prepare and sanctify his **saints so they will be able to see his face, here and now,***
as well as to bear the glory of his presence in the eternal worlds."
Bruce R. McConkie, *The Promised Messiah: The First Coming of Christ* [162]

Within the temple, participants are taught the truths, tokens, and keys necessary to overcome the Fall and be redeemed of the Lord. The ceremony provided in the temple is a practice dress rehearsal meant to prepare us for the actual event.

The Real Endowment

"In general terms the endowment is not exclusively a temple ceremony.
*The temple endowment is a sacred ordinance that **prefigures an actual Endowment of power***
***from God which occurs much later**, and probably outside of an actual temple…The temple and the*
scriptures teaches us that a time may (come), if we are faithful, (when we) pierce the veil, enter the divine
presence, and be allowed to request an actual Endowment, a gift, from the hands of God…
This is The Endowment, the greatest outcome of mortality that occurs in mortality; a gift so glorious
that nobody but God could bestow it. It is this Endowment that the temple ordinance is prefiguring,
and which is the focal point of almost everything we experience within those sacred walls…
The reason the temple experience is so repetitive isn't to bless the departed, it is to super-
saturate the living with the message of how to righteously approach the veil.
The ceremony we call the endowment prefigures the mortal journey from the earliest stages
of spiritual childhood in the pre-mortal world, to the loftiest stages of spiritual maturity
in the natural world, which includes penetrating the veil, speaking with Christ,
and being endowed with power."
John Pontius, *Call to Zion* [163]

The endowment drama shown in the temple is actually the story of our own personal exaltation. During the presentation each character represented is symbolic of various aspects within the soul. For example, each of us possesses an Adam, Eve, and Lucifer tendency. Those willing to "awaken" and see the complexity of the internal universe are then invited to "cast out" all that is dark through the power of Christ Jesus. To successfully complete this process results in being personally sealed unto the Fathers forever. (see Truth #67).

Sealed in the Arms of Jesus

*"**The temple is the narrow channel through which one must pass to reenter the Lord's presence**.*
A mighty power pulls us through that channel, and it is the sealing power of the at-one-ment of the Lord
Jesus Christ. The Savior's at-one-ment is another word for the sealing power. By the power of the
*at-one-ment, **the Lord draws and seals his children to himself in the holy temples**. In scripture we*
can study how the ancient great ones were drawn through that narrow channel to find their heart's desire:
we find, for example, Adam, cast out, bereft of his Lord's presence, searching relentlessly in the lonely
world until he finds the keys to that passage to the Lord. Abraham searches for his priesthood privileges
(see Abraham 1:1) and after a diligent quest exclaims, "Thy servant has sought thee earnestly; now I have
found thee" (Abraham 2:12). Moses on Horeb, Lehi at the tree, Nephi on the mountain top all these men
*conducted that search which is outlined and empowered in the temple endowment, **gradually increasing***
the hold, the seal, between themselves and their Lord. This was the very search for which they
were put on earth: to rend the veil of unbelief, to yield to the pull of the Savior's sealing power,
***to stand in the Lord's presence, encircled about in the arms of his love.** (see D&C 6:20; 2 Nephi*
1:15). This then is the temple endowment: having been cast out, to search diligently according to the
*revealed path, and at last to **be clasped in the arms of Jesus.** (Mormon 5:11)."*
M. Catherine Thomas, *The Brother of Jared at the Veil* [164]

Through Christ's Atonement we can overcome all sin and live each day in harmony with eternal law. It is possible to consecrate our entire souls to God. Admittedly, we will still fail and fall short, but our loving Savior remains eager to accept our sincere attempt at full repentance. The essential question is how long will we make Him wait by keeping ourselves separated in the chains of sin.

Our Choice

"Moses sought diligently to bring Israel to the point where they "might behold the face of God."
But Israel failed and they could not receive the Second Comforter. The lesser priesthood was instituted,
and the possibility of seeing God was closed to them. But in our time, the possibility has been renewed.
Understand, Moses did see the face of God…Moses individually accepted the offer. The rank and file did
not. This unfortunate historic failing of Israel should not be repeated by us. The reason the ordinances are
universally available now, and the Temple rites are open to all, and the dialogue at the veil is open to all,
and the priesthood is so generally spread among all the Church members is to avoid this prior failing by
our ancestors. We are supposed to be doing better than they did. We, unlike them,
are supposed to behold the face of God."
Denver Snuffer, *Conversing with the Lord through the Veil* [165]

Through the cleansing blood of the Atonement, we become candidates to have an audience with Jesus Christ. Even then, despite our best efforts, it will still be necessary for Him to forgive us just prior to our entering into His presence, for *"no unclean thing can dwell with God."* (1 Nephi 10:21).

Therefore, sanctify yourselves that your minds become single to God, and the days will come
that you shall see him; for he will unveil his face unto you, and it shall be in his own time,
and in his own way, and according to his own will.
Doctrine and Covenants 88:67-68

Only the omniscient Master can determine when an adequate surrender and sacrifice has been offered. Until that day, let all who desire to be embraced by the Lord find peace in knowing that He will come in His own time, and in His own way, but come He will!

"A man had been praying for some time to meet one of the three Nephites. The Spirit spoke to him and said
in substance, "Why pray to meet one of them? Why not pray to meet the Savior?" So he began to pray
to meet the Savior. Not long thereafter his new prayer was answered at which time his calling and election
was also made sure. This man subsequently explained to my friend who told me this story that the Savior
loves us so much, it's like a child who wants a new bike that costs $150 but the child only has $1.
Simply by putting forth a sincere effort and putting up the $1, the Savior then makes up the difference.
We think it also worth noting that the Lord did not simply appear to him,
he had to ask for it before the Lord appeared."
Anonymous, *Experiencing the Mighty Change of Heart* [166]

To have Jesus visit in the flesh and relate to us as Savior and friend requires that our imperfect human desires be swallowed up in the wisdom of Father. By surrendering our very lives into the hands of God, we glorify Him and become candidates for receiving the Second Comforter.

The Death of "Self"

"It may appear more obvious to desire the Second Comforter to exult in the presence of our Savior;
to worship at his feet; to have the privilege of beholding his face, and tearfully thanking Him
for the gift of his atoning blood shed for our expense. But, as righteous as these things are,
such a motivation is nowhere listed as sufficient to part the heavens. There is a greater purpose,
one which powers the mighty mainspring of eternity and engages the gears of everlasting law,
and that purpose, when it is the only light that burns in our hearts, not just one of many flickering desires,
but when our eye becomes single to this aspect of the glory of God, then our hearts will be pure indeed;
then the heavens will open, and the One whom holy writ calls Wonderful, Counselor, the Mighty God,
the Everlasting Father, the Prince of Peace, will step through the veil.
The exact process to so obtaining cannot be annotated here, simply because it will be different
for each of us, aligning with our pre-mortally covenanted calling, and also with the divine genome that
uniquely defines each soul. But, in addition to these indefinable specifics, there will be a common theme;
like an exquisite melody whose harmonies are the lives of the righteous.
This common desire is that we might, like John, whom the Savior called Beloved, prolong our service
to our master beyond the scope of mortality, and beyond the ability of mortals,
to do far more than the laws of opposition allow; to sacrifice ourselves in
Christ-like grace to the cause of His glory. (3 Nephi 28:6)."
John Pontius, *The Triumph of Zion* [167]

To assist us in making whatever sacrifice is required, and that we might be prepared for our own personal day of salvation, the parable of the ten virgins is provided.

Then shall the kingdom of heaven be likened unto ten virgins, which took their lamps,
and went forth to meet the bridegroom. And five of them were wise, and five were foolish.
They that were foolish took their lamps, and took no oil with them: But the wise took oil in their vessels
with their lamps. While the bridegroom tarried, they all slumbered and slept.
And at midnight there was a cry made, Behold, the bridegroom cometh; go ye out to meet him.
Then all those virgins arose, and trimmed their lamps. And the foolish said unto the wise,
Give us of your oil; for our lamps are gone out. But the wise answered, saying,
Not so; lest there be not enough for us and you: but go ye rather to them that sell, and buy for yourselves.
And while they went to buy, the bridegroom came; and they that were ready went in with him
to the marriage: and the door was shut. Afterward came also the other virgins, saying,
Lord, Lord, open to us. But he answered and said, Verily I say unto you, I know you not.
Watch therefore, for ye know neither the day nor the hour wherein the Son of man cometh.
Matthew 25:1-13

Initially, we may assume it is "non-members" or the "inactive" who represent the "unwise virgins." But careful analysis reveals that *all ten* had been invited to the marriage feast, *all ten* were supposedly seeking the Bridegroom, and *all ten* had personally been introduced to temple symbolism.

One interpretation of the parable is that only a portion of even the active Saints will have the oil of the Holy Spirit burning in their souls. These are they who watch closely for the day of their own personal Second Coming.

"Thus, of divine necessity, the supporting circle around Jesus gets smaller and smaller and smaller, giving significance to Matthew's words: 'All the disciples left him, and fled.' Peter stayed near enough to be recognized and confronted. John stood at the foot of the cross with Jesus' mother. Especially and always the blessed women in the Savior's life stayed as close to Him as they could. But essentially His lonely journey back to His Father continued without comfort or companionship…This Easter week and always, may we stand by Jesus Christ " at all times and in all things, and in all places that we may be in, even until death," for surely that is how He stood by us when it was unto death and when He had to stand entirely and utterly alone."

Jeffrey R. Holland, *None Were with Him*[168]

A fundamental growth step occurs when we grow from wanting to be with Jesus in the next life to seeking His loving face in this life. Those who will believe the necessary doctrine choose to gain knowledge from the temple and become purified from the blood and sins of this generation. These are they who can be received of the Lord while still on the earth. This glorious and holy event has occurred many times to many souls.

Am I Ready?

"Jesus has been upon the earth a great many more times than you are aware of. When Jesus makes his next appearance upon the earth, but few of this Church will be prepared to receive him and see him face to face and converse with him; but he will come to his temple."

Brigham Young, *Discourses of Brigham Young* [169]

Heaven and Hell

*"You are talking about heaven and about earth, and about hell, but let me tell you, **you are in hell now, and you have got to qualify yourselves here in hell to become subjects for heaven; and even when you have got into heaven, you will find it right here where you are on this earth**. When we escape from this earth, we suppose we are going to heaven? Do you suppose you are going to the earth that Adam came from? That Eloheim came from? Where Jehovah the Lord came from? No. When you have learned to become obedient to the Father that dwells upon this earth, to the Father and God of this earth, **and obedient to the messengers He sends**—when you have done all that, remember **you are not going to leave this earth. You will never leave it until you become qualified, and capable, and capacitated to become a father of an earth yourselves. Not one soul of you ever will leave this earth, for if you go to hell, it is on this earth; and if you go to heaven, it is on this earth; and you will not find it anywhere else."***

Heber C. Kimball, *Journal of Discourses* [170]

In the pre-mortal realm, Satan rebelled against God and was cast out with a third part of the hosts of heaven. When pondering the location where Satan and these spirits were evicted, scripture reveals that the adversary was *cast out into the earth* (Revelations 12:8) and that he is now the temporary *"god of this world."* (2 Corinthians 4:4).

"Neither was there place found in heaven for the great dragon, who was cast out; that old serpent called the devil, and also called Satan, which deceiveth the whole world; he was cast out into the earth; and his angels were cast out with him."

JST Revelation 12:8

These scriptures, as well as the state of the world today, invite us to accept that **the world in which we currently live is indeed "hell."**

Welcome to Hell

"And it came to pass that Adam, being tempted of the devil—for, behold, the devil was before Adam, for he rebelled against me, saying, Give me thine honor, which is my power; and also a third part of the hosts of heaven turned he away from me because of their agency; And they were thrust down, and thus came the devil and his angels; And, behold, there is a place prepared for them from the beginning, which place is hell."

Doctrine and Covenants 29:36-38

When we embody onto the earth we initially see *"through a glass darkly."* (1 Corinthians 13:12). We perceive ourselves to be completely separated from God. This illusion is not without merit, for in forgetting Father's glory, as well as our own true and eternal identity, we are provided with a context to experience good and evil objectively.

108

"And it must needs be that the devil should tempt the children of men, or they could not be agents unto themselves; for if they never should have bitter they could not know the sweet."
Doctrine and Covenants 29:39

Most of us spend years in the "bitter," reinforcing the spiritual bars that keep us imprisoned. Instead of turning to Jesus Christ and finding a freedom that can only be found in Him, we allow the deceiver to seduce us into choosing actions that separate us from the Divine. This is sin. The result is a life of stress, anger, despair, and pain. Thus, "hell" is *both* a physical location and an internal state of being that results from our continued spiritual ignorance.

"Hell is a disease in the human mind.
The whole world is a hospital."
Don Miguel Ruiz, *Beyond Fear* [171]

As our eye becomes single to the glory of God, the veil thins and we begin to see things *"as they really are."* (Jacob 4:13). How paradoxical it is that in the awakening, we finally sense the horror and depth of our individual fall. Once we accept the seriousness of our spiritual predicament, we can begin to work out our salvation with real fear and trembling. Coming to know Jesus Christ as Savior and friend reveals that He is our only chance for escaping the lone and dreary world of the natural man. Surely there is no other way.

"Spirituality, our true aim, is the consciousness of victory over self, and of communion with the Infinite.
Spirituality impels one to conquer difficulties and acquire more and more strength.
To feel one's faculties unfolding, and truth expanding in the soul, is one of life's sublimest experiences."
David O. Mckay, *Conference Report* [172]

On earth God uses experiences of good and evil, light and darkness, and joy and sorrow to strengthen the soul and awaken us to the Christ essence within. In this sense, *all* that we experience here in mortality will eventually be seen as useful. Thus, we should literally *"thank the Lord…in all things."* (D&C 59:7).

Individually we have chosen to subject ourselves to specific scenarios involving fear, challenge, and temptation. We agreed to this refining process that in **submitting to all things, we might transcend all things**. Although difficult at times to appreciate, it is during the sorrowful shattering of the broken heart that we learn to *walk the way of The Christ.*

Flow in Christ
"But in reality, the life of the disciple of Christ can become very simple – he need only hold his mind to one main idea: to abide in Christ, to be in position: "God gives the wind, and the water, and the heat; man but puts himself in the way of the wind, fixes his water-wheel in the way of the river, puts his piston in the way of the steam; and so holding himself in position before God's Spirit, all the energies of Omnipotence course within his soul…Such is the deeper lesson to be learned from considering the lily. It is the voice of nature echoing the whole evangel of Jesus, 'Come unto Me, and I will give you rest." Of course there must be doing, but the doing must flow from the tranquil mind, seeking nothing for itself in the doing; rather, open to present beauties, desiring to bless this moment with Peace. So, it appears then that for one to grow up in Christ, one need only yield to that flow of energy

*and life that leads from one blessing to another, that opens the eyes to Divinities. The fruits of this
awareness may keep us just as busy as a person who is trying to save himself by his own works,
but it will have a different flavor, a sweeter fragrance, a deeper serenity. Life is happening through us.
Let us stand back and let the Christ-stream flow."*
M. Catherine Thomas, *Christ-Stream-Why are We So Anxious?*[173]

Those willing to be on the Lord's errand request that the heavens lead them in their daily
ministry. They consistently question, "How might I truly know God? And what is specifically
required of me that I might overcome the Fall and complete my telestial probation here on earth?
Disciple Alan Cook summarizes the answer, *"Not that much-just everything!"* This includes all of
our time, talents, efforts, desires, intentions, words, works, thoughts, ambitions, dreams...The
entirety of our agency, breath after breath...year after year. The complete soul, nothing left but
the *"mind of Christ."* (1 Corinthians 2:16).

On Earth, As It Is In Heaven
*"I will put my own definition to the term sanctification, and say it consists in **overcoming every
sin** and **bringing all into subjection to the law of Christ**. God has placed in us a pure spirit;
when this reigns predominant, without let or hindrance, and **triumphs over the flesh
and rules and governs and controls as the Lord controls the heavens and the earth,**
this I call the blessing of sanctification."*
Brigham Young, *Teachings of Latter Day Prophets* [174]

When we surrender our desires into the Lord's will and then act as He directs, one level
of discipleship has been achieved. His heaven the comes into our hell.

Consecrating the Flesh
*"The highest achievement of spirituality comes as we conquer the flesh...As givers gain control
of their desires and properly see other needs in light of their own wants, then the powers of the gospel
are released in their lives. They learn that by living the great law of consecration
they insure not only temporal salvation, but also spiritual sanctification."*
Spencer W. Kimball, *Conference Report* [175]

When the law of consecration is no longer just doctrinal theory, but an actual daily practice,
all that we have, and all that we are, accumulates into a peaceful obsession for Christ.
By communing with God in our private closets and on the top of sacred mountains, spiritual
tools practiced in the temple become alive and valid. We transcend this lone and dreary
world...literally.

*"Prayer is how we knock. But it is not just any kind of prayer that "knocks."
Knocking reminds us of the series of taps given in sacred places and which symbolically allows
us to enter into the presence of the Lord. Recall how prayer is offered prior to that ceremonial entrance.
Nevertheless, this is how an individual can actually knock at the real veil –
through the true order of prayer, and if he is ready to come to God (clean and pure),
then God is ready to open the heavens and tell all about it."*
Craig Mills, *Home Sanctuary* [176]

The gospel of Jesus Christ invites us to awake and arise. Those who do so fully overcome the Fall, complete their telestial probation, and become kings and queens unto the Most High God. These souls enter into the Church of the Firstborn and the next stage of their unfolding exaltation. (see Truth #23).

The manner in which we grow and advance is similar to the cosmic progression of the earth. After the transgression of Adam and Eve, the earth was also cursed and "fell" out of her paradisiacal glory into its current telestial orbit. Similar to how personal redemption requires overcoming temptation, sorrow, and sin, so too must Mother Earth endure the cleansing of destruction, war, and natural disaster. Eventually both the souls of men and spirit of this planet will be redeemed and dwell within a *"new heaven and a new earth."* (Revelations 21:1).

"This earth is our home, it was framed expressly for the habitation of those who are faithful to God,
and who prove themselves worthy to inherit the earth when the Lord shall have sanctified,
purified and glorified it and brought it back into his presence, from which it fell far into space…
When the earth was framed and brought into existence and man was placed upon it, it was near the throne
of our Father in heaven. And when man fell—though that was designed in the economy, there was nothing
about it mysterious or unknown to the Gods, they understood it all, it was all planned—
but when man fell, the earth fell into space, and took up its abode in this planetary system,
and the sun became our light. When the Lord said—"Let there be light," there was light,
for the earth was brought near the sun that it might reflect upon it so as to give us light by day,
and the moon to give us light by night. This is the glory the earth came from, and when it is glorified
it will return again unto the presence of the Father, and it will dwell there, and these intelligent beings
that I am looking at, if they live worthy of it, will dwell upon this earth."
Brigham Young, *Journal of Discourses* [177]

Comparing the currently un-exalted earth *we live on*, to the un-exalted soul *we live in*, provides a spiritual parallel for both personal and global transformation. It is fascinating to consider how the Gods of the Eloheim are utilizing this telestial realm to bring both people and the planet "out of hell" and into paradisiacal glory. This cosmic perspective, and others like it, encourage us to consider that the plan of salvation may entail much more than we previously imagined.

But remember that all my judgments are not given unto men;
and as the words have gone forth out of my mouth even so shall they be fulfilled, that the first
shall be last, and that the last shall be first in all things whatsoever I have created
by the word of my power, which is the power of my Spirit.
D&C 29:30

Nine years after the church was organized, and seven years after it came under condemnation, the Prophet Joseph Smith said, *"I never have had the opportunity to give them the plan that God has revealed to me."*[178] This curious statement encourages us to ponder what other elements the plan of salvation might entail.

"…It is said that those of the terrestrial glory will be ministered unto by those of the celestial; and those of the telestial will be ministered unto by those of the terrestrial – that is, those of the higher glory minister to those of a lesser glory. I can conceive of no reason for all this administration of the higher to the lower, unless it be for the purpose of advancing our Father's children along the lines of eternal progression…"
B.H. Roberts, *New Witnesses for God* [179]

Today, the church teaches that *"life is a test"* provided for *spiritual progression*, and that mortality has been provided for us so we can grow *"line upon line."* (2 Nephi 28:30). Despite these solid truths, most of the culture has *also* determined that God, in the name of "justice," is required to place His less valiant souls in a telestial or terrestrial kingdom forever—without any hope of increase. Once this "final judgment" has occurred, there is supposedly no hope for that soul to progress beyond the assigned kingdom. Elder Bruce R. McConkie, reinforced this belief by teaching that it was heresy to believe *"there is progression from one kingdom to another in the eternal worlds or that lower kingdoms eventually progress to where higher kingdoms once were.*[180]

In response to these mainstream ideas concerning what God can and cannot do throughout all eternity, we should remember each of us lives within a veil of incomplete understanding. Determining the final destiny of souls, based on our current interpretation of scripture, only serves to reinforce human ignorance concerning God and His infinite and eternal plan.

Eternal Is His Name
For, behold, the mystery of godliness, how great is it! For, behold, I am endless, and the punishment which is given from my hand is endless punishment, for Endless is my name. Wherefore-Eternal punishment is God's punishment. Endless punishment is God's punishment.
D&C 19:10-12

The manner in which the Mormon mainstream usually interprets this verse requires us to ask, should we take a deeper look at how we perceive God and His plan of salvation? Do our cultural assumptions about justice and the three degrees of glory accurately represent who Father is, and what He has planned for our eventual exaltation? Surely in relation to eternal compassion and spiritual logic, there must be more to the story.

"It is reasonable to believe, in the absence of direct revelation…that, in accordance with God's plan of eternal progression, advancement from grade to grade within any kingdom, and from kingdom to kingdom, will be provided for. But if the recipients of a lower glory be enabled to advance, surely the intelligences of higher rank will not be stopped in their progress; and thus we may conclude, that degrees and grades will ever characterize the kingdoms of our God. Eternity is progressive; perfection is relative; the essential feature of God's living purpose is its associated power of eternal increase."
James E. Talmage, *The Articles of Faith* [181]

From scripture, we are provided an essential clue for understanding how God teaches His children about salvation and eternity.

And surely every man must repent or suffer, for I, God, am endless.
Wherefore, I revoke not the judgments which I shall pass, but woes shall go forth, weeping, wailing
and gnashing of teeth, yea, to those who are found on my left hand. Nevertheless, it is not written
that there shall be no end to this torment, but it is written endless torment. Again, it is written eternal
damnation; wherefore it is more express than other scriptures, that it might work upon the hearts
of the children of men, altogether for my name's glory. Wherefore, I will explain unto you this mystery,
for it is meet unto you to know even as mine apostles.
D&C 19:4-8

How fascinating, that according to this scripture, God allows us to believe in our current interpretation of scripture, *"that it might work upon the hearts of the children of men,"* until we are eventually prepared to receive the greater paradigm.

Jesus had not finished his work when his body was slain, neither did he finish it after his resurrection
from the dead; although he had accomplished the purpose for which he then came to the earth,
he had not fulfilled all his work. And when will he? Not until he has redeemed and saved
every son and daughter of our father Adam that have been or ever will be born upon this earth
to the end of time, except the sons of perdition. That is his mission.[3]
Joseph F. Smith, *Gospel Doctrine* [182]

Because Latter Day Saints believe that the soul continues to progress after physical death, it becomes relevant to question, how, where, and in what manner the growth occurs.

"I am not a strict constructionalist, believing that we seal our eternal progress by what we do here.
It is my belief that God will save all of His children that he can: and while, if we live unrighteously here,
we shall not go to the other side in the same status, so to speak, as those who lived righteously;
nevertheless, the unrighteous will have their chance, and in the eons of the eternities that are to follow,
they, too, may climb to the destinies to which they who are righteous and serve God,
have climbed to those eternities that are to come."
J. Reuben Clark, *Church News* [183]

Most Mormons have decided that God can only send a soul to earth one time, but as will be briefly summarized here, early church leaders had a different perspective concerning salvation and what is now termed "multiple mortalities." Admittedly, a full discussion of "re-mortalization" and what a *"continuation of the lives"* might entail, is beyond the scope of this text. (D&C 132:22-25). What will be stated here, is that there are key differences between the doctrine of "re-incarnation," (which is a false teaching offensive to the divinity within), and God's wise utilization of multiple probations. (To further explore this doctrine see, *"Teachings of the Doctrine of Eternal Lives"*[184]).

"Upon the same principle, supposing I have a lump of clay which I put upon my wheel, out of which clay
I want to make a jug; I have to turn it into as many as 50 or 100 shapes before I get it into a jug.
How many shapes do you suppose you are put into before you become Saints,
or before you become perfect and sanctified to enter into the celestial glory of God?"
Heber C. Kimball, *Journal of Discourses* [185]

Apparently, those who are able to "graduate" from this lone and dreary world are "shaped" until they have become *"clean from the blood and sins of this generation."* For most, accomplishing this high level of righteousness, would require more than just one mortal experience. (D&C 76:50-70).

"Here then is eternal life- to know the only wise and true God;
and you have got to learn howto be Gods yourselves, *and to be kings and priests to God,*
the ***same as all Gods have done before you,*** *namely, by going from one small degree to another,*
and from a small capacity to a great one; ***from grace to grace, from exaltation to exaltation..."***
Joseph Smith, *Teachings of the Prophet Joseph Smith* [186]

It seems reasonable to at least consider that there are multiple climbs as we grow from exaltation to exaltation. And if this realm provides the needed opposition and opportunity to choose between good and evil, isn't it possible that Father might send His growing children back to Earth to continue their progression? Perhaps we magnify from probation to probation until we have transcended this telestial world and are able to enter into a terrestrial realm. Brigham Young taught, *"This world is a poor miserable hell...The Lord will* ***bring every person*** *to their covenant* ***either sooner or later*** *if it must be that they serve a probation in hell, he has to make atone in hell* ***and bring them back*** *to comply with it."*[187]

"Joseph always told us that we would have to pass by sentinels that are placed between us
and our Father and God. Then, of course, we are conducted along ***from this probation***
to other probations, *or from one dispensation to another..."*
Heber C. Kimball, *Journal of Discourses* [188]

In truth, this fallen realm is perfect for providing the context needed to demonstrate deep faith, offer real sacrifice, and experience the broken heart and contrite spirit necessary to obtain salvation.

Eternity to Eternity

"The Lord said to Jeremiah the Prophet...the clay that marred in the potters hands was
thrown back into the unprepared portion, to be prepared over again. So it will be with every wicked man
and woman, and every wicked nation, kingdom, and government upon the earth, sooner or later;
they will be thrown back to the native element from which they originated,
to be worked over again, and be prepared to enjoy some sort of kingdom."
Brigham Young, *Journal of Discourses* [189]

Perhaps if we die in our sins, without having been fully *"born of God"* (Alma 36:24), the Lord is required, in relation to eternal justice to say, *"Depart from me, ye that work iniquity."* (Matthew 7:23). Could it also be true that when the physical body dies unprepared or prematurely, our loving Heavenly Father reviews our spiritual progress, and in mercy offers us another chance to return and try again?

Going Back to Hell?

And they who remain shall also be quickened; nevertheless, they shall return again to their own place,
(the telestial kingdom or world in which we now live?), *to enjoy that which they are willing
to receive, because they were not willing to enjoy that which they might have received.*
D&C 88:32

The principle of "re-mortalization" can also bring great comfort concerning those who have died entwined in the chains of sin. Although mercy cannot rob justice (Alma 42:25), "*God's punishment*" may center around Him tailoring the next perfect life scenario.

"You that are mourning about your children straying away will have your sons and your daughters. If you succeed in passing through these trials and afflictions and receive a resurrection, you will, by the power of the Priesthood, work and labor, as the Son of God has, until you get all your sons and daughters in the path of exaltation and glory. This is just as sure as that the sun rose this morning over yonder mountains. Therefore, mourn not because all your sons and daughters do not follow in the path that you have marked out to them, or give heed to your counsels. Inasmuch as we succeed in securing eternal glory, and stand as saviors, and as kings and priests to our God, we will save our posterity. When Jesus went through that terrible torture on the cross, He saw what would be accomplished by it; He saw that His brethren and sisters the sons and daughters of God would be gathered in, with but few exceptions those who committed the unpardonable sin. That sacrifice of the divine Being was effectual to destroy the powers of Satan. I believe that every man and woman who comes into this life and passes through it, that life will be a success in the end. It may not be in this life. It was not with the antedeluvians. They passed through troubles and afflictions; 2,500 years after that, when Jesus went to preach to them, the dead heard the voice of the Son of God and they lived. They found after all that it was a very good thing that they had conformed to the will of God in leaving the spiritual life and passing through this world."
Lorenzo Snow, *Collected Discourses* [190]

In comparison to how traditional Christianity promotes "punishment and hell," we Latter Day Saints are blessed to be taught of a loving and merciful God. And yet when we, living in a veil of illusion, feel comfortable determining what God can and can't do for eternity, we have imagined a very puny and impotent God. The reality is that God and His glorious plan is much grander than our common religious understanding.

Plural Probations
*"…When the sun goes down, I lay down to sleep, which is typical of death;
and in the morning I rise and commence my work where I left it yesterday.
That course is typical of **the probations** we take."*
Heber C. Kimball, *Journal of Discourses* [191]

For those who understand the high spiritual standard required for celestial glory, but are heavy laden with sin and weakness, the doctrine of multiple probations offers a spiritual lifeline of hope. Although the Mormon mainstream may recoil at the idea, the possibility of returning to earth to continue our progression honors both eternal justice and divine mercy.

And the scribes and Pharisees brought unto him a woman taken in adultery; and when they had set her
in the midst, They say unto him, Master, this woman was taken in adultery, in the very act.
Now Moses in the law commanded us, that such should be stoned: but what sayest thou?…
But Jesus stooped down…and said unto them, He that is without sin among you,
let him first cast a stone at her. And again he stooped down, and wrote on the ground.
And they which heard it, being convicted by their own conscience, went out one by one,
beginning at the eldest, even unto the last: and Jesus was left alone, and the woman standing
in the midst. When Jesus had lifted up himself, and saw none but the woman, he said unto her,
Woman, where are those thine accusers? hath no man condemned thee?
She said, No man, Lord. And Jesus said unto her, Neither do I condemn thee: go, and sin no more.
John 8: 3-11

Even earthly parents, flawed and selfish, rarely give up on their children. So why do we imagine a perfect and eternal Heavenly Father and Mother would have such a limited plan of salvation? In reality the efforts of the Gods to redeem us never end, for "now" is the day of salvation—and it always will be.

Never Give Up

"There is never a time when the spirit is too old to approach God. All are within the reach
of pardoning mercy, who have not committed the unpardonable sin, which hath no forgiveness,
neither in this world, nor in the world to come. There is a way to release the spirits of the dead;
that is by the power and authority of the Priesthood—by binding and loosing on earth.
This doctrine appears glorious, inasmuch as it exhibits the greatness of divine compassion
and benevolence in the extent of the plan of human salvation."
Joseph Smith, *History of the Church* [192]

How comforting to know that the spirit is never too old to approach God, and that His mercy endures beyond the grave. Praise be unto Almighty God for the gift of His most majestic Son!

In relation to justice, the reality is that until we have been fully redeemed from the Fall and experienced our own personal "second coming," we are not yet ready for the promise of a glorious resurrection in Christ. However, if we are willing to keep changing, He will keep inviting us into His immortality and eternal life. Worlds without end.

Behold, I say unto you, that there is no resurrection—or, I would say, in other words,
that this mortal does not put on immortality, this corruption does not put on incorruption—
until after the coming of Christ. Behold, he bringeth to pass the resurrection of the dead.
But behold, my son, the resurrection is not yet. Now, I unfold unto you a mystery…
*Behold, there is a time appointed that **all shall come forth from the dead**. Now when this time cometh*
*no one knows; but God knoweth the time which is appointed. Now, **whether there shall***
be one time, or a second time, or a third time, that men shall come forth from the dead,
it mattereth not; *for God knoweth all these things; and it sufficeth me to know that this is the case-*
*that there is a time appointed that **all shall rise from the dead**.*
Alma 40:2-10

The "coming of Christ" Alma referred to is a personal visit from Jesus, which occurs to all who were once spiritually "dead," but now live in Him! (see Truth #21). The promise by Alma that *"all shall rise from the dead,"* (physically and eventually spiritually), contains an implied message of hope for those who insist on trusting in a God who is available *"eternity to eternity."* (D&C 76:2-8).

For behold, this is my work and my glory—to bring to pass
the immortality and eternal life of man."
Moses 1:39

Great is his wisdom, marvelous are his ways,
and the extent of his doings none can find out.
His purposes fail not, neither are there any who can stay his hand.
D&C 76: 2-3

God does not fail, but we can delay His victory if we insist on remaining in our sins. The Lord has said, *"Behold, ye are little children and ye cannot bear all things now; ye must grow in grace and in the knowledge of the truth. Fear not, little children, for you are mine, and I have overcome the world, and you are of them that my Father hath given me;* **And none of them that my Father hath given me shall be lost."** (D&C 50:40-42). This does not mean the requirements of salvation will be lowered, only that God will continue to accept our ongoing repentance and apply the blood of the infinite and eternal Atonement, experience after experience…life after life…until finally we are transformed into the nature of godliness.

In truth, God has a specific plan for each soul that spans many lifetimes and involves numerous experiences. Jesus Christ has always been the solution and continues to be our one-way ticket out of hell. He is our escape and the only source of true salvation. Although the death of the natural man does not usually come quickly, mortal life is the gift provided to assist us in overcoming any sin that might require us to again return to a telestial probation. During our progression, Father allows the serpent to bruise our heel, until we are able to "crush its head!"

"The Church is full of very good people who believe in Jesus Christ.
They, however, have not been "valiant" in the testimony of Christ even if they think they have.
There are varying degrees of resurrection, infinite numbers really, but at the time of mortal death
there is a division into only two: life or death. Many will have done good works in this life,
even in the name of Christ, but will have not yet qualified for a resurrection to life,
thus they remain in the rounds of telestial existence."
Anonymous Saint

One way to conceptualize the *"one eternal round,"* (1 Nephi 10:19), is that our "current life" becomes the "pre-mortal life" for the next mortality. In that sense, our present life experience should be respected with great importance, for this would be **our only chance** to work out our salvation and be loyal to Christ in this ***unique and specific set of circumstances.*** If we are to be *"saviors on Mount Zion"* to our current family and loved ones, now is the day to be redeemed in Him! This sobering reality partially explains why *"Ye cannot say, when ye are brought to that awful crisis, (physical death) that I will repent, that I will return to my God. Nay, ye cannot say this; for that same spirit which doth possess your bodies at the time that ye go out of this life, that same spirit will have power to possess your body in that eternal world."* (Alma 34:34). This is why we must repent now and not *"procrastinate the day of our repentance"* (Alma 34:33), *"for after this day of life, which is given us to prepare for eternity, behold, if we do not improve our time while in this life, then cometh the night of darkness wherein there can be no labor performed."* (Alma 34:33).

No wonder the modern-day church doesn't teach about multiple mortalities any longer. With so much apathy and procrastination already occurring, this "mystery" should only be understood by those already serious about receiving complete redemption in Christ.

Another reason this topic should be approached with wisdom is that whenever we work toward grasping the mysteries, whatever is being considered inevitably correlates with other gospel truths. To blend greater light into a more complex paradigm requires aligning pieces of the doctrinal puzzle simultaneously. Specifically in relation to considering multiple mortalities, and how God may use that gift to facilitate salvation, an understanding of the "intelligence" and how the "higher self" embodies is essential. (see Truth #62 for further clarification).

It has been this author's experience that most souls seeking Zion and the greater glories of God eventually come to believe in multiple probations. However, most go through an initial stage where they consider the principle, feel some initial "spiritual dissonance," and then eventually come to terms with the teaching. The doctrine does require some re-ordering and re-conceptualizing of how we previously perceived the plan of salvation. To some the idea is extremely disturbing. To others it becomes a lifeline of hope, a motivator, and a key principle for magnifying their performance in this lifetime. Perhaps the difference between the reactions is whether or not the principle applies to the unique life path of that particular soul. For many, it may not be relevant at all, while for others, it may assist them in completing their errand from the Lord.

> *"God has fulfilled His promises to us, and our prospects are grand and glorious.*
> *Yes, in the next life we will have our wives, and our sons and daughters.*
> *If we do not get them all at once, we will have them some time,*
> *for every knee shall bow and every tongue shall confess that Jesus is the Christ."*
> Lorenzo Snow, *The Teachings of Lorenzo Snow*, p 195.

When pondering all that salvation, exaltation, and eternity may entail, terms come to our mind such as "one eternal round," "eternal progression," and "eternal lives." What remains consistent is that as a seeker of truth, you just never quite get to the bottom…With God, the story always expands and deepens. Often what is revealed challenges the assumptions of the previous understanding. This is how it should be, worlds without end…

"There is much which appears mysterious in the plan of salvation, and there is an eternity of mystery to be unfolded to us; and when we have lived millions of years in the presence of God and angels, and have associated with heavenly beings, shall we then cease learning? No, or eternity ceases. There is no end. We go from grace to grace, from light to light, from truth to truth."
Brigham Young, *Journal of Discourses*[193]

It appears self-evident that in relation to eternity and salvation, there are numerous truths, principles, gifts, and powers, that due to our current fallen state, simply are not yet relative to our spiritual progression. (translation, transfiguration, time travel, trans-relocation, etc…) But as we grow in our spirituality, if we are serious about Zion and celestial glory, all truth and power must eventually become personally relevant.

A Peculiar People?

We Mormons are a peculiar people. We say we believe in the mysteries of God,
but when we are introduced to one, we usually reject the new information.

We Mormons are a peculiar people. We say life is a "test," and that we are here to grow
line upon line, but when a greater "line" is explained, we frequently condemn the perspective
as a being deception.

We Mormons are a peculiar people. We say we believe in eternal progression,
but when a partial explanation of how that is to occur is suggested,
we proclaim it to be false-doctrine.

Indeed,
We are a peculiar people.

As was discussed in Truth #18, we should avoid denying something just because it initially makes us uncomfortable. Temporary bewilderment is a normal part of being stretched into a greater view of God and His universe.

As always, the Holy Spirit is our sure witness of truth. If it is God's will for us to have increased perspective, He will lead us into greater light. Therefore, we need not live in constant fear of being *tossed to and fro, and carried about with every wind of doctrine* (Ephesians 4;14), but can instead trust in Him to teach us of His ways.

Life After Life

"As I thought about it I remarked that we do use words rather loosely when we speak of the 'life before this, and this life, and the next life,' as though we were a cat of nine lives, when as a matter of fact, we only have one life. This life we speak of did not begin with mortal birth. This life does not end with mortal death…immortality means to eventually gain a body that will no longer be subject to the pains of mortality, no longer subject to another mortal death, and no longer disillusioned."
Harold B. Lee, *Teachings of the Presidents of the Church* [194]

Regardless of how many probations we may have personally experienced, *remember, it is this current life that matters most and that we need not wait for the "next life" to repent and come into the fullness of salvation.* The often implied, but always urgent message is: Awake! Come unto Jesus Christ! For *"now is the day of salvation."* (2 Corinthians 6:2). For when we have had enough sorrow and tutoring in this world of choice and experience, and the desire for Jesus outweighs everything the planet has to offer, the soul turns skyward and shouts, "Hosanna to His name! Glory to the Almighty God for the gift of His most merciful Son! For surely, now and forever, He is the way, the truth, and the life!"

But behold, the Lord hath redeemed my soul from hell; I have beheld his glory, and I am encircled about eternally in the arms of his love.
2 Nephi 1:13-15

"Mother Teresa's mission to serve others unable to meet their own needs burned deep in her heart. Finally, at the age of thirty nine, she was allowed to pursue her passion in poverty stricken Calcutta. On her first day, she encountered a man lying in the gutter, so covered with disease and insects that everyone avoided him. Mother Teresa knelt down next to him and began cleaning his infested body. He was so astounded at her caring, he asked her, "Why are you helping me?" Mother Teresa smiled and replied, "Because I love you."
Joan Rawlusyk, *Reach Out and Touch Someone* [195]

Disciples of Jesus Christ love and serve all people in and out of the church. The result of being filled with the *"pure love of Christ"* (Moroni 7:47-48) is an all-encompassing desire to love God and bless others. These are the souls who become eligible to grow from membership in the LDS church, to spiritual inclusion within the *"Church of the Firstborn."* (D&C 76:94).

*And thus we saw **the glory of the celestial**, which excels in all things—where God, even the Father, reigns upon his throne forever and ever; Before whose throne all things bow in humble reverence, and give him glory forever and ever. **They who dwell in his presence are the church of the Firstborn**; and they see as they are seen, and know as they are known, having received of his fullness and of his grace.*
D&C 76:92-94

When hearing the phrase *"Church of the Firstborn,"* most assume that because Jesus Christ is the *"firstborn,"* the title must be referring to His restored Church. This interpretation is sufficient until we begin to pursue a true fullness of the gospel and desire to transcend this lone and dreary world.

*"**What is the difference, if there is a difference between the Church of the Firstborn and The Church of Jesus Christ of Latter-day Saints**, or of any day saints? Well, the members of the Church of the Firstborn are members of the Church of Jesus Christ, but not all those who are members of the Church of Jesus Christ become members of the Church of the Firstborn, for they are they unto whom the Lord has given all things. They are priests and kings. They are they who have received the exaltation, they who are made equal in power, and in might, and in dominion, who attain to the fullness and become the sons, and for the sisters, the daughters of God…**Brethren and sisters, we cannot be satisfied with just membership in this Church**. We should live to be worthy of and pray for the fullness of the blessings of our Father's kingdom."*
Joseph Fielding Smith, *Seek Ye Earnestly* [196]

Entering into the *"Church of the Firstborn"* requires sanctification to the degree that the natural man is cast off and the soul is fully redeemed from the Fall. Those Saints who accomplish this degree of righteousness are not only ordained *to someday* become kings and queens, but have actually received their full endowment. These are they who have parted the veil, completed their telestial probation, and are now able to enter into the terrestrial/celestial "Church."

> *"The scriptures speak of those who qualify for exaltation as being the church of the Firstborn (see D&C 76:54, 67, 102).* **The church of the Firstborn is the inner circle of faithful Saints** *who have proven true and faithful to their covenants. As baptism is the gate to membership in the church of Jesus Christ on earth, so celestial marriage opens the door* **to membership in the heavenly church***...*
> **The church of the Firstborn is the Church beyond the veil,** *the organized body of Saints who qualify for exaltation. It is made up of those who qualify for the blessings of the Firstborn."*
> Joseph Fielding McConkie, *Joseph Smith: The Choice Seer* [197]

Participation in *The Church of Jesus Christ of Latter Day Saints* is an essential stepping-stone on our journey to exaltation. Our future entrance into the *Church of the Firstborn* will be determined in part by whether we believe, accept, and magnify the gospel as restored through the Prophet Joseph Smith.

> **"The churches of Nephi and Alma were churches of anticipation.** *They were admonished to look forward to the coming and redemptive mission of the Holy One in America (1 Nephi 12:6). But while their prophets and leaders were dedicated men of God, the general membership was often unstable, being prone to vacillate between fervent repentance and ungrateful apostasy... Being a mixture of wheat and tares, sheep and goats, these churches were doctrinally and authoritatively true but morally and spiritually imperfect...* **The Church of Jesus Christ of Latter-day Saints is also a church of anticipation.** *It, too, anticipates additional revelation, the institution of higher principles, the establishment of Zion, the perfecting of the Saints, and the coming of the Son of Man... In the meantime the sheep and the goats, the wheat and the tares continue to dwell side by side. Consequently, we are not without some contention and dissension. Nor have we wholly escaped the plagues of selfishness, dishonesty, worldliness, immorality, family upheaval, and spiritual apathy that beset Babylon (Revelation 18:4; D&C 133:5). Thus,* **we comprise those wise and foolish virgins foretold by the Lord** *(Matthew 25:1-13; D&C 45:56-57; 133:10)."*
> Paul R. Cheesman, *The Book of Mormon: The Keystone Scripture* [198]

The *Church of the Firstborn* has been spoken of for decades by those who hunger for more than membership in the LDS Church can provide. It is important Latter Day Saints understand that membership in this meek and lowly group is requisite for celestial glory.

> *"It should be remembered, however, that* **only 'they who are the church of the Firstborn' are heirs of celestial glory** *(see D&C 76:54), and they are the ones 'he shall bring with him, when he shall come in the clouds of heaven to reign on the earth over his people' (verse 63) and the ones 'who shall have part in the first resurrection.' (verse 64; see also D&C 45:54). Hence the gospel is to be preached to every creature that all might obtain celestial glory if they will."*
> Legrand Richards, A Marvelous Work and a Wonder [199]

One way to conceptualize the two churches is that the LDS church provides the gateway to *"see the kingdom"* (John 3:3), until after time and transformation, we are prepared to *"enter the kingdom."* (John 3:5). From the LDS Church, we receive the preparatory principles and ordinances of the gospel until we are able to comprehend and align ourselves with the greater mysteries of the kingdom.

LDS Church	Church of Firstborn
Gospel of Jesus Christ	Gospel of the Father
Telestial realm	Terrestial-celestial realm
Telestial probation	Terrestial probation
LDS Missionaries	144,000 born-again missionaries
Physical and visible	Spiritual and initially "invisible"
Preparatory gospel/access to fullness	Fullness of gospel/access to all truth
Married in the temple	Sealed by the Holy Spirit of Promise
Aaronic/Melchizedek Priesthood	Holy Order of God
Born to see the kingdom	Born to enter the kingdom
Born of the water	Born of the Spirit
Gift of Holy Ghost	Gift of translation
Mind of the natural man	Just men and women made perfect
Justified	Sanctified
Anointed to become kings and queens	Anointed as kings and queens

Begotten in Him?

And now, verily I say unto you, I was in the beginning with the Father, and am the Firstborn;
*And **all those who are begotten through me are partakers of the glory of the same,** *
***and are the church of the Firstborn**.*
Doctrine and Covenants 93:21-23

CHAPTER THREE: APOSTASY BY OMISSION

And thus ye shall become instructed in the law of my church,
and be sanctified by that which ye have received,
and ye shall bind yourselves to act in all holiness before me—
That inasmuch as ye do this, glory shall be added to the kingdom
which ye have received. Inasmuch as ye do it not,
it shall be taken, even that which ye have received.

Doctrine and Covenants 43:9-10

TRUTH #24 THE CHURCH OF JESUS CHRIST OF LATTER-DAY SAINTS IS THE LORD'S TRUE CHURCH.

A Perfect Beginning

And after having received the record of the Nephites, yea, even my servant Joseph Smith, Jun.,
might have power to translate through the mercy of God, by the power of God, the Book of Mormon.
And also those to whom these commandments were given, might have power to lay the foundation
of this church, and to bring it forth out of obscurity and out of darkness, the only true and living church
upon the face of the whole earth, with which I, the Lord, am well pleased,
speaking unto the church collectively and not individually—
For I the Lord cannot look upon sin with the least degree of allowance;
Doctrine and Covenants 1:29-31

The Church of Jesus Christ of Latter Day Saints provides the laws and ordinances necessary to receive salvation. It is the Lord's true church here in the telestial world.

Members are *offered access* to priesthood power, temple truths, daily revelation, ongoing scripture, and inspired doctrine. Being a member of the LDS church can be a great blessing if the institution is utilized to learn and live the gospel of Jesus Christ.

During religious gatherings, the declaration that *"the Church is true"* is often repeated. This mantra is arguably the most frequently used statement in the entire organization. Therefore, it would be wise to ask, "What exactly does this phrase mean?" Is the church a building? Is it just another 501c3 corporation? Does it represent a group of people with common beliefs?

When members refer to "the church," are they conceptualizing a tool of salvation God utilizes to assist us in finding Jesus Christ? Or are they referring to the church as if it were the same as the gospel of Jesus Christ? Is this perspective accurate and wise? Perhaps how we individually define "church" depends on the role, purpose, and meaning we have been taught.

In 1984, Elder Ronald E. Poelman of the Seventy provided valuable council during general conference concerning why we need to differentiate between *"church"* and *"gospel."*

"The gospel of Jesus Christ is a divine and perfect plan. It is composed of eternal, unchanging principles,
laws, and ordinances which are universally applicable to every individual regardless of time, place,
or circumstance. Gospel principles never change. The Church of Jesus Christ of Latter-day Saints
is a divine institution, administered by the priesthood of God. The Church has authority to teach correctly
the principles and doctrines of the gospel and to administer its essential ordinances.
The gospel is the divine plan for personal, individual salvation and exaltation. The Church is the delivery
system that provides the means and resources to implement [God's] plan in each individual's life.
Procedures, programs, and policies are developed within the Church to help us realize gospel blessings
according to our individual capacity and circumstances. Under divine direction, these policies, programs,
and procedures do change from time to time as necessary to fulfil gospel purposes. Underlying every aspect
of Church administration and activity are the revealed eternal principles contained in the scriptures.
As individually and collectively we increase our knowledge, acceptance, and application of gospel
principles, we become less dependent on Church programs. Our lives become gospel centered.

Sometimes traditions, customs, social practices and personal preferences of individual Church members may, through repeated or common usage be misconstrued as Church procedures or policies. Occasionally, such traditions, customs and practices may even be regarded by some as eternal gospel principles. Under such circumstances those who do not conform to these cultural standards may mistakenly be regarded as unorthodox or even unworthy. In fact, the eternal principles of the gospel and the divinely inspired Church do accommodate a broad spectrum of individual uniqueness and cultural diversity. The conformity we require should be according to God's standards. The orthodoxy upon which we insist must be founded in fundamental principles and eternal law, including free agency and the divine uniqueness of the individual. It is important therefore to know the difference between eternal gospel principles which are unchanging, universally applicable and cultural norms which may vary with time and circumstance..."
Ronald E. Poelman, *The Gospel and the Church* [200]

The culturally created axiom *"the church is perfect, but the people are not,"* would be more accurate if instead we referred to the gospel of Jesus Christ as being "perfect." Study of the word "perfect" in the original Hebrew helps us understand that it means *"to be or make complete."*[201]
If we are going to merge "perfection" and "completion" into how we conceptualize the LDS Church, we ought to also ponder what it means that many aspects of the original Restoration are not even present in the church today. (United Order, School of the Prophets, full endowment, original garment, office of church patriarch in its full and appropriate capacity, gathering of Israel, council of fifty, plural marriage, spiritual adoption, Zion, etc...)

Observing that the LDS church, (in its current form) only offers members partial access to what Joseph Smith worked to restore, is essential so we do not overestimate our religious status and mistakenly imply that *"all is well in Zion."* (2 Nephi 28:21).

"It seems that too many of us have overestimated our virtues by underestimating the Lord's standards. Therefore, the Bridegroom has yet to claim his bride—the Church. But he does not delay his coming; it is right on schedule... Christ will have a pure people, a Zion people." (D&C 82:14; 97:21; 100:16)."
Paul Cheesman, *The Book of Mormon: The Keystone Scripture* [202]

In truth, the gospel of Jesus Christ is perfect and complete, but the church, (as currently manifested) is not. Referring to the LDS Church as "perfect" is correct only in the sense that it provides a context to practice service, meekness, patience, and long suffering.

When members imply that the church is identical to the gospel, they reinforce a religious dynamic where the Creator and the created are **blurred by association**. The result is a graying of our belief system where God, His gospel, and the LDS church are related to as if they were categorically the same. Some members seem especially prone to project the **infallible nature of God onto the church and it's leaders.**

When we imply that church and gospel are identical we reinforce false traditions and incomplete beliefs. Most active members have received a type of social conditioning that can later lead to a crisis of faith when they learn of the many doctrinal and cultural problems present in the church.

Although the earthly church may struggle, the ultimate eternal meaning of *"the Church"* refers to the celestial council of the Elohim. This definition includes all principles, powers, truths, laws, ordinances, and glories that exist in unison with Father and His eternal life. In comparison to the gospel of Jesus Christ—which is eternal and unchanging, the LDS Church is specific to this telestial sphere and will not survive into the eternities. This invites us to understand that churches come and go, but the sacred gospel of Jesus Christ—as empowered by Holy Priesthood of God, is innately "eternal." (see Truth #8).

"The Priesthood of God, that was given to the ancients and is given to men in the latter days,
is co-equal in duration with eternity—is without beginning of days or end of life.
It is unchangeable in its system of government and its Gospel of salvation.
It gives to Gods and angels their supremacy and power, and offers wealth, influence, posterity,
exaltations, power, glory, kingdoms and thrones, ceaseless in their duration,
to all who will accept them on the terms upon which they are offered."
Brigham Young, *Contributor* [203]

Elder Ronald E. Poelman attempted to accelerate our understanding when he taught, *"Both the gospel of Jesus Christ and the Church of Jesus Christ are true and divine. However there is a distinction between them which is significant and it is very important that this distinction be understood…**Failure to distinguish between the two and to comprehend their proper relationship may lead to confusion and misplaced priorities with unrealistic and therefore failed expectations.**"* [204] (see Truths #3, #9, and #48).

Constantly reminding everyone *"the Church is true"* may give temporary mental assurance to the masses, but in the long run the meaning we apply to the mantra may not lead us to Jesus Christ. Instead, we would be wise to proclaim, "Yes, the gospel is true, but the more important question is are we being true to the gospel!"

Passion for Christ

*"You have been baptized;—you have had the laying on of hands; and some have been ordained, and some anointed with a holy anointing. A spirit has been given you. And you will find, **if you undertake to rest,** it will be the hardest work you ever performed. I came home from a foreign mission. I presented myself to our President, and inquired what I should do next;— rest;—said he. If I had been set to turn the world over,— to dig down a mountain, to go to the ends of the earth, or traverse the deserts of Arabia, it would have been easier than to have undertaken to rest, while the Priesthood was upon me. **I have received the holy anointing and I can never rest, till the last enemy is conquered, death destroyed, and truth reigns triumphant!"***
Parley P. Pratt, *Deseret News* [205]

Being a member of the Lord's church does not negate the eternal principle of agency. Every soul on earth, as well as every religious culture, determines the degree to which they will internalize the gospel of Jesus Christ. To accept and magnify, or omit and distort, is a personal and institutional choice.

*"The Lord has stated that **His Church will never again be taken** from the earth because of apostasy. But He has also stated that **some members of His Church will fall away**. There has been individual apostasy in the past, **it is going on now**, and there will be* ***an even increasing amount in the future.*** *While we cannot save all the flock from being deceived, we should, without compromising our doctrine, strive to **save as many as we can**. For, as President J. Reuben Clark said, 'We are in the midst of the **greatest exhibition of propaganda** that the world has ever seen.' **Do not believe all you hear.**"*
Ezra Taft Benson, BYU Speeches of the Year [206]

Many in Mormonism trust that "things are going just fine" (2 Nephi 28:21). In support of this view, they refer to growing membership rolls and numerous temples being built. Positive and hopeful comments from the brethren are interpreted to mean the church is progressing and that God is pleased with the cumulative effort.

In contrast, Jesus warned that using external performance to determine internal righteousness, is not an effective approach for accurately assessing spiritual worthiness.

Not every one that saith unto me, Lord, Lord, shall enter into the kingdom of heaven; but he that doeth the will of my Father which is in heaven. Many will say to me in that day, Lord, Lord, have we not prophesied in thy name? and in thy name have cast out devils? and in thy name done many wonderful works? And then will I profess I never knew you: depart from me, ye that work iniquity.
Matthew 7:21-23

In truth, there is no "church salvation." God has warned that if we as a Mormon people do not become instructed and sanctified in the law, the gospel *"shall be taken, even that which ye have received."*(D&C 43:9-11). Imagining ourselves worthy of celestial glory because of being "active in the church" does not alter universal law. The divine elements of both justice and mercy will be applied to the entire human race.

As this final dispensation comes to a close, every soul, family, church, institution, government, nation, and planet will be assessed in relation to eternal law and the level of truth received. This is simply how it is...worlds without end.

"When God offers a blessing or knowledge to a man, and he refuses to receive it, he will be damned.
The Israelites prayed that God would speak to Moses and not to them;
in consequence of which he cursed them with a carnal law."
Joseph Smith, *Teachings of Presidents of the Church,*[207]

In God's universe nothing is static. As independent souls we are either progressing toward exaltation and the truth of all things, or digressing toward the darkness of spiritual annihilation. Likewise the church as a religious entity is either receiving and magnifying divine revelation, or falling into denial, omission, and apostasy. There is no sustainable "neutral ground."

Temple changes enacted by the institution over the past 185 years provide an important example of how spiritual knowledge must be preserved and practiced...or it will be lost.

TEMPLE DIGRESSION:

1839

"If there is no change of ordinances, there is no change of Priesthood."
"Where there is no change of priesthood, there is no change of ordinances...."
Joseph Smith, *Teachings of the Prophet Joseph Smith* [208]

1912

"No jot, iota, or tittle of the temple rites is otherwise than uplifting and sanctifying.
In every detail the endowment ceremony contributes to covenants of morality of life, consecration of person to high ideals, devotion to truth, patriotism to nation, and allegiance to God."
James E. Talmage, *The House of the Lord* [209]

1965

"The Gospel can not possibly be changed...the saving principles must ever be the same.
They can never change...the Gospel must always be the same in all of its parts...no one can change the Gospel...if they attempt to do so, they only set up a man-made system which is not the Gospel, but is merely a reflection of their own views...if we substitute "any other Gospel" there is no salvation in it...the Lord and His Gospel remain the same-always."
The Prophets Message, *Church News* [210]

1979

"We explained briefly the Apostasy and the Restoration: that there is vast evidence and history of an apostasy from the doctrine taught by Jesus and his Apostles, that the organization of the original Church became corrupted, and sacred ordinances were changed to suit the convenience of men..."
David B. Haight, *Joseph Smith the Prophet* [211]

1990

The earth also is defiled under the inhabitants thereof; because they have transgressed the laws,
changed the ordinance, broken the everlasting covenant.
Therefore hath the curse devoured the earth, and they that dwell therein are desolate:
therefore the inhabitants of the earth are burned, and few men left.
Isaiah 24:1-6

2005

"The church recently altered the initiatory aspect of the endowment.
Several beautiful elements previously included in the "washing and anointing" were deleted
and a few applicable verses from Exodus chapter forty were added. At the end of the initiatory
the patron is told that he or she has now been "symbolically" washed and anointed,
and that the temple garment is now "authorized."
Anonymous Saint

2008

"Possibly out of consideration for the elderly and disabled,
initiates are no longer instructed to stand while making covenants."
LDSendowment.org

2013

"The new temple film is the first update in more than 20 years.
There have been no changes to the script."
Ruth Todd, *LDS Church statement* [212]

Brigham Young understood that the spirituality of the church would always be in a state of fluctuation. He warned, *"This people I say are very tardy. Can we stand still, receive so much pertaining to the blessings of the kingdom of God, receive so much knowledge, just so much wisdom, just so much power, and then stop and receive no more?... I can answer this people must go forward, or they will go backward."* [213] (see Truth #33).

No matter what the world, or the world of religion chooses, every individual determines the amount of light they will assimilate during their mortal journey. For those who desire the truth of all things, now is the day. God and His abundant universe is waiting!

What I the Lord have spoken, I have spoken, and I excuse not myself; and though the heavens and the earth
pass away, my word shall not pass away, but shall all be fulfilled, whether by mine own voice or by the
voice of my servants, it is the same. For behold, and lo, the Lord is God, and the Spirit beareth record,
and the record is true, and the truth abideth forever and ever. Amen.
Doctrine and Covenants 1:38-39

TRUTH #26 WE AS A PEOPLE CAN RECEIVE A MUCH GREATER MESSSAGE FROM THE BOOK OF MORMON IF WE APPLY THE PROPHECIES AND WARNINGS DIRECTLY TO OURSELVES.

Behold, I speak unto you as if ye were present, and yet ye are not. But behold, Jesus Christ hath shown you unto me, and I know your doing. And I know that ye do walk in the pride of your hearts; and there are none save a few only who do not lift themselves up in the pride of their hearts, unto the wearing of very fine apparel, unto envying, and strifes, and malice, and persecutions, and all manner of iniquities; and your churches, yea, even every one, have become polluted because of the pride of your hearts.
Mormon 8:35-36

Although we have been counseled to *"liken all scripture"* unto ourselves, (1 Nephi 19:23), it is more comfortable to apply the difficult verses to the "non-members" and "inactives." This trend is particularly popular when revelation condemns our spiritual performance.

To the Tribe of Ephraim

*Woe to the crown of pride, **to the drunkards of Ephraim**, whose glorious beauty is **a fading flower**, which are on the head of the fat valleys of them that are overcome with wine!...But they also have erred through wine, and through strong drink are out of the way; the priest and the prophet have erred through strong drink, they are swallowed up of wine, they are out of the way through strong drink; **they err in vision, they stumble in judgment. For all tables are full of vomit and filthiness, so that there is no place clean**...Wherefore hear the word of the Lord, ye scornful men, that rule this people which is in Jerusalem...Because ye have said, **We have made a covenant with death, and with hell are we at agreement; when the overflowing scourge shall pass through, it shall not come unto us:** for we have made lies our refuge, and under falsehood have we hid ourselves: **And your covenant with death shall be disannulled, and your agreement with hell shall not stand; when the overflowing scourge shall pass through, then ye shall be trodden down by it.***
Isaiah 28:1-18

Surely Isaiah was not suggesting that those with the blood of Ephraim in their veins would become drunk with Babylon's money and power. Why would Isaiah predict we would prefer vomiting up the precepts of men rather than following the Holy Spirit? To interpret Isaiah literally is just so drastic and discouraging when we can instead bask in the glory of being God's chosen people! (see Truth #7 on being Gentile).

"Christ also used the name "Gentile" to identify those through whom the gospel would go to the Lamanites. (3 Nephi 21:2-4). If Church members from Gentile nations will bear in mind that the term "Gentile" when used in the Book of Mormon includes them, the prophecies therein will have much greater meaning and be more disturbing."
H. Verlan Andersen, *Apostasy of the Latter Days* [214]

With stiff necks and closed minds, the Gentile tares read the blunt verses and then re-assure themselves that the Lord's rebuke could not pertain to them. First, "because we have a living prophet" and second, because we are "members of the true church." It is unclear how these beliefs change our personal need for redemption, but in Mormonism today, any interpretation which is unusual, uncomfortable, or places the church and its culture in an unfavorable light is conveniently ignored or considered to be a misinterpretation. Unfamiliar perspectives are rationalized away and any view that challenges the mainstream mindset is quickly set aside as "negativity" or "false doctrine."

> *"It is obvious today that we extol Joseph Smith as a great prophet, and truly He is, but do we know what he actually taught? And then what are we to do when those same teachings, from the man we claim to love and adore, contradict our cultural assumptions and church as manifested today? Will we still love and support the Prophet of this final dispensation when we understand he lived polygamy and polyandry (married to women who were married to other men). When we consider who taught Brigham Young about the doctrines of Adam-God and the prohibition against the Canaanites receiving the priesthood? What about Joseph's establishment of the council of fifty, patriarch of the church, and the Holy Order he established. How many are willing to study and receive knowledge concerning his true nature and office in a Godhead. What was Joseph really saying about eternal progression with God's eternal round during the King Follett Discourse? Sadly we are more comfortable with prophets who tell us what we want to hear, who reinforce our assumptions and assure us of our righteousness. Prophets that actually invite revolution and change are just too uncomfortable and must be mentally stoned, rejected, avoided, or silenced."*
> Denver Snuffer [215]

Those who love the truth, more than the comfortable traditions they have been taught, awaken to the reality that the Book of Mormon was written to us, for us, and about us.

> *And thus commandeth the Father that I should say unto you: At that day when the Gentiles shall sin against my gospel, and shall reject the fulness of my gospel, and shall be lifted up in the pride of their hearts above all nations, and above all the people of the whole earth, and shall be filled with all manner of lyings, and of deceits, and of mischiefs, and all manner of hypocrisy, and murders, and priestcrafts, and whoredoms, and of secret abominations; and if they shall do all those things, and shall reject the fulness of my gospel, behold, saith the Father, I will bring the fulness of my gospel from among them.*
> 3 Nephi 16:10

Careful examination of 3 Nephi 16 reveals that we LDS are the only people to have actually received access to the fullness of the gospel. Thus we are the only people who could reject it. (see Truth #37). As will be discussed in Truth #33, it is important to observe that scripture does not predict we will deny *all* of the gospel, but that as a result of our pride and ignorance, we will reject a true *fullness of the gospel.*

"Must Be Somebody Else"

They wear stiff necks and high heads; yea, and because of pride, and wickedness,
and abominations, and whoredoms, they have all gone astray save it be a few,
who are the humble followers of Christ; nevertheless, they are led,
that in many instances they do err because they are taught by the precepts of men.
2 Nephi 28:14

Those willing to apply the warnings of the Book of Mormon directly to themselves can awaken to a deeper repentance. In this sense, there is a telestial, terrestrial, and celestial manner for reading and applying scripture.

The telestial approach is to apply revelation to the world and the "non-members." This is the most comfortable interpretation when reading scripture because it only requires us to judge others. The slightly more useful "terrestial" perspective is to relate scripture to the church and its members. This too is relatively easy because there are so many problems and the disease of fault-finding can be quite addictive. The celestial level, and the way God intended for us to read His word, is to apply the warning directly to our own souls. For in the end, we will fall at the feet of the Master, and *know to our core* that this is the only level that really mattered.

"Be the change you want to see in the world."
Mahatma Gandhi, [216]

To be part of the *"humble few"* (2 Nephi 28:14) requires constant repentance. This allows Jesus Christ and His Holy Spirit to slowly eradicate the traditions of men from our minds and hearts. A celestial application of scripture does not involve projecting the parables of the wheat and tares, ten virgins, and prodigal son onto those poor "non-members," but instead involves relating the message directly to the natural man within.

This know also, that in the last days perilous times shall come. For men shall be lovers of their own selves,
covetous, boasters, proud, blasphemers, disobedient to parents, unthankful, unholy…
Having a form of godliness, but denying the power thereof: from such turn away…
2 Timothy 3: 1-2, 5

Refusing to apply scripture to ourselves and our Mormon culture delays the opportunity to change and receive the truth. Zion has been waiting for 185 years and with Babylon starting to crumble at the edges, isn't it time we acknowledge and live all that scripture requires us to be?

And many great destructions have I caused to come upon this land, and upon this people, because of their
wickedness and their abominations. O all ye that are spared because ye were more righteous than they,
will ye not now return unto me, and repent of your sins, and be converted, that I may heal you?
Yea, verily I say unto you, if ye will come unto me ye shall have eternal life. Behold, mine arm of mercy
is extended towards you, and whosoever will come, him will I receive; and blessed are those
who come unto me. Behold, I am Jesus Christ the Son of God…
3 Nephi 9 12-15

"The kingdom of the father is like a certain woman who was carrying a jar full of meal.
While she was walking on the road, still some distance from home, the handle of the jar broke
and the meal emptied out behind her on the road. She did not realize it; she had noticed no accident.
When she reached her house, she set the jar down and found it empty."
Gospel of Thomas [217]

The gospel of Jesus Christ is perfect, eternal and infallible. The church and its members are not. Initially new converts and social Mormons may not perceive any serious problems in the organization, but with study and tutoring from the Spirit, it becomes obvious that religious history is about to cycle and repeat.

"The church" at the time of Christ was nearly in a complete state of apostasy. It appears that most of
the Jews were living a lie, thinking that they were the Lord's valiant covenant people, but history has
revealed otherwise. The church's leadership refused the role of John the Baptist and Christ himself and
even demanded His crucifixion. This condition resulted from many years of man's wisdom creeping
into the doctrine and laws of God. Just a handful of people could see things for what they really were.
Do you suppose the general membership of the Jewish church thought there was something wrong
with the doctrine as taught to the leadership of the church? They didn't even dare think of such a thing!
Only those few humble believers could see something wasn't right."
Anonymous Saint

When God establishes or restores a church, the teachings and doctrines are initially pure and pristine. Satan provides continual opposition until over time, he is slowly able to corrupt the system and integrate the philosophies of men into the doctrine. This infiltration minimizes the degree of light being shared until only limited spiritual power exists. Once this weakened level of spirituality becomes "the norm," false traditions can be mainstreamed down for generations under the guise of "teaching truth." When local leaders speak of *"keeping the doctrine pure"* they know not what they say, but this lack of understanding is in harmony with all of the great cultures which have fallen. For in refusing to acknowledge the loss of spiritual power and instead continually reminding themselves of their "blessed" and "chosen" status, they re-enact the tragedy.

Time Marker: 1874
"Do you think that this people called Latter-Day Saints are traveling in the path that they
should go in? Do you think that they offer their oblations and sacrifices to the Lord as they should?
What do you think about it? What is the general expression through our community?
It is that the Latter-day Saints are drifting as fast as they can into idolatry,
drifting into the spirit of the world and into pride and vanity."
Brigham Young, *Journal of Discourses* [218]

Rarely do we consider the possibility that history could be repeated in the Lord's only true church. Ironically, just as a large portion of Nephites, Jaredites, and Jews became arrogant, wealthy, and influential, many now imagine the modern-day church to be immune from the possibility of apostasy.

> *"Some go to church to actually learn and repent. Most go to be assured, told all is well*
> *and that they are the righteous because they are "active", pay their tithing and have*
> *current temple recommends. We have the Church we want, not the one the Lord had in mind.*
> *But such is the history of apostasy throughout the dispensations."*
> Anonymous Saint

The benefit of perceiving our true religious status is that we become candidates to hear the Lord's ongoing invitation to *"go ye out of Babylon."* (D&C 133:5-7). None of us will be judged for the collective performance of the church, but all of us will answer for our own delusions and decisions.

Even as the institution builds high-rise apartments, establishes billion-dollar malls, dedicates banks, and spends millions of dollars on various Babylonian investments, each of us can be the broken widow who offers her little mite unto Christ. (Mark 12:41-44).

Scripture warns that *"the whole world lieth in sin,"* because *"it is not given that one man should possess that which is above another."*(D&C 84:49, D&C 49:20). As Saints, we can either enable the sickness, or separate ourselves from the lust for power through generosity and sacrifice. All that is of this world will fall, but we need not stay on the Titanic. Those willing to get on the "life boat of Christ," are doing so now, before the financial iceberg arrives.

Maintaining confidence in the church and its leaders may be more comfortable, but it also prohibits us from overcoming spiritual blindness and entering into a greater consecration.

Time Marker: 1873
> *"But I will prophesy concerning this Church and the people, that all who will not come*
> *into that order of things, when God, by his servants, counsels them so to do, will cease growing*
> *in the knowledge of God, they will cease having the Spirit of the Lord to rest upon them,*
> *and they will gradually grow darker and darker in their minds, until they lose the Spirit and power of God,*
> *and their names will not be numbered with the names of the righteous.*
> *You may put that down and record it."*
> Orson Pratt, *Journal of Discourses* [219]

Over the years true prophets have tried to awaken us, but with little success. Despite their best efforts, we as a people continue to be soiled with the blood and sins of this generation. In choosing the world we continue to break the everlasting covenant.

Time Marker: 1936
> *"Are we not too much inclined to blame the generations that are past for the breaking of the*
> *new and everlasting covenant, and to think it is because of the great apostasy which followed*
> *the Apostles in primitive times? Perhaps we should wake up to the realization that it is because of*

the breaking of covenants, especially the new and everlasting covenant which is the fullness of the gospel that the world is to be consumed by fire and few men left. Since this punishment is to come at the time of the cleansing of the earth when Christ comes again, should not the Latter-Day Saints take heed unto themselves? We have been given the new and everlasting covenant, and many among us have broken it."
Joseph Fielding Smith, *Deseret News* [220]

In truth, a cultural apostasy has been brewing for several decades. Today's *"falling away"* correlates with the same pattern of pride described in the Book of Mormon and seems to be more prevalent where the church has been established the longest. (see Truth #48).

Time Marker: 1938
*"It is a very apparent fact that we have traveled far and wide in the past 20 years. What the future will bring I don t know . **But if we drift as far from the fundamental things in the next 20 years, what will be left of the foundation laid by the Prophet Joseph Smith? It is easy for one who observes to see how the apostasy came about in the primitive church of Jesus Christ. Are we not traveling the same road?"***
Joseph Fielding Smith, *Joseph Fielding Smith Journal* [221]

Time Marker: 1969
"Let us consider some of the precepts of men that may and do cause some of the humble followers of Christ to err. Christ taught that we should be in the world but not of it. Yet there are some in our midst who are not so much concerned about taking the gospel into the world as they are about bringing worldliness into the gospel. They want us to be in the world and of it. They want us to be popular with the world even though a prophet has said that this is impossible, for all hell would then want to join us.
"Through their own reasoning and a few misapplied scriptures, they try to sell us the precepts and philosophies of men. They do not feel the Church is progressive enough- they say that it should embrace the social and socialist gospel of apostate Christendom."
Ezra Taft Benson, *A Divided Church? or the Destructive Precepts of Men* [222]

Today the warnings of President Benson have come to fruition. Doctrine has been minimized to the point of corruption, while a focus on achieving acceptance from the world overshadows a pure and simple passion for Zion. Many in the church appear to be continuing their slide into the pride, immorality, and the ways of Babylon. Today only a few stand for Jesus Christ and proclaim the difficult truths. These cultural trends mirror exactly what Book of Mormon prophets warned would occur.

Time Marker: Today
"For they saw and beheld with great sorrow that the people of the church began to be lifted up in the pride of their eyes, and to set their hearts upon riches and upon the vain things of the world, that they began to be scornful, one towards another, and they began to persecute those that did not believe according to their own will and pleasure. And thus, in this there began to be great contentions among the people of the church; yea, there were envyings, and strife, and malice, and persecutions, and pride, even to exceed the pride of those who did not belong to the church of God."
Alma 4:8-9

> **TRUTH #28** THE WORLD IS FULL OF DARKNESS AND SUBTLE DECEPTION.
> EVEN AT CHURCH WE MUST BE ABLE TO DISCERN TRUTH FROM ERROR.
> GOD'S HOLY SPIRIT IS OUR SURE GUIDE.

For we wrestle not against flesh and blood, but against principalities, against powers,
against the rulers of the darkness of this world, against spiritual wickedness in high places.
Ephesians 6:12

In the pre-mortal realm, Satan rebelled, had a spiritual temper tantrum, and was cast out of Father's presence. As the temporary *"god of this world"* (2 Corinthians 4:4), he attempts to wreak havoc upon the righteous—even appearing at times as an *"angel of light."* (2 Corinthians 11:14).

In general, the adversary will use every scheme available to distract, destroy, and if possible, *"deceive the very elect."* (Matthew 24:24). For those who want *"religion,"* he is pleased to provide *"the philosophies of men mingled with scripture."* The current status of our world would suggest his devious plans have been quite effective.

And the great dragon was cast out, that old serpent, called the Devil, and Satan,
which deceiveth the whole world: *he was cast out into the earth,*
and his angels were cast out with him.
Revelation 12:9

When the adversary or his minions begin to work on a soul, they usually start with the common "in your face" type of temptations involving "good and evil." If greed, lust, materialism, anger, and selfishness do not work, they will try to magnify pride within the believer. Satan supports those who judge others in a spirit of self-righteousness. Religious pride also makes it easier for him to lull a "righteous saint" into carnal security, by assuring them *"all is well in Zion."* (2 Nephi 28:21).

By mingling religious tradition with cultural assumption, the enemy knows he can distract the novice Saint from an accurate perception of their true standing with the Lord. The deception is reinforced with a type of "herd mentality" where the Mormon mainstream assumes, "we have a living prophet and can't be led astray!"

"People who regard themselves as members of the only true Church have the fatal tendency
to consider themselves immune from the disease of deception."
H. Verlan Andersen, *The Great and Abominable Church of the Devil* [223]

If the normal attempts involving direct temptation don't succeed, the adversary (in desperation) will often make a "last-ditch" effort. By using others who are already under his influence, he may offer the naïve and uneducated some of the mysteries of the kingdom—mingled with subtle discrepancies. Compared to the "milk" on Sunday, some of these spiritual teachings, curious half-truths, and misleading miracles can be quite attractive. If the deceiver can use the deeper mysteries of the kingdom to lure in a growing believer—especially by promoting

137

those philosophies which minimize the Atonement of Christ—a beginning foundation of false worship has been laid by the enemy.

*"The religion of the ancient Zoramites in the Book of Mormon is paralleled by much of the religion practiced in our modern world: it was **false, superficial, undemanding, impotent, and Christless.** Consequently, the message of God's prophets to that misguided people is as relevant now as it was over two thousand years ago."*
Rodney Turner, *Studies in Scriptures* [224]

In truth, the forces of opposition will readily reveal the deeper glories of the kingdom if that light can then be promoted in such a way as to diminish reliance on the Atonement of Jesus Christ. The adversary knows if he can get us to *"look beyond the mark"* of the Savior, our misplaced focus will eventually crumble on a sandy foundation. (3 Nephi 18:13).

Even more insidious than saying "Christ is not coming" is the implication that "Christ is not needed." Presently, there is a growing number of "spiritual movements" that accept the goodness of Jesus, but deny any personal need for redemption through His sacred blood. These trendy beliefs are not supported by dark or evil people, but rather by good and honorable individuals who have been *"blinded by the craftiness of men."* (D&C 76:75). These intelligent and wholesome people fall for a type of "relative deception," (wherein they believe in, and experiencing terrestrial goodness-at the expense of celestial greatness).

And many false prophets shall rise, and shall deceive many. And because iniquity shall abound, the love of many shall wax cold...Then if any man shall say unto you, Lo, here is Christ, or there; believe it not. For there shall arise false Christs, and false prophets, and shall shew great signs and wonders; insomuch that, if it were possible, they shall deceive the very elect.
Matthew 24:11-12, 23-24

As prophesied, the world is now swarming with *"false-christs"* (Mark 13:22) and *"false-spirits."* (D&C 50:2). These are not just individuals claiming to be a political or spiritual messiah, but also include any movement or religion promoting a false plan of salvation. Pseudo-spirituality that diminishes the role of the Redeemer has been used in the past and is flourishing again in a world which has been seduced in the name of "light, love, and acceptance."

In this world there are many willing to promote an *"anything but the Atonement of Jesus Christ"* **mentality. How ironic that nothing less than Jesus Christ will do.**

And this Anti-Christ, whose name was Korihor, (and the law could have no hold upon him) began to preach unto the people that there should be no Christ. And after this manner did he preach, saying: O ye that are bound down under a foolish and a vain hope, why do ye yoke yourselves with such foolish things? Why do ye look for a Christ? For no man can know of anything which is to come. Behold, these things which ye call prophecies, which ye say are handed down by holy prophets, behold, they are foolish.
Alma 30:12-14

To successfully differentiate between that which is Godly, and the insidious imitations of an anti-Christ, requires that we ask for and receive the gift of discernment.

For behold, my brethren, it is given unto you to judge, that ye may know good from evil;
and the way to judge is as plain, that ye may know with a perfect knowledge, as the daylight is
from the dark night. For behold, the Spirit of Christ is given to every man, that he may know
good from evil; wherefore, I show unto you the way to judge; for every thing which inviteth to do good,
and to persuade to believe in Christ, is sent forth by the power and gift of Christ;
wherefore ye may know with a perfect knowledge it is of God.
Moroni 7:15-16

When introduced to unfamiliar teachings, members tend to be cautious so they are not carried about *"with every wind of doctrine."* (Ephesians 4:14). This hesitation is wise, and yet those who quickly succumb to fear may be easily enticed to avoid or deny that which is truly of God. Without a strong doctrinal base and continual tutoring from the Holy Spirit, it can be difficult to determine what is a "beautiful mystery" and what is a "deceptive distraction." Thankfully, God has given us the sure source to make the distinction.

*"...**There is one major question we should ask ourselves**. Assuming we are living a life*
*so we can know, then **what does the Holy Ghost have to say about it?***
We are under obligation to answer this question. God will hold us responsible.
Let us not be deceived** in the sifting days ahead. **Let us rally together on principle
***behind the prophet as guided by the promptings of the Spirit**."*
Ezra Taft Benson, *The Teachings of Ezra Taft Benson* [225]

To avoid a doctrinal "Leaning Tower of Pisa" and still benefit from the valuable spirituality of others, requires we independently be in tune with the *"Spirit of Truth."* (D&C 50:17). Even at church, we must determine what is doctrinally correct and what is just "religious rhetoric" handed down through the generations. For example...

"I testify that if we shall look to the First Presidency and follow their counsel and direction,
no power on earth can stay or change our course as a church, and as individuals we shall gain peace in this
life and be inheritors of eternal glory in the world to come."
Joseph Fielding Smith, *Eternal Keys and the Right to Preside* [226]

In the days of religious drama ahead, many of our incorrect cultural assumptions will be tested and shown to be inadequate. The limitations of habitually following religious leaders will be revealed. A fundamental separation will occur between those who primarily look to other men and those who deeply *trust God.*

*"**Jesus Christ is the only beacon on which we can rely**. The message of The Church of Jesus*
Christ of Latter-day Saints is that there is but one guiding hand in the universe, only one truly
infallible light, one unfailing beacon to the world. That light is Jesus Christ, the light and life of
the world, the light which one Book of Mormon prophet described as "a light that is endless,
that can never be darkened. (Mosiah 16:9)."
Howard W. Hunter, *The Teachings of Howard W. Hunter* [227]

When considering new perspectives on the gospel, God has provided a formula to assist us with receiving the truth and avoiding deception. Father desires for us to grow into the "truth of all things." He is eager to confirm additional truths as we become willing to receive them. In Him we need not fear, for through the peace of His Spirit, we can assuredly differentiate between that which is "false doctrine," and that which is "forgotten doctrine."

Truth Standard

If any man will do his will, he shall know of the doctrine,
Whether it be of God, or whether I speak of myself.
John 7:17

1) Does the principle, teaching, or religious movement explicitly or implicitly diminish the role of Jesus Christ and His Atonement? Is Jesus honored as Savior and King? (Moroni 7:15-18).

2) Do the new teachings bring me closer to Jesus Christ? (John 7:17).

3) Are the principles being shared ratified by the Holy Spirit? Have I experienced the actual Spirit of God confirming what is taught, or is it just emotion? (2 Nephi 28:1).

4) In relation to any teaching, what does it mean if I am experiencing a *"stupor of thought?"* (D&C 9:9). Is it possible that some things are "true," but I am not yet prepared for the increase?

5) Does this new teaching or scriptural interpretation contradict the words of the Prophet Joseph Smith? (D&C 52:9).

6) Am I avoiding or denying a particular teaching because it is uncomfortable or unfamiliar to me? If so, is it because I am simply avoiding the pain of changing? (Helaman 16:2).

7) Am I accepting or rejecting the teaching based on cultural assumption and the traditions of men, or am I relying on prophecy in scripture to determine what is accurate and true.   (D&C 1:38).

8) Whether I accept, reject, or decide to wait and study more before making a decision, do I feel peace in my decision? (Galatians 5:22).

9) Is it possible to "try the fruit" to see if "it is good" without breaking the commandments? (John 7:17).

10) Do I own the truth in my soul? Do I possess a simple and sure knowing that cannot be removed or degraded? (Joseph Smith History 1:25).

Possessing spiritual discernment has always been essential for overcoming spiritual death, but In the days to come, it will also become a matter of life and death. To perceive, and then act on what is accurate and of God, will be essential when the Lord gathers His surviving Saints. A true prophet of God has blessed us to know the difference between what is real and what is deception.

"I bless you with increased discernment to judge between Christ and anti-Christ.
I bless you with increased power to do good and to resist evil. I bless you with increased
understanding of the Book of Mormon. I promise you that from this moment forward,
if we will daily sup from its pages and abide by its precepts, God will pour out upon each child
of Zion and the Church a blessing hitherto unknown and we will plead to the Lord
that He will begin to lift the condemnation the scourge and judgment.
Of this I bear solemn witness."
Ezra Taft Benson, *A Sacred Responsibility* [228]

TRUTH #29 RELIGIOUS TRADITION AND LIMITED DOCTRINAL UNDERSTANDING HAS RESULTED IN THE PHILOSOPHIES OF MEN BEING MINGLED WITH SCRIPTURE.

Beyond Tradition

*"This is "Mormonism's" message to the world—**It calls upon the Christian world and upon all men to abandon their lifeless, worn-out creeds; to throw away all that is false and worth-less— the doctrines of men and the doctrines of devils, and come back into the light, into the path that God has marked out. That is all;** and this is what brought about the death of Joseph Smith— not the abatement of the Nauvoo Expositor, nor the calling out of the Legion to defend the city against mobs and despoilers. That is only the surface reason. The deep-rooted, fundamental reason is this: **The world was unwilling, as ever, to give up its false traditions,** to believe all that God had revealed, that it might be prepared for what He will yet reveal before man can be made perfect and the kingdom of God firmly established."*
Orson F. Whitney, *Conference Report* [229]

The Prophet Joseph taught that overcoming false tradition was essential for understanding celestial law and receiving God's exaltation. Joseph found it difficult to eradicate the incorrect beliefs that lingered in the hearts and minds of the early Saints.

*"I have tried for a number of years to get the minds of the Saints prepared to receive the things of God; but we frequently see some of them, after suffering all they have for the work of God, will fly to pieces like glass as soon as anything comes that is **contrary to their traditions**: they cannot stand the fire at all. **How many will be able to abide a celestial law,** and go through and receive their exaltation, I am unable to say, as many are called, but few are chosen." (HC 6:183-85).*
Joseph Smith, *Discourses of the Prophet Joseph Smith* [230]

In the early days of the church, most converts to Mormonism had been involved with some previous denomination. These new members brought with them various ideologies concerning God, life, and salvation.

Through revelation, God provided corrective guidance, but as a whole, those joining the newly established religion struggled to embrace pure doctrine.

"It is often the case that young members in this church, for want of better information, carry along with them their old notions of things and sometimes fall into egregious errors."
Joseph Smith, *Discourses of the Prophet Joseph Smith* [231]

Despite Joseph's best efforts, not all incorrect beliefs were removed from the testimonies of the church and its members. An unbiased study of church history reveals that with the death of Joseph Smith, and the Saints failing to complete the Nauvoo temple in sufficient time to again receive the fullness of the priesthood (D&C 124:28-37), the Restoration was not finished and the condemnation announced in 1832 was never lifted. (D&C 84:54-55). As mentioned previously, Joseph Smith stated in 1839, *"I never have had the opportunity to give them the plan that God has*

142

revealed to me."[232] Understanding that what the Lord provided to the Saints was true but incomplete, leads us to conclude that for almost two centuries, we as a people have struggled to adequately understand and live the degree of light that was provided. The implication being that each new generation has only been able to pass on to their children a decreasing portion of what God intended to restore.

This "inherited condemnation" has fostered decades of incomplete and misleading rhetoric. Today some of what is assumed to be "truth," should more actually be termed "religious tradition." (see Truth #34).

Cultural Assumption
"The Lord will never again let His Church go astray."

After Joseph was martyred, Brigham Young continued to encourage the Saints to eradicate error. He stated, *"I told the people that as God lived, if they would not have truth they would have error sent unto them and they would believe it. If they would not believe the revelations that God had given he would suffer the devil to give revelations that they would follow after."* [233]

It has been approximately 140 years since Brigham issued this warning. This leaves us to ponder which false precepts and incorrect traditions we have insisted on keeping.

"A long habit of not thinking a thing wrong, gives it a superficial appearance of being right, and raises at first a formidable outcry in defense of custom. But the tumult soon subsides. Time makes more converts than reason."
Thomas Paine, *Common Sense* [234]

Those who delve into church history and then analyze scripture find inconsistent traditions in several aspects of our religious experience. (Sacrament, temple endowment, priesthood, Word of Wisdom, etc...) This ongoing phenomenon is reinforced by members who incorrectly assume that because "the church is true," every principle is being taught and conceptualized correctly.

"There are also apostate doctrines that are sometimes taught in our classes and from our pulpits and that appear in our publications. And these apostate precepts of men cause our people to stumble."
Ezra Taft Benson, *Conference Report* [235]

One of the incorrect assumption is that because "we have a living prophet" there can't be any serious doctrinal problems. The belief is that if adjustments and clarifications were needed, the prophet and brethren would surely make the corrections. This attitude negates the reality that when a cultural belief is passed down for generations "as truth," new statements of re-affirming testimony are habitually spoken, even if the teaching was incomplete or erroneous from the start.

Without a shadow of a doubt...

"It has been necessary to circumvent the inconvenient barriers of scripture and conscience
by the use of the tried and true device of rhetoric, defined by Plato as the art of making true things
seem false and false things seem true by the use of words...This invaluable art has,
since the time of Cain, invested the ways of Babylon with an air of high purpose,
solid virtue, and impeccable respectability..."
Hugh Nibley, *Approaching Zion* [236]

In the temple we are warned that Satan will utilize religion to teach the philosophies of men mingled with scripture. Despite this warning, general conference and the *Ensign* include regular references to philosophers such as William James, William Shakespeare, and Ralph Waldo Emerson. (see January 2012 *Ensign*).

Throughout church history some inspired leaders attempted to clarify truth from tradition, but in the end the responsibility to learn correct doctrine rests with each individual.

Cultural Agency

"Parents are cautioned against establishing false traditions in the home,
You will remember the Jewish people were so steeped in their traditions before the days of Jesus,
they did not recognize the Christ when He came among them. False traditions in Church families
could also find us unprepared to receive the Christ when He comes again."
Delbert L. Stapley, *BYU Speeches of the Year* [237]

As humans we become comfortable in our habits, rituals, and current doctrinal understanding. The natural man is addicted to "being right," and it prefers not to have its assumptions about God and salvation challenged.

"Some have reached provincial conclusions and do not really want to restructure
their understandings of things. Some wish to be neither shaken nor expanded by
new spiritual data...most are quite content with a superficial understanding
or a general awareness of spiritual things."
Neal A. Maxwell, *Meek and Lowly* [238]

Hugh Nibley addressed the problem and quoted Joseph Smith as saying, *"If we get puffed up by thinking that we have much knowledge, we are apt to get a contentious spirit, and what is the cure? Correct knowledge is necessary to cast out that spirit. The cure for inadequate knowledge is "ever more light and knowledge."* **But who is going to listen patiently to correct knowledge if he thinks he has the answers already?** *There are a great many wise men and women too in our midst who are too wise to be taught; therefore they must die in their ignorance."* [239]

What will you choose: Truth or Tradition?
Are you willing to accept that often they are not compatible?

TRUTH #30 THE BOOK OF MORMON WARNS THAT IN RELATION TO PURE DOCTRINE THE HOLY WORD OF GOD WILL BE TRANSFIGURED.

O ye wicked and perverse and stiffnecked people, why have ye built up churches unto yourselves to get gain? **Why have ye transfigured the holy word of God**, *that ye might bring damnation upon your souls?* **Behold, look ye unto the revelations of God**; *for behold, the time cometh at that day when all these things must be fulfilled.*
Mormon 8:33

Could this warning from Moroni really apply to the Lord's Church and the Mormon culture? Who was the Book of Mormon written to? Is it possible that over the past 185 years, the meaning applied to certain words has been diluted or altered to the degree that our current interpretations are limited or even incorrect? Could it be that some of what is being taught from the pulpit today is widely accepted, but doctrinally inaccurate? And if we, in the Lord's Church, are the stewards of God's true scripture, what other institution or culture even has the influence necessary to transfigure the holy word of God?

Transfigure: To change in outward form or appearance; To transform.[240]

When the holy word of God is "transfigured," it can relate to a literal change in linguistics, or apply to *the interpretation and meaning* given to a particular scripture, principle, or teaching.

Misconstrue: To misunderstand the meaning of; take in a wrong sense; misinterpret.[241]

Pointing out that some of our traditional beliefs and interpretations are not congruent with scripture is not comfortable or popular. But it is essential if we are to become one with God, Jesus Christ, and the Truth of All Things.

"To become a joint heir of the heirship of the Son, one must put away all his false traditions."
Joseph Smith, *History of the Church* [242]

When the mind and heart are securely anchored in the gospel of Jesus Christ, it becomes safe to ask the tough questions:
1) Why do I believe what I believe?
2) Has everything I *"know without a shadow of a doubt"* been confirmed by the Holy Spirit?
3) Have I specifically asked God what is really true—one teaching at a time?
4) Is there a deeper level of truth He desires to reveal unto me?
5) Are the testimonies heard at church on Sunday mostly cultural rhetoric?
6) Are the teachings taught in our "fine congregations" supported by scripture?
7) Is there a way to keep what is correct, and still eradicate the precepts of men from my testimony?
8) Who do I trust as the final source of all truth?

Members who believe leaders can be unequivocally trusted concerning doctrinal matters have not studied church history and the many contradictions which have occurred.

"If any man writes to you, or preaches to you, doctrines contrary to the Bible, or Book of Mormon, or the Book of Doctrine and Covenants, set him down as an impostor."
Joseph Smith, *Times and Seasons* [243]

Today there are many *"accidental imposters."* These good Saints unknowingly promote religious beliefs which are not supported in scripture.

Religious Rhetoric

"The Church is perfect, but the people aren't." (see Truth #24).
"I never said it would be easy, I only said it would be worth it." (see Truth #29).
"We need to set more goals." (see Truth #35).
"Odds are, you're going to be exalted." (see Truths #13 and #14).
"Family is the most important thing." (see Truth #3).
"We are teaching the fullness of the gospel." (see Truths #12 and #14).
"Follow your leaders and even if they're wrong-you will be blessed." (see Truth #36).
"The church is the kingdom of God on Earth." (see Truth #76).
"The Prophet cannot lead us astray."   (see Truth #36).
"Obedience to the law will save us." (see Truth #9).

Today the Sunday experience is cluttered with cultural assumption, false tradition, and the *"precepts of men."*(2 Nephi 28:14). Doctrine that was once considered sacred and essential is now often perceived as unnecessary. Somehow "positive encouragement" has replaced an honest and blunt call to repentance.

Feel Good Fuzzies

"How many articles do you find in the LDS Church News, Ensign and New Era which are positive, flattering and reassuring? How many articles confront you, call you to repent, warn you of the judgment and the duration of eternity? (Enos 1: 23.) Why is the Book of Mormon constantly calling upon us to repent? Why are we not called relentlessly to repentance by our current leaders? Is there a disconnection between the message of the Book of Mormon and our modern messages? Has the Lord changed His mind? Was Nephi just a crank? Is the Book of Mormon a negative book not relevant to an enlightened people who are specially chosen by God for endless happiness and promised they will never be led astray? Why would the Book of Mormon be a message for us? Why do we have a book so negative in tone, pessimistic in its view of us, while we sit atop the promises of never again having to face an apostasy?"
Denver Snuffer, *Removing the Condemnation* [244]

Accepting the ramifications of our Latter Day status can be uncomfortable. Members tend to shy away from acknowledging serious error and instead focus on the security of tradition.

Comfortable

*"Here we see that the new churches retained their traditions, of course. They were not seeking to be original. They claimed to be the old true church…There were many churches which professed to know the Christ, and **yet they did deny the more parts of his gospel**. They took some parts. They kept parts of the gospel, but **they got rid of others they didn't like. Well, we do that the same way**. They did deny the more parts of this gospel, insomuch that they did receive all manner of wickedness. And they went further than that. **They had the gospel. They denied most of it**, though, but they **still had the forms and the ordinances and they administered them**. They professed to know the Christ. They accommodated their doctrines to the market…**It was very popular. The church grew phenomenally** as a result of this. **Remember, this is the church we're talking about. This is not apostates**…the phenomenal growth of the church is no proof that it's true at all, or that it's on the true path. It grew faster than anything because it was very popular. **So don't use popularity as a gauge either.**"*
Hugh Nibley, *Teachings of the Book of Mormon* [245]

Reviewing church history and then attempting to synthesize 19th and 20th century Mormonism reveals an abundance of doctrinal contradiction. (see Truths #29, #31, and #33) Those who compare the fullness of the gospel, (as taught in scripture and by Joseph Smith), with what is reviewed in the church today, find hundreds of variations and minimizations. The result is that each true seeker is required to turn directly to God and His revelations as the final authority.

The Standard

*"Whenever you find any doctrine, any idea, any expression from **any source** whatsoever that is in conflict with that which the Lord has revealed and **which is found in the holy Scriptures**, you may be assured that it is **false and you should put it aside** and stand firmly grounded in the truth in prayer and in faith, relying upon THE SPIRIT OF THE LORD."*
Joseph F. Smith, *Conference Report* [246]

After a certain interpretation is passed on from generation to generation, it becomes accepted by that particular culture as "the truth." This phenomenon creates one of life's great ironies. For when an awakening Saint tries to correct or clarify that which over time has been "transfigured," those who have only been taught the mainstream narrative—and are only familiar with the prevalent interpretation, may ironically accuse the one sharing, *"of taking the scriptures of out of context."* Thus, all Mormons who hunger for truth are left to learn from the Holy Spirit and scripture to the greatest possible depth our testimonies will allow. It is our choice whether to trust the incomplete interpretations given to us by well-intentioned men, or go directly to God and learn of Him. (Matthew 28:29).

Truth or Tradition?

"The early customs and teachings of parents and friends, to a greater or lesser degree,
influence the minds of children, but when they are disposed to inquire at the hands of Him
who has eternal intelligence to impart to them, when their understandings are enlarged,
when their minds are enlightened by the Spirit of Truth, so that they can see things that are unseen
by the natural eye, they may then be corrected in their doctrine and belief,
and in their manner of life, but not until then."
Brigham Young, *Salvation* [247]

The reality that God, Jesus, and the Holy Spirit represent our sure source is part of what makes changing even a small aspect of God's word so serious. One of the most interesting adjustments involves only adding a simple comma to the text. Here is the current version of Doctrine and Covenants 89:12-13.

Yea, flesh also of beasts and of the fowls of the air, I, the Lord, have ordained
for the use of man with thanksgiving; nevertheless they are to be used sparingly;
And it is pleasing unto me that they should not be used,
only in times of winter, or of cold, or famine.
D&C 89:12-13

Apparently the comma after the word "used" was inserted into the 1921edition of the Doctrine and Covenants. According to the historian T. Edgar Lyons, when Joseph Fielding Smith was shown the new comma, he remarked, *"Who put that in there?"*[248]

Removing the comma reverses the meaning of the revelation and suggests that although meat should still be used sparingly, the use of meat in all seasons is permissible. Consider the original message.

Yea, flesh also of beasts and of the fowls of the air, I, the Lord, have ordained for the use of man with
thanksgiving; nevertheless they are to be used sparingly; And it is pleasing unto me that they should not
be used only in times of winter, or of cold, or famine.
D&C 89:12-13

The fact that one comma could change the message so dramatically suggests that we also consider the meaning of other grammatical changes made to scripture. Does it matter that content in the Book of Mormon has been changed, and what new perspectives would we gain by reading the original version of each revelation?

1830 Edition of the Book of Mormon

"And the angel said unto me, behold the Lamb of God, yea, even the Eternal Father!..."
1 Nephi 11:21

1981 Edition of the Book of Mormon

"And the angel said unto me: Behold the Lamb of God,
yea, even the Son of the Eternal Father!..."
1 Nephi 11:21

1830 Edition of the Book of Mormon

"...and shall make known to all kindreds, tongues, and people, that the Lamb of God
is the Eternal Father and the Savior of the world..."
1 Nephi 13:40

1981 Edition of the Book of Mormon

"...and shall make known to all kindreds, tongues, and people that the Lamb of God
is the Son of the Eternal Father, and the Savior of the World..."
1 Nephi 13:40

Other examples of scripture being altered could be provided here, but these two verses were chosen because they relate directly to how we perceive the very nature of "GOD!"

On June 16, 1844, just eleven days before the Prophet was martyred, Joseph Smith spoke to the people concerning eternity and the plurality of the gods. According to the exact hand-written notes that Thomas Bullock scribed, the Prophet stated, *"my object was to preach the Scrip--& preach the doctrine there being a God above the Far. of our Ld. J.C.--I am bold to declare I have taut. all the strong doctrines publicly--& always stronger that what I preach in private."*[249] Considering the subject of the talk, it seems likely Thomas Bullock recorded the message correctly and that Joseph was revealing the "strong" doctrine of, *"... there being a God above the Father of our Lord Jesus Christ."*

Decades later, Joseph Fielding Smith would edit the text by adding a comma. The quote was changed in the *Teachings of the Prophet Joseph Smith* to read, *"My object was to preach the scriptures, and preach the doctrine they contain, there being a God above, the Father of our Lord Jesus Christ. I am bold to declare I have taught all the strong doctrines publicly, and always teach stronger doctrines in public than in private."*[250] This added comma after the word "above" resulted in the message being interpreted in a way that now supports contemporary Mormon doctrine.

For those who think changes like this are irrelevant, we should remember Joseph Smith stated, *"If any man inquire, what kind of a being is God...he will realize that unless he knows God, he has not eternal life for there can be eternal life on no other principle."*[251] In addition the gospel warns that we cannot be saved in ignorance (D&C 131:6) and that it is impossible to have effectual faith in a belief that is not eternally correct. (See Truth # 5). These teachings suggest that it is wise to be **intense and exact** in our studies, especially in relation to the eternal nature of Almighty God!

And I, John, bear record, and lo, the heavens were opened, and the Holy Ghost descended upon him in the form of a dove, and sat upon him, and there came a voice out of heaven saying: This is my beloved Son. And I, John, bear record that he received a fulness of the glory of the Father; And he received all power, both in heaven and on earth, and the glory of the Father was with him, for he dwelt in him. And it shall come to pass, that if you are faithful you shall receive the fulness of the record of John. I give unto you these sayings that you may understand and know how to worship, and know what you worship, that you may come unto the Father in my name, and in due time receive of his fulness. For if you keep my commandments you shall receive of his fulness, and be glorified in me as I am in the Father; therefore, I say unto you, you shall receive grace for grace.
D&C 93:15-20

These verses teach us that Jesus received "*a fullness of the glory of the Father; and that he received all power both in heaven and on earth, and that the glory of the Father was with him, for he dwelt in him.*" (D&C93:16-17). These sayings are given unto us that we "*may understand and know **how to worship**, and know **what you worship**, that you may come unto the Father...and in due time receive of his fullness.*" If we are serious about receiving celestial glory, we need to possess a *physical and meta-physical* understanding of whom we worship. (see D&C 131:7 and Lecture on Faith #5).

In 1835 the church published the first Doctrine and Covenants. Included at the beginning of the text was "*The Lectures on Faith,*" which compromised the "doctrine" aspect of the book. These seven lectures were approved by the Prophet Joseph Smith and considered "scripture" after being ratified through the process of common consent. Lecture five is particularly relevant for receiving a correct understanding of what represents "GOD."

LECTURE FIVE

*"...We shall in this lecture speak of the Godhead; we mean the Father, Son, and Holy Spirit. **There are two personaages** who constitute the great, matchless, governing, and supreme power over all things – by whom all things were created and made that are created and made, whether visible or invisible; whether in heaven, on earth, or in the earth, under the earth, or throughout the immensity of space. They are the Father and the Son: **The Father being a personage of spirit,** glory, and power, possessing all perfection and fullness. The Son, who was in the bosom of the Father, a personage of tabernacle, made or fashioned like unto man, or being in the form and likeness of man - or rather, man was formed after his likeness and in his image. He is also the express image and likeness of the personage of the Father, possessing all the fullness of the Father, or the same fullness with the Father, being begotten of him; and was ordained from before the foundation of the world to be a propitiation for the sins of all those who should believe on his name; and **is called the Son because of the flesh**- and descended in suffering below that which man can suffer, or in other words, suffered greater sufferings, and was exposed to more powerful contradictions than any man can be. But notwithstanding all this, he kept the law of God and remained without sin; showing thereby that it is in the power of man to keep the law and remain also without sin. And also, that by him a righteous judgment might come upon all flesh, and that all who walk not in the law of God, may justly be condemned by the law, and have no excuse for their sins. And he being the Only Begotten of the Father, full of grace and truth, and having overcome,*

*received a fullness of the glory of the Father – **possessing the same mind with the Father;** **which Mind is the Holy Spirit,** that bears record of the Father and the Son; and these three are one, or in other words, these three constitute the great, matchless, governing, and supreme power over all things; by whom all things were created and made, that were created and made: and these three constitute the Godhead and are one: **the Father and the Son possessing the same mind,** the same wisdom, glory, power, and fullness; filling all in all – **the Son being filled with the fullness of the Mind, glory, and power; or in other words the Spirit, glory, and power of the Father** - possessing all knowledge and glory, and the same kingdom; sitting at the right hand of power, in the express image and likeness of the Father - a Mediator for man – **being filled with the fullness of the Mind of the Father, or in other words, the Spirit of the Father;** which Spirit is shed forth upon all who believe on his name and keep his commandments; and all those who keep his commandments shall grow up from grace to grace, and become heirs of the heavenly kingdom, and joint heirs with Jesus Christ; possessing the same mind, being transformed into the same image or likeness, even the express image of him who fills all in all; being filled with the fullness of his glory, and become one in him, even as the Father, Son, and Holy Spirit are one. From the foregoing account of the Godhead, which is given in his revelations, the saints have a sure foundation laid for the exercise of faith unto life and salvation, through the atonement and mediation of Jesus Christ, by whose blood they have a forgiveness of sins, and also a sure reward laid up for them in heaven-even that of partaking of the fullness of the Father and the Son, through the Spirit. As the Son partakes of the fullness of the Father through the Spirit, so the saints are, by the same Spirit, to be partakers of the same fullness, to enjoy the same glory; for as the Father and the Son are one, so in like manner the saints are to be one in them through the love of the Father, the mediation of Jesus Christ, and the gift of the Holy Spirit; they are to be heirs of God and joint heirs with Jesus Christ."*

In relation to the Godhead, lecture five promises, *"the saints have a sure foundation laid for the exercise of faith unto life and salvation."* And yet in 1921, a committee of prominent church leaders decided to re-print the Doctrine and Covenants without the Lectures on Faith included. Their omission and minimization of what Joseph Smith considered to be the very *"doctrine of salvation,"*[252] does not change the truth that the Lectures on Faith remain accurate scripture.

"Now these statements that I now read were in part written by the Prophet and in whole approved by him and taught by him in the school of the prophets. They're taken from the Lectures on Faith... this in effect is a creed announcing what Deity is. And in my judgment, it is the most comprehensive, intelligent, inspired utterance that now exists in the English language—that exists in one place defining, interpreting, expounding, announcing, and testifying what kind of a being God is. It was written by the power of the Holy Ghost, by the spirit of inspiration. And it is, in effect, eternal scripture; it's true."
Bruce R. McConkie, *The Lord God of Joseph Smith* [253]

Over the past 185 years, the church has altered its teachings concerning even the nature of Deity. The version of the "Godhead" promoted today has a more "western-friendly" mindset and makes conversion for Protestant Christians more compatible. But in relation to fully *"knowing God,"* it is essential to understand our religious digression so that any serious student of truth can reclaim the original teaching.

Elohim and Jehovah in Mormonism and the Bible
Boyd Kirkland [254]

"Currently the Church of Jesus Christ of Latter-day Saints defines the Godhead as consisting of three separate and distinct personages or Gods: Elohim, or God the Father; Jehovah, or Jesus Christ, the Son of God both in the spirit and in the flesh; and the Holy Ghost. The Father and the Son have physical, resurrected bodies of flesh and bone, but the Holy Ghost is a spirit personage. Jesus' title of Jehovah reflects his pre-existent role as God of the Old Testament. These definitions took official form in "The Father and the Son: A Doctrinal Exposition by the First Presidency and the Twelve" (1916) as the culmination of five major stages of theological development in Church history (Kirkland 1984):

1. Joseph Smith, Mormonism's founder, originally spoke and wrote about God in terms practically indistinguishable from then-current protestant theology. He used the roles, personalities, and titles of the Father and the Son interchangeably in a manner implying that he believed in only one God who manifested himself as three persons. The Book of Mormon, revelations in the Doctrine and Covenants prior to 1835, and Smith's 1832 account of his First Vision all reflect "trinitarian" perceptions. He did not use the title Elohim at all in this early stage and used Jehovah only rarely as the name of the "one" God.

2. The 1835 Lectures on Faith and Smith's official 1838 account of his First Vision both emphasized the complete separateness of the Father and the Son. The Lectures on Faith did not consider the Holy Ghost to be a personage at all, but rather defined it to be the mind of God: "There are two personages who constitute the great, matchless, governing, and supreme power over all things.... the Father and the Son--the Father being a personage of spirit, glory and power, possessing all perfection and fullness, the Son. . . a personage of tabernacle . . . possessing the same mind with the Father, which mind is the Holy Spirit, that bears record of the Father and the Son, and these three are one . . ." (Lundwall, 48). The names Elohim and Jehovah were both used in association with God the Father, who was also considered to be the God of the Old testament (Kirkland 1984,37).

3. Between 1838 and 1844, Joseph Smith introduced the concept of an infinite lineal hierarchy of Gods. The book of Abraham describes the creation as being performed by "the Gods" (4:1), and the King Follett Discourse further describes these Gods as a council presided over by a "head God" clearly a patriarchal superior to God the Father (Larson 1978, 202-03; Hale 1978, 212-18; Kirkland 1984, 38). Elohim was used variously as the name of God the Father, the name of a "Head God" who directed the Father in the creation of the world, and as a plural representing the Council of the Gods. The name Jehovah was also still associated with the Father, not with Jesus. The Holy Ghost was now generally referred to by Joseph Smith as being a personage.

4. In the 1854 general conference of the Church and on many other occasions throughout his life, Brigham Young taught that God the Father was also known as Michael. After creating the earth under the direction of Elohim and Jehovah, his patriarchal superiors in the Council of the Gods, Michael descended from his exalted, immortal status to become Adam, the first man, to provide his spiritual progeny with physical tabernacles. While in this fallen condition, his Father Elohim, the "grandfather" of mankind, presided over the earth in his stead. Following his "death," Adam returned to his exalted status and presided over Israel using both titles, Elohim and Jehovah. Jesus was begotten by this personage both spiritually and in the flesh (Kirkland 1984, 38-40; Buerger 1982, 14-58).

5. Between Brigham Young's death and the turn of the century, a mixture of all of the previously discussed theological positions circulated within the Church causing much conflict and confusion. To achieve some semblance of harmony between these widely varying ideas, as well as to quell external attacks from anti-Mormon critics at the "Adam-God" doctrine, Mormon leaders carefully reformulated Mormon theology around the turn of the century and articulated it in 1916 (Kirkland 1984, 39-41). These adjustments remain as the current doctrine of the Church today. As a result, much of the original meaning and context of the various godhead references in earlier Mormon scripture and teachings were lost as they were redefined or discarded during this harmonizing process. The Bible was used only as a secondary "prooftext" source for this reformulation of theology, as Mormon sources (regardless of their own extreme diversities) were considered to be more doctrinally sound and pure." (Boyd Kirkland, *Elohim and Jehovah in Mormonism and the Bible).*

Several examples of how the holy word of God has been transfigured could be provided here, but the heavens prefer we discover the truth individually-as we are prepared and willing to receive it. For those who desire the pure and undefiled gospel of Jesus Christ, being able to differentiate between eternal truth and religious tradition is essential.

The glory of God is intelligence, or, in other words, light and truth...And that wicked one cometh and taketh away light and truth, through disobedience, from the children of men,
*and **because of the tradition of their fathers.***
Doctrine and Covenants 93:36, 39

By implementing small omissions and discrepancies into our gospel comprehension, the deceiver twists and minimizes, (here a little and there a little) until over time, the interpretation and meaning applied to a gospel principle is gradually distorted. Eventually, cultural misinterpretation leads to incorrect religious application.

The degree that a member is able eradicate false traditions from their testimonies is the same degree to which he or she can receive a true gospel fullness.

"Fast-Food Mormonism"
"What does it mean when much of today's spirituality involves inspirational stories and quotes from general conference, but without any scriptural substance? Should cute stories from the Ensign supplant the words of Jesus? And what does it mean that Deseret Book is willing to promote and sell vampire books, along with spiritual self-help material, while refusing to print many books of doctrinal substance- even when what has been written is true and accurate? Is popular replacing essential? If not, then why the constant reminder that the words of the living prophet are more important than past scripture? Are the ancient and sacred words of mighty Isaiah, noble Enoch, and beloved Joseph, Really supposed to take a backseat to cute stories about shoveling snow and baking cookies?"
Anonymous Saint

The wheat of the church seek correction and clarification concerning the gospel of Jesus Christ. They acknowledge every verse in scripture and hunger for the correct interpretation, not just those which reinforce the common narrative. They seek out and receive truth which enlarges gospel understanding-even when it challenges the mainstream view.

*"When we learn the true definition of a word, especially if the word is found in scripture, our understanding increases. For example: **Unbelief** doesn't mean you don't believe, it means the form of your belief is not correct (i.e. you have the wrong kind of understanding). **Vanity** is not a slave to fashion, it means ineffective or lacking power. (i.e. your faith is vain)...**Wicked** can be defined as "acting in the name of the Lord, when you really aren't. Wickedness is deviating from correct doctrine. A wicked generation is a religious group of people who are unrepentant. A wicked leader teaches the commandments of men. He has a form of Godliness without the power. Wickedness leads people astray. An act of wickedness is similar to taking the Lord's name in vain. Which includes pretending you are speaking on behalf of the Lord when they are not His word's. We have been warned and forewarned that wickedness will increase...Today, we use the word wicked and evil interchangeably. However, they are two completely different words. Evil is outward, and can be seen with the natural eye. Wicked is inward, and is usually hidden, and disguised. Evil produces fear, sorrow, distress, injury or calamity, Wicked produces a false hope in something that can not save you. It is the religious who are convinced they know what is "right", and are the ones who can be the most wicked. It was the religious, temple-working Jews who crucified their Savior. Despite being religious, moral, and chaste virgins, the five who do not know the Lord are called foolish and wicked. Doctrine and Covenants 63:54 states, "And until that hour there will be foolish virgins among the wise; and at that hour cometh an entire separation of the righteous and the wicked."*
Anonymous Saint

Adjusting the doctrine by changing scripture and omitting the teachings of Joseph Smith has also led to a misapplication of how the church administers the gospel on a structural level. (see Truth #33). Examples where religious protocol contradicts scripture include the manner in which tithing is defined and acquired, how the Word of Wisdom is practiced, and even the method of administering the sacrament. (see Truth #31). Perhaps the most significant "transfiguration" has occurred in relation to changing the temple endowment.

In the temple, participants are warned Lucifer is willing to provide *"the philosophies of men mingled with scripture."* His distortions and subtle deceptions make it necessary to acquire pure knowledge, receive the truth as confirmed by the Holy Spirit, and then differentiate between what is eternally correct and that which has been altered and corrupted. How ironic that parsing out false philosophy is now applicable even to the temple endowment itself.

"If there is no change of ordinances, there is no change of Priesthood."
"Where there is no change of priesthood, there is no change of ordinances..."
Joseph Smith, *Teachings of the Prophet Joseph Smith* [255]

Observing that temple ordinances have been changed several times is not the angry ranting of some "anti-Mormon," but rather the concerned voice of those who understand there is a divine correlation between salvation, temple, and the power of creation.

"The temple, as we have seen, represented the whole creation...The eternal covenant was... imagined as the system of bonds that held the creation in being. The Hebrew words for covenant, creation and binding are closely related. Sin was, by definition, anything that broke those bonds, whether done deliberately or in ignorance, and so one of the duties of a priest was to protect the covenant by giving right teaching. The priest was an angel [a messenger, the same word in Hebrew] of the LORD, and so a priest who neglected his teaching or gave false teaching was a fallen angel. Isaiah was one of many prophets who had a vision of the covenant collapsing. He saw the heavens and the earth wilting under the weight of pollution...because people had transgressed the laws, violated the statutes, and broken the eternal covenant. Therefore a curse was devouring the earth. Since the temple represented the creation, any sin against the creation was deemed to pollute the temple,"
Margaret Barker, *Our Great High Priest. The Church as the New Temple,* [256]

To break the covenant is to pollute the temple and offend God and Mother Earth. Although today's liberal media is obsessed with global warming and saving the planet, the Lord has identified what truly defiles the earth and brings destruction upon the people.

Changing the Ordinances
Behold, the LORD maketh the earth empty, and maketh it waste, and turneth it upside down, and scattereth abroad the inhabitants thereof. And it shall be, as with the people, so with the priest; as with the servant, so with his master; so with the seller; as with the lender, so with the borrower...The land shall be utterly emptied, and utterly spoiled: for the LORD hath spoken this word. The earth mourneth and fadeth away, the world languisheth and fadeth away, the haughty people of the earth do languish. The earth also is defiled under the inhabitants thereof; because they have transgressed the laws, changed the ordinance, broken the everlasting covenant. Therefore hath the curse devoured the earth, and they that dwell therein are desolate: therefore the inhabitants of the earth are burned, and few men left.
Isaiah 24:1-6

According to Isaiah none are spared from the curse when God's children break the everlasting covenant. This process, which includes idolatry, changing ordinances, and polluting the Lord's temple, has traditionally been applied to **the apostasies of other churches.** In 1979 Apostle David B. Haight stated:

"We explained briefly the Apostasy and the Restoration: that there is vast evidence and history of an apostasy from the doctrine taught by Jesus and his Apostles, that the organization of the original Church became corrupted, and sacred ordinances were changed to suit the convenience of men..."
David B. Haight, *Joseph Smith the Prophet* [257]

In addition to the historical pattern explained by Elder Haight, Joseph Smith prophetically addressed the temptation to change temple ordinances when he stated,

"Ordinances instituted in the heavens before the foundation of the world, in the priesthood, for the salvation of men, are not to be altered or changed. All must be saved on the same principles."
Joseph Smith, *History of the Church* [258]

Ironically, even church educational manuals explain the spiritual relevance of breaking covenants and changing ordinances.

Apostasy from the True Church

"What does the term apostasy mean? Throughout history, evil people have tried to destroy the work of God. This happened while the Apostles were still alive and supervising the young, growing Church. Some members taught ideas from their old pagan or Jewish beliefs instead of the simple truths taught by Jesus. Some rebelled openly...More and more error crept into Church doctrine, and soon the dissolution of the Church was complete. The period of time when the true Church no longer existed on earth is called the Great Apostasy. Soon pagan beliefs dominated the thinking of those called Christians...Many of the ordinances were changed because the priesthood and revelation were no longer on the earth...There were no Apostles or other priesthood leaders with power from God, and there were no spiritual gifts. The prophet Isaiah had foreseen this condition, prophesying, 'The earth also is defiled under the inhabitants thereof; because they have transgressed the laws, changed the ordinance, broken the everlasting covenant' (Isaiah 24:5). It was the Church of Jesus Christ no longer; it was a church of men...."
Gospel Principles Manual, *The Church of Jesus Christ in Former Times* [259]

We fail to apply this standard to ourselves. When unenlightened men changed the ordinances after the death of Jesus, it was considered "apostasy." But when the same categorical choices are made today, it is considered "revelation."

When local leaders are questioned concerning temple changes, the usual response is "We have a living prophet today." In response to this answer it is unclear how having a religious leader changes our personal need to access the full endowment. Does having prophetic leadership somehow make the losses acceptable? Are we supposed to pretend that losing key elements of the original endowment, such as the penalties, five points of fellowship, and the complete true order of prayer is irrelevant?

Do the Changes Really Matter?

"No jot, iota, or tittle of the temple rites is otherwise than uplifting and sanctifying. In every detail the endowment ceremony contributes to covenants of morality of life, consecration of person to high ideals, devotion to truth, patriotism to nation, and allegiance to God."
James E. Talmage, *The House of the Lord* [260]

All of Father's commandments?

"Zion will not and cannot be built until a people is found who are zealous of good works and are striving to live all the commandments. That is the crux of the whole issue, and why it matters when covenants are slandered, brought low, and become anything less than an exalting principle for the children of men."
Dan Mead, *Zion* [261]

A Slippery Slope

"Does an absolute God view as "His" a Church which does not keep all His commandments, preserve and preach all His words, and follow all His instructions? If He "cannot look upon sin with the least degree of allowance" then how are we doing when we neglect, discard and reject things He has instructed us to do, believe and follow?"
Denver Snuffer [262]

Are We Becoming Catholic?

"Now, what have the Christians got that the Latter-day Saints have not got? Has the holy Catholic Church got faith in Jesus that we have not got? Not a particle that is true and pure. But as for the ordinances of the House of God , we say, and we say it boldly, and here is the standard of our faith-The Old and New Testament-that the mother church and all her daughters have transgressed the laws, everyone of them; they have changed almost every ordinance in the house of God; and not only so, but like the children of Israel in olden days, they have broken the covenants made with the fathers."
Brigham Young, *The Essential Brigham Young* [263]

Could the current temple experience be incomplete-but still effective? And if so, is it possible for an individual to diligently seek and privately receive all that was once offered?

One Gospel

"The Gospel can not possibly be changed…the saving principles must ever be the same. They can never change…the Gospel must always be the same in all of its parts…no one can change the Gospel…if they attempt to do so, they only set up a man-made system which is not the Gospel, but is merely a reflection of their own views…if we substitute "any other Gospel" there is no salvation in it…the Lord and His Gospel remain the same-always."
The Prophet's Message, *Church News* [264]

A complete review of changes made by the church is beyond the scope of this text. But a review of church history reveals the endowment has been changed several times. (1893, 1919, 1936, 1990, 2005, 2008, 2013).[265] Members have generally responded to the changes in the following manner:

1) We have a true prophet who leads us. The changes were directed by God and a sign of the church's progress. All who question the appropriateness of the changes demonstrate a lack of faith.

2) We have a prophet who leads us. If we are losing parts of the endowment, we should examine the reasons why God would impress the brethren to make the changes. The losses may relate directly to the spiritual performance of the people.

3) By changing the ordinances and breaking the everlasting covenant, we are fulfilling the prophecies of Isaiah. These ongoing losses represent a minimization of light and are a sign of our ongoing condemnation. (D&C 84:55-56).

Those who believe the President of the church was directed by God to omit and modify temple content may want to ponder the following questions: For what purpose would God direct this? Are the people no longer worthy of a true fullness? Could it be a sign of our ongoing apathy and disobedience? Or is it due to the reality that the church is increasingly vulnerable to legal dispute? Was direct contact at the veil ended to diminish the possibility of the church being sued? Was it primarily a business decision? Perhaps temple changes were enacted to appease the people and give them the *convenience* Elder Haight mentioned in the previous quote? Did surveys and polling data gathered from members before the 1990 temple changes have any influence on the brethren? Is it possible leaders simply gave members what they wanted by eradicating symbolism they didn't like and didn't understand? And what about those Saints who mourn the changes and still desire to partake of the full endowment?

The Beginning of the End

"After chosen people lose their connection with God, they no longer receive regular or consistent revelation to increase their knowledge and add to their sacred records. The body of scripture first becomes static. Then, because of wickedness, men deliberately suppress, alter, and discard past revelations which they are no longer willing to accept. Their canon of scriptures actually diminishes over time. Despite all this, God's patience with His chosen people persists until finally they alter and reject His ordinances."
Denver Snuffer, *Come Let Us Adore Him* [266]

In truth, everything that is required to part the veil and be redeemed of the Lord remains available. Regardless of policy adjustments and doctrinal loss, the eternal gospel of Jesus Christ never changes.

"...We stand ready to bear off this Gospel to the nations of the earth, this great plan of salvation devised by our Father. There has never been any other, and there never will be.
Men have tinkered at it; but their efforts do not change God's plan, it is like its author-
'the same yesterday, today and forever.' God is the fountain of truth, righteousness and grace."
Daniel H. Wells, *The Saving Ordinances of the Gospel* [267]

Despite institutional limitations, it remains our individual responsibility to turn to the Master and *"seek learning even by study and also by faith."* (D&C 109:7). Those who turn to God will be blessed with an abundance of temple light concerning altars, the true order of prayer, penalties, five points of fellowship, the second washing and anointing, and sealing power.

Our Father and His Son are the greatest teachers in the universe. And even though some important aspects of the original endowment have been temporarily lost or gone dormant, they remain ready to deliver all that we are willing to receive.

> *Give ear, O ye heavens, and I will speak; And hear, O earth, the words of my mouth.*
> *My doctrine shall drop as the rain…and as the showers upon the grass.*
> Deuteronomy 32:1-2

Those hungry for truth can study older versions of the endowment, ponder what the changes mean, and then receive further light and knowledge from God, angels, and His true messengers. To be tutored directly from heaven has always been the invitation.

The Sure Source

> *"I do not want men to come to me or my brethren for testimony as to the truth of this work; but let them **take the Scriptures of divine truth**, and there the path is pointed out to them as plainly as ever a guideboard indicated the right path to the weary traveler. There **they are directed to go, not to Brothers Brigham, Heber, or Daniel, to any apostle or elder in Israel, but to the Father in the name of Jesus, and ask for the information they need…what is revealed by the Lord from Heaven is sure and steadfast,** and abides for ever. **We do not want the people to rely on human testimony,** although that cannot be confuted and destroyed; still, there is a more sure word of prophecy that all may gain if they will seek it earnestly before the Lord."*
> Brigham Young, *Journal of Discourses* [268]

In contrast to what Brigham Young taught, the institution for several decades has encouraged members to rely on human testimony. By *constantly* emphasizing the importance of current leadership, the church has been able to enact numerous changes while simultaneously maintaining the illusion that the church is teaching what Joseph Smith revealed.

Today, the truth is coming out. Members feel betrayed by an organization that they have given their lives to. For those who love Jesus Christ and the Restoration, the challenge is to not let the church's "transfiguration" result in a personal apostasy. The church may be struggling, but God is not. In HIM, all can be made right. All is well. The truth remains.

> *The Lord of hosts is with us; the God of Jacob is our refuge…*
> *Be still, and know that I am God…*
> Psalms 46:7,10

TRUTH #31 THE PROPHET MORONI EXPLICITLY WARNS THAT IN THE LAST DAYS, THE LORD'S CHURCH WILL BE POLLUTED.

And my vineyard has become corrupted every whit; and there is none which doeth good save it be a few; and they err in many instances because of priestcrafts, all having corrupt minds.
D&C 33:4

For over 200 years America has existed as a symbol of freedom throughout the world. For just under 200 years, The Church of Jesus Christ of Latter Day Saints has existed as a beacon of religious truth. This reality has made both America and The Church of Jesus Christ the target of evil.

"History seems to show that the powers of evil have won their greatest triumphs by capturing the organizations which were formed to defeat them, and that the devil has thus changed the contents of the bottles, he never altered the labels. The fort may have been captured by the enemy, but it still flies the flag of its defenders."
Admiral Ben Moreel, *Prophet Principles and National Survival* [269]

Satan knows that the most effective way to destroy something is from the inside. Similar to when Jesus knew Judas would betray him but still chose him to be an apostle, we must understand that the Lord allows corruption to exist within His church to fulfill His wise and holy purposes.

"It is important to realize that while the Church is made up of mortals, no mortal is the Church. Judas, for a period of time, was a member of the Church-in fact, one of its apostles- but the Church was not Judas...Sometimes we hear someone refer to a division in the Church. In reality, the Church is not divided. It simply means that there are some who, for the time being at least, are members of the Church but not in harmony with it. These people have a temporary membership and influence in the Church; but unless they repent, they will be missing when the final membership records are recorded."
Ezra Taft Benson, *To the Humble Followers of Christ* [270]

Good and faithful members may find it difficult to comprehend our Latter Day situation, but part of the adversary's continual efforts to deceive include reassuring members that mass corruption could never happen within the Lord's church.

"People who regard themselves as members of the only true Church have the fatal tendency to consider themselves immune from the disease of deception. Knowing that they belong to the Lord's Church and have His scriptures and His prophets to guide them, they blindly assume that this adequately protects them against false beliefs. All history teaches the folly of such an assumption, and the scriptures specifically deny its validity..."
H. Verlan Andersen, *The Apostasy of the Latter Days* [271]

Today the Lord allows the tares to thrive within the Church. These members are not "bad people," they simply have not yet come to certain realizations. Personal honesty requires us to acknowledge that all of us have played the part of "tare" in various scenarios during our life. Thus, making observations about the church being polluted is not about being judgmental or negative, but rather about having the knowledge necessary to rectify our own personal pollution. In truth, focusing on the problems of the church is wasted energy unless it motivates us to perceive our own individual weaknesses and then repent.

> *"It is well that our people understand this principle, so they will not be misled by those apostates*
> *within the Church who have not yet repented or been cut off. But there is a cleansing coming.*
> *The Lord says that his vengeance shall be poured out "upon the inhabitants of the earth…*
> *And upon my house shall it begin, and from my house shall it go forth, saith the Lord;*
> *First among those among you, saith the Lord, who have professed to know my name*
> *And have not known me…(D&C 112:24-26.) I look forward to that cleansing;*
> *its need within the Church is becoming increasingly apparent."*
> Ezra Taft Benson, *To the Humble Followers of Christ* [272]

This prophetic statement about a coming cleansing was issued in 1969 by President Benson. Decades later, his warning requires us to ask whether the tares have now corrupted the church to the degree that it is significantly distorted and ineffective as compared to its original purpose.

To "pollute" something involves desecrating that which was once clean, virtuous, and approved of God. (D&C 1:30). The possibility that the Lord's church has been tragically polluted is also congruent with revelation recorded in the Book of Mormon. The prophet Moroni witnessed in vision *our day* and mourned the depleted status of the *Holy Church of God.*

> *Behold, I speak unto you as if ye were present, and yet ye are not. But behold, Jesus Christ hath shown you*
> *unto me, and* **I know your doing**. *And I know that ye do walk in the* **pride of your hearts**;
> *and there are none save a few only who do not lift themselves up in the pride of their hearts,*
> *unto the* **wearing of very fine apparel**, *unto envying, and strifes, and malice, and* **persecutions**,
> *and* **all manner of iniquities; and your churches, yea, even every one, have become polluted**
> *because of the pride of your hearts. For behold, ye do* **love money, and your substance**,
> *and your fine apparel, and the adorning of your churches, more than ye love* **the poor and the needy,**
> **the sick and the afflicted**. *O ye pollutions, ye hypocrites, ye teachers, who sell yourselves for that which*
> *will canker,* **why have ye polluted the holy church of God? Why are ye ashamed to take upon you**
> **the name of Christ?** *Why do ye not think that greater is the value of an endless happiness*
> *than that misery which never dies—because of the* **praise of the world?**
> *Why do ye adorn yourselves with that which hath no life, and yet suffer the hungry, and the needy,*
> *and the naked, and the sick and the afflicted to pass by you, and notice them not?*
> Mormon 8:35-39

Mormons usually skip over these verses or conveniently interpret them to be referring to the initial apostasy and the Roman Catholic Church. This introductory interpretation works well until we remember Moroni saw *our doing,* and that the Book of Mormon was written specifically to us-not another religion. The Catholic church *never was* the *"holy church of God,"* making it impossible to "pollute" something that was corrupt from the beginning.

In addition to these obvious clues, disciple Dan Mead points out that at the beginning of Mormon chapter nine, Moroni begins to speak to *"those who do not believe in Christ."* (Mormon 9:1). This verse makes it clear that the message previously recorded in Mormon chapter eight is addressed to those *who do believe in Christ* and are part of the Lord's once-holy church.

Listed below are some quotes that relate to the spiritual challenges Moroni observed in vision.

Pride

"…The Book of Mormon is the "record of a fallen people." (D&C 20:9). Why did they fall? This is one of the major messages of the Book of Mormon. Mormon gives the answer in the closing chapters of the book in these words: "Behold, the pride of this nation, or the people of the Nephites, hath proven their destruction." (Moro. 8:27.) And then, lest we miss that momentous Book of Mormon message from that fallen people, the Lord warns us in the Doctrine and Covenants, "Beware of pride, lest ye become as the Nephites of old." (D&C 38:39).

Ezra Taft Benson, *Beware of Pride* [273]

"There is irony about being the Lord's "chosen people" which often escapes us. More often than not, the blessing of being "chosen" turns into a burden which the chosen fail in their attempt to carry. It turns them into an example of what not to do, how not to live, and how to disappoint God…Almost without exception, being a "chosen" group is a statement of God's patience, commitment and long suffering. It has little to do with the worthiness of the group itself…Those who are "chosen" presume this means they are right with God. This presumption of superiority feeds pride, haughtiness and arrogance. The chosen people are blind to their actual condition. They never realize they are on display, exhibiting foolishness, excess, pride and disobedience. From a distance, later in time, or from outside, the glaring weaknesses of the chosen become the great lesson to be learned from chosen people. These weaknesses exhibited by those chosen of the Lord teach a valuable lesson to those who are willing to see. In each generation of those chosen by God, there are individuals who are shown by revelation the pride and arrogance of those who ignorantly celebrate God's peculiar delight in them. These few individuals are the ones upon whom the Lord lays the obligation to declare repentance. These characters are generally outcasts who are disliked and rejected."

Denver Snuffer, *Come Let Us Adore Him* [274]

Wearing Fine Apparel

For behold, ye do love money and your substance, and your fine apparel, and the adorning of your churches, more than ye love the poor and the needy, the sick and the afflicted.

Mormon 8:37

"The Lord was gregarious, but we've turned Him into a caricature. The leaders of the church have themselves become imprisoned by an image which requires them to be holy from birth and never stray from a sort of "plastic-fantastic" single, dimensional, cardboard persona. Inside this trap you see them living as if on constant display (which they are),

wearing the uniform of a white shirt, dark suit and power tie to see a movie, (should they ever attend a movie). The Saints want it, the Brethren deliver, and everyone moves about judging motive from conduct when it is utter rubbish."
Anonymous Saint

But the LORD said unto Samuel, Look not on his countenance, or on the height of his stature; because I have refused him: for the LORD seeth not as man seeth; for man looketh on the outward appearance, but the LORD looketh on the heart.
1 Samuel 16:7

Envy, Strife, and Malice

This people draweth nigh unto me with their mouth, and honoureth me with their lips; but their heart is far from me.
Matthew 15:8

For they saw and beheld with great sorrow that the people of the church began to be lifted up in the pride of their eyes, and to set their hearts upon riches and upon the vain things of the world, that they began to be scornful, one towards another, and they began to persecute those that did not believe according to their own will and pleasure. And thus, in this there began to be great contentions among the people of the church; yea, there were envyings, and strife, and malice, and persecutions, and pride, even to exceed the pride of those who did not belong to the church of God.
Alma 4:8-9

Persecuting God's Humble Elect

"...You will live to see men rise in power in the church who will seek to put down your friends and the friends of our Lord and Savior, Jesus Christ. Many will be hoisted because of their money and the worldly learning which they seem to be in possession of; and many who are the true followers of our Lord and Savior will be cast down because of their poverty."
Joseph Smith, *Mosiah Hancock Journal* [275]

Blessed are ye, when men shall revile you, and persecute you, and shall say all manner of evil against you falsely, for my sake. rejoice, and be exceedingly glad: for great is your reward in heaven: for so persecuted they the prophets which were before you.
Matthew 5:11-12

Love of Money and Substance

"The Lord has blessed us as a people with a prosperity unequaled in times past.
The resources that have been placed in our power are good, and necessary to our work
here on the earth. But I am afraid that many of us have been surfeited with flocks and herds
and acres and barns and wealth and have begun to worship them as false gods,
and they have power over us. Do we have more of these good things than our faith can stand?
Many people spend most of their time working in the service of a self image that includes
sufficient money, stocks, bonds, investment portfolios, property, credit cards, furnishings,
automobiles, and the like to guarantee carnal security throughout, it is hoped,
a long and happy life. Forgotten is the fact that our assignment is to use these many resources
in our families and quorums to build up the kingdom of God — to further the missionary effort
and the genealogical and temple work; to raise our children up as fruitful servants unto the Lord;
to bless others in every way, that they may also be fruitful. Instead, we expend these blessings on
our own desires, and as Moroni said, "Ye adorn yourselves with that which hath no life, and yet
suffer the hungry, and the needy, and the naked, and the sick and the afflicted to pass by you,
and notice them not. (Mormon 8:39)."
Spencer W. Kimball, *The Teachings of Spencer W. Kimball* [276]

For what is a man profited, if he shall gain the whole world, and lose his own soul?
Or what shall a man give in exchange for his soul?
Matthew 16:26

Ashamed to Take On the Name of Christ

Nevertheless among the chief rulers also many believed on him; but because of the Pharisees
they did not confess him, lest they should be put out of the synagogue:
For they loved the praise of men more than the praise of God.
John 12:42-43

For these are they who are of Paul, and of Apollos, and of Cephas. These are they who say
they are some of one and some of another--some of Christ and some of John, and some of Moses,
and some of Elias, and some of Esaias, and some of Isaiah, and some of Enoch;
But received not the gospel, neither the testimony of Jesus,
neither the prophets, neither the everlasting covenant.
D&C 76:99-101

164

Idolatry and Worshipping False Gods

*"…when I review the performance of this people in comparison with what is expected,
I am appalled and frightened. If we insist on spending all our time and resources building
up for ourselves a worldly kingdom, that is exactly what we will inherit. In spite of our delight
in defining ourselves as modern, and our tendency to think we possess a sophistication
that no people in the past ever had–in spite of these things, we are, on the whole,
an idolatrous people–a condition most repugnant to the Lord."*
Spencer W. Kimball, *Ensign* [277]

*"Among the Lord's people, worship of the true God is rarely done away with.
Rather, they often* **worship the true God alongside the false Gods***. They maintain careful
equilibrium in order to preserve an identity with the national God, the God of Israel or of
the Fathers. At the same time, the people follow their own Gods as they please. This compromise
enables people to satisfy both their carnal instincts and their spiritual aspirations…
Ironically appearances of true worship persist in every stage of apostasy."*
Avraham Gileadi, *Modern Idolatry:12 Diatribes* [278]

Seeking and Achieving the Praise of Babylon

*"There were many churches which professed to know the Christ, and yet they did deny
the more parts of his gospel. They took some parts. They kept parts of the gospel, but they got rid
of others they didn't like…They accommodated their doctrines to the market…It was very popular.
The church grew phenomenally as a result of this. Remember, this is the church were talking about.
This is not apostates…the phenomenal growth of the church is no proof that it's true at all,
or that it's on the true path. It grew faster than anything because it was very popular.
So don't use popularity as a gauge either."*
Hugh Nibley, *Teachings of the Book of Mormon* [279]

*"There are at least three dangers that threaten the Church within, and the authorities need to
awaken to the fact that the people should be warned unceasingly against them. As I see these, they
are* **flattery of prominent men in the world***, false educational ideas, and sexual impurity."*
Joseph F. Smith, *Gospel Doctrine: Selections from the Sermons and Writings of Joseph F. Smith* [280]

*"For several decades there seems to have a been a consistent effort to be "accepted" by the world.
In direct contrast to being a "peculiar people" a consistent public relations effort has been enacted
in an attempt to be included in "mainstream Christianity." To the wise observer there seems to be
a fine line between advancing missionary work through social interaction, and selling our soul
for popularity and ongoing condemnation. We know that many are called, and few are chosen,
but why are they not chosen? Because their hearts are set so much upon the things of this world,
and they aspire to the honors of men. (D&C 121:34)."*
Anonymous Saint

Reviewing the words of scripture requires us to admit a stark reality: The prophet Moroni prophesied that the Gentile church would be polluted—and it has been.

"For they saw and beheld with great sorrow that the people of the church began to be lifted up in the pride of their eyes, and to set their hearts upon riches and upon the vain things of the world, that they began to be scornful, one towards another, and they began to persecute those that did not believe according to their own will and pleasure. And thus, in this there began to be great contentions among the people of the church; yea, there were envyings, and strife, and malice, and persecutions, and pride, even to exceed the pride of those who did not belong to the church of God".
Alma 4:8-9

One of the most symbolic examples of how pride, wealth, contention, doctrinal ignorance, and unrighteous dominion, have polluted the Holy Church of God can be observed in the manner in which the sacrament is administered today. One Latter Day Saint offers the following perspective.

Becoming a Sacrament
By Anonymous

With the Savior in their midst…

One by one they approached Him, touched the wounds in His hands and were enfolded by Him in a sacred embrace. They then fell on His feet and wept.

They gazed upon His face and heard His words.
They bore witness as He took the little children and blessed them and wept.

They watched as angels ministered to the children with love.
They witnessed the Savior healing the sick and afflicted among them.

They, each one, partook of the sacrament He offered them,
He was moved with compassions for them and wept and prayed to the Father

Each one had been through much pain and suffering,
Each broken and contrite soul did hear, did see, did partake.

In 3 Nephi 18:3-13, the Savior administered the sacrament to approximately two thousand men, women, and children. He gave them bread in remembrance of His holy body and wine in remembrance of His sacred blood.

The significance of the wine should not be ignored. Jesus commanded us to partake of the sacrament using bread *and* wine. Why wine? Why is water not sufficient? Wine is essential because it holds qualities and characteristics of the Atonement that water does not. Wine is bitter to the taste. It is not necessarily a pleasant experience at first and the bitterness of it lingers in the mouth, resting there in burning remembrance and solemn contemplation of Him. The wine is swallowed and the burning spreads through the body, cleansing it with its heat. Then, somehow, the sweetness of the grape comes to the senses and the burning becomes a glowing warmth that embraces and forgives.

And when the disciples had come with bread and wine, he took of the bread and brake and blessed it and…he commanded his disciples that they should take of the wine of the cup and drink of it, and that they should also give unto the multitude that they might drink of it.
3 Nephi 18:3,8

Partaking of the bread and wine allows a broken heart to touch the Lord and accept His gift, which is *all that the Father hath.* There is great power in loving the Savior with full purpose of heart and partaking of the sacrament as the Savior demonstrated. Doing so is a step toward receiving the Second Comforter. Jesus came to the Jews and Nephites. He will do the same for us. Let us go and fully partake. (*Becoming a Sacrament).*[281]

Receiving this ordinance, as defined by the Savior, is clearly significant to our salvation. For Jesus commanded it of us, and said that if we do *"more or less"* than this, then *"the gates of hell are ready open to receive (us)."* (3 Nephi 18:13).

So…why do we no longer partake of wine during the sacrament? There is no verse in scripture directing us to replace "wine" with "water," and yet the dominant belief is that partaking of wine contradicts the Word of Wisdom. The irony is that *by not allowing* the use of wine we are actually *non-compliant* with D&C 89. The Word of Wisdom explains that it is not good to drink wine or strong drink **except** when *"assembling yourselves together to offer up your sacraments before him."*(D&C 89:5). What might be the reasons that we no longer partake of the sacrament as Jesus originally intended? Could it be that culturally we are not prepared or qualified to receive the full ordinance?

In the early church, administration of the sacrament was done differently, with the entire congregation kneeling for the sacramental prayer, (D&C 20:76) and then sitting quietly while meditating to hymns. In compliance with 3 Nephi 18:28-30, anyone considered unworthy was to be prayed for, but not allowed to partake of the sacrament.

In today's church, the sacred duty to *"administer bread and wine-the emblems of the flesh and blood of Christ"* (D&C 20:40) has been relegated to the Aaronic Priesthood. This practice is also contrary to revelation which explains that when an elder is present, the sacrament is to be administered by someone holding the Melchizedek Priesthood. (D&C 20: 40,50).

For Mormons, there are just so many things *"that have always been that way."* Very few question why our religious practice does not fully align with the example of Jesus and His scripture.

Today's method for administering the sacrament may not be perfect, but the current ordinance does demonstrate that truth and meaning are still present within the LDS church. Even with the limitations, accessing the Holy Spirit and renewing our covenants remains possible. It is that same Spirit which then invites those who are ready into a deeper symbolism and power. When we partake of the sacrament in the manner Jesus intended, we can then *know personally* that when we are ready to come to Him, He is ready to come to us. In that moment, we grow from *taking* the sacrament, to *becoming a sacrament.* Our consecration is completed in Christ.

Some still dream of a time and place when broken-hearted souls simply gather to worship God. They envision a worthy Melchizedek Priesthood holder inviting the entire congregation to kneel and partake of the Lord's supper. (D&C 20:76-77). With arm raised to the square, the humble disciple blesses the unleavened bread which has been carefully kneaded with adoration for the Messiah. Next, the wine is blessed as a sacred emblem of the blood of our Lord's new testament. Holy emblems are individually shared as each person ponders with joy and meditation their continued surrender unto the Master.

The personal cleansing symbolized in the sacrament is also representative of the religious cleansing to come. For *"God will not be mocked,"* and in the end He will purge and perfect His Saints.

> *"The Church should be cleansed from bad men,*
> *and the Lord will take His own way to cleanse the Church"*
> Orson Spencer, *History of the Church* [282]

Regardless of what the mainstream currently believes about "the church," the day will come when the Lord will correct the pollution and purify His house. (see Truth #48). All that has been lost or gone dormant since the death of Joseph will be re-restored, and the higher laws will again be established. (see Truth #41).

Awaiting the Final Cleanse

> *"In our own dispensation the law of Enoch was offered to the Church, but the Latter-day Saints failed to live it and therefore it was taken away and a lesser law instituted until such time as Christ shall come to cleanse the Church, along with the rest of the world, of its wickedness and disobedience, by removing all things that offend."*
> Joseph Fielding Smith, *The Progress of Man* [283]

TRUTH #32 ENDOWED MEMBERS HAVE COVENANTED NOT TO SPEAK EVIL OF THE LORD'S ANOINTED. IT IS WISE TO LOVE ALL PEOPLE AS WE SEEK THE UNITY AND PURITY OF ZION.

Let your communication be, Yea, yea; Nay, nay:
for whatsoever is more than these cometh of evil.
Matthew 5:37

Every church leader on a both a global and local level has been called to be a witness of Jesus Christ. Each deserves our prayers and support while they do the best they can to magnify a spiritually demanding calling.

In today's complicated religious environment, we need to remember the apostles are under extreme political and spiritual pressure. They have problems and weaknesses, and so do we. The choices they make for the collective church are mostly irrelevant in relation to personal salvation and own specific stewardship. We should be focused on our own repentance, not the limitations and errors of others.

"...We can safely assume that the Brethren will be held responsible for any personal mistakes.
To use the supposed errors of others, including the Brethren, as an excuse for our
lessened devotion is a most grave error! All of us are in the process of becoming
including prophets and General Authorities."
Neal A. Maxwell, *All Things Shall Give Thee Experience* [284]

Today many choices are being made by the corporate church which are difficult to understand and accept. Nevertheless, every endowed member has covenanted to refrain from *"evil speaking of the Lord's anointed."* For those who understand scripture and watch for the historical warning signs of apostasy, this can be a difficult covenant to keep.

Wisdom suggests focusing on individual weaknesses instead of institutional corruption. Fault finding or publicly disagreeing with church policy may feel therapeutic, but it is unlikely to bring us closer to Christ.

To Have Mercy on Ourselves
"Accusing someone is Satanic. One of the titles for Satan is "the accuser of the Brethren."
Satan's accusations are not said to be unwarranted or unsupported. He is not necessarily accusing
his victims unjustly. It is probable some if not all of the accusations were, or are, just. If any of us were
measured by an absolute standard of obedience, faithfulness, and virtue, we would all necessarily fail.
Satan does not need to use an unfair standard to accuse and condemn us...the negative and condemned
*role of accusing belongs to Satan. **Those who take it upon themselves to do the condemning***
***are acting the part of Satan.** "Joseph Smith taught in DHC 4:445: "If you do not accuse each other,*
god will not accuse you."...It is in this sense that Joseph taught, "A man is his own tormentor and his
own condemner." In the great Day of Judgment, men will have to face their accusers...
for us to pass the test, we must not accuse our offenders. It does not matter who will accuse you.

What matters is whether or not you will accuse another…. Show charity to the Saints. Give it to the Church authorities. **Rather than judge or dismiss them, pray for, sustain and support them. It will please God and relieve you of yet another difficult self-imposed test that might prevent you from surviving the Day of Judgment.** *If we show mercy to our fellow man, we merit mercy from Our Lord. If we show love to our fellow man, we merit love from Our Lord. With what measure we measure, it will be measured again to us; pressed down and overflowing….***Our mercy shown to others is really mercy being shown to ourselves. We set the standard for our own judgment. Christ's counsel pleads for us to set that standard mercifully low for others, so we can meet that standard ourselves.***"*
Denver Snuffer, *The Second Comforter-Conversing with the Lord Through the Veil* [285]

It can be difficult to be spiritually aware and still contribute to social unity by minimizing conflict. The mind of the natural man does not want to meekly submit, but would rather justify the illusion of its own self-importance. When negativity is spoken about leadership, especially in public, pride increases and the Spirit shrinks. Very little good results from speaking evil of the Lords anointed, even when what is spoken is accurate.

"The rhetorical criticism seems to raise a notch when some pseudo-intellectual Saints speak about the presiding authorities of the Church. The Brethren who preside over the Church of Jesus Christ of Latter Day Saints deserve your support, prayers and confidence, not your judgment and criticism. If they fail or err, forgive them and sustain them with your prayers. You fail. You err. If you want to be forgiven of that in your life, then forgive them for their failings and errors. The Seriousness of this issue is reflected in the Temple covenants. Refraining from "evil speaking of the Lord's anointed" should be given its broadest possible application. Calling Church authorities into question is an unnecessary distraction from the issues you should be dealing with. Work on the things in your life that need attention. Criticism of Church leaders or members from afar is just not one the things you need to crowd into your life. Let them go in peace, and without your judgment and censure. Support them with your prayers. They will do better with your charity than they will with your complaints. The inspired leaders of the Church of Jesus Christ of Latter day Saints are assigned by the Lord to lead his Saints in these latter days. They are entrusted with keys and authority which is necessary for salvation. If you want to make personal covenants with God, you must do so through His established systems for allowing that. And those who are chosen by Him to preside in His Church are entitled to receive the voice of inspiration to assist them in the process. When they do speak with the voice of inspiration, you should hear them as the "voice of the Lord."
Denver Snuffer, *The Second Comforter-Conversing with the Lord Through the Veil* [286]

Growing Saints who feel micro-managed, spiritually starved, or consistently overlooked should turn to the Lord for peace and guidance. What the brethren determine to be best for the global church may or may not be the Lord's will for your specific situation. Remembering this spiritual dynamic can assist each Saint in following the Holy Spirit as directed-while still being externally supportive of general church policy. The fact that others may not understand or agree with this perspective does not change the value of the approach.

Then went the captain with the officers, and brought them without violence: for they feared the people, lest they should have been stoned. And when they had brought them, they set them before the council: and the high priest asked them, Saying, Did not we straitly command you that ye should not teach in this name? and, behold, ye have filled Jerusalem with your doctrine, and intend to bring this man's blood upon us. Then Peter and the other apostles answered and said,
We ought to obey God rather than men.
Acts 5: 26-29

If local leadership accidentally slips into priestcraft and unrighteous dominion, it may help to remember the love Jesus demonstrated during His mortal ministry. Just as Jesus submitted to Caiaphas, Pilate, and the Pharisees, those who are humble at heart practice love in their own wards and branches. By choosing to model the same self-control Jesus demonstrated toward His local leaders, the remnant of Christ exemplifies real power.

And straightway in the morning the chief priests held a consultation with the elders and scribes and the whole council, and bound Jesus, and carried him away, and delivered him to Pilate. And Pilate asked him, Art thou the King of the Jews? And he answering said unto him, Thou sayest it. And the chief priests accused him of many things: but he answered nothing. And Pilate asked him again, saying, Answerest thou nothing? behold how many things they witness against thee. But Jesus yet answered nothing; so that Pilate marvelled.
Mark 15:1-5

Elder Neal A. Maxwell knew that demonstrating obedience to leadership would be especially difficult during the final dispensation. He stated, *"Among the requirements that God has laid upon us is to pay heed to his living prophets. In our dispensation this has been described as "following the Brethren." It is a dimension of obedience that has been difficult for some in every dispensation. It will be particularly hard in ours, the final dispensation."*[287]

The temptation to fault leadership stems in part from placing unrealistic expectations on the brethren. The Apostles at the time of Jesus were not without error, and the brethren today do not claim to be above reproach. Unfortunately, cultural assumption and religious tradition continues to imply that church leaders are practically infallible. Many members interpret *"not speaking evil of the Lord's anointed"* to mean there is no evil occurring. They imagine the Lord to be intricately involved in daily church decisions.

When those who are awake then make the obvious-but difficult to accept observations, local leaders may react to sincere questioning by condemning these members for being faithless and disobedient. Sometimes leaders who wish to deny stark realities are quick to dismiss genuine concerns as *"speaking evil of the Lord's anointed."* Applying this accusation as a broad generalization implies that something "true" could be "evil," but in reality ***"the truth" is never evil-even when it makes us uncomfortable.***

"As a young missionary the truth was always good and I usually thought of the peace and good news of the gospel in reference to the truth. What I didn't know at the time was that the truth can also be very painful, even excruciating. I now know that the truth is always preferable, but not always pain free. So, why is truth always preferable, even if painful? Why not live in a state of ignorance and bliss,

171

free from worry and concern? (Don't worry, be happy). Why not stay in the Garden of Eden where all
was "sweetness and light"? Because, as the scripture says, we can never be free until we know
the whole truth. And freedom is necessary if we are to achieve our full potential, our exaltation
and ultimate happiness. In reality it is not the truth that is painful, it is our waking up from a deep sleep
or coma that is painful…We yearn to go back to sleep and not face the cruel reality. But if we go back to
sleep, we continue to atrophy, deteriorate and eventually die. So it is with eternal truths. We must
"awake and arise" and face the pain of waking up. The gospel "good news" is not that everything is
"sweetness and light" and that we can live in our comfortable homes, go to our comfortable churches
in our comfortable cars to later have our comfortable Sunday dinner and then eventually die and go to
our comfortable mansion in heaven. The good news is that once we do wake up to our awful reality or
awful situation, Christ will be there to help us through the transition, the labor pains. The pains can't
be avoided, but the pain of loneliness can be avoided. There is an enumerable host of beings
who have already gone through this painful awakening and have now entered into the rest
of the Lord. They are waiting for us to wake up so that we too can be made free,
go through the necessary pain and then enter into His rest…"
Anonymous Saint

Today, anyone who compares the sacred and mighty gospel of Jesus Christ, to what is occurring on a typical Sunday at church, cannot help but feel the fire of a righteous indignation. The trends, patterns, and choices being enacted require all to remember the Lord's admonition, *"Behold, I sent you out to testify and warn the people, and it becometh every man who hath been warned to warn his neighbor.* (D&C 88:81). The question is, what should a disciple of Christ do when it is the church itself that members must be warned against? The answer comes from the Lord.

…Wherefore, be subject to the powers that be, until he reigns whose right it is to reign,
and subdues all enemies under his feet.
D&C 58:22

This verse is applicable to our current political and religious environment. The answer is to live righteously, follow meekly, and allow God to determine the rest.

"When Christ commented on the corrupt and worldly hierarchy of His own day would He say,
"All they bid you do, that do ye." (See Matt. 23:3-4) True prophets may teach, but they do not supplant.
Hierarchies established by Dispensation Heads are allowed to go forward without being molested or made
afraid by those who receive sub-dispensations of the Gospel. This pattern has been true throughout.
When Lehi finished crying repentance, he departed. His sub-dispensation functioned without any attempt
to supplant. God Himself then intervened to discipline Jerusalem.
His prophets fled; but His presiding priestly class was forcibly removed to Babylon."
Denver Snuffer, *Come Let Us Adore Him* [288]

Many have egotistically tried (without success), to "fix the church." In comparison God wisely watches and allows the storm to rage upon the just and the unjust. He knows the perfect method and timing for the wheat to be gathered, the tares burned, and the house of God set in order (D&C 85:7). Only He can *"steady the ark."* Until that time, let us focus on our own personal repentance and refuse to create division in the church by speaking evil of the Lord's anointed.

"We see increased conflict between peoples in the world around us.
Those divisions and differences could infect us. That is why my message of hope today is that
a great day of unity is coming. The Lord Jehovah will return to live with those who have become
His people and will find them united, of one heart, unified with Him and Heavenly Father."
Henry B. Eyring, Our Hearts Knit As One [289]

> **TRUTH #33** SINCE THE DEATH OF THE PROPHET JOSEPH SMITH, A SIGNIFICANT LOSS OF LIGHT HAS OCCURRED BY OMISSION AND NEGLIGENCE. OVER THE PAST 185 YEARS, ESSENTIAL ELEMENTS OF THE RESTORATION HAVE BEEN MISINTERPRETED, DISTORTED, OR ABANDONED. THE DEGREE TO WHICH THIS HAS OCCURRED COULD BE CONSIDERED AN APOSTASY BY OMISSION.

"We have lost numerous important elements of the restoration such as Zion itself, the law of consecration and stewardship, the United Order, the Holy Order of the Priesthood, patriarchal marriage, the office of Patriarch to the Church, the common administration of the second washings and anointings, the general convention of the School of the Prophets, and the practice of prayer circles outside the temple. Also important emblems of the patriarchal order have vanished from the temple ceremony and we no longer have access to the garment of the holy priesthood as it was revealed from heaven. This may seem like a criticism of the Church and its authority, but it is not. It is simply the recognition of the disposition and propensities of the Saints…Through negligence, distortion, disbelief, and a general lack of understanding, we have violated those lost principles and commandments."
James Custer, *The Unspeakable Gift* [290]

To accurately evaluate our collective performance requires more than counting temples and convert baptisms. If the benchmark we are going to use for comparison is our ever-darkening and suicidal world, then perhaps all really is well in Zion. If however, the glory and power of Zion is the standard we seek, it appears much of the Mormon culture, at least in America, is quickly slipping into full fellowship with Babylon. This spiritual tragedy was foreseen by Elder Neal A. Maxwell.

"Only reform and self-restraint, institutional and individual, can finally rescue society! Only a sufficient number of sin-resistant souls can change the marketplace. As Church members, we should be part of that sin-resistant counterculture. Instead, too many members are sliding down the slope, though perhaps at a slower pace."
Neal A. Maxwell, *Behold the Enemy is Combined* [291]

During the Restoration Joseph pleaded with the Saints to receive every aspect of the gospel. History records that the Saints struggled to embrace the increase. And when comparing what Joseph Smith taught to our common gospel diet, we cannot help but mourn all that has been lost or neglected generation after generation. Some are concerned this accumulating loss will eventually evolve into a full apostasy.

"Religious history testifies that, with the single exception of the inhabitants of the City of Enoch, no people to whom the gospel has been given have remained faithful to their covenants for more than a few generations…This cycle of human folly which so many prophets have noted, has repeated itself with such consistent regularity that any group which finds itself to be the favored recipients of the gospel would do well to assume that their apostasy is certain, and the only question about it is how long it will take."
H. Verlan Andersen, *The Great and Abominable Church of the Devil* [292]

174

History warns that most cultures can only endure the brilliance of the gospel for a few decades. Eventually, pride and corruption enter into a society-until the masses are slowly engulfed by the subtle disease of apostasy.

> *"This is a world filled with change and decay. All things here are touched by entropy.*
> *Even truth dissipates unless it is continually renewed by effort...*
> *Latter Day Saints must guard the truths we possess or they will vanish.*
> *All past dispensations of the Gospel have decayed, finally resulting in apostasy.*
> *Without vigilance and great care, we can meet the same fate."*
> Denver Snuffer, *Beloved Enos* [293]

Some choose to blame Church leadership for the losses, but all leaders are sustained by common consent and it is the spiritual standing of the general membership, (from which leaders were selected), that should stand accountable. The loss of doctrinal depth and the accompanying reduction in spiritual power has not occurred because it was the *"will of the Lord,"* but because the performance of the people required the minimization.

> *And thus ye shall become instructed in the law of my church, and be sanctified by that which ye have received, and ye shall bind yourselves to act in all holiness before me—**That inasmuch as ye do this,** **glory shall be added to the kingdom which ye have received. Inasmuch as ye do it not,** **it shall be taken, even that which ye have received.** Purge ye out the iniquity which is among you; sanctify yourselves before me...*
> D&C 43:9-11

Today, if members want to study calling and election, Second Comforter, Church of the Firstborn, the Holy Order, return of the ten tribes, the gospel being taken from the Gentiles to the house of Israel, miracles and spiritual gifts, additional scripture and prophecy, translation, and the literal building of Zion, they must search for the light themselves. Public teaching of the so-called "mysteries," and what is required to become Zion is almost non-existent.

Zion on Hold

> *"It came to us as a Revelation from God, in the same manner as the one to the Prophet Joseph regarding the building of Center Stake of Zion and the Temple in Jackson Co, Missouri.*
> *The people failed to carry out the Order of Enoch and God gave a command to suspend the law."*
> Heber J Grant, *Diary Excerpts* [294]

As members of the Lord's Church, we are not above universal law. (see Truth #25). If we choose to omit and negate greater light and knowledge from our testimonies, God will allow. If we choose to assume the prophet will tell us all that is needed to gain celestial glory, God will accept. And if we choose to delay Zion, even while secret combinations of darkness gather around us, God will weep.

The Next Cycle of Apostasy?

"You don't have to be a Latter-day Saint—you don't even have to be religious—to see the repeating pattern of history in the lives of God's children as recorded in the Old Testament. Time and again we see the cycle of righteousness followed by wickedness. Similarly, the Book of Mormon records that ancient civilizations of this continent followed exactly the same pattern: righteousness followed by prosperity, followed by material comforts, followed by greed, followed by pride, followed by wickedness and a collapse of morality until the people brought calamities upon themselves sufficient to stir them up to humility, repentance, and change. In the relatively short span of years covered by the New Testament, the historic pattern repeats itself again. This time the people turned against Christ and His Apostles. The collapse was so great we have come to know it as the Great Apostasy, which led to the centuries of spiritual stagnation and ignorance called the Dark Ages…One of the great lessons of this historical pattern is that our choices, both individually and collectively, do result in spiritual consequences for ourselves and for our posterity…Does any of this sound familiar, my young brothers and sisters? Do you see the historical pattern emerging again—the pattern of righteousness followed by prosperity, followed by material comforts, followed by greed, followed by pride, followed by wickedness and a collapse of morality—the same pattern we've seen again and again within the pages of the Old and New Testaments and the Book of Mormon? *More importantly, what impact will the lessons of the past have on the personal choices you make right now and for the rest of your lives? The voice of the Lord is clear and unmistakable. He knows you. He loves you. He wants you to be eternally happy. But according to your God-given agency, the choice is yours. Each one of you has to decide for yourself if you are going to ignore the past and suffer the painful mistakes and tragic pitfalls that have befallen previous generations, experiencing for yourself the devastating consequences of bad choices. How much better your life will be if you will follow the noble example of the faithful followers of Christ such as the sons of Helaman, Moroni, Joseph Smith, and the stalwart pioneers—and choose, as they did, to remain faithful to your Heavenly Father's commandments…And so it returns, as it always does, to your own personal faith and testimony."*
M. Russell Ballard, *Learning the Lessons of the Past* [295]

Those who believe *"all is well in Zion"* deceive themselves and maintain their own condemnation. In relation to our collective status, there have been several key moments in church history when the spiritual needs of "the few" were sacrificed to meet the needs of "the many." For example was it truly the will of the Lord that the law of consecration be replaced with the law of tithing? Was plural marriage just an embarrassing mistake that the church could end without spiritual consequence? (See 77truths.com). Did God really want the temple endowment changed, or due to their lack of understanding, was He simply giving the people what they wanted?

Samuel Principle

And the Lord said unto Samuel, Hearken unto the voice of the people in all that they say unto thee: for they have not rejected thee, but they have rejected me, that I should not reign over them.
1 Samuel 8:7

This fundamental decision of whether to have God or man "reign" over us is at the heart of today's spiritual dilemma. What is a disciple of Christ to do when he or she yearns for a true fullness, but is not allowed to believe, teach, and practice the truth due to the condemnation of the general membership? Should a true believer obey the voice of Christ or the global policies that men have deemed appropriate for the general population?

The Leadership We Deserve

"And if He (The LORD) should suffer him (Joseph Smith) to lead the people astray,
it would be because they ought to be led astray. If He should suffer them to be chastised,
and some of them destroyed, it would be because they deserved it..."
Brigham Young, *Journal of Discourses* [296]

An honest review of Mormon history reveals several examples where doctrine that was once viewed as *"essential,"* is now considered *"inconsequential."* (Adam-God, United Order, celestial marriage, full garment, office of patriarch, blacks and the priesthood, literal gathering to Israel, spiritual adoption, Second Anointing, calling and election, etc...).

The key question is whether these changes enacted by the church were the will of God or the choices of men. And if it was the voice of God, why would He require the loss? In some instances (such as abandoning the United Order, postponing Zion, and changing the temple ordinances), it may have indeed been the will of God, but only because the members required the decrease in light, not because it was God's greater intention. In other situations political and financial realities appear to have influenced institutional choices.

"There are at least three dangers that threaten the Church within, and the authorities need to awaken
to the fact that the people should be warned unceasingly against them. As I see these, they are flattery
of prominent men in the world, false educational ideas, and sexual impurity."
Joseph F. Smith, *Gospel Doctrine* [297]

The relevant question today is, do these losses, omissions, distortions, delays, and transfigurations, accumulate to represent a "Latter Day falling away?" And if so, isn't it amazing that God has again allowed a spiritual context to be created where every soul must choose whether they will stand with truth or tradition, scripture or policy, God or man?

"Latter-day Saints believe that apostasy occurs whenever an individual or community rejects
the revelations and ordinances of God, changes the gospel of Jesus Christ, or rebels against
the commandments of God, thereby losing the blessings of the Holy Ghost and of divine authority.
The rise of revelatory communities, apostasies, and restorations has happened cyclically throughout
the history of mankind, in a series of dispensations from the time of Adam and Enoch (Moses 7)
to the present...The English word "apostasy" derives from the Greek apostasía or apóstasis
("defection, revolt")... It can mean "to stand away from," or the active 'to cause to stand away from.'
Thus an apostasy can be an active, collective rebellion or a "falling away."
Todd Compton, *Encyclopedia of Mormonism* [298]

This definition suggests that if we are assessing whether someone or something is in a state of "apostasy," it must be determined from what they have apostatized. In other words if someone is "standing apart," what have they separated themselves from? Have they "apostatized" from the teachings of the modern-day church? Is the "apostasy" occurring in contrast to the original teachings of Joseph Smith? Or is it in relation to the eternal gospel of Jesus Christ and the truth of all things?

Socially, some members seem to consider "apostasy" to be learning or believing anything the current brethren are not teaching. Because it is assumed everything the brethren do is in complete harmony with God's will, the brethren and the church are often conceptualized as "the truth" itself. The church policy manual supports this religious perspective by defining apostasy as those who, *"Repeatedly act in clear, open, and deliberate public opposition to the Church or its leaders." And/or to "persist in teaching as Church doctrine information that is not Church doctrine after they have been corrected by their bishops or higher authority. Continue to follow the teachings of apostate sects (such as those that advocate plural marriage) after being corrected by their bishop or higher authority. In such cases, excommunication may be necessary if repentance is not evident after counseling and encouragement. Priesthood leaders must take disciplinary action against apostates to protect Church members. The Savior taught the Nephites that they should continue to minister to a transgressor, but "if he repent not he shall not be numbered among my people, that he may not destroy my people" (3 Nephi 18:31; see also Mosiah 26:36). Total inactivity in the Church or attending or holding membership in another church does not constitute apostasy."*[299]

This definition of apostasy does not concern itself with what is actually true and doctrinally correct, but instead insists that whatever the church is currently teaching (even though the doctrine has changed many times) is beyond reproach. The current policy requires "repentance" from the accused, but how can someone repent of something that is true and isn't even a sin?

> **Truth is knowledge of things as they are,**
> **and as they were, and as they are to come.**
> D&C 93:24

Instead of defining "apostasy" as error existing in opposition to God and His eternal truth, the handbook implies the current understanding and teaching of leadership is the basis for what is correct and infallible. According to policy, the institution, not God and His eternal gospel, is the unfailing standard from which a person is judged. **Ironically, this definition of apostasy is apostasy itself.**

Defining Apostasy

Telestial Definition: Church Policy and the Brethren.
"Repeatedly act in clear, open, and deliberate public opposition to the Church or its leaders."[300]

Terrestial Definition: Traditional Religious Belief.
"An abandonment of one's religious faith, a political party, or one's principles."[301]

Celestial Definition: God and Eternal Truth.
"To exist in opposition to that which has been, is now, and always will be, true."[302]

In reality, the truth cannot be apostasy to God. An accurate and binding definition of "apostasy" can only be defined as something that exists in direct opposition to that which is eternally true. God's gospel, as provided through prophecy, revelation, and scripture, should be the standard utilized, not the philosophies of men mingled with current policy.

In 2008, a general authority taught, *"The Church, with all its organizational structure and programs, offers many important activities for its members aimed at helping families and individuals to serve God and each other. Sometimes, however, it can appear that these programs and activities are closer to the center of our heart and soul than the core doctrines and principles of the gospel. Procedures, programs, policies, and patterns of organization are helpful for our spiritual progress here on earth, but let's not forget that they are subject to change. In contrast, the core of the gospel-the doctrine and the principles-will never change...*[303]

This wise counsel is true, but does not address what we Latter Day Saints are to do when essential doctrine is minimized, changed, or omitted by the church. The implied message is that leaders would never alter the teaching of core gospel principles, but our own religious history confirms that is exactly what has happened on several occasions. (The nature of Deity, temple ordinances, blacks and the priesthood, law of consecration, sacrament, celestial marriage, word of wisdom, gathering of Israel, role of leadership, blood atonement, spiritual adoption, Adam-God, Zion, etc).

"It is your privilege and duty to live so that you know when the word of the Lord is spoken to you and when the mind of the Lord is revealed to you. I say it is your duty to live so as to know and understand all these things. Suppose I were to teach you a false doctrine, how are you to know it if you do not possess the Spirit of God?"
Brigham Young, *Journal of Discourses* [304]

"Follow" the Scriptures

"Some prophets—I say it respectfully—know more and have greater inspiration than others.
Thus, if Brigham Young, who was one of the greatest of the prophets, said something about Adam
which is out of harmony with what is in the book of Moses and in section 78, it is the scripture
that prevails. This is one of the reasons we call our scriptures the standard works. They are the standards
of judgment and the measuring rod against which all doctrines and views are weighed, and it does not
make one particle of difference whose views are involved. The scriptures always take precedence."
Bruce R. McConkie, *The Parable of the Unwise Builder* [305]

Within Mormonism today, there is a prevalent attitude that even if there are problems and errors, members should still obey current leadership without question. This attitude is not in harmony with the teachings of the Prophet Joseph Smith.

"We have heard men who hold the priesthood remark that they would do anything they were told
to do by those who preside over them [even] if they knew it was wrong; but such obedience as this is
worse than folly to us; it is slavery in the extreme; and the man who would thus willingly
degrade himself, should not claim a rank among intelligent beings, until he turns from his folly.
A man of God would despise the idea. Others, in the extreme exercise of their almighty authority
have taught that such obedience was necessary, and that no matter what the saints were told do
by their presidents they should do it without any questions. When Elders of Israel will so far indulge
in these extreme notions of obedience as to teach them to the people, it is generally because
they have it in their hearts to do wrong themselves."
Joseph Smith, *Millennial Star* [306]

If questioning, disagreeing, and even condemning the mainstream culture is the correct definition of "apostasy," then the prophets Moroni, Samuel, and Isaiah would certainly be excommunicated today. Admittedly there are real apostates in the Church, but often they are not the ones being persecuted.

Religious Irony

"Culturally we have made the word "apostate" a four-letter word. I think adulterer, liar, addict
(even murderer) might be preferred in Mormon circles. You might as well tie a millstone around
your neck if you are labeled an apostate (or at least carry a big red letter "A" on your chest).
It is blasphemous to speak out against the institution. That is why in the time of Christ the Pharisees
and Sadducees hated Jesus so much because Christ was basically an "apostate."
The road ahead will be interesting. Actually the more banks we dedicate, the more shopping malls
and luxury apartment complexes we build around the temple, and the more honorary degrees we give
to Gadiantons at our university-the better. It makes things more black and white."
David Christenson, *Building Babylon* [307]

In summary, "truth" cannot be manipulated or transfigured for religious or political expediency. Mormonism was intended to be inclusive of *"all truth,"*[308]and the temple teaches *"all truth may be circumscribed into one great whole."*[309] This universal definition ironically includes "truth" about the LDS church that the faithful wish was not accurate. To identify and work through today's spiritual dilemma is not a new test, for mankind has always had a fundamental choice between alignment with God, or incrementally avoiding and rationalizing that which is difficult to accept.

Spiritual stagnation occurs when a culture maintains their religious assumptions for so long that most in the mainstream are unable to differentiate between truth and tradition. If an awakening soul then brings attention to the cold reality of religious contradiction, it usually brings the ire of those wishing to maintain their Mormon comfort. How predictable it is that the messenger must then be silenced by labeling him or her as "the apostate."

Despite the onslaught of ignorance and unrighteous dominion about to be inflicted upon the wheat of the church, let all understand: **The truth is never apostasy!** (see Truth #38).

"The Standard of Truth has been erected. No unhallowed hand can stop the work from progressing. Persecutions may rage, mobs may combine, armies may assemble, calumny may defame. But the truth of God will go forth boldly, nobly, and dependent till it has penetrated every continent, visited every clime, swept every country, and sounded in every ear, until the purposes of God shall be accomplished and the Great Jehovah will say, 'The work is done.'"
Joseph Smith, *The Wentworth Letter* [310]

The fact that the *"standard of truth"* Joseph promoted is now only partially available is a spiritual reality many are not willing to hear. The old saying, ***"No evidence will convince you of a truth you don't want"*** applies today, but an honest study of church history does reveal a tragic digression in spiritual light.

 This religious fact leaves those who love the gospel to meekly wait upon the Lord to fix the problems in His way and His time. Until that time arrives, every soul can work privately within their own families to reclaim a true gospel fullness.

A Real Fullness Required
"Better suffer a thousand deaths than succumb to the force of persecution by promising to discard a single principle which God has revealed for our glory and exaltation. Our character, as Latter-day Saints, should be preserved inviolate, at whatever cost or sacrifice."
Lorenzo Snow, *Journal of Discourses* [311]

When looking at an overview of church history it becomes obvious that the greatest moment of tragedy and transition occurred when beloved Joseph was martyred. His willingness to die for the cause of Christ, combined with the members lack of faith and commitment, contributed to his early martyrdom. We will never know what *could have been* if the Saints had only received a true fullness, avoided condemnation, finished the Nauvoo Temple on time, lived the United Order, established Zion, and joined Joseph in migrating to the Rocky Mountains…We will just never know what could have been.

For those who love Joseph and yearn to partake of all that God offered through him, today's religious context presents a spiritual conundrum. Specifically, how to interact and serve among a people whose collective needs are not yet congruent with receiving a true fullness.

Peace and a partial answer can come when we ponder: Has the Lord allowed this religious scenario to occur so as to strengthen the wheat? Is it possible today's *"famine in the land"* is useful in the sense that a if a member remains solely dependent on the church, he or she will spiritually starve? But as a soul turns directly to Jesus Christ, He begins to provide light until doctrinal losses are incrementally regained! Usually this "remembering" includes the *dark night of the soul*," that in coming to sense the misery and depth of the fall, we can shout out in desperation and praise, ***"I want God and all of His Gospel!"*** (see Truth #41).

Valiant members may find comfort in Josephs original encouragement to stay with a majority of the Twelve. In the October 1994 general conference Elder James E. Faust reiterated this spiritual guideline.

> *"Today I speak of keys other than those of metal. The keys I speak of never rust.*
> *These are the keys of life and salvation in the kingdom of God. The Prophet Joseph Smith said,*
> *"I will give you a key that will never rust, if you will stay with the majority of the Twelve Apostles,*
> *and the records of the Church, you will never be lead astray."*
> James E. Faust, *General Conference* [312]

If staying with a majority of the Twelve is "a key that will never rust" it seems logical to apply that standard to past, current, and future leadership. However, let us understand that when Joseph Smith made this statement, the standard for being an Apostle was to have personally received the Second Comforter.[313]

True Apostleship
> *"Never cease striving until you have seen God face to face. Strengthen your faith; cast off your doubts,*
> *your sins, and all your unbelief; and nothing can prevent you from coming to God.*
> ***Your ordination is not full and complete till God has laid His hand upon you.***
> ***We require as much to qualify us as did those who have gone before us;*** *God is the same.*
> *If the Savior in former days laid His hands upon His disciples, why not in latter days?"*
> Oliver Cowdery, *History of the Church* [314]

This standard supports the conclusion that it would indeed be wise to listen to a majority of those true apostles who have personally received the Second Comforter in the flesh.

Joseph's counsel to follow the majority also includes an implied message about the minority of the brethren. Remembering the example of Judas, as well as the apostasy of some of the early Apostles, reminds us that we need to posses inspired discernment concerning all matters.

> *"Six of the original Twelve Apostles apostatized, and three of their successors apostatized,*
> *making nine apostates that once had hands laid upon them, ordaining them to the Apostleship."*
> Brigham Young, *Journal of Discourses* [315]

Joseph also instructed the Saints to stay with *"the records of the Church."* This requires us to interpret whether he was referring to the actual physical pages, most of which are owned and controlled by the church, or was he suggesting the faithful stay with the gospel of Jesus Christ as recorded in revelation? In other words, was Joseph advising us to stay with the men who control the records, or to stay with the truth written on the records?

"No quorum in the Church was entirely exempt from the influence of those false spirits who are striving against me for the mastery; even some of the Twelve were so far lost to their high and responsible calling as to begin to take sides secretly with the enemy."
Joseph Smith, *The Historical Record* [316]

To Mormons who are content in their self-assured beliefs, these perspectives and concerns will be interpreted as being ridiculous and false. To write about these and other valid problems will be deemed by the mainstream as Satan's deceptions. Those wishing to maintain the status quo will buttress their view by quoting Orson Hyde, who claimed Joseph Smith taught, *"Brethren, remember that the majority of this people will never go astray; and as long as you keep with the majority you are sure to enter the celestial kingdom."*[317]If this quote is accurate and Joseph really did say this, then a spiritual quandary is revealed by comparing this belief with what scripture states is required for celestial glory. (see D&C 76, Moses 6, D&C 132, Alma 5, etc…). For how can we as a people remain under condemnation, appear to be *growing* in pride, even while *decreasing* in light—and still qualify for celestial glory?

Analyzing scripture and then comparing it to this quote by Orson Hyde leads this author to conclude that Joseph Smith was either misquoted or he was referring to a majority of Saints who were still alive after the church had been cleansed.

ONLY A FEW...

*They wear stiff necks and high heads; yea, and because of pride, and wickedness,
and abominations, and whoredoms, they have all gone astray save it be a few,
who are the humble followers of Christ…*
2 Nephi 28:14

ONLY A FEW...

*Behold, there are many called, but few are chosen. And why are they not chosen?
Because their hearts are set so much upon the things of this world,
and aspire to the honors of men…*
D&C 121:34-35

ONLY A FEW....

*For strait is the gate, and narrow the way that leadeth unto the exaltation and continuation
of the lives, and few there be that find it, because ye receive me not in the world
neither do ye know me. But if ye receive me in the world, then shall ye know me,
and shall receive your exaltation; that where I am ye shall be also.*
D&C 132:22-23

ONLY A FEW...

That by keeping the commandments they might be washed and cleansed from all their sins,
and receive the Holy Spirit by the laying on of the hands of him who is ordained and sealed unto this
power; And who overcome by faith, and are sealed by the Holy Spirit of promise, which the Father sheds
forth upon all those who are just and true. They are they who are the church of the Firstborn.
They are they into whose hands the Father has given all things—They are they who are priests and kings,
who have received of his fulness, and of his glory; And are priests of the Most High,
after the order of Melchizedek, which was after the order of Enoch, which was after the order of the
Only Begotten Son. Wherefore, as it is written, they are gods, even the sons of God...
These are they who are just men made perfect through Jesus the mediator of the new covenant,
who wrought out this perfect atonement through the shedding of his own blood. These are they whose
bodies are celestial, whose glory is that of the sun, even the glory of God, the highest of all,
whose glory the sun of the firmament is written of as being typical.
D&C 76: 52-58, 69-70

Regardless of how small "the few" becomes, the sure place is to *"know God."* For in the end all will admit the church could never save us, and that He alone is the author and finisher of our faith!

In the Church, but Not of the Church

"For the soul seeking redemption in Christ, it becomes relevant to ask: Am I coming closer to God and the truth by aligning myself with the mainstream of the Church? Is the culture as a whole moving closer or farther away from Zion? And if Babylon is overcoming the Mormon culture-as many within the church seem to be seeking money, power and fame,
is there a way I can be in the Church, but not of the Church?"
Anonymous Saint

Religious and Political Apostasy

*"Important in the record of the dispensations is that when men depart from God's way and substitute their own ways in it's place they usually do not admit that that is what they are doing; often they do not deliberately or even consciously substitute their ways for God's ways; on the contrary, they easily and largely **convince themselves that their way is God's way. The apostasy described in the New Testament is not a desertion of the cause, but a perversion of it, a process by which the righteous are removed and none perceives it.** The Wedding of the Christian Church and the Roman State was a venture in political dialectics, a restatement of the age-old political exercise of demonstrating that our way is God's way...The Lord told the Apostles that in time "whosoever killeth you will think that he doeth God service" (John 16:2). The horrible fiasco of the Crusades went forward under the mandate of "Deus Vult"-God wills it: it is his idea; the Inquisition was carried out by selfless men "for the greater glory of God."*
Hugh Nibley, *Beyond Politics* [318]

Very few question the political maneuvers, financial dealings, and doctrinal omissions which the church has enacted over the past 185 years. Members assume that because this is the Lord's true church, everything is being handled according to Father's will.

"Some go to Church to actually learn and repent. Most go to be assured, told all is well and that they are the righteous because they are "active", pay their tithing and have current temple recommends. We have the Church we want, not the one the Lord had in mind. But such is the history of apostasy throughout the Dispensations."
Anonymous Saint

Very few seem concerned that another "falling away" could occur within the culture of Mormonism. Leaders have assured everyone that the church is "on course" and that the Lord is "hastening the work." None of this wishful thinking changes the reality that the patterns of religious apostasy, as demonstrated by the Jews, Nephites, and Jaredites, are repeating right before our eyes.

For the Lord hath said: This is my church, and I will establish it; and nothing shall overthrow it, save it is the transgression of my people.
Mosiah 27:13

When pride, doctrinal compromise, and looking past the mark of Christ is repeatedly chosen, the Holy Spirit withdraws and religious protocols become stagnant. ***The very power we so desperately need is absent***. Without an accurate understanding of our true status, followed by an intense call to repentance, the tragedy deepens.

"Part of the apostasy process involves the slow and tragic withdrawal of God's Spirit. As meetings become more bureaucratic and dogmatic, participants feel the Spirit in lesser degree, and are thus less likely to repent. The real tragedy is in observing the people rarely even notice, as "the norm" continues to be accepted. During these "winding down" years, a few may offer the voice of warning-often to be rejected as being "judgmental" or "radical."
Anonymous Saint

Members tend to ostracize anyone who challenges mainstream assumptions. Particularly hot-button topics include priesthood authority, prophetic presence, and the overall status of the church.

"There are two approaches to preserving a belief system. Scholars refer to these as "sophic" and "mantic," but the scriptural language would be "the priestly" and "the prophetic." Priests deal with rites, ordinances, commandments and procedures. This durable approach to preserving a belief system allows a dispensation of the Gospel to continue to have a presence, long after a founder has died. Moses, for example, established a system of rites and observances which then became the religious fare of priests who perpetuated the system from the time of Moses until the coming of Christ. Prophets deal with God and angels. They receive new insight, promises and covenants. Their conduct can even appear to violate the traditions of the religion they follow, but that is only because they are not bound to the tradition as practiced by the priests. Instead they have penetrated into the underlying meaning, the original power, the purpose of the rites. Dispensations are founded by those who combine both traditions. Moses was a prophet, and established priestly rites. Christ was a prophet and more, and He also established priestly rites. Similarly, Joseph Smith was an authentic Dispensation Head who was both a prophet and established priestly rites. The reason an apostasy can be concealed from the view of religious believers is because they confuse the presence of continuing priestly tradition with both. They do not notice the prophetic presence has left. Concealing the fact that the prophetic presence is gone is possible because priests focus on authority and make that idea the central, even controlling issue for salvation."
Denver Snuffer, *The Prophetic and the Priestly* [319]

The curriculum chosen for the 2014 Priesthood/Relief Society manual consisted of the summarized teachings of Joseph Fielding Smith. In the text, the church uses the words of President Smith to remind the Saints,"...*If we shall look to the First Presidency and follow their counsel and direction, no power on earth can stay or change our course as a church, and as individuals we shall gain peace in this life and be inheritors of eternal glory in the world to come.*" [320] Not only is obedience to the brethren reinforced, but it is suggested that doing so correlates with eternal glory. The same lesson then re-assures the Saints, "*The gospel itself has been the same in all dispensations; the plan of salvation is the same for all our Father's children in every age. From time to time it has been lost by apostasy...But there is one great added thing we have received in this age that has never been had before. In this dispensation the Lord has decreed that the Church shall never again be led astray; this time the gospel is here to stay. This time the revealed truth is destined to prepare a people for the second coming of the Son of Man, and the Church will be established in all parts of the earth when the Lord comes to usher in the millennial era of peace and righteousness.*" [321]

How wonderful it must feel to members to be promised that they cannot be led astray! And how blatantly inconvenient it is to learn the guarantee is false. Nowhere in scripture has the Lord decreed that the church shall never again be led astray. Nowhere in scripture is it stated that looking to the First Presidency and following their counsel will result in peace in this life and *"eternal glory in the world to come."* How delusional we are to imagine trusting in other men is sufficient! But we as a people are eager to believe in a God that is willing to suspend eternal agency, just so we can feel comfortable congratulating ourselves with false self assurance! How tragic that we have interpreted scripture and a few quotes in such a way that we conflate God, gospel, and the church, into one spiritual entity. No wonder there will be such weeping and wailing and gnashing of teeth after this life-for it will not be until then that we wake up to the full tragedy of our gospel performance.

In response to the idea that we as a collective people cannot be led astray, H. Verlan Anderson, member of the Quorum of the Seventy, provides the following warning.

<u>The Failure of People to Recognize the Signs of Apostasy</u>
by H. Verlan Anderson

"In the great majority of cases where apostasy has occurred, it appears that the people became wicked while believing themselves to be righteous. This happened time and again to the Children of Israel and the Nephites, and was plainly evident in the case of the Jews at the time of Christ. There are recorded exceptions to this rule. For example, when the Nephites apostatized immediately prior to Christ's visit we are told: Now they did not sin ignorantly, for they knew the will of God concerning them, for it had been taught unto them; therefore they did willfully rebel against God. (3 Nephi 6:18). But the typical situation is described thus by Mormon as he commented on the frequency and rapidity with which a people who have been blessed forsake the Lord:...they do harden their hearts, and do forget the Lord their God, and do trample under their fee the Holy One-yea, and this because of their ease, and their exceedingly great prosperity (Helaman 12:2) Prophecies regarding the Gentile Apostasy of the latter days indicate that it will be the typical one wherein Church members will be led away by false beliefs into evil practices. Nephi had much to say regarding the event. Among other things he predicted that:

1) *"Because of pride, and because of false teachers, and false doctrine, their churches have become corrupted..."* (2 Nephi 28:12)
2) *"the humble followers of Christ" will err in many instances because they are taught by the precepts of men.* (2 Nephi 28:14)
3) *Some will be lulled away into carnal security, that they will say: All is well in Zion; yea, Zion prospereth, all is well-and thus the devil cheateth their souls, and leadeth them away carefully down to hell."* (2 Nephi 28:21)
4) *Others will be deceived into believing that there is no devil and no hell.* (2 Nephi 28:22)
5) *There will be many who say...*

"Eat, drink, and be merry: nevertheless, fear God-he will justify in committing a little sin; yea, lie a little, take the advantage of one because of his words, dig a pit for thy neighbor; there is no harm in this; and do all these things, for tomorrow we die; and if it so be that we are guilty, God will beat us with a few stripes, and at last we shall be saved in the kingdom of God. Yea, and there shall be many which shall teach after this manner, false and vain and foolish doctrines..."
2 Nephi 28:8-9

"People who regard themselves as members of the only true Church have the fatal tendency to consider themselves immune from the disease of deception. Knowing that they belong to the Lord's Church and have His scriptures and His prophets to guide them, they blindly assume that this adequately protects them against false beliefs. All history teaches the folly of such an assumption, and the scriptures specifically deny its validity. In fact, it is those who have the truth "plainly manifest unto them" who have the most to fear as the following scriptures state:

"Behold here is the agency of man, and here is the condemnation of man; because that which was from the beginning is plainly manifest unto them, and they receive not the light (D&C 93:31 and 2 Nephi 32:7)
For of him unto whom much is given much is required; and he who sins against the light shall receive the greater condemnation. (D&C 82:3 and 2 Nephi 9:27)."
H. Verlan Andersen, *The Apostasy of the Latter Days* [322]

The wheat of Christ acknowledge these collective challenges. They know that to get honest about the our true spiritual standing, and then to change those problems within the soul, represents our only chance of becoming true disciples of Jesus Christ.

Do not say: O God, I thank thee that we are better than our brethren; but rather say:
O Lord, forgive my unworthiness, and remember my brethren in mercy—
yea, acknowledge your unworthiness before God at all times.
Alma 38:14

Due to the complicated nature of Mormonism today, trying to explain our current apostasy over the pulpit would likely be ineffective and unhelpful. If the Lord desires this type of rebuke to occur, He will cause it to happen by calling and anointing those who are willing to prophecy like Samuel the Lamanite. Until that day, instead of trying to "wake up the Mormons" and "save the church," the wise alternative is to study, ponder, pray, and worship in private. This is the approach Joseph Smith chose, and the result was a personal visit from Deity. During this holy experience, the Father and the Son directed Joseph Smith concerning how to avoid the religious apostasy of his day. Perhaps the pattern the Prophet demonstrated is the answer to all of our religious dilemmas.

An Eternal Pattern
"In accordance with this, my determination to ask of God, I retired to the woods to make the attempt.
It was on the morning of a beautiful, clear day, early in the spring of eighteen hundred and twenty.
It was the first time in my life that I had made such an attempt, for amidst all my anxieties
I had never as yet made the attempt to pray vocally. After I had retired to the place where
I had previously designed to go, having looked around me, and finding myself alone,
I kneeled down and began to offer up the desires of my heart to God..."
Joseph Smith, *Joseph Smith History,* [323]

When we are ready to fall before God, He is ready to receive us. At that time Father and His Holy Spirit may enlarge our previous gospel understanding. Perceiving our own personal apostasy allows us to see the Mormon situation more clearly, but in the end it will not matter what the church did, only that we awakened unto *The Christ.*

And it came to pass also on another sabbath, that he entered into the synagogue and taught: and there was a man whose right hand was withered. And the scribes and Pharisees watched him, whether he would heal on the sabbath day; that they might find an accusation against him. But he knew their thoughts, and said to the man which had the withered hand, Rise up, and stand forth in the midst. And he arose and stood forth. Then said Jesus unto them, I will ask you one thing; Is it lawful on the sabbath days to do good, or to do evil? to save life, or to destroy it? And looking round about upon them all, he said unto the man, Stretch forth thy hand. And he did so: and his hand was restored whole as the other. And they were filled with madness; and communed one with another what they might do to Jesus.

Luke 6:6-11

THE GOSPEL OF JESUS CHRIST is a living-breathing-gospel of Love. His marvelous light is fascinating, fluid, surprising, and abundant! The teachings of Jesus were designed to guide us through the deep and complex situations of life. To obey God's voice with exactness eventually requires that we possess the capacity to act beyond the predictable. During life all are subjected to various scenarios involving surprise, irony, paradox, and apparent contradiction.

Final Answer

"From scripture we observe that when God told Nephi to cut off Laban's head, he did not wait until he could go and check the church policy manual to see if Lehi would approve. Because Nephi was raised to be obedient to the law of Moses, he did struggle internally and was concerned about what to do. Then Nephi obeyed the Spirit, while technically breaking the lower law in favor of being obedient to God's higher voice and purpose. We might remember that Abraham lied to King Abimelech that Sarah was his sister-thus breaking the law-so as to accomplish the greater purpose of preserving his own life. (Genesis 20:1-3). Other common examples include Abraham being commanded to violate the law of Moses by killing Isaac and Joseph being commanded to live plural marriage. These examples, (and there are several more) are not offered as excuses for breaking the law, but as examples that in reality God's voice in each moment and in each unique context is supreme."

Anonymous Saint

Religion tries to make truth "neat and tidy," but life is not always an *Ensign* story with a predictable ending. Many situations cannot be answered by church policy. This is why it is essential to **be Spirit led instead of tradition dependent.** Wisdom requires flexibility and inspired creativity. "Following the Spirit" must be more than lip service. Similar to how legislating morality in politics doesn't work, applying global policy to each unique situation tends to be limiting.

The letter killeth, but the spirit giveth life.

2 Corinthians 3:6

Some focus on the letter of the law to such an extreme that "the rules" overshadow the *meaning, power, and purpose* of the gospel. Various elements of the church, (home teaching, ward parties, young men/women activities, Boy Scouts, etc.), are emphasized to the point that they unintentionally *"omit the weightier matters of the law,* (such as) *judgment, mercy, and faith…* (Matthew 23:23). Many church leaders are aware of this problem.

> *"The Church, with all its organizational structure and programs, offers many important activities for its members aimed at helping families and individuals to serve God and each other. Sometimes, however* ***it can appear that these programs and activities are closer to the center of our heart and soul than the core doctrines and principles of the gospel. Procedures, programs, policies, and patterns of organizations are helpful for our spiritual progress here on earth, but let's not forget that they are subject to change****…As we strive to understand, internalize, and live correct gospel principles, we will* ***become more spiritually self reliant.***"
> Dieter F. Uchtdorf, *Christlike Attributes-The Wind Beneath our Wings* [324]

The program of the Church was designed to be *a means to an end*. It was meant to guide us along on our journey to Jesus Christ. Unfortunately an ever-growing focus on performance, statistics, and annual reports has become a religion unto itself.

In *1899* the church penned a booklet of policies which could be considered the first church policy manual. It was fourteen pages in length.[325] Today, the current church policy manual is over four hundred pages and includes global and local policies concerning minute details. We might ask, have we missed the point?

What is the "member percentage" for successfully accessing the Atonement of Jesus Christ?

Sitting in meetings week after week will not save us. Replacing true worship with a focus on dogma and policy cannot transform the soul. Minimizing the miracle of Christ, while maximizing the church and its programs, is not God's definition of "righteousness."

Are we becoming Latter Day Jews?

"This matter of a devout and seemingly religious people becoming spiritually blind "by looking beyond the mark" illustrates perfectly how true and saving religion can become a damning burden. For generations that went before, and then in the day of our Lord's ministry, his Israelite brethren, by "looking beyond the mark," turned the truth of heaven into a system that led them to hell. That is to say, they took the plain and simple things of pure religion and added to them a host of their own interpretations; they embellished them with added rites and performances; and they took a happy, joyous way of worship and turned it into a restrictive, curtailing, depressive system of rituals and performances. The living spirit of the Lord's law became in their hands the dead letter of Jewish ritualism."
Bruce R. McConkie, *The Mortal Messiah* [326]

Is the disease of micro-management overcoming a ministry once rooted in a love for salvation? As a culture, are we spiraling down into the same mindset that seduced the Jews into misjudging, and eventually crucifying Jesus Christ?

But behold, the Jews were a stiff-necked people; and they despised the words of plainness, and killed the prophets, and sought for things that they could not understand. Wherefore, because of their blindness, which blindness came by looking beyond the mark, they must needs fall…
Jacob 4:14

Today, some local leaders refer to the policy manual as if it were scripture. Rules, regulations, codes, and protocols are accessed first instead of immediately turning to Jesus Christ for specific guidance. Global policies supposedly trump local inspiration, and universal conformity is expected regardless of unique purpose and context. Of what value is the mantra to "follow the Spirit" if local leaders think the brethren have already decided all the answers? There are of course, many leaders doing the best they can in their unique stewardships. The problem is usually not the heart of the local leader, but the hierarchal management system they labor within.

The process for obtaining a temple recommend offers one example of how religious standardization and uninspired uniformity can at times negate the will of God. Perhaps with membership growing in so many third-world countries, there's just no other practical method for young local leaders to determine worthiness. And yet passing a questionnaire with "yes" and "no" answers is incredibly similar to the laws of rote obedience enforced by the Jewish Pharisees. Included in this global litmus test are questions about a member's willingness to sustain other men in their callings. The person being interviewed must agree, (even though there is no real evidence of seership, prophecy, or additional revelation), that the church is indeed led by prophets, seers, and revelators. Very few notice *how odd it is that a member's "worthiness" is imagined to be directly connected to the effectiveness of the brethren in fulfilling their apostolic calling.* Despite a church history where previous leaders struggled spiritually and/or apostatized, a broad stroke of support and agreement must be professed by the member—or the result is to be banned from the temple.

What is a soul to do when he or she prefers to stand in the truth and "please God," rather than just be "recommended" of men? It has been the experience of some that simply observing that we as a church have not received additional prophecy or scripture for many years, will result in losing temple privileges. It is unclear how mentioning the truth makes a member "unworthy," but perhaps the greater problem is the assessment tool utilized by other men to determine "worthiness."

Dead Devotion
"Ironically appearances of true worship persist in every stage of apostasy.
Laying stress on outward observances is often a symptom of alienation from the true God.
When false Gods are the order of the day, **people feel the need to scrupulously preserve**
the exterior of true worship. *People who reach this point confuse righteousness with actively*
congregating and religiously performing ecclesiastical duties. In such worship, institutional
convention may become the enemy of spontaneity, resulting in dead, stereotypical devotion."
Avraham Gileadi, *Modern Idolatry:12 Diatribes* [327]

Structure, conformity, and intolerance for the unorthodox, has combined to drain the spiritual life out of today's Sunday experience. What was once a spiritual buffet of light is now usually a diet of gospel "left-overs." This bleak and tragic decrease has been gradually occurring for so many decades that very few members miss the life and authenticity the Mormon culture once offered.

J. Golden Kimball: The Real Deal

"Cut me off from the Church? They can't do that! I repent too damn fast!" [328]

"There are not enough general authorities to do all the thinking
for the membership of the Church." [329]

To curb J. Golden's occasional use of cuss words, the brethren prepared a speech for him to read
in general conference. Growing frustrated at the podium, he stopped halfway and said,
"Hell, Heber, I can't read this damn thing!" [330]

How wonderful it would be to again have the brethren stand in general conference and speak freely as inspired by the Holy Ghost. Putting away the teleprompters and pre-approved talks might allow God to communicate through His Apostles on a deeper level. Unfortunately, unrealistic expectations and cultural norms hinder the brethren's ability to speak bluntly and with personality. The result is "canned inspiration," pre-packaged for mass delivery. What we hear is useful, but oh so constricted.

"There are limits to what the Spirit permits us to say."
Boyd K. Packer, *The Twelve Apostles* [331]

Today those who believe in unorthodox views are often "sent to the bishop's office." Entrance into church leadership is usually reserved for those who "fit the mold." The fruit of this trickle-down bureaucracy is dogma, tradition, and stagnation in the ward trenches. What could be termed "corporate religion" offends the Spirit. Often at church there is so much focus on "goals," "programs," and "hastening the work" that local meetings start to feel like multi-level marketing events.

The prophets from the Book of Mormon took a different approach when conducting meetings.

And their meetings were conducted by the church after the manner of the workings of the Spirit, and by the power of the Holy Ghost; for as the power of the Holy Ghost led them whether to preach, or to exhort, or to pray, or to supplicate, or to sing, even so it was done.
Moroni 6:9

It is reported that President Gordon B. Hinkley was speaking to a group of leaders and held up a copy of the new church policy manual. He then proclaimed, *"This is the problem with the Church!"* Whether this is accurate, rumor, or wishful thinking, this alleged comment summarizes how business and bureaucracy appear to be taking over the institution.

MONEY, POWER, POLICY, AND INFLUENCE:

The Early Approach
"Never do another day's work to build up a Gentile city. Never lay out another dollar while you live, to advance the world in its present state; it is full of wickedness and violence; no regard is paid to the prophets, nor the prophesyings of the prophets, nor to Jesus nor his sayings, nor the word of the Lord that was given anciently, nor to that given in our day. They have gone astray, and they are building up themselves, and they are promoting sin and iniquity upon the earth..."
Brigham Young, *Journal of Discourses* [332]

Slightly Peculiar
"Have we separated ourselves from the Nations? Yes. And what else have we done? Ask yourselves the question. Have we not brought Babylon with us? Are we not promoting Babylon here in our midst? Are we not fostering the spirit of Babylon that is now abroad on the face of the whole earth? I ask myself this question, and I answer, Yes, yes...we have too much of Babylon in our midst."
Brigham Young, *Journal of Discourses* [333]

Money Minded
*"So money is the name of the game by which the devil cleverly decoys the minds of the Saints from God's work to his. "Why does the Lord want us up here in the tops of these mountains?" Brigham asked twenty years after the first settling of the Valley. **"He wishes us to build up Zion. What are the people doing? They are merchandizing, trafficking and trading..."***
Hugh Nibley, *Approaching Zion* [334]

One True Master
"Every step in the direction of increasing one's personal holdings is a step away from Zion…
one cannot serve two masters…so it is with God and business, for mammon is simply
the standard Hebrew word for any kind of financial dealing."
Hugh Nibley, *Approaching Zion* [335]

Seeking Mammon?
"In October of 2006 the LDS Church announced major plans to invest in huge development
on two blocks in the heart of downtown Salt Lake City. The investment includes a destination
retail development, along with high quality housing and office space…
Nearly $2 billion will be invested in the project during the next five years."
"Some of the most sacred ground for the church … is immediately adjacent to this project
and part of the reason we are proceeding with it," Bishop Burton said…A mix of condominiums,
townhouses and apartments will provide a "wide variety of accommodations
for people who desire to live, work, shop and worship downtown."
David H. Burton, *Downtown Rising* [336]

The Multi-Billion Dollar Mall
"City Creek Reserve is spending more than $1 million a day on construction,
and the project ultimately will cost around $3 billion, said Chris Redgrave, a KSL executive
who also chairs the Salt Lake Chamber's Can-Do Coalition,
which is looking for ways to jump-start the downtown economy."
Deseret News, *Salt Lake City High Rise is Ready For Occupancy on Main* [337]

Spiritual Re-Runs
*And it came to pass that king Noah **built many elegant and spacious buildings**;*
and he ornamented them with fine work of wood, and of all manner of precious things,
of gold, and of silver…And he also built him a spacious palace, and a throne in the midst thereof,
all of which was of fine wood and was ornamented with gold and silver and with precious things.
And he also caused that his workmen should work all manner of fine work within the walls
of the temple, of fine wood, and of copper, and of brass.
And it came to pass that he built a tower near the temple; yea, a very high tower…
Mosiah 11:8,9,10,12

194

Legitimate Concerns

"What does it mean when the Lord's Church is involved in dedicating banks, establishing housing for gay and lesbian tenants, focused on providing environmentally friendly buildings, and inviting Gaddianton robbers to speak at BYU? Are we being wise as serpents and harmless as doves-keeping our friends close and enemies closer? Or have we sold our soul to Babylon and joined them in their ways? Perhaps the real issue is that asking these honest and reasonable questions is considered a sign of apostasy itself. In today's church all are required to convince their local ecclesiastical leader that they know the emperor has his clothes on…
or else his or her temple clothing will be taken away."
Anonymous Saint

When in Rome?

"You are moving into the most competitive age the world has ever known.
All around you is competition. You need all the education you can get. Sacrifice a car; sacrifice anything that is needed to be sacrificed to qualify yourselves to do the work of the world. That world will in large measure pay you what it thinks you are worth, and your worth will increase as you gain education and proficiency in your chosen field."
Gordon B. Hinckley, *A Prophet's Counsel and Prayer for Youth* [338]

Guiding the Next Generation…into Babylon

"Master the mysteries of money. Try to gain experience with money. It may seem mysterious, but you can start small. Balance a budget (it's simple—don't spend more than you earn), and learn about checking accounts, credit cards, and loans."
David A. Edwards, *Practically Out the Door, New Era* [339]

Worshipping Idols?

"Idols: The work of men's hands on which the people set their hearts.
That which human resources have been promoted and sold for gold and silver (Isaiah 44:9, 46:6). The entire production of idols is erroneous and vain (Jeremiah 51:17-18) because it causes the people to become like the idols themselves. It constitutes the "wine" that makes people drunk with the wine of Babylon."
Dan Mead, *Worshipping False Gods* [340]

Fulfilling Isaiah's Prophecy?
Wine: money and false doctrine
Strong drink: false revelation

But they also have erred through wine, and through strong drink are out of the way;
the priest and the prophet have erred through strong drink, they are swallowed up of wine,
they are out of the way through strong drink; they err in vision, they stumble in judgment.
Isaiah 28:7

Prophetic Apologies
"I am sorry that this people are worldly-minded...Their affections are upon...their farms,
upon their property, their houses and possessions, and in the same ratio that this is the case,
the Holy Spirit of God – the spirit of their calling – forsakes them,
and they are overcome with the spirit of the evil one."
Brigham Young, *Journal of Discourses* [341]

Modern Day Warning
"If we lust...for the riches of the world, and spare no pains [hard work] to obtain and retain them,
and feel 'these are mine,' then the spirit of the anti-Christ comes upon us. This is the danger...
[we] are in." Many people spend most of their time working in the service of a self-image
that includes sufficient money, stocks, bonds, investment portfolios, property, credit cards,
furnishings, automobiles, and the like to guarantee carnal security throughout,
it is hoped, a long and happy life."
Spencer W. Kimball, *Teachings of Spencer W. Kimball* [342]

Nephite Cycle
"The Church does have substantial assets, for which we are grateful. These assets are primarily in
buildings in more than eighty nations. They are in ward and stake meeting facilities.
They are in schools and seminaries, colleges and institutes. They are in welfare projects.
They are in mission homes and missionary training centers. They are in temples, of which we
have substantially more than we have ever had in the past, and they are in genealogical facilities.
But it should be recognized that all of these are money-consuming assets and not money-
producing assets...They are physical facilities to accommodate the programs of the Church
in our great responsibility to teach the gospel to the world, to build faith and activity among
the living membership, and to carry forward the compelling mandate of the Lord concerning
the redemption of the dead. We have a few income-producing business properties, but the return
from these would keep the Church going only for a very short time. Tithing is the Lord's law
of finance. There is no other financial law like it. It is a principle given with a promise spoken

by the Lord Himself for the blessing of His children. ... the business assets which the Church has today are an outgrowth of enterprises which were begun in the pioneer era of our history when we were isolated in the valleys of the mountains of western America....Merchandising interests are an outgrowth of the cooperative movement which existed among our people in pioneer times. The Church has maintained certain real estate holdings, particularly those contiguous to Temple Square, to help preserve the beauty and the integrity of the core of the city...

I repeat, the combined income from all of these business interests is relatively small and would not keep the work going for longer than a very brief period. I should like to add, parenthetically for your information, that the living allowances given the General Authorities, which are very modest in comparison with executive compensation in industry and the professions, come from this business income and not from the tithing of the people. When all is said and done, the only real wealth of the Church is the faith of its people."

Gordon B. Hinckley, *"Questions and Answers"* [343]

In the World and of the World

"This people is embedded in the business practice and the seeking and earning, laboring for money. We have our money and investments invested in babylonian businesses, in the stock market, in real estate. We put our money and backing in Babylonian banking institutions, like the one with the name Zion on it. We build up those who wear their nice clothes and fancy apparel, we command each other to do the same. We only allow tithes and offerings to be paid in the form of Babylonian paper currency, with no real backing besides the words of men in excess. We thus force our people to labor in Babylon for money in order to get by day to day, showing we have no charity according to 2 Nephi 26:28-32. We discourage the Zionistic movement of gathering out, in favor of staying where we are to change where we are.

If a man were to labor today, in Babylon, for the welfare of others, accepting no payment, would mean financial and personal ruin. They would end up a vagabond, however enriched. A beggar on the street unable to be a "provident provider" for his family. In today's society, and under the direction of our leaders, he would become a destitute of sorts unable to support a family.

In Zion, this same man who labored for others would be exalted through inheritance, and increased in family. As Nephi points out; "Wherefore, if they should have charity they would not suffer the laborer in Zion to perish." But force them to perish we do.

Thus they have not charity, forcing those who seek Zion to do the same, instructing them to seek babylonian education, that they might excel according to their genius and hard work. The tools of Babylon, Goal setting, Hard work to advance, getting gain, and Education that you might prosper. As the Anti Christ said, "every man fared in this life according to the management of the creature (goals, organize); therefore every man prospered according to his genius (get an education), and that every man conquered according to his strength."

Dan Mead, *Apostasy, Are You In It?*[344]

197

The longer a church has been established, the more susceptible it becomes to the effects of money, power, and "institutionalization." In the Lord's church, conformity and obedience to that which "has been determined" is expected without argument. This attitude, when enforced for decades, results in a religion that is unavoidably ritualistic. In the name of consistency and uniformity, religious gatherings become dogmatic and dead. This is the slow and tragic descent of all corrupted religions.

And now I say unto you that it was expedient that there should be a law given to the children of Israel, yea, even a very strict law; for they were a stiffnecked people, quick to do iniquity, and slow to remember the Lord their God; Therefore there was a law given them, yea, **a law of performances and of ordinances**, *a law which they were to observe strictly from day to day, to keep them in remembrance of God and their duty towards him. But behold, I say unto you, that* **all these things were types of things to come.**
Mosiah 13: 28-31

Goal setting, opinion polling, statistical reports, data analysis, surveys, and motivational speaking techniques, convolute and drown out the simple whisper of the Holy Spirit. None of the bureaucracy and strategic planning going on in the church at this time will result in the establishment of Zion. The reality is, Zion cannot be managed—it must be manifested.

"If we would establish Zion in our homes, branches, wards and stakes, we must rise to the standard. We cannot wait until Zion comes for these things to happen- Zion will come only as they happen."
D. Todd Chistofferson *Come to Zion* [345]

In contrast to Zion, a constant emphasis on policy and structure can turn even good leaders into "yes-men," and power hungry men into tyrants. When "corporatism" is promoted from the top, it breeds the disease of unrighteous dominion, until over time a type of false power poisons the entire body of Christ. Usually it is "middle management" that administers the wounds, but in some cases there actions are simply the fruit of trying to climb the corporate ladder.

From D&C 121 we know humans are tempted to aspire to the honors of men. Unfortunately, even sincere leaders with noble motives, can slip into unrighteous dominion-thus bringing an "amen" to their priesthood. (D&C 121:37).

Hugh Nibley observed some of the key differences between functioning as a religious manager, and providing true leadership.

The Fatal Shift

"Leaders are movers and shakers, original, inventive, unpredictable, imaginative, full of surprises that discomfit the enemy in war and the main office in peace. For the managers are safe, conservative, predictable, conforming organization men and team players, dedicated to the establishment…
The leader, for example, has a passion for equality. For the manager, on the other hand, the idea of equality is repugnant and even counterproductive. Where promotion, perks, privilege, and power are the name of the game, awe and reverence for rank is everything, the inspiration and motivation of all good men. Where would management be without the inflexible paper processing, dress standards, attention to proper social, political, and religious affiliation? "If you love me," said the greatest of all leaders,

198

"you will keep my commandments." "If you know what is good for you," says the manager,"
"you will keep my commandments and not make waves." That is why the rise of management
always marks the decline, alas, of culture."
Hugh Nibley, *Leaders to Managers: The Fatal Shift* [346]

Managers usually become obsessed with "proper church procedure" and thrive on using tradition, rules, and policies as a means of maintaining order. They are usually dogmatic about attending meetings, white shirts, and the word of wisdom. These members may know a great deal about church policy, but very little about people and the pure love of Christ.

"Usually the Lord gives us the overall objectives to be accomplished and some guidelines to follow,
but he expects us to work out most of the details and methods. The methods and procedures are usually
developed through study and prayer and by living so that we can obtain and follow the promptings
*of the Spirit. **Less spiritually advanced people, such as those in the days of Moses,***
***had to be commanded in many things**. Today those spiritually alert look at the objectives,*
check the guidelines laid down by the Lord and his prophets, and then prayerfully act —
without having to be commanded in all things. This attitude prepares men for godhood."
Ezra Taft Benson, *The Teachings of Ezra Taft Benson* [347]

In truth, just as the Holy Spirit encourages an abundant life of freedom and joy, bureaucracy breeds oppression and control. Once a leader is seduced into the mindset of the Pharisee, the manipulations and punishments inflicted will seem justified-and even required. In their minds they are "protecting the flock," or "magnifying their calling," but in reality they are only re-enacting the same patterns inflicted against Jesus and all true disciples. In time, the unrighteous dominion will backfire, but not until spiritual stagnation has slowly crept in and lulled away the masses. Year after year…meeting after meeting…policy after policy…slowly down to hell…(2 Nephi 28).

At that time Jesus went on the sabbath day through the corn; and his disciples were an hungred,
and began to pluck the ears of corn, and to eat. But when the Pharisees saw it, they said unto him,
Behold, thy disciples do that which is not lawful to do upon the sabbath day. But he said unto them,
Have ye not read what David did, when he was an hungred, and they that were with him;
How he entered into the house of God, and did eat the shewbread, which was not lawful for him to eat,
neither for them which were with him, but only for the priests? Or have ye not read in the law,
how that on the sabbath days the priests in the temple profane the sabbath, and are blameless?
But I say unto you, That in this place is one greater than the temple.
Matthew 12:1-6

In contrast to the Pharisees, we have the meek and mighty example of Jesus. His life demonstrates how to humbly inspire and uplift the masses. His way is love and longsuffering, practice and patience, truth and transparency. These are not common attributes promoted in corporate America today.

The Lord's Way

"Our modern social systems depend on control, dominion and compulsion for success. Between boycotts, picketing, public ridicule, social ostracism, political correctness and peer pressure, our day has little need to rely on meekness, kindness, gentleness, love unfeigned and pure knowledge to convince another to change their lives. The methods used by the sons of God are considered weak when compared to modern management techniques. In the end, however, it is only the tools of the meek which actually produces change in the hearts of men. If compulsion is used, as soon as compulsion is removed the modern management techniques fail. None of it will survive the grave. Those who delude themselves into thinking they have "magnified their calling" by using such tools to increase statistical performance in their ward or stake or mission will likely never understand the meekness of our Lord."

Denver Snuffer, *Beloved Enos* [348]

Did God want His church to look like a country club for Saints, or a half-way house for sinners? Running the church like a Fortune-500 company may appear to bring "short-term membership dividends," but in the end it won't produce the spiritual power necessary to establish Zion.

"We cannot run the Church as we would run a business."

David O. McKay, *David O. McKay and the Rise of Modern Mormonism* [349]

Perhaps our religious situation is exactly as it should be. For now is the day of our decision: worldly wealth or eternal riches, false authority or real power?

What choose ye this day?

And, behold, one came and said unto him, Good Master, what good thing shall I do, that I may have eternal life?...Jesus said unto him, If thou wilt be perfect, go and sell that thou hast, and give to the poor, and thou shalt have treasure in heaven: and come and follow me. But when the young man heard that saying, he went away sorrowful: for he had great possessions.

Matthew 19:16, 21-22

Reader's Note: Again the purpose of this chapter is not to criticize the brethren or speak evil of the Lord's anointed. There is a difference between being intentionally negative to hurt and destroy the church versus providing light and truth that encourages us to obtain a proper hierarchy of worship.

"The fundamental principles of our religion are the testimony of the Apostles and Prophets, **concerning Jesus Christ, that He died, was buried, and rose again the third day, and ascended into heaven; and all other things which pertain to our religion** *are only appendages to it."*
Joseph Smith, *Discourses of the Prophet Joseph Smith* [350]

Any principle, doctrine, code, policy, or person who is focused on more than God, and/or places an explicit or implicit limitation on the Atonement of Jesus Christ, will eventually be shown to be preparatory in nature. When we focus on *anything,* as if it were more important than GOD ALMIGHTY and His son JESUS CHRIST, we are lingering in idolatry.

"Therefore, in all ages when men have fallen under the power of Satan and lost the faith, **they have put in its place a hope in the arm of flesh,** *and in gods of silver and gold…* **whatever thing a man sets his heart and his trust in most is his god;** *and if his god doesn't also happen to be the true and living God of Israel, that man is laboring in idolatry."*
Spencer W. Kimball, *The Teachings of Spencer W. Kimball* [351]

Should we be concerned that according to President Kimball's definition of idolatry, many in the church appear to worship prophet, church, and family? Active members say they believe in having an eye single to the glory of God, but if this is really true, why are fast and testimony meetings dominated with repetitious statements such as: "I know we are led by a living prophet," "I love my family," and "I know the Church is true?" What does it mean that in many talks and testimonies the Lord Jesus Christ is mentioned as an afterthought? Is it possible that an emphasis on "following the prophet" has replaced a sincere plea to "come unto Christ?"

Worship: "Reverent honor and homage paid to God or a sacred personage, or to any object regarded as sacred. Adoring reverence or regard."[352]

To comprehend why there is so much focus on the prophet and brethren requires understanding the changes that were implemented during the Wilford Woodruff administration.

For years the church had wanted the Utah territory to obtain statehood. Preventing this political accomplishment was a moral/legal backlash in the United States against plural marriage.[353] The United States government wanted the church to suspend the practice before allowing statehood. The dilemma for the church was that for decades, it had taught that living plural marriage was essential for obtaining the highest exaltation in heaven.[354] For the church to abandon this aspect of the Restoration would represent a monumental shift in doctrine and lifestyle.

After President Woodruff determined to sign the Manifesto, he apparently felt the need to re-assure those Saints who were concerned. He stated,

A New Promise
"The Lord will never permit me or any other man who stands as President of the Church to lead you astray. It is not in the program. It is not in the mind of God. If I were to attempt that, the Lord would remove me out of my place, and so he will any other man who attempts to lead the children of men astray from the oracles of God and from their duty."
Wilford Woodruff, *General Conference* [355]

This new doctrinal assurance was destined to become a growing pillar of belief. How appealing it must have been for the Saints to be promised they could not be led astray! With the once "essential" doctrine of plural wives now supposedly banned by God, the Utah territory could achieve statehood and persecution from the government would likely subside.

What most have not been taught is the context and meaning behind President Woodruff's spiritual guarantee. Even after releasing the first Manifesto in 1890, the president had no intention of permanently abandoning plural marriage—as witnessed by many of his statements and the tacit permission granted to some to continue the principle.[356] Telling the government what they wanted to hear was in part a charade to ensure the political and financial survival of the church.[357] Although the church prefers to suggest the Lord wrote the Manifesto, several years later in 1908, Charles W. Penrose of the Quorum of the Twelve admitted that he himself had actually written the Manifesto and that President Woodruff had signed the document to *"beat the Devil at his own game."*[358]

In reality, the church wasn't sincerely committed to ending the practice until 1904 when Joseph F Smith wrote the *"Second Manifesto."*[359] By that time the roots of what would become "prophetic infallibility" had already taken hold. The Mormons had their promise, and they intended to apply the comfort of that teaching whenever spiritual re-assurance was needed.

The purpose in providing this brief summary is not to debate the merits of plural marriage, but to provide the context from which today's belief concerning church leadership originated. As generations passed, that one statement by President Woodruff became a doctrinal mainstay—even though it has very little scriptural basis and contradicts what the Prophet Joseph Smith taught.

Thus saith the Lord?

*"If anything should have been suggested by us, or any names mentioned,
except by commandment, or thus saith the Lord, we do not consider it binding…"*
Joseph Smith, *Teachings of the Prophet Joseph Smith* [360]

*"If any man preaches to you, doctrines contrary to the Bible, the Book of Mormon, or the Book of Doctrine
& Covenants, set him down as an imposter…**Try them by the principles contained in the
acknowledged word of God;** if they preach, or teach, or practice contrary to that, disfellowship them;
cut them off from among you as useless and dangerous branches."*
Joseph Smith, *Times & Seasons* [361]

Joseph Smith instructed us to compare all teaching to the word of God, but the institution found Wilford Woodruffs promise irresistible and useful. Now whenever new policies or doctrinal changes were likely to cause upheaval, the guarantee could be utilized to validate the institution and help members accept the changes.

The relevance of this century-old belief came to the forefront in December of 2013 when the church released a document titled, *"Race and the Priesthood."* [362] This document and others were released to quell the uneasiness that had been spreading throughout the church in relation to church doctrine and its ambiguous history.

A fascinating contradiction is revealed in reading *"Race and the Priesthood."* While addressing the topic of priesthood throughout church history, the article states, *"The Church was established in 1830, during an era of great racial division in the United States. At the time, many people of African descent lived in slavery, and racial distinctions and prejudice were not just common but customary among white Americans…In 1852, President Brigham Young publicly announced that men of black-African descent could no longer be ordained to the priesthood, though thereafter blacks continued to join the Church through baptism and receiving the gift of the Holy Ghost. Following the death of Brigham Young, subsequent Church presidents restricted blacks from receiving the temple endowment or being married in the temple. **Over time, Church leaders and members advanced many theories to explain the priesthood and temple restrictions. None of these explanations is accepted today as the official doctrine of the Church…Today, the Church disavows the theories advanced in the past…**Church leaders today unequivocally condemn all racism, past and present, in any form."(LDS Newsroom, Race and the Priesthood).* [363]

This statement from the church helps us to understand that according to leaders today, the same prophet who promised, *"The Lord will never permit me or any other man who stands as President of the Church to lead you astray,"* is the same man who was also influenced by *"great racial division in the United States,"* and *"advanced theories"* which the brethren now *"unequivocally"* condemn as racist.

Those who have eyes to see will see.

The reality is that by allowing the promise made in 1890 by Wilford Woodruff to be hard-wired into the testimonies of the members, the church has painted itself into a doctrinal corner. As additional information about the church and its history becomes public, members willing to learn the truth are often left feeling betrayed and confused. The problem is not that our inspired leaders made mistakes, but that the church suggested God wouldn't let them.

How ironic that the cultural obsession to trust in leaders isn't even in harmony with many of the directives from the brethren themselves!

*"Do not, brethren, put your trust in man though he be a Bishop, an Apostle or a President; if you do, they will fail you at some time or place; they will do wrong or seem to, and your support be gone; but **if we lean on God, he never will fail us**. When men and women depend on God alone and trust in Him alone, their faith will not be shaken if the highest in the Church should step aside. They could still see that He is just and true, that truth is lovely in His sight and the pure in heart are dear to Him."*
George Q. Cannon, *Gospel Truth* [364]

Common sense requires all to ask, if the head of the church could never lead the people astray, why does scripture provide direction concerning what to do if the President transgresses?

There is not any person belonging to the church who is exempt from this council of the church. And in as much as a President of the High Priesthood shall transgress, he shall be had in remembrance before the common council of the church, who shall be assisted by twelve counselors of the High Priesthood; And their decision upon his head shall be an end of the controversy concerning him.
D&C 107: 81-83

The Prophet Joseph Smith made errors, but as a testimony to his greatness, he was humble enough to confess his mistakes, so that others might learn from his example. Perhaps Joseph knew that if the people continued to rely on leaders more than God, they would fall.

"The people should each one stand for himself and depend on no man or men... If the people departed from the Lord, they must fall."
Joseph Smith, *Words of Joseph Smith* [365]

After the promise made by President Woodruff, what began as righteous support for inspired leadership, slowly digressed into a subtle suggestion of infallibility. As the church became larger and more powerful, this cultural attitude mutated into implied worship. What occurs in testimony meeting today often represents a disturbing demonstration of *"looking beyond the mark of Christ."*

Part of the Test
*"Brethren and sisters, be faithful, live so that the Spirit of the Lord will abide within you, then you can judge for yourselves. I have often said to the Latter-day Saints---"Live so that you will know whether I teach you truth or not." Suppose you are careless and unconcerned, and give way to the spirit of the world, and **I am led, likewise, to preach the things of this world and to accept things that are not of God, how easy it would be for me to lead you astray!** But I say to you, live so that you will know for yourselves whether I tell the truth or not."*
Brigham Young, *Journal of Discourses* [366]

The idea of prophetic infallibility is not scriptural, but the notion has become a core belief for most Latter Day Saints. Through repetition, rhetoric, and wishful thinking, *"not speaking evil of the Lord's anointed"* has been translated into the perception that when it comes to leading the church, the Lord will not let the brethren make mistakes.

Some wonder why leaders allow these attitudes to persist when they could speak bluntly and curtail the onslaught of human worship. In the 1996 August *Ensign*, the First Presidency did state, *"We make no claim of individual infallibility or perfection as the prophets, seers, and revelators. Yet I humbly state that I have sat in the company of these men and I believe their greatest desire is to know and do the will of our Heavenly Father. I pray that we may be responsive to His Spirit and be found listening to the oracles He has appointed. I so pray because I know that we mortals, without the aid of revelation, cannot know the purposes of God."*[367]

Despite occasional clarification from the brethren, many Mormons seem to have watered the entire gospel down to one simple principle: "Follow the prophet." For them, this convenient phrase supposedly quells all contradiction and resolves every legitimate dispute. When members ask, "why have temple ordinances been changed?" "Did Brigham Young really teach "Adam-God?" And, "when will we again receive real revelation and prophecy in the church," these and hundreds of other similar questions are frequently answered, "we have a living prophet today."

It is unclear how having a "living prophet" rectifies the level of light lost since the days of Joseph and what is required for salvation. Neither is there any legitimate answer concerning how being led by a prophet decreases the ongoing condemnation of the church and its people. We should observe that the apostate Zoramites had a prophet in the land, but that did not stop them from ascending the rameumptom and proclaiming self-righteousness. (Alma 31:21).

Once a member accepts the *"just follow the prophet"* mindset, they usually feel justified in picking and choosing which prophecy, truths, and scriptural warnings they will apply to themselves and the Mormon culture. Scripture which could be unsettling (Mormon 8, 2 Nephi 28, D&C 84, etc), is rationalized away with the reassurance, "We can't be led astray." Those who need additional reassurance **repeatedly** quote an obscure verse in Amos 3 which promises that the Lord God will supposedly *do nothing* without first notifying the prophets. Somehow this scripture in Amos, mixed with and a great deal of religious rhetoric, has resulted in an attitude of "prophetic infallibility."

> In Catholicism, the doctrine is that the Pope is infallible, but the Catholics don't believe it.
>
> In Mormonism, the doctrine is that the Prophet is fallible, but the Mormons don't believe it

Rock Stars

"Any time you place a prophet on a pedestal, the only thing they can generally do is fall off – the only direction they can go is down. It is reasonable to assume that eventually they will fall off in some way or other. As President George Q. Cannon once taught, Do not, brethren, put your trust in man though he be a Bishop, an apostle or a president; if you do, they will fail you at some time or place; they will do wrong or seem to, and your support will be gone; but if we lean on God, He will NEVER fail us. When men and women depend upon GOD ALONE and trust in HIM ALONE, their faith will not be shaken if the highest in the Church should step aside. (DW 43:322 [Mar 7, 1891]). Unfortunately, we seem to have difficulty following President Cannon's advice. People in general want to view prophets as perfect – as the ideal examples for us to follow. This is often one of the first challenges new ultra-Mormons face. If they were previously faithful social Mormons, then they generally held the prophets and apostles in very high regard. Indeed, to a large extent their faith was likely directed at these men, rather than the Lord. When they discover that these men may not be as perfect as all that, it becomes a difficult challenge to their misdirected faith. Good men, who probably have far fewer flaws than most, can become viewed as hypocrites and deceivers. This is not because they are bad people or have terrible flaws, but mostly just because they are people with normal flaws. One could even say that they possess characteristics and attributes of above average people. Yet, they will never be able to live up to our expectations or remain on the pedestal upon which we have placed them.
Hence, we tend to judge them far more harshly than we should."
Curtis Portitt, *Apostasy of the LDS Church* [368]

It has been the experience of this author that when trying to sincerely discuss these cultural problems and doctrinal inconsistencies, members tend to get angry and defensive. Often they revert to, "I support the brethren-end of story." This reaction is beautiful on one level, but seems to occur even when the discussion isn't about the prophet or the brethren. Somehow everything in this amazing and expansive gospel gets watered down to one basic thing: "Follow the prophet."

"When the prophet speaks,… the debate is over."
Elaine Cannon, *Ensign* [369]

When this type of mindset becomes the religious norm, the effects of "institutionalism" accelerate. Believers become dogmatic, and only a few remain willing to question, is having so much faith in leadership really wise and effective? For what is a disciple to do when so many key doctrines are no longer discussed or explained by the current brethren? Is it possible that trusting in the arm of flesh can prevent a soul from having an eye single to the glory of God? Could trusting in the prophet be "preparatory" until we are spiritually able to actually know God for ourselves?

A More Excellent Way
We must not just "follow the prophet," but follow Jesus Christ the way true prophets do.
We must not just "follow the brethren," but follow the brethren unto Christ.
We must not just "trust our leaders," but trust righteous leaders when they are inspired.
We must not just "obey without question," but question and then obey all that is of God.
We must not "worship men," but worship only the true and living God!

Today the standard view is, "Obey your leaders and even if they are wrong, you will be blessed." This agreement is probably good for the daily functioning of the institution, but in reality it is a false precept that grates against the agency of man and delays a personal salvation that can be found only in Jesus Christ. It also supports the anti-Mormon argument that members are blind sheep.

"There is nothing in the scriptures that urges, admonishes, counsels, or advises the Saints to support apostasy, false doctrine, political correctness, courting the kings of Babylon, idol worship or any other form of corruption. We are repeatedly counseled to seek, to ask, to knock… to learn for ourselves so that we will not be deceived."
Dan Mead, *The Kings of Babylon* [370]

In contrast to our cultural attitude, the Prophet Joseph Smith taught, *"We have heard men who hold the priesthood remark that they would do anything they were told to do by those who preside over them (even) if they knew it was wrong; but such obedience as this is worse than folly to us; it is slavery in the extreme; and the man who would thus willingly degrade himself, should not claim a rank among intelligent beings, until he turns from his folly. A man of God would despise the idea. Others, in the extreme exercise of their almighty authority have taught that such obedience was necessary, and that no matter what the saints were told to do by their presidents, they should do it without any questions. When the Elders of Israel will so far indulge in these extreme notions of obedience as to teach them to the people, it is generally because they have it in their hearts to do wrong themselves."* [371] Brigham Young accepted this warning and advised the Saints to do the same.

"If a bishop or any other officer in this church shall counsel the people to violate any of the laws of God and to sustain and build up the kingdom of this world, the Lord will justify them in refusing to obey that counsel."
Brigham Young, *Journal of Discourses* [372]

Today members of the church live within a "who said" culture. Often the focus is not centered on whether something is true as confirmed by the Holy Spirit, but rather, what is the calling and church position of the one speaking? When a man is called to a high position in the church—such as a Seventy or Apostle, it is assumed everything he speaks and teaches is doctrinally correct. The qualifier provided by Joseph Smith has long been forgotten that, ***"a prophet was a prophet only when he was acting as such."*** [373]

Perplexed

"After watching conference I realized there were many inspirational stories, pleasantries, and humor mixed in with the usual counsel to pay our tithing, get married and go to the temple, as well as serve one another. One of the main themes of the last two conferences has been the importance of following the Living Prophet. One of our more dynamic speakers is President Uchtdorf. In his talk, he testified to us that The Church of Jesus Christ of Latter-day Saints is on course and that we have a living prophet. This should be very comforting to us. We tend to like to hear that we are doing well. We have the security that all we need to do is look towards our "modern day Moses." President Monson was referred to over and over again as our

"Beloved Prophet" and was pointed out as an example and one we should follow. In the last conference, there were several talks that quoted the 14 Fundamentals in Following the Prophet.
The top two fundamentals are: first, The prophet is the only man who speaks for the Lord in everything; and second, the living prophet is more vital to us than the standard works. The correlation department also emphasizes the importance of following our living prophet in our manuals. Here is a quote from the Aaronic Priesthood Manual 3-Lesson 24 "Testify of the blessings that come to those who rely on the words of the living prophet. Explain that life is full of dangers but that if we read, study, pray, and follow the living prophet and the Church leaders who preside over us, we can travel safely to our destination, the celestial kingdom." I am somewhat perplexed though when I read my scriptures (which we have been told isn't as vital as listening to President Monson).. I read that reaching the Celestial Kingdom is more than just reading, studying, and praying and following President Monson and the other Church Leaders. I read, "there is no other way or means whereby man can be saved, only in and through Christ." While President Monson is a remarkable man as he referenced himself as being a bishop at a young age to a ward of 1,080 members with 84 widows is remarkable.... It is only Jesus Christ that can save me. I personally know that I need to have a personal relationship with the Savior here in THIS WORLD. This means to actually KNOW HIM, not just knowing about Him…or following others who possibly might know Him better than me."For strait is the gate, and narrow the way that leadeth unto the exaltation and continuation of the lives, and FEW there be that find it, because ye receive me not in the world neither do ye know me. (D&C 132:22)."
David Christenson, *Perplexed* [374]

Stating observations like this tend to challenge cultural assumption and make members who worship the brethren uncomfortable. When reading these religious realities, many are quick to cry out, "It's all a deceptive plan to pull members away from the church!"

In relation to not speaking evil of the Lord's anointed, the author clearly states that the brethren should be supported, prayed for, and obeyed when they speak by the power of the Holy Ghost. The purpose of this summary is not to encourage anyone to negate the brethren, but that we listen to those called and then put our unyielding trust in the one sure source!

"We must all learn to depend upon God and upon Him alone. Why, the very man upon whom we think we can rely with unbounded confidence, and trust with all we possess, may disappoint us sometimes, but trust in God and He never fails."
George Q. Cannon, *Journal of Discourses* [375]

In relation to this essential decision, disciple Curtis Porrit summarizes the religious dilemma both church leaders and members face.

The Apostasy of the Church of Jesus Christ of Latter Day Saints
By Curtis Porrit

"If the Latter-day Saints are struggling with righteousness, as this work claims they are, then we must ask ourselves how the Lord would go about taking away that which has already been revealed to them. What has been revealed that can easily be taken away from us? How would He do it? How would He use his prophets under such circumstances?"

" As mentioned earlier, one seemingly obvious area involves the temple ordinances. It is fairly easy for the Lord to take away parts of the endowment, for example. This He has done multiple times and, for the most part, most social Mormons are relatively unaware of these changes. Generations of Mormons have grown up without any knowledge at all about the teachings in the early temple ceremonies. Most of these teachings are available to those who search for them, but generally only those who search for them will find them. Thus, it seems a likely place for the Lord to take away even that which they have been given. But what about the other doctrines that were plainly taught during the early years of the church – doctrines with associated "thus saith the Lord" authority attached to them? It seems to be a difficult chore for the Lord to completely take these truths away from his people. How do you stop talking about or, in some cases, completely discount, doctrines that are clearly accessible and even published within our own canon of scriptures? How would you handle it if you were the Lord? How would you handle it if you were the prophet of the church? What seems ideal would be to take the higher doctrines away from some while somehow making them available to others. This seems to be what the verses in 2 Nephi indicate. Ideally, the Lord would want to find a way to meet the need for milk among the masses, while at the same time allowing the meat to be available to those few who truly seek it, thus allowing all people to progress as much as possible and at their own level without "perishing" due to too much or too little meat. The fact that the LDS church has difficulty accomplishing both goals seems obvious. In fact, the ability to successfully deal with both the milk and the meat seems to be almost an impossibility – a task the Lord has never been able to accomplish with any of the churches he has organized throughout history. Why should we expect any more from the Lord's church today? Yet, as we follow Joseph Smith's council to "search deeper and deeper into the mysteries of Godliness," we are faced with a dilemma regarding our responsibility to the Lord. What do we do about these higher doctrines and the apparent state of the LDS church? What do we do when Joseph Smith said one thing and the current prophet says another? At this point a story from the Old Testament may help to evaluate our current situation.

In 1 Kings, chapter 13 we find a story about two prophets of God. The first prophet was told directly by God not to eat or drink in the kingdom of Israel, nor to linger in that land after his mission there was completed. Yet, as he was leaving Israel, the second prophet stopped the first and invited him to tarry in the land of Israel and to eat with him there. The first prophet explained that he was not allowed to do so, as commanded by God. At this response, the second prophet explains, I am a prophet also as thou art; and an angel spake unto me by the word of the LORD, saying, Bring him back with thee into thine house, that he may eat bread and drink water. (1 Kings 13:18) Having no reason to doubt the old prophet or the angel who spoke with him, the first prophet obeys or "follows" the admonition of the second and went back with him, and did eat bread in his house, and drank water. But then a strange thing occurs. And it came to pass, as they sat at the table, that the word of the LORD came unto the prophet that brought him back: And he cried unto the man of God that came from Judah, saying, Thus saith the LORD, Forasmuch as thou hast disobeyed the mouth of the LORD, and hast not kept the commandment which the LORD thy God commanded thee, But camest back, and hast eaten bread and drunk water in the place, of the which the LORD did say to thee, Eat no bread, and drink no water; thy carcase shall not come unto the sepulcher of thy fathers. (1 Kings 13:20-22.)."

" The first prophet was actually cursed for following the counsel of the second prophet, even though he was a true prophet and stated that this counsel came from an angel of God. He was actually deceived by the second prophet on purpose as a test to see what he would do. To put it another way, the first prophet was punished because he placed his trust in the "arm of flesh" rather than his own personal knowledge of God's commandments. There are a few lessons to be learned from this story. The first is that we should *always look directly to God for our surest answers, not to any man on earth, even if he is a true prophet. We should place God's word above anything we hear or see from any of his servants. Personal revelation has always been the highest form of authority and truth. It reigns above the words of other prophets. This thought was echoed by the words of President George Q. Cannon when he stated, Perhaps it is his own design that faults and weaknesses should appear in high places in order that his saints may learn to trust in him and not in any man or men. (Millennial Star 53:658, 1891) As strong as this lesson is, we also learn other important truths from the account in 1 Kings. According to this story, is it possible that a true prophet of God might actually say things that are not true in order to test us? Is it possible that the Lord may use this approach to find out who will be faithful to what they know is true and who will blindly "follow the brethren?" According to this story, I think this possibility clearly exists. Could the Lord take an approach similar to this today? Could He be using his prophets today in such a way as to appease and progress the masses with milk, lest they perish, while at the same time testing those who know better to see what they will do? I think this is clearly possible. Would this mean that they are false prophets? No it would not. In fact, it would be a great way to meet the needs of the social Mormons while providing a very good test for the ultra-Mormons – those who are truly interested in the higher principles. This approach may meet multiple needs the Lord has today in helping his children progress on different levels."*

"It is important to note that both of the prophets spoken of in 1 Kings were true prophets of God. The second prophet was obeying the Lord when he said things that were not altogether true. The fact that he "lied" to the first prophet is no indication whatsoever that he was a false prophet. That said, it should also be recognized that believing a principle and openly living and/or preaching it are two different things. It is one thing, for example, to gain a testimony of plural marriage or the Adam-God doctrine. It is completely another to begin living or preaching these principles without God's approval or calling.

This should be clear by now. Yet, the choice of what one believes, prays about, and desires in his heart, regardless of what "the brethren" are saying about it, provides for an excellent test of our character, testimony, and willingness to accept what God has revealed. When modern prophets make statements which seem contradictory to the revelations given to earlier prophets, it usually has to do with higher or difficult doctrines. Whenever this happens we have a choice. We can choose to simply reject one or both of the prophets. We can "settle down in a state of blind self-security, trusting our eternal destiny in the hands of our leaders with a reckless confidence that in itself would thwart the purposes of God in our salvation." Or we can choose to study, ponder, and pray about the issues, as the scriptures direct us to do, realizing that contradictory or even false statements do not necessarily imply that a false prophet is at work and that we may have a similar responsibility when it comes to living or preaching these doctrines. I feel the latter choice is clearly the wisest. In past dispensations the Lord has often used his prophets to preach lower doctrines to his people. In many cases He has used them to enforce lower doctrines even when knowledge of higher laws existed. Such was the case with Moses as well as several of the Book of Mormon prophets. That the Lord can use modern prophets in this same manner should go without saying. In our day, taking this approach would provide a way for some truths to be "taken away" from the masses while still allowing those who "hearken unto my precepts, and lend an ear unto my counsel" to receive more, just as Nephi stated. In fact, the current course of the church may be the only way to allow for both milk and meat to exist on earth at the same time. It may be the only way to do world-wide missionary work while still allowing some saints to pursue the path of perfection, at least to some extent."

"Here lies the great choice for the modern church and it's leaders, namely, to choose between missionary work and perfecting the saints. You simply can't have it both ways. Within the entire cannon of scriptures and throughout all dispensations of the gospel you will not find an adequate solution to this problem.

You can either preach milk and put off perfecting the saints, or you can teach meat and leave people behind. The LDS church seems to have clearly chosen the former at the expense of the latter, at least for the time being. This, however, is no indication of apostasy among church leadership. The Lord has taken this approach countless times in the past. And, given the prophecies concerning the church in the last days, there is every reason to believe that He is taking this approach again in our day. The greatest prophets on earth, including Joseph Smith and the Savior Himself, never overcame this problem of milk vs. meat. Some people they exalted and others they lost. It is just so today.

"Again we must cry for personal revelation on the matter. The modern leaders of the church simply cannot be pronounced as false prophets based solely on their teachings or apparent contradictions alone. There is a scriptural and/or historical precedent for almost everything the modern prophets have said and done."

"That the church is on a downward path is clear. That some of the modern leaders of the church are contributing to this downward path seems equally clear. What is less clear is the will of the Lord concerning his church and what the roles of the modern prophets are regarding the church. Are they commanded to reach higher to perfect the saints, as was Enoch? Or have they been commanded to lower themselves to the masses, as was Moses? If the latter, are they true prophets or false prophets? If the latter, what is our responsibility regarding the church and its leaders? What is our responsibility concerning the higher doctrines of the gospel as taught by Joseph Smith, Brigham Young, and others? These are important questions, the answers to which may be as unique and individual as the role of a prophet itself."
(Curtis Porritt, *The Apostasy of the Church of Jesus Christ of Latte Day Saints*).[376]

Is it possible that *"the church,"* has been focused for so long on *"the church,"* that it has unintentionally-but systematically inverted the hierarchy of worship?

What would happen today if Joseph Smith returned to the earth, attended a sacrament meeting and preached the same sermons he once taught the Saints? Isn't it likely he would now be severely ostracized for not supporting church leadership? And what if Jesus Christ Himself attended one of our gospel doctrine classes? Would He again be cast out as a blasphemous apostate who was not supporting the prophet?

> *Then said the lord of the vineyard, What shall I do? I will send my beloved son:*
> *it may be they will reverence him when they see him. But when the husbandmen saw him,*
> *they reasoned among themselves, saying, This is the heir: come, let us kill him,*
> *that the inheritance may be ours. So they cast him out of the vineyard, and killed him.*
> *What therefore shall the lord of the vineyard do unto them?*
> Luke 20:13-15

Long ago... the Messiah stood on a hill far away. He looked down tenderly upon those, who in just a few days would reject His divinity and choose to crucify Him.
He mourned, *"O Jerusalem, Jerusalem, thou that killest the prophets, and stonest them which are sent unto thee, how often would I have gathered thy children together, even as a hen gathereth her chickens under her wings, and ye would not!"* (Matthew 23:37).

Oh well...it doesn't matter..."we have a living prophet."

TRUTH: #37 BEFORE ZION IS FULLY ESTABLISHED, THE GOSPEL WILL BE TAKEN FROM THE GENTILES AND RETURNED TO THE HOUSE OF ISRAEL.

*"In this dispensation the **Gentiles** have their day for the gospel first,
and when they refuse, it will be taken to the Jews."*
Joseph Fielding Smith, *Answers to Gospel Questions* [377]

Who has been provided access to the fullness of the gospel in these latter days?

*Behold, because of their belief in me, saith the Father, and because of the unbelief of you,
O house of Israel, **in the latter day shall the truth come unto the Gentiles,
that the fulness of these things shall be made known unto them.***
3 Nephi 16:7

*Yea, even my father spake much **concerning the Gentiles, and also concerning the house of Israel**,
that they should be compared like unto an olive-tree, whose branches should be broken off
and should be scattered upon all the face of the earth…And after the house of Israel should be scattered
they should be gathered together again; or, in fine, **after the Gentiles had received the fulness
of the Gospel**, the natural branches of the olive-tree, or the remnants of the house of Israel,
should be grafted in, or come to the knowledge of the true Messiah, their Lord and their Redeemer.*
1 Nephi 10:12,14

Will the Gentiles receive the fullness of the gospel?

*And in that day shall be heard of wars and rumors of wars, and the whole earth shall be in commotion,
and men's hearts shall fail them, and they shall say that Christ delayeth his coming until
the end of the earth. And the love of men shall wax cold, and iniquity shall abound.
And when the times of the Gentiles is come in, a light shall break forth among them that sit in darkness,
and it shall be the fulness of my gospel; **But they receive it not; for they perceive
not the light, and they turn their hearts from me because of the precepts of men.
And in that generation shall the times of the Gentiles be fulfilled.***
Doctrine and Covenants 45:26-30

The Gentiles spoken of in the Book of Mormon are not only those who reject the missionaries, but also include members of the church who have made an everlasting covenant with God and then failed to receive the fullness. (see Truth #7).

*"The Book of Mormon contains many predictions of a falling away
among the "Gentiles" in the latter days."*
Verlan H. Anderson, The Apostasy of the Latter Days [378]

Those who insist the church and its mainstream are on track may want to carefully examine scriptural warnings.

*And thus commandeth the Father that I should say unto you: At that day when the Gentiles shall sin against my gospel, and shall **reject the fullness of my gospel**, and shall be lifted up in the **pride of their hearts above all nations**, and above all the people of the whole earth, and shall be filled with all manner of lyings, and of deceits, and of mischiefs, and all manner of hypocrisy, and murders, and priestcrafts, and whoredoms, and of secret abominations; and if they shall do all those things, and shall **reject the fullness of my gospel**, behold, saith the Father, **I will bring the fullness of my gospel from among them.** And then will I remember my covenant which I have made unto my people, O house of Israel, and I will bring my gospel unto them.*
3 Nephi 16:10-11

Members usually interpret this verse to be referring to "non-members." But those who study and are willing to learn soon realize a soul can't sin against a gospel that he or she hasn't been taught. The reality is, we LDS are *the only ones* who even have access to the fullness of the gospel as provided in the temple and modern-day scripture.

...In the latter day shall the truth come unto the Gentiles, that the fullness of these things shall be made known unto them.
3 Nephi 16:7

The *fullness of the gospel* was offered by God, but slowly rejected by the Saints decade after decade. Please understand, Book of Mormon prophets did not predict that we would deny *gospel basics*, but rather a genuine fullness involving every gospel truth.

Rejecting the Fullness
*"As we have observed before, **the rejection isn't of the gospel per se it is of the Fullness of my Gospel.** In other words, even though we do embrace a portion of the word, we must not reject the fullness, the mysteries of God which would bring us into the presence of the Master, and enable us to at last build Zion."*
John Pontius, *The Triumph of Zion* [379]

What will cause the Gentiles to reject the fullness?

Pride
"Pride can be characteristic of a whole race and will cause one of the hingepoint happenings in human history. As far as the spread of the gospel is concerned, the time will come when the Lord will take his gospel elsewhere from the proud and resistant Gentiles."
Neal A. Maxwell, *Meek and Lowly* [380]

Love of Riches

*For they saw and beheld with great sorrow that the people of the church began to be lifted up in the **pride of their eyes**, and to set their **hearts upon riches and upon the vain things of the world**, that they began to be scornful, one towards another, and they began to persecute those that did not believe according to their own will and pleasure. And thus, in this eighth year of the reign of the judges, there began to be great contentions among the people of the church; yea, there were envyings, and strife, and malice, and persecutions, and pride, even to exceed the pride of those who did not belong to the church of God.*

Alma 4:8-9

Priestcraft

*He commandeth that there shall be no priestcrafts; for, behold, **priestcrafts** are that men preach and set themselves up for a light unto the world, that they may get gain and praise of the world; but **they seek not the welfare of Zion.***

2 Nephi 26:29

Idolatry

*"Therefore, in all ages when men have fallen under the power of Satan and lost the faith, they have put in its place a **hope in the arm of flesh, and in gods of silver and gold**… whatever thing a man sets his heart and his trust in most is his god; and if his god doesn't also happen to be the true and living God of Israel, that man is laboring in **idolatry**."*

Spencer W. Kimball, *The Teachings of Spencer W. Kimball* [381]

Those willing to get brutally honest apply scripture and prophecy directly to their own souls. Once humbled and broken, the disciple perceives a more accurate view of how things really are and what we as a people have done with the fullness offered. Making this sobering acknowledgement creates a hunger in the soul to receive *all* that God once offered through the prophet Joseph Smith.

"So it was that the Father determined and Christ taught that the Gentiles would be the ones to whom the Gospel message would first come in our day. Now we have it. (Or had it anyway.) This movement from Israel to Gentile and from Gentile to Israel is evening the playing field. This is balancing out the record of history. It is not that one is more favored than another. Rather it is that each one will have a suitable turn and opportunity to receive what the Lord offers…The promise is that the "fullness of these things" will come to the Gentiles. What things? What does it mean that the "fullness" will be coming to the Gentiles? Have the Gentiles in fact received it? If we received it, what have we done with it? Do we still have it…? What will happen if we have not retained that fullness?"

Denver Snuffer, *Removing Condemnation* [382]

America and the Gentile Church

At that day when the Gentiles shall sin against my gospel, and shall reject the fulness of my gospel...
I will bring the fulness of my gospel from among them. And then will I remember my covenant which
I have made unto my people, O house of Israel, and I will bring my gospel unto them.
And I will show unto thee, O house of Israel, that the Gentiles shall not have power over you;
but I will remember my covenant unto you, O house of Israel, and ye shall come unto
the knowledge of the fulness of my gospel.
3 Nephi 16:10-12

When the time of the Gentiles is fulfilled, a cleansing of the wicked will occur throughout the world and within the church. During that process the gospel will be taken to the house of Israel.

In the Mirror

"The scenario in 3 Nephi 16 also matches other scriptures on the same subject.
For example, in chapter 5 of Jacob we find the allegory of the vineyard.
This allegory discusses the history of the Lord's people clear up to the millennium. A careful reading
of the chapter indicates rather clearly that the gospel will be given to the Gentiles (the wild branches)
and that they will eventually "overrun the roots" and bring forth "evil fruit." (Jacob 5:37)
The Lord deals with this problem by restoring the house of Israel (the natural branches)
to the gospel. (Jacob 5:54-56) The allegory goes on to say that as the house of Israel
receives the gospel, the apostate Gentiles are "cast away. (Jacob 5:65, 69, 73-74)."
Curtis R. Porritt, *The Apostasy of the Church of Jesus Christ of Latter Day Saints* [383]

There are many views concerning how this monumental shift may occur. Some believe the gathering will involve small Zion-like communities already living throughout Central and South America. Others have speculated about the role Lamanite Saints will play when destruction comes and the gospel is again "re-restored" in its fullness. (see Truth #75).

Gather to the Rockies

"You will gather many people into the fastness of the Rocky Mountains as a center for the gathering
of the people ...you will yet be called upon to go forth and call upon the free men
to gather themselves together to the Rocky Mountains; and the Redmen from the West
and all people from the North and from the South and from the East, and go to the West,
to establish themselves in the strongholds of their gathering places, and there you will gather with the
Redmen to their center from their scattered and dispersed situation, to become the strong arm of Jehovah,
who will be a strong bulwark of protection from your foes."
Joseph Smith, A Prophecy of Joseph the Seer [384]

Today, political and financial instability is increasing throughout America, Central America, and Mexico. The problem of illegal immigration along the southern border of the U.S. is mostly ignored and/or intentionally exacerbated. Integrating the populations of America, Mexico, and Canada has long been the intention of those who promote a one-world order. With poverty and desperation now escalating throughout North America, a perfect context is being created where scripture can be fulfilled-and the American Gentiles will again be scourged unto repentance.

A Lamanite Scourging

And inasmuch as ye shall keep my commandments, **ye shall prosper, and shall be led to a land of promise; yea, even a land which I have prepared for you; yea, a land which is choice above all other lands.** *And inasmuch as thy brethren shall rebel against thee, they shall be cut off from the presence of the Lord. And inasmuch as thou shalt keep my commandments, thou shalt be made a ruler and a teacher over thy brethren. For behold, in that day that they shall rebel against me, I will curse them even with a sore curse, and they shall have no power over thy seed except they shall rebel against me also. And* **if it so be that they rebel against me, they shall be a scourge unto thy seed, to stir them up in the ways of remembrance.**
1 Nephi 2:20-24

There are two choices for America and the Gentile Church. Repent and return to the Lord Jesus Christ, or continue to reject *the fullness of the gospel* and be torn down by the house of Israel.

Hope for the Mormons

But if the Gentiles will repent *and* **return unto me, saith the Father,** *behold* **they shall be numbered among my people, O house of Israel.** *And I will not suffer my people, who are of the house of Israel, to go through among them, and tread them down, saith the Father. But if they will not turn unto me, and hearken unto my voice, I will suffer them, yea, I will suffer my people, O house of Israel, that they shall go through among them, and* **shall tread them down, and they shall be as salt that hath lost its savor,** *which is thenceforth good for nothing but to be cast out, and to be trodden under foot of my people, O house of Israel. Verily, verily, I say unto you, thus hath the Father commanded me—that I should give unto this people this land for their inheritance.*
3 Nephi 16:13-16

Regardless of the details the Lord uses to fulfill prophecy, it seems likely that the surviving Saints will be gathered from several different cultures and religious backgrounds.

For *the time cometh that he shall manifest himself unto all nations, both unto the Jews and also unto the Gentiles; and after he has manifested himself unto the Jews and also unto the Gentiles, then he shall manifest himself unto the Gentiles and also unto the Jews, and the last shall be first, and the first shall be last.*
1 Nephi 13:42

When the time of transition and gathering arrives, the Lord will remember His covenant people. This will include those who are of pureblood descent, as well as the repenting Gentiles who are *"humble followers of Christ."* (2 Nephi 28:14).

216

Restoring the Jews

"I thank God that the day is at hand when the Jews will be restored. I have felt to pray for them; I feel interested in their behalf, for they are of the seed of Abraham and a branch of the house of Israel, and the promises of God still remain with them. It is true they fell through unbelief, and the kingdom was taken from them and given to the Gentiles, and when it came from them, it came clothed with all its gifts, powers, and glory, Priesthood and ordinances which were necessary for the salvation of men, and to prepare them to dwell in the presence of the Gods; **and when the kingdom was given to the Gentiles, they for a while brought forth the natural fruits of the kingdom. But they, like the Jews, HAVE FALLEN through the same example of unbelief, and now, in the last days, the kingdom of God has to be taken from the Gentiles, and restored back to every branch and tribe of the house of Israel;** *and when it is restored to them, it must go back with all its gifts, and blessings, and Priesthood which it possessed when it was taken from them."*
Wilford Woodruff, *Journal of Discourses* [385]

It is interesting to note that over a century ago President Wilford Woodruff considered the Gentiles to have already fallen. This requires us to ask, at what point was the fullness of the gospel considered to have been rejected by the Latter Day Saints?

Why are the scriptures not interpreted this way in the LDS culture?

Fullness or Fail

"When we have our names sealed in the Lamb's Book of Life we have Perfect Love and then it is impossible for false Christ's to deceive us. God has often sealed up the heavens because of covetousness in the Church. Except the Church "receive" the fullness they will yet fail."
Joseph Smith, *Teachings of the Prophet Joseph Smith* [386]

In our day of pride and vanity, explaining to the general membership that we are actually Gentiles who are in the process of rejecting the fullness of the gospel, may not be well received. Perhaps similar to many other important truths recorded in scripture, the Lord allows each of us to apply revelation to the degree we are prepared to receive it.

"And he said, Go, and tell this people, Hear ye indeed, but understand not; and see ye indeed, but perceive not. Make the heart of this people fat, and make their ears heavy, and shut their eyes; lest they see with their eyes, and hear with their ears, and understand with their heart, and convert, and be healed. Then said I, Lord, how long? And he answered, Until the cities be wasted without inhabitant, and the houses without man, and the land be utterly desolate."
Isaiah 6: 9-11

217

TRUTH #38 DURING THE TIME OF CLEANSING, THE TARES WILL CONTINUE TO CHOKE THE WHEAT. TRUE PROPHETS HAVE ALWAYS BEEN PERSECUTED AND REJECTED BY THE MAJORITY.

*"Many men will say, "I will never forsake you, but will stand by you at all times."
But the moment you teach them some of the mysteries of the kingdom of God that are retained in the heavens and are to be revealed to the children of men when they are prepared for them they will be the first to stone you and put you to death. It was this same principle that crucified the Lord Jesus Christ, and will cause the people to kill the prophets in this generation."*
Joseph Smith, *Teachings of the Prophet Joseph Smith* [387]

Both Jesus and Joseph organized churches containing greater light than their culture could embrace. During their respective ministries, they were consistently misjudged and persecuted by the tares of their day. The Lord Jesus was called *"Beelzebub"*(Matthew 10:25) and accused of being a *gluttonous wine-bibber.* (Matthew 11:19). Joseph Smith was degraded as *"old Joe Smith-the false prophet,"*[388] and Enoch was considered a *"wild man."* (Moses 6:38). The apostle Paul was assumed to be a *"mad"* and *"pestilent fellow."* (Acts 24:5, 26:24).

Throughout history social oppression and personal attacks unavoidably occur whenever ***God invites a culture within a culture to accept greater light.***

"I have tried for a number of years to get the minds of the Saints prepared to receive the things of God; but we frequently see some of them, after suffering all they have for the work of God, will fly to pieces like glass as soon as anything comes that is contrary to their traditions: they cannot stand the fire at all. How many will be able to abide a celestial law, and go through and receive their exaltation, I am unable to say, as many are called, but few are chosen."
Joseph Smith, *Teachings of the Prophet Joseph Smith* [389]

Believers who repeatedly obey the gospel of Jesus Christ eventually experience the mighty change of heart. (Alma 5:12-14). These are they who have been personally cleansed by the blood of the Lamb. Others who have not yet experienced the miracle of redemption may accidentally mis-judge those who have awakened. This spiritual dichotomy is recorded in scripture as the parable of the "wheat and tares."

Another parable put he forth unto them, saying, The kingdom of heaven is likened unto a man which sowed good seed in his field: But while men slept, his enemy came and sowed tares among the wheat, and went his way. But when the blade was sprung up, and brought forth fruit, then appeared the tares also. So the servants of the householder came and said unto him, Sir, didst not thou sow good seed in thy field? from whence then hath it tares? He said unto them, An enemy hath done this. The servants said unto him, Wilt thou then that we go and gather them up? But he said, Nay; lest while ye gather up the tares, ye root up also the wheat with them. Let both grow together until the harvest: and in the time of harvest I will say to the reapers, Gather ye together first the tares, and bind them in bundles to burn them: but gather the wheat into my barn.
Matthew 13: 24-30

Usually when we think of Mormons being persecuted, we mentally refer to the 1800s, when angry mobs burned houses, harassed children and families, and killed the faithful.

Since that dark era, another type of slow and subtle persecution has been growing within the church. Paradoxically, the new persecution only occasionally comes from the outside world, but instead is delivered by Mormons…against the Saints.

> *"So also in our day the Lord has told us of the tares within the wheat that will eventually be hewn down when they are fully ripe. But until they are hewn down, they will be with us, amongst us."*
> Ezra Taft Benson, *Conference Report* [390]

Social neglect demonstrated toward those who "don't fit the mold" often results in profound religious loneliness. Some who love truth and dare to question tradition are prone to receive a type of "silent choking" from the mainstream. How ironic that the same religious people who were once persecuted are now the ones who often do the persecuting.

> *"Mortal man is here to be tested. The test is not whether they can conform to the expectations of a broad, mainstream, self-congratulating "chosen" people. The test is far more individual than that. It is a lonely quest to find the Chosen One of Israel. Those who really find Him, not an imaginary version of the Living God, but actually meet the Risen Lord, the Savior of mankind, generally do not rely at all upon their chosen status. Rather they are usually somewhat at odds with the chosen mainstream."*
> Denver Snuffer, *Come let us adore Him* [391]

Members who do not reaffirm mainstream beliefs are frequently overlooked, minimized, or avoided. Those who are spiritually awake often report that due to the level of spirituality present in their local congregations, they are prohibited by the Holy Spirit from speaking deeper truths. We can assume God does this to avoid overwhelming His growing flock as well as prevent a premature persecution coming upon His willing wheat.

> *Nevertheless among the chief rulers also many believed on him; but because of the Pharisees they did not confess him, lest they should be put out of the synagogue:*
> *For they loved the praise of men more than the praise of God.*
> John 12:42-43

When a dilemma arises between obeying God or appeasing man, it is important to remember that **TRUTH IS ITS OWN AUTHORITY.** Even though our "who said" culture usually requires all spiritual teachings to be confirmed by a General Authority, God is the final authority of all that is true. He is the trusted source! When neither comment or clarification is available from the current brethren, many shrink and determine the principle being considered must be irrelevant or false. (see Truth #18).

In comparison, disciples who love Jesus Christ and celebrate in His power and peace eventually grow to where they can "stand in the truth" independent of any other person. They might continue to learn from inspired teachers, but they also believe Father when He says, *"it is given to abide in you; the record of heaven; the Comforter; the peaceable things of immortal glory; the truth of all things; that which quickeneth all things…that which knoweth all things…"* (Moses 6:61).

219

In Christ and His Spirit, all who internalize this process can differentiate between the undefiled truths of the kingdom and the philosophies of men mingled with scripture over the pulpit.

> *"Not only are there apostates within our midst, but there are also apostate doctrines*
> *that are sometimes taught in our classes and from our pulpits and that appear in our*
> *publications. (See March 2003 Ensign for an example) And these apostate precepts of men cause*
> *our people to stumble. As the Book of Mormon, speaking of our day, states: ". . . they have all*
> *gone astray save it be a few, who are the humble followers of Christ; nevertheless, they are led,*
> *that in many instances they do err because they are taught by the precepts of men. (2 Ne. 28:14)."*
> Ezra Taft Benson, *Conference Report* [392]

In truth, a lack of doctrinal understanding on the part of a local leader does not necessarily make a person "apostate." People in general don't like having their assumptions questioned, so when contradictions between scripture and church history are highlighted, leaders sometimes become fearful and slip into unrighteous dominion. When those wielding religious influence become threatened, they may revert to using punishment and control to try and maintain the status quo for their "flock." Frequently, what is perceived as being, *"best for the church,"* overrides a careful analysis of what is actually true.

With good intentions, some leaders may feel it is their duty to rebuke or silence what they currently perceive as false doctrine, even when the message they are attacking is doctrinally correct, valid, and commanded of God.

To take an honest look at what Joseph Smith taught and then compare it to church doctrine today, requires a fierce loyalty to Father, Jesus Christ, and the original Restoration. It's just so much easier to attack the growing member, than to re-organize cherished beliefs held true for generations.

The misunderstanding of one leader does not make someone on God's errand an "apostate."

None of the unrighteous dominion happening in today's church changes what is really true, but it does provide the accused with the essential experience of being falsely persecuted. This is what Jesus Christ responded to with love, and this is what all true servants of Christ must endure as they progress into full discipleship.

Often, the degree of light allowed in church meetings (and in church courts) is a direct commentary on the spiritual capacity of those in attendance. Despite this reality, those who love God will obey the Holy Spirit when directed to speak, even if their testimony results in personal persecution.

And when they had brought them, they set them before the council: and the high priest
asked them, Saying, Did not we straitly command you that ye should not teach in this name?
And, behold, ye have filled Jerusalem with your doctrine, and intend to bring
this man's blood upon us. Then Peter and the other apostles answered and said,
We ought to obey God rather than men.
Acts 5:28-29

When the Holy Spirit prompts an individual to provide additional light and/or issue a call to repentance, that person is likely to be misunderstood, ridiculed, and rejected. The invitation to change is never popular with the masses, but on a personal level, the rejection that follows is an essential aspect of the Christ pattern and something that all true prophets must endure.

Enoch the Seer

And they came forth to hear him, upon the high places, saying unto the tent-keepers:
Tarry ye here and keep the tents, while we go yonder to behold the seer, for he prophesieth,
and there is a strange thing in the land; a wild man hath come among us.
Moses 6:38

Similar to those who condemned Enoch as a "wild man," many rank and file Mormons are quick to conclude that anyone teaching "deep doctrine," must be sharing "false doctrine."

"We have the most interesting Church, unlike any other. We are in the unique position of having to be careful what we quote from the founders of our Church. Quoting the "wrong thing" can get you into lots of trouble and if you persist, will get you asked out of the Church. Imagine another church, where if you quoted the wrong scripture or if you quoted the "wrong quote" by the founder or originator of that church, the next thing you know, the current leaders are asking you to shut up or to not come back. To me, it borders on sheer lunacy. If I want to stir things up all I have to do is read from Teachings of the Prophet Joseph Smith which was compiled by the tenth President of the Church, Joseph Fielding Smith. Having made that "mistake", I will be asked politely the first time to "stick to the manual" and the second time, asked to be quiet and reminded that we have "living prophets" who give us "current revelation," whatever that is."
Anonymous Saint

When truth is written or spoken that is unfamiliar or difficult to hear, some may get offended and defend cultural norms. When members give *"carte blanche"* support to *anything and everything* the church does, they unknowingly mimic Laman and Lemuel who inaccurately testified, *"We know that the people who were in the land of Jerusalem were a righteous people, for they kept the statutes and judgments of the Lord, and all his commandments."* (1 Nephi 17:22). This type of spiritual rationalization comes not only from "inactives," but also from those who have been ordained with priesthood authority. Some leaders, who honestly believe they are doing God's will by "protecting the flock," may be tempted to enforce their current understanding by making threats of taking away temple recommends or pursuing disciplinary action.

"The ravening wolves are amongst us, from our own membership, and they, more than any others, are clothed in sheep's clothing, because they wear the habiliments of the priesthood."
President J. Reuben Clark, *Conference Report* [393]

To maintain the illusion that everything is progressing appropriately, local leaders may enact incorrect judgments when faced with the difficult situations. The social tares of the church may try to quiet or discredit a member who does not have a notable church position, but has nonetheless been commanded of God to proclaim repentance. (D&C 88:81). Our religious assumption that only those with religious "keys" would ever be called to proclaim such a message is incorrect and at odds with scriptural history. (Jesus Christ, John the Baptist, Lehi, Abinadi, Enos, Samuel the Lamanite, etc). The reality is that *Jesus Christ has all the keys, and can personally assign whomsoever He chooses to deliver His message.* All are free to assess and determine whether a message is from God or a deception, but in the end, the pretenders will be revealed, while the Lord's true servants kneel at His feet and stand by His side. (Moses 1:25-26).

Behold, I am Alpha and Omega, even Jesus Christ. Wherefore, let all men beware how they take my name in their lips—For behold, verily I say, that many there be who are under this condemnation, who use the name of the Lord, and use it in vain, having not authority. Wherefore, let the church repent of their sins, and I, the Lord, will own them; otherwise they shall be cut off.
D&C 63: 60-64

Many of the leaders who persecute the wheat are good men who sincerely feel justified in their religious actions. In their minds they have erroneously determined the messengers to be the real "wolves" in sheep's clothing. (Alma 5:59). When this dynamic occurs, all who are falsely accused should **meekly and sincerely** return love to the offender, praying as Jesus did, ***"Father, forgive them; for they know not what they do."*** (Luke 23:34).

God loved the birds and invented trees.
Man loved the birds and invented cages.
Jacques Deval

The most catalytic realization of God is that He is within you (Luke 17). To know that He isn't a static pool of water but rather, growing, evolving, expanding, as we exalt him, is liberating and peaceful. Permanence is damnation, becoming is progression. Yet, in principle, in passion, in love, he does not change. We must connect to His unchanging principles, the one eternal God, for they are the very catalyst for change within us. Understanding this paradox will place us in the humble state of knowing that what we are now cannot be enough, but what we are becoming will always be. That kingdom, within you, is the light of Christ, designed to exalt all. This is where He speaks to us, where He converts us, constantly, and thus exalts the kingdom of God, within you. Through the instrumentality of the Holy Ghost our baseness, our course beastly desires, the dust from whence we came, can quicken Christ within us, by The Christ who has put all our enemies beneath His feet. We don't have to go far to find God. In fact, if you do, you won't. The kingdom of God is within you, the lunch is provided, so where are we going? You are there, a Kingdom waiting for burgeoning growth. This places those who would set up fences for others in the most awkward position. Since man's real authority is only found in his relationship with God. It is individual and personal, over his kingdom. That authority is his own and only pertains to him. That authority is called agency. Exercising authority over others, outside of this influence, is the biggest illusion. It is the very trickery with which Satan gains control over men. The appearance of authority is just that, appearance. Once 'authority' is manifest by gaining control, compulsion or dominion over another persons kingdom, we can plainly see the error of that arrangement. By placing walls in belief and action for another man we place his kingdom in bondage, no longer fully free to grow and stretch.

Dan Mead, *Authority* [394]

This trend of making false accusations and implementing unjust discipline stems from human pride, cultural assumption, good intentions, and a lack of doctrinal understanding. Assuming this type of spiritual choking continues to increase within the Lord's church, it will represent the ongoing fulfillment of prophecy.

...Even Satan, sitteth to reign—behold he soweth the tares; **wherefore, the tares choke the wheat and drive the church into the wilderness***...But the Lord saith unto them, pluck not up the tares while the blade is yet tender (for verily your faith is weak), lest you destroy the wheat also.*

D&C 86: 3,6

> # The Mormon culture does not always *follow* scripture,
> ## but it is consistently *fulfilling* scripture.

In relation to D&C 86, James Custer writes, *"There is also a tendency to regard the active element of the church membership as the wheat and the in-active element as the tares. A thoughtful examination of the latter day application of the parable will however bring one to the realization that the in-actives have virtually no influence in church affairs and therefore, no significant ability to choke the wheat and drive the church into the "wilderness." The wilderness being a state of general apostasy among the membership."*[395](D&C 15:14, 33:4).

Being "choked" is especially hurtful when respected church leaders—or even family members are inflicting the wounds. Nathan Shackelford observes, *"Choking is a very intimate process. The fact that this is the analogy used is both alarming and revealing. Choking involves intimacy, calculation, touch, shutting off of the windpipe or origin of voice and speaking. Metaphorically, it is the* **shutting off of a person's soul voice.** *Choking is not instant, but progressive. Because of the nature of the act, and the medium, the two (wheat and tare) will have had a relationship and know each other. Choking denotes that what the person (the wheat) is saying, their behavior and even their very nature, activates such a source of internal suffering in the tare, revealing a gaping chasm between who they truly are and what they have become in this mortality, it is such that it is not enough for the tare just to get rid of them (an act of non-attachment), but they must be intimately silenced, and by using their own hands."*[396]

There are many reasons why a prophet is generally not accepted in his own country, his own church, or even his own family (Matthew 10:25-42 and Luke 4:24). One reason family members struggle to hear the message is that they are intimately familiar with the weaknesses of the messenger. Another reason rejection occurs is simply because people in general don't like to change.

> *...if a prophet come among you and declareth unto you the word of the Lord, which testifieth of your sins and iniquities, ye are angry with him, and cast him out and seek all manner of ways to destroy him; yea, you will say that he is a false prophet, and that he is a sinner, and of the devil, because he testifieth that your deeds are evil. But behold, if a man shall come among you and shall say: Do this, and there is no iniquity; do that and ye shall not suffer; yea, he will say: Walk after the pride of your own hearts; yea, walk after the pride of your eyes, and do whatsoever your heart desireth and if a man shall come among you and say this, ye will receive him, and say that he is a prophet. Yea, ye will lift him up, and ye will give unto him of your substance; ye will give unto him of your gold, and of your silver, and ye will clothe him with costly apparel; and because he speaketh flattering words unto you, and he saith that all is well, then ye will not find fault with him.*
> Helaman 13:25-28

Mormons usually assume that church callings correlate with actual righteousness. Reading about the General Authorities who apostatized in the early days of the church demonstrates this belief is not always accurate. In addition scripture provides historical patterns that are relative today, (Judas, Herod, King Noah, etc...). Despite these spiritual examples, observing unpleasant realities within Mormonism is usually not well received.

> *"How great and terrible is God's work among every generation. How similar are the methods by which He separates His sheep, who hear His voice, from the goats, who are merely religious.*
> *Daily, weekly or annual outward observances of religious forms can never save a soul.*
> *To be saved mankind must accept His messengers. Those whom He inspires and then sends point to the path back to Him. They alone will point to Him, and not to themselves. They alone will encourage people to come to Him, and not take honor for themselves. Invariably it is the religious who are responsible for persecuting and killing the ones actually sent by God."*
> Denver Snuffer, *Come, Let Us Adore Him* [397]

Just as the Jews railed against Jesus and killed Him, persecution is always part of the Christ pattern. To prophesy and be rejected by the mainstream is usually a required aspect of being fully accepted of the Lord.

> *"God's servants are almost never found at the head of society. They are often like Abinadi or Samuel the Lamanite-belittled, persecuted, and violently opposed. They always pay their tithing, but rarely collect it. It is not likely this pattern will ever change."*
> Denver Snuffer, *Come Let Us Adore Him* [398]

From the warnings in D&C 121, we know how difficult it is for men to avoid slipping into unrighteous dominion. Despite this spiritual challenge, the church is full of good men, doing the best they can to lead members in the manner in which they have been trained. In some instances, *real apostasy is occurring,* and in those cases local leadership remains essential for protecting the flock.

In addition, the Lord places all of His children in the spiritual context they individually need to overcome deficits and grow. What leaders may not yet understand is that many of them have been placed in their ecclesiastical positions to see how *they* will respond to the power and prestige. Denver Snuffer summarizes, *"Since the Lord reserves to Himself alone the final judgment (3 Nephi 27:27) I think we overstep our privileges when we presume our judgment of others is our right. **In fact, the irony of judging while holding priesthood office is that the one judging may be the one really on trial.** They hold office, are given "keys" and are upheld by other saints to see whether they will execute the assignment in conformity with D&C 121, using gentleness, meekness, persuasion, kindness and love unfeigned. If they don't, they fail the test, and in the process establish the criteria and means by which they will be judged."* [399]

Currently, the wheat being persecuted exist as a mostly silent, but growing minority. Perhaps the day will come when God's remnant will finally be allowed to speak openly and with power and authority. If and when the Lord facilitates this glorious time of open discourse, the historical patterns of religious persecution and rejection will again intensify within the walls of our own chapels. At that great and dreadful day, every member will have to choose to whom they offer their spiritual allegiance.

Watching for Samuel

But as many as there were who did not believe in the words of Samuel were angry with him; and they cast (doctrinal) stones at him upon the wall, and also many shot (mental) arrows at him as he stood upon the wall; but the Spirit of the Lord was with him, insomuch that they could not hit him with their stones neither with their arrows.

Helaman 16:2

> Is there a Samuel getting ready to the climb the wall?
> Will there be another Abinadi? And who will be the next Alma to listen?

Similar to when Samuel the Lamanite climbed the wall and called the distracted and idolatrous Nephites to repentance, there will be social Mormons who respond to the "God-ordained" messengers by throwing spiritual rocks and shooting religious arrows. Even now, God allows unrighteous dominion to be inflicted upon His servants, to test the broken-hearted, and to allow those who are sleeping to be reassured *"all is well in Zion."* (2 Nephi 28:21).

How comforting it is to know that in the reality of heaven, any incorrect judgments based in pride and unrighteous dominion are not binding. Nothing can change the truth, and in the end all who have been persecuted for Christ, (especially when it was done in the name of "keys" and religious authority), will be justified in Him.

Blessed are Ye

Blessed are they which are persecuted for righteousness' sake: for theirs is the kingdom of heaven. Blessed are ye, when men shall revile you, and persecute you, and shall say all manner of evil against you falsely, for my sake. Rejoice, and be exceeding glad: for great is your reward in heaven: for so persecuted they the prophets which were before you.

Matthew 5:10-12

> **TRUTH #39** ABANDONING THE CHURCH AND ITS MEMBERS IS USUALLY NOT THE ANSWER. THE WHEAT MUST HOLD FAST TO THE PROPHECIES AND TEACHINGS RECORDED IN SCRIPTURE. THIS INCLUDES SERVING OTHERS WITH WISDOM, PATIENCE, AND LOVE.

"Our Savior gave Himself in unselfish service. He taught that each of us should follow Him by denying ourselves of selfish interests in order to serve others.
"If any man will come after me, let him deny himself, and take up his cross, and follow me. "For whosoever will save his life shall lose it: and whosoever will lose his life for my sake shall find it. (Matthew 16:24-25)."
Dallin H. Oaks, *Unselfish Service* [400]

Those who love Jesus Christ and His gospel sometimes have a hard time staying in His Church. Many have served for years with passion and commitment only to find themselves increasingly dissatisfied with the social, cultural, and doctrinal problems present. The following letter summarizes the doctrinal concerns a growing number of members appear to be experiencing.

Conflicted and Confused

"For years we attempted to work it all out so that it all made sense. The more we studied and prayed, the less the pieces of the puzzle seemed to fit, and the greater became our concern and our dismay. Eventually, however, we came to realize that the reason the pieces did not fit was because they were pieces to different puzzles. The Church had changed so much from its 19th Century origins that it was no longer the same. To list the changes of which I speak and to document them would lengthen this epistle into a volume of unwieldy size. Some of the more outstanding areas of concern, however, include the identity of and nature of Deity ("Adam God"); Jehovah of the Old Testament and Christ; consecration, united order and tithing; the nature of eternal progression; the temple endowment; eternal marriage, polygamous and monogamous; Negro and priesthood; the priesthood garment; priesthood offices, particularly that of Seventy; blood atonement; preaching by the Spirit vs. written speeches; method of missionary work; trusting our salvation to human leaders; world and national politics, government and friendship with the world; infallibility of the President of the Church; the nature of revelation; gathering of Israel; rebaptism; adoption; laws of God and laws of man; establishment of the Kingdom of God; sacrament; and more. In all of these areas, the present teachings of the Church are not the same as they were before the great transition in Mormonism which occurred just after the turn of the century."
Anonymous Saint [401]

Those who perceive today's ever-deepening apostasy must possess the spiritual maturity necessary to avoid a personal apostasy at heart. Understanding how much has been lost does create legitimate sorrow, but frustration does not justify breaking personal covenants made with God. Every baptized member has covenanted *to mourn with those that mourn, yeah, and comfort those that stand in need of comfort, and to stand as witnesses of God at all times and in all things, and in all places that ye may be in...*(Mosiah 18:9). Surely a Mormon congregation would be one of those places where we are to stand as a witness of Christ and minister to others with love.

To assist those considering becoming inactive, leaving the church, or saying truths that could result in excommunication, it might be wise to ponder why the Lord allows the church to remain in its current state. Surely the Creator of the universe has power to rectify the problems, so it seems reasonable to ask, why doesn't He? How could God allow righteousness to coincide with, and even be dominated by, apathy, ignorance, pride, and priestcraft? Why would God allow true doctrine to be ignored, minimized, and even eradicated from within His only true church?

In response to these understandable questions, let us remember the Lord's work is to *"bring to pass the immortality and eternal life of man"* (Moses 1:39). To further spiritual growth, He often sanctifies His children by subjecting them to difficult and unjust circumstances. In this sense, the Church, (and life) is ***perfect in its imperfection.***

> Is it possible that the "perfect storm" brewing in the Church today
> provides the "perfect context" for increased spiritual transformation?

Scripture teaches there must be *"opposition in all things."* (2 Nephi 2:11). In harmony with this truth, "the world" has provided abundant opposition to the church. But what is the "opposition" to the literal establishment of Zion? Could it paradoxically be the church? Is it possible that the institution is valuable for coming out of the world while *simultaneously* providing *unintentional opposition* for those who truly seek Zion? Perhaps the Lord in His wisdom first invites souls to come unto Christ through baptism into His church, only to then use the same organization as a trial of faith for those seeking a true fullness of the gospel. If so, how remarkably wise and clever of our God!

Just as the Jewish culture, with its religious fanaticism and blind legalism, provided the perfect context for the Messiah to manifest His divine role as Savior, disciples of Christ are currently offered a religious environment valuable for true spiritual growth. In this sense, "the Church," as both solution and problem, is "perfect" for providing the appropriate setting needed for spiritual progression.

"People are often unreasonable, illogical, and self-centered; Forgive them anyway.
If you are kind, People may accuse you of selfish, ulterior motives; Be kind anyway.
If you are successful, you will win some false friends and some true enemies; Succeed anyway.
If you are honest and frank, people may cheat you; Be honest and frank anyway.
What you spend years building, someone could destroy overnight; Build anyway.
If you find serenity and happiness, they may be jealous; Be happy anyway.
The good you do today, people will often forget tomorrow; Do good anyway.
Give the world the best you have, and it may never be enough;
Give the world the best you've got anyway. You see, in the final analysis,
it is between you and God; It was never between you and them anyway."
Kent M. Keith, *The Paradoxical Commandments* [402]

Wisdom requires letting the Lord relate to the LDS Church as He determines. This includes patiently submitting to the tares while the Lord allows them to flourish among the membership. (Matthew 13:24-30). Instead of trying to fix what God is using to stretch His wheat and identify

227

His tares, we can adopt the counsel of 17ᵗʰ century Christian Jeanne Guyon, who states, *"Do not be anxious and do not be so eager for action. The purest love you can ever know is that love which comes to you when the Lord is working on your soul. So let Him work. You must just remain in the place He assigns to you."*[403] This advice is also congruent with Elder Uchdorf's solid counsel in the October 2008 General Conference to, *"Lift where you stand."*[404]

Whether a soul is working to come out of the world and into the LDS church, or to come out of religious condemnation and into the Church of the Firstborn, the LDS church offers a perfect environment to practice unconditional love, patience, service, meekness, humility, wisdom, and long suffering.

> *"The more we repent, the less tolerant we become of sin, and the more tolerant we become of sinners. The less we repent, the more tolerant we become of sin, and the less tolerant we become of sinners."*
> Richard Brady, *Orem Cascade Stake Conference* [405]

Admittedly, it can be difficult for the natural man to be involved week after week. The ego wants to delay personal repentance by instead focusing on "what's wrong with the church." The solution is to remember that each of us is responsible for our own personal transformation, not the institution's.

In the Mirror

> *"The blame for the condition we each find our selves in this world today falls squarely in one place only - upon me - this natural man enemy to God. I have chosen it. It is not about "the church", or "the brethren" or the failings and weaknesses of others. It is about whether I choose to be stripped completely of my vanity and pride and ego and self, and "see" that there is only one way out of this self-created Hell, to turn back to Him, repent and receive His fullness."*
> Jeff Ostler, *My Choice* [406]

Instead of resenting the church for its flaws, we should ask, Have I been born of God? Have I received my calling and election? Am I a member of the Church of the Firstborn? What needs to be changed in my heart and mind that I may part the veil and be received of the Lord in the flesh?

For those who justify leaving the Church due to its many problems, it would be wise to remember the life of Jesus and ponder: Did the Master abandon His Jewish family? What would have happened if He had stopped teaching the Jews because they "just weren't getting it?" Did the mercy and longsuffering that Christ displayed have a time limit? And in relation to His followers, accusers, and even those who would eventually crucify Him, did His love for them end?

> *And when they were come to the place, which is called Calvary, there they crucified him... Then said Jesus, Father, forgive them; for they know not what they do...*
> Luke 23:33-34

In truth, we *"serve whom we love and love whom we serve."* Those who are like Christ demonstrate faith, charity, and long-suffering. Even in our moments of resentment and frustration, we can *"pray unto the Father with all the energy of heart, that ye may be filled with this love…that when he shall appear we shall be like him…"* (Moroni 7:48).

In the April 2010 General Conference, President Henry B. Eyring shared this approach for being a true minister of Jesus Christ.

> *"When I find myself drawn away from my priesthood duties by other interests and when my body begs for rest, I give to myself this rallying cry: "Remember Him." The Lord is our perfect example of diligence in priesthood service. He is our captain. He called us. He goes before us. He chose us to follow Him and to bring others with us… I remember His example in the days before. Out of love for His Father and for us, He allowed Himself to suffer beyond the capacity of mortal man. He told us some of what that infinite sacrifice required of Him. You remember the words: "For behold, I, God, have suffered these things for all, that they might not suffer if they would repent; "But if they would not repent they must suffer even as I; "Which suffering caused myself, even God, the greatest of all, to tremble because of pain, and to bleed at every pore, and to suffer both body and spirit—and would that I might not drink the bitter cup, and shrink—"Nevertheless, glory be to the Father, and I partook and finished my preparations unto the children of men." From the cross on Calvary, the Savior announced, "It is finished."*
>
> *Then His spirit left His body, and His mortal remains were placed lovingly in a tomb. He taught us a lesson by what He did in three days in the spirit world, before His Resurrection, which I remember wheneverI am tempted to feel that I have finished some hard task in His service and deserve a rest. The Savior's example gives me courage to press on. His labors in mortality were finished, but He entered the spirit world determined to continue His glorious work to save souls. He organized the work of the faithful spirits to rescue those who could still be made partakers of the mercy made possible by His atoning sacrifice."*
>
> Henry B. Eyring, *Act In All Diligence* [407]

Although the merciful act of the Atonement "is finished," Jesus Christ is not. According to Joseph F. Smith, even after the Lord had been resurrected, He *"had not fulfilled all his work. And when will he? Not until he has redeemed and saved every son and daughter of our father Adam that have been or ever will be born upon this earth to the end of time, except the sons of perdition. That is his mission."*[408] This reality requires all who honor the Messiah to shout, how amazing is the Christ! How Glorious is our God! And should we not be mirroring the nobility of Jesus in some miniscule degree? Should we not interact with all people in the same way Jesus ministered to the Jews?

> *"I speak of the loneliest journey ever made and the unending blessings it brought to all in the human family. I speak of the Savior's solitary task of shouldering alone the burden of our salvation. Rightly He would say: 'I have trodden the winepress alone; and of the people there was none with me… I looked, and there was none to help; and I wondered that there was none to uphold [me].' Now I speak very carefully, even reverently, of what may have been the most difficult moment in all of this solitary journey to Atonement. I speak of those final moments for which Jesus must have been prepared intellectually and physically but which He may not have fully anticipated emotionally and spiritually—that concluding descent into the paralyzing despair of divine withdrawal when He cries in ultimate loneliness, 'My God, my God, why hast thou forsaken me?'"*
>
> Jeffrey R. Holland, *None were with Him* [409]

After Jesus triumphantly completed the horror of Gethsemane and Calvary, He did not stop, but continued to minister to the children of God with kindness and wisdom. This reaffirms that He doesn't give up on anyone, and neither should we. In this spirit, leaving the church and missing the opportunity to meekly serve is usually not the answer.

The Way, The Truth, and the Life

"A great example of unselfish service is the late Mother Teresa of Calcutta, whose vow committed herself and her fellow workers to "wholehearted free service to the poorest of the poor." She taught that "one thing will always secure heaven for us—the acts of charity and kindness with which we have filled our lives."

"We can do no great things," Mother Teresa maintained, "only small things with great love."

When this wonderful Catholic servant died, the First Presidency's message of condolence declared, "Her life of unselfish service is an inspiration to all the world, and her acts of Christian goodness will stand as a memorial for generations to come." That is what the Savior called losing our lives in service to others. Each of us should apply that principle to our attitudes in attending church. Some say "I didn't learn anything today" or "No one was friendly to me" or "I was offended" or "The Church is not filling my needs." All those answers are self-centered, and all retard spiritual growth. In contrast, a wise friend wrote, "Years ago, I changed my attitude about going to church. No longer do I go to church for my sake, but to think of others. I make a point of saying hello to people who sit alone, to welcome visitors, . . . to volunteer for an assignment. . . ."In short, I go to church each week with the intent of being active, not passive, and making a positive difference in people's lives. Consequently, my attendance at Church meetings is so much more enjoyable and fulfilling." All of this illustrates the eternal principle that we are happier and more fulfilled when we act and serve for what we give, not for what we get. Our Savior teaches us to follow Him by making the sacrifices necessary to lose ourselves in unselfish service to others. If we do, He promises us eternal life, "the greatest of all the gifts of God" (D&C 14:7), the glory and joy of living in the presence of God the Father and His Son, Jesus Christ."

Dallin H. Oaks, *Unselfish Service* [410]

Those who feel alienated, frustrated, or offended will find many valid reasons to justify leaving the Mormons. The alternative is to personally repent, listen, love, obey, learn, surrender, serve, and love without condition.

"The nearer we get to our Heavenly Father, the more we are disposed to look with compassion on perishing souls; we feel that we want to take them upon our shoulders, and cast their sins behind our backs. If you would have God have mercy on you, have mercy on one another."

Joseph Smith, *Teachings of the Prophet Joseph Smith* [411]

Personal pride about religious pride is still sin. When the natural man is in control, there is a dark satisfaction that comes from judging those who worship false idols, but in the end, making enmity from those who seem less spiritual is still ungodly. If there must be drama and conflict, let the judgment and separation come from the Pharisees and not the soul of the repentant.

And then shall many be offended, and shall betray one another, and shall hate one another.
And many false prophets shall rise, and shall deceive many.
And because iniquity shall abound, the love of many shall wax cold.
But he that shall endure unto the end, the same shall be saved.
Matthew 24:10-13

The alternative to being offended, cold, and distant is to love without condition and to acknowledge our own unworthiness before God at all times.

Do not pray as the Zoramites do, for ye have seen that they pray to be heard of men,
and to be praised for their wisdom. Do not say: O God, I thank thee that we are better than our brethren;
but rather say: O Lord, forgive my unworthiness, and remember my brethren in mercy-
yea, acknowledge your unworthiness before God at all times.
Alma 38:13-14

Focusing on Church problems instead of our own weaknesses can seduce a growing member to determine they have "graduated from the program." But have any of us "graduated" from the gospel of Jesus Christ? Do we not all lack to some degree Christ-like charity, compassion, and humility? And while it is true that an active member may not learn any new doctrine on Sunday, isn't service within the LDS Church usually the pathway for entering into the Church of the Firstborn?

Real Progression

"What is the mission field for The Church of Jesus Christ of Latter-day Saints?
Who is not included? If all the world is the mission field for the church, what, then, becomes the mission field for the Church of the Firstborn?...Would members of the Church of the Firstborn not pay tithes to The Church of Jesus Christ of Latter-day Saints? Would they not attend its meetings?
Would they not support its programs? Would they not use The Church of Jesus Christ of Latter-day Saints to assist them in raising their children? Would they not have their families baptized into The Church of Jesus Christ of Latter-day Saints? Even if they held authority given them directly from the Lord, would they not continue to be faithful members of The Church of Jesus Christ of Latter-day Saints?
To uphold and respect the authorities who are given the duty to preside?"
Denver Snuffer, *Removing the Condemnation* [412]

For a disciple of Christ desiring to be in the Church of the Firstborn, the daily choices we make accumulate to represent monumental decisions. Will I be selfish or lose myself upon the cross of Christ? Can I avoid judging others for their weakness and instead focus on my own desperate need for redemption? And if I am impatient, arrogant, and self-righteous, won't that be the standard of intolerance the Lord is then required to apply to my soul? (Matthew 7:1-3).

"Now I tend to judge others, those that, for lack of a better word, are presently the way that I used to be. I judge those that judge others, I judge those that think a white shirt is a small part of the path to salvation, I judge those that follow silent prophets, I judge those that set up suggestions as commandments and commandants as suggestions. The truth of the matter is that neither position will bring me salvation, much less exaltation. While I might be more "justified" in my current beliefs, I am no less damning myself by choosing to continue to judge. Christ does not want me to judge, he just wants me to love. Having more truth, but still lacking love will not act to save me..."

Troy Hallaway, *Judging* [413]

When the day of judgment arrives, if we have procrastinated away our own repentance, do we imagine we can stand before the Lord and rationalize, "But the Mormons were so pathetic!" When we kneel at the feet of the Master, do we really want to stammer, "But...but...it's the bishop's fault!" Will it matter?

Why We Should Stay

"I've said several times in several ways that we have an obligation to support the church's leaders and the programs of the church. I believe that with all my heart. The Lord is going to hold us all accountable. No one is going to be relieved from their respective responsibilities. Pay tithes, attend your meetings. Keep a current temple recommend and use it. Serve when asked to do so. You will have a great influence on others for the good when you provide service. Not merely by what you say, but by the example you provide. There is a great deal of unrest in the church. Oftentimes the result is inactivity. I believe that is a mistake. If all those who continued to care about the Gospel persisted in attending meetings and serving, it would do more to help the church than drifting into inactivity. Those who are sensitive to the troubles which beset the church need to be there, faithfully serving. If only those who are blinded to the troubles remain active, then the organization becomes narrower and narrower, less and less aware of its situation, and prone to continue in a course that will discard yet more of what matters most. I wish I could inspire thousands of inactive Saints to return to activity. I know I have helped hundreds to return. Those who are most troubled are the ones who the church can use right now. Those who keenly sense that all is not well with Zion are the ones who need to be filling the pews. Until they fill the pews they won't be filling the leadership positions. And until they fill the leadership positions, there won't be any changes made to the course we are on at present. If you love Zion and want her redemption, then serve her cause. Faithfully serve her cause. Don't sever yourself from her. There is no question the Lord will hold accountable those who are in leadership positions for every word, every thought, and every deed. (Alma 12: 14.) They aren't spared. This is why we should pray for them, uphold them, and do what we can to relieve them of the terrible burdens and consequences of being accountable for their callings. (D&C 107: 22.) When you withdraw from the church you cut yourself off from necessary ordinances, including the sacrament. You imperil your capacity to keep the Sabbath day holy. You limit your capacity to serve others. Even a bad lesson makes you consider what the teacher and manual is ignoring, misstating or mangling. You needn't be argumentative or unpleasant. But by being there you have a time to reflect upon the subject being addressed by the class and to contemplate what that subject means to you. Use it meditatively and gratefully. It is a gift.

If you see more clearly than others, then thank the Lord for that and stop being impatient with your fellow Saint. You are a gift to the church. Your talents and your abilities belong to and were intended to be a part of the church. Serve there. Patiently and kindly. You needn't start an argument in every class to make a difference. Quietly going about serving and occasionally providing a carefully chosen insight is important and will garner you far more blessings than withdrawing and letting your light grow dim. We're all in this together. This is our dispensation. You are responsible for helping it be preserved and passed along to the rising generation. Do not grow weary in this fight. We share a common enemy, and it is not the leadership of the church. It is the one who stirs people up to anger. (2 Ne. 28: 20.) I'd like to open people's eyes only so as to permit them to save their own souls and those of others. I would never want anyone to walk away from the church as a result of seeing its weaknesses. Be wise, but harmless. (Matt. 10: 16.) Be patient with anyone's shortcomings, no matter whether they serve in the nursery or in the presidency of an organization."
Denver Snuffer, *Be Firm and Steadfast* [414]

Apostasy in the Church will continue to deepen. The challenge for the remnant today is not just to endure the apostasy, but to sincerely love those who don't even think there is one. Becoming a "Pharisee," about the "Pharisees," is not the way of The Christ.

"In the practice of tolerance, one's enemy is the best teacher."
Dali Lama [415]

During the journey to salvation all who love Jesus and His gospel come to various spiritual crossroads. At these key moments numerous choices exist. The individual can choose to remain at a religious plateau and become stagnant, including a digression into complacent inactivity and dis-association, or he or she can seek peace and direct tutoring from God.

Overcome the fall, part the veil, and be sealed to Jesus Christ.
Personal righteousness increases/fulfillment of temple promises.
Unselfishly work toward spiritual rebirth and calling and election.
Participate in miracles and spiritual gifts. Experience visions and healings.
From study and faith receive knowledge concerning the greater gospel.
KEY MOMENT:
Boredom.
Frustration and blame.
Anger, judgment, and resentment.
Antagonism toward church and gospel.
Departure and disassociation/breaking temple covenants.
Spiritual digression and confusion. Loss of spiritual purpose.

Various sub-cultures within Mormonism appear to be more susceptible to disagreement and disassociation with the church. Educational scholars sometimes become "too wise" for the simplicity of the gospel and instead promote the philosophies of men. Theologians who study church history often struggle to rectify the gaping holes between the church Joseph Smith restored and the institution today. These students of truth often feel betrayed by an organization that continues to deny by omission its many historical flaws and failures. (Something the church has tried to address to some degree with various documents released on lds.org).

Others have been seduced by the ever-slipping morality of the world. Due to their eagerness to promote homosexuality, "social justice", and a twisted view of gender equality, these members often become disaffected when the institution works to maintain some degree of morality.

BYU

*"I attended sessions of meetings for the **institute teachers**, held in the assembly room on the fourth floor of the Church Office Building. I cannot say that I was very greatly edified. Too much **philosophy of the worldly nature** does not seem to mix well with the fundamentals of the gospel. In my opinion many of our teachers employed in the church school system have absorbed too much of the **paganism of the world**, and have accepted too readily the views of the **uninspired educators** without regard for the revealed word of the Lord. What to do about it I do not know. It is a problem for the Presidency to consider."*
Joseph Fielding Smith, *Joseph Fielding Smith Journal* [416]

Another group susceptible to disassociation from the church involves those with spiritual gifts. These intuitive souls often lack an LDS audience to minister to and bless. In America a predominantly western mindset hinders embracing the metaphysical nature of the Universe. Some determine that spiritual gifts involving energy and healing are taboo or of the devil. This premature judgment is compounded when the gifted individual is female. (see Truth #61).

Regardless of personal preference, and even if the church as an institution is not healthy, the gospel of Jesus Christ remains perfect. Regardless of various beliefs and life experiences, making separation from the church, (which still offers some of that perfect gospel), is rarely the answer. Love instead of judgment, forgiveness instead of condemnation, and unity instead of separation is the way of *The Christ*.

BE ONE

"If we are to have unity, there are commandments we must keep concerning how we feel. We must forgive and bear no malice toward those who offend us. The Savior set the example from the cross: "Father, forgive them; for they know not what they do."(Luke 23:34). We do not know the hearts of those who offend us. Nor do we know all the sources of our own anger and hurt. The Apostle Paul was telling us how to love in a world of imperfect people, including ourselves, when he said, "Charity suffereth long, and is kind; charity envieth not; charity vaunteth not itself, is not puffed up, doth not behave itself unseemly, seeketh not her own, is not easily provoked, thinketh no evil" (1 Corinthians 13:4–5). And then he gave solemn warning against reacting to the faults of others and forgetting our own when he wrote, "For now we see through a glass, darkly; but then face to face: now I know in part; but then shall I know even as also I am known. (1 Corinthians 13:12)."
Henry B. Eyring, *Be One* [417]

Paradoxically, on rare occassions there do seem to be certain life paths that do not require being actively involved with the organization. For a few, (not the angry or offended ones), there appears to be a "spiritual line" that gets crossed where the soul must either stand for truth or spiritually shrink into oblivion. Only the Lord and that particular soul can accurately determine if and when that time has come. The great prophet Mormon referred to this dilemma and wrote about his changing relationship with the Lord's people.

And it came to pass that I, Mormon, did utterly refuse from this time forth to be a commander and a leader of this people, because of their wickedness and abomination.
Mormon 3:11

And it came to pass that I did go forth among the Nephites, and did repent of the oath which I had made that I would no more assist them.
Mormon 5:1

It is the perspective of this author that unity with the church should be sought first, patience and long-suffering should follow, and then if there must be a separation from the LDS Church, let the Pharisees make that choice and invoke their own condemnation.

An Abinadi Moment

"There are some who would have us believe that the final test of the rightness of a course is whether everyone is united on it. But the church does not seek unity, simply for unities sake. The unity for which the Lord prayed and which President McKay speaks is the only unity which God honors – that is, "unity in righteousness," unity in principle. We cannot compromise good and evil in an attempt to have peace and unity in the Church, any more than the Lord could have compromised with Satan in order to avoid the War in Heaven."
Ezra Taft Benson. *Our Immediate Responsibility* [418]

Social Mormons cannot fathom that God would direct or allow a family to go inactive or leave the church. Although the directives of God are not always neat and tidy, they consider such claims to be the voice of deception.

Until a day of physical destruction and natural separation arrives, (either personally or among the masses), let us all focus on the covenants that encourage, and even require, members to stay involved as the Spirit directs. There are many valid reasons to stay and serve within the Lord's organization. In addition to loving others as Christ loves us, children and families are usually blessed by the spiritual education they receive in Primary and Sunday School. Even when the doctrine isn't completely correct, a degree of the Holy Spirit is usually still present on Sunday. Those who attend church with a serving heart often go home happy in Christ.

In most situations a disciple is not as effective or useful to the Lord outside of the Church. Staying "active" also allows Christ-centered comments to be made, inspired lessons to be taught, and heart-felt testimonies to be given. If the wheat are not present in the church, who will the Lord use to fulfill prophecy? It would therefore seem essential that those who have awakened remain to publish the message of Jesus Christ and His Zion!

Wanted: Humble Wheat

"The Church has never been more in need of those who love her, who support her with the Lord's spirit and with his true teachings. We, as members, must mature spiritually like the wheat.
We need to pray night and day and rebuke Satan from the church and from the leadership of the church.
If you think we, out here, are squeezed and choked by the tares of our wards, think about the wheat among the leadership of the church. I think literally they live on Ground Zero of the war between Satan and Jesus.
Believe me there never was more intrigue, strategy, pain, suffering and struggling.
If we love Brother Joseph, we will support His church with all our might, strength, faith, prayers.
We cannot give it over to Satan, especially by default. We must be valiant until Joseph and the Lord come to cleanse the church, but they can't do that until we become mature spiritually –
D&C defines mature wheat as those who receive revelations, visions, prophecy, visitation of angels, and the Second Comforter. We must have one single focus on accomplishing this."
Jeanene Custer, *Stay with the Lord in His Church* [419]

In truth, the sincere ministry of just one disciple, in just one ward, can minimize and delay the religious apostasy occurring in others. Speaking the truth, when directed by God and His Holy Spirit, can literally save families who otherwise would just continue coasting along with the status quo. Leaving the church prematurely, either due to pride or an unwillingness to suffer for Christ, negates the opportunity to save those whom you might have assisted. It also hinders the growing disciple from fulfilling the measure of his or her creation.

Today, dissatisfaction with the church and its culture is growing. Thousands are leaving the church or going inactive. Both President Benson and President Hinkley were aware of this growing trend and simply invited all to "come back."

Perhaps the essential questions for those who have left the church should be, what is the will of God at this time? Should I now return to assist a wounded and growing flock?

AN INVITATION FROM THE FIRST PRESIDENCY OF THE
CHURCH OF JESUS CHRIST OF LATTER-DAY SAINTS
December 25, 1985

Come back, Come back and
feast at the table of the Lord, and taste again
the sweet and satisfying fruits of
fellowship with the Saints.

"We rejoice in the blessings that come of membership and activity in this Church whose head is the Son of God, the Lord Jesus Christ. In deep sincerity we express our love and gratitude for our brethren and sisters everywhere. We are aware of some who are less active, of others who have become critical and are prone to find fault, and of those who have been disfellowshipped or excommunicated because of serious transgressions. To all such we reach out in love. The Lord said: "I, the Lord, will forgive whom I will forgive, but of you it is required to forgive all men." (D&C 64:10) We encourage members to forgive those who may have wronged them. To those who have ceased activity and to those who have become critical, we say, "Come back. Come back and feast at the table of the Lord, and taste again the sweet and satisfying

236

fruits of fellowship with the saints."We are confident that many have longed to return, but have felt awkward about doing so. We assure you that you will find open arms to receive you and willing hands to assist you. We know there are many who carry heavy burdens of guilt and bitterness. To such we say, "Set them aside and give heed to the words of the Savior, who gave His life for the sins of all. "Come unto me, all ye that are heavy laden, and I will give you rest. Take my yoke upon you, and learn of me; for I am meek and lowly in heart; and ye shall find rest unto your souls. "For my yoke is easy, and my burden is light."
(Matt. 11:28-30). We plead with you. We pray for you.
We invite and welcome you with love and appreciation.
Sincerely your brethren,"

Ezra Taft Benson
Gordon B. Hinckley
Thomas S. Monson [420]

Eventually the season of the wheat and tares growing together will come to an end. The church will be cleansed and our individual opportunity to be heroic for Christ will be over. Until that time, let us focus on loving others as He loves us, that when the house of God is set in order (D&C 85:7), we will have individually contributed to the Lord's harvest.

ONE HEART

"We see increased conflict between peoples in the world around us.
*Those divisions and differences could infect us. That is why my message of hope today is that **a great day of unity is coming**. The Lord Jehovah will return to live with **those who have become His people and will find them united, of one heart, unified with Him and with our Heavenly Father**. The joy of unity He wants so much to give us is not solitary. We must seek it and qualify for it with others. It is not surprising then that **God urges us to gather so that He can bless us.** He wants us to gather into families. He has established classes, wards, and branches and commanded us to meet together often. In those gatherings, which God has designed for us, lies our great opportunity. We can pray and work for the unity that will bring us joy and multiply our power to serve. To the Three Nephites, the Savior promised joy in unity with Him as their final reward after their faithful service. He said, "Ye shall have fulness of joy; and ye shall sit down in the kingdom of my Father; yea, your joy shall be full, even as the Father hath given me fulness of joy; and **ye shall be even as I am, and I am even as the Father; and the Father and I are one.** (3 Nephi 28:10)."*
Henry B. Eyring, *"Our Hearts Knit as One"*[421]

TRUTH #40 THE LDS CHURCH CONTINUES TO PROVIDE SACRED ORDINANCES, ANCIENT SCRIPTURE, AND INSPIRED DOCTRINE.

THE CHURCH OF JESUS CHRIST of Latter Day Saints is the Lord's true church here in the telestial world. Those actively participating in the church are blessed to be taught inspired doctrine and participate in sacred ordinances. Regardless of the many problems, the church as a spiritual entity continues to assist souls in returning to God's presence.

Our Path to Father

*Abraham received the priesthood from Melchizedek…And this greater priesthood administereth the gospel and holdeth the **key of the mysteries of the kingdom, even the key of the knowledge of God**. Therefore, in the ordinances thereof, the power of godliness is manifest. And **without the ordinances thereof, and the authority of the priesthood, the power of godliness is not manifest unto men in the flesh; For without this no man can see the face of God, even the Father, and live.***
Doctrine and Covenants 84:14-22

At church and in the temple members are taught the spiritual tools Adam and Eve used to receive further light and knowledge. The organization that builds churches and temples cannot exalt us, but through the keys, tokens, powers, principles, and ordinances provided, we are invited to commune with a God who can.

Power in the Priesthood

*"The fullness of the gospel consists in those **laws, doctrines, ordinances, powers, and authorities** needed to enable men to gain the fullness of salvation. Those who have the gospel fullness do not necessarily enjoy the fullness of gospel knowledge or understand all of the doctrines of the plan of salvation. But they do have the fullness of the priesthood and sealing power by which men can be sealed up unto eternal life. **The fullness of the gospel grows out of the fullness of the sealing power and not out of the fullness of gospel knowledge.**"*
Bruce R. McConkie, *Mormon Doctrine*[422]

Through the Prophet Joseph Smith we have been blessed to learn the laws and ordinances of the gospel. Principles advanced in scripture continue to represent a "pearl of great price." The church also publishes the Book of Mormon, where the principles, prophecies, warnings, and solutions we need for salvation are provided. For these contributions, as well as the social and cultural blessings associated with being "Mormon," we should eternally praise God!

But Ammon said unto him: I do not boast in my own strength, nor in my own wisdom; but behold, my joy is full, yea, my heart is brim with joy, and I will rejoice in my God. Yea, I know that I am nothing; as to my strength I am weak; therefore I will not boast of myself, but I will boast of my God, for in his strength I can do all things…
Alma 26:11-12

Relative to our quickly decaying world, the LDS church remains a positive force for good. Despite institutional problems, the gospel of Jesus Christ continues to heal souls and we should do everything in our power to maximize righteousness upon the earth. The following story demonstrates the simple goodness many members of the church continue to demonstrate.

"Humble isn't usually the first word that comes to mind when describing a star athlete,
but it's the one most often used by people who have been around Jabari…Eyes might be on him most of all
at the end of his freshman year in college, when he has to decide whether he will declare for the NBA draft-
or like thousands of other Mormon men who turn 19-embark on a two-year mission to spread the faith…
Jabari wakes up each morning at five and says a simple prayer, thanking God for another day. By 5:30
he's off to church for Bible study. "I realize why I'm in the position I'm in right now," says Jabairi..
"It's not because of me. It's because of God."
Jeff Benedict, *Mormon Faith More Important to Jabari Parker than NBA stardom* [423]

Acknowledging the hand of God in all things can help us avoid judging others who are currently benefiting from the Mormon experience. In reality, the LDS church continues to provide a spiritual context for members to learn about God and then demonstrate faith, compassion, and service.

When a member awakens to our cultural apostasy, he or she may be tempted to minimize or negate the goodness that is still present in the church. Disciple Daniel Rogers explains that this is not how the Lord views His growing flock, and that when we choose to be critical or condescending toward other church members, we are acting from a place of pride and ignorance.

The True Standard of Righteousness

Regarding righteousness, a person can try to live up to every law and commandment both cultural
and scriptural and it will be insufficient. At the end of the day, after all we can do, we are saved
by Christ's grace. Why did Nephi labor so diligently to teach of Christ? Why did he and his people
believe in Christ and talk about Him so much? Nephi spoke of Christ because all we do amounts
to basically nothing. No amount of compliance with any law will be sufficient to save us.
Assume your height was a visible measure of your righteousness. You could compare yourself
to others and say, "Look, I'm six feet tall and everyone else is five feet, therefore I am
righteous." This is in essence what we do; we compare ourselves to others and find comfort
in being "taller". Christ is the Empire State Building or Mt. Everest. From His perspective
the difference between the best of us and the worst of us is so insignificant that we all equally
fall short. You can't even tell from the top of the Empire State Building just who is taller
than the other. This is the standard of righteousness that heaven uses. We all fall so far short
of it that it is purely by Christ's grace that we are saved. *You will not save yourself by saving up*
for that bicycle. The amount you offer is nothing compared to the standard of Righteousness.
The only thing you can offer is a broken heart and contrite spirit.
You must be willing to set aside anything and everything to know Him."
Daniel Rogers, *The Second Comforter, My Testimony* [424]

Anyone, who has kneeled before God and begged, *"Please don't give up on me,"* should extend that same kindness to all of mankind. Jesus never gave up on His Jewish family, and we as Latter Day Saints should not give up on ours. Instead of condemning those who lack understanding, we would be wise to acknowledge-and then magnify, the degree of light that still remains in the Lord's church.

> **TRUTH #41** THROUGHOUT HISTORY EVERY APOSTASY HAS RESULTED IN ANOTHER RESTORATION. DURING THIS FINAL DISPENSATION, THOSE CALLED TO FULFILL PROPHECY WILL RECLAIM ALL THAT HAS BEEN LOST OR GONE DORMANT SINCE THE DEATH OF THE PROPHET JOSEPH SMITH.

"It is in the order of heavenly things that God should always send a new dispensation into the world when men have apostatized from the truth and lost the priesthood."
Joseph Smith, *History of the Church* [425]

When what has been minimized, abandoned, and distorted over the past 185 years is compared to what is required for Zion, the need for a "re-restoration" becomes obvious. As early as 1856, Brigham Young spoke of the need for a "reformation' in the Church. He proclaimed, *"we need a reformation in the midst of this people; we need a thorough reform, for I know that very many are in a dozy condition with regard to their religion...You are losing the Spirit of the Gospel..."* [426] Apostle Orson Pratt agreed, *"There must be a reformation. There will be a reformation among this people, but He will plead with the stronger ones of Zion, He will plead with this people, He will plead with those in high places, He will plead with the priesthood of this church, until Zion shall become clean before him. I do not know but what it would be an utter impossibility to commence and carry out some principles pertaining to Zion right in the midst of this people."* [427]

LDS missionaries teach new converts that during "the Apostasy" many plain and precious parts of the gospel were changed or omitted. They point out that after the death of Jesus Christ, religious corruption included losing priesthood authority, changing doctrine, and altering sacred ordinances. Missionaries then explain that these spiritual losses in the early church justified the need for a Restoration through the Prophet Joseph Smith.

*"Through time and apostasy following Christ's Resurrection and Ascension, however, the divine authority of the priesthood and **the sacred ordinances were changed or lost**, and the associated covenants were broken. **The Lord revealed His displeasure over this situation in these words:** 'For they have strayed from mine ordinances, and have broken mine everlasting covenant; They seek not the Lord to establish his righteousness,** but every man walketh in his own way, and after the image of his own god.' This situation required a restoration of knowledge pertaining to the importance, significance, and appointed administration of sacred gospel ordinances, both live and vicarious, as well as the divine authority of the priesthood and priesthood keys to administer them."*
Dennis B. Neuenschwander, *Ordinances and Covenants* [428]

In relation to our current status today, some have wondered how God would respond if a young boy with real faith again walked into a grove of trees and asked, *"Which of all the sects is right?"* Since Father is a God of exactness and cannot look upon sin with the least degree of allowance, would He again declare, *"They draw near to me with their lips, but their hearts are far from me, they teach for doctrines the commandments of men, having a form of godliness, but they deny the power thereof?"* [429]

In 1829 the Almighty Father told Joseph Smith that, *"A marvelous work is about to come forth."* (D&C 4:1). Since that time the work of the Lord has occurred through His church to some degree, but in relation to what is required to establish Zion, some have wondered, **was the initial *"marvelous work and a wonder," the only "marvelous work and a wonder?"***

How would the Mormon culture respond today
if the Prophet Joseph Smith returned to finish the Restoration?

Is it possible that when the times of the Gentiles are fulfilled and the gospel is again taken to the house of Israel, that the work will again "commence?" Could it be that the "marvelous work" Joseph initiated is about to intensify with an even greater scope and vigor?

And then shall the work of the Father commence at that day, even when this gospel shall be preached among the remnant of this people. Verily I say unto you, at that day shall the work of the Father commence among all the dispersed of my people, yea, even the tribes which have been lost, which the Father hath led away out of Jerusalem. Yea, and then shall the work commence, with the Father among all nations in preparing the way whereby his people may be gathered home to the land of their inheritance.
3 Nephi 21: 26, 28

Even though the work did "commence" in 1830, the church has always struggled to teach and convert Lamanite-Israel. When the time arrives for Zion to be literally established, it will be the descendents of those who were once led *"out of the land of Jerusalem"* who will be leading the charge to Zion. (1 Nephi 17:14 and Truths #7 and #37). At that time the ten tribes will return and the restoration of all things that Joseph Smith initiated will be completed and implemented.

But behold, there shall be many—at that day when I shall proceed to do a marvelous work among them, that I may remember my covenants which I have made unto the children of men, that I may set my hand again the second time to recover my people, which are of the house of Israel…
2 Nephi 29:1

And the Lord will set his hand again the second time to restore his people from their lost and fallen state. Wherefore, he will proceed to do a marvelous work and a wonder among the children of men.
2 Nephi 25:17

Concerning the possibility of another "sub-dispensation" occurring within the umbrella of this "final dispensation," scripture provides historical patterns worth observing. When Jesus came among the Jewish culture He did not seek to fix or overtake the religious structure of the day. Instead, He established a power and truth which superceded it. The Lord knew His Jewish family would not receive Him, but He intends to offer them another chance.

And behold, according to the words of the prophet, the Messiah will set himself again The second time to recover them; wherefore, he will manifest himself unto them in power and great glory, unto the destruction of their enemies, when that day cometh when they shall believe in him; and none will he destroy that believe in him.
2 Nephi 6:14

Whether Jew or Gentile, we are the offspring of a God who simply will not give up on us. Because He is omniscient and can see all things, He institutes small and simple measures that have beneficial influence for generations to come.

For example, when Lehi was commanded to leave Jerusalem, Jeremiah was the prophet of the day. To someone living in Jerusalem at that time, the prophet Lehi, (who had also been called of God-and was required to leave the mainstream that he might begin a mighty work), would have appeared obscure and irrelevant.

Hundreds of years after Lehi arrived in the promised land, with the Nephites constantly waffling in their spirituality, Zeniff was a Nephite leader fighting to guide his people into righteousness. (Mosiah 9:17-18). Before Zeniff died he conferred the kingdom upon his son Noah. As a spiritual and political leader, King Noah *did not walk in the ways of his father,* but instead led the people into apathy and apostasy. (Mosiah 11:1-2). To save the pure in heart, the Lord sent Abinadi to rebuke the king and his wicked priests. Alma accepted Abinadi's message, and after personally repenting, was able to lead the Lord's remnant into the wilderness where they could reclaim the teachings of the earlier prophets. (Mosiah 18:20). This scriptural pattern could be viewed as a "re-restoration" of what the Lord had previously provided through His prophets. It is also analogous of what is occurring in the church today.

Re-baptized with Real Power

And now it came to pass that Alma took Helam, he being one of the first, and went and stood forth in the water, and cried, saying: O Lord, pour out thy Spirit upon thy servant, that he may do this work with holiness of heart. And when he had said these words, the Spirit of the Lord was upon him, and he said: Helam, I baptize thee, having authority from the Almighty God, as a testimony that ye have entered into a covenant to serve him until you are dead as to the mortal body; and may the Spirit of the Lord be poured out upon you; and may he grant unto you eternal life, through the redemption of Christ, whom he has prepared from the foundation of the world. And after Alma had said these words, both Alma and Helam were buried in the water; and they arose and came forth out of the water rejoicing, being filled with the Spirit.
Mosiah 18:12-14

These examples and others suggest that the manner in which God will reinstate a true fullness will not involve creating another church. Rather He will gather souls who know the voice of God and are willing to return to the original offering. Perhaps only a smattering of broken Saints will survive the day of cleansing, that they might organize themselves into righteous family kingdoms and receive the restored fullness. (see Truth #67).

Because most imagine "church" and "priesthood" to be synonymous, they logically conclude that the church as currently manifested, will never change form. This reassuring, but incorrect assumption negates Joseph's warning, "*until we have perfect love we are liable to fall...God has often sealed up the heavens because of covetousness in the church. Except the church receive the fullness they will yet fail.*" [430] The reality that we as a people have not received and lived a true fullness suggests that "the church" as we know it may change form. And that in the future how God perceives "His Church" may be very different from the institutional structure we observe today.

Spiritual "Re-Run"

"How few or many of us will be permitted to participate in the ongoing process of the Restoration remains to be seen. However, when the fullness returns, those who become the heirs will look back on the era of the Latter-day Saints with much the same reaction as we look back on the Jewish era in which Christ lived. They will be astonished at the great principles of truth we discarded, neglected or ignored. They will wonder in astonishment at our groveling to gain acceptance from a doomed and ignorant religious tradition calling itself "Christianity." They will find it utterly incomprehensible that we argued we should be regarded as one of them, rather than proclaiming their doctrines are the commandments of men, having a form of godliness but lacking any power. They will wonder why we would trade the power of God for acceptance and popularity; particularly when we were told that pandering for popularity is at the heart of priestcraft. Our failure will be clear to them, although we find it quite opaque. We still think we're approved by the Lord, even though our condemnation is set out in scripture."
Anonymous Saint

In truth, the fullness was offered, the Saints rejected it, and now only a "few" are striving to access the level of light required to establish Zion. These are they who will be honored to participate in the restoration of all things.

The Next Cycle?

*And in that day there shall be a root of Jesse, which shall stand for an ensign of the people...
and it shall come to pass in that day that the Lord shall set his hand again the second time
to recover the remnant of his people which shall be left...*
2 Nephi 21:10-11

*And the day that he shall set his hand again the second time to recover his people, is the day,
yea, even the last time, that the servants of the Lord shall go forth in his power,
to nourish and prune his vineyard; and after that the end soon cometh.*
Jacob 6:2

*And blessed are they who shall seek to bring forth my Zion at that day, for they shall have the gift
and the power of the Holy Ghost; and if they endure unto the end they shall be lifted up at the last day,
and shall be saved in the everlasting kingdom of the Lamb; and whoso shall publish peace, yea,
tidings of great joy, how beautiful upon the mountains shall they be.*
1 Nephi 13:37

- A majority of Gentiles, both in and out of the church, will choose the comforts of Babylon over the standard of righteousness required for Zion. (2 Nephi 28).

- The Mormon culture will continue to reject by omission the fullness of the gospel as offered by God through the Prophet Joseph Smith. The church as a whole will remain under condemnation and slowly digress into the wilderness of full apostasy, (D&C 84:54-59, D&C 86:1-3).

- No other temporal church shall rise to take the place of *The Church of Jesus Christ of Latter Day Saints*, but eventually, all that is unclean within and beyond the religion shall fall and be burned (D&C 86:7, 2 Nephi 23:22).

- Because Zion cannot be redeemed by a people under condemnation, only a righteous and humble "few" will survive the destructive cleansing. (2 Nephi 28:14). The remnant of Christ will have the privilege of fulfilling latter-day prophecy. (D&C 43:28-32).

- The purging of the Gentiles shall continue until many cities lie desolate and the land is ravaged. Only a small remnant, a holy offspring unto God, will survive to establish the Lord's Holy City. (Isaiah 1:27-29, 6:11-14, D&C 86:7).

- When the time of cleansing arrives, the gospel will be taken from the Gentiles and returned to the House of Israel. (3 Nephi 16:10-15). Those Gentiles who "repent and return" shall be part of this transition to Israel. The progression will include those of pure-blood decent, Lamanite-Israel, and the cleansed Gentile remnant. Only those who are sanctified will be allowed to participate in the redemption of Zion (D&C 64:33-40).

- Until the time of this monumental shift, the tares will continue to control and maintain the corporate church. Sadly, the institution will become an increasing hull of empty tradition and bureaucracy. During this time, the Lord's true servants, both within and beyond the institution, will wield real power as they prepare Zion for the redemption of Israel. (D&C 113:7-8).

- At the appropriate time, the Lord will send one mighty and strong to gather the wheat, redeem Zion, and complete *the restoration of all things.* (D&C 101:55-62, 85:7). Many will eagerly anticipate the arrival of this leader and desire to be sealed to him for eternity through spiritual adoption. (see Truth #67). Although God will enact the specific manner in which prophecy will be fulfilled, scripture and common sense seem to suggest that an "authorized re-restoration" would likely involve the Prophet Joseph Smith. (D&C 103:18-22; 105:14-19, 26-27, 34-37). (see Truth #75).

- With Jesus Christ acting as King of Kings and Lord of Lords, and with Joseph at His side, all who *know God* will praise *The Christ* for His Holiness and wisdom! All that God once offered the Saints will again be restored, and literal Zion will be established. (D&C 101:43-62, 64:33-36). Additional ordinances of a higher order will be revealed to those entering into the Church of the Firstborn. Millions will receive a true fullness of the priesthood, and all doctrine which has gone dormant will be revived. The United Order, law of consecration, and the entire political arm of the kingdom (as introduced through the council of fifty) will be established. A true "Kingdom of God" with real spiritual teeth will reign supreme. Truth, light, and justice will permeate the planet. Angels will openly walk the earth and miracles of healing will be commonplace. Dreams, visions, visitations, and prophecy will be a daily occurrence and many will be proficient at speaking in tongues, using seer stones, and every other spiritual gift. The sealed portion of the plates will provide additional teaching, and true messengers sent from Father will consistently tutor and bless the people. All that is considered "religion" will be complete, active, and authorized by Father and His Holy Spirit of Promise. Those who choose to do so will reclaim and righteously live plural marriage. The lost ten tribes will arrive in power as Joseph's Zion from below, welcomes Enoch's Zion from above! All that is Holy and of God will accumulate into the manifestation of something "great and terrible:" Jesus Christ and His Zion!
- During the Millennium, the earth will fully transition from a telestial existence into a terrestrial realm. As part of the "re-restoration" of all things, every doctrine, element, and ordinance, relating to the same ancient gospel Adam and Eve once enjoyed-will again be taught and practiced among the family of God. In receiving this ancient gospel, life on earth will be known throughout the universe as "Heaven on Earth."

The Final Cleansing

*"In our own dispensation the law of Enoch was offered
to the Church, but the Latter-day Saints failed to live it
and therefore it was taken away and a lesser law instituted
until such time as Christ shall come to cleanse the Church,
along with the rest of the world, of its wickedness and
disobedience, by removing all things that offend."*

Joseph Fielding Smith, *The Progress of Man* [431]

The Promise of Freedom

*Behold, **this is a choice land, and whatsoever nation shall possess it shall be free from bondage, and from captivity, and from all other nations under heaven, if they will but serve the God of the land, who is Jesus Christ,** who hath been manifested by the things which we have written. And this cometh unto you, O ye Gentiles, that ye may know the decrees of God—**that ye may repent, and not continue in your iniquities until the fullness come,** that ye may not bring down the Fullness of the wrath of God upon you as the inhabitants of the land have hitherto done. For behold, this is a land which is **choice above all other lands;** wherefore he that doth possess it **shall serve God or shall be swept off;** for it is the everlasting decree of God. And it is **not until the Fullness of iniquity** among the children of the land, that they are swept off. And now, we can behold the decrees of God concerning this land, that it is a land of promise; and whatsoever nation shall possess it **shall serve God, or they shall be swept off when the fullness of his wrath shall come upon them.** And the fullness of his wrath cometh upon them when they are ripened in iniquity. And he had sworn in his wrath unto the brother of Jared, that whoso should possess this land of promise, from that time henceforth and forever, should serve him, the true and only God, **or they should be swept off when the fullness of his wrath should come upon them.***

Ether 2:12-8 (verses presented in reverse order for consideration)

America is a sacred land with a divine destiny. For generations the United States Constitution has stood as a backbone for the administration of proper government. The result of establishing a nation based on the principles of faith, freedom, and self-determination is a society which has been blessed and protected for over 230 years.

"I sought for the key to the greatness of America in her harbors; in her fertile fields and boundless forests; in her rich mines and vast world commerce; in her public school system and institutions of learning. I sought for it in her democratic Congress and in her matchless Constitution. Not until I went into the churches of America and heard her pulpits aflame with righteousness did I understand the secret of her genius and power. America is great because America is good, and if America ever ceases to be good, America ceases to be great."

Alexis de Tocqueville

Those wishing to maintain freedom in America must understand the conditions set forth by God in the Book of Mormon, *"And now we can behold the decrees of God concerning this land, that it is a land of promise; and whatsoever nation shall possess it shall serve God, or they shall be swept off when the fulness of his wrath shall come upon them. And the fulness of his wrath cometh upon them when they are ripened in iniquity. For behold, this is a land which is choice above all other lands; wherefore he that doth possess it shall serve God or shall be swept off; for it is the everlasting decree of God. And it is not until the fulness of iniquity among the children of the land, that they are swept off."* (Ether 2:9-10).

History demonstrates that when a nation or people begin to set at naught the commandments of God, that particular people is in danger of losing political and religious liberty.

247

"For behold, thus saith the Lord: I will not show unto the wicked of my strength, to one more than the other, save it be unto those who repent of their sins."(Helaman 7:23). *"And for this cause wo shall come unto you except ye shall repent. For if ye will not repent, behold...all those great cities which are round about, which are in the land of our possession, shall be taken away that ye shall have no place in them; for behold, the Lord will not grant unto you strength, as he has hitherto done, to withstand against your enemies."* (Helaman 7:22). *"And if the time comes that the voice of the people doth choose iniquity, then is the time that the judgments of God will come upon you; yea, then is the time he will visit you with great destruction even as he has hitherto visited this land."* (Mosiah 29:27).

Some have romanticized the Book of Mormon to the point that they love to read about miracles, missionary work, and service, but prefer to omit the difficult messages that relate to war, secret combinations, and political corruption. Our lack of understanding concerning darkness and intrigue does not change the reality that when a majority of people choose evil, the promise of safety and freedom is over.

> *And it came to pass that in this same year, behold, Nephi delivered up the judgment seat...*
> *for as their laws and their governments were established by the voice of the people,*
> *and they who chose evil were more numerous than they who chose good, therefore they were*
> *ripening for destruction, for the laws had become corrupted. Yea, and this was not all;*
> *they were a stiffnecked people, insomuch that they could not be governed by the law nor justice,*
> *save it were to their destruction.*
> Helaman 5:1-3

This historical pattern should motivate us to be actively involved in preserving freedom for our posterity. True Americans know that freedom is always under attack from the enemy of all righteousness, and that the result of electing "modern-day Gaddianton robbers" is control, destruction, and death.

America's Warning
> *And whatsoever nation shall uphold such secret combinations, to get power and gain,*
> *until they shall spread over the nation, behold, they shall be destroyed; for the Lord will not suffer*
> *that the blood of his saints, which shall be shed by them, shall always cry unto him*
> *from the ground for vengeance upon them and yet he avenge them not.*
> Ether 8:22

The Book of Mormon explains how the nations of the earth can avoid destruction. Both on a national and global level, there is only one real solution: The Lord Jesus Christ.

Gun control is looming…
Gay marriage is spreading…
Inflation is arriving…
Years of desolation are starting…
But no matter what the world chooses,
Jesus Christ is our Savior and King!

When a person, family, church, or nation turns to the Lord Jesus Christ, they delay the heartache and reciprocity the masses may be inviting upon the whole. To bring even one soul to Christ really does matter on a personal and planetary level. For when a child of God comes home to the Father and Mother who gave him or her life, the Lord and His angels of destruction again pause and wait…Eventually, over time, all who can be saved-will have been saved, and the tipping point of wickedness will be reached upon the earth. Until that time, all who know the divine solution must offer one simple plea to all who will listen, "Come unto Christ!"

Oh all ye that are spared…will ye not now return unto me, and repent of your sins,
and be converted, that I may heal you? Yea, verily I say unto you,
if ye will come unto me ye shall have eternal life.
Behold, mine arm of mercy is extended towards you,
and whosoever will come, him will I receive…
Behold I am Jesus Christ.
3 Nephi 9: 13-15

> ## TRUTH: #43: MANY MEMBERS AND NON-MEMBERS ARE POLITICALLY DECEIVED. SOME ARE TEACHABLE, BUT KNOW NOT WHERE TO FIND THE TRUTH.

*"I apprehend no danger to our country from a foreign foe…Our destruction, should it come at all, will be from another quarter-**from the inattention of the people to the concerns of the government**…I fear that they may place too implicit a confidence in their public servants, and fail properly to scrutinize their conduct; that in this way they may be made dupes of designing men, and become the instruments of their own undoing…."*
Daniel Webster [432]

Many citizens within the United States have been lulled into a false security. Distracted by numerous forms of superficial and obscene entertainment, they have unknowingly allowed the shackles of subtle control to be silently woven into the laws of mainstream society. This gradual deception includes being conditioned to overlook-and even support, unconstitutional legislation.

"The Constitution established four federal crimes. Today the experts can't even agree on how many federal crimes are now on the books—they number into the thousands. No one person can comprehend the enormity of the legal system—especially the tax code. Due to the ill-advised drug war and the endless federal expansion of the criminal code we have over 6 million people under correctional suspension, more than the Soviets ever had, and more than any other nation today, including China. I don't understand the complacency of the Congress and the willingness to continue their obsession with passing more Federal laws…The federal register is now 75,000 pages long and the tax code has 72,000 pages, and expands every year. When will the people start shouting, "enough is enough," and demand Congress cease and desist."
Ron Paul, *The Proliferation of Federal Crimes* [433]

For years church leaders have urged *"members to play a role as responsible citizens in their communities, including becoming informed about issues and voting in elections."*[434] Despite this encouragement Latter Day Saints often appear to prefer avoiding uncomfortable political realities. By maintaining political ignorance, they continue *"walking in darkness at noon day."* (D&C 95:6). Sadly, this refusal to see, challenge, and confront evil only intensifies the tragedy to come.

*"Too often we bask in our comfortable complacency and rationalize that the ravages of war, economic disaster, famine, and earthquake cannot happen here. Those who believe this are either not acquainted with the revelations of the Lord, or they do not believe them. **Those who smugly think these calamities will not happen, that they somehow will be set aside because of the righteousness of the Saints, are deceived and will rue the day they harbored such a delusion.** The Lord has warned and forewarned us against a day of great tribulation and given us counsel, through His servants, on how we can be prepared for these difficult times. Have we heeded His counsel?"*
Ezra Taft Benson, *The Teachings of Ezra Taft Benson* [435]

Those choosing to awake and arise understand that today's secret combinations are not reported in the mindless fluff of the mainstream press. The deterioration of freedom should be the constant concern of the national media, but no matter how large the atrocity enacted against the righteous and the naïve, "the truth" is consistently disguised or omitted by those who control the mainstream media. The former chief of staff for the *New York Times* once stated,

Media Propaganda

"There is no such thing…in America as an independent press. You know it and I know it. There is not one of you who dares to write your honest opinions, and if you did you know beforehand it would never appear in print…The business of the journalist is to destroy the truth; to lie outright; to pervert; to vilify; to fawn at the feet of mammon, and to sell the country for his daily bread… We are the tools and vassals of rich men behind the scenes…We are the jumping jacks, they pull the strings and we dance…We are intellectual prostitutes."
John Swinton [436]

A Controlled Message

"We are grateful to The Washington Post, The New York Times, Time Magazine and other great publications whose directors have attended our meetings and respected their promises of discretion for almost forty years (since 1952). It would be impossible for us to develop our plans for the world if we had been subject to the bright lights of publicity during those years. But the world is now more sophisticated and prepared to march towards a world government. The supra-national sovereignty of an intellectual elite and world bankers is surely preferable to the national auto determination practiced in past centuries."
David Rockefeller, *U.N. Blue Print for World Control* [437]

The real news of today can be found in scripture. Especially applicable are the prophecies recorded in the book of Isaiah, Matthew 24, Ether 8, Helaman chapters 6-12, D&C 29, 38, 45, and the book of Revelations. Scripture helps us to "see the darkness" and still focus on God's glory.

Is it All Just a Conspiracy?

"I testify that wickedness is rapidly expanding in every segment of our society. (See D&C 1:14-16; 84:49-53.) It is more highly organized, more cleverly disguised, and more powerfully promoted than ever before. Secret combinations lusting for power, gain, and glory are flourishing. A secret combination that seeks to overthrow the freedom of all lands, nations, and countries is increasing its evil influence and control over America and the entire world. (See Ether 8:18-25.). (Ensign, November 1988, p. 87.) "Yes, there is a conspiracy of evil. The source of it all is Satan and his hosts. He has a great power over men to 'lead them captive at his will, even as many as would not hearken' to the voice of the Lord. (Moses 4:4.) His evil influence may be manifest through governments; through false educational, political, economic, religious, and social philosophies; through secret societies and organizations; and through myriads of other forms. His power and influence are so great that, if possible, he would deceive the very elect. As the second coming of the Lord approaches, Satan's work will intensify through numerous insidious deceptions."
Ezra Taft Benson, *Ensign* [438]

For generations those who lust for power have used money and political influence to place their hand-picked tyrants in positions of influence. Over time, those willing to "sell-out" have come to dominate *both* major political parties. The Nephites faced the same predicament when the Gaddiantons systematically took control of their government.

> *And thus they **did obtain the sole management of the government**, insomuch that they did trample under their feet and smite and rend and turn their backs upon the poor and the meek, and the humble followers of God. And thus we see that they were in an awful state, and ripening for an everlasting destruction.*
> Helaman 6: 39-40

The disturbing reality is that global bankers have established a dialectical system which controls each supposedly opposing force. Often the tensions reported to exist in Washington between Democrats and Republicans is only an imaginary argument...an entertaining facade to continue the illusion of democracy in America.

> *"Control over government also gives him (Satan) control over radio and television, over newspapers and magazines...Only those who will write, speak, and portray the lies he wants told will be permitted to use these powerful communication media...Furthermore, control of government also puts Satan in a position to destroy families and the Lord's Church..."*
> H. Verlan Anderson, The Great and Abominable Church of the Devil,[439]

Because voting for the "lesser of two evils" is still voting for evil, the powers that control what happens in government laugh when citizens argue republican-democrat, conservative-liberal, or capitalism-communism. The reality is that for years

Step by Step...
"In politics nothing happens by accident. If it happens, you can bet it was planned that way."
Franklin Roosevelt, *U.N. Blue Print for World Control* [440]

Church members, who tend to be honest and sincere in their good intentions, often have a hard time comprehending such pernicious evil, but without proper education and the ability to wade through the media propaganda, these sincere Saints may unknowingly repeat patterns warned against in the Book of Mormon.

Vote Republican!
*And it came to pass on the other hand, that the Nephites did build them up (the Gaddiantons) and support them, beginning at the more wicked part of them, until they had overspread all the land of the Nephites, and had **seduced the more part of the righteous until they had come down to believe in their works and partake of their spoils**, and to join with them in their secret murders and combinations.*
Helaman 6:38

In truth, there is no political messiah to save us. In the end, only the real Savior will reign as King of Kings and Lord of Lords! Some believe that if Mitt Romney had become the president of the United States, our country would have been spared. And while it is true that the principles he publicly espoused may have delayed the destruction, all must understand that in the end, only obedience to God's commandments could have saved America. (Ether 2: 8-10).

"This past 4th of July we attended a sacrament meeting at a nearby LDS ward and I heard something that disturbed me very much. What I heard in this ward was probably not anything unique, sadly, to this ward alone but similar things may have been said last Sunday at many other wards. In fact, in my own ward, back in 2008 one man bore his testimony of how wonderful it would be "to have a righteous Stake President like Mitt Romney in the White House and how blessed we were to have that man in the public eye." Well - in this fast and testimony meeting – a little old lady stood up and said basically this (paraphrasing but not exaggerating): "I've been reading a wonderful book by Mitt Romney called "No Apologies" and I am so grateful for Mitt Romney. He is so wonderful. I don't know how it is possible for God to bless one man with so much knowledge, goodness and wisdom. If we follow Mitt Romney's teachings that you will find in his book - America will return to its greatness and its position as the sole World Superpower." She went on and on about militarism and how the military is the source of all of our freedom. She went on about our great "Caucasian heritage" in this nation. She went on and on for about 15 minutes and NOT one word about Jesus Christ or the Book of Mormon or the Founding Fathers. Needless to say I was flabbergasted and dismayed. I felt like I had attended the Church of Mitt Romney."
Mark Hudson, *False Hope* [441]

Those who watch must carefully ponder: Should the church be encouraging members to comply with laws that destroy freedom and increase control? For example, why does the church verbally support the Constitution in public, and then at other inconvenient times fail to support the standard? (The church's relationship/cooperation with the NSA spying center in Bluffdale, Utah.). What does it mean when politicians who are advancing a one-world order are honored with accolades at BYU? (Dick Cheney and Zbigniew Brzezinski). Should we be concerned when a freedom-loving professor at the "Lord's University" speaks the truth about 9-11 and is then ridiculed, avoided, and forced to retire? Is there a valid reason the institution chooses to advance and promote the same propaganda that various government agencies promote? (FEMA responses during emergencies and the World Health Organization promoting unsafe vaccines).

These, and other disturbing examples could be given, but is it possible we have done "all the wrong things" for all the right reasons? Does the end always justify the means? And if so, to what degree, and when will the compromise and capitulation end?

"Odd that we can pretend to raise a 'voice of warning' and at the same time pretend all is well is Zion."
Dan Mead

When it comes to the LDS church and political issues, the faithful hope we are simply "keeping our friends close, and our enemies closer." Others worry that in failing to take a stand against blatant corruption, the church has sold its soul for political power and influence.

Politically Deceived

"There is no guarantee that the devil will not deceive a lot of men who hold the priesthood. Free agency is the principle against which Satan waged his war in heaven. It is still the front on which he makes his most furious, devious, and persistent attacks. That this would be the case was foreshadowed by the Lord. When Satan "was cast out of heaven," his objective was (and still is) 'to deceive and to blind men, and to lead them captive at his will.' This he effectively does to as many as will not hearken unto the voice of God. His main attack is still on free agency. When he can get men to yield their agency, he has them well on the way to captivity. 'We who hold the priesthood must beware concerning ourselves, that we do not fall in the traps he lays to rob us of our freedom.

We must be careful that we are not led to accept or support in any way any organization, cause or measure which in its remotest effort, would jeopardize free agency, whether it be in politics, government, religion, employment, education, or in any other field. It is not enough for us to be sincere in what we support. We must be right!' (Elder Marion G. Romney.) Now this is crucial for us to know, for as President John Taylor said, 'Besides the preaching of the Gospel, we have another mission, namely, the perpetuation of the free agency of man and the maintenance of liberty, freedom and the rights of man.' It was the struggle over free agency that divided us before we came here. It may well be the struggle over the same principle which will deceive and divide us again."

Ezra Taft Benson, *BYU Speeches of the Year* [442]

It appears that the adversary has convinced some of the Mormon faithful that because of the twelfth article of faith, they are required to automatically obey every law of land—no matter how immoral and unconstitutional a specific law or policy may be.

Before considering what scripture actually states, let us ponder whether God, who inspired Joseph Smith to write the Articles of Faith, really intends for us to sin against eternal law in favor of complying with man's lower reasoning.

THE LAW OF THE LAND
by James Custer

"There is a great deal of rhetoric lately with respect to our obligation to render obedience to all the laws promulgated by government. There are those among the LDS people who cite D&C 58:21-22 as the requirement, and proclaim an obligation incumbent upon us all:

Let no man break the laws of the land, for **he that keepeth the laws of God hath no need to break the laws of the land**. *Wherefore, be subject to the powers that be, until he reigns whose right it is to reign, and subdues all enemies under his feet.*
D&C 58:21-22

This scripture does not, however, support the contentions of those who quote it for the purpose of quelling any and all dissent against present law and government. Those who rend the scriptures in this way are guilty of misleading and exercising unrighteous dominion. And they are either guilty of counseling in ignorance or they are guilty of deliberate deception.

It is true, *"he that keepeth the laws of God hath no need to break the laws of the land,"* but how does God define "laws of the land?" D&C 98:4-7 clearly and unambiguously answers that question for us; and should forever put all contention to rest.

And now, verily I say unto you concerning the laws of the land, it is my will that **my people should observe to do all things whatsoever I command them. And that law of the land which is constitutional**, *supporting that principle of freedom in maintaining rights and privileges, belongs to all mankind, and is justifiable before me. Therefore, I, the Lord, justify you, and your brethren of my church, in* **befriending that law which is the constitutional law of the land; and as pertaining to law of man, whatsoever is more or less than this, cometh of evil.**
D&C 98:4-7

God is plain and concise, *"My people should observe to do all things whatsoever I command them."* God defines the law of the land as being only that which is constitutional. All the rest are laws of men and therefore evil. A law is constitutional or unconstitutional by virtue of its intrinsic nature. A prejudiced decision of the Supreme Court does not alter that intrinsic nature.

This government under which we presently endure is not the government established by the Constitution. The Constitution provided for a republic and we now have an incorporated social democracy—there's a BIG difference! This is not the government our fore-fathers gave their blood, honor and fortunes to establish. This corporate social democracy is not in all things bound by the Constitution, and is not of the people, nor by the people, nor for the people." (James Custer, *The Law of the Land*). [443]

The prophet Joseph Smith clearly prioritized God's truth above the lower laws of man. For example he and a few of the early Saints chose to obey God and live the law of plural marriage even when it was illegal under the Illinois anti-bigamy statutes.[444] Later when Wilford Woodruff finally acquiesced to the pressures of an unjust government, several church leaders, including President Woodruff himself, continued to secretly encourage and allow celestial marriage.[445]

After the Second Manifesto banning plural marriage was released in 1904, apostles John W. Taylor and Matthias F. Cowley refused to abandon their wives and the principles of

Celestial marriage. As a result Elder Taylor was excommunicated and Elder Cowley eventually had his priesthood suspended.[446] This brief commentary has not been provided to explain or justify plural marriage, but to demonstrate that these men and others prioritized their conscience above what other leaders believed was in the best interest of the church.

Throughout history many men and women of various faiths have demonstrated that being aligned with eternal truth is more noble than mediocre compliance to secular law.

Today, disciples of Christ question: Have we as a Mormon people lost the faith and commitment necessary to put God's commandments above the secular codes which govern this telestial world? Are we as a people willing to receive our spiritual marching orders directly from God? And who is ready to be persecuted for the truth, regardless of the suffering which is sure to be inflicted by both members and non-members?

Those who intend to stand for truth must understand the difference between being obedient to God's law versus enabling the laws of men because of apathy and ignorance. Possessing the ability to navigate through today's moral and legal dilemmas will be an important skill in preparation for the establishment of God's Zion. Disciple Tom Hulet teaches a simple indicator of whether a law is moral and thus "constitutional," *"If you as a individual don't have the right under God's law to do it, then you may not delegate that particular right to government."*[447] This wise standard is being repeatedly violated today.

Thankfully a number of Americans, including some LDS, are awakening to our *"awful situation."* (Ether 8:24). These souls are like Captain Moroni and are willing to die in the defense of truth, family, and freedom. (Alma 62:5). They come from various backgrounds, but all work to oppose the dark plans of globalization and a one-world government.

As secret combinations continue to be enacted against America and its citizens, members will face a tidal wave of religious and moral complexity. Those who expect to just "follow the brethren" should consider the warning from Apostle J. Reuben Clark when he stated, *"There will be a lot of vacant places among those who guide and direct, not only this government, but also this Church of ours."*[448]

In the future, many will sell out to political pressure and social convenience, while others stand valiant for truth in the face of persecution. As always, the choice is ours.

The Helmuth Hubener Story

"Helmuth, Karl-Heinz, and Rudi were members of The Church of Jesus Christ of Latter-day Saints. Members of minority faith communities had good reason to feel threatened by the politics and policies of the Third Reich. The Third Reich was brutal in its approach to numerous religious sects. The Latter-day Saints were not generally a part of the German Christian community that mixed politics, Aryan racial theory, and Christianity, so Latter-day Saints may have felt a bit exposed at times. The Latter-day Saints and the Third Reich did share an interest in genealogy and Christian traditions that may have kept the Mormon Church from becoming a target of the government, despite the fact that it was not a mainstream German faith community. Many Latter-day Saints elders, including leaders in Helmuth and Karl-Heinz's own congregation, were members of the Nazi Party. The structure and disciplines of the Latter-day Saints Churches did not attract the attention of the National Socialist Party the way the Jewish faith and Gypsy traditions did. The ethnic makeup of the Latter-day Saints in Germany was quite similar to the German nation as a whole and the National Socialist Party and that probably also provided some protection to the members. The Hubener Group owed much credit to their Church and families for the principles and values that drove them to risk everything and oppose their own government in wartime, but it seems likely that the organizing principle for this group of young people was Helmuth's keen intellect, dedication to the truth, and his disdain for the propaganda lies of the German government." (R. Blair Holmes, *When Truth was Treason*)[449]

"The youthful Helmuth had, since a small child, been a member of the Boy Scouts, an organization strongly supported by his church, but in 1935 the Nazis banned scouting from Germany. He then joined the Hitler Youth, as required by the government, but would later disapprove of *Kristallnacht*, the "night of the broken glass," when the Nazis, including the Hitler Youth, destroyed Jewish businesses and homes. When one of the leaders in his local congregation, a new convert of under two years, undertook to bar Jews from attending its religious services, Hübener found himself at odds with the new policy, but continued to attend services with like-minded friends as the Latter-day Saints locally debated the issue. (His friend and fellow resistance fighter, Rudi Wobbe would later report that of the two thousand Latter-day Saints in the Hamburg area, seven were pro-Nazi, but five of them happened to be in his and Helmuth's St. Georg Branch (congregation); thus stirring controversy with the majority who were non- or anti-Nazis.)

After Hübener finished middle school in 1941, he began an apprenticeship in administration at the Hamburg Social Authority (*Sozialbehörde*). He met other apprentices there, one of whom, Gerhard Duwer, he would later recruit into his resistance movement. At a bathhouse he met new friends, one of whom had a communist family background and, as a result, he began listening to enemy radio broadcasts; these were strictly forbidden in Nazi Germany, being considered a form of treason. In the summer of that same year, Hübener discovered his brother Gerhard's shortwave radio in a hallway closet and began listening to the BBC on his own, and used what he had heard to compose various anti-fascist texts and anti-war leaflets, of which he also made many copies. The leaflets were designed to bring to people's attention how skewed the official reports about World War II from Berlin were, as well as to point out Adolf Hitler's, Joseph Goebbels', and other leading Nazis' criminal behavior. Other themes covered by Hübener's writings were the war's futility and Germany's looming defeat. He also mentioned the mistreatment sometimes meted out in the Hitler Youth. In the autumn of 1941, he managed to involve three friends in his listening: Karl-Heinz Schnibbe and Ruddi Wobbe, who were fellow Latter-day Saints, and later Gerhard Duwer. Hübener had them help him distribute about 60 different pamphlets, all containing material from the British broadcasts, and all consisting of typewritten copies. They distributed them throughout Hamburg, using such methods as surreptitiously pinning them on bulletin boards, inserting them into letterboxes, and stuffing them in coat pockets."[450]

"Hübener was arrested by German authorities and two days later was excommunicated by local authorities of the LDS Church. When the Church leadership in the U.S. were informed of the excommunication, they revoked it. Hübener was posthumously reinstated in the LDS Church in 1946, with the note "excommunicated by mistake",[451] because the specific process required for excommunication from the LDS Church was not followed by Hübener's local church leader at the time. The local church leader, Arthur Zander, was a fervent member of the Nazi Party, even to the extent of affixing notices to the church door stating "Jews not welcome".

Zander had attempted to protect others of his religious group and thus had excommunicated the young man, but in his haste and likely fear had done so without proper authority, because he had not first obtained his district president's permission. That district president was Otto Berndt, who, in fact, was sympathetic to Hübener and was suspected of assisting and encouraging the boy. Berndt was soon after questioned by the Gestapo and released with an ominous warning: "After Jews, you Mormons will be next."[452]

Hübener's activities could be seen as conflicting with the LDS Church's twelfth article of faith, which states, "We believe in being subject to kings, presidents, rulers, and magistrates, in obeying, honoring, and sustaining the law." However, his behavior could also be seen as justified by his faith, as he was fighting in defense of rights supported by the LDS Doctrine & Covenants Section 134."[453]

"On 5 February 1942, Helmuth Hübener was arrested by the Gestapo at his workplace in the Hamburger Bieberhaus. While trying to translate the pamphlets into French, and trying to have them distributed among prisoners of war, he had been noticed by Nazi Party member Heinrich Mohn, who had denounced him."

"On 11 August 1942, Hübener's case was tried at the *Volksgerichtshof* in Berlin. Hübener was found guilty of conspiracy to commit high treason and treasonous furthering of the enemy's cause. He was sentenced not only to death, but also to permanent loss of his civil rights, which means he could be (and was) mistreated in prison, with no bedding or blankets in his cold cell, etc.[454] On 27 October, at the age of 17, he was beheaded by guillotine at Plötzensee Prison in Berlin. His two friends, Schnibbe and Wobbe, who had also been arrested, were given prison sentences of five and ten years respectively."[455]

"Perhaps one of the most notable statements he made regarding the matter was to a fellow member of his church showing his belief that his actions were right in the beliefs of his religion. The day of his execution he wrote to the fellow branch member, *"I know that God lives and He will be the Just Judge in this matter... I look forward to seeing you in a better world!"*[456]

Those loyal to Jesus Christ should ask, how might this story relate to the future? Will history cycle? And what will be my role in the great Latter Day drama? In Christ, do I personally possess the wisdom and spiritual metal necessary to discern eternal truth from political error?

The Voice of Deception.

"No, it is not we that have deserted Christianity, it is those who came before us who deserted Christianity. We have only carried through a clear division between politics which have to do with terrestrial things, and religion, which must concern itself with the celestial sphere. There has been no interference with the doctrine (Lehre) of the Confessions or with their religious freedom (Bekenntnisfreiheit), nor will there be any such interference. On the contrary the State protects religion, though always on the one condition that religion will not be used as a cover for political ends... National Socialism neither opposes the Church nor is it anti-religious, but on the contrary it stands on the ground of a real Christianity....
For their interests cannot fail to coincide with ours alike in our fight against the symptoms of degeneracy in the world of to-day, in our fight against a Bolshevist culture, against atheistic movement, against criminality, and in our struggle for a consciousness of a community in our national life...
These are not anti-Christian, these are Christian principles!...
for the result of our political battle is surely not unblest by God."
Adolf Hitler, *Speech to the Germans* [457]

As Latter Day Saints, we have been commanded to *"waste and wear out our lives in bringing to light all the hidden things of darkness…*(D&C 123:13). It is our spiritual duty to warn all people about political intrigue and the prophecies of destruction that await the disobedient. (D&C 88:81).

By choosing to be anxiously engaged in our own family stewardships, we can contribute to the Lord's spiritual harvest, even if the majority chooses to go the way of all the world…

Consecrating Thy Life

*"…I testify that the God of heaven sent His choice spirits to lay the foundation of this government, and He has sent other choice spirits-you-to preserve it. This is the land reserved for the **establishment of Zion and the second coming of our Lord and Savior**. When all events are finished and written, we will look back and see that "**There's a Divinity that shaped our ends**," that this and other crises which preceded the glorious events of Christ's return were foreknown to God. Yes, we will see that he sent **special spirits willing to give their blood to defend our freedoms**."*
President Ezra Taft Benson, *The Crisis of our Constitution* [458]

Secret Combinations

And again, I say unto you that the enemy in the secret chambers seeketh your lives. **Ye hear of wars in far countries, and you say that there will soon be great wars in far countries, but ye know not the hearts of men in your own land.** *I tell you these things because of your prayers; wherefore, treasure up wisdom in your bosoms, lest the wickedness of men reveal these things unto you by their wickedness, in a manner which shall speak in your ears with a voice louder than that which shall shake the earth; but if ye are prepared ye shall not fear. And that ye might escape the power of the enemy, and be gathered unto me a righteous people, without spot and blameless…*
D&C 38: 28-31

God is freedom. Satan is control. God is choice. Satan is force. All that is true and loving leads to Jesus Christ and His Father. All that is distortion, deception, and hate is of Satan. The adversary lives in an emotional, mental, and spiritual hell and wishes all God's children to suffer with him. To further his dark agenda he seeks to end all personal agency on the earth.

The Enemy is Combined

"I testify that wickedness is rapidly expanding in every segment of our society. (See D&C 1:14-16; 84:49-53.) It is more highly organized, more cleverly disguised, and more powerfully promoted than ever before. Secret combinations lusting for power, gain, and glory are flourishing. A secret combination that seeks to overthrow the freedom of all lands, nations, and countries is increasing its evil influence and control over America and the entire world. (See Ether 8:18-25)."
Ezra Taft Benson, *Ensign* [459]

Today, the world is one continual scene of chaos, destruction, and pain. Traumatic violence, motivated by hunger and desperation, is breaking out in various countries across the globe. Any attempt to try and specifically summarize the horror in writing is immediately outdated. Sadly, this moment in time (2015), is only a prelude for the fulfillment of prophecy as nations continue to rise up against nation and men begin to take up their swords in earnest. (D&C 45:33). Similar to how King Benjamin could not list the *"divers ways and means"* in which we might sin (Mosiah 4:29), it is impossible to fully communicate the mounting details of political corruption, economic manipulation, and moral degradation.

Those desiring an accurate description of today's secret combinations can learn the truth from prophecy in the Book of Mormon and Doctrine and Covenants.

Today

"The Book of Mormon narrative is a chronicle of nations long since gone. But in its descriptions of the problems of today's society, it is as current as the morning newspaper and much more definitive, inspired, and inspiring concerning the solutions of those problems.
I know of no other writing which sets forth with such clarity the tragic consequences to societies

that follow courses contrary to the commandments of God. Its pages trace the stories of two distinct civilizations that flourished on the Western Hemisphere. Each began as a small nation, its people walking in the fear of the Lord. **But with prosperity came growing evils.** *The people succumbed to the wiles of ambitious and scheming leaders who oppressed them with burdensome taxes, who lulled them with hollow promises, who countenanced and even encouraged loose and lascivious living.* **These evil schemers led the people into terrible wars that resulted in the death of millions** *and the final and total extinction of two great civilizations in two different eras. No other written testament so clearly illustrates the fact that* **when men and nations walk in the fear of God and in obedience to His commandments, they prosper and grow, but when they disregard Him and His word, there comes a decay that, unless arrested by righteousness, leads to impotence and death.**
The Book of Mormon is an affirmation of the Old Testament proverb:
Righteousness exalteth a nation: but sin is a reproach to any people. *(Prov. 14:34)."*
Gordon B. Hinkley, *A Testimony Vibrant and True* [460]

Some members believe political issues should not be discussed at all in church. They are especially uncomfortable talking about political corruption and interpret the church's "neutral" stance as being justification for political avoidance.

In contrast, President Ezra Taft Benson stood in general conference and warned...."*In the ancient American civilization there was no word which struck greater terror to the hearts of the people than the name of the Gadiantons. It was a secret political party which operated as a murder cult. Its object was to* **infiltrate legitimate government,** *plant its* **officers in high places,** *and then seize power and live off the spoils appropriated from the people. It would start out as a small group of dissenters, and by using secret oaths with the threat of death for defectors, it would gradually gain a* **choke hold on the political and economic life of whole civilizations.** *The object of the Gadiantons, like modern communists, was to destroy the existing government and set up a ruthless criminal dictatorship over the whole land. One of the most urgent, heart-stirring appeals made by Moroni as he closed the Book of Mormon was addressed to the gentile nations of the last days.* **He foresaw the rise of a great worldwide secret combination among the gentiles which** *"seeketh to overthrow the freedom of* **all lands, nations, and countries.**" *(Ether 8:25.) He warned each gentile nation of the last days* **to purge itself of this gigantic criminal conspiracy which would seek to rule the world.** *The prophets, in our day, have continually warned us of these* **internal threats in our midst**—*that our greatest threat from socialistic communism lies* **within our country**.*"* [461]

This message from President Benson was not popular then, and is mostly ignored now. The struggle to awaken to our *"awful situation"* (Ether 8:24) has resulted in millions of good and decent people unknowingly contributing to the *church of the devil.* (D&C 18:20).

Supporting the Gadiantons
And it came to pass on the other hand, that the Nephites did build them up (the Gadiantons) and support them, beginning at the more wicked part of them, until they had overspread all the land of the Nephites, and had seduced the more part of the righteous until they had come down to believe in their works and partake of their spoils, and to join with them in their secret murders and combinations.
Helaman 6:38

For generations war, taxation, and debt have been used to bankrupt countries and enslave the masses. To further the purpose of ending all national sovereignty, evil and traumatic scenarios, (like 9-11), have been covertly implemented. The anticipated result of these "false flags" is a scared and desperate population turning to the government for another "easy solution." The cost is lost freedom and increased dependency.

> *"The government seems too anxious to give, give, give to the poor, to the aged, to the schools,*
> *to everyone.... And every time a gift returns to the people—a so-called gift—*
> *it comes with fetters binding and tying and enslaving.*
> *For every block of funds given to the people, they lose a bigger block of liberty."*
> Spencer W. Kimball, *Biography* [462]

Disciple Mark Hudson explains, *"Babylon is the religious term for all things worldly and physical. Money is a huge part of Babylon – indeed it is the driving force of Babylon. You can buy anything in this world with money. In Hebrew, the word for Mammon means "financial dealings." This is the central theme of Babylon. We cannot serve God and Mammon both. The world we live in is completely and totally run on "financial dealings" of some sort or another. The United States today is a Corporation – it is no longer a free republic where the power remains with the people. Truthfully we are all effectively the chattel property of the powerful and elite international bankers. They have done this by creating a "Debt Empire" where the entire monetary system is solely created on illusion and debt. God warned us about this in the scriptures and it is how conspiring men have always sought to control the world for ages. During times of war governments spend extreme amounts of money. They accumulate more and more debt, which requires added taxation in order to pay for the debt. What greater or more efficient way is there to "murder and get gain" than through war?"* [463]

> *And Cain said: Truly I am Mahan, the master of this great secret, that I may murder and get gain.*
> *Wherefore Cain was called Master Mahan, and he gloried in his wickedness.*
> Moses 5:31

During World War II, Heber J. Grant and the First Presidency wrote a letter to the U.S. Treasury which stated, *"**We believe that our real threat comes from within and not from without,** and it comes from the underlying spirit common to Nazism, Fascism, and Communism, namely the spirit which would array class against class, **which would set up a socialistic state of some sort,** which would rob the people of the liberties which we possess under the Constitution, and would set up such a reign of terror as exists now in many parts of Europe..."**We confess to you that it has not been possible for us to unify our own people even upon the necessity of such a turning about,** and therefore we cannot unfortunately, and we say it regretfully, make any practical suggestion to you as to how the nation can be turned about."* [464]

Despite President Grant's warning many of the Saints in that era apparently liked the appeal of socialist policies. Now over 75 years later, with the middle class being successfully manipulated into food stamps, government-sponsored health care, and poverty, and with Social Security on the brink of insolvency, America will soon suffer the consequences of fraud, greed, and deceit.

"...unless the people of America forsake the sins and the errors, political and otherwise, of which they are now guilty and return to the practice of the great fundamental principles of Christianity, and of Constitutional government, there will be no exaltation for them spiritually, and politically we shall lose our liberty and free institutions."
Heber J. Grant, *First Presidency Letter* [465]

Damaging schemes are now in place that will result in the general population pleading with the government to "save them." Crisis after crisis will be enacted that supposedly justify decreasing personal freedom and national sovereignty.

All the Right Reasons to Do All the Wrong Things...
"I wish to say with all the earnestness I possess that when you youth and maidens see any curtailment of these liberties I have named, when you see government invading any of these realms of freedom which we have under our Constitution, you will know that they are putting shackles on your liberty, and that tyranny is creeping upon you, no matter who curtails these liberties or who invades these realms, and no matter what the reason and excuse therefore may be."
James R. Clark, *First Presidency Message* [466]

Once American citizens are fully enslaved in a state of financial gluttony, desperation will overtake the country. Global inflation, national violence, and local crime will escalate. The Holy Spirit will withdraw and the love of many shall wax cold. (Matthew 24:12). New politicians, proclaiming another false brand of "salvation," will be elected, only to increase the corruption already present within our failed two-party system. Law by law, crisis after crisis, an ever-growing oppression will engulf the masses until all national and global stability is fully eroded.

Change of Government
"Now I tell you it is time the people of the United States were waking up with the understanding that if they don't save the Constitution from the dangers that threaten it, we will have a change of government."
Joseph Fielding Smith, *Doctrines of Salvation* [467]

It is difficult for those who love America and freedom to watch the country slowly slip toward martial law and communism. Personal repentance and a commitment to fight for freedom can delay and minimize the heartache, but revelation warns that eventually there will be *"a full end of all nations."* (D&C 87:6). This cleansing of America and the world is tragic, but also represents an essential part of God's plan. For when the time arrives that the wicked are destroying themselves with fire, it is then that the Holy City can be established! (2 Nephi 30:10).

The purpose of reviewing these political elements is not to encourage fighting a battle that cannot be won politically. We live on "enemy ground," and trying to "win" by electing the right candidate will not succeed in the end. The only sure hope is to seek spiritual escape in Jesus Christ and His Zion. We should thank all those who have fought for freedom, acknowledging that without these patriotic souls, America would not have endured this long. While also understanding that the "battle" for America must be temporarily "lost," that the "war" involving Zion and the entire Earth might be forever won!

The End of All Nations

And thus, with the sword and by bloodshed the inhabitants of the earth shall mourn;
and with famine, and plague, and earthquake, and the thunder of heaven, and the fierce and
vivid lightning also, shall the inhabitants of the earth be made to feel the wrath, and indignation,
and chastening hand of an Almighty God, until the consumption decreed hath made a
***full end of all nations**...Wherefore, **stand ye in holy places**, and be not moved,*
until the day of the Lord come; for behold, it cometh quickly, saith the Lord. Amen.
Doctrine and Covenants 87:6,8

Our Father once baptized the earth with water. In the future the Lord and His angels will come to purge the planet with fire. Our challenge is to be spiritually pure enough to withstand the day of His glory. (see Truth #70).

A Voice of Warning

"I stand before the Church this day and raise the warning voice. It is a prophetic voice, for I shall say only what the apostles and prophets have spoken concerning our day. . . . It is a voice calling upon the Lord's people to prepare for the troubles and desolations which are about to be poured out upon the world without measure. For the moment we live in a day of peace and prosperity but it shall not ever be thus. Great trials lie ahead. All of the sorrows and perils of the past are but a foretaste of what is yet to be. And we must prepare ourselves temporally and spiritually. . . . Peace has been taken from the earth, the angels of destruction have begun their work, and their swords shall not be sheathed until the Prince of Peace comes to destroy the wicked and usher in the great Millennium. . . . There will be wars in one nation and kingdom after another until war is poured out upon all nations and two hundred million men of war mass their armaments at Armageddon. . . . Bands of Gadianton robbers will infest every nation, immorality and murder and crime will increase, and it will seem as though every man's hand is against his brother."
Bruce R. McConkie, *Ensign* [468]

The future of America will include violent terrorism, planned pandemics, and natural disasters. These and other events will be used to justify eliminating individual liberty and increasing government control. As America implodes morally, economically, and militarily, only the righteous will know the peace of God.

What will eventually occur within the Unites States of America?

"It is hard to believe that a nation as large and as prosperous and as powerful as the United States is today could lose the power to govern. Even though there are serious problems in this country today, it still has a great governing power and is a world leader in its influence. What conditions could bring such a nation to the brink of destruction? What kinds of crises could strike with such power as to destroy the United States? Although there is much that is not known concerning the specific events that will bring the Lord's prophecies to fulfillment, he has given several indications of what is to come.
In a scripture quoted in the previous chapter, the Lord said that when the times of the Gentiles were fulfilled, there would be men standing in that generation which would not pass away until they saw an "overflowing scourge cover the land." The Lord often spoke of this scourge coming upon the people, and the devastating results of what would follow. In March of 1829, even before the Church was organized, he said: For a desolating scourge shall go forth among the inhabitants of the earth, and shall continue to be poured out from time to time, if they repent not, until the earth is empty, and the inhabitants thereof are consumed away and utterly destroyed by the brightness of my coming. Webster defines a scourge as "an instrument of punishment or criticism; a cause of widespread or great affliction." This scourge seems to involve many forms of terrible calamities, including great hailstorms,

tempests, plagues, pestilence, and war. Such terrible disasters will be such that they will lay to waste those
who fight against God and will actually leave mighty cities desolate of their populations.
The Lord warned some specific cities, particularly Boston, New York and Albany,
of the desolation awaiting them if they did not repent."
Gerald Lund, *The Coming of the Lord* [469]

During the next few years God will allow a variety of scenarios to occur. These political, moral, and financial traumas will encourage those who believe in God to seek an even greater repentance.

Satan will also attempt to use *the same* corruption and horror to establish his one-world order. In the end, his schemes will not succeed, but initially global suffering will increase, and the faith of all who believe will be tested.

Our World Today
"All that is yet to be shall go forward in the midst of greater evils and perils and desolations
than have been known on earth at any time. . . . Amid tears of sorrow—our hearts heavy with
forebodings—we see evil and crime and carnality covering the earth. Liars and thieves and adulterers
and homosexuals and murderers scarcely seek to hide their abominations from our view.
Iniquity abounds. There is no peace on earth. We see evil forces everywhere uniting to destroy the family,
to ridicule morality and decency, to glorify all that is lewd and base. We see wars and plagues and
pestilence. Nations rise and fall. Blood and carnage and death are everywhere. Gadianton robbers fill
the judgment seats in many nations. An evil power seeks to overthrow the freedom of all nations
and countries. Satan reigns in the hearts of men; it is the great day of his power."
Bruce R. McConkie, *General Conference* [470]

Those positioned by Lucifer to advance one-world control know the masses are much easier to manipulate when they are SCARED, COLD, HUNGRY, SICK, UNARMED, and DESPERATE.

Waiting for the Next False Flag
"Today Americans would be outraged if U.N troops entered Los Angeles to restore order;
tomorrow they will be grateful! This is especially true if they were told there was an outside threat
from beyond whether real or promulgated, that threatened our very existence. It is then that all peoples
of the world will pledge with world leaders to deliver them from evil. The one thing that man fears is
the unknown. When presented with this scenario, individual rights will be willingly relinquished
for the guarantee of their well being granted to them by their world government."
Henry Kissenger, *Hiding in Plain Sight* [471]

A full and complete summary of last-day events is beyond the scope of this text. What will be provided here is an overview of the political, legal, social, moral, economic, religious, and spiritual trends occurring in America and throughout the world today.

Working for a One-World Order
"Out of these troubled times a New World Order can emerge...We are now in sight of a United Nations
that performs as envisioned by its founders."
George H.W. Bush, *U.N. Blue Print for World Control* [472]

Legalizing Sin

And seeing the people in a state of such awful wickedness, and those Gadianton robbers
filling the judgment-seats—*having usurped the power and authority of the land;*
laying aside the commandments of God, and not in the least aright before him;
doing no justice *unto the children of men;* ***condemning the righteous*** *because of their righteousness;*
letting the guilty and the wicked go unpunished because of their money;
and moreover to be held in office at the head of government, to rule and do according to their wills,
that they might get gain and glory of the world, and, moreover, that they might the more easily
commit adultery, and steal, and kill, and do according to their own wills....
Helaman 7:4-5

A Planned Economic Collapse

And behold, the time cometh that he curseth your riches, that they become slippery,
that ye cannot hold them; and in the days of your poverty ye cannot retain them. And in the days
of your poverty ye shall cry unto the Lord; and in vain shall ye cry, for your desolation is already
come upon you, and your destruction is made sure; and then shall ye weep and howl in that day,
saith the Lord of Hosts. And then shall ye lament, and say: O that I had repented, and had not killed
the prophets, and stoned them, and cast them out. Yea, in that day ye shall say: O that we had remembered
the Lord our God in the day that he gave us our riches, and then they would not have become slippery
that we should lose them; for behold, our riches are gone from us.
Helaman 13:31-33

Hyper-Inflation Coming to U.S.

"If the American people ever allow private banks to control the issue of their money,
first by inflation and then by deflation, the banks and corporations that will grow up around,
will deprive the people of their property until their children will wake up homeless
on the continent their fathers conquered."
Thomas Jefferson, *Hiding in Plain Site* [473]

One-World Banking

"The Vatican has called for a "global public authority" and a world central bank to rule
over financial affairs in the wake of the engineered economic collapse. The planned implosion of
the global economy "has revealed behaviors like selfishness, collective greed and hoarding of goods
on a great scale." The 18-page document, entitled "Towards Reforming the International Financial and
Monetary Systems in the Context of a Global Public Authority," declares global economics needs an
"ethic of solidarity" among rich and poor nations. In response, the Vatican is calling for
"a supranational authority" with worldwide scope and "universal jurisdiction" to guide economic
policies and decisions. The authority will be run by the United Nations, according to the document.
It will take time to replace economic policies and in the process destroy national sovereignty,
according to the Vatican. "Of course, this transformation will be made at the cost of a gradual,
balanced transfer of a part of each nation's powers to a world authority and to regional authorities,
but this is necessary at a time when the dynamism of human society and the economy and the progress
of technology are transcending borders, which are in fact already very eroded in a globalized world."
Kurt Nimmo [474]

Disappearing Middle Class

"I see in the near future a crisis approaching that unnerves me and causes me to tremble
for the safety of my country. Corporations have been enthroned. An era of corruption in
High places will follow, and the Money Power of the Country will endeavor to prolong its reign
by working upon the prejudices of the People, until the wealth is aggregated in a few hands,
and the Republic is destroyed."
Abraham Lincoln, just prior to his assassination[475]

Pandemic

And when the times of the Gentiles is come in, a light shall break forth among them that sit in darkness,
and it shall be the Fullness of my gospel; But they receive it not; for they perceive not the light,
and they turn their hearts from me because of the precepts of men. And in that generation shall the
times of the Gentiles be fulfilled. And there shall be men standing in that generation, that shall not pass
until they shall see an overflowing scourge; for a desolating sickness shall cover the land.
But my disciples shall stand in holy places, and shall not be moved; but among the wicked,
men shall lift up their voices and curse God and die.
Doctrine and Covenants 45:28-32

Political and Religious Persecution

"We stand in danger of losing our liberties, and that once lost, only blood will bring them back;
and once lost, we of this church will, in order to keep the Church going forward,
have more sacrifices to make and more persecutions to endure than we have yet known. . . ."
J. Rueben Clark, *Conference Report* [476]

Religious Treason

"There is a strongly felt need... for a reform of the United Nations Organization,
and likewise of economic institutions and international finance,
so that the concept of the family of nations can acquire real teeth...
there is urgent need of a true world political authority."
Pope Benedict, *Caritas in Veritate* [477]

The Scourge of Illegal Immigration

O all ye that are pure in heart, lift up your heads and receive the pleasing word of God,
and feast upon his love; for ye may, if your minds are firm, forever. But, wo, wo, unto you that are not
*pure in heart, that are filthy this day before God; **for except ye repent** the land is cursed for your sakes;*
*and **the Lamanites**, which are not filthy like unto you, nevertheless they are cursed with a sore cursing,*
***shall scourge you even unto destruction.** And the time speedily cometh, that except ye repent*
they shall possess the land of your inheritance, and the Lord God will lead away the righteous
out from among you.
Jacob 3:2-4

Gentiles to be Treaded Down

And I say unto you, that if the Gentiles do not repent after the blessing which they shall receive, after they have scattered my people—Then shall ye, who are a remnant of the house of Jacob, go forth among them; and ye shall be in the midst of them who shall be many; and ye shall be among them as a lion among the beasts of the forest, and as a young lion among the flocks of sheep, who, if he goeth through both treadeth down and teareth in pieces, and none can deliver.
3 Nephi 20:15-16

Another Famine

*And there came prophets in the land again, crying repentance unto them—that they must prepare the way of the Lord or there should come a curse upon the face of the land; yea, **even there should be a great famine**, in which they should be destroyed **if they did not repent.***
Ether 9:28

Desperation, and Violence

For nation shall rise against nation, and kingdom against kingdom; there shall be famine and pestilences, and earthquakes in divers places. And again, because iniquity shall abound, the love of men shall wax cold...
JST Matthew 24:30

Storms and Natural Disasters

For after your testimony cometh the testimony of earthquakes, that shall cause groanings in the midst of her, and men shall fall upon the ground and shall not be able to stand. And also cometh the testimony of the voice of thunderings, and the voice of lightnings, and the voice of tempests, and the voice of the waves of the sea heaving themselves beyond their bounds. And all things shall be in commotion; and surely, men's hearts shall fail them; for fear shall come upon all people.
Doctrine and Covenants 88:89-91

Cosmic Events

For not many days hence and the earth shall tremble and reel to and fro as a drunken man; and the sun shall hide his face, and shall refuse to give light; and the moon shall be bathed in blood; and the stars shall become exceedingly angry, and shall cast themselves down as a fig that falleth from off a fig-tree.
Doctrine and Covenants 88:87

And there shall be a great hailstorm (small asteroids?) sent forth to destroy the crops of the earth.
Doctrine and Covenants 29:16

Illegal Wars

"The Constitution explicitly states that only Congress has the power to declare war. We, as a nation, have capitulated that right to our new Imperial Presidency…From now on the President, as he pleases, will commit American troops to fight wars he considers necessary. It is up to us to demand that Congress reclaim that right. The founders made the Congress responsible, not the president for committing Americans to war, because they feared that America would become like the Roman Empire again, with Caesar able to conduct wars as he saw fit. The ability to unilaterally wage war is a huge usurpation of power. Not many republics have survived long after the fact."
Ken Bowers, *Hiding in Plain Site* [478]

War in America

For verily I say unto you, that great things await you; **Ye hear of wars in foreign lands; but, behold, I say unto you, they are nigh, even at your doors, and not many years hence ye shall hear of wars in your own lands.** *Wherefore I, the Lord, have said, gather ye out from the eastern lands, assemble ye yourselves together ye elders of my church; go ye forth into the western countries, call upon the inhabitants to repent, and inasmuch as they do repent, build up churches unto me. And with one heart and with one mind, gather up your riches that ye may purchase an inheritance which shall hereafter be appointed unto you. And it shall be called the New Jerusalem, a land of peace, a city of refuge, a place of safety for the saints of the Most High God; And the glory of the Lord shall be there, and the terror of the Lord also shall be there, insomuch that the wicked will not come unto it, and it shall be called Zion.* **And it shall come to pass among the wicked, that every man that will not take his sword against his neighbor must needs flee unto Zion for safety. And there shall be gathered unto it out of every nation under heaven; and it shall be the only people that shall not be at war one with another.** *And it shall be said among the wicked: Let us not go up to battle against Zion, for the inhabitants of Zion are terrible; wherefore we cannot stand. And it shall come to pass that the righteous shall be gathered out from among all nations, and shall come to Zion, singing with songs of everlasting joy.*
D&C 45: 62-71

The Next Civil War

*"****The whole government is gone; it is as weak as water.****" I heard Joseph Smith say nearly thirty years ago, 'They shall have mobbings to their hearts content, if they do not redress the wrongs of the Latter-day Saints.'* **Mobs will not decrease but will increase until the whole government becomes a mob, and eventually it will be State against State, city against city, neighborhood against neighborhood…"**
Brigham Young quoting Joseph Smith [479]

Social Chaos and Turmoil

"Mobs will not decrease but will increase until the whole government becomes a mob, and eventually it will be State against State, city against city, neighborhood against neighborhood, Methodists against Methodists, and so on. It will be the same with other denominations of professing Christians, and it will be Christian against Christian, and man against man, and those who will not take up the sword against their neighbors, must flee to Zion."
Brigham Young, *The Coming of the Lord* [480]

Prophecy is being fulfilled on a daily basis. The message to prepare spiritually and temporally has been a religious mainstay within the LDS church for decades. Only a few seem to have taken the warnings seriously.

Prophetic Warnings

"I warn future historians to give credence to my history; for my testimony is true, and the truth of its record will be manifest in the world to come. All the words of the Lord will be fulfilled upon the nations, which are written in this book. The American nation will be broken in pieces like a potter's vessel, and will be cast down to hell if it does not repent—and this, because of murders, whoredoms, wickedness and all manner of abominations, for the Lord has spoken it."
Wilford Woodruff, *The Coming of the Lord* [481]

Those who love God, America, and the truth need not despair. Scripture promises that in time, the great and abominable church will fall and Babylon will be cast down (2 Nephi 28:18, D&C 29:21). Until that time, all who have faith can rejoice in the anticipated establishment of Zion.

Within her walls of safety an "economy" of love, prosperity, and generosity will flourish! Money will cease to exist and Satan will be bound. (D&C 88:110). This state of peace and happiness will not be the result of political maneuvering or religious positioning, but rather the fruit of spiritual enlightenment.

A Modern-Day Captain Moroni

"Political action, to be truly beneficial, must be directed toward changing the hearts and minds of the people, recognizing that it's the virtue and morality of the people that allow liberty to flourish. The Constitution or more laws per se, have no value if the people's attitudes aren't changed. To achieve liberty and peace, two powerful human emotions have to be overcome. Number one is "envy" which leads to hate and class warfare. Number two is "intolerance" which leads to bigoted and judgmental policies. These emotions must be replaced with a much better understanding of love, compassion, tolerance and free market economics. Freedom, when understood, brings people together. When tried, freedom is popular... I have come to one firm conviction after these many years of trying to figure out "the plain truth of things." The best chance for achieving peace and prosperity, for the maximum number of people world-wide, is to pursue the cause of LIBERTY."
Ron Paul, *Farewell Address to Congress* [482]

As America continues her descent into moral relativity, political corruption, and social collapse, it is essential to understand the role and purpose of darkness. Instead of "fearing" the opposition in an unproductive manner, or attributing all that we do not yet understand to the power of the devil, we should remember **"all things work together for good to them that love God..."**(Romans 8:28). And that in the end, both the effects of good and evil are used to **"work upon the hearts of the children of men."** (D&C 19:7). Part of the reason scripture warns of so much heartache and sorrow is to reinforce our faith when challenged to the core.

Regarding the suffering and destruction which surely will come, peace can be found in knowing the Lord will gather and preserve His true disciples. (see Truths #50 and #64).

Gathering the Elect

*For verily, verily, I say unto you that ye are called to lift up your voices as with the sound of a trump, to declare my gospel unto a crooked and perverse generation. For behold, the field is white already to harvest; and **it is the eleventh hour**, and the last time that I shall call laborers into my vineyard. And my vineyard has become corrupted every whit; and there **is none which doeth good save it be a few**; and they err in many instances **because of priestcrafts**, all having corrupt minds. And even so will **I gather mine elect from the four quarters of the earth**, even as many as will believe in me, and hearken unto my voice. Open your mouths and they shall be filled, and you shall become even as Nephi of old, who journeyed from Jerusalem in the wilderness.*
D&C 33:2-4, 6, 8

Before the cleansing arrives, those who love God and His gospel will have already separated themselves from Babylon and her secret combinations. These are they who are ready, and even eager, to *"flee unto Zion for safety."*(D&C 45:68). (see Truth #65).

The Zion Escape

*"A terrible revolution will take place in the land of America, such as has never been seen before; for the land will be literally left without a supreme government, and every species of wickedness will run rampant. Father will be against son, and son against father, mother against daughter, and daughter against mother. The most terrible scenes of murder and bloodshed, and raping that have ever been looked upon will take place. **Many will come with bundles under their arms to escape the calamities, and there will be no escape except by fleeing to Zion.**"*
Joseph Smith, *White Horse Prophecy* [483]

*"The message of The Church of Jesus Christ of Latter-day Saints is that there is but **one guiding hand in the universe, only one truly infallible light**, one unfailing beacon to the world. That light is Jesus Christ, the light and life of the world, the light which one Book of Mormon prophet described as "a light that is endless, that can never be darkened" (Mosiah 16:9). As we search for the shore of safety and peace, whether we be individual women and men, families, communities, or nations, **Christ is the only beacon on which we can ultimately rely.**"*
Howard W. Hunter, *The Teachings of Howard W. Hunter* [484]

The emphasis to "follow the brethren" is usually rationalized by interpreting D&C 1:38 literally which states, *"whether by mine own voice or by the voice of my servants, it is the same."* When the one who is speaking is truly a "servant of God," and speaks by the power of the Holy Ghost, then this precept is doctrinally correct. But even then, those who have personally talked with Deity know that in relation to raw power and pure love, only the Gods deserve our unconditional trust.

*"**Do not, brethren, put your trust in man though he be a bishop; an apostle, or a president;** if you do, they will fail you at some time or place, they will do wrong or seem to, and your support be gone; but if we lean on God, He never will fail us. **When men and women depend on God alone, and trust in Him alone, their faith will not be shaken if the highest in the Church should step aside.** They could still see that He is just and true, that truth is lovely in His sight, and the pure in heart are dear to Him. Perhaps it is His own design that faults and weaknesses should appear in high places in order that His Saints may learn to trust in Him and not in any man or men. **Therefore, my brethren and sisters, seek after the Holy Spirit and His unfailing testimony of God and His work upon the earth. Rest not until you know for yourselves** that God has set His hand to redeem Israel, and **prepare a people for His coming.**"*
George Q. Cannon, *Collected Discourses* [485]

In truth, "follow the prophet" was never meant to be an excuse for spiritual apathy. Particularly in relation to surviving the last days, many assume that the prophet will tell them all that is necessary to protect their families.

Cultural Assumption
"To survive the future I only need to follow church leadership."

This cultural belief assumes that every member will *have access* to continuing revelation through the organizational prophet. It minimizes the stark reality that when the world and church are cleansed of wickedness, only a sampling of true prophets and apostles will remain scattered throughout the earth. Those local leaders who survive will undoubtedly do their best to lead the people, but where a member lives geographically, and in what manner the secret combinations are inflicted, will determine in part how much access a soul has to true prophetic leadership. It seems likely that every surviving soul will eventually have to determine in whom they trust. When that time arrives, what we believe, and who we know, will literally become a life-or-death decision.

"For the leaders of this people cause them to err;
and they that are led of them are destroyed."
Isaiah 9:16

There is however a sure alternative: to personally possess the ability to hear the voice of God independent of any other human being, that when the days of destruction arrive and inspired leadership is not readily available, survivors can still walk forward into the will of the Father.

"The time will come when no man or woman will be able to endure on borrowed light.
Each will have to be guided by the light within himself. If you do not have it, how can you stand?
Do you believe this? How is it now? You have the First Presidency, from whom you can get counsel to
guide you, and you rely on them. **The time will come when they will not be with you.** *Why?*
Because they will have to flee and hide up to keep out of the hands of their enemies. You have the Twelve
now. **You will not always have them,** *for they, too, will be hunted and will have to keep out of the way*
of their enemies. You have other men to who you look for counsel and advice. **Many of them will not be**
amongst you. You will be left to the light within yourselves. If you do not have it,
you will not stand; therefore seek for the Testimony of Jesus and cleave to it,
that when the trying time comes, you may not stumble and fall."
Heber C. Kimball, *Life of Heber C Kimball* [486]

J. Reuben Clark, a member of the First Presidency, tried to help prepare the Saints for the loss of freedom coming to America. He also knew that in the last days there would be a shortage of true leadership within the church. He prophesied,

"Brethren, I do not suppose that any of you have had communistic leanings. I suppose that all of you love
your country, love the Constitution, love the free institutions under which we live, love our freedoms.
But if there be any, may I ask you, prayerfully and humbly, think this thing over, because if it comes here
it will probably come in its full vigor and **there will be a lot of vacant places among those who guide**
and direct, not only this government, but also this Church of ours."
J. Reuben Clark, Jr., *Conference Report* [487]

When the anticipated destructions arrive, being led of the Spirit will be life saving. The cultural assumptions and incomplete traditions we have promoted will be seen as misleading. In this time of crisis the pertinent questions will be: Can I personally hear the voice of God? Am I able to differentiate between the voice of peace and the fearful ranting of my mind? And similar to Lehi, am I prepared and willing to follow the Holy Spirit, even when persecuted by the people?

"... **Some people fancy because we have the Presidency and Apostles of the Church they will do**
the thinking for us. *There are men and women so mentally lazy that they hardly think for themselves.*

*To think calls for effort, which makes some men tired and wearies their souls. Now, brethren and sisters, we are surrounded with such conditions that it requires not only thought, **but the guidance of the Holy Spirit**. Latter-day Saints, you must think for yourselves. **No man or woman can remain in this Church on borrowed light.** I am a strong believer in the following statement made by my father in the House of the Lord in 1856: "**We think we are secure in the chambers of the everlasting hills, but the time will come when we will be so mixed up that it will be difficult to tell the face of a Saint from the face of an enemy to the people of God. Then, brethren, look out for the great sieve, for there will be a great sifting time, and many will fall; for I say unto you there is a test, a test, a TEST coming, and who will be able to stand?"**
J. Golden Kimball, Conference Report [488]*

A key aspect of our test is will whether we will be leadership dependent or Spirit led? The choice is ours, but must be made before the day arrives.

"Now you won't survive spiritually unless you know how to receive revelation... I don't know whether you know how to receive revelation but you won't survive without it... it's a noisy world, and you're going to have to learn personally, and privately and individually that revelation will come when the Lord can speak to our feelings."
Boyd K. Packer, BYU Devotional [489]

When Gordon B. Hinkley was the president of the church, he counseled members to know the voice of the Holy Spirit. Rarely did he warn of specific dangers which were about to come upon the planet. Instead, he taught correct principles and let the people determine the meaning of his message. After Hurricane Katrina afflicted New Orleans in 2005, President Hinkley referred to D&C 88:90 which warns of *"the waves of the sea heaving themselves beyond their bounds."* His general conference talk, *"If Ye Are Prepared, Ye Shall Not Fear,"* also reconfirmed that spiritual warnings offered *before* the actual calamities are usually **general** in nature. (Matthew 24, D&C 29, 38, 45). Those wanting **specific details** before and during the event must get the information directly from the Lord, (and then keep it to themselves). Those who can access immediate direction from above are the ones who will survive to fulfill Latter Day Prophecy. These are they who will abide the day, not because they are "members of the church," but because they know the voice of God!

*And at that day, when I shall come in my glory, shall the parable be fulfilled which I spake concerning the ten virgins. For they that are wise and have received the truth, and **have taken the Holy Spirit for their guide**, and have not been deceived—verily I say unto you, they shall not be hewn down and cast into the fire, **but shall abide the day.***
D&C 45:56-57

In the days to come those dependent on the church and its leaders, rather than the Lord Jesus Christ and His Holy Spirit, will be sorely disappointed.

Are we to "follow the prophet," or are we to follow Jesus Christ the way true prophets do?

We must learn to trust God with full abandon. Leaning on leaders when we could go directly to the Lord stifles spiritual progression. Some have become so dependent on church leadership that they get angry and defensive when the cultural trend is discussed honestly. **To them, it is a sign of apostasy not to be dependent on church leaders.**

Disciple Dan Mead responds, *"The first step to real apostasy is putting an idol between me and my Lord! We don't want or need another mediator between us and Jesus Christ. The result of cultural assumption and dependence on other human beings has resulted in a mindset where some bishops, stake presidents, and other general authorities are under the illusion a member is dependent on them to access Jesus Christ and his salvation."*[490]

Thankfully we can have an eye single to the glory of God and still support the brethren, but it must be done with an accurate hierarchy. God is first, all else is secondary. (see Truth #3).

> *The Preparing Wheat* follow the prophet and believe in Jesus Christ. (D&C 1:38).
> *The Wheat of God* follow the Lord Jesus Christ and believe in His true prophets. (D&C 135:3).

It is wise to follow the council of true apostles and prophets. As messengers of the Lord, their words and directives assist those who will listen and obey. All should learn from their counsel while also seeking a greater communion with the Holy Spirit. Any man who suggests a different order of emphasis is not a true apostle or prophet of the Lord.

Those willing to rely *"wholly upon the merits of him who is mighty to save"*(2 Nephi 31:19), understand the need for direct tutorship from the Holy Spirit. These Saints remember a sacred place within where *"ye need not that any man teach you."* (1 John 2:27). This does not mean we cannot learn from God's true apostles, only that our spiritual progression should be primarily, and if necessary solely, focused on the Lord Jesus Christ.

O Lord, I have trusted in thee, and I will trust in thee forever. I will not put my trust in the arm of flesh; for I know that cursed is he that putteth his trust in the arm of flesh. Yea, cursed is he that putteth his trust in man or maketh flesh his arm. Yea, I know that God will give liberally to him that asketh. Yea, my God will give me, if I ask not amiss; therefore I will lift up my voice unto thee; yea, I will cry unto thee, my God, the rock of my righteousness. Behold, my voice shall forever ascend up unto thee, my rock and mine everlasting God. Amen.
2 Nephi 4:34-35

> **TRUTH #47:** POLITICAL INFLUENCE, ECONOMIC CORRUPTION, AND MORAL RELATIVITY WILL COMBINE AGAINST ALL TRUE BELIEVERS OF JESUS CHRIST. THE FULFILLMENT OF PROPHECY WILL INCLUDE THE LORD'S HOUSE BEING CLEANSED AND A SEPARATION OF THE WHEAT FROM THE TARES.

In the Mirror

"Indeed, even now we observe an acceleration of the prophesied polarization of the forces of good and evil. (Doctrine and Covenants 1:35-36). This process will continue for some years until it reaches its climax at the Savior's coming…The destructions which prepared the way for Christ's appearance to the Nephites and Lamanites will have their counterpart in these last days. In due time the Redeemer's wrath will be felt by all mankind. **'And upon my house shall it begin, and from my house shall it go forth,' saith the Lord.'** *(Doctrine and Covenants 112:23-26; 133:2).* **The eventual result will be 'an entire separation of the righteous and the wicked'—both in the Church and in the world.** *(D&C 63:54)."*
Paul Cheesman, The Book of Mormon: The Keystone Scripture [491]

The gospel of Jesus Christ is not a popularity contest. When disciples of Christ teach the truth they are not widely accepted, but instead are misrepresented, persecuted, and even killed for the cause of Christ. If rejection from the world is not occurring against the church and its members, it is likely a sign that the collective culture has been seduced into the superficial ways of Babylon. The result of capitulating to the whims of the world is the withering of real priesthood power.

"There is nothing that would so soon weaken my hope and discourage me as to see this people in full fellowship with the world, and receive no more persecution from them because they are one with them. In such an event, we might bid farewell to the Holy Priesthood with all its blessings, privileges and aids to exaltations, principalities and powers in the eternities of the Gods."
Brigham Young, Journal of Discourses [492]

Currently the wheat in the church, (those who have been "born-again" and continually cry repentance), and the tares of the church, (those who have not yet awakened and believe all is well in Zion), function together. According to prophecy, a day of separation will arrive.

"Sometimes we hear someone refer to a division in the Church. In reality, the Church is not divided. It simply means that there are some who, for the time being at least are members of the Church but not in harmony with it. These people have a temporary influence in the Church; but unless they repent, they will be missing when the final membership records are recorded. It is well that our people understand this principle so as to not be misled by those apostates within the Church who have not yet repented or been cut off. But there is a cleansing coming. The Lord says that his vengeance shall be poured out upon the inhabitants of the earth… And upon my house shall it begin, and from my house shall it go forth, saith the Lord; First among those among you who have professed to know my name and have not known me….(D&C 112:24-26). I look forward to that cleansing; its need within the Church is becoming increasingly apparent."
Ezra Taft Benson, To The Humble Followers of Christ [493]

277

More than forty years has passed since President Ezra Taft Benson proclaimed this warning. Some have wondered if those who are "*not in harmony*" with the gospel have actually overtaken the day-to-day functioning of the church. And if so, is the day of anticipated cleansing fast approaching?

Cleansing the Church

*"In our day the Lord has established his Church. He is desirous that there be no iniquity in the Church and that the **members be clean and pure before him.** He said this is "the only true and living church upon the face of the whole earth, with which I, the Lord, am well pleased, speaking unto the church collectively and not individually—For **I, the Lord cannot look upon sin with the least degree of allowance**" (D&C 1:30-31). On another occasion he said, "Purge ye out the iniquity which is among you; sanctify yourselves before me" (D&C 43:11). He said, "Behold, I, the Lord, have looked upon you, and **have seen abominations in the Church** that profess my name. But blessed are they who are faithful and endure" (D&C 50:4-5). His command is, **"Wherefore, let the Church repent of their sins, and I the Lord, will own them; otherwise they shall be cut off. (D&C 63:63)."***
Monte S. Nyman and Charles D. Tate, Jr, *Alma, the Testimony of the Word* [494]

Succumbing to religious pride results in being "cut off" from the Lord. This can happen on an individual or institutional level. But in relation to when the Creator will purge pride from the earth on a global level, only God in His perfect state of omniscience can determine when the spiritual breaking point has been reached.

"For years we have been counseled to have on hand a year's supply of food...
***Should the Lord decide at this time to cleanse the Church—and the need for that cleansing seems to be increasing—**a famine in this land of one year's duration* could *wipe out a large percentage of slothful members, including some ward and stake officers. Yet we cannot say we have not been warned."*
Ezra Taft Benson, *Conference Report* [495]

Many who are "active in the church" consider themselves to be the "wheat," but historically a distinction exists between those who are actually pure in heart, and those who due to tradition and religious status, mistakenly think they are.

Is Being "Active" Enough?

*"The season of the world before us will be like no other in the history of mankind. Satan will unleash every evil scheme, every vile perversion ever known to man in any generation. As parents, spouses, children, and members of Christ's church, we must find safety. Unfortunately, many will struggle mightily before recognizing this bitter truth: there is no safety in this world—wealth cannot provide it, enforcement agencies cannot ensure it, **even membership in the Church will not guarantee it.**"*
Vaughn J. Featherstone, *The Incomparable Christ: Our Master and Model* [496]

In July of 1833 a mob gathered at Independence, Missouri to harass the Mormons. In their anger they traumatized children, destroyed property, and assaulted Bishop Edward Partridge. In response to this persecution, Oliver Cowdery wrote, *"This great tribulation would not have come upon Zion had it not been for rebellion...it was necessary that these things should come upon us; not only justice demands it, but there was no other way to cleanse the church."*[497]

The church has been cleansed before; it will happen again. In the future the thinning will involve modern-day details, but the pattern of sifting and removing all that is unclean will be the same. (see Truth #48).

Those who watch the church closely observe increasing turmoil within the organization. For decades, the adversary has worked to gradually pollute the Lord's church, and now with the details of church history becoming public knowledge, those who love what the church was supposed to be, can only wonder how such a disturbing metamorphosis occurred?

Despite noble efforts by a few faithful members to make a real difference, (2 Nephi 28:14), patterns in scripture suggest that the Lord's people will again cross a line that requires massive cleansing. Some have wondered if homosexuality and the issue of gay marriage will be the final catalyst that instigates the destruction drama.

HOMOSEXUALITY AND GAY MARRIAGE

1995: Standing for Truth
"THE FAMILY is ordained of God. Marriage between man and woman is essential to His eternal plan. Children are entitled to birth within the bonds of matrimony, and to be reared by a father and a mother who honor marital vows with complete fidelity. Happiness in family life is most likely to be achieved when founded upon the teachings of the Lord Jesus Christ."
The Family, A Proclamation to the World [498]

The first commandment given to Adam and Eve and their posterity was to *"Be fruitful, and multiply, and replenish the Earth."* (Genesis 1:28). In response to this profound edict, the evil one uses every temptation, scheme, and mutation possible to derail the purposes of God. In support of his rebellion, most of the government, the media, and a growing number of activist judges are currently obsessed with promoting homosexuality and gay marriage.

2004: Staying Strong
"The Church of Jesus Christ of Latter-day Saints favors a constitutional amendment preserving marriage as the lawful union of a man and a woman."
The First Presidency, *Constitutional Amendment* [499]

A few years after the church made this important proclamation a significant political victory for truth and the traditional family occurred in the 2008 California election. The church and its members were largely responsible for passing "Proposition 8," which defined marriage, even in the liberal-leaning state of California, as being between one man and one woman. Prior to the vote, Latter Day Saints from many states made a stand for truth. The backlash from gay rights advocates included anger, violence, vandalism, and assault. How wonderful that in this particular circumstance, the Church and its members were again worthy of persecution!

"Temple Grounds Vandalized by Protesters"
November 13, 2008

"But shall we not be persecuted?" Yes, and does not Jesus say, Blessed are ye when men revile you and persecute you, etc.,—would you be deprived of that blessing. "But we have had enough of it." O, have you? No matter, you will have to put up with it. "But," say you, "have we not certain constitutional rights?" Yes, on paper, but when you get through with them, the paper does not amount to much; it is like pie-crust, easily broken. We do not pay much attention to these things. Honorable men will be governed by constitutions, and laws, and principles, but dishonorable persons will not."
John Taylor, *Journal of Discourses* [500]

For years, liberal forces have tried to influence the brethren to compromise on this key doctrine. Those promoting Satan's agenda have attempted to use homosexuality to morally and politically destroy the Church.

Due to the institution's constant effort to be viewed by the public in a favorable light, capitulating to the media appears to be a growing temptation. And to those who think such a possible betrayal by the church could never happen, a different perspective is obtained by reviewing church history in relation to several key doctrines. Examples where the church has waffled on key doctrine include changes made to scripture, blacks and the priesthood, plural marriage, church finances, and even how we conceptualize Deity. (see Truths #30 and #33).

Currently America is being morally gutted by an onslaught of immoral legislation. Over the past decade Satan has accelerated his constant and vicious attack on purity and religious freedom. Because our personal salvation relates to staying loyal to God and truth, we should watch closely how the church as an institution chooses to respond to the propaganda.

"Mormon Church Softening on Gay Marriage"
Washington Post [501]

Obviously the LDS church cannot control how a biased and corrupt media chooses to represent the institution. And yet in 2009, an ordinance in Salt Lake City involving gay rights and housing discrimination came onto the political stage. The church, which had previously opposed similar legislation, surprisingly modified its official position regarding the same-gender ordinance. It was the first time the church had supported a pro-gay policy. The director of public affairs for the church made the following announcement explaining the reason for the change.

Trying to Please Two Masters

"There are going to be gay advocates who don't think we've gone nearly far enough, and people very conservative who think we've gone too far; the vast majority of people are between those polar extremes and we think that's going to resonate with people on the basis of fair-mindedness."
Michael Otterson, Director of Public Affairs [502]

Assessing what people consider to be *"fair-minded"* implies that how the gospel of Jesus Christ is interpreted and implemented is subject to cultural opinion and moral relativity. Those watching with wisdom can only mourn what is occurring and question whether these decisions are "revelation," or simply the outcome of opinion polling and political compromise.

2010: Slippery Slope

"A newly published compilation of LDS guidelines — used by all church leaders worldwide when dealing with their members — has softened the language about gay Mormons.
The book, known as the Church Handbook of Instructions, lays out the Utah-based faith's policies on everything from baptism to running a worship service to counseling troubled marriage partners....Like most recent LDS Church statements, this new handbook makes a clear distinction between same-sex orientation and behavior. It eliminates the suggestion, mentioned in the previous 2006 edition, that same-sex relationships "distort loving relationships" and that gays should repent of their "homosexual thoughts or feelings." It also says that celibate gay Mormons who are worthy and qualified in every other way should be allowed to have callings or church assignments, and to participate fully in temple rituals."
Salt Lake Tribune, *Updated LDS Handbook Softens Language on Gays* [503]

In May of 2013 the Boy Scouts of America changed their policy to openly accept gay scouts into their troops. The church determined to support the change.

2013: Boy Scout Sell-Out

"For the past 100 years, The Church of Jesus Christ of Latter-day Saints has enjoyed a strong relationship with Boy Scouts of America, based on our mutual interest in helping boys and young men understand and live their duty to God and develop upright moral behavior.

As the Church moves forward in its association with the Boy Scouts of America, Church leaders will continue to seek the most effective ways to address the diverse needs of young people in the United States and throughout the world. The Church's long-established policy for participation in activities is stated in the basic instructional handbook used by lay leaders of the Church: "young men …who agree to abide by Church standards" are "welcomed warmly and encouraged to participate." This policy applies to Church-sponsored Scout units. Sexual orientation has not previously been—and is not now—a disqualifying factor for boys who want to join Latter-day Saint Scout troops. Willingness to abide by standards of behavior continues to be our compelling interest. These standards are outlined in the booklet For the Strength of Youth and include abstinence from sexual relationships. We remain firmly committed to upholding these standards and to protecting and strengthening boys and young men."
LDS Newsroom, *Church Responds to Boy Scouts Policy Vote* [504]

It is not honest to imply that accepting the changes made by the Boy Scouts represents no change in church policy. To support the change sent an implied message to the world that the Mormon church is softening its stance against homosexuality.

"Mormons Endorse Plan to Admit Gay Scouts"
New York Times, *Mormons Endorse Plan to Admit Gay Scouts* [505]

"LDS Church Accepts New Boy Scout Policy on Gay Members"
Christian Post, *LDS Church Accepts New Boy Scout Policy on Gay Members* [506]

In reality, there is no neutrality concerning this issue, and no middle ground to be found through "reasonable compromise." The Lord *"cannot look upon sin with the least degree of allowance,"* (D&C 1:31), and neither should we.

It is important to acknowledge that some of God's children are born with homosexual tendencies and urges. These psychological aspects are categorically similar to the varied weaknesses present in every human being. In reality, each of us sins and falls short of the glory of God. But regardless of the specific weaknesses and deficits, all can be overcome through Jesus Christ! Each of us arrives on this earth with specific life path issues to face and conquer! Even more destructive than pretending homosexuality is not a sin, is the insidious message that it cannot be overcome in Christ.

When God Calls…He Calls in Love

"Let me share my testimony, as I tell how God called me out of homosexuality. I believe that what God has done for me, He can also do for you. If you are struggling with homosexuality, I'm living proof that there is hope through Jesus Christ.
Janet Boynes, *Called out* [507]

Until an individual has experienced a good friend or family member succumbing to- or choosing the gay or bi-sexual lifestyle, the complexity of this moral issue may be underestimated. Many of those choosing to be involved in homosexual relationships have experienced horrific abuse as a child, or a lack of solid parenting in their lives. None of these valid aspects of the problem changes the reality that God has given us commandments which have been crafted for our personal long- term happiness.

Wisdom requires being patient and loving, but also taking a firm stand against the ignorance of society. For in reality, eternal law cannot be changed to appease the masses.

Natural Law

For this cause God gave them up unto vile affections: for even their women did change the natural use into that which is against nature: And likewise also the men, leaving the natural use of the woman, burned in their lust one toward another; men with men working that which is unseemly, and receiving in themselves that recompence of their error which was meet.
Romans 1:26-27

In the 2006 policy manual, the church suggests that gays should repent of their *"homosexual thoughts and feelings."* [508] How subtle and sad it is that the current manual no longer encourages this effort, even though the core of all sin remains internal.

Thou shalt love thy wife with all thy heart, and shalt cleave unto her and none else. And he that looketh upon a woman to lust after her shall deny the faith, and shall not have the Spirit; and if he repents not he shall be cast out.
D&C 42:22-23

If lusting upon another woman and not repenting is a sin worthy of being cast out, then surely lusting upon another person of the same gender is also of considerable significance. The root of the problem is spiritual and internal—not just behavioral. For the church to try to soften the definition of sin by now focusing primarily on external behavior could be the seed of a future "sell-out."

283

2013: Where the Church Stands (currently)

"The experience of same-sex attraction is a complex reality for many people. The attraction itself is not a sin, but acting on it is. Even though individuals do not choose to have such attractions, they do choose how to respond to them. With love and understanding, the Church reaches out to all God's children, including our gay and lesbian brothers and sisters."

Mormonsandgays.org

The requirement and opportunity to love all people is part of the Christ path, and the natural response demonstrated by anyone who has tasted the mercy of Jesus Christ. The deception promoted in this misleading argument centers around what truly represents "love?" Satan has succeeded in convincing the general public that "love" equates with moral and legal acceptance.

In contrast, the gospel of Jesus Christ requires we love the offender by providing an ongoing invitation to change and repent. This occurs by demonstrating true compassion, wise patience, and an ongoing hope that all of those entangled in this sin will yet find victory in Christ.

In response to the idea that requiring repentance is "judgmental," there is an old prayer that says, "Please God forgive me for sinning in different ways than other people do." This type of approach allows the disciple to focus on his or her own sins-and avoid judgment, while still being loyal to the truth of God's law.

The reality that homosexual tendencies are complicated and difficult to overcome does not change the fact that through the Lord Jesus Christ all things can be done! (Philippians 4:13).

In 1993, the *Association of Mormon Counselors and Psychotherapists* published a scientific journal titled, *"Understanding Homosexuality."* LDS therapists provided perspective and research which focused on treating homosexuality and assisting clients who wanted to transcend the gay lifestyle. In addition to challenging the liberal propaganda being actively promoted, editors of the journal pointed out that explaining alternative perspectives, (which were aligned with the gospel of Jesus Christ), was desperately needed.

"The topic of homosexuality is controversial. I am sure we will not please everyone with the contents of this issue. Some will probably say, "It isn't balanced enough. You only represent one perspective." Perhaps this is true, but my response is, "The professional literature is not balanced. Only one perspective gets published right now-the gay affirmative one. Someone needs to present alternative perspectives."
P. Scott Richards, *Editorial* [509]

Twenty years later, those who analyze religious trends can only wonder what happened to that desperately needed message. Do we as a people bluntly, honestly, and lovingly speak the truth? Or do we cower in the fear that being misrepresented and persecuted will result in bad public relations? Who remains willing to cry out to all the world that homosexuality remains a serious sin that can be overcome in Jesus Christ? Is the LDS church providing that voice today?

President Kimball was willing in 1969 when he wrote *The Miracle of Forgiveness* and taught, *"Let it therefore be clearly stated that the seriousness of the sin of homosexuality is equal to or greater than that of fornication or adultery…"*[510]

When the church today instead chooses to water down the message, it appears it is trying to buy friends and appease enemies. Sending mixed messages may seem more "loving," but it can also distract those struggling with same-gender attraction from the Atonement of Christ.

Protestants Embracing Freedom

"Former homosexuals joyfully point to one definitive Scripture that mentions them and the redemptive process they are embracing: "Neither fornicators, nor idolaters, nor adulterers, nor homosexuals, nor sodomites … will inherit the kingdom of God. And such were some of you. But you were washed, but you were sanctified, but you were justified in the name of the Lord Jesus and by the Spirit of our God." (1 Corinthians 6:9-11). When I met and married my wife, Dee, almost 12 years ago, she and I both were clueless about what my post-homosexual life would be like. As painful as my past sin was to me, my wife was not the cause of my change; rather, she was the fruit of my change... Our responsibility as Christians is to pour love out without measure on those who struggle to overcome homosexuality. Compassion was the hallmark of the Chief Shepherd, and as His disciples, we should be characterized by it too as we encourage them to embrace the freedom Christ offers."
Pastor D.L. Foster, *Sex, Lies, and the Gay Debate* [511]

Complete and Permanent Change

"I came out of homosexuality after a powerful encounter with Jesus Christ and a desire to serve and obey Him. I can say with complete honesty that I NEVER have homosexual desires of any sort - physical or emotional."
Ex-lesbian Yvette Cantu Schneider, *Americans for Truth about Homosexuality* [512]

Instead of helping homosexuals turn to Jesus Christ for repair and healing, many in the United States have decided to accept and even promote the gay lifestyle. Under the guise of "social justice," the tragedy of gay marriage is now overtaking the country.

"Gay Marriage Approval Continues Sweep Across the Country" [513]

In the near future, the so-called "fundamental rights" of homosexuals will likely be used to assault religious freedom. The black robes sitting on the bench of the Supreme Court may eventually make catastrophic decisions affecting morality in America and the Church.

The Fight for Religious Freedom

"My dear young friends, I am pleased to speak to this BYU-Idaho audience…
I ask your understanding as I speak to a very diverse audience. In choosing my subject
I have relied on an old military maxim that when there is a battle underway, persons who desire
to join the fray should "march to the sound of the guns." So it is that I invite you to march with
me as I speak about religious freedom under the United States Constitution. There is a battle over
the meaning of that freedom. The contest is of eternal importance, and it is your generation
that must understand the issues and make the efforts to prevail."
Dallin H. Oaks, *Religious Freedom* [514]

During the past decade, relentless propaganda from the media, as well as numerous legal setbacks, have combined to sway public opinion. Initially, true Christians fought to maintain God's definition of marriage, but now after years of struggle, many churches are starting to capitulate to the corruption.

Setting a Dangerous Precedent

"In the Church News there is an article about religious freedom being eroded by encroaching social
and cultural "rights" which conflict with religious freedom. The case of Perry v. Schwartzenegger
in California, which challenges the Proposition 8 vote was cited by Elder Lance Wickman, the Church's
General Counsel (lawyer). In that case the public's decision to prohibit same-sex marriage is being
challenged on the basis that voters cannot negate a fundamental right. The Church is alarmed about
the growing potential for conflict between social and cultural "rights" on the one hand, and the free
exercise of religion on the other. The deeper problem the Church has with their position on this legal
conflict in California, is the position taken on the Salt Lake City ordinance the Church endorsed several
weeks ago. In that decision, the Church announced that employment and housing were "fundamental
rights" which same-sex attraction could not forfeit. The Church endorsed the use of coercive governmental
power to compel employers and property owners to permit homosexual employees and renters,
upon pain of punishment by the Courts. This was an extraordinary departure from past positions
of the Church, and represented the first time the Church approved governmental compulsion against
employers and property owners to protect homosexual conduct. The effect of the Church's change in view
on the Salt Lake City ordinance was almost immediate. A follow-on state-wide survey after the Church's
changed position showed that there was a dramatic shift in Utah's view of tolerance toward homosexual
behavior. Essentially, Mormons all over Utah fell in line behind the Church's new attitude.
Now the Church is attempting to sound the alarm about legal encroachment of cultural/social views
(read homosexuality) into other areas which will inevitably conflict with religious liberty.
But the Church has already conceded the argument. By extension of the Church's position with respect
to housing and employment, the only question to answer is what to define as a "fundamental right."

If housing and employment, then why not marriage? How does that distinction get made? And if any judge, anywhere, or ultimately five of the nine Supreme Court Justices, decide that marriage is a "fundamental right," then the result will follow that religion cannot prevent the practice. And if religion cannot prevent the practice of this "fundamental right" to marry despite a couple's homosexual orientation, then the LDS Church cannot prohibit or limit homosexual marriage practices anywhere. Not even in their own marriage ceremonies. For to do so would invade a "fundamental right" of the persons involved. It will take time for the arguments to wend their way through the courts. But ultimately the Church's position on the "fundamental right" of homosexuals to be employed and housed without discrimination, using the coercive force of the government to protect that "right" against employers and property owners, will be the same reason the government will force the LDS Church to be coerced into acceptance of homosexual marriage. The LDS Church's own words/press release and public relations spokesman's words will be the reason cited by the Court against the Church, at the time the decision is reached. The Court will announce that the LDS Church has already recognized the need for governmental power to be used to protect fundamental rights of housing and employment. The Court will rule the Church must, therefore, accept as a fundamental right marriage, as well."
Denver Snuffer, *Social and Cultural "Rights"* [515]

If Satan is able to use corrupt judges to force gay marriage upon the LDS church, the day of moral destruction will have fully arrived. In an effort to avoid this scenario, it seems the church has backed away from its original and unapologetic stand for truth, and is now only arguing for "fairness" and a "religious exemption."

"Mormons Join Hawaii's Gay-Marriage Fight, But With A New Approach" [516]

In September of 2013, LDS leaders wrote a letter to church members in Hawaii who were about to vote on gay marriage. In the letter they stated, *"Whether or not you favor the proposed change, we hope that you will urge your elected representatives to include in any such legislation a strong exemption for people and organizations of faith. Such an exemption should: "Protect religious organizations and officials from being required to support or perform same-sex marriages or from having to host same-sex marriages or celebrations in their facilities; and "Protect individuals and small businesses from being required to assist in promoting or celebrating same-sex marriages."[517]*

Currently those who control the U.S. government are obsessed with promoting gay marriage. State by state, law by law, gay marriage is being forced upon the people through legislation and the legal system. In liberal states, a majority of people are voting to legalize gay marriage, and in conservative states where citizens want to maintain traditional values, activist judges are forcing acceptance of gay marriage by legislating from the bench.

"Same Sex Marriage Imposed on Utah" [518]

And now behold, I say unto you, that the foundation of the destruction of this people is beginning to be laid by the unrighteousness of your lawyers and your judges.

Alma 10:27

Legally inconsistent rulings concerning this issue have placed the nation at the edge of moral destruction. The same church that once bluntly and openly condemned homosexuality, is now depending on other judges to rectify the legal oppression enacted.

The Writing on the Wall

The Church of Jesus Christ of Latter-day Saints issued the following statement Friday after a court ruling on same-sex marriage in Utah: The Church has been consistent in its support of traditional marriage while teaching that all people should be treated with respect.
This ruling by a district court will work its way through the judicial process.
We continue to believe that voters in Utah did the right thing by providing clear direction in the state constitution that marriage should be between a man and a woman and we are hopeful that this view will be validated by a higher court.
LDS Newsroom, *Church Statement on Court Ruling Regarding Same-Sex Marriage in Utah*[519]

It seems essential to ask, what will we do as a church and as a people when it becomes "illegal" to obey the gospel of Jesus Christ? What will happen if and when the Supreme Court rules gay marriage is a constitutional right, and that all churches must marry homosexuals or be charged with "discrimination?"[520] Will we as a people stand strong in the face of intense persecution? Have we in the past? Do we know our own history in relation to Zion, blacks and the priesthood, blood atonement, avenging the death of Joseph Smith, plural marriage, our definition of "God," and a host of other teachings that were too unpopular to maintain?

Legal Corruption leads to Religious Betrayal

Stages of Betrayal

Stout proclamation for truth: (Proclamation on the Family)
Dismay at the moral collapse: (Response to Supreme Court decision)
Attempts at compromise and political bargaining: (SLC ordinance)
Omission of a blunt call to repentance: (Hawaiian vote on gay marriage)
Subtle acceptance: (Accepting Boy Scout policy change)
Betrayal of eternal truth: (Future religious rationalizations?)

Those who believe it is always appropriate to obey the laws of the land should remember that "legal" does not necessarily mean "moral." (see Truth #43). No matter what various governments enact throughout the world, the church should choose to stand strong for God's truth. This is what makes the changes in church attitude and policy so disturbing. (See mormonsandgays.com).

What will the Lord's church do when it becomes illegal to obey the gospel of Jesus Christ?

What has the church done in the past?

What will you do?

Younger members of the church seem to be buying into Satan's deceptions. In relation to Mormons becoming more *"tolerant,"* the *Salt Lake Tribune* reported, *"When Salt Lake City embraced anti-discrimination ordinances for gay and transgender residents last fall snagging a landmark endorsement by the LDS Church and widespread support from city officials more shifted than public policy. Public opinion throughout Utah jumped, too. Support for some gay rights, short of marriage, climbed 11 percentage points across the state from a year ago, according to a new Salt Lake Tribune poll, and shot up by 10 percent among Mormons. Two-thirds of Utahns (67 percent) favor employment protections and safeguards for same-sex couples such as hospital visitation and inheritance rights, up from 56 percent in January 2009, when pollsters asked the same question…Opposition dropped, overall, from 40 percent to 23 percent. Among LDS respondents, it plummeted from 48 percent to 28 percent. 'This isn't a gradual change of attitudes. This is a fairly dramatic jump,' says Matthew Burbank, chairman of the University of Utah's political science department. 'Clearly, the fact that the LDS Church was officially endorsing this position had an impact on people."* [521]

Similar to other moral-political choices made by the institution during the past 185 years, it seems realistic to expect that another day of decision will face the church. The choice will again center around denying God and His eternal gospel, or standing faithful in the face of intense persecution. The decision will be made on an individual and institutional level, but the reciprocity coming from that decision is not negotiable.

Behold, vengeance cometh speedily upon the inhabitants of the earth, a day of wrath,
a day of burning, a day of desolation, of weeping, of mourning, and of lamentation;
and as a whirlwind it shall come upon all the face of the earth, saith the Lord.
And upon my house shall it begin, and from my house shall it go forth, saith the Lord;
First among those among you, saith the Lord, who have professed to know my name and have not
known me, and have blasphemed against me in the midst of my house, saith the Lord.
D&C 112:24-26

This author prophesies in the name of Jesus Christ, that an era of monumental decision is coming upon the church and its members. The complexities that have already begun to divide the wheat from the tares will continue to increase until Babylon falls. Most reading this text will live to see issues of great moral significance face America and the LDS Church.

"Because of pride, and because of false teachers, and false doctrine, their churches have become corrupted, and their churches are lifted up; because of pride they are puffed up."
2 Nephi 28:12

Pride is replaced with humility and awe when we sense that everything the Holy Father and Mother does is abundantly creative! The essence of Eternal life itself includes magnificent and universal expansion. In God, the divine masculine and the divine feminine unify to reign supreme! This is the "yin and yang" of all reality—which together comprise a glory, light, and magnification which is incompatible with the sin of homosexuality.

In contrast, everything within the realm of evil is divisive and constrictive. Darkness is a mutation that hides and destroys, minimizes and distorts...For America to embrace gay marriage and consider it a "constitutional right" is a twisted perspective that invites heavenly correction. (D&C 86:5). For the church to play both sides of the fence will not work and is another sign of our Latter Day Apostasy.

Into the Wilderness
Verily, thus saith the Lord unto you my servants, concerning the parable of the wheat
and of the tares: Behold, verily I say, the field was the world, and the apostles were the sowers
of the seed; And after they have fallen asleep the great persecutor of the church, the apostate,
the whore, even Babylon, that maketh all nations to drink of her cup, in whose hearts the enemy,
even Satan, sitteth to reign—behold he soweth the tares; wherefore, the tares choke the wheat
and drive the church into the wilderness.
D&C 86:2-3

In relation to the sin of homosexuality, as well as many other spiritual-political issues, each of us will individually determine whether they will fade into the wilderness of apostasy, or stand firm for God and His unchanging truth! Those who determine to honor the cause of Christ must be prepared to sacrifice and suffer for His Holy name.

No Persecution = No Perfection

"The Lord's church will not be persecuted into oblivion. The only reason we have peace and calm is because of our wickedness. Nothing more. We are at one with the exchangers.
We need persecution and suffering in this existence to reach perfection as a society.
We need the separation and division that the word of God brings. As Paul said, our suffering brings perfection. And as Joseph said true prophets have never existed without it.
As Alma said, all those who desire to follow Christ must come out from the wicked, be separate, touch not unclean things. As Gentiles, our scenario and calling is not presently to cover the earth anyway. It is to gather out the elect from the wicked. From Daniel's vision of the stone cut without hands, the stone doesn't grow and fill the earth until after the destruction of Babylon. Throughout history the doctrine of God is that a small group of people stand up for what is right and spend their lives defending it and their families. When this people rise up, becoming better in heart and mind, stronger in character, and choose to get out of Babylon, the Lord will prepare a cloud by day and a pillar of fire by night to protect them. I want no other society than this."
Dan Mead, *Nothing Less Will Do* [522]

Some will stand tall for the Lord, but be knocked low into the ground. Others will be deceived and surrender to the whims of the culture. Reviewing the recent concessions of the corporate church in relation to *several* moral and political issues, and then comparing those choices to the Book of Mormon, reveals the political maneuvering of the institution can no longer be fully trusted as representing "God's will." The wheat of the church perceive this reality, but ironically are then deemed to be the "apostates."

Sending Mixed Messages

"Since BYU is run by the Church and has the First Presidency and Quorum of the Twelve as its Board of Directors...If you oppose having Dick Cheney at BYU to receive an Honorary Doctorate for "Humanitarian Service"...or Zbigniew Brzezinski (co-founder of the Trilateral Commission with David Rockefeller) speaking to highly impressionable BYU students...
If you wonder why the prophet is dedicating a new Zion's bank financial complex...
If you wonder why the Church decided to side with the homosexuals on legislation against "discrimination" in housing in Salt Lake City...If you oppose illegal amnesty and the open border policy...If you question or disagree with the Church's position on any issue the Church has injected itself into in our Babylonian culture...
then brother....you are an apostate."
Jim Uhl, *Political Apostasy* [523]

Monumental choices are now being presented within the Mormon culture. The core of these spiritual, political, and moral decisions is simple: Truth or acceptance? Persecution or popularity? Freedom or control? Babylon or Zion? The choice is yours.

A Day of Decision

"Are we to go hand and glove with the world? No, we are not of the world; God has chosen us out of the world to be His people, that we may be subject to His laws and bow to His authority."

Brigham Young, *Journal of Discourses* [524]

"God will have a humble people. Either we can choose to be humble or we can be compelled to be humble. Alma said, Blessed are they who humble themselves without being compelled to be humble. Let us choose to be humble. (Alma 32:16)."
Ezra Taft Benson, *Beware of Pride* [525]

A wise seminary teacher once taught, *"the world is struggling and we are struggling with the world."* [526] The core of this challenge seems to be our inability-or unwillingness, to separate ourselves from Babylon and come unto the Lord Jesus Christ with full repentance. This spiritual challenge seems to be particularly prevalent in areas where wealth and political influence are dominant among the Saints.

Our Choice

*"It is not always easy to live in the world and not be a part of it. We cannot live entirely with our own or unto ourselves, nor would we wish to. We must mingle with others. In so doing, we can be gracious. We can be inoffensive. We can avoid any spirit or attitude of self-righteousness. But we can maintain our standards. The natural tendency will be otherwise, and many have succumbed to it. In 1856, when we were largely alone in these valleys, some thought we were safe from the ways of the world. To such talk, President Heber C. Kimball responded: 'I want to say to you, my brethren, the time is coming when we will be mixed up in these now peaceful valleys to that extent that it will be **difficult to tell the face of a Saint from the face of an enemy** to the people of God. Then, brethren,"* he went on, *"look out for the great sieve, **for there will be a great sifting time, and many will fall; for I say unto you there is a test, a Test, a TEST coming, and who will be able to stand?'"***
Gordon B. Hinckley, *Teachings of Gordon B. Hinckley* [527]

Particularly in cities where the Mormon culture has been established the longest, symptoms of pride, vanity, materialism, dishonesty, white-collar crime, bankruptcy, depression, and addiction are increasing. Political maneuvering, acquiring material gain, and seeking social acceptance, appear to have become mainstays in wealthy areas. Like a virus, the depravity of the world has infected many within America. This slow and steady decline among members is rooted in trying to please both God and mammon—and is exactly what the prophets warned would occur.

Falling with Babylon

"Instead of raising themselves to the standard of the Gospel, they are content to descend to the level of the wicked and corrupt. Many of the Elders of Israel who have responsibilities resting upon them, with which they will find they cannot trifle with impunity, are taking this course all the time. What wonder, then, that the Spirit of the Lord is grieved? What wonder that the Latter-day Saints need to be preached to continually? It is no wonder to me when I contemplate the condition of the people of these valleys, and especially Salt Lake City, Ogden, and our cities contiguous to the railways."
Joseph F. Smith, *Journal of Discourses* [528]

It can be observed that many who live along the Wasatch Front are good people living a decent life. However, the Lord did not invite His people to simply build up another large metropolitan city. In relation to Babylon, we have been commanded to *come out of her, my people, that ye be not partakers of her sins, and that ye receive not of her plagues.* (Revelations 18:4). For people who have been invited to come unto Zion, to then instead embrace, integrate, and even promote the ways of the world, is not an inconsequential choice.

What To Do?

"Our sons and daughters must live pure lives so as to be prepared for what is coming.
*After a while **the gentiles will gather by the thousands to this place, and Salt Lake City will be classed among the wicked cities of the world. A spirit of speculation and extravagance will take possession of the Saints, and the results will be financial bondage. Persecution comes next** and all true Latter-day Saints will be tested to the limit. **Many will apostatize and others will be still not knowing what to do.** Darkness will cover the earth and gross darkness the minds of the people. The judgments of God will be poured out on the wicked to the extent that **our Elders from far and near will be called home,** or in other words the gospel will be taken from the Gentiles and later on carried to the Jews."*
Heber C. Kimball [529]

Social patterns recorded in scripture (Helaman 12), as well as numerous dreams and visions reported by those with spiritual gifts (Joel 2), confirm to all that enabling sin will eventually result in accumulative destruction. (D&C 112). Both prophecy and common sense remind us that an intensified call to repentance is needed throughout the world and within the church.

And thus we see that except the Lord doth chasten his people with many afflictions, yea, except he doth visit them with death and with terror, and with famine and with all manner of pestilence, they will not remember him.
Helaman 12:3

We must love everyone and avoid casting stones of judgment. Simultaneously, it must be acknowledged that sin brings suffering and that God will not be mocked. As recipients of the Lord's gospel, we cannot forget the sacred invitation to become a Zion people. (see Truth #68).

To assist us in fulfilling our divine heritage, God will invite the Mormons through "tough love" to come back to Jesus Christ and receive a true fullness. According to scripture, this divine invitation will manifest first among those who have blasphemed against the Lord in His house.

*Verily, verily, I say unto you, **darkness covereth the earth, and gross darkness the minds of the people, and all flesh has become corrupt before my face.** Behold, vengeance cometh speedily upon the inhabitants of the earth, a day of wrath, a day of burning, a day of desolation, of weeping, of mourning, and of lamentation... **And upon my house shall it begin, and from my house shall it go forth, saith the Lord; First among those among you, saith the Lord, who have professed to know my name and have not known me, and have blasphemed against me in the midst of my house, saith the Lord.** Therefore... purify your hearts before me; and then go ye into all the world, and preach my gospel unto every creature who has not received it.*
Doctrine and Covenants 112:23-28

This warning is directed to those who profess to know His name, but do not really know Him. In connection with this prophecy, those who pretend to speak for the Lord-when in reality they do not, are guilty of "taking the Lord's name in vain."

"False prophets claim they speak for the Lord, but He has not spoken to them. (Eze.13:6-8).
God intends to deal with the false prophets, and as a result all will know that He is the Lord. (Eze. 13:9).
Those false prophets who cry "peace" when there is no peace will be overthrown and
a great, violent storm will overtake them. (Eze. 13:10-14). They had become a wild vine,
not bringing forth fruit worthy to preserve, and therefore, were to be burned. (Eze. 15:6-8).
The false prophets who led them were only interested in feeding themselves, getting praise and
amassing power. They were not interested in teaching righteousness. (Eze 22: 25-26).
They claimed to speak for the Lord when the Lord had never spoken to them. They used the Lord's name
to oppress people. (Eze. 22: 28-29). But the destruction which would come upon them would
leave them astonished, even drunk with the desolation that was to come (Eze. 23:32-34)."
Denver Snuffer, *Passing the Heavenly Gift* [530]

Thus the sin of blaspheming in the midst of the Lord's house will eventually result in destruction in Utah, as well as other corrupted areas of the church.

A Sign of the Destruction To Come

"On August 11, 1999, an F2 tornado touched down in the metropolitan area of Salt Lake City.
The tornado lasted ten minutes and killed one person, injured more than 80 people, and caused more than
$170 million in damages. It was the most destructive tornado in Utah's history,
and awakened the entire state's population to the fact that the Beehive State does experience tornadoes."
National Weather Service, *A Scientific Report* [531]

In truth, the "beginning of the end" will start in Utah. (D&C 112:23-28). After the Lord cleanses His house, the devastation will spread into heavily populated areas throughout America and the world.

Large Cities

And this work of destruction did also continue in the seventy and fifth year. For the earth was
smitten that it was dry, and did not yield forth grain in the season of grain; and the whole earth
was smitten, even among the Lamanites as well as among the Nephites, so that they were smitten
that they did perish by thousands in the more wicked parts of the land.
Helaman 11:6

When chaos and anarchy begin in the large cities, the basic need for food, water, and shelter will overwhelm millions. Fear and selfishness will result in constant turmoil and irrational violence. Horrific trauma will afflict the innocent as terrified children suffer for the sins of their parents.

Ether was a prophet of the Lord…and began to prophesy unto the people, for he could not be restrained because of the Spirit of the Lord which was in him. For he did cry from the morning, even until the going down of the sun, exhorting the people to believe in God unto repentance lest they should be destroyed…And it came to pass that Ether did prophesy great and marvelous things unto the people, which they did not believe, because they saw them not.
Ether 12:2-5

History teaches that during times of spiritual decline, a subtle division grows between those who will listen, demonstrate faith, and take action, and those who simply will not heed the warnings. When the cleansing begins, it will shock the masses, but their lack of preparedness will not stop the economic hardship, earthquakes, terrorism, and plagues.

A Desolating Sickness

"I was immediately in Salt Lake City wandering about the streets in all parts of the City and on the door of every house I found a badge of mourning, and I Could not find a house but what was in mourning. It seemed strange to me that I saw no person [on] the street in my wandering about through the City. They seemed to be in their houses with their Sick and Dead. I saw no funeral procession, or any thing of that kind, but the City looked very Still and quiet as though the people were praying and had control of the disease what ever it was. I then looked in all directions over the Territory, East west North and South, and I found the same mourning in every place throughout the Land."
John Taylor, *Spiritual Survival in the Last Days* [532]

In 2005, President Gordon B. Hinkley fortified the Tabernacle on Temple Square to withstand a severe earthquake. This practical preparation is congruent with those who have seen in vision the Wasatch Front being afflicted with multiple earthquakes and severe flooding.

Regardless of how and when the Lord cleanses His church, all who now currently live in Utah can prepare for the upcoming atrocities by "pre-determining" they will leave the area when directed by the Holy Spirit. Similar to Lehi and Nephi, those willing to act in faith can be warned to flee prior to the destruction. Others may also be directed to stay, either to serve and protect others, or possibly find safety in the temples.

*"…in the summer of 1862 the foundation of the Salt Lake temple, owing to some defect in its structure, was taken out and re-laid. Considering the fact that the foundation was 16 feet deep, and 16 feet broad; and that the building is 186 1/2 feet by 99 feet—this was no small undertaking; and nine years had been occupied in laying it. **President Young said he expected this temple to stand through the millennium,** and the brethren would go in and give the endowments to the people during that time; "and this," he added, **"is the reason why I am having the foundation of the temple taken up."***
B. H. Roberts, *A Comprehensive History of The Church of Jesus Christ of Latter-day Saints* [533]

In truth, a day of desolation and separation is coming. *"For all flesh is corrupted before me; and the powers of darkness prevail upon the earth, among the children of men, in the presence of all the hosts of heaven-which causeth silence to reign, and all eternity is pained, and the angels are waiting the great command to reap down the earth, to gather the tares that they may be burned…"*(D&C 38:11-12).

Some souls actually look forward to the cleansing, not because they desire for their brethren to suffer, but because their hunger for Zion is so intense. Thankfully, it is the Lord who decides when, where, and how His people are to be spiritually strengthened.

Those who act in His humility and power, will then be blessed to succeed as they perform the bidding of the Lord.

*"We shall yet face greater perils, we shall yet be tested with more severe trials, and we shall yet weep more tears of sorrow than we have ever known before… We tremble because of the **sorrows and wars and plagues** that shall cover the earth. We weep for **those in the true Church who are weak and wayward and worldly and who fall by the wayside as the caravan of the kingdom rolls forward**…"*
Bruce R. McConkie, *General Conference* [534]

*"**There will be a people raised up**, if we will not be that people—*
there will yet be a people raised up whose lives will embody in perfection the revelations...
*and **such a people will have to be raised up before Zion can be fully redeemed,***
and before the work of our God can be fully established in the earth."
George Q. Cannon, *Journal of Discourses* [535]

Due to our ongoing condemnation and the reality of collective free agency, some have wondered if there is still time for us to become a pure and holy people? Will darkness overtake the earth before Zion can be established? And how many Saints today are even seeking a true fullness of the gospel?

Although asking these questions may seem justified, the Lord's remnant can find hope, as well as a partial answer from Apostle Orson Pratt who stated, *"in the midst of all these conflicting opinions, the humble servant of God comes forth and boldly declares with authority that **all the promises of Jesus will be fulfilled** while there is one believer upon the face of the earth to be perfected and saved."*[536]

Regardless of how severe the persecution and destruction becomes, and no matter how small Zion's population in numbers may be, *"the words of the Lord, which have been spoken by the holy prophets, shall all be fulfilled; and ye need not say that the Lord delays his coming unto the children of Israel. And ye need not imagine in your hearts that the words which have been spoken are vain, for behold, the Lord will remember his covenant which he hath made unto his people of the house of Israel."* (3 Nephi 29:2-3).

Currently, God is preparing a meek and humble people to fulfill His prophecies. As spiritual history marches forward, the valiant must remember that overwhelming oppression and sorrow does not mean truth and goodness have lost. As stated previously, ***God provides and/or allows various experiences to occur that we might heal and transcend all ungodliness within ourselves.***

Wherefore, be not weary in well-doing, for ye are laying the foundation of a great work.
And out of small things proceedeth that which is great. Behold, the Lord requireth the heart
and a willing mind; and the willing and obedient shall eat the good of the land of Zion
in these last days.
Doctrine and Covenants 64:33-34

The wheat can find hope and comfort in knowing that the Gentiles will not be utterly destroyed. (2 Nephi 30:1). And that *a remnant of Ephraim shall survive and assist in carrying forth the gospel unto the House of Israel.* (see Truth #37). Those appointed and ordained to fulfill prophecy can have faith that God will indeed protect His people. This includes those who will personally dwell within the peace and safety of Zion, be present in the flesh to welcome the return of the Ten Tribes, and shout praises to God at the joyful return of Enoch's City. (Moses 7:63).

And righteousness and truth will I cause to sweep the earth as with a flood, to gather out
mine elect from the four quarters of the earth, unto a place which I shall prepare, an Holy City, that my
people may gird up their loins, and be looking forth for the time of my coming;
for there shall be my tabernacle, and it shall be called Zion, a New Jerusalem.
And the Lord said unto Enoch: Then shalt thou and all thy city meet them there, and we will receive them
into our bosom, and they shall see us; and we will fall upon their necks,
and they shall fall upon our necks, and we will kiss each other;
And there shall be mine abode, and it shall be Zion.

Moses 7:62-64

Unite to Survive

"In this dispensation there is a principle or commandment peculiar to it. What is that?
*It is **the gathering of the people to one place**. The gathering of this people is as necessary to be observed by believers, as faith, repentance, baptism, or any other ordinance. **It is an essential part of the Gospel of this dispensation,** as much so as the necessity of building an ark by Noah for his deliverance, was a part of the Gospel in his dispensation."*
Brigham Young, *Journal of Discourses* [537]

Today, the LDS Church invites all to come unto Christ and enjoy the fellowship of the Saints. However, the message sent out today is not to "gather unto Zion," but rather to come and "join the church."

"And so today the Lord's people are gathering "out from among the nations"
as they gather into the congregations and stakes of the Church of Jesus Christ of Latter Day Saints...
The Lord calls upon us to be beacons of righteousness to guide those who
seek the safety and blessings of Zion."
D. Todd Christofferson, *Come to Zion* [538]

Missionary work could be considered a type of "institutional gathering," but referring to our LDS wards and branches as if they were "Zion," is offensive to the light and glory of true Zion.

With the World

"How can we say that there is any protection for saints in teaching watered down and false doctrines, scattering the saints, teaching idol worship and using Zion's resources to build up Babylon?
Where do we get the notion that the job of a prophet is to protect the church? If by protect you mean warn I could see that. The only protection, the only safety, that the saints have available to them is in keeping the commandments, in the Holy One of Israel. The only safety is in becoming clean from the world, not in quietly dispersing amongst them. Oh well, we are gentiles, that's what we do.
The Lord will cleanse us eventually. All the while though, he will plead with us to repent.
We are in the phase that the Lord described as being chastened and tried, that little season. Now we are being chastened. Gathering out and being persecuted is what qualifies us for His protection. Without it we stand to be chastened, driven out from the land of our inheritance. Even now we are being destroyed, chastened and tried. We are at this moment cast out and in bondage. And we will remain as long as we are taught to be in the world, rather then to come out of it and be clean. That is when we will be safe, though the world will be in turmoil and destruction."
Dan Mead, *Cast Out* [539]

Prior to the start of the Civil War, a special invitation was offered to the elect of the Church. The Lord stated, *"Therefore let my servant Joseph Smith, Jun. say unto **the strength of my house...Gather yourselves together unto the land of Zion**, upon the land which...has been **consecrated unto me.**"* (D&C 103:22). Then in 1838 the Lord explained, *"that the **gathering** *together* upon the land of Zion, and upon her stakes, may be for a defense, and **for a refuge from the storm**, and from wrath when it shall be poured out without mixture upon the whole earth." (D&C 115:6).

From history we know that most of the Saints did not accept the invitation to come to Zion. After the death of Joseph Smith, the principle of "gathering" slowly faded from the mindset of the people. By 1859 Apostle Heber C. Kimball was concerned about the loss of focus on gathering and admitted, *"Yes, I feel many times to weep and am sorrowful, and I can hardly sleep at night; and if I had Gabriel's trump, I would speak to the Saints of all nations, and I would say, **Gather! gather!** and do not wait even for a handcart to be made. I feel this in my soul. Do the world believe it? Do the Latter-day Saints believe it? No."* [540]

Despite the reality that to establish a literal Zion requires a literal gathering, the emphasis to unify in holiness was first delayed, and then ignored. Currently the principle has been indefinitely postponed until "further notice."

Changing Focus

"In our day, the Lord has seen fit to provide the blessings of the gospel, including an increased number of temples, in many parts of the world. Therefore, we wish to reiterate the long-standing counsel to members of the Church to remain in their homelands rather than immigrate to the United States. Experience has shown that those who relocate to the United States often encounter language, cultural, and economic challenges, resulting in disappointment and personal and family difficulties."
First Presidency, *Remain in Homelands* [541]

"The place of gathering for the Mexican saints is in Mexico, the place of gathering for the Guatemalan saints is in Guatemala; the place of gathering for the Brazilian saints is in Brazil, and so it goes throughout the length and breadth of the whole earth."
Bruce R. McConkie, *Church News* [542]

Despite the practical reasons the church selected this approach, the principle of a literal gathering remains an essential aspect of the Restoration yet to be fulfilled.

THE GATHERING:

"In various dispensations there are various differences in regard to certain requirements of the Gospel. For instance, in the day of Noah, when he preached the Gospel to the antediluvian world, he was given a special commandment, to build an ark, that in case the people would reject him and the message sent unto them, that himself and all who believed on him might be saved from the destruction that awaited them. In this dispensation there is a principle or commandment peculiar to it. What is that? **It is the gathering the people unto one place. The gathering of this people is as necessary to be observed by believers, as faith, repentance, baptism, or any other ordinance. It is an essential part of the Gospel of this dispensation, as much so, as the necessity of building an ark by Noah, for his deliverance, was a part of the Gospel of his dispensation."**
Brigham Young, Journal of Discourses [543]

If we want to get in the Latter Day ark, we need to be like Noah and separate ourselves from all that is corrupt. Contrary to religious assumption, the current functioning and righteousness of the Mormon mainstream is not sufficient to survive the cleansing and establish Latter Day Zion.

"There are remnant people in every religion, even the Mormon splinter groups , but right now we are like a symphony warming up before the conductor comes, each playing our own squeaky tune. But when the Master comes, we will play beautiful Celestial music together. We can't be gathered until we are mature wheat - until we have repented and become submissive enough to be part of Him - until we live in Him."
Jeanene Custer, *Seeking Zion* [544]

To hear the call, awaken to our difficult situation, and then deepen our personal discipleship, is essential for the literal survival of God's children upon the earth.

"Take away the Book of Mormon and the revelations, and where is our religion? We have none; **for without Zion, and a place of deliverance, we must fall;** *because the time is near when the sun will be darkened, and the moon turn to blood, and the stars fall from the heaven, and the earth reel to and fro. Then, if this is the case,* **and if we are not sanctified and gathered to the places God has appointed…we must fall; we cannot stand; we cannot be saved; for God will gather out his Saints from the Gentiles, and then comes desolation and destruction, and none can escape except the pure in heart who are gathered."**
Joseph Smith, *History of the Church* [545]

True prophets have always invited believers to gather together and spiritually strengthen one another prior to destruction. The most successful example is Enoch, who, over a period of many years, unified an entire city in righteousness. Noah was able to preserve his "family Zion" before the flood destroyed the masses. Moses led the children of Israel out of bondage, and Joseph Smith unified the Saints to some degree in Ohio, Illinois, and Missouri.

This pattern of gathering the righteous prior to destruction will again be implemented when the Lord determines the time is right.

Even so will I gather mine elect from the four quarters of the earth, even as many as will believe in me, and hearken unto my voice.
D&C 33:6

Until the day of the global gathering arrives, believers can individually choose to place themselves under the protection of divine guidance. Obedient disciples have the promise that the Holy Spirit will even now direct them to the appropriate location for their specific family. God will not forget His listening children, but instead will lead them out from among the horrors of Babylon.

As a shepherd seeketh out his flock…among his sheep that are scattered; so will I seek out my sheep, and will deliver them out of all places where they have been scattered in the cloudy and dark day.
Ezekiel 34:12

CHAPTER FIVE: THE FALL OF BABYLON

*And there came one of the seven angels which had the seven vials, and talked with me, saying unto me, Come hither; I will shew unto thee the judgment of **the great whore that sitteth upon many waters:** With whom the **kings** of the earth have committed **fornication**, and the inhabitants of the earth have been made drunk with the wine of her **fornication**. For all nations have drunk of the wine of the wrath of her fornication, and **the kings of the earth have committed fornication with her**, and **the merchants of the earth are waxed rich through the abundance of her delicacies.** And **the kings** of the earth, who have committed **fornication** and lived deliciously with her, shall bewail her, and lament for her, when they shall see the smoke of her burning...*
Revelations 17:1-2, 18:3,9

TRUTH #51 THE FATE OF THE GADIANTONS WILL BE TO FALL INTO THE PIT THEY DUG FOR THE SAINTS. THE GREAT AND ABOMINABLE CHURCH WILL FAIL AND SATAN'S ONE-WORLD ORDER WILL NOT STAND.

"There is no peace on earth. We see evil forces everywhere uniting to destroy the family,
to ridicule morality and decency, to glorify all that is lewd and base. We see wars and plagues
and pestilence. Nations rise and fall. Blood and carnage and death are everywhere.
Gadianton robbers fill the judgment seats in many nations. An evil power seeks to overthrow
the freedom of all nations and countries. Satan reigns in the hearts of men;
it is the great day of his power."
Bruce R. McConkie, *General Conference* [546]

Secretly....subtly....and consistently....America's government is being manipulated away from the principles of a free republic and into the tyranny of socialism, communism, and a one-world order.

Nephi was shown this great and abominable church in vision. (1 Nephi 14:9). This pseudo "church" is described as the *"whore of all the earth"* and the *"mother of all abominations."* (1 Nephi 14:9-10). Those striving to endure the oppression of the beast need to understand that even if Satan's plan appears to be succeeding, in the end, Babylon will fall.

"The time is approaching when the nations will be broken up, on account of their wickedness.
The Latter-day Saints are not going to war against them—they will destroy themselves with their
immorality and abominations. They will quarrel and contend one with another, State with State,
and nation with nation, until they are broken up; and thousands, tens and hundreds of thousands,
will, undoubtedly, come for protection at the hands of the servants of God..."
Lorenzo Snow, *Biography and Family Record of Lorenzo Snow* [547]

Watching the Nephite cycle repeat in America and the Church can be extremely discouraging. Peace is found in the Lord's promise that the wicked will destroy the wicked and eventually fall into "the pit" they dug for the Saints. (1 Nephi 14:3, D&C 109: 25).

THE PIT
And that great pit, which hath been digged for them by that great and abominable church,
which was founded by the devil and his children, that he might lead away the souls of men
down to hell—yea, **that great pit which hath been digged for the destruction of men**
shall be filled by those who digged it, unto their utter destruction...
1 Nephi 14:3

Scripture prepares the faithful to understand that Satan will have his short-term illusion of success, but only to the point of fulfilling the Lord's greater purposes.

*And it came to pass that the angel spake unto me, Nephi, saying: Thou hast beheld that **if the Gentiles repent it shall be well with them**; and thou also knowest concerning the covenants of the Lord unto the house of Israel; and thou also hast heard that **whoso repenteth not must perish.***
1 Nephi 14:5

Ironically, the fruit of Satan's harassment will be the refining of a righteous remnant. This will include true disciples who have been fully sanctified and are prepared to dwell with the Lord Jesus Christ at His Second Coming. (see Truth #74).

*But, behold, I say unto you that **before this great day shall come** the sun shall be darkened, and the moon shall be turned into blood, and the stars shall fall from heaven, and **there shall be greater signs in heaven above and in the earth beneath**; And there shall be weeping and wailing among the hosts of men; And there shall be a great hailstorm sent forth to destroy the crops of the earth. And it shall come to pass, because of the wickedness of the world, that I will take vengeance upon the wicked, for they will not repent; **for the cup of mine indignation is full**; for behold, **my blood shall not cleanse them if they hear me not**. And **the great and abominable church, which is the whore of all the earth, shall be cast down by devouring fire,** according as it is spoken by the mouth of Ezekiel the prophet, who spoke of these things, which have not come to pass but surely must, **as I live, for abominations shall not reign.***
Doctrine and Covenants 29:14-17, 21

For a time it will seem all is lost, but the dark agenda of those who seek total control will eventually struggle and collapse. Those who refuse to align themselves with the mark of the Beast will be pushed to the limit, but in the end God's covenant people will overcome the evil promoted in this sick and suicidal world.

Babylon Falling

"…By-and-by the Spirit of God will entirely withdraw from those Gentile nations, and leave them to themselves…And when that day comes, the Jews will flee to Jerusalem, and those nations will almost use one another up, and those of them who are left will be burned; for that will be the last sweeping judgment that is to go over the earth to cleanse it from wickedness…And I saw there were wars and rumors of wars among the Gentiles, and the angel said to me, Behold the wrath of God is upon the mother of harlots; and when that day comes then shall the work of the Father commence in preparing the way to gather in all his covenant people, and then great Babylon will come down."
Orson Pratt, *Journal of Discourses* [548]

In the end the Globalists will discover they have deluded themselves. Their dark commander will betray them, and their conniving schemes will implode. Then they will be left to acknowledge that the Holy One of Israel is the *only God* who determines the destiny of this earth.

And when that day shall come, it shall come to pass that kings shall shut their mouths; for that which had not been told them shall they see; and that which they had not heard shall they consider. For in that day, for my sake shall the Father work a work, which shall be a great and a marvelous work among them; and there shall be among them those who will not believe it, although a man shall declare it unto them.
3 Nephi 21:8-9

Concerning this prophecy in the Book of Mormon, Denver Snuffer writes, *"Christ is quoting from Isaiah and applying the words to a specific time frame. It is post-gentile receipt of the Book of Mormon, post-delivery of that book to the remnant, and post-opportunity for gentiles to repent and know of the true points of His doctrine. When that happens, the Lord will be freed up to fulfill the covenants of the Father. When the Father's covenants are being fulfilled, "kings shall shut their mouths." That is, the noble of this world will not know what to say. They will be at a loss of words because of the Father's acts. Things that haven't been "told them" will take place, and they will not understand.Things that they never had taught to them will unfold, and they cannot comprehend, cannot get their hands around it all. It will dumbfound them. Even when people who understand that the events are according to the Father's plan, and the Lord's covenant, they will not be able to believe it. Too much! Too distressing! Too unexpected! Too great to take in! It will be confusion and distress, and the idea that God is behind it all will be unbelievable to them. (Isa. 52: 15.) Their plans for managing the world will be dashed and end. Their great investments will be lost. The control they imagined they had as "kings" will fade to dust. (Hag. 2: 22.) How can such splendor, such great and masterful arrangements, such glory in mankind become nothing? How can it all fall to the dust? (Rev. 14: 7-8.) It will be "great and marvelous" because it shows the Father's power and might. But it will be inconvenient and distressing, unbelievable and terrible. (Malachi 4: 1.) What is coming will leave proud men speechless and believing people vindicated. Everything will change."*[549]

The wheat can find peace and strength in knowing that the current political, social, and religious happenings of today are fully known to the Lord. The challenges we face, as well as the solutions we need, are clearly documented in the prophecies of the Book of Mormon.

THE FALL OF THE GREAT AND ABOMINABLE CHURCH

Wherefore, the Lord God will proceed to make bare his arm in the eyes of all the nations,
in bringing about his covenants and his gospel unto those who are of the house of Israel.
Wherefore, he will bring them again out of captivity, and they shall be gathered together to the
lands of their inheritance; and they shall be brought out of obscurity and out of darkness;
and they shall know that the Lord is their Savior and their Redeemer, the Mighty One of Israel.
*And **the blood of that great and abominable church, which is the whore of all the earth,***
shall turn upon their own heads; for they shall war among themselves, and the sword of their
***own hands shall fall upon their own heads,** and they shall be drunken with their own blood.*
And every nation which shall war against thee, O house of Israel, shall be turned one against another,
and they shall fall into the pit which they digged to ensnare the people of the Lord.
And all that fight against Zion shall be destroyed, and that great whore, who hath perverted the
right ways of the Lord, yea, that great and abominable church, shall tumble to the dust and
***great shall be the fall of it.** For behold, saith the prophet, the time cometh speedily that Satan shall have*
*no more power over the hearts of the children of men; for the day soon cometh that all the **proud and they***
***who do wickedly shall be as stubble;** and the day cometh that they must be burned. For the time soon*
cometh that the fullness of the wrath of God shall be poured out upon all the children of men;
*for **he will not suffer that the wicked shall destroy the righteous.***
1 Nephi 22:11-16

> **TRUTH #52** SURVIVING THE FUTURE WILL REQUIRE ACCESSING SPIRITUAL POWERS INTRODUCED IN THE LORD'S HOLY HOUSE. WHEN ACCESS TO LDS TEMPLES IS NO LONGER AVAILABLE, INDIVIDUALS WILL CONTINUE TO UTILIZE DIVINE KNOWLEDGE TO COMMUNE WITH HEAVEN.

Walls of Safety

"Before the Savior comes the world will darken. The time will come when even the elect will begin to lose hope if they do not come often to the temples. I believe that the Saints will come to the temples not only to do vicarious work but also to find a God-given haven of peace. True and faithful Latter-day Saints the world over will long to bring their children to the temple for service and for safety... There are great unseen hosts in the temple. Joseph told the brethren, "And I beheld the temple was filled with angels." (History of the Church, 2:428.) I believe deceased prophets of all dispensations visit the temples. Those who attend the temple will feel their strength and companionship. We will not be alone in the house of the Lord...The Savior will come and honor His people. Those who are prepared and therefore spared on that glorious, triumphant day will be a temple-loving people. They will know Him and see Him "red in his apparel, and his garments like him that treadeth in the wine-vat. . .They will cry out, "Blessed be the name of he that cometh in the name of the Lord. . . . Thou art my God, and I will praise thee: thou art my God, I will exalt thee." (Psalm 118:26, 28.) Then we will all join in one grand hosanna that will ring from one end of eternity to the other, a hosanna shout to God and the Lamb...Those who live in that day—whether that be us, our children, our children's children, or some future generation—will bow down at His feet and worship Him as the Lord of lords, King of kings. They will bathe His feet with their tears, and He will weep and bless them for having suffered through some of the greatest trials ever known to man. His bowels will be filled with compassion, His heart will swell wide as eternity, and He will love them as no mortal can love. He will bring peace that will last a thousand years, and they who have become his children of the covenant will dwell with Him...Let us prepare this special future generation with faith to surmount every trial and every condition. We will do it in our holy, sacred temples. Come, oh, come up to the temples of the Lord and walk in His edifices wherein there is truly "holiness to the Lord...As the evil night darkens on this generation, we must come to the temple for light and safety. Only in the house of the Lord will we find quiet, sacred havens where the storm cannot penetrate. There unseen sentinels watch over us. So it was that the Prophet Joseph pled with God during the dedicatory prayer of the Kirtland Temple: "And we ask thee, Holy Father, that thy servants may go forth from this house [temple] armed with thy power and that thy name may be upon them . . . and thine angels have charge over them." (D&C 109:22.) The Lord has promised: "I will go before your face. I will be on your right hand and on your left, and my Spirit shall be in your hearts, and mine angels round about you, to bear you up." (D&C 84:88.) Surely angelic attendants guard the temples of the Most High God. It is my conviction that as it was in the days of Elisha, so it will be for us: 'Fear not: for they that be with us are more than they that be with them."
Vaughn J. Featherstone, *The Incomparable Christ: Our Master and Model* [550]

When storms rage, famine tortures, crime escalates, and anarchy threatens to destroy the entire earth, God will provide protection for His Saints in the House of the Lord.

307

A Temple Refuge

*"…In light of the **current raging of the adversary**…We do now and will yet face great challenges to the work of the Lord. But like the pioneers who found the place which God for them prepared, so we will fresh courage take, knowing our God will never us forsake. Today temples dot the earth as sacred places of ordinances and covenants, of edification, and of **refuge from the storm**."*
David A. Bednar, *Honorably Hold a name and Standing* [551]

Temple worship blesses participants with access to priesthood keys, sacred altars, and the true order of prayer. Utilizing these spiritual technologies results in the power of God being made manifest! (D&C 84:20-21). During the temple ceremony we are accustomed to being shown these tools and gifts in a "packaged version," but accessing divine power does not always occur in an orthodox manner.

Midnight Worship

"August 27, 1844 Tuesday At 12 o clock at night in company with Mrs. Woodruff, Br A. O. Smoot, Sisters Smoot, and Hannah Ells, we walked to the Temple of the Lord in Nauvoo…After gazing a few moments upon her magnus walls, and examining her capitols which were Completed, standing on the ground, we all as of one accord ascended the ladders unto the top of the walls. Several of the police and friends followed our example, among which was Gen C. C. Rich and Elder Godard. We repaired to the South west corner of the Temple and their in company with Mrs. Woodruff & the above named brethren and sisters, we bowed our knees upon the top corner stone which was prepared to receive its Capitol, And their with up lifted hands towards heaven, I called upon the God of Abraham, Isaac, Jacob and Joseph by Prayer and supplication to except the gratitude of our hearts for his mercies and blessings unto us in preserving our lives giving us power to build the Temple thus far. Prayed that the Saints might have power to finish the Temple according to the pattern given, and accepted at their hands, that the Saints might receive their endowment, and be prepared to plant the work of God in all the world. I asked my heavenly father in the name of Jesus Christ and by virtue of the Holy Priesthood and the Keys of the kingdom of God that he would speedily avenge the blood of Joseph the Prophet Seer and Revelator, and Hiram the Patriarch, which had been shed by the hands of the American gentile nation, upon all the heads of the Nation and State that have aided, abetted or perpetrated the horrid deed, of shedding the blood of those righteous men even the Lords anointed…I prayed that God would preserve our lives and enabled us to fill our mission in righteousness and be enabled to again return to this land and tread the courts of the Lords house in peace and receive blessings at his hand…I dedicated myself my family, and all appertaining unto me, unto God committing my all into his hands for the mission. Praying for his blessing to rest upon me through the mission appointed unto me in the name of Jesus Christ Amen. After Prayers we again descended to the ground returned to our homes with Joy and peace in our hearts."
Wilford Woodruff, *Journal* [552]

The early Saints climbed to the top of the unfinished temple at midnight, praised God with great passion, and then pled with Him to preserve their lives. This pattern of utilizing temple protocols to supplicate God for mercy and protection will be life-saving in the days to come. Petitioning God and His angels for specific assistance will also decrease the likelihood that the Saints will be required to become violent in the defense of their families.

"If this people will take this course, and live their religion in all things, I can prophecy in the name
of Israel's god that you will never have to fire a gun, for the Lord will send his angels
to do the work of destruction among the wicked."
Heber C. Kimball, *Journal of Discourses* [553]

In the House of the Lord participants are taught the pattern for casting out evil-that they might not be hindered in receiving true messengers from Father. Learning how to dismiss the darkness in us, and around us, results in experiencing greater light and power.

Worthy and Protected

*"Faithful, endowed members of the Church who **keep all their covenants** and **properly wear***
*their sacred coverings will be **safe as if protected behind temple walls**. The covenants and ordinances*
*are filled with **faith as a living fire**. In a day of desolating sickness, scorched earth, barren wastes,*
sickening plagues, disease, destruction, and death (see Joel 2:2-6; also D&C 29 and 133),
we as a people will rest in the shade of trees. We will drink from the cooling fountains.
We will abide in places of refuge from the storm. We will mount up as on eagles' wings;
we will be lifted out of a wicked, insane, and evil world.
We will be as fair as the sun and clear as the moon."
Vaughn J. Featherstone, *The Incomparable Christ: Our Master and Model* [554]

Joseph Smith emphasized the importance of using the endowment to its fullest potential when he stated, *"Now the great and grand secret of the whole matter, and the summum bonum of the whole subject that is lying before us, consists in obtaining the powers of the Holy Priesthood. For him to whom these keys are given there is no difficulty in obtaining a knowledge of facts in relation to the salvation of the children of men..."* [555] Throughout history the faithful have always gathered around consecrated altars to access the power of the holy priesthood and worship with sacred keys.

"From the expulsion of Adam and Eve from the garden, to the present day the Lord
has commanded us to build altars, that we may worship Him and make an offering unto the Lord.
The focal point of religious worship throughout the ages, and in most cultures, has been the altar-
a natural or man-made elevation used for prayer, sacrifice, and related purposes...
The altar was built that people might kneel by it to communicate
and make covenants with their God."
Encyclopedia of Mormonism [556]

In the early days of the church it was common for Latter Day Saints to worship around the home altar. Righteous families, clothed in the robes of the Melchizedek Priesthood, would gather at home or in the countryside to pray for revelation and strength.

Personal Power

"The prayer circle had several functions. Here the brethren dressed in temple clothing or the robes
of the priesthood and offered special prayers. Often bottles of oil were consecrated for the healing of the sick.
A member might give a brief talk on some principle, followed by the informal, spontaneous testimonies
of other brethren. Members took turns being "mouth" or voice in the prayers and ordinances."
Craig Mills, *Home Sanctuary* [557]

Although utilizing altars and the true order of prayer outside of the LDS temple is no longer officially allowed, what has not changed is the method for accessing eternal truth. An awakening Saint who wishes to remain anonymous asks the obvious questions.

"Why would people be taught the True Order of Prayer in an Endowment if they should never use it personally to benefit their own personal lives or the lives of their families?

Is the True Order of Prayer merely ceremony or ritual only in an endowment?

Is the Endowment prayer circle merely a time to thank Heavenly Father for a nice Endowment session?

If the True Order of Prayer is taught in the endowment for "instruction only"(which it is) to what end is this instruction given?"

In the future, altars and the true order of prayer will again be utilized as God intended. When destruction and chaos spread throughout the world, citizens will be overwhelmed and society will be desperate for God's help. Social disruption will also effect the day-to-day functioning of the church, and many will be surprised when they do not have access to an LDS temple. When the conveniences of organized religion are no longer available, those who have not already done so will be required to transition into a greater level of spirituality.

"Finally, prayer is how we knock. But it is not just any kind of prayer that "knocks."
Only through the true order of prayer can a person knock. Knocking reminds us of the series of taps given in sacred places and which symbolically allows us to enter into the presence of the Lord.
Recall how prayer is offered prior to that ceremonial entrance. Nevertheless, this is how an individual can actually knock at the real veil - through the true order of prayer, and if he is ready to come to God, then God is ready to open the heavens and tell all about it."
Craig Mills, *Home Sanctuary* [558]

Acquiring spiritual knowledge through the use of sacred altars and the true order of prayer is a spiritual method that transcends any particular culture or religion. The light of eternity is available to every child of God. To the exact degree faith, knowledge, and purity can be presented before the Lord is the same degree to which God and the blessings of His holy priesthood can be revealed. It is really quite upsetting, but we Mormons don't own eternal truth! God and His universe are abundantly more magnificent than His church, but because most have a limited view on "keys," and promote an "institutionalized" view of the gospel, they incorrectly imagine the LDS temple to be the only place God can deliver His ordinances.

Freedom in the Early Church

*"I was asked if certain ordinances could be performed in different places. I told them,
yes, under certain circumstances. Where, I was asked. 'Anywhere besides in temples?' Yes.
Anywhere beside the Endowment House?" Yes. 'Where, in some other house?' In another house
or out of doors, as the circumstances might be. Why did I say that?…It is the authority of the Priesthood,
not the place that validates and sanctifies the ordinance. I was asked if people could be sealed outside. Yes!
I could have told them I was sealed outside, and lots of others…I will say that man was not made
for temples, but temples were made for man…The temples are places that are appropriated for a great
many ordinances, and among these ordinances that of marriage; but, then, if we are interrupted by men
who do not know about our principles, that is all right, it will not impede the work of God,
or stop the performance of ordinances. Let them do their work, and we will try and do ours."*
John Taylor, *Journal of Discourses* [559]

In comparison to what was taught in the early church, Joseph Fielding Smith summarizes the current Mormon perspective, but with an important caveat concerning how the Lord delivers priesthood in times of trouble. He states, "*Joseph Smith said, 'if a man gets a fullness of the Priesthood of God, he has to get it in the same way that Jesus Christ obtained it, and that was by keeping all the commandments and obeying all the ordinances of the house of the Lord.'*[560] "*I hope we understand that. If we want to receive the fullness of the Priesthood of God, then we must receive the fullness of the ordinances of the house of the Lord and keep His commandments…Let me put this in a little different way. I do not care what office you hold in this Church, you may be an apostle, you may be patriarch, a high priest, or anything else, and you cannot receive the fullness of the Priesthood unless you go into the temple of the Lord and receive these ordinances of which the Prophet speaks. No man can get the fullness of the Priesthood outside of the temple of the Lord. There was a time when that could be done, for the Lord could give these things on the mountain tops—no doubt that is where Moses got it, that is no doubt where Elijah got it—and the Lord said that in the days of poverty, when there was no house prepared in which to receive these things, that they can be received on the mountain tops. But now you will have to go into the house of the Lord, and you cannot get the fullness of the priesthood unless you go there.*" [561]

Just as Jesus once endowed His prophets in the mountains, He will do so again. Even now, before the days poverty afflict America, the Lord can be found in the tops of the mountains! **He has all of the keys** and can ordain whomsoever He chooses. Most of our rhetoric about "keys" is irrelevant due to the "amen" we have placed upon our own priesthood because of unrighteous dominion (D&C 121: 37). And in relation to President Smith's teaching that there must be a "*house prepared in which to receive these things,*" we might ask, are we not the temple of God? (1 Corinthians 3:16). Can the Lord still deliver the fullness of the priesthood to whomsoever He determines is prepared? And if so, cannot the Creators of this universe also select any location, (similar to the sacred grove) and make it holy unto the glory of the Fathers? (see Truth #67).

The sad reality is many of the LDS temples have been spiritually polluted. Those with spiritual gifts often report that angels rarely come to the temples anymore. This invites us to consider whether the time has arrived for the wheat to again return to the mountains and receive a true fullness. Is it possible that true believers, who have engraved temple symbolism upon their heart and mind, even now understand how to turn mountains, meadows, rivers, and canyons into sacred temple sites? And if so, doesn't it seem likely that in the future hundreds of mountain altars will again dot the Western United States? Will it not be a glorious day for Mother Earth when the remnant of Christ reaches up-and a loving Father and Mother reaches down?

The ability to turn an unrefined and primitive space into a "sacred temple" is a spiritual skill Joseph Smith demonstrated when he cried out for assistance in Liberty Jail.

Prison Plea

O God, where art thou? And where is the pavilion that covereth thy hiding place?
How long shall thy hand be stayed, and thine eye, yea thy pure eye, behold from
the eternal heavens the wrongs of thy people and of thy servants, and thine ear be penetrated
with their cries? Yea, O Lord, how long shall they suffer these wrongs and unlawful oppressions,
before thine heart shall be softened toward them, and thy bowels be moved with compassion
toward them? O Lord God Almighty, maker of heaven, earth, and seas, and of all things
that in them are, and who controllest and subjectest the devil, and the dark and benighted
dominion of Sheol—stretch forth thy hand; let thine eye pierce; let thy pavilion be taken up;
let thy hiding place no longer be covered; let thine ear be inclined; let thine heart be softened,
and thy bowels moved with compassion toward us. Let thine anger be kindled against
our enemies; and, in the fury of thine heart, with thy sword avenge us of our wrongs.
Remember thy suffering saints, O our God; and thy servants will rejoice in thy name forever.
Doctrine and Covenants 121:1-6

The Lord's Answer

My son, peace be unto thy soul; thine adversity and thine afflictions shall be but a small moment;
And then, if thou endure it well, God shall exalt thee on high; thou shalt triumph over all thy foes.
(Doctrine and Covenants 121:7-8)…If thou art called to pass through tribulation; if thou art
in perils among false brethren; if thou art in perils among robbers; if thou art in perils by land
or by sea; If thou art accused with all manner of false accusations; if thine enemies fall upon thee;
if they tear thee from the society of thy father and mother and brethren and sisters; and if with
a drawn sword thine enemies tear thee from the bosom of thy wife, and of thine offspring,
and thine elder son, although but six years of age, shall cling to thy garments,
and shall say, My father, my father, why can't you stay with us? O, my father, what are the men
going to do with you? And if then he shall be thrust from thee by the sword, and thou be dragged
to prison, and thine enemies prowl around thee like wolves for the blood of the lamb;
And if thou shouldst be cast into the pit, or into the hands of murderers, and the sentence of
death passed upon thee; if thou be cast into the deep; if the billowing surge conspire against thee;
if fierce winds become thine enemy; if the heavens gather blackness, and all the elements
combine to hedge up the way; and above all, if the very jaws of hell shall gape open the mouth
wide after thee, know thou, my son, that all these things shall give thee experience,
and shall be for thy good. The Son of Man hath descended below them all.
Art thou greater than he?
Doctrine and Covenants 122:5-8

Joseph allowed His Lord to turn the oppression of bondage into a personal heaven of revelation, peace, and worship. Jesus did not only see a broken and suffering man living in filthy rags, He saw purity and passion...true temple worthiness.

> *"It was more temple than prison, so long as the Prophet was there.*
> *It was a place of meditation and prayer. A temple, first of all, is a place of prayer;*
> *and prayer is communion with God. It is the "infinite in man seeking the infinite in God."*
> *Where they find each other, there is holy sanctuary—a temple.*
> *Joseph Smith sought God in this rude prison, and found him.*
> *Out of the midst of his tribulations he called upon God in passionate earnestness..."*
> B.H. Roberts, *Comprehensive History of the Church of Jesus Christ of Latter-day Saints* [562]

The Prophet demonstrated how to walk the path that all must endure. Disciple Alan Cook explains, *"It is strange but true, that Jesus and his 12 apostles were all prisoners—falsely accused by Herod's temple workers, betrayed by false friends, arrested, and convicted on perjured testimony by the very people who claimed to be waiting for the promised Messiah...All willing to stand for Christ must ask, will history cycle again?*[563]

As sanctification deepens, we grow from "going to the temple" to "becoming the temple." In Christ, a Holy of Holies awakens within our soul until we realize that what constitutes "a temple" transcends a physical building. This realization entices those who are hungry for God to cry out, "break me, destroy me," "do whatever it takes to free me from the suffering of the natural man." Those who bleed in this manner find the Father willing to answer their broken offering. With boldness they begin to work out their salvation with real fear and intense trembling. With time and experience, the result is an internal temple that is capable of creating an external temple. For in that day, GOD and man have become ONE.

TRUTH #53 DESPITE INTENSE PERSECUTION AND HARSH DESTRUCTION THE RIGHTEOUS WILL ENDURE. REGARDLESS OF WHAT THE FUTURE HOLDS, GOD'S TRUE SAINTS WILL TRANSCEND THIS LONE AND DREARY WORLD.

And there came one of the seven angels…saying unto me, Come hither; I will shew unto thee the judgment of the great whore that sitteth upon many waters: **With whom the kings of the earth have committed fornication,** *and the* **inhabitants of the earth have been made drunk** *with the wine of her fornication… And upon her forehead was a name written, MYSTERY, BABYLON THE GREAT, THE MOTHER OF HARLOTS AND ABOMINATIONS OF THE EARTH. And I saw the woman* **drunken with the blood of the saints, and with the blood of the martyrs of Jesus***…*
Revelation 17:1-6

Whether challenges come as a result of personal sin, religious persecution, or political injustice, every soul and family will experience mental, emotional, and physical adversity in the days ahead. All will be subjected to the fire of sanctification.

"Nor are the days of our greatest sorrows and our deepest sufferings all behind us.
They too lie ahead. We shall yet face greater perils, we shall yet be tested with more severe trials, and we shall yet weep more tears of sorrow than we have ever known before. . . .
We tremble because of the sorrows and wars and plagues that shall cover the earth.
We weep for those in the true Church who are weak and wayward and worldly and who fall by the wayside as the caravan of the kingdom rolls forward. . . . All that is yet to be shall go forward in the midst of greater evils and perils and desolations than have been known on earth at any time. . . . Amid tears of sorrow—our hearts heavy with forebodings—we see evil and crime and carnality covering the earth. Liars and thieves and adulterers and homosexuals and murderers scarcely seek to hide their abominations from our view. Iniquity abounds."
Bruce R. Mckonkie, *The Coming Tests and Trials and Glory* [564]

God's remnant will endure persecution, false imprisonment, and the death of loved ones. To survive all that Satan inflicts upon the righteous—and still remain on the earth to fulfill your errand from the Lord, will require a deep and abiding faith.

A Difficult But Required Persecution
"Time is rapidly rolling on, and the prophecies must be fulfilled. The days of tribulation are fast approaching, and **the time to test the fidelity of the Saints has come.** *Rumor with her ten thousand tongues is diffusing her uncertain sounds in almost every ear; but in these times of sore trial,* **let the Saints be patient and see the salvation of God. Those who cannot endure persecution, and stand in the day of affliction, cannot stand in the day when the Son of God shall burst the veil, and appear in all the glory of His Father, with all the holy angels."**
Joseph Smith, *History of the Church* [565]

When the day of war, disease, and turmoil arrives, there will be some who taunt true Christians, saying, *"It is vain to serve God, and what doth it profit that we have kept his ordinances and that we have walked mournfully before the Lord of Hosts!"*(3 Nephi 24:14). The journey however is not without merit, for in sacrificing all that we have, for all that He is, we enter into the family of Christ.

For ye have not received the spirit of bondage again to fear; but ye have received the Spirit of adoption, whereby we cry, Abba, Father. The Spirit itself beareth witness with our spirit, that we are the children of God: And if children, then heirs; heirs of God, and joint-heirs with Christ; if so be that we suffer with him, that we may be also glorified together.
Romans 8:15-17

In truth, some of the most valiant will die for the cause of Christ. As martyrs for Jesus, these souls will endure mortal suffering that they might receive the joy of exaltation!

*And all they who **suffer persecution for my name**, and endure in faith, though **they are called to lay down their lives** for my sake yet shall they partake of all this glory. Wherefore, **fear not even unto death; for in this world your joy is not full, but in me your joy is full**. Therefore, care not for the body, neither the life of the body; but care for the soul, and for the life of the soul. And **seek the face of the Lord always**, that in patience ye may possess your souls, and **ye shall have eternal life**.*
D&C 101:35-38

Martyrdom of the Original Apostles:
Peter: Crucified head down in Rome, 66 A.D.
Andrew: Bound to death. He preached until his death in 74 A.D.
James: Son of Zebedee. Beheaded in Jerusalem by the sword. (Acts 12:1-9).
John: Banished to the Isle of Patmos, 96 A.D. (Rev. 1- 9).
Phillip: Crucified at Heirapole, Phryga, 52 A.D.
Bartholomew: Beaten, crucified, and beheaded by the command of a king, 52 A.D.
Thomas: Run through by a lance at Corehandal, East Indies, 52 A.D.
Matthew: Slain by the sword in the city of Ethiopia about 60 A.D.
James: Son of Alphaeus. Thrown from a pinnacle, then beaten to death, 60 A.D.
Thaddeus: Shot to death by arrows, 72 A.D.
Simon: Crucified in Persia, 74 A.D.

Eventually we all will walk through the *"valley of the shadow of death."* (Psalms 23:4). But God's disciples will *"fear no evil,"* and instead minister to all with compassion, patience, and love. (Psalms 23:4).

"The great challenge is to refuse to let the bad things that happen to us do bad things to us. That is the crucial difference between adversity and tragedy."
Neal A. Maxwell, *Ensign* [566]

When persecution and injustice occur, feelings of resentment and a desire for revenge may arise within the soul. Some will be become bitter and others will succumb to violent hatred, but retribution enacted by humans is not of God, for it is the Lord who has declared, *"vengeance is mine, and I will repay."*(Mormon 3:15).

From the Book of Mormon we observe at least two different models for relating to our "enemies." Scripture repeatedly demonstrates that usually it is noble to defend our families even unto bloodshed and death. (3 Nephi 3). In contrast, as demonstrated by the Anti-Nephi-Lehies, (Alma 24), there may also be a time we are required to meekly surrender and lay down our weapons of war. It appears both responses are appropriate, depending on the will of the Lord in each unique circumstance.

To Love Thy Enemies...

*For behold, they had rather **sacrifice their lives** than even to take the life of their enemy;*
*And they have buried their weapons of war deep in the earth, **because of their love towards their brethren.** And now behold I say unto you, has there been so great love in all the land?*
*Behold, I say unto you, Nay, there has not, even among the Nephites. For behold, they would take up arms against their brethren; they would not suffer themselves to be slain. But behold how many of these have laid down their lives; and we know that they have gone to their God, **because of their love and of their hatred to sin.***
Alma 26:32-34

A Righteous Defense

*And it came to pass that the people of Limhi began to drive the Lamanites before them; yet they were not half so numerous as the Lamanites. **But they fought for their lives, and for their wives, and for their children**; therefore they exerted themselves and like dragons did they fight.*
Mosiah 20:11

Defending Your Family

And again, the Lord has said that: Ye shall defend your families even unto bloodshed. Therefore for this cause were the Nephites contending with the Lamanites, to defend themselves, and their families, and their lands, their country, and their rights, and their religion. And it came to pass that when the men of Moroni saw the fierceness and the anger of the Lamanites, they were about to shrink and flee from them. And Moroni, perceiving their intent, sent forth and inspired their hearts with these thoughts— yea, the thoughts of their lands, their liberty, yea, their freedom from bondage. And it came to pass that they turned upon the Lamanites, and they cried with one voice unto the Lord their God, for their liberty and their freedom from bondage. And they began to stand against the Lamanites with power; and in that selfsame hour that they cried unto the Lord for their freedom, the Lamanites began to flee before them...
Alma 43:47-50

Grateful in All Things

"In the practice of tolerance, one's enemy is the best teacher."
Dali Lama [567]

In the future, those seeking the safety of Zion will be faced with spiritual and ethical dilemmas. Survivors will have to determine when to fight, when to submit, and when to withdraw. Each unique scenario will require God's specific guidance. In general survivors will be required to confront, avoid, diminish, and dismiss evil as directed by the Holy Ghost.

Many who have "prepared" for the future have already pre-determined that they will use their weapons to protect the innocent. This attitude is noble, but let us remember that according to God's word, only He can justify the choice of violence and war. (D&C 98:21-33).

Even if God requires certain souls to die in silence as a martyrs, while others are commanded to be aggressive in defense, *all* can find hope in the eventual justice of God. Through the miraculous and merciful gift of Jesus, *all things* will eventually be made right.

PRESS ON SAINTS: VICTORY IN CHRIST!

"For His Atonement to be infinite and eternal, He had to feel what it was like to die not only physically but spiritually, to sense what it was like to have the divine Spirit withdraw, leaving one feeling totally, abjectly, hopelessly alone. But Jesus held on. He pressed on. The goodness in Him allowed faith to triumph even in a state of complete anguish. The trust He lived by told Him in spite of His feelings that divine compassion is never absent, that God is always faithful, that He never flees nor fails us.
When the uttermost farthing had then been paid, when Christ's determination to be faithful was as obvious as it was utterly invincible, finally and mercifully, it was "finished." Against all odds and with none to help or uphold Him, Jesus of Nazareth, the living Son of the living God, restored physical life where death had held sway and brought joyful, spiritual redemption out of sin, hellish darkness and despair. With faith in the God He knew was there,
He could say in triumph, "Father, into thy hands I commend my spirit."
Jeffrey R. Holland, *None Were With Him* [568]

During World War II, Apostle John A. Widtsoe assured the Saints that the Lord is ever victorious in His cause! Today as our world marches ever closer to World War III, the same promises apply. Elder Widtsoe proclaimed, *"Every individual may carry the blessings of Zion with him wherever he goes. Our boys who have been called into our country's service, if they keep themselves clean and undefiled, carry Zion with them. It is my faith that they will be protected by divine power. Should they fall in action or from disease it will be with the consent of our Father in heaven. Besides, to all Latter-day Saints, time and eternity are closely associated. Our sons who live righteously, yet who may lose their lives in this devil-engendered war (and may they be few in number, I pray) will enter into the glory prepared for the righteous. The Lord has so declared. "Therefore, whosoever belongeth to my church need not fear, for such shall inherit the kingdom of heaven." (D. & C. 10 55) And also, "fear not even unto death; for in this world your joy is not full, but in me your joy is full." (D.& C. 101:36) In this world upheaval, in this day of wanton destruction, we, as a people must look upward. There must be trust and faith in our hearts. Hope must walk by our side. We must remember charity also. We must treasure the warm words of the Father to His Church, "Be of good cheer, and do not fear, for I the Lord am with you, and will stand by you." (D&C 68: 6) We who have been called to leadership in the Church of Christ must lead our people from anxiety and fear and doubt, to trust and faith in the Lord, and certainty in the outcome of the Lord's plan of salvation. We must repeat with gladness the words of the Lord, "Fear not, let your hearts be comforted; yea, rejoice evermore, and in everything give thanks." (D&C 98:1)* **Above the roar of cannon and airplane, the maneuvers and plans of men, the Lord always determines the** *tide of battle. So far and no farther does He permit the evil one to go in his career to create human misery. The Lord is ever victorious; He is the Master to whose will Satan is subject. Though all hell may rage, and men may follow evil, the purposes of the Lord will not fail.* The God of Israel, "He slumbers not nor sleeps." It is well to remember the admonition of old: "Be still and know that I am God." It is our destiny as a people to purify the world; to lead men from evil to good; to win the nations to the realm of everlasting truth; to prepare the earth for the coming of the Lord. We are called to establish the kingdom of God on earth. If we accept our mission with faith and the courage born of faith, the Lord will make us victorious in our labors in his cause. Happiness will wait upon us. The protection of heaven will be about us. At this time in our history, let us teach as never before. "If ye are prepared, ye shall not fear."[569]

In and through the resurrection of Jesus Christ, the sting of death can be made sweet. Gratitude can replace resentment-as hope overcomes despair. All who love God can and will transcend this world of sin, selfishness, and fear. The path is sure. Jesus is the victory.

O LORD, thou art my God; I will exalt thee, I will praise thy name;
for thou hast done wonderful things…He will swallow up death in victory;
and the Lord GOD will wipe away tears from off all faces;
and the rebuke of his people shall he take away from off all the earth…
Isaiah 25:1,8

I am perfect; suffer and do as I suffer and do, and ye shall be perfect.
And ye shall be even as I am, and I am even as the Father; and the Father and I are one.
3 Nephi 28:10

The day is approaching when the whole earth will be in commotion. The love of men will wax cold and gross iniquity shall abound. (D&C 45:26-27). During these tumultuous times, when the streets are filled with blood and chaos, it will be essential to remember *"all things work together for good to them that love God."*(Romans 8:28).

…if so be that we suffer with him, that we may be also glorified together.
For I reckon that the sufferings of this present time are not worthy
to be compared with the glory which shall be revealed in us.
Romans 8:17-18

Whether called to endure personal tragedies, family betrayal, or global massacre, all of God's children will be invited to depend on Him with complete surrender. Various life scenarios will occur that will require the soul to be completely aligned with Jesus Christ.

And they that have been scattered shall be gathered. And all they who have mourned
shall be comforted. And all they who have given their lives for my name shall be crowned.
Therefore, let your hearts be comforted concerning Zion; for all flesh is in mine hands;
Be still and know that I am God.
D&C 101:13-16

Let us remember that the existence of suffering and death does not mean God and the truth have lost. These sacred experiences are provided that we might observe, heal, and transcend all ungodliness within ourselves. To participate in this sacred journey is to walk the way of the Christ.

"It is the fire of suffering which will bring forth the gold of godliness."
Jeanne Guyon, *Experiencing the Depths of Jesus Christ* [570]

Those willing to endure all things for Christ in this life, are blessed to receive the Lord's commendation in the worlds to come.

*And all they who suffer persecution for my name, and endure in faith, though they are called to
lay down their lives for my sake yet shall they partake of all this glory. Wherefore, fear not even unto death;
for in this world your joy is not full, but in me your joy is full. Therefore, care not for the body,
neither the life of the body; but care for the soul, and for the life of the soul. And seek the face of
the Lord always, that in patience ye may possess your souls, and ye shall have eternal life.*
D&C 101:35-38

God's disciples understand that the pain and persecution of the present moment is necessary for cleansing the earth and establishing a Zion society.

*"We contemplate a people who have embraced a system of religion, unpopular, and the adherence
to which has brought upon them repeated persecutions. A people who for their love of God,
and attachment to His cause, have suffered hunger, nakedness, perils, and almost every privation.
A people who, for the sake of their religion have had to mourn the premature death of parents,
husbands, wives and children. A people, who have preferred death to slavery and hypocrisy,
and have honorably maintained their characters, and stood firm and immovable,
in times that have tried men's souls ... Your names will be handed down to posterity
as Saints of God and virtuous men."*
Joseph Smith, *Teachings of the Prophet Joseph Smith* [571]

As Babylon teeters and begins to fall, disciples ordained to survive the destruction will receive the understanding and power they need to fulfill their personal errand from the Lord. With broken hearts and contrite spirits, the Lord's people will enter Zion singing songs of everlasting joy! (see Truth #63).

Peace in the Zion Promise

*Zion shall not be moved out of her place, notwithstanding her children are scattered.
They that remain, and are pure in heart, shall return, and come to their inheritances,
they and their children, with songs of everlasting joy, to build up the waste places of Zion.*
Doctrine and Covenants 101:17-18.

Love Comes Quickly

"No one is born hating another person because of the color of his skin, or his background,
or his religion. People must learn to hate, and if they can learn to hate, they can be taught to love,
for love comes more naturally to the human heart than its opposite."
Nelson Mandela, *Autobiography* [572]

God is love, and those who know Him are filled with the pure love of Christ. When we love our enemies, bless them that curse us, do good to them that hate us, and pray for them which despitefully use and persecute us, we have walked the way of the Christ. (Matthew 5:44).

"Let's Pray"

"Eve Carson, a 20-year-old popular student at the University of North Carolina, was kidnapped from
her home in Chapel Hill about 3.35am on March 5, 2008. Lovette's longtime friend, Jayson McNeil,
stated Lovette had told him about the kidnapping and shooting...she pleaded for her life saying,"
they didn't have to do what they were doing." "I asked him, so what led to you all murdering her?"
"He explained to me because she had seen their faces. He explained he shot her five times with a .25 caliber.
"She took the bullets. She ate them. She was still alive and talking." He then stood over Ms. Carson and
shot her in the chest. "He explained to me he no longer heard anything else." McNeil also told the court
Ms. Carson asked them to pray. "Even before he shot her, she said,
'Let's pray.' She wanted them to pray together."
Beth Velliquette, *The Herald Sun* [573]

During times of obscene injustice, loss, and trial, we can find comfort in remembering that Father uses difficult consequences, (tough love), as well as experiences we prefer, (tender compassion), to shape our progression. Whatever principle or experience is "showing up" (patience, persecution, faith, endurance, joy, forgiveness, etc) is "perfect" in the sense of what is needed and appropriate to facilitate spiritual growth. From an eternal perspective, and in Christ, all is blessing, all is benevolent, and all will eventually be seen as "LOVE."

"An old man and his son worked a small farm, with only one horse to pull the plow.
One day, the horse ran away. "How terrible," sympathized the neighbors. "What bad luck."
"who knows whether it is bad luck or good luck", the farmer replied. A week later, the horse returned
from the mountains leading five wild mares into the barn. "what wonderful luck!" said the neighbors.
"Good luck? Bad luck? Who knows? Answered the old man. The next day, the son trying to tame
one of the horses, fell and broke his leg. "How terrible. What bad luck!" "Bad luck, Good luck?"
The army came to all the farms to take the young men for war, but the farmer's son
was of no use to them, so he was spared. Good luck? Bad?"
Dan Millman, *The Way of the Peaceful Warrior* [574]

In truth, both His "mercy" and "justice" represent different aspects of the *same love*. As humans living within a veil, everything we perceive as "good" or "bad" is consumed within Father's compassionate and eternal purposes. His incomprehensible and omniscient love is evidenced by the Father weeping over His wayward children who were about to be destroyed.

And it came to pass that the God of heaven looked upon the residue of the people, and he wept;
and Enoch bore record of it, saying: How is it that the heavens weep, and shed forth their tears
as the rain upon the mountains? And Enoch said unto the Lord: How is it that thou canst weep,
seeing thou art holy, and from all eternity to all eternity? The Lord said unto Enoch:
Behold these thy brethren; they are the workmanship of mine own hands…And unto thy brethren
have I said, and also given commandment, that they should love one another, and that they should
choose me, their Father; but behold, they are without affection, and they hate their own blood;
Moses 7:28-29, 32-33

When the cleansing of the earth starts in earnest, it will be traumatic to watch the suffering. Fear will overcome many, but the remnant of Christ will find hope in knowing that even mighty Moses *"feared"* and saw the *"bitterness of hell."* (Moses 1:20). Like this great prophet, we too can perceive the adversary, receive strength in the Lord, and then roar out with power, *"In the name of the Only Begotten, depart hence, Satan!"* (Moses 1:21). From the example of Moses we are taught the pattern for releasing and removing evil from our presence. The key is to be personally aligned with the power of God until we too, in Christ, can look upon the darkness and proclaim:

How art thou fallen from heaven, O Lucifer, son of the morning! Art thou cut down to the ground,
which did weaken the nations! For thou hast said in thy heart: I will ascend into heaven,
I will exalt my throne above the stars of God; I will sit also upon the mount of the congregation,
in the sides of the north; I will ascend above the heights of the clouds; I will be like the Most High.
Yet thou shalt be brought down to hell, to the sides of the pit. They that see thee
shall narrowly look upon thee, and shall consider thee, and shall say:
Is this the man that made the earth to tremble, that did shake kingdoms?
2 Nephi 24:12-16

Those who have experienced heartache know that wisdom is the answer to hate, and that when we act within the power of pure love, we need not wait until death to see things as they really are. For it is in the very moment that we offer pure compassion that we can do *"all things"* in Christ Jesus. (Philippians 4:13).

"Love is so strong. It may not win a battle,
but it will always win a heart."
Tiegan Corbridge, *Winning the Heart* [575]

Do I not hold the destinies of all the armies of the nations of the Earth?
Therefore will I not make solitary places to bud and to blossom,
and to bring forth in abundance? Saith the Lord.
D&C 117:6-7

THE VICTORY has been, is now, and forever will be in, *The CHRIST.* Even when economic collapse, disease, and death come upon family and friends, all who are faithful to God's plan can look forward to the promised day when we are reunited with the heavens. Because of Jesus Christ the righteous who lose loved ones can still cry out, *"O death, where is thy sting? O grave, where is thy victory? Thanks be to God, which giveth us the victory through our Lord Jesus Christ."* (1 Corinthians 15: 55).

He that seeketh me early shall find me, and shall not be forsaken.
D&C 88:83

Jesus Christ is our Savior in this life *and* in the worlds to come. No matter how long and deep the journey ahead, we know the Father's *"wisdom is greater than the cunning of the devil,"* and that in the end, His sons and daughters will be triumphant! (3 Nephi 21:10).

"This Spirit of Christ fosters everything that is good, every virtue (see Moroni 7:16).
*It stands in brilliant, **indestructible opposition** to anything*
that is coarse or ugly or profane or evil or wicked."
Boyd K. Packer, *The Light of Christ* [576]

As the world becomes increasingly violent, true Christians everywhere will be pushed to the brink of despair. Believers can take comfort in the Lord's promise, *"I do not require at their hands to fight the battles of Zion; for, as I said in a former commandment, even so will I fulfil—**I will fight your battles**.* (D&C 105:14).

"Love is the final conqueror of all battles."
Carleen Taylor, *Call Me Dad* [577]

Those who question God's ability to prevail against evil should ask, who can stand against the Mighty Creator of this Universe and His angels of wrath? For surely He has promised that in the end, *"wickedness shall not be upon the earth… and the great and abominable church, which is the whore of all the earth, shall be cast down by devouring fire…"*(D&C 29:9,21).

I, the Lord, am angry with the wicked; I am holding my Spirit from the inhabitants of the earth.
*I have sworn in my wrath, and decreed wars upon the face of the earth, and **the wicked shall***
***slay the wicked**, and **fear shall come upon every man**; And the **saints also shall hardly escape**;*
*nevertheless, **I, the Lord, am with them**, and will come down in heaven*
*from the presence of my Father and **consume the wicked with unquenchable fire.***
Doctrine and Covenants 63:32-34

When the destruction intensifies, God will protect His humble elect by instructing those holding true priesthood power to organize the elements.

"Those holding the sealing power have, at the behest of the Lord, the elements fight their battles for them.
This was the power Moses called upon to defeat the Pharaoh. This was the power that protected
Enoch's City. It will be this same power that will defend the New Jerusalem."
Denver Snuffer, *Passing the Heavenly Gift* [578]

The promise of God's protection does not mean all of the righteous will be spared from physical death, but we can rejoice that the Gentiles will not be utterly destroyed. (2 Nephi 30:1). Through the grace and wisdom of the Lamb, the surviving remnant will enter into the *"one heart and one mind"* of Zion. (Moses 7:19). Whether in life or death, God is the victory!

Now, what do we hear in the gospel which we have received? A voice of gladness! A voice of mercy from
heaven…Brethren, shall we not go on in so great a cause? Go forward and not backward. Courage, brethren;
and on, on to the victory! Let your hearts rejoice, and be exceedingly glad.
Let the earth break forth into singing…and let all the sons of God shout for joy!
D&C 128:19, 22-23

When the city of Zion is established, the earth will shout with joy and her righteous sons and daughters will dwell in safety and peace. Those contributing to the unity of Zion will possess complete purity and power in the Lord.

And, now, behold, if Zion do these things she shall prosper, and spread herself and become very glorious,
very great, and very terrible. And the nations of the earth shall honor her, and shall say:
Surely Zion is the city of our God, and surely Zion cannot fall, neither be moved out of her place,
for God is there, and the hand of the Lord is there; And he hath sworn by the power of his might to be her
salvation and her high tower. Therefore, verily, thus saith the Lord, let Zion rejoice, for this is Zion —
the pure in heart; therefore, let Zion rejoice, while all the wicked shall mourn. For behold,
and lo, vengeance cometh speedily upon the ungodly as the whirlwind; and who shall escape it?
D&C 97: 18-22

If the wicked do attempt to attack the Holy City, Mother Earth will roar like a protective lion, and the angels of wrath will use the elements of nature to protect God's people.

Come Roar with Me!
"The Lord is near, and he justifieth me.
Who will contend with me? Let us stand together.
Who is mine adversary? Let him come near me, and I will smite him
with the strength of my mouth."
2 Nephi 7:8

The Prophet Joseph Smith demonstrated how to petition the Lord for protection and justice during dangerous times of violence and chaos.

Nothing to Fear

…We ask thee, Holy Father, that **thy servants may go forth from this house armed with thy power,** *and that thy name may be upon them, and thy glory be round about them, and* **thine angels have charge over them; That no weapon formed against them shall prosper; that he who diggeth a pit for them shall fall into the same himself;** *That no combination of wickedness shall have power to rise up and prevail over thy people upon whom thy name shall be put in this house; And* **if any people shall rise against this people, that thine anger be kindled against them;** *And if they shall smite this people thou wilt smite them;* **thou wilt fight for thy people as thou didst in the day of battle, that they may be delivered from the hands of all their enemies.**
Doctrine and Covenants 109:22, 25-28

In truth, the moment of glory is fast approaching. Our choice is between Zion or Babylon, truth or deception, eternal meaning or the superficial. Even during times when it appears Satan is ahead, God's covenant people will trust that in the end the Lord Jesus will rule and reign forever.

A Kingdom of Triumph

"There is now another empire. It is the empire of Christ the Lord. It is the empire
of the restored gospel. It is the kingdom of God. And the sun never sets on this kingdom.
It has not come of conquest, of conflict, or of war. It has come of peaceful persuasion,
of testimony, of teaching, one here and another there."
Gordon B. Hinkley, *General Conference* [579]

When the hour of sorrow arrives, the tender Lamb will comfort the delicate soul. Even if some are required to die in His name, those who have stood strong for Him will not be forsaken, but will be welcomed home by Jesus with compassion and tears of gratitude.

Then shalt thou call, and the Lord shall answer;
thou shalt cry, and he shall say, Here I am.
Isaiah 58:9

CHAPTER SIX: GATHERING THE REMNANT

Lift ye up a banner upon the high mountain...
that they may go into the gates of the nobles.
I have commanded my sanctified ones,
I have also called my mighty ones...
even them that rejoice in my highness.
Isaiah 13:2-3

*Now I, Moroni…have not as yet perished; and I make not myself known to the Lamanites lest they should destroy me. For…because of their hatred they put to death every Nephite that will not deny the Christ. And **I, Moroni, will not deny The Christ…***
Moroni 1:1-3

Disciples who love Jesus will not implicitly or explicitly, by commission or omission, verbally or behaviorally, *"deny the Christ."*

Let no man be afraid to lay down his life for my sake;
for whoso layeth down his life for my sake shall find it again.
D&C 103: 27

Throughout his life, and even on the road to martyrdom, Joseph Smith exemplified loyalty to righteousness and the cause of truth. Regardless of the circumstances he was called to endure, he refused to disappoint or betray his Savior Jesus Christ.

*"O ye Twelve and all saints…in all your trials troubles, temptations, afflictions, bonds, imprisonment, and death, **See to it that you do not betray heaven, that you do not betray Jesus Christ**, that you do not betray your Brethren, and that you **do not betray the revelations of God** whether in the Bible, Book of Mormon, or Doctrine and Covenants or any of the word of God. Yea **in all your kicking and floundering** see to it that you do not this thing lest innocent blood be found in your skirts and you go down to hell…but whatever you do do not betray your friend… remember brethren that if you are imprisoned Brother Joseph has been imprisoned before you. If you are placed where you can only see your Brethren though the gates of a window while in Irons because of the gospel of Jesus Christ **remember Brother Joseph has been in like circumstances also**…"*
Joseph Smith, *The Words of Joseph Smith* [580]

Like Joseph and Moroni, *those willing to sacrifice all they have, for all He is,* obey all directives from the Holy Spirit-even when it is not convenient or popular.

*"To get salvation we must not only do some things, but **everything** which God has commanded. Men may preach and practice everything except those things which God commands us to do, and will be damned at last. We may tithe mint and rue, and all manner of herbs, and still not obey the commandments of God. The object with me is to obey and teach others to obey God in just what He tells us to do. **It mattereth not whether the principle is popular or unpopular, I will always maintain a true principle, even if I stand alone in it.**"*
Joseph Smith, *Teachings of the Prophet Joseph Smith* [581]

Today this same "spiritual autonomy" defines all true disciples of the Lord. Those who love pleasing Father more than hearing praise of men are often required to stand alone.

> *"The Standard of Truth has been erected; no unhallowed hand can stop the work*
> *from progressing; persecution may rage, mobs may combine, armies may assemble,*
> *calumny may defame, but the truth of God will go forth boldly, nobly, and independent,*
> *till it has penetrated every continent, visited every clime, swept every country,*
> *and sounded in every ear, till the purposes of God shall be accomplished,*
> *and the Great Jehovah shall say the work is done."*
> Joseph Smith, *The Wentworth Letter,* [582]

For those who intend to contribute to the fulfillment of Latter Day prophecy, now is the time to be heroic for Christ. Regardless of what the mainstream chooses, this is the day to make an irrefutable stand for truth, both in the world and in the Lord's Church.

> *"A good man will endure all things to honor Christ,*
> *and even dispose of the whole world, and all in it, to save his soul."*
> Joseph and Hyrum Smith, *History of the Church* [583]

Those willing to separate themselves from the blood and sins of this generation learn to *walk the way of The Christ.* These are they who teach as He teaches, heal as He heals, and love as He loves.

> *"He preached the gospel; so can we. He spoke by the power of the Holy Ghost; so can we.*
> *He served as a missionary; so can we. He went about doing good; so can we. He performed*
> *the ordinances of salvation; so can we. He kept the commandments; so can we.*
> *He wrought miracles; such also is our privilege if we are true and faithful in all things…*
> *We are his agents; we represent him; we are expected to do and say what he would do and say if*
> *he personally were ministering among men at this time…We have power to become the sons*
> *of God, to be adopted into the family of the Lord Jesus Christ, to have him as our Father,*
> *to be one with him as he is one with his Father…'Thou art after the order of him who*
> *was without beginning of days or end of years, from all eternity to all eternity,'*
> *the Lord said to Adam. 'Behold, thou art one in me, a son of God;*
> *and thus may all become my sons.'(Moses 6:67–68)."*
> Bruce R. McConkie, *The Ten Blessings of the Priesthood* [584]

> **TRUTH #58** THOSE WHO PERSONALLY "KNOW GOD" HAVE A BROKEN HEART AND CONTRITE SPIRIT. THESE SAINTS ARE THE RIGHTEOUS "FEW" WHO WILL BE GATHERED HOME TO ZION.

...I gather mine elect from the four quarters of the earth,
even as many as will believe in me, and hearken unto my voice.
D&C 33:6

When considering the existence of a Latter Day remnant, we must remember that God loves all of His children perfectly. He is not a *"respecter of persons."* (Acts 10:34). Relative terms such as "the elect," "wheat and tare," "sheep and goats," and "the righteous" should only be used in the spirit of observation, not as a judgment of eternal worth. In truth, every spirit is an irreplaceable aspect of God's eternal soul and is precious in their current, but temporary stage of progression.

Paradoxically, being the *"elect of God"* (D&C 84:34) requires sincere humility and the absence of pride toward our brothers and sisters. The wheat know that in relation to the majesty of God, we truly are *"less than the dust of the earth."* (Mosiah 4: 2,11).

"The antidote for pride is humility, meekness, submissiveness...We can choose to humble ourselves
by conquering enmity toward our brothers and sisters, esteeming them as ourselves,
and lifting them as high or higher than we are."
Ezra Taft Benson, *Conference Report* [585]

The idea of a righteous branch existing within the mainstream culture is a foreign concept to most members. However, researching Book of Mormon patterns, as well as the words of the early brethren, quickly reveals the expectation, and need, for an LDS remnant.

*"God will preserve **a portion of this people**, of the meek and humble, to bear off the kingdom*
to the inhabitants of the earth, and will defend His Priesthood;
for it is the last time, the last gathering time."
Brigham Young, *Contributor* [586]

"And if we, as a people, do not hold ourselves on the altar ready to be used, with our means and all
that God has bestowed upon us, according to the Master's bidding, for the upbuilding of his kingdom
*upon the earth, he will pass on and get somebody else; because **he will get a people that will do it.***
*I do not mean to say, that he will pass on and leave this people; no, **there will come up from the midst***
***of this people that people** which has been talked so much about."*
Daniel H. Wells, *Journal of Discourses* [587]

"If my brethren and sisters do not walk up to the principles of the holy Gospel
of life and salvation, they will be removed out of their places,
and others will be called to occupy them."
Brigham Young, *Journal of Discourses*[588]

Perhaps the Apostles understood that despite the Lord's continual invitation, the Mormon people as a whole would remain under condemnation, (D&C 84: 54-55) and that only a small portion of the membership would become Zion at heart.

"There will be a people raised up, if we will not be that people—there will yet be a people raised up whose lives will embody in perfection the revelations contained in this book...and such a people will have to be raised up before Zion can be fully redeemed, and before the work of our God can be fully established in the earth. In this book, as I have said, is the pattern of the Zion of God. Here are embodied the doctrines, precepts, laws, ordinances, everything in fact that is necessary in order to make us a perfect people before the Lord."
George Q. Cannon, *Journal of Discourses* [589]

Although today's LDS remnant is <u>not</u> an apostate group or movement, they also do not pretend *"all is well in Zion."* These members love God and His gospel more than they love His Church. They are willing to be ostracized if necessary so as to fulfill their errand from the Lord.

"...the kingdom will not be taken from this people and given to another, but a people will come forth from among us who will be zealous of good works, willing to do the bidding of the Lord, who will be taught in his ways, and who will walk in his paths. We, if we are willing, may be humble instruments in the hands of God, in bringing to pass his great and glorious kingdom."
Daniel H. Wells, *Journal of Discourses* [590]

Men and women, wielding the power of His holy priesthood, are now making the required sacrifices to contribute to futuristic Zion. A growing few are reclaiming gospel truths once offered through Joseph Smith—and then inviting anyone who will listen to do the same. These souls are God's remnant. Fiercely loyal to Jesus Christ, they praise the Father by demonstrating obedience in all things great and small.

Invited
Lift ye up a banner upon the high mountain, exalt the voice unto them, shake the hand, that they may go into the gates of the nobles. I have commanded my sanctified ones, I have also called my mighty ones...even them that rejoice in my highness.
Isaiah 13:2-3

As prophecy unfolds, the existence of a growing LDS remnant will come to be of great spiritual significance. Humanity is now at a crucial crossroads which will eventually require a type of "remnant pattern" to again be re-enacted. (see Truths #49 and #50). **Soon** *"the Lord shall set his hand again the second time to recover the remnant of his people."* (2 Nephi 21:11, 25:17, 29:1, Jacob 6:2). Only this time, the final cleansing of the wheat and tares will occur throughout the world, as well as within the Lord's Church. (see Truth #47).

"The day will come when the Lord will choose a people out of this people, upon whom he will bestow his choicest blessings."
Heber C. Kimball, *Journal of Discourses* [591]

From "church" to "temple" to "Zion," the Lord is now refining a *"people out of this people,"* who are eager and willing to grow from "Mormon" to "Saint" to "Remnant."

*"I have frequently said, and say again, that there are and always have been a great many in this Church that are not Saints. **There are more "Mormons" than Saints**; and **there are different degrees and grades of "Mormons" and of Saints.** There are many that are "Mormons" that are not Saints; and **so it will be until Jesus comes to separate the sheep from the goats;** This must be; this we all believe and understand."*
Brigham Young, *Journal of Discourses* [592]

When considering the parable of the ten virgins and observing the temple symbolism of the wedding supper, we are left to conclude that only a portion (of even the active, temple-worthy Saints) will know the Lord to the required degree. All who desire to "enter in" must individually possess the sacred oil of His Holy Spirit burning within their souls.

"I believe that the Ten Virgins represent the people of the Church of Jesus Christ and not the rank and file of the world. All of the virgins, wise and foolish, had accepted the invitation to the wedding supper; they had knowledge of the program and had been warned of the important day to come. They were not the gentiles or the heathens or the pagans, nor were they necessarily corrupt and reprobate, but they were knowing people who were foolishly unprepared for the vital happenings that were to affect their eternal lives. They had the saving, exalting gospel, but it had not been made the center of their lives. They knew the way but gave only a small measure of loyalty and devotion. I ask you: What value is a car without an engine, a cup without water, a table without food, a lamp without oil?"
Spencer W. Kimball, *Faith Precedes the Miracle* [593]

All members are *offered access* to authorized priesthood, temple ordinances, inspired doctrine, and divine revelation. The degree to which participants study, believe, and actually live the fullness of the gospel is an individual and collective choice. (see Truths #15 and #25).

Instead of choosing God, many now seek for the acceptance and praise of our ever-darkening world. Some members seem to be falling into the pride, greed, immorality, contention, and overall lure of Babylon. This cultural reality mirrors exactly what the prophets in the Book of Mormon warned against.

"For they saw and beheld with great sorrow that the people of the church began to be lifted up in the pride of their eyes, and to set their hearts upon riches and upon the vain things of the world, that they began to be scornful, one towards another, and they began to persecute those that did not believe according to their own will and pleasure. And thus, in this there began to be great contentions among the people of the church; yea, there were envyings, and strife, and malice, and persecutions, and pride, even to exceed the pride of those who did not belong to the church of God."
Alma 4:8-9

Over the past decade several church leaders have made a plea that we maintain "unity in the church."[594] But what good is unity if it means conforming to mediocrity? Analyzing the messages which are promoted in sacrament meeting would suggest that many are content with our current spiritual status. Most members seem to implicitly promote a salvation where being "active in the church" is imagined to be sufficient. This type of wishful thinking is not congruent with common sense or God's scripture.

ONLY A FEW…

Behold, there are many called, but few are chosen. And why are they not chosen?
Because their hearts are set so much upon the things of this world,
and aspire to the honors of men…
D&C 121:34-35

ONLY A FEW….

For strait is the gate, and narrow the way that leadeth unto the exaltation and continuation
of the lives, and few there be that find it, because ye receive me not in the world neither
do ye know me. But if ye receive me in the world, then shall ye know me,
and shall receive your exaltation; that where I am ye shall be also.
D&C 132:22-23

ONLY A FEW…

They wear stiff necks and high heads; yea, and because of pride, and wickedness,
and abominations, and whoredoms, they have all gone astray save it be a few,
who are the humble followers of Christ…
2 Nephi 28:14

In truth, revelation confirms that only "a few" will repent to the degree that they can be received of Jesus Christ in this life, as well as endure celestial glory in the worlds to come. (see Truths #21 and #23). This is a high and daunting standard that can be met.

As explained within in this text, Latter Day Saints who achieve this level of holiness, represent the Gentile remnant who are adopted into the House of Israel and sealed unto the Fathers. (See Truth #7 #37, and #67). In this sense, to be "remnant" is not necessarily related to being Jew, Gentile, or Lamanite-Israel, but rather in becoming one with God and His gospel.

The preparing remnant knows the "church is true" and believes in Jesus Christ. (D&C 1:30).
The Remnant of God knows the Lord Jesus Christ and believes in His church. (D&C 76: 22).

The preparing remnant follows the prophet and believes in the Lord Jesus Christ. (D&C 1:38).
The Remnant of God follows the Lord Jesus Christ and believes in his prophet. (D&C 135: 3).

The preparing remnant is proud to be a member of the only true and living Church.
(D&C 1: 30).
The Remnant of God is humbled to be a servant of the Lord Jesus Christ. (Mosiah 2:21).

The preparing remnant is content to review the preparatory gospel and lesser portion of the word. (Alma 12:10).

The Remnant of God is engaged in receiving the mysteries of God and greater portion of the word. (D&C 19:10).

The preparing remnant is focused primarily on being obedient and doing good works of service. (Mosiah 2:17).

The Remnant of God seeks to become the pure love of Christ and love all people unconditionally. (Moroni 7:47).

The preparing remnant is focused on earning salvation through good works, service, and the law of carnal commandments. (Philippians 2:12, D&C 84:27).

The Remnant of God is focused on becoming purified, receiving salvation through the grace of Jesus Christ, and eventually being exalted as a god. (D&C 132:19-20).

The preparing remnant experiences God and His Holy Spirit almost exclusively in relation to the church and its program. (D&C 101:22).

The Remnant of God perceives all of life to be divine and considers a religious context as being only one place where God and His Holy Spirit can be manifest. (Mosiah 18:9 and D&C 29: 34).

The preparing remnant makes church on Sunday a regular part of their life. (Exodus 20:8).

The Remnant of God makes the gospel of Jesus Christ the sum purpose of their entire life. (D&C 88:67).

The preparing remnant follows the arm of flesh and the Holy Spirit when possible. (2 Nephi 4: 34).

The Remnant of God follows the Holy Spirit and the arm of flesh when possible. (D&C 93:26).

The preparing remnant is focused on feeling the Holy Spirit. (Galatians 5:22).

The Remnant of God is seeking to receive all of the ordinances and have each one ratified by the Holy Spirit of Promise. (D&C 76:53).

The preparing remnant receives their callings from inspired leaders of the church. (Alma 8:29).

The Remnant of God receives their personal life assignments directly from the Lord Jesus Christ. (1 Nephi 3:7).

The preparing remnant seeks the approval of church leaders and other members. (Mosiah 17:12).

The Remnant of God seeks and receives approval from God. (Matthew 25:23).

The preparing remnant is content to believe and act as if all is well in Zion. (2 Nephi 28:21).

The Remnant of God understands the inspired meaning of 3 Nephi 16. (3 Nephi 16:10-15).

The preparing remnant applies the Nephite cycle to "in-actives" and the world. (1 Nephi 11:36).
The Remnant of God applies the Nephite cycle to self, country, and the culture of Mormonism. (D&C 85:7).

The preparing remnant is often lulled away into false security. (Helaman 6:38).
The Remnant of God sees the signs of the times and offers a voice of warning. (D&C 88:81).

The preparing remnant views the Mormon culture as a "chosen people." (Alma 31:28).
The Remnant of God knows that we are often the "salt that has lost its savor." (D&C 103:10).

The preparing remnant focuses on religious success in comparison to the world. (2 Nephi 28:21).
The Remnant of God focuses on spiritual challenges and limitations in comparison to the Zion standard. (D&C 136:31).

The preparing remnant follows rules and obeys the program of the Church. (D&C 82:10).
The Remnant of God follows the Lord Jesus Christ and obeys His gospel. (Genesis 22:1-13).

The preparing remnant is dogmatic about the church policy manual. (Luke 6:1-5).
The Remnant of God lives in compliance with daily promptings from the Holy Spirit. (1 Kings 19:11-12).

The preparing remnant relates to the church as if it were "God." (Alma 31:17-23).
The Remnant of God knows GOD is more than His church. (D&C 35:1).

The preparing remnant believes many of the scriptures apply primarily to the world and other churches. (Mormon 8: 33-41).
The Remnant of God understands that scripture, especially the Book of Mormon and Isaiah, was written directly for us and about us. (Alma 37: 2).

The preparing remnant believes that cultural interpretation is actually the gospel of Jesus Christ. (D&C 9:7).
The Remnant of God understands that in some instances, the holy word of God has been transfigured. (Mormon 8:33).

The preparing remnant is reviewing that which has been publicly revealed to all members. (Alma 12:10).
The Remnant of God is seeking that which has not yet been revealed to the masses. (D&C 76:7).

The preparing remnant omits scripture that is difficult to hear, understand, and interpret correctly. (Mormon 8:33).
The Remnant of God is grateful to be taught that which is difficult to comprehend and requires a greater repentance. (Proverbs 9:8).

The preparing remnant applies the parable of the prodigal son to the non-members and "in-actives" of the church. (Luke 15:11-32).
The Remnant of God applies the parable of the prodigal son to every soul upon the face of the earth. (Luke 15:11-32).

The preparing remnant is content with that which is good. (JST Revelations 3:16).
The Remnant of God appreciates that which is good and yearns to receive all that is great. (1 Corinthians 12:31).

The preparing remnant is proud to be a full tithe payer. (Matthew 6:1-4).
The Remnant of God is humbled in their attempt to live the law of consecration. (Luke 21:1-4).

The preparing remnant obeys the commandments so they can be blessed. (D&C 82:10).
The Remnant of God understands that all things are a blessing. (D&C 59:7).

The preparing remnant is progressing toward an awareness of the Intelligence. (D&C 98:12).
The Remnant of God is seeking reconciliation with the Intelligence, and thereby with God. (Alma 40:11).

The preparing remnant is mostly unaware of true reality and is thus prone to boast in his or her own strength. (Mosiah 11:19).
The Remnant of God has some awareness of true reality and is naturally humbled by the "nothingness" of man. (Helaman 12: 7).

The preparing remnant conceptualizes repentance as something we do or don't do. (Exodus 20:3-17).
The Remnant of God conceptualizes repentance as an internal shift that centers on becoming. (Moses 8:25).

The preparing remnant utilizes the Melchizedek Priesthood as a prayer. (2 Nephi 32:9).
The Remnant of God administers the will, word, and power of Almighty God within the stewardship of the Melchizedek Priesthood. (Acts 9:40-41).

The preparing remnant attends the LDS temple on a regular basis and mistakenly believes they hold the fullness of the Melchizedek Priesthood. (D&C 109:8-13).
The Remnant of God has become the temple. They have personally received the live endowment, and under the hands of Jesus have received the sealing power and actual fullness of the priesthood. (D&C 93:1).

The preparing remnant is commanded not to enter into temptation. (3 Nephi 18:18).
The Remnant of God is commanded not to be tempted. (3 Nephi 18:15).

The preparing remnant is hoping to bind Satan during the millennium. (D&C 88:110).
The Remnant of God through righteousness has already bound Satan in their own lives. (John 14:30).

The preparing remnant does not truly believe miracles and gifts can be manifested today. (1 Corinthians 14:22).
The Remnant of God is actively seeking to magnify the gifts of the Spirit. (1 Corinthians 12:4-10).

The preparing remnant is content to have their names on the record of the church. (D&C 128:4).
The Remnant of God is focused on having their names written in the "Lamb's book of life." (D&C 132:19).

The preparing remnant is anointed to someday become Kings and Queens. (Temple endowment).
The Remnant of God has been called and chosen to be Kings and Queens, Priests and Priestesses. (Endowed personally by Jesus Christ).

The preparing remnant is focused primarily on The Church of Jesus Christ of Latter Day Saints. (D&C 1:30).
The Remnant of God contributes to the LDS church while seeking membership in The Church of the Firstborn. (D&C 77:11).

Someone once taught that after Jesus selected His Twelve Apostles, there was another called and ordained in private. The religious world was never to know about this mighty disciple, but among the friends of Jesus, he came to be known as the "Thirteenth Apostle."

Today, in like manner, some worship and serve in an obscure and seemingly irrelevant manner. Only the Father, Mother, and their Beloved Son perceive the ministry of these dedicated disciples. And so to those whom the world rejects, to those whom the church will never acknowledge…to the lonely and those who are cast out, and to those who simply love *The Christ,*

I salute you in the name of the Lord Jesus Christ, in token or remembrance
of the everlasting covenant, in which covenant I receive you to fellowship,
in a determination that is fixed, immovable, and unchangeable,
to be your friend and brother through the grace of God in the bonds of love,
to walk in all the commandments of God blameless,
in thanksgiving, forever and ever. Amen.
Doctrine and Covenants 88:133

Wherefore I, Jacob, gave unto them these words as I taught them in the temple,
having first obtained mine errand from the Lord.
Jacob 1:17

When we embody onto this planet, we enter into a veil of forgetfulness. All that we previously covenanted to accomplish for the Lord is taken from our remembrance. This is as it should be until, through the power of the Holy Ghost, the veil thins and we remember our specific life assignments. Those who remember, reclaim, and then accomplish these spiritual assignments, are privileged to return home in victory.

"Jesus was a god before he came into the world and yet his knowledge was taken from him.
He did not know his former greatness, neither do we know what greatness we had attained to before
we came here, but he had to pass through an ordeal, as we have to, without knowing or realizing
at the time the greatness and importance of his mission and works."
Lorenzo Snow, *Journal of Lorenzo Snow* [595]

The personal gifts we bring into this life, as well as the synchronistic events we experience, prepare us to fulfill our assigned ministry. What may appear in the moment to be needless suffering often becomes the perfect lesson needed for the future. The tutoring the Lord provides for His servants often involves years of heartache, hardship, and shaping, *"for whom the Lord loveth he chasteneth, and scourgeth every son whom he receiveth."* (Hebrews 12:6). Such was the case for John the Baptist, who lived several seasons in the wilderness before the time finally arrived for his ministry. Jesus Himself grew *"grace to grace"* before being allowed to complete the infinite and Holy Atonement.

Throughout our mortal lives, God allows us to be pushed to capacity. He wisely facilitates our unique spiritual path, requiring exactness so that when the moment of ministry arrives, we are prepared to implement God's will with power and success!

Paul: A Well-Lived life
But watch thou in all things, endure afflictions, do the work of an evangelist,
make full proof of thy ministry. For I am now ready to be offered, and the time of my departure is at hand.
I have fought a good fight, I have finished my course, I have kept the faith: Henceforth there is
laid up for me a crown of righteousness... *which the Lord, the righteous judge, shall give me*
at that day: and not to me only, but unto all them also that love his appearing.
2 Timothy 4:5-8

For those intent on fulfilling their specific life assignments, the questions become quite intense and deeply personal.

1) What is my unique errand from the Lord?
2) Am I willing to sacrifice all that is required, even my very life if need be, that I might be found *"true and faithful in all things?"*
3) What exists within my soul that is preventing me from fully consecrating my life to God?
4) What do I need to "do" and "become" to successfully complete my life mission?
5) Do I have the ability to hear the guiding voice of God's Spirit in every moment? Am I spirit led or tradition dependent? Do I trust in Him above all else?
6) What spiritual and temporal preparations must I make today-so as to fulfill my sacred duty tomorrow?
7) Am I committed to doing the will of the Father at all costs that I might be a friend unto Jesus?
8) Whether experiencing joy or sadness, peace or turmoil, life or death, will I stand firm in the testimony of Jesus Christ?

Those who comprehend the magnitude of the journey may be intimidated by the sheer difficulty of the climb. With fear, trembling, awe, and respect, they may be allowed to fall at the feet of the Master, pleading with Him for the endurance required to fulfill their life mission and glorify Father.

A Disciple's Journey
We are fools for Christ's sake, but ye are wise in Christ; we are weak, but ye are strong;
ye are honourable, but we are despised. Even unto this present hour we both hunger, and thirst,
and are naked, and are buffeted, and have no certain dwelling place; And labour, working with
our own hands: being reviled, we bless; being persecuted, we suffer it: Being defamed, we intreat:
we are made as the filth of the world, and are the off scouring of all things unto this day.
I write not these things to shame you, but as my beloved sons I warn you…
for in Christ Jesus I have begotten you through the gospel.
1 Corinthians 4:10-15

God knows each weakness and strength. He clearly perceives the various aspects of our soul that must yet be purged, cleansed, and transformed. Like Paul, we all have a *"thorn in the flesh."* (2 Corinthians 12:7). But our weaknesses and failures are not without purpose, for in realizing our desperate need for Christ, we become candidates to fulfill the measure of our creation.

The Weak and Simple
*The **weak things of the world shall come forth and break down the mighty and strong ones,***
*that man should not counsel his fellow man, neither trust in the arm of flesh—But that **every man might***
***speak in the name of God the Lord**, even the Savior of the world; That faith also might increase in the*
earth; That mine everlasting covenant might be established;
*That **the fullness of my gospel might be proclaimed by the weak and the simple***
unto the ends of the world, and before kings and rulers.
Doctrine and Covenants 1:19-23

Paradoxically, being weak and simple often correlates with being deep and strong. In the eyes of the Lord, the meek are majestic, the humble powerful, the lowly exalted.

Seeking True Success

"God help us my brethren and sisters, to make our calling and election sure.
God help us to do our duty, and to build up Zion in His own appointed way;
perfect ourselves and our families, and have a forgiving spirit in our hearts,
not a spirit to find fault with everything we see. That God may help us in all things requisite
to make us perfect in the day of the Lord."
Brigham Young, Jr., *General Conference* [596]

"I am only one
But I am One.

I cannot do everything
But I can do something.

And what I can do
That I ought to do.

And what I ought to do
By the Grace of God,

I will do."

Edward Everett Hale [597]

"There is your will; there is God's will. There is your plan; there is God's plan. There is your prayer; there is His prayer. You must agree to His plans. He takes from you all your own workings so that His may be substituted in their place."
Jeanne Guyon, *Experiencing the Depths of Jesus Christ* [598]

When we align ourselves with Father's will, we experience being in harmony with heaven. Once touched by His love and wisdom, we no longer desire to betray Him-or ourselves, through any type of sin. To sense even a small portion of what the Lord suffered in Gethsemane and on the cross, and then choose to add to His agony through personal transgression, becomes unbearable.

"I thank the Savior personally; for bearing all which I added to His hemorrhaging at every pore for all humanity in Gethsemane. I thank Him for bearing what I added to the decibels of His piercing soul cry atop Calvary."
Neal A. Maxwell, *Ensign* [599]

To redeem our soul is the Lord's daily work and passion. He will not rest until He has saved all who are willing to believe and follow Him. Could there be a more trusted friend than Jesus? In agony, He suffered for us that He might bring to pass our personal immortality and eternal life. He submitted to *all things* that we too might receive *all things* and enter into the rest of God. (see Truth #2) To surrender our will into the majesty, compassion, and wisdom of *"The Christ,"* represents an essential element of growing from believer to servant to friend.

*Henceforth I call you not servants; **for the servant knoweth not what his lord doeth**: but **I have called you friends**; for all things that I have heard of my Father I have made known unto you. Ye have not chosen me, but **I have chosen you, and ordained you, that ye should go and bring forth fruit, and that your fruit should remain** that whatsoever ye shall ask of the Father in my name, he may give it you. These things I command you, that ye love one another.*
John 15:15-17

The Sergeant Wint Story

I was twenty-one and newly married when the United States Army drafted me into the war. I was assigned a tour of duty in Vietnam and would be shipping out in a few days. My precious wife and I savored every moment as I prepared to leave. Little did we understand the horror I would experience in the days to come.

One afternoon as I was leaving the military base, an intense dread came over me concerning the future and the unknown mystery of what lay ahead. A darkness washed through me like ice and in desperation I finally began to pray. Immediately my fear was swallowed up in the warmth of an assuring spirit. A gentle whisper came directly into my soul and confirmed to me that I would not be alone. This would be the same power I would again call upon in a few short days as I lay on the battlefield bleeding…

Easter morning, April 6, 1969, dawned quietly as my motley crew of forty-eight men gathered together. Their strength and courage lay unseen beneath their battle-torn attire. In sacred brotherhood, we stood solemnly as the Army chaplain offered a simple prayer to God. As he prayed the nearby helicopters sat ominously silent, waiting to transport us into hostile territory.

The countryside was deceptively peaceful as we landed, but as the helicopters flew out of sight the Viet Cong opened fire. Deadly bullets sliced through the air as we scrambled for protection in the open rice paddy. Suddenly searing pain shot through my face as bullets entered several areas of my body. Death seemed moments away as I slipped between agony and the blessed state of unconsciousness. Lying wounded and helpless in the open field I needed assistance. Several of my men had already been wounded trying to save me from the barrage of continuous gunfire. Lying in a pool of my own blood I heard the sound of yet another soldier pushing his way through the marshy soil towards me. My battlefield savior was on a self-appointed mission and he did not give up. As he strained to reach me, a final shot ripped through the air and then all was still, all was silent. I listened as he offered the ultimate sacrifice and released his last breath.

Many years have passed since that sacred moment. The physical wounds have scarred, healed, and faded, but I have not forgotten. And sometimes on a quiet Easter morning, I recall the man who died for me that I might live again. It is in these moments I am reminded of the mercy of our Savior, and how I too can now walk, the Way of The Christ.

TRUTH #61 ALL OF GOD'S CHILDREN HAVE THE INNATE ABILITY TO DEVELOP SPIRITUAL GIFTS. SURVIVING THE APOCALYPSE WILL REQUIRE ACCESSING GIFTS OF THE SPIRIT.

For behold, I am God; and I am a God of miracles; and I will show unto the world
that I am the same yesterday, today, and forever; and I work not among the children of men
save it be according to their faith.
2 Nephi 27:23

The presence, and/or absence of spiritual gifts, is a direct commentary on the spiritual status of any given people. In relation to simple faith, what we expect, we experience.

"How vital, therefore, for us to know the realities: There is a plan of salvation; there was an apostasy;
and now there has been a restoration. God has given man moral agency, leaving him free to believe
or disbelieve, or to disregard the divine and spiritual evidence. Thus an incredible irony emerges:
As people become less believing there are fewer spiritual experiences,
and this is twisted by the disbeliever into confirmation of his premises."
Neal A. Maxwell, *Men and Women of Christ* [600]

The church teaches that we worship a God of miracles. This provides a context for us to experience the fruit of real faith. However, there seems to be an imaginary and unspoken line concerning "what is appropriate or possible." For when a young believer mentions wanting to see an angel, or enacting a great miracle of healing, there are many ready to discourage such hope. Apparently, they are afraid members will get disappointed, or that they will place their testimonies on "*signs and wonders.*" (Matthew 16:4).

Although these concerns are well intentioned, the views they promote contribute to a people who are of "*little faith.*" (Matthew 8:26). As a result, many in the church have never even considered that an angel would come to them personally, or that they could individually develop the "*gift of healing.*" (Moroni 10:11).

Do I Really Believe?

"Today we prefer our miracles at a distance. When we do accept the occasional miracle,
we want it to be separated by culture, time and reduced to written accounts from the deceased.
We think it's safer that way. Society trusts that when the miraculous has been reduced to history alone
*it can then safely be the stuff from which PhD's and theologians extract the **real** meanings.*
After all, our scientific society only trusts education, certification and licensing; not revelation, visitation
and ministering of angels. Well, even if that is not as it should be, it is at least as Nephi said it would be:
"They deny the power of God, the Holy One of Israel; and they say unto the people: Hearken unto us,
and hear ye our precept; for behold there is no God today, for the Lord and the Redeemer hath done
his work, and he hath given his power unto men. Behold, hearken ye unto my precept;
if they shall say there is a miracle wrought by the hand of the Lord, believe it not;
for this day he is not a God of miracles; he hath done his work. (2 Nephi 28: 5-6)."
Denver Snuffer, *Jumping Out a Window* [601]

Growing beyond cultural norms and our own internal doubt results in receiving spiritual gifts. The Prophet Joseph Smith educated the Saints concerning how to detect a true angel or messenger from a false one, because he expected members to be communicating with them. (D&C 129:1-9).

Thankfully, the opportunity to receive angels and their message has not ended. There is still time to enlarge our mental capacity and increase our spiritual abilities. In Christ, we can become the mechanism God uses in the future to receive essential revelation, as well as provide heroic healings.

Real Priesthood Power

"Consider a priesthood blessing where a willing individual steps forth to perform that ordinance without having opened the channels of intimate revelation through the walk of his own life. For such an individual, the words will lack power and conviction, and the promises will be tentative and conditional not unrighteous, but without power. Such blessings often include admonition, beseeching of the Lord, and escape clauses that give both the priesthood holder, and the recipient, a place to hang their faith if it doesn't come to pass, as neither of them truly expect. At the end of such blessings we are often not surprised, and oddly, not disturbed, when our desires are not realized as promised. We just accept that the answer from the heavens was no or that someone didn't have the faith necessary and we're OK with that. Brother Joseph made this statement regarding haphazard priesthood healings. Brother Joseph, while in the Spirit, rebuked the Elders who would continue to lay hands on the sick from day to day without the power to heal them. Said he: 'It is time that such things ended. Let the Elders either obtain the power of God to heal the sick or let them cease to minister the forms without the power.' (Autobiography of Parley P. Pratt)…[602] In line with Josephs counsel, consider the same priesthood holder who has obtained the voice of Christ as his guide, who has fasted and prayed diligently to obtain righteous priesthood power, who is familiar with the workings of revelation, and is fearless in speaking the truths that come into his heart. As the blessing progresses, let us assume that the voice of heaven instructs him to invoke a very powerful healing. To the extent that that individual has faith Christ, and faith in his own ability to correctly hear the Holy Spirit, the resulting blessing will flow with power. Words of eternal worth will be spoken. Prophecy will tumble from his lips, and power will heal and sanctify the recipient of the blessing. There will be no fine print; no escape clauses, just the blessing and the palpable power. Both will walk away with greater faith, and the words will be fulfilled to the letter."
John Pontius, *The Triumph of Zion* [603]

Faith, knowledge, priesthood, and gifts of the Spirit, are all interconnected. However, accessing the spiritual power that God offers His children is not gender-specific. The common Mormon assumption that spiritual healings and manifestations must primarily occur through a man holding the priesthood is doctrinally incorrect and spiritually limiting. Throughout the earth numerous males and females from every faith and background have received and developed gifts of the Spirit. This reality invites us to understand that manifestations of the Spirit **are fueled by faith—not priesthood status.**

Cultural Assumption
"Only male priesthood holders can give blessings of healing."

*"It appears that we have taken some miracles which belong in the category of faith-powered,
and transplanted under the heading of priesthood-powered. In computer terms, we cut and pasted
where we should have copied and pasted. By recasting such miracles as being by-priesthood-
only we have excluded a high percentage of faithful members from believing it proper to request and receive
such miracles by their faith, and we have limited our belief regarding what miracles are available
through the priesthood. That these miracles belong to the priesthood is undeniable. We have all witnessed
such things under the administration of righteous priesthood holders, and can only believe that the fact
that these miracles do occur stamps them as approved of God. What we have perhaps done is to overlook
the fact that even priesthood miracles are a by product of faith. Please note the following verse:
"For God having sworn unto Enoch and unto his seed with an oath by himself; that every one being
ordained after this order and calling should have power, by faith, to break mountains, to divide the seas,
to dry up waters, to turn them out of their course; (JST Genesis 14:30). In other words,
even when it is by the authority of the priesthood that someone places their hands on the sick
and commands them to recover, it is faith that fuels the miracle from heaven."*
John Pontius, *Call to Zion* [604]

Pondering the grandeur of Mother Earth, the majesty of the moon, the nobility of childbirth, and the depth and mystery of Heavenly Mother, reveals the raw power of the divine feminine.

To then unify Father's knowledge with Mother's wisdom, reveals an ever-deepening view of that which represents "GOD."

WOMEN and SPIRITUAL GIFTS

When the gospel of Jesus Christ was restored, it was Joseph's perspective that the sisters would be involved in utilizing the power of the priesthood. Although the Prophet's vision was never realized, he explained before his death what God's intentions were for the sisters.

*"On April 28, 1842, Joseph Smith records in his history (DHC 6:602-607) that he met with the members
of the newly organized "Female Relief Society and gave a lecture on the Priesthood, **showing how the
sisters would come in possession of the privileges, blessings, and gifts of the Priesthood,
and that the signs should follow them, such as healing the sick**... and that they might attain
unto these blessings by a virtuous life, and diligence in keeping all the commandments." According to the
synopsis of his remarks on that occasion, as reported by Eliza R. Snow, the Prophet Joseph Smith quoted
I Corinthians 12th and 13th chapters and Mark 16:15-18. His commentary on these scriptures to the ladies
of the "Female Relief Society" were, in part, as follows: **"No matter who believeth these signs,
such as healing the sick, casting out devils, etc., should follow them that believe,
whether male or female. He asked the Society if they could not see by this sweeping promise,
that ...if the sisters should have faith to heal the sick, let all hold their tongues,
and let everything roll on. ..."Respecting females administering for the healing of the sick,**

344

he further remarked, there could be no evil in it, if God gave His sanction by healing;
that there could be no more sin in any female laying hands on and praying for the sick
than in wetting the face with water; it is no sin for anybody to administer that has faith,
or if the sick have faith to be healed by their administrations." (DHC 4:602-604).
Joseph Smith continued instructions by saying that "it was according to revelation that the sick
should be nursed with herbs and mild food, and not by the hand of an enemy. (D&C 42:43)."
Messages of the First Presidency of The Church of Jesus Christ of Latter-day Saints [605]

Every Woman's Calling

"The Lord designs that the principle of knowledge shall be developed in every heart,
that ALL may stand before Him, not depending upon nor being blindly led by their priests
or leaders, as is the universal custom. The genius of the kingdom with which we are associated
*is to disseminate knowledge through all the ranks of the people, **and to make every man a prophet***
and every woman a prophetess…"
George Q. Cannon, *Journal of Discourses* [606]

A Different Church

"My wife (is doing) poorly…Sister Richards sent for us to clothe in the robes of the Holy Order
and pray for her as she felt as she should not live long. We offered up the Signs and prayed for my wife;…
Returned home found my wife quite sick… Sister Whitney came in anointed her and sung in tongues.
I also sang. The Lord blessed us."
Heber C. Kimball, *Heber C. Kimball Diary* [607]

In the Old Testament several female prophets are mentioned. (Exodus 15:20, Judges 4:4, 2 Kings 22:14, 2 Chronicles 34:22, Nehemiah 6:14, Isaiah. 8:3). The Bible also identifies Anna as a prophetess (Luke 2:36) and Philip as the father of four unmarried daughters who prophecy. (Acts 21:7-9). In relation to 1 Corinthians 11:4-5, it is clear that at the time of Jesus both men and women did pray and prophecy within the Jewish culture.

These historical clues, as well as the examples of Eliza R. Snow, Emmeline B. Wells, and others, encourage us to conclude that in the future both men and women will administer with power to all who desire blessing and healing. Surely our current beliefs will be magnified as the Saints grow closer to receiving the Zion once envisioned.

Power in Unity

"The Church teaches that a woman may lay on hands upon the head of a sick child and ask the Lord
*to bless it, in the case when those holding the priesthood cannot be present. **A man might under such***
***conditions invite his wife to lay on hands with him in blessing their sick child.** This would be*
merely to exercise her faith and not because of any inherent right to lay on hands. A woman would have
no authority to anoint or seal a blessing, and where elders can be called in, that would be the proper way
to have an administration performed. (Doctrines of Salvation, 3:178)."
Joseph Fielding McConkie, *Answers: Straightforward Answers to Tough Gospel Questions* [608]

Today only a few elect sisters seem interested in participating in the power of the priesthood and the associated gifts of the Spirit. Perhaps the other loving, faithful, and frequently overwhelmed women, fear having one more responsibility upon their shoulders. Or maybe they simultaneously under-estimate their spiritual abilities along with the cultural norm. Whatever the reason, all who seek Zion need to understand that although each gender is unique and different, both are equally capable of accessing God's holy priesthood.

A Mother's Faith

"I am preaching to you practical religion. Learn to take proper care of your children.
If any of them are sick, the cry now, instead of "Go and fetch the Elders to lay hands on my child!" is,
"Run for a doctor." Why do you not live so as to rebuke disease? It is your privilege to do so without
sending for the Elders. You should go to work to study and see what you can do for the recovery
of your children…Study and learn something for yourselves. It is the privilege
of a mother to have faith and to administer to her child; this she can do herself,
as well as sending for the Elders to have the benefit of their faith."
Brigham Young, *Journal of Discourses* [609]

As children of God, both men and women can recover from the disease of unbelief and magnify their spiritual ability. Today the invitation from Father and Mother is to come and partake of the universal mystery and power of godliness!

ONENESS

"One of the Savior's strengths was that instead of adapting himself to cultural traditions he adapted
himself (he submitted) to the righteous designs of his Heavenly Father. This is why Jesus Christ is not only
the way and the model for men of the Church, but for the women also. There is only one way,
and Jesus is that way. Some women bemoan the fact that there is no female model.
They seek the wrong image. Male is not the model. Female is not the model.
Divine Oneness is the model."
Jan Ostler, *Men and Women* [610]

In the future there will be thousands in need of physical and emotional comfort. These survivors will not care about an official declaration of "who has the priesthood." Instead, the criteria will be, who is able to lay hands on those who are suffering and command with real power, "In the name of Jesus Christ…arise and walk!"

Now there was at Joppa a certain disciple named Tabitha, which by interpretation is called Dorcas:
this woman was full of good works and alms deeds which she did. And it came to pass in those days,
that she was sick, and died: whom when they had washed, they laid her in an upper chamber.
And forasmuch as Lydda was nigh to Joppa, and the disciples had heard that Peter was there,
they sent unto him two men, desiring him that he would not delay to come to them.
Then Peter arose and went with them. When he was come, they brought him into the upper chamber:
and all the widows stood by him weeping, and shewing the coats and garments which Dorcas made,
while she was with them. But Peter put them all forth, and kneeled down, and prayed; and turning him
to the body said, Tabitha, arise. And she opened her eyes: and when she saw Peter, she sat up.
And he gave her his hand, and lifted her up, and when he had called the saints and widows,
presented her alive. And it was known throughout all Joppa; and many believed in the Lord.
Acts 9:36-42

Joseph taught the early Saints to align themselves with the will of Father, apply faith through mental exertion, and then command "the miracle" to be enacted.

"Let us here offer some explanation in relation to faith, that our meaning may be clearly comprehended. We ask, then, what are we to understand by a man's working by faith? We answer, we understand that when a man works by faith, he works by mental exertion instead of physical force; it is by words, instead of exerting his physical powers, with which every being works when he works by faith. God said, let there be light and there was light."
Joseph Smith, *Lectures on Faith* [611]

Perhaps our greatest spiritual awakening occurs when we realize just how little we actually believe, and that although we profess to *"know without a shadow of a doubt,"* our faith is like a mustard seed. (Luke 17:6). Acknowledging our struggle to demonstrate real faith creates space within our testimonies, so that eventually we can be filled with the light of a deeper *"knowing."*

> Do I truly believe I can heal the sick, raise the dead,
> and move mountains?
>
> Am I willing to begin seeking true power in Christ?

Only sin, doubt, and fear prevent us from walking on water, healing cancer, and restoring sight to the blind. Manifesting miracles to this degree is the natural fruit of walking the way of the Christ.

"The born again powers exhibited by Jesus are manifest by all those who are born of the Spirit: Power to move about uninhibited, power to ask and receive, the power of life and death, power over the elements, to move mountains or create them…Then are we atoned with our intelligence and redeemed…This implies that being born to enter the Kingdom of God is not an endpoint, but rather a fantastic new beginning."
James Custer, *The Unspeakable Gift* [612]

It is the amazing Christ who modeled for us how to perform with great power and majesty! His life and ministry is a profound demonstration of what occurs when a soul dwells in oneness with the FATHER, MOTHER, and the TRUTH OF ALL THINGS.

OM

And there arose a great storm of wind, and the waves beat into the ship, so that it was now full.
And he was in the hinder part of the ship, asleep on a pillow: and they awake him, and say unto him,
Master, carest thou not that we perish? And he arose, and rebuked the wind, and said unto the sea,
Peace, be still. *And the wind ceased, and there was a great calm. And he said unto them,*
Why are ye so fearful? How is it that ye have no faith? And they feared exceedingly,
and said one to another, What manner of man is this, that even the wind and the sea obey him?
Mark 4:38-41

In truth, healings, miracles, and visions are part of the "Christ pattern" that Jesus is eager for all to experience. How humbling, that eventually we too will manifest divine power, for the Lord has promised, *"Verily, verily, I say unto you, He that believeth on me, the works that I do shall he do also; and greater works than these shall he do..."* (John 14:12). Father is even now providing the experiences we need so that eventually we too can organize matter with the Gods.

Divine Potential

"One day President Snow noticed a group of children working with clay. After watching the children for several minutes he then stated, 'these children are now at play, making mud worlds, the time will come when some of these boys, through their faithfulness to the gospel, will progress and develop in knowledge, intelligence and power, in future eternities, until they shall be able to go out into space where there is unorganized matter and call together the necessary elements, and through their knowledge of and control over the laws and powers of nature, to organize matter into worlds on which their posterity may dwell, and over which they shall rule as gods."
Lorenzo Snow, *Improvement Era* [613]

Obviously we are not yet prepared to organize our own universe. First, we must learn to master the internal galaxy in our own mind, body, and spirit. This process is accelerated when we learn how to maneuver light and energy through the energetic systems of the human body.

"In the resurrection, men who have been faithful and diligent in all things in the flesh, have kept their first and second estate, and are worthy to be crowned Gods, even the Sons of God, will be ordained to organize matter."
Brigham Young, *Discourses of Brigham Young* [614]

In truth, we need not wait for mortal death to organize matter. As children of light we are even now baby creators living in a sea of spiritual energy.

There is no such thing as immaterial matter. All spirit is matter, but it is more fine or pure, and can only be discerned by purer eyes; We cannot see it; but when our bodies are purified we shall see that it is all matter.
D&C 131: 7-8

We often read, *"faith is the substance of things hoped for, the evidence of things not seen,"*(Hebrews 11:1). But have we considered that *faith is a literal substance* existing within and around our physical bodies? Is it possible the presence of "faith" is an energetic substance that literally fuels the organization of matter? Would this not explain why the light of Christ is *"in all and through all things"* (D&C 88:6-7) and is the building block of all existence? (D&C 88:13).

> *"Man should know the everywhereness of God through the projection of "the light of truth,"*
> *from the presence of God, which is "the same light" that quickeneth the minds of men; "*
> *which light proceedeth forth from the presence of God to fill the immensity of space.*
> *The light which is in all things, which giveth life to all things, which is the law (i.e. power)*
> *by which all things are governed, even the power of God*
> *who is in the bosom of eternity, who is in the midst of all things."*
> Alvin R. Dyer, *The Meaning of Truth* [615]

One way to conceptualize the energy of faith is to compare it to an ever-growing or diminishing ball of fire within the soul. Initially this power is "unseen," but significant faith does provide the evidence for that which we hope. In other words, what exists internally, manifests externally. By obtaining knowledge concerning God's will, and then combining the faith of our spirit with the works of our body, a spiritual event or "miracle" is produced. Whatever depth and intensity is present within our soul, is the same degree to which we are able to perform Father's work.

LAZARUS

> *Jesus said, Take ye away the stone. Martha, the sister of him that was dead, saith unto him,*
> *Lord, by this time he stinketh: for he hath been dead four days. Jesus saith unto her, Said I not unto thee,*
> *that, if thou wouldest believe, thou shouldest see the glory of God? Then they took away the stone from*
> *the place where the dead was laid. And Jesus lifted up his eyes, and said, Father, I thank thee that thou hast*
> *heard me. And I knew that thou hearest me always: but because of the people which stand by I said it,*
> *that they may believe that thou hast sent me. And when he thus had spoken, he cried with a loud voice,*
> *Lazarus, come forth.*
> John 11:39-43

From a spiritual/scientific viewpoint, we should ponder, "how did Jesus raise Lazarus?" What is the method He used for healing leprosy (Matthew 8:3), escaping His enemies untouched (Luke 4:30), and providing the hungry multitude with loaves and fishes? (Matthew 15:32-38). Is there a formula available that can bolster our knowledge and spiritual power?

Part of the answer includes understanding the difference between a mature exalted God, and a growing child of God. (see Truth #62). When the faith of an individual is perfected, (as it is with Jesus), the soul no longer dwells in the realm of being separated from FATHER and the TRUTH OF ALL THINGS. The result of "dwelling" in this "ONE-NESS" includes the ability to organize universal substance instantaneously.

Hearken unto me, O Jacob and Israel, my called; I am he; I am the first, I also am the last.
*Mine hand also hath laid the foundation of the earth, and **my right hand hath spanned***
the heavens: when I call unto them, they stand up together.
Isaiah 48:12-13

In God, Love…Light…and Faith are the fundamental energies of the Universe. Emanating from the Totality of the Eloheim is the very energy and glory of all existence.

"There is life in all matter, throughout the vast extent of all the eternities; it is in the rock, the sand, the dust, in water, air, the gases, and in short, in every description and organization of matter, whether it be solid, liquid, or gaseous, particle operating with particle."
Brigham Young, *Discourses of Brigham Young* [616]

In the metaphysical community, the "life" Brigham Young referred to is called "energy." Eastern traditions term the light of Christ as "chi" or "prana." Regardless of the terminology used, it is inspiring to consider that the essence of Deity is present within every molecule of God's endless universe.

"Split a piece of wood, and I am there.
Lift a rock, and you will see me."
Gospel of Thomas [617]

When an individual stands in the power of Christ and commands cells which have been corrupted by cancer to "be thou clean," (Matthew 8:3), the energy of that particular disease is required to re-organize or depart. Whether referring to loaves, leukemia, or autism, *the intelligence, consciousness,* or *light of Christ* contained within those elements is required to obey under the jurisdiction of universal law. Thus as children of the Divine, we are blessed with the privilege to act and not just be acted upon. (2 Nephi 2:26). We too have the choice to literally magnify or diminish the Holy Intelligence dwelling within out soul.

"These intelligences are grades, from the lowest to the highest and the highest of all is God's intelligence himself and we are in-between. And some intelligences were assigned to the elements, and some were assigned to plant life, and some were assigned to animals.
And those that were his very special superior super deluxe intelligences were given bodies in his image and you are they. You are very, very special people."
Cleon Skousen, *A Personal Search for the Meaning of the Atonement* [618]

By understanding the formula for performing miracles, (knowledge + faith + sanctification = spiritual power to perform God's will), we accept that whether home teaching or raising the dead, the pattern is the same. In each unique circumstance, only that which represents the will of God, the degree of faith available, and subsequent miracle manifested is varied. Over time, God tutors us until we become personally capable of participating in healings, visions, and visitations. Instead of imagining these events as only happening to "someone else," *the power to interact on both sides of the veil becomes possible.* God's gospel, in all its mystery and depth, becomes real and personal.

Spiritual Gifts

"Does God interact with man as He once did in the days of Joseph and Paul? Do you believe that the great spiritual manifestations, blessings and outpouring of the gifts of the spirit have nearly ceased or become so much more toned down than they were in days of old because we are more mature in spiritual matters? Is this all because we have matured so much in the practice being a Zion people that we just don't need these special gifts anymore? or, is it simply because of the historical type and shadow of the unbelief of man?"
Anonymous Saint

Because of our fallen nature we labor within the limitations of spiritual death and struggle to manifest miracles. Our sins, (which eventually will be viewed as learning experiences where we missed the mark), maintain our temporary separation from Father in this realm and make it difficult to remember our spiritual nature. In truth, man is separate. God is One.

To meekly minister *"in the name of God"* requires those acting as conduit to at least temporarily span the apparent bridge between God and self. A partial "family reunion" must occur if the will and word of the Father is to be revealed and enacted.

*"Now, my brethren those are the parameters within which this priesthood must find expression. It is not as a cloak that we put on and take off at will. It is, when exercised in righteousness, as **the very tissue of our bodies**, a part of us at all times and in all circumstances."*
Gordon B. Hinkley, *Personal Worthiness to Exercise the Priesthood* [619]

The priesthood is not a prayer. It is the power of God unto salvation! Participating in the sacred ordinance of giving real priesthood blessings should not include vain repetitions. While we grow in our ability to speak true revelation, Father is patient with our weakness. He knows that we are little children doing the best we can and that initially we all display a mixture of faith and doubt. Over time faith increases until a relationship of trust is established with God. He leads the message and the miracle. We learn to speak His will with exactness. We are nothing, He is All.

Real Priesthood

"I find no cause for boasting in my priesthood—nothing is easier than conferring it upon one, but that is only the beginning; for it to be a real power requires a degree of concentration, dedication, and self-discipline which few ever attain to, and for the rest priesthood is not a blessing but a terrible risk. Very few men on earth, including those in the Church are really qualified. In terms of prestige, status, power, and authority and riches, the priesthood has absolutely nothing to offer. The world laughs at it, the latter-Day saints abuse or ignore it, those who take it seriously do so in "fear and trembling."
Hugh Nibley, *Priesthood* [620]

As Latter Day Saints all are offered access to true priesthood power. Whether male or female all are invited to develop various spiritual gifts while in mortality. Those who receive God's priesthood and the associated gifts are then able to demonstrate real faith, power, and healing. In so doing they fulfill prophecy.

And it shall come to pass afterward, that I will pour out my spirit upon all flesh; and your sons and your daughters shall prophesy, your old men shall dream dreams, your young men shall see visions…

Joel 2:28

As growing sons and daughters of God, all love, all healing, and all power is available to us. Perhaps the angels among us are bored, waiting to be asked for divine assistance that they may enact God's work with greater effectiveness. Today the invitation remains: Who will offer great sacrifice that faith may increase? Who is willing to develop the gift of healing? Will we stand and minister with love amongst a torn and bleeding world? Who can part the veil of illusion and receive the "one-ness" of *The Christ*? God is waiting, the world is suffering, the choice is ours.

A God of Power and Love

"One of the greatest miracles we can imagine is for someone to be brought back to life after being dead for a time. So it was with Lazarus, whom Jesus raised (see John 11:17, 39–44). So it has been with others in our day…It happened while Elder 'Iohani Wolfgramm and his wife were serving a mission in their native Tonga, presiding over a branch on an outlying island. Their three-year-old daughter was accidentally run over by a loaded taxi. Four of the occupants of the taxi sorrowfully carried her lifeless body to her parents. "Her head was crushed and her face was terribly disfigured." The sorrowing helpers offered to take the little girl's body to the hospital so the doctors could repair her severely damaged head and face for the funeral. I now quote the words of her father, Elder Wolfgramm: "I told them I did not want them to take her but that I would ask God what I should do and, if it was possible, to give her life back." The helpers took the little girl's body into the chapel. Elder Wolfgramm continued: "I asked them to hold her while I gave her a priesthood blessing. By then the curious people of the village were flocking in to see our stricken little daughter. As I was about to proceed with the administration, I felt tongue-tied. Struggling to speak, I got the distinct impression that I should not continue with the ordinance. It was as if a voice were speaking to me saying: 'This is not the right time, for the place is full of mockers and unbelievers. Wait for a more private moment.' "My speech returned at that moment and I addressed the group: 'The Lord has restrained me from blessing this little girl, because there are unbelievers among you who doubt this sacred ordinance. Please help me by leaving so I can bless my child." The people left without taking offense. The grieving parents carried the little girl to their home, put her body on her own bed, and covered her with a sheet. Three hours passed, and her body began to show the effects of death. The mother pleaded with the father to bless her, but he insisted that he still felt restrained. Finally, the impression came that he should now proceed. I return to his words: "All present in the home at that moment were people with faith in priesthood blessings. The feeling of what I should do and say was so strong within me that I knew Tisina would recover completely after the blessing. Thus, I anointed her head and blessed her in the name of Jesus Christ to be well and normal. I blessed her head and all her wounds to heal perfectly, thanking God for his goodness to me in allowing me to hold his priesthood and bring life back to my daughter. I asked him to open the doors of Paradise, so I could tell her to come back and receive her body again and live. The Lord then spoke to my heart and said, 'She will return to you tomorrow. You will be reunited then." The parents spent an anxious night beside the body of the little girl, who appeared to be lifeless. Then, suddenly, the little girl awoke, alive and well. Her father's account concludes: "I grabbed her and examined her, her head and face. They were perfectly normal. All her wounds were healed; and from that day to this, she has experienced no complications from the accident. Her life was the miraculous gift from Heavenly Father during our missionary labors in Fo'ui."

Dallin H. Oaks, *Miracles* [621]

352

> **TRUTH #62** EVERY SON AND DAUGHTER OF GOD IS OF DIVINE WORTH. TO APPRECIATE THE INFINITE AND ETERNAL NATURE OF THE SOUL REQUIRES AN UNDERSTANDING OF "THE INTELLIGENCE" OR "HIGHER SELF." EACH AWAKENS TO THEIR PERSONAL POTENTIAL AND IDENTITY AT VARIOUS TIMES AND IN DIFFERENT WAYS.

"In the Church of Jesus Christ of Latter Day Saints, the individual, the human soul, is of utmost importance. We are the sons and daughters of God. He loves us…We need to constantly remember that faith in God is reflected in faith in oneself."
Marvin J. Ashton, *Faith* [622]

Initially, many of us conceptualize "the veil" as being like a blanket that covers the entire earth. However the veil is more of an individual mental phenomenon, a type of spiritual amnesia-which when in full force, filters out an accurate perception of God, life, and self.

**In the Culture of Religion,
Tradition is Greatness**

**In Life,
Love is Greatness**

**In God,
You are Greatness**

Looking into the eyes of a tiny infant often reveals a deep and holy "knowing." As the baby adjusts to mortality the veil intensifies, until sometime during the toddler years, awareness of visits from Heavenly Mother and the angels usually starts to wane. Over time the veil settles into full force and we become like Adam, "having forgotten all."

During mortality if we allow the Holy Spirit to repeatedly sanctify us, the veil "thins" and we begin to see God, life, and self more clearly. Incrementally, our true identity and divine potential is revealed until we begin to remember and reclaim our divine heritage. In Christ, we come to understand that *we are not* the fallen and flawed beings we previously imagined ourselves to be. We awaken.

Remembering the True Self

"We turn our minds to what has happened to us since we left that pre-mortal world of Light and entered this narrower, darker world, reduced from our pre-mortal capacities, and our memory veiled. **We see that without the memory of who we really are, we begin to create something of an artificial self, a mortal overlay, where false perceptions and distortion layer over the brilliant, eternal, pre-mortal spirit. As this artificial overlay accumulates with stuff, our fears, our personality distortions, our weaknesses, our pride, our blindness, our contraction of spirit, our controlling behaviors, our un-love, all these begin to lodge in the overlay, acting like mists and clouds over our brilliance and beauty, troubling our behavior and experience.** *But the Savior lifts the veil for us* **when He tells us who we really are***: "Ye were also in the beginning with the Father; that which is Spirit, even the Spirit of truth" (D&C 93:23); and, "The day shall come [that you shall know] . . . that I am the true light that is in you, and that you are in me; otherwise ye could not abound." Because we are of the Spirit of Truth, and because Christ's Light of Truth gives our soul life,* **there are many transcendent and divine qualities in us***. We can't help it – that's just who we are.* **Our problem lies in our identifying more with our artificial self than with our eternal self. But we can choose to stop identifying with this false self's doubt and negativity, and awaken more to our eternal self which holds these transcendent qualities. These qualities include Reverence for All Life, Pure Love, Perfect Faith, and an innate ability to Commune with the Lord."*

M. Catherine Thomas, *Shifting our Thinking: the Second Shift* [623]

A great awakening occurs when we realize we have not only forgotten the glory of God, but also *our own true and eternal nature.* Parting the veil helps us stop identifying with the "false-self" or "little-me," and instead put our faith in an omniscient God who sees our eventual exaltation!

The Christ Essence Within

"He preached the gospel; so can we. He spoke by the power of the Holy Ghost; so can we. He served as a missionary; so can we. He went about doing good; so can we. He performed the ordinances of salvation; so can we. He kept the commandments; so can we. He wrought miracles; such also is our privilege if we are true and faithful in all things...We are his agents; we represent him; we are expected to do and say what he would do and say if he personally were ministering among men at this time... We have power to become the sons of God, to be adopted into the family of the Lord Jesus Christ, to have him as our Father, to be one with him as he is one with his Father...the Lord said to Adam. "Behold, thou art one in me, a son of God; and thus may all become my sons. (Moses 6:67–68)."

Bruce R. McConkie, *The Ten Blessings of the Priesthood* [624]

Those devoted to modeling the life of Jesus Christ are invited to consider a more complex and comprehensive view concerning God and His universal nature. The effect of wanting to *"know Him,"* is an invitation to truly *"know self."*

The Organization of a Holy Intelligence

Man was also in the beginning with God.
Intelligence, or the light of truth, was not created or made, neither indeed can be.
Doctrine and Covenants 93:29

In what we term "the beginning," a divine organization of eternal and uncreated substance occurred. From the totality of all things, the Eloheim organized a unique reality where opposition, duality, relativity, and distinction could co-exist. The "up" was divided from "down," the "here" from the "there."

And God saw the light, that is was good: and God divided the light from the darkness.
And God called the Light Day, and the darkness he called Night…And God saw everything
that he had made, And behold it was very good.
Genesis 1: 4,5,31

When duality was established within this universe, (termed by science as the "Big Bang") the *"Intelligence of man"* was organized from the Holy Spirit of Mother and Father. (D&C 93:29). Manifested through the divine power of creation, a fundamental differentiation of energy occurred, resulting in the formation of spirit element.

"The intelligence out of which we were created might just as accurately be referred to as
the "word" or "thought" of God. In Genesis 1:3 we read that God speaks light into existence.
Or we might describe it as God imagining or conceiving light into existence. Since we are made of
light, or truth, or the glory of God, it would be equally true that He conceives or imagines us
into existence. It was both a creative act and an act of faith for God to conceive of us."
Denver Snuffer, *Beloved Enos* [625]

While the "All-ness," "Is-ness," and "Totality" of absolute reality remains, (pointed to in Mormonism with terms such as "omniscience," "eternity to eternity," and the "celestial realm."), a relative reality was also organized to bring to pass *the immortality and eternal life of man* (Moses 1:39). This realm includes the telestial world in which we now live.

"Hence, we infer that God Himself had materials to organize the world out of chaos —
chaotic matter — which is element and in which dwells all the glory. Element had an existence
from the time He had. The pure principles of element are principles that never can be destroyed.
They may be organized and reorganized, but not destroyed. Nothing can be destroyed.
They never can have a beginning or an ending; they exist eternally."
Joseph Smith, *The King Follett Discourse* [626]

The "Intelligence," from which our spirit body was derived, is uncreated, eternal, and infinite. It is god-like in nature, (with a small "g"), and exists as spirit element. Intelligence, or *who you really are*, is nothing less than a god in ascension.

Now the Lord had shown unto me, Abraham, the intelligences that were organized before the world was;
and among all these there were many of the noble and great ones;
Abraham 3:22

This "Higher-Self" cannot be adequately contained within a finite physical body, but rather exists **within and beyond the flesh.** Although we often imagine the spirit to be inside the physical body, it is actually the spirit that "holds" or contains the physical body within its stewardship.

Both the spirit body and the physical body are organized from eternal and uncreated "matter." Because the divine substance used to organize our physical body vibrates at a slower rate, the physical body is observable and touchable to the basic senses. What has been termed "spirit" or "aura" is more subtle and requires a thinning of the veil to be perceived with the natural eye. (D&C 131:7-8).

By organizing existence in this manner, a type of "virtual reality" was created for God's children. Spirit element could now embody and have the opportunity to experience good and evil, love and joy, pleasure and pain. Once embodied upon the mortal playground of earth, the intelligence could magnify, that in tasting the "bitter," we might become the "sweet."

The Organization of the Spirit Body

"God made the tabernacle of man out of the earth and put into him Adam's spirit (Michael),
and then he became a living body or human soul. Man existed in spirit; the mind of man—
the intelligent part-is as immortal as, and is coequal with, God Himself.
I know that my testimony is true."
Joseph Smith, *The King Follett Discourse* [627]

In truth, "we" are travelers here, organized from the same energetic material as Father and all existence. Mortal life is merely a context the Gods use to provide spiritual progression to their developing children. To facilitate the joyous and eternal increase that exaltation offers, Adam and Eve chose transgression, *"that man may be."*[628]

Each of "us" is similar to Adam-in the sense that just as his spirit was derived from/and is "Michael," the "I" that we know ourselves to be here on earth has also been organized directly from an Intelligence. This holy and eternal light is the "God-spark" that burns within us, and represents the *Christ essence within.*

...the day shall come when you shall comprehend even God, being quickened in him and by him.
*Then shall ye know that ye have seen me, that I am, and that **I am the true light that is in you,***
***and that you are in me;** otherwise ye could not abound.*
Doctrine and Covenants 88:49-50

One way to conceptualize our composite identity is to compare the spiritual and physical nature of the Intelligence to ice and water. Both have been organized from the same energetic element, (H_2O) but are manifest in different forms.

All things are created "spiritually" before they manifest "physically." Both the visible, (physical-observable matter) and the "invisible," (spiritual-often unobservable matter), are literally organized from the eternal and uncreated light of Christ. This ongoing process of *energetic re-organization* allows the Intelligence to *act and be acted upon.* (2 Nephi 2:14).

Similar to how our physical bodies have cells, organs, and systems that function, our spirit body also has an energetic anatomy organized to fulfill the measure of its creation. In true reality we exist as *divine energy* capable of housing a physical body when preferable. For we are *literally* in the Father and the Father is *literally* in us. (D&C 88:41).

For ye are the temple of the living God; as God has said, I will dwell in them, and walk in them; and will be their God, and they shall be my people.
2 Corinthians 6:16

The Intelligence of God is composed of the nature and matter of God's universal soul. Unlike the fallen mind, the Intelligence, from which we were derived, exists on both sides of the veil and is not limited to time in the way "we" conceptualize reality. During the experience of mortality the Intelligence remains connected with Father, while the "self" we initially imagine ourselves to be experiences spiritual death. Living in a difficult, fallen soul, dealing with a difficult, fallen world, can be, well…difficult. But how abundantly glorious it is to learn that the mortal self is only a small portion of our true and complete existence. The temporal self is the aspect we remember, see, and touch while living here within the veil, but it is not the full "I Am," whose composite sum only dwells within the realm of eternity.

At first, this concept may seem strange and unusual, but each of "us" (The Intelligence) knew in the pre-mortal realm that to partake of exaltation would require our spirit body receive a physical tabernacle and then grow through experience toward perfection.

The Intelligence is Eternal
It is the "I AM" of who you are

In summary, the Intelligence is the "true-self," "god-self," or "me without the veil." To understand this perspective reveals a partial view of how God sees us in eternity.

*"…when we can see ourselves as God sees us and comprehend ourselves as he comprehends us, and understand our position as he understands it, we should have different views of ourselves than we have when unenlightened by the Spirit. No wonder that Joseph Smith should say that he felt himself shut up in a nutshell, there was no power of expansion, it was difficult for him to reveal and communicate the things of God, because there was **no place to receive them**. What he had to communicate was so much more comprehensive, enlightened and dignified than that which the people generally knew and comprehended, it was difficult for him to speak; he felt fettered and bound to speak, in every move he made, and so it is to the present time. Yet this being a fact and these being part of the things we expect to accomplish, there must be a beginning somewhere; and if the chips do fly once in a while when the hewer begins to hew, and **if we do squirm once in a while it is not strange, because it is so difficult for the people to comprehend the things which are for their benefit***

We have been brought up so ignorantly and our ideas and views are so contracted it is scarcely possible to receive the things of God as they exist in his bosom."
John Taylor, *Journal of Discourses* [629]

As we awaken to the deeper reality of God and our true nature, a fundamental choice is revealed. To remain in the fallen state of the "small-self," (Ego-natural man), or to become purified that we might be redeemed and enter into the collective Glory of God!

"Spirituality, our true aim, is the consciousness of victory over self, and of communion with the Infinite. Spirituality impels one to conquer difficulties and acquire more and more strength. To feel one's faculties unfolding, and truth expanding in the soul, is one of life's sublimest experiences."
David O. Mckay, *Conference Report* [630]

For those who have been entwined in the chains of sin, it is a great relief to find out we are not who we once thought we were! (fallen mortal self). And that in the end we will go home to the Intelligence, or *"God who gave us life."* (Alma 40:11).

"The indwelling intelligence expands within us to our fullness and to our perfection in all things. We are reconciled and atoned with God, his universe, and therefore with the intelligence who animates us and loves us, and has labored with us through our mortal probationary ordeal and who is now fulfilled in oneness with us. There is no longer any dichotomy between the infinite intelligence and the finite body; we are whole, having fulfilled the Christ pattern. We are like Jesus the Christ and capable of performing the same works."
James Custer, *The Unspeakable Gift* [631]

The reality of our true identity is pointed to by the profound saying, *"we are not human beings having a spiritual experience, we are spiritual beings having a human experience."*[632] Members often say that they want to "feel the Spirit," but life is actually more about the spirit "feeling the body." This perspective, (and others like it) tend to sooth the soul and enliven the mind. The awakening reveals that *all truth* points toward God and our true identity.

Sensing the "I AM"

"That which "acts," the Lord says, is called "intelligence" or "light."
So we ask, what then is an "intelligence?"
There is no description, except that it's like "light." And everything that exists,
which is "truth," is filled with intelligence. Everything is filled with it.
Perhaps the best way for you to know about "intelligence" is to find out about it
the way I found out about it. I said to Brother Widtsoe,
"What is an "intelligence" like?" He said to me, "Well, look in the mirror and tell him-
you are an intelligence. "Oh that's right, that's good! Yes, I am an intelligence." I said.
Then he asked, "How big are you?
Where are you?" I said I'm right here. "
No," he said, "you're not down there-did you notice?
Isn't that *down* from where you are? Take a hold of your chin and shut your eyes....
Is that below you or above you? Now take hold of your ears....Is that beside you?
Where is your little "I Am?" I replied, "Its way in there isn't it?"
He said, "I think so. It's a little tiny "I Am."
It is self knowing, self determining, anticipatory, and it can learn.
It is a little *intelligence.* Fascinating!
And this little *intelligence* has always existed
as an independent entity-a little "I Am."
W. Cleon Skousen, *A Personal Search for the Meaning of the Atonement* [633]

For those willing to restructure and magnify their beliefs concerning God, life, and self, a marvelous paradox is revealed through the doctrine of the Intelligence. In our fallen state we represent beings who are *"less than the dust of the earth,"* (Helaman 12:7), while simultaneously existing as a little god in ascension. (Psalms 82:6).

"If we take man, he is said to have been made in the image of God, for the simple reason
that he is a son of God, and being his son, he is, of course, his offspring, an emanation from God,
in whose likeness, we are told, he is made. He did not originate from a chaotic mass of matter,
moving or inert, but came forth possessing, in an embryonic state, all the faculties and powers
of a God. And when he shall be perfected, and have progressed to maturity,
he will be like his Father — a God."
John Taylor, *The Gospel Kingdom* [634]

When the portion of the Intelligence which is embodied sins, the natural man or woman suffers, while our true essence remains *eternally* connected to God. This spiritual arrangement has been organized that "we," (as baby gods in ascension, but not yet exalted), might utilize the experiences of mortality to magnify the soul. By experiencing *"opposition in all things,"* (2 Nephi 2:11), we learn to *transcend all things*. In this sense, the "I AM" of self is able to "have its cake," (dwelling in union with God), and "eat it too," (magnification through experience and sanctification).

> *"As finite creatures, we are the only begotten and therefore the firstborn of the intelligences*
> *to whom we belong. The intelligences are in essence, father or mother types in the sense*
> *that they have nurtured us from the beginning. We belong to our intelligence;*
> *our intelligence does not belong to us, as we commonly think."*
> James Custer, *The Unspeakable Gift* [635]

One way to grasp this spiritual arrangement is to consider the "mind-body-spirit" we know ourselves to be in this life, to be only a part or portion of the Intelligence. After physical death occurs and the mortal journey is completed, that same "mind-body-spirit" returns home to be integrated into the Intelligence from whence it came! (Alma 40:11). Similar to "uploading a computer," the individual personality and growth of that particular person remains, while simultaneously contributing to the ongoing collective increase of the Intelligence.

> *"The Intelligence came first. It is the "I AM" of each of us, the first manifestation; it is the mind, source,*
> *and center of all consciousness, intellect, and awareness. The finite spiritual physical body is simply*
> *a useful appendage, a creative and reproductive tabernacle for the intelligence."*
> James Custer, *The Unspeakable Gift* [636]

This wise configuration has been accomplished that the Intelligence, or *"glory of God,"* (D&C 93:36), might expand through the vehicle of mortal life. By participating in *"that which has been done in other worlds,"*[637] the Intelligence achieves eternal and ongoing increase. No wonder God said *"let there be light,"* and saw that *"it was good."* (Genesis 1:3-4).

Understanding the glory and reality of the Intelligence results in asking one fundamental question: Who am I?

I Am the Soul

I AM that I AM
I AM not the body
I AM not the emotions
I AM not the thoughts
I AM not the mind.
The mind is only a subtle instrument
Of the Soul.

I AM a Spiritual being of Divine Intelligence
Divine Love, Divine Power,
I AM one with the Higher Soul
I AM that I AM

I AM one with the Divine Spark
I AM a Child of God
I AM connected with God.
I AM one with God.
I AM one with All.

Master Choa Kok Sui, *Achieving Oneness with the Higher Soul* [638]

The Greatest Revelation

I have said, Ye are gods; and all of you are children of the most High.
Psalms 82:6

When Jesus proclaimed, "I AM THAT I AM" (Exodus 3:14), He was describing *The Christ* nature of His Father, *The Christ* nature of Himself, and *The Christ* nature existing within each of us.

Molding a Masterpiece

You are a "marvelous work and wonder" that cannot be accurately defined
by how much you "do or don't do" in mortality.
Only in the realm of "divine being"
can we begin to receive an accurate view of our true eternal worth.

To assist us in awakening to our divine potential, God often provides or allows the "dark night of the soul." These difficult and heart-wrenching experiences are necessary to curtail the natural man. Stemming from the pain we suffer, we begin to differentiate between the thoughts we have, and the spirit we simply know. Instead of being controlled by the ranting of the mind, we start to dwell in the peace of the soul.

This process of awakening is metaphorical to the experience of wicked Laban, whose head/ego was severed by the sharpness of a two-edged sword. (God's Holy Word). For it is better that the mind of the natural man should "perish," than a nation of kings and queens dwindle in unbelief. Thus all are left to determine whether they will be a "Laban" or a "Nephi?"

Have you heard "the Voice?"

Can you differentiate between the confusion and shouts of the natural man
and the peaceful guidance of the Holy Spirit that dwells within?

Will you begin to notice that your thoughts are a very small aspect
of who you really are?

Have you ever observed your thoughts from a distance,
utilizing the ones that are loving, useful, and true
while allowing that which is negative, selfish, or dark to be released?

To facilitate a deeper integration of the embodied spirit with the eternal Intelligence, Father encourages His children to listen to the *still small voice.* Like a wise parent, the "Holy Spirit" of the "Higher Self" uses the voice of conscience to provide the perfect sermon at the perfect moment.

"The Spirit of Christ can be likened unto a "guardian angel" for every person."
Boyd K. Packer, *The Light of Christ* [639]

As we grow beyond what we believe, to *who* we know, the soul seeks reconciliation with that which simply "IS." Those who reach this "Holy of Holies" experience a "vibrant peace" that transcends the common doldrums of this world. They know Jesus meant it when He smiled and said, *"for behold the kingdom of God is within you!"* (Luke 17:21).

Remembering this reality, even for a brief moment, helps us realize God and the Intelligent Spirit, from whom "we" are derived, is always around us, in us, and with us. Consequently, our understanding is enlarged concerning who and what the "Holy Ghost" really is.

Hereby know we that we dwell in him, and he in us, because he hath given us of his Spirit.
And we have seen and do testify that the Father sent the Son to be the Savior of the world.
*Whosoever shall confess that Jesus is the Son of God, **God dwelleth in him, and he in God**.*
*And we have known and believed the love that God hath to us. God is love; and **he that dwelleth in love***
***dwelleth in God, and God in him**. Herein is our love made perfect, that we may have boldness*
*in the day of judgment: because **as he is, so are we in this world**.*
1 John 4:13-17

In truth, all of life, with its challenges and lessons, invites us to be reconciled to God and the god within. Father is eager to reveal our true identity, with its accompanying name and sign, but only after we have integrated sufficiently with all that is "GOD." Joseph Smith understood the glory and power of this relationship when he stated, *"If men do not comprehend the character of God, they do not comprehend themselves."* [640]

His Sacred Invitation
Behold, here is the agency of man, and here is the condemnation of man; because that which was from
the beginning is plainly manifest unto them, and they receive not the light. And every man whose spirit
*receiveth not the light is under condemnation. **For man is spirit. The elements are eternal,***
and spirit and element, inseparably connected, receive a Fullness of joy; And when separated,
***man cannot receive a fullness of joy.** The elements are the tabernacle of God;*
yea, man is the tabernacle of God, even temples; and whatsoever temple is defiled,
*God shall destroy that temple. **The glory of God is intelligence,***
***or in other words, light and truth**.*
D&C 93:31-36

*For behold, the Lord God hath sent forth the angel crying through the midst of heaven,
saying: Prepare ye the way of the Lord, and make his paths straight, for the hour of his coming is nigh—
When the Lamb shall stand upon Mount Zion, and with him a hundred and forty-four thousand,
having his Father's name written on their foreheads. Wherefore, prepare ye for the coming of
the Bridegroom; go ye, go ye out to meet him. For behold, he shall stand upon the mount of Olivet,
and upon the mighty ocean, even the great deep, and upon the islands of the sea, and upon the land
of Zion. And he shall utter his voice out of Zion, and he shall speak from Jerusalem, and his voice
shall be heard among all people; And it shall be a voice as the voice of many waters, and as the voice
of a great thunder, which shall break down the mountains, and the valleys shall not be found.
He shall command the great deep, and it shall be driven back into the north countries, and the islands
shall become one land; And the land of Jerusalem and the land of Zion shall be turned back into their own
place, and the earth shall be like as it was in the days before it was divided. And the Lord, even the Savior,
shall stand in the midst of his people, and shall reign over all flesh.*
D&C 133:17-25

Powerful and illuminating events will soon transform the earth. In addition to the prophesied darkness and destruction, the future will also include abundant light and amazing miracles. What will be considered by some as *"the end of the world,"* will be for others the *"beginning of heaven on earth."* All that is to be enacted will work together to fulfill the Lord's eternal purposes. The question is, are we ready?

*"On the last night of the play, a whole cast and stage crew stay in the theater until the small,
or not so small, hours of the morning striking the old set. If there is to be a new opening soon,
as the economy of theater requires, it is important that the new set should be in place and ready
for the opening night; all the while the old set was finishing its usefulness and then being taken down,
the new set was rising in splendor to be ready for the drama that would immediately follow.
So it is with this world. It is not our business to tear down the old set-the agencies that do that are already
hard at work and very efficient-the set is coming down all around us with spectacular effect.
Our business is to see to it that the new set is well on the way for what is to come-and that means
a different kind of politics, beyond the scope of the tragedy that is now playing its closing night.
We are preparing for the establishment of Zion."*
Hugh Nibley [641]

Those who survive taking down the "old set" will be blessed to observe, participate, and contribute to the "new set" and the fulfillment of latter-day prophecy. The following scriptures, quotes, and comments identify a few of the key spiritual events yet to occur.

Receive the Sealed Portion of the Plates

"Question: When will we receive more of the mind and will of the Lord, and when will the great doctrinal restoration be completed?"

"Answer: We have a revealed answer as to **when we shall receive the sealed portion of the Book of Mormon. What we have so far received is to test our faith. When we repent of all our iniquity and become clean before the Lord, and when we exercise faith in him like unto the brother of Jared, then the sealed portion of the ancient word will be translated and read from the housetops...** *Why should the Lord give us more of the biblical word if we are indifferent to what he has already revealed? Does anyone think the Lord should give us the words of Zenos when we are ignoring the words of Isaiah? There are revelations without end that are available to the faithful at any time they are prepared to receive them.* **As a matter of practical reality, however, the great doctrinal restoration is to be Millennial.** *Of that day Nephi said: Then "the earth shall be full of the knowledge of the Lord as the waters cover the sea. Wherefore, the things of all nations shall be made known; yea, all things shall be made known unto the children of men. There is nothing which is secret save it shall be revealed; there is no work of darkness save it shall be made manifest in the light; and there is nothing which is sealed upon the earth save it shall be loosed.* **Wherefore, all things which have been revealed unto the children of men shall at that day be revealed;** *and Satan shall have power over the hearts of the children of men no more, for a long time. (2 Nephi 30:15-18)."*

"Question: What are the vehicles of the Restoration?"

"Answer: **First, the Book of Mormon***, which was translated by the gift and power of God; second, the Doctrine and Covenants, whose contents are revealed, coupled with such inspired utterances as the King Follett Sermon; and, third, the so-called Translations, which include the book of Abraham, the book of Moses (itself part of the Inspired Version), and the whole Joseph Smith Translation of the Bible. None of these vehicles have given us their full load.* **We have only about a third of the Book of Mormon; the field of revelation is without bounds or limits;** *and the Bible restoration has scarcely been commenced."*
Bruce R. McConkie, *The Doctrinal Restoration* [642]

Join the Gathering at Adam-ondi-Ahman

"This **council in the valley of Adam-ondi-Ahman** *is to be of the greatest importance to this world. At that time there will be a transfer of authority from the usurper and imposter, Lucifer, to the rightful King, Jesus Christ. Judgment will be set and all who have held keys will* **make their reports and deliver their stewardships,** *as they shall be required...Our Lord will then assume the reigns of government; directions will be given to the Priesthood; and He, whose right it is to rule, will be installed officially by the voice of the Priesthood there assembled. This grand council of Priesthood will be composed, not only of those who are faithful who now dwell on this earth, but also of the prophets and apostles of old, who have had directing authority. Others may also be there, but if so they will be there by appointment, for this is to be an official council called to attend to the most momentous matters concerning the destiny of this earth. When this gathering is held, the world will not know of it;*

the members of the Church at large will not know of it, yet it shall be preparatory to the coming in the clouds of glory of our Savior Jesus Christ as the Prophet Joseph Smith has said. **The world cannot know of it. The Saints cannot know of it-except those who officially shall be called into this council-** *for it shall precede the coming of Jesus Christ as a thief in the night, unbeknown to all the world."*
Joseph Fielding Smith, *The Way to Perfection* [643]

Behold, this is the preparation wherewith I prepare you...That through my providence, **notwithstanding the tribulation which shall descend upon you,** *that the church may stand independent above all other creatures beneath the celestial world; That* **you may come up unto the crown prepared for you, and be made rulers over many kingdoms,** *saith the Lord God, the Holy One of Zion, who hath established the foundations of* **Adam-ondi-Ahman;** *Who hath appointed Michael your prince, and established his feet, and set him upon high, and given unto him the keys of salvation under the counsel and direction of the Holy One, who is without beginning of days or end of life. Verily, verily, I say unto you, ye are little children, and ye have not as yet understood how great blessings the Father hath in his own hands and prepared for you; And ye cannot bear all things now;* **nevertheless, be of good cheer, for I will lead you along. The kingdom is yours and the blessings thereof are yours, and the riches of eternity are yours.**
D&C 78:13-18

Greet the Ten Tribes at Their Return

"We believe in the literal gathering of Israel and in the restoration of the Ten Tribes; that Zion (the New Jerusalem) will be built upon the American continent; that Christ will reign personally upon the earth; and, that the earth will be renewed and receive its paradisiacal glory."
Joseph Smith, *Article of Faith Ten* [644]

After this vision closed, the heavens were again opened unto us; and Moses appeared before us, and **committed unto us the keys of the gathering of Israel** *from the four parts of the earth, and the* **leading of the ten tribes from the land of the north.**
D&C 110:11

"If there's anything that sets the gospel of Jesus Christ apart from all other religions of the world...it's the literal, matter-of-fact view it takes of realities in this life and beyond this life, the view resting on the experience of very real and vivid contacts between men upon the earth and beings from higher spheres. This sense of literal reality is most clearly set forth in our Tenth Article of Faith. The other articles have to do with our beliefs, principles, ordinances, and divine gifts: they are timeless in their application and could belong to any dispensation. But Article Ten deals explicitly with our time and our space and sets forth the steps by which God intends to consummate this great latter-day work."
Hugh Nibley, *Approaching Zion* [645]

"There are five such steps:
(1) The literal gathering of Israel.
(2) The restoration of the Ten Tribes.
(3) The building of Zion (the New Jerusalem) upon the American continent.
(4) Christ's personal reign upon the earth.
(5) The renewal of the earth in its paradisiacal glory."

"In each of these steps earthly time and place are implicit. The statement does not pinpoint either,
but it leaves no doubt at all that things are going to happen in a definite temporal order and involve people
living in definite places on this particular planet. The Latter-day Saints have often become confused
about the "game plan" of unfolding processes in these latter days by giving undue priority to one event
over another or by arbitrarily shifting the order of events to suit some preconceived plans of their own.
But one thing is clear: the Lord has given us here an outline of the whole plan as far as it concerns us.
It behooves us, therefore, to keep the whole plan in mind and, as in all great projects, never to lose sight
of the ultimate goal while we are working toward the necessary intermediate goals or steps.
Here the final step in the whole progression is that the earth will be renewed and receive
its paradisiacal glory. Quite literally, "heaven is our destination."
Hugh Nibley, *Approaching Zion* [646]

Be Ordained as Part of 144,000 High Priests

Q. What are we to understand by sealing the one hundred and forty-four thousand,
out of all the tribes of Israel—twelve thousand out of every tribe?

A. We are to understand that those who are sealed are high priests, ordained unto the holy order of
God, to administer the everlasting gospel; for they are they who are ordained out of every nation,
kindred, tongue, and people, by the angels to whom is given power over the nations of the earth,
to bring as many as will come to the church of the Firstborn.
Doctrine and Covenants 77:11

Today LDS missionaries invite souls to come unto Christ and be baptized into The *Church of Jesus Christ of Latter Day Saints*. In the future, the Lord's messengers will canvass the earth one final time to gather out the righteous from *"every nation, kindred, tongue and people."* (1 Nephi 19:16-17). These born-again emissaries will invite the righteous who remain to gather unto Zion and enter into the *Church of the Firstborn*. (D&C 76:52-60).

Those who are part of the 144,000 will risk their lives to preach the Gospel and gather the wheat. To overcome the evil they face will require possessing great spiritual power. (see Gift of Translation in Truth #70).

And I will give power *unto my two witnesses, and they shall prophesy a thousand two hundred and threescore days, clothed in sackcloth. And if any man will hurt them, fire proceedeth out of their mouth, and devoureth their enemies: and if any man will hurt them, he must in this manner be killed.*
These have power to shut heaven, that it rain not in the days of their prophecy: and have power over waters to turn them to blood, and to smite the earth with all plagues, as often as they will. And when they shall

have finished their testimony, the beast that ascendeth out of the bottomless pit shall make war against them, and shall overcome them, and kill them. And their dead bodies shall lie in the street of the great city, which spiritually is called Sodom and Egypt, where also our Lord was crucified. And they of the people and kindreds and tongues and nations shall see their dead bodies three days and an half, and shall not suffer their dead bodies to be put in graves. And they that dwell upon the earth shall rejoice over them, and make merry, and shall send gifts one to another; because these two prophets tormented them that dwelt on the earth. And after three days and an half the Spirit of life from God entered into them, and they stood upon their feet; and great fear fell upon them which saw them. And they heard a great voice from heaven saying unto them, Come up hither. And they ascended up to heaven in a cloud; and their enemies beheld them.

Revelations 11: 3, 5-12

Establish the Holy City of Zion

"She (Zion) will be great because she will be glorious and beautiful, powerful and unassailable. Her enemies will try and fail to distress her. She will glow with the power of God day and night and will set at defiance the armies of nations, defending herself even by fire from heaven. She will be beautiful because there will be no struggle within her walls, no pain or illness, neither sorrow nor death. And within her sacred environs the Son of God will dwell."

John Pontius, *The Triumph of Zion* [647]

*And the Lord said unto Enoch: As I live, even so **will I come in the last days**, in the days of wickedness and vengeance, to fulfil the oath which I have made unto you concerning the children of Noah; And the day shall come that the earth shall rest, but before that day the heavens shall be darkened, and a veil of darkness shall cover the earth; and the heavens shall shake, and also the earth; and great tribulations shall be among the children of men, **but my people will I preserve; And righteousness will I send down out of heaven; and truth will I send forth out of the earth, to bear testimony of mine Only Begotten;** his resurrection from the dead; yea, and also the resurrection of all men; and righteousness and truth will I cause to sweep the earth as with a flood, **to gather out mine elect from the four quarters of the earth, unto a place which I shall prepare, an Holy City,** that my people may gird up their loins, and be looking forth for the time of my coming; for there shall be my tabernacle, and **it shall be called Zion, a New Jerusalem.***

Moses 7:60-62

Welcome the Translated City of Enoch

*And the Lord said unto Enoch: **Then shalt thou and all thy city meet them there, and we will receive them into our bosom, and they shall see us; and we will fall upon their necks, and they shall fall upon our necks, and we will kiss each other; And there shall be mine abode, and it shall be Zion,** which shall come forth out of all the creations which I have made; and **for the space of a thousand years the earth shall rest.***

Moses 7:63-64

*"We have no business here other than to build up and establish the Zion of God. It must be done according to the will and law of God, **after that pattern and order by which Enoch** built up and perfected the former-day Zion, which was taken away to heaven, hence the saying went abroad that Zion had fled. **By and by it will come back again**, and as Enoch prepared his people to be worthy of translation, so we, through our faithfulness, **must prepare ourselves to meet Zion from above** when it shall return to earth, and to abide the brightness and glory of its coming."*
Brigham Young, *Discourses of Brigham Young* [648]

Shout with Joy at the Global Return of the Lord Jesus Christ

For the hour is nigh and the day soon at hand when the earth is ripe; and all the proud and they that do wickedly shall be as stubble; and I will burn them up, saith the Lord of Hosts, that wickedness shall not be upon the earth; For the hour is nigh, and that which was spoken by mine apostles must be fulfilled; for as they spoke so shall it come to pass; For I will reveal myself from heaven with power and great glory, with all the hosts thereof, and dwell in righteousness with men on earth a thousand years, and the wicked shall not stand.
Doctrine and Covenants 29:9-11

And then shall appear the sign of the Son of man in heaven: and then shall all the tribes of the earth mourn, and they shall see the Son of man coming in the clouds of heaven with power and great glory. And he shall send his angels with a great sound of a trumpet, and they shall gather together his elect from the four winds, from one end of heaven to the other.
Matthew 24:30-31

And another trump shall sound…unto all nations, kindreds, tongues, and people; And this shall be the sound of his trump, saying to all people, both in heaven and in earth, and that are under the earth— for every ear shall hear it, and every knee shall bow, and every tongue shall confess, while they hear the sound of the trump, saying: Fear God, and give glory to him who sitteth upon the throne, forever and ever; for the hour of his judgment is come.
Doctrine and Covenants 88:103-104

The faithful know that all prophecy will be fulfilled and that the work of the Lord will succeed. To contribute to and participate in this future "marvelous work and a wonder" is a great honor that makes any momentary sacrifice for Christ a personal privilege.

TRUTH #64 PRIOR TO THE WORLD BEING AFFLICTED WITH SEVERE DESTRUCTION, HEAVENLY FATHER WILL GATHER AND PROTECT HIS CHILDREN.

Ready to Gather?

"In this dispensation there is a principle or commandment peculiar to it. What is that? It is the gathering of the people to one place. The gathering of this people is as necessary to be observed by believers, as faith, repentance, baptism, or any other ordinance. It is an essential part of the Gospel of this dispensation, as much so as the necessity of building an ark by Noah for his deliverance, was a part of the Gospel in his dispensation. Then the world was destroyed by a flood, now it is to be destroyed by war, pestilence, famine, earthquakes, storms, and tempests, the sea roiling beyond its bounds, malarious vapors, vermin, disease, and by fire and the lightnings of God's wrath poured out for destruction upon Babylon."
Brigham Young, *Journal of Discourses* [649]

Before the world is afflicted into oblivion, the children of God will be given a chance to repent and turn to God. Scripture predicts that the general population will reject the truth and eventually digress to the point that God's "tough love" is required. Only the righteous who enter into Zion will be provided with an escape.

*Behold, the Lord hath created the earth that it should be inhabited…And he raiseth up a righteous nation, and destroyeth the nations of the wicked. **And he leadeth away the righteous into precious lands, and the wicked he destroyeth, and curseth the land unto them for their sakes.***
1 Nephi 17:36-38

When hardship, trial, and death occurs within our own families, trusting in God's purpose during our moment of sorrow can bring some comfort. Because of Jesus Christ, the temporary separation of physical death is not the end.

Thank You Mommy, I Love You!

"I was widowed in July 1993 when I lost both my husband and our twelve-year-old son in a drowning accident. By the time I met the missionaries, I was at a point in my life where I didn't care what happened to me. I simply wanted to know whether I would ever see my child again. When the missionaries assured me I would, I joined the Church. Shortly after my own baptism, I was able to have my son baptized by proxy. I sat all alone at the edge of the baptismal font in the basement of the Toronto Canada Temple. My youngest son was doing the baptism for both my son Christopher and my husband. As the officiator said Christopher's name, I felt a pair of arms wrap around my neck and hug me tight. I was startled, because I was the only the one sitting there. As I turned to see who it was, I saw the image of my son; he whispered, "Thank you, Mommy. I love you! I immediately started to cry; he wiped away my tears and waved good-bye. I was so startled I couldn't speak. I watched as he faded away and was joined by my husband and many angels. From that day on I never worried whether I'd ever see him again; I knew I would. And I know that in the meantime, he's in a good place."
Meli Cardullo, *Chicken Soup for the Latter Day Saint Soul* [650]

Without faith and an eternal perspective, it is natural to interpret life's tragedies, (especially those involving children), to mean that God is uncaring and cruel. The reality is that sometimes bringing His little ones home is the most loving thing Heavenly Father can do. Such was the case in Noah's day, when the people had become so completely depraved and hardened past feeling, that the most loving course Father could enact was to end their mortal probation.

But as the days of Noe were, so shall also the coming of the Son of man be. For as in the days that were before the flood they were eating and drinking, marrying and giving in marriage, until the day that Noe entered into the ark, And knew not until the flood came, and took them all away; so shall also the coming of the Son of man be. Then shall two be in the field; the one shall be taken, and the other left.
Two women shall be grinding at the mill; the one shall be taken, and the other left.
Watch therefore: for ye know not what hour your Lord doth come.
Matthew 24:37-42

When sin and darkness reach "critical mass," the wicked and unsuspecting will again be removed from the earth. In contrast, those who demonstrate exact obedience and are personally ordained to survive, will live to fulfill prophecy. These are they who are sanctified and thus will be provided a place of refuge before and during the annihilation. This is the promise.

"The Lord has power over his Saints and thus we should have hope. I promise you tonight
in the name of the Lord whose servant I am that God will always protect and care for his people.
We will have our difficulties the way every generation and people have had difficulties...
But with the gospel of Jesus Christ you have every hope and promise and reassurance.
The Lord has power over his Saints and will always prepare places of peace, defense,
and safety for his people. When we have faith in God we can hope for a better world—
for us personally and for all mankind."
Howard W. Hunter, *The Teachings of Howard W. Hunter* [651]

Examples include Enoch and his righteous city being taken into heaven *before* the flood. (Moses 7:23). The brother of Jared and his family remaining intact at the tower of Babel. (Genesis 11:6). And Moses leading God's remnant out of Egypt and away from Pharaoh. Even the Lord Jesus Christ had to be preserved through divine warning and evacuation.

Behold, the angel of the Lord appeareth to Joseph in a dream, saying, Arise, and take the young child
*and his mother, and **flee into Egypt**, and be thou there until I bring thee word:*
for Herod will seek the young child to destroy him. When he arose,
*he took the young child and his mother by night, and **departed into Egypt**:*
Matthew 2:13-14

In truth, internal separation from the world must precede a literal external escape. This is a key part of the gospel paradigm in every dispensation. During His ministry, the Lord Jesus invited the Jews to *come out* from religious superstition into a living-breathing gospel of love. Those who chose to follow Him were blessed to *see and then leave* the dogma of Jewish tradition.

The word *"church"* in the original Greek actually means, *"that which is called out."*[652] But even after a group of believers has made the initial step of coming out of the world, God still allows each culture to determine to what degree they will overcome and abandon the world, (Nephites, Jaredites, Children of Israel, Latter Day Saints).

Scripture illustrates that leaving Babylon and fleeing to an area of refuge usually involves entering into a literal "wilderness" and dwelling in "tents." Examples include Moses leading the children of Israel, Alma escaping King Noah, and Lehi leaving Jerusalem.

> *And it came to pass that* **the Lord commanded my father, even in a dream,** *that he should take his family and depart into the wilderness. And it came to pass that* **he was obedient** *unto the word of the Lord, wherefore he did as the Lord commanded him. And it came to pass* **that he departed into the wilderness**. *And* **he left his house,** *and the land of his inheritance, and his gold, and his silver, and his precious things, and* **took nothing with him, save it were his family, and provisions, and tents, and departed into the wilderness.**
> 1 Nephi 2:2-4

From the Book of Mormon we know Lehi and his family escaped the political and religious culture of their day. The Lord required this separation that they might establish a righteous family kingdom and inherit the land of promise.

Separating from Unbelief and Apathy

> *And it came to pass that the Lord did warn me, that I, Nephi, should* **depart from them and flee into the wilderness,** *and* **all those who would go with me.** *Wherefore, it came to pass that I, Nephi, did take my family, and also Zoram and his family, and Sam, mine elder brother and his family, and Jacob and Joseph, my younger brethren, and also my sisters, and all those who would go with me.*
> *And* **all those who would go with me were those who believed in the warnings and the revelations of God;** *wherefore, they did hearken unto my words. And we did take our tents and whatsoever things were possible for us, and did journey in the wilderness for the space of many days.*
> **And after we had journeyed for the space of many days we did pitch our tents.**
> 2 Nephi 5:5-7

The "tents" recorded in scripture represent a symbolic-and sometimes literal escape from the world. Those eager to leave Babylon usually find themselves *first* living in a spiritual wilderness until God eventually relocates them into a literal wilderness.

Wilderness = A sacred context provided for escaping political corruption and religious apostasy.
Tents   = Symbolic of leaving Babylon in favor of honoring temple covenants.

The wheat of the church observe the condition of our deteriorating world and look forward to a day of separation. These Saints are willing to flee Babylon as directed by the Spirit and have already pre-determined to obey the Lord when that essential moment arrives.

Knowing His Voice

"In these latter days, as in the times of old, we must avoid being acted upon by acting for ourselves to avoid evil. The Holy Ghost will prompt us. Joseph was told to flee from Potiphar's wife. Abraham obeyed the commandment to flee out of the land of Ur. Lehi was instructed to flee Jerusalem before it was destroyed. And to protect the Savior's life, Mary and Joseph were prompted to flee into Egypt. The promptings that come to us to flee evil reflect our Heavenly Father's understanding of our particular strengths and weaknesses and His awareness of the unforeseen circumstances of our lives. When these promptings come, they will not generally stop us in our tracks, for the Spirit of God does not speak with a voice of thunder. The voice will be as soft as a whisper, coming as a thought to our minds or a feeling in our hearts. By heeding its gentle promptings, we will be protected from the destructive consequences of sin."
Robert D. Hales, *To Act for Ourselves: The Gift and Blessing of Agency* [653]

*And the time speedily cometh, that except ye repent they shall possess the land of your inheritance, and **the Lord God will lead away the righteous out from among you.***
Jacob 3:4

And this was their faith, that by so doing God would prosper them in the land, or in other words, if they were faithful in keeping the commandments of God that he would prosper them in the land;
yea, warn them to flee, or to prepare for war, according to their danger;
Alma 48:15

"The cry of the angel unto the righteous of this dispensation is, "Come out of (Babylon) O my people, that ye partake not of her sins, and that ye receive not of her plagues."
Brigham Young, *Journal of Discourses* [654]

Even now the warning siren is being sounded. Many of those led by the Holy Spirit are already "pre-gathering" into areas that in the future will exist as "cities of light." This process will continue until the Lord determines it is time for the full cleansing and separation to occur. Today is our opportunity to re-locate our families as directed—and then warn any who will listen. (D&C 88:81).

*And that every man should take righteousness in his hands and faithfulness upon his loins, and lift a warning voice unto the inhabitants of the earth; and **declare both by word and by flight** that desolation shall come upon the wicked.*
D&C 63:37

The Lord in His tender mercy invites every child to come out of Babylon before it's too late. Those who will not listen will face great difficulty.

Take the Leap of Faith

*"I prophesy, that **that man who tarries after he has an opportunity of going**, will be afflicted by the devil. Wars are at hand; we must not delay...We ought to have the building up of **Zion as our greatest object**. When wars come, we shall have to flee to Zion. The cry is to make haste..."*
Joseph Smith, *Discourses of the Prophet Joseph Smith* [655]

> If Joseph Smith taught that we ought to have the building up of Zion
> as our greatest objective,
> why is the establishment of Zion not even part of today's
> four-fold mission of the church?

Without a literal Zion to escape to, increasing economic violence and political persecution will continue to afflict the Saints. Just as the oppression approaches the "tipping point," those who are led by the Lord will escape to freedom.

Political Repeat

*But the king was more wroth, and caused that Alma should be cast out from among them, and sent his servants after him that they might slay him. But he fled from before them and hid himself that they found him not. And he being concealed for many days did write all the words which Abinadi had spoken…And now **the king said that Alma was stirring up the people to rebellion against him; therefore he sent his army to destroy them**. And it came to pass that Alma and the people of the Lord were apprised of the coming of the king's army; therefore they **took their tents and their families and departed into the wilderness.** And they were in number about four hundred and fifty souls.*
Mosiah 17:3-4, 18:33-35

The Lord allows the required "rain" to fall on the just and the unjust. (Matthew 5:45). He also provides a refuge from the storm at the appropriate time. His people will be tried, tested, and broken to capacity, but in the end all will know that Jesus Christ never abandons His flock.

*And the LORD will create upon every dwelling place of mount Zion, and upon her assemblies, **a cloud and smoke by day, and the shining of a flaming fire by night:** for **upon all the glory shall be a defense**. And there shall be a tabernacle for a shadow in the daytime from the heat, and for **a place of refuge,** and for a covert from storm and from rain.*
Isaiah 4:5-6

Are You Coming?

Examples from the Book of Mormon

Lehi and family separated from Jerusalem

Nephi from his brothers Laman and Lemuel

King Mosiah from the land of Nephi to Zarahemla

Alma and followers from King Noah

King Limhi, the son of Noah, from the Lamanites

Ammonites from the Lamanites

The humble from the city of Ammonihah

Lachoneus from the Gadiantons

Jaredites from the tower of Babel

Examples from the Old Testament

Adam and Eve from the Garden of Eden

Enoch separated from the world to the city of Zion

Noah and seven others separated

Abraham from his father

Lot and his family from the cities of Sodom and Gomorrah

Isaac from Esau

Joseph sold into Egypt away from his family

Jacob from Canaan to Egypt

Moses/Israel from Egypt

See also: Omni 1:12-13, 2 Nephi 5:5-7, Alma 26:6-7, Alma 39:14, Mosiah 22:8-13, Mosiah 24:20, Helaman 13:14, 3 Nephi 3:22-26, 3 Nephi 20:41-42, D&C 29:8, D&C 37, D&C 38:31, D&C 38:42, D&C 61:24-25, D&C 63:24, D&C 101: 67-69, D&C 103:16-19, D&C 133:4-7, Matthew 2:13-14.1 Nephi 1:1-4 and 3 Nep 20:41, 42, Isaiah 56:8-12, 57:1-2, Isaiah 13:11-16.

TRUTH #65 FLEEING TO THE MOUNTAINS WILL BE AN INTIAL STEP FOR ESCAPING THE DESTRUCTION. DURING THIS TIME OF CLEANSING, THE SURVIVING SAINTS WILL BEGIN TO ESTABLISH ZION.

Safety in the Mountains

"Before the Lord destroyed the old world, he directed Noah to prepare an ark; before the cities of Sodom and Gomorrah were destroyed, he told Lot to "flee to the mountains" before Jerusalem was destroyed, Jesus gave his disciples warning, and told them to "flee out of it;" and before the destruction of the world a message is sent; after this, the nations will be judged, for God is now preparing his own kingdom for his own reign, and will not be thwarted by any conflicting influence, or opposing power...The whole world is in confusion, morally, politically, and religiously; but a voice was to be heard, "Come out of her, my people, that you partake not of her sins, and that ye receive not of her plagues."
John Taylor, *The Government of God* [656]

For over 185 years a portion of Latter Day Saints have worked to spiritually come out of condemnation, leave Babylon, and become a Zion people. To separate ourselves from the sin and darkness of this world has always been the sacred challenge and opportunity.

Invited from the Beginning

*"I do not know but that it would be an utter impossibility to commence and carry out some principles pertaining to Zion right in the midst of this people. They have strayed so far that to get a people who would conform to heavenly laws, **it may be needful to lead some from the midst of this people** and **commence anew somewhere in the regions round about these mountains**."*
Orson Pratt, *Journal of Discourses* [657]

The wheat of Christ perceives the political and spiritual deception present within today's society. The depravity and cruelty they observe among the people encourages them to be ever-ready for the day when the Lord directs them to flee to the mountains.

A Promise to the Remnant

*But behold, I, Jacob, would speak unto **you that are pure in heart**. Look unto God with firmness of mind, and pray unto him with exceeding faith, and he will console you in your afflictions, and he will plead your cause, and **send down justice upon those who seek your destruction**...And the time speedily cometh, that except ye repent they shall possess the land of your inheritance, and **the Lord God will lead away the righteous out from among you**.*
Jacob 3:1,4

Escaping into the wilderness has always been a pattern the Lord uses to spare His people from complete destruction. When the time arrives, those who trust in Christ will accept the Lord's invitation to flee to areas of safety.

Yea, let the cry go forth among all people: Awake and arise and go forth to meet the Bridegroom;
behold and lo, the Bridegroom cometh; go ye out to meet him. Prepare yourselves for the great day
of the Lord. Watch, therefore, for ye know neither the day nor the hour. Let them, therefore, who are
among the Gentiles flee unto Zion. And let them who be of Judah flee unto Jerusalem,
unto the mountains of the Lord's house.
D&C 133:10-13

Scripture relates that when the prophet Nephi visited an *"exceedingly high mountain,"* (1 Nephi 11:1), he was able to see *"things as they are."* (D&C 93:24). These phrases are both figurative and literal, for once the spiritual mountain had been climbed, the soul qualifies to dwell in the safety of a physical mountain wilderness.

Before Wilford Woodruff died, he shared a vision of the last days where he saw survivors fleeing to the mountains for safety.

Escape to Zion
"The next I knew I was just this side of Omaha. It seemed as though I was above the earth,
and looking down at it. As I passed along upon my way east, I saw the road full of people,
mostly women, with just what they could carry in bundles on their backs
traveling to the mountains on foot."
Wilford Woodruff, *Prophetic Years* [658]

Similar to when the early Saints relocated to Utah, God's people will again escape to the mountains in preparation for Zion and the arrival of the Master.

"This people will go into the Rocky Mountains; they will there build temples to the Most High.
They will raise up a posterity there, and the Latter Day Saints who dwell in these mountains
will stand in the flesh until the coming of the Son of Man.
The Son of Man will come to them while in the Rocky Mountains."
Wilford Woodruff, *Conference Report* [659]

Although it may appear that this prophecy has been fulfilled, some still look forward to a future time when the Lord will appear to His people who have gathered to the Rocky Mountains. These secluded gatherings will include those who have established mountain temples, are teaching and living the fullness of the gospel, and possess a determination to do the will of the Lord in all things.

Are We Ready to Fulfill This Prophecy?

"The United States will spend her strength and means warring in foreign lands until other nations will say, "Let's divide up the lands of the United States", then the people of the U. S. will unite and swear by the blood of their fore-fathers, that the land shall not be divided. Then the country will go to war, and they will fight until one half of the U. S. army will give up, and the rest will continue to struggle. They will keep on until they are very ragged and discouraged, and almost ready to give up — **when the boys from the mountains will rush forth** *in time to save the American Army from defeat and ruin. And they will say, 'Brethren, we are glad you have come; give us men, henceforth, who can talk with God'. Then you will have friends, but you will save the country when its liberty hangs by a hair, as it were."*
Joseph Smith, *Mosiah Hancock Autobiography* [660]

Today the wheat are preparing for a separation that will precede the great and dreadful day of the Lord. For many, this involves relocating to areas of refuge *before* the cleansing begins. Others will travel to sacred locations as the Spirit directs. Those who see the signs and heed the warnings are prepared to obey the Lord when He proclaims, *"depart ye unto the mountain which I have prepared for you."*

Standing in Holy Places

But my disciples shall stand in holy places, and shall not be moved; *but among the wicked, men shall lift up their voices and curse God and die. And there shall be earthquakes also in divers places, and many desolations; yet men will harden their hearts against me, and they will take up the sword, one against another, and they will kill one another. And now, when I the Lord had spoken these words unto my disciples, they were troubled. And I said unto them: Be not troubled, for, when all these things shall come to pass,* **ye may know that the promises which have been made unto you shall be fulfilled.**
D&C 45:32-35

"We believe in the literal gathering of Israel and in the restoration of the Ten Tribes; that Zion (the New Jerusalem) will be built upon the American continent; that Christ will reign personally upon the earth; and, that the earth will be renewed and receive its paradisiacal glory."
Joseph Smith, *Article of Faith Ten* [661]

From scripture we know that whenever a Zion is established, the gathering exists as a *"City of Holiness."*(Moses 7:19). In addition to a centralized location, Joseph Smith also prophesied that Latter Day Zion would eventually increase until it had filled North and South America.[662]

"There has been great discussion in relation to Zion--where it is, and where the gathering of the dispensation is, and which I am now going to tell you. The prophets have spoken and written upon it; but I will make a proclamation that will cover a broader ground. The whole of America is Zion itself from north to south, and is described by the Prophets, who declare that it is the Zion where the mountain of the Lord should be, and that it should be in the center of the land."
Joseph Smith, *History of the Church* [663]

To conceptualize where Zion will be stationed in the future, requires understanding why God initially directed the Saints to gather to the *"the center of the land."*[664]

When Joseph received the revelation to establish Zion in Missouri, that area of the nation represented the edge of civilization. Jackson County was considered to be a "frontier to the west" and was the ideal location for Mormon missionaries to obtain access to the Lamanites and convert the House of Israel.

In 1831 the Lord stated, *"Hearken, O ye elders of my church, saith the Lord your God, who have assembled yourselves together…in this land, which is the land of Missouri, which is the land which I have appointed and consecrated for the gathering of the saints. Wherefore, this is the land of promise, and the place for the city of Zion. And thus saith the Lord your God, if you will receive wisdom here is wisdom. Behold, the place which is now called Independence is the center place; and **a spot for the temple is lying westward**…Wherefore, it is wisdom that the land should be purchased by the saints, and also every tract lying westward, **even unto the line running directly between Jew and Gentile**…Behold, this is wisdom, that they may obtain it for an everlasting inheritance."*(D&C 57:1-5).

One reason the Lord wanted a line directly between the Jews (Native Americans) and Gentiles (Americans, including the LDS), was to facilitate the conversion of the House of Israel into His church. It was hoped that by settling close to Adam-ondi-Ahman and starting to build a Holy City, the literal blood of Israel could be integrated into the church through conversion and marriage. Once the Lamanites had been reclaimed, the Mormon Gentiles could then fulfill prophecy by assisting the remnant of Jacob in building Zion.

379

And they shall assist my people, the remnant of Jacob, and also as many of the house of Israel
as shall come, that they may build a city, which shall be called the New Jerusalem. And then shall
they assist my people that they may be gathered in, who are scattered upon all the face of the land,
in unto the New Jerusalem.
3 Nephi 21:23-24

To understand the significance of this verse requires accepting that when the Lord refers to *"my people,"* He is speaking about the remnant of Jacob. The *"they"* mentioned are the LDS Gentiles who have actually repented. (see Truths #7 and #37).

Contrary to our "chosen people" mindset, early Mormon prophets knew that the Latter Day Saints were Gentiles and that it would be our role *to assist* the House of Israel in gathering the elect.

Privileged to Assist
"What says the Book of Mormon in relation to the building up of the New Jerusalem
on this continent one of the most splendid cities that ever was or ever will be built on this land?
Does not that book say that the Lamanites are to be the principal operators in that important work,
and that those who embrace the Gospel from among the Gentiles are to have the privilege of assisting
the Lamanites to build up the city called the New Jerusalem? This remnant of Joseph, who are now
degraded, will then be filled with the wisdom of God; and by that wisdom they will build that city;
by the aid of the Priesthood already given, and by the aid of Prophets that God will raise up in their midst,
they will beautify and ornament its dwellings; and we have the privilege of being numbered with them,
instead of their being numbered with us. It is a great privilege indeed that we enjoy of being associated
with them in the accomplishment of so great a work."
Orson Pratt, *Journal of Discourses* [665]

It was never intended that the Gentiles would preside over the establishment of Zion, but rather that those Gentiles who repented would be privileged to assist in the process. Initially, the role of the early Saints was to re-locate to Missouri, convert and marry worthy Lamanites, and then assist Israel in establishing a blossoming community.

After the Lord directed the Saints to go to Missouri approximately a thousand valiant families migrated to the new Zion.[666] This sudden influx of northerners into a southern state was not well received, and in July of 1833, a mob gathered at Independence to destroy Church property. Bishop Edward Partridge was tarred and feathered, and the Saints were forced to sign an agreement stipulating that they would leave the county.[667]

The mobbing, violence, and persecution became so intense that **another location for Zion was suggested.** Oliver Cowdery wrote a letter to the Saints in Missouri advising, *"It is wisdom that you look out another place to locate on. Be wise in your selection and commence in the best situation you can find…**Another place of beginning will be no injury to Zion in the end**…There was no other way to save the lives of all the church in Zion, or the most; and any who are dissatisfied with that move are not right…**This great tribulation would not have come upon Zion had it not been for** rebellion…It was necessary that these things should come upon us; not only justice demands it, but **there was no other way to cleanse the Church."**[668]

This letter clarifies that the Saints, although faithful enough to relocate to Missouri, still needed to complete their sanctification process. In addition, Oliver Cowdery believed that choosing another place instead of Jackson County would *"be no injury to Zion in the end."* Apparently, achieving the required holiness was primary, and the external location of Zion secondary. Brother Cowdery's council to the Saints to find another location for Zion was also supported by Joseph Smith, who at the end of the letter, added his own personal note of encouragement.

"P.S. Brethren if I were with you I should take an active part in your sufferings & although nature shrinks yet my spirit would not let me forsake you unto death God helping me. Oh be of good cheer for our redemption draweth near. Oh God save my Brethren in Zion. Oh brethren give up all to God, forsake all for Christ sake."
Joseph Smith, *Oliver Cowdery Letter* [669]

Within the church today, an almost universal expectation exists that Zion will yet be built in Jackson County, Missouri. In many ways this belief has been faith promoting, but when the day of gathering arrives, there may be some monumental surprises!

Remembering that Zion is above all a standard of spiritual holiness, and not necessarily based on literal location, encourages us to consider that our traditional references to Zion being in Missouri may be mostly symbolic-rather than literal.

"O Babylon…O Babylon…We bid thee farewell.
We are going to the mountains of Ephraim to Dwell."
"Ye Elders of Israel," *Hymns of The Church of Jesus Christ of Latter-day Saints* [670]

Even though almost all members have been taught that the faithful will eventually return to Jackson County, a careful analysis of scripture indicates that Zion will not be built upon the plains and prairies, but rather in the tops of the mountains.

And it shall come to pass in the last days, that the mountain of the LORD's house shall be established in the top of the mountains, and shall be exalted above the hills; and all nations shall flow unto it.
And many people shall go and say, Come ye, and let us go up to the mountain of the LORD, to the house of the God of Jacob; and he will teach us of his ways, and we will walk in his paths: for out of Zion shall go forth the law, and the word of the Lord from Jerusalem.
Isaiah 1:2-3

This prophecy from Isaiah is usually interpreted as having been fulfilled when the Saints migrated to the Salt Lake Valley. But is it possible that *"mountain of the Lord's house,"* which Isaiah prophesied would be established in the *"top of the mountains,"* is both symbolic and literal? In remembering that Zion must also be established on sacred soil that has not be defiled by man, what if, on a deeper level, these sacred prophecies have not yet been fulfilled?

Mountain Movements

But in the last days it shall come to pass, that the mountain of the house of the LORD shall be established in the top of the mountains, and it shall be exalted above the hills; and people shall flow unto it.
Micah 4:1

381

"There will be tens of thousands of Latter-day Saints who will be gathered in the Rocky Mountains,
and there they will open the door for the establishing of the Gospel among the Lamanites...
This people will go into the Rocky Mountains; they will there build temples to the Most High."
Joseph Smith, *Millennial Star* [671]

Just a few days prior to the martyrdom of Joseph and Hyrum Smith, the brothers counseled together and determined to journey west to escape their enemies. This leaves us to question what the Prophets knew that influenced their decision. With the Saints evicted from Missouri and struggling in Nauvoo, what could have been the Lord's new strategy for establishing Zion? The following extract from Mosiah Hancock's journal gives a possible explanation.

ZION IN THE SOUTHWEST?

"The next day the Prophet came to our home and stopped in our carpenter shop and stood by the turning lathe. I went and got my map for him. "Now", he said, "I will show you the travels of this people."
He then showed our travels through Iowa, and said, "Here you will make a place for the winter;
and here you will travel west until you come to the valley of the Great Salt Lake! You will build cities to the North and to the South, and to the East and to the West; and you will become a great and wealthy people in that land. But, the United States will not receive you with the laws which God desires you to live, and you will have to go to where the Nephites lost their power. They worked in the United Order for 166 years, and the Saints have got to become proficient in the laws of God before they can meet the Lord Jesus Christ, or even the city of Enoch". He said we will not travel the shape of the horse shoe for there we will await the action of the government. Placing his finger on the map, I should think about where Snowflake, Arizona is situated, or it could have been Mexico, he said,
"The government will not receive you with the laws that God designed you to live,
and those who are desirous to live the laws of God will have to go South..."
Joseph Smith, *Mosiah Hancock Journal* [672]

In 1861, Willliam W. Phelps wrote a letter to Brigham Young which included a revelation which he attributed to Joseph Smith concerning marriage and the Native Americans. According to Brother Phelps, Joseph Smith stated, *"It is my will, that in time, ye should take unto you wives of the Lamanites and Nephites, that their posterity may become white, delightsome, and just, for even now their females are more virtuous than the gentiles. Gird up your loins and be prepared for the mighty work of the Lord to prepare the world for my second coming to meet the tribes of Israel according to the predictions of all the holy prophets since the beginning; Be patient, therefore, possessing your souls in peace and love, and keep the faith that is now delivered unto you for the gathering of scattered Israel, and lo, I am with you, though ye cannot see me, till I come: even so. Amen."* [673]

Within this same document William Phelps reported, *"About three years after this was given...I asked brother Joseph, privately, how "we," that were mentioned in the revelation could take wives of the "natives" as we were all married men? He replied instantly "In the same manner that Abraham took Hagar and Keturah; and Jacob took Rachel, Bilhah and Zilpah; by revelation—the saints of the Lord are always directed by revelation."* [674]

It appears that one reason God commanded the controversial practice of taking plural wives was to facilitate the blood of Lamanite-Israel being integrated into the church. Unfortunately, the Saints struggled to live the principle correctly, and the U.S. government refused to acknowledge the validity of this spiritual law. Eventually, the church acquiesced to political pressure and abandoned the practice of plural marriage. The opportunity for the Gentiles to assist in building Zion was put on hold until a future day when the Lamanites would yet blossom as a rose.

But before the great day of the Lord shall come, Jacob shall flourish in the wilderness, and the Lamanites shall blossom as the rose. Zion shall flourish upon the hills and rejoice upon the mountains, and shall be assembled together unto the place which I have appointed.
D&C 49:24-25

For centuries Native Americans have been repeatedly uprooted from their lands. Currently, Lamanite-Israel is mostly scattered throughout the west, southwest, and Rocky Mountain regions, with various cultures also dwelling in Mexico and Central America.

Both Joseph and Brigham worked to establish Mormon communities near the Lamanite-remnant, that both Jew and Gentile might work together to build the New Jerusalem.

"Joseph said it was the voice of the Spirit for him to go to the West among the Natives and take Hyrum and several others along with him and look out a place for the Church.'[675] The other accounts say that Joseph received a revelation that he had to go to the west to escape martyrdom, and he had to find the New Jerusalem among the Natives in the American Southwest-beginning in 1830, Joseph was looking to the Rocky Mountains, even as he sent out the first four missionaries (Bushman's Joseph Smith: Rough Stone Rolling). I quote from a review of Bushman's book: Professor Bushman continues, 'Church members were thrilled to think that Cowdery's band of missionaries was to locate the exact spot (of the New Jerusalem).[676] The four missionaries did not set out to go specifically to Independence, Missouri, but rather "among the Lamanites" to find the site of the New Jerusalem. They were to be the locators; they were searching for the spot. It was not a cut-and-dried mission to Independence, at all. If we do not understand that concept, we cannot understand the focus of the coming forth of the Book of Mormon and the entire impetus of the Restoration in those first two years and the "fixation" of both Joseph and Brigham on the Rocky Mountains through the remainder of their lives."[677]
Stephen Markham, *Letter to Wilford Woodruff* [678]

The early brethren believed the remnant spoken of in the Book of Mormon was located in the west and southwest areas of the United States. This initial understanding is rarely talked about today, but it is one of the symbolic reasons the Nauvoo Temple faces west.

The Chosen
"Brigham Young did not take the Church east so that it could be among the Remnant. He took it west so that it would be as close to the Remnant as he could get. Brigham Young did not send for a Navajo, a Cherokee, a Piaute, a Ute, a Sioux, a Shoshone, etc., to participate in the very first live endowment session to ever be conducted in a totally completed temple in this dispensation. (St. George) NO, he sent for the "chief" priest of the Hopi in Oraibi - the "mother" village of all other Hopi villages. Chief Tuva and his wife Katsinmana were in that very first live endowment company because Brigham Young wanted to fulfill the requirement of the Book of Mormon that the Gentiles help the Remnant get themselves "redeemed" again."
Stephen Markham, *Letter to Wilford Woodruff* [679]

It was Joseph's intention to move the Saints west to Zion. When his life was once again threatened, the Prophet wanted to turn west for his escape. Just five days before his murder, the Prophet remarked, *"There is no mercy here—no mercy here."* Hyrum said, *"No; just as sure as we fall into their hands we are dead men."* Joseph replied, *"Yes; what shall we do, Brother Hyrum?"* He replied, *"I don't know."* All at once Joseph's countenance brightened up and he said, *"The way is open. It is clear to my mind what to do. All they want is Hyrum and myself; then tell everybody to go about their business, and not to collect in groups, but to scatter about. There is no doubt they will come here and search for us. Let them search; they will not harm you in person or property, and not even a hair of your head. We will cross the river tonight, and go away to the West."*[680]

Escaping West

"Saturday June 22, 1844, about 9 p.m. Hyrum came out of the Mansion and gave his hands to Reynolds Cahoon, at the same time saying, "A company of men are seeking to kill my brother Joseph, and the Lord has warned him to flee to the Rocky Mountains to save his life. Good-by, Brother Cahoon, we shall see you again." In a few minutes afterwards Joseph came from his family. His tears were flowing fast. He held a handkerchief to his face, and followed after Brother Hyrum without uttering a word."
Joseph Smith, *Teachings of the Prophet Joseph Smith* [681]

After Joseph and Hyrum left for the west, a pregnant and weary Emma Smith requested that her husband return to Nauvoo. In addition, some of the Prophet's closest friends accused him of being a *"coward."* Joseph's reply was that *"If my life is of no value to my friends it is of none to myself."*[682] After weighing their options, Joseph and Hyrum determined to return to Nauvoo. The fate of the prophet-brothers was set.

Martyrs for Christ

*"Well do I remember the Prophet's speech from a frame in front of his mansion--where he said, "Brethren, I now roll this work onto the shoulders of the Twelve; and they shall bear and send this Gospel to every nation under Heaven". He asked the Legions if they were not all his boys, and they shouted "Yes!" I stood on the rail of the fence in front of the mansion.
When the Prophet said, "Brethren, the Lord Almighty has this day revealed to me something I never comprehended before! That is--I have friends who have at a respectful distance been ready to ward off the blows of the adversary. (He brought his hand down on my father's head as he was acting as body-guard to the Prophet) While others have pretended to be my friends, and have crept into my bosom and become vipers, and have been my most deadly enemies. I wish you to be obedient to these true men as you have promised. ARE YOU WILLING TO DIE FOR ME?" Yes! was the shout. "You have said you are willing to die for me--".
Then he drew his sword and cried, "I WILL DIE FOR YOU!
If this people cannot have their rights, my blood shall run upon the ground like water."*
Joseph Smith, *Mosiah Hancock Journal* [683]

Joseph's death at Carthage brought an immediate and sudden decrease in revelation. The previous focus of becoming a Zion people and establishing a literal city was overshadowed by the dilemma of succession. With Joseph III too young to lead and both Brigham and Sydney wanting the mantle, a time of confusion and uncertainty replaced the Lord's invitation to become Zion.

In this religious environment, the prior emphasis to build Zion in Jackson County, Missouri, (which had been perfect and appropriate at the time), became cemented into the belief system of the members. After the Prophet Joseph was lost, *the most recent choice for Zion—became the only choice for Zion.*

Members, who were educated in this lingering mindset, then repeated these same religious expectations for many generations. The question is, are the traditions we've been taught accurate?

Maintaining Tradition

"Zion, as used in this scripture (Isaiah 2:2-3), means America. In fact, America is Zion.
At times the term is used to include both the North and South American continents.
In some references the word Zion is used to designate the area in and about Jackson County, Missouri,
where the New Jerusalem will be built, which city is itself sometimes called Zion.
From Zion the law of God shall eventually go forth into all the world."
Marion G. Romney, *America's Fate and Ultimate Destiny* [684]

Several years before the Prophet Joseph was martyred, he spoke at the home of Jared Carter. According to historical records, the Prophet read the second chapter of Joel and then stated:

"It is very difficult for us to communicate to the churches all that God has revealed to us,
in consequence of tradition; for we are differently situated from any other people that ever
existed upon this earth; consequently those former revelations cannot be suited to our conditions;
they were given to other people, who were before us; but in the last days, God was to call
a remnant, in which was to be deliverance, as well as in Jerusalem and Zion.
Now if God should give no more revelations, where will we find Zion and this remnant?
The time is near when desolation is to cover the earth, and then God will have a place
of deliverance in his remnant, and in Zion…"
Joseph Smith, *Teachings of the Prophet Joseph Smith* [685]

Today's true prophets have the same dilemma early leaders faced, how to invite souls to come unto Jesus Christ and His Zion-when so many have already determined all of the answers.

"You will gather many people into the fastness of the Rocky Mountains as a center for the gathering
of the people …you will yet be called upon to go forth and call upon the free men from Maine to gather
themselves together to the Rocky Mountains; and the Redmen from the West and all people from the
North and from the South and from the East, and go to the West, to establish themselves in the
strongholds of their gathering places, and there you will gather with the Redmen to their center
from their scattered and dispersed situation, to become the strong arm of Jehovah,
who will be a strong bulwark of protection from your foes."
Joseph Smith, *A Prophecy of Joseph the Seer* [686]

Today, "Zion" is often referred to as a national park, a bank in Utah, or a spiritual reality that will someday-somehow just magically appear. Over time, a doctrine that was once considered absolutely essential is now referred to as a distant ideal. Admittedly, some church leaders do continue to speak of a literal return to Jackson County, but we should each ask the Lord directly, has the time passed for the flatlands of Missouri to become the Mountain of the Lord? Will the Savior still use the same location He once chose, or will He provide new and additional areas of refuge for those who have awakened and become Israel?

Several Gatherings

"There will be gatherings, and a great gathering, and at last a distribution of the survivors into their respective promised lands. Between the time of the great upheavals, and the time of the final distribution, there will be a season in which there will a great gathering in the "Mountains" (2 Ne. 12: 2) where it will be a fearsome, even terrible thing for the wicked to contemplate. (D&C 45: 68-70.) This will be in "the tops of the mountains." (Micah 4: 1; 2 Ne. 12:2; Isa. 2: 2.) This will be where the New Jerusalem will exist. This will be before the final distribution into the various places of inheritance of the Lord's people. Before the return to the lands of inheritance, however, there will be terrible days, the likes of which have only been seen in the final pages of the Nephite record. (Mormon 6: 6-22)."
Denver Snuffer, *Removing the Condemnation* [687]

In the future, economic destruction, war, and social anarchy will increase. Many have dreamed dreams and seen visions where the Lord in response leads His children to isolated and undefiled "cities of light." These sacred and protected areas will mostly be scattered throughout the western United States. Those who can hear the voice of the Lord and gather to these small gatherings will be provided with the initial "Zion" needed to survive.

Preserved in Holy Places

"Verily, I say unto you, that the day of vexation and vengeance is nigh at the doors of this nation, when wicked, ungodly, and daring men will rise up in wrath and might, and go forth in anger, like as the dust is driven by a terrible wind; and **they will...cause the death and misery of many souls; but the faithful among my people shall be preserved in holy places during all these tribulations."**
Joseph Smith, *Joseph Smith Collection, Church Historian's Office* [688]

Hiking to Zion

"Years ago, when the Spirit opened up to the mind of the Prophet Brigham, the visions of the future, he plainly foresaw that the time must come, when the saints would rejoice in the privilege of going to Zion on foot, not only with handcarts, but without them; that they would be glad to escape from the nations with their lives."
Millennial Star [689]

For many, questioning the future location of Zion is deceptive nonsense. They assume that if something as monumental as the future location of Zion were to be clarified, the organizational prophet would surely direct them. Beyond this assumption, appropriate and essential questions remain. Could it be that after remaining under condemnation for 185 years, the Lord allows His people to remain in the beliefs they prefer? It seems probable that the issue of Zion's location will be a "litmus test" separating those who trust in tradition, from those who independently know the voice of God? Perhaps only a "few" will grow to understand: *Wherever God dwells…there is Zion.*

Zion's Outcasts

And he shall set up an ensign for the nations, and shall assemble the outcasts of Israel,
and gather together the dispersed of Judah from the four corners of the earth.
2 Nephi 21: 12

The Lord's invitation to become Zion included gathering the elect into one location. This process, both then and now, was to involve men and women who had endured the refining fire, excelled spiritually, and become kings and queens in Christ. (see Truth #67).

Temple Mountains

"In February of 1844 Joseph Smith met with the Twelve and discussed the Oregon and California
Exploring Expedition, and stated that he wanted "every man that goes to be a king and a priest.
When he gets on the mountains he may want to talk with his God."
Joseph Smith, *History of the Church* [690]

When the unity of Zion is again offered, these kings and queens will hear the voice of *Messiah*…These are they who will be personally led by Jesus into a metaphorical and literal *"mountain of the Lord."* These Saints will rear their children in the undefiled and unpolluted *"top of the mountains!"* (Isaiah 2:2). To *know Christ* and live secluded from the world will be a personal Zion for them. They will dwell with angels, and the Lord Jesus Christ will teach and minister to them frequently. With Him in their midst, it will be heaven on earth.

These gatherings will include those who were once considered obscure, peculiar, and *"on the fringe."* Ironically, most of the souls in Zion will have been cast out and deemed unworthy. As *strangers and pilgrims* upon the earth, (Hebrews 11:13), these are they who will be privileged to shout praises unto Christ the King!

BEAUTIFUL UPON THE MOUNTAINS:

Behold I say unto you, that whosoever has heard the words of the prophets, yea,
all the holy prophets who have prophesied concerning the coming of the Lord—I say unto you,
that all those who have hearkened unto their words, and believed that the Lord would redeem
his people, and have looked forward to that day for a remission of their sins, I say unto you,
that these are his seed, or they are the heirs of the kingdom of God. And these are they who
have published peace, who have brought good tidings of good, who have published salvation;
and said unto Zion: Thy God reigneth! And O how beautiful upon the mountains were their feet!
And again, how beautiful upon the mountains are the feet of those that are still publishing peace!
…And behold, I say unto you, this is not all. For O how beautiful upon the mountains are the
feet of him that bringeth good tidings, that is the founder of peace, yea, even the Lord,
who has redeemed his people; yea, him who has granted salvation unto his people; For were it not
for the redemption which he hath made for his people, which was prepared from the foundation
of the world, I say unto you, were it not for this, all mankind must have perished.
Mosiah 15:11,14-19

> **TRUTH #67** ESTABLISHING AN ETERNAL FAMILY KINGDOM WAS THE PASSION OF JOSEPH SMITH AND AN ESSENTIAL ASPECT OF THE ORIGINAL CHURCH. AS WE ACCEPT AND LIVE THE FULLNESS OF THE GOSPEL, WE CAN BECOME THE KINGS AND QUEENS GOD INTENDS US TO BE.

Pilate therefore said unto him, Art thou a king then?
Jesus answered, Thou sayest that I am a king.
To this end was I born, and for this cause came I into the world,
that I should bear witness unto the truth.
John 18:37

The endowment is the story of our own personal exaltation. During the temple presentation a progression is revealed that involves advancing from raw intelligence into a child of God. Once born into mortality, we determine the degree of our spiritual advancement.

Ever present within this journey is an invitation to awake and arise, that through the Atonement of Jesus Christ we might reclaim our true and eternal nature. Those who prove themselves faithful in all things-become clean from the blood and sins of this generation. These are they who are chosen, called up, and anointed kings and queens, priests and priestesses unto the Most High God!

A Personal Kingdom

"Whenever the Lord has a people on earth he offers to make them a nation of kings and priests —
not a congregation of lay members with a priest or a minister at the head — but a whole Church
in which every man is his own minister, in which every man stands as a king in his own right,
reigning over his own family-kingdom. The priesthood which makes a man
a king and a priest is thus a royal priesthood."
Bruce R McConkie, *Doctrinal New Testament Commentary* [691]

Once endowed in the temple, the realization of these blessings is conditional upon our faithfulness and the depth of our repentance. Joseph's vision of the three degrees of glory makes it clear that qualifying for celestial glory requires we achieve the spiritual title of king or queen.

Worthy of Celestial Glory?

*They are they who received the **testimony of Jesus**, and believed on his name...That by keeping the commandments they might be washed and cleansed from all their sins, and **receive the Holy Spirit** by the laying on of the hands of him who is ordained and sealed unto this power; And who overcome by faith, and are **sealed by the Holy Spirit of promise**, which the Father sheds forth upon all those who are just and true. They are they who are the **church of the Firstborn**. They are they into whose hands **the Father has given all things** — They are they who are priests and kings, who have received of his fullness, and of his glory; And are priests of the Most High, after the order of Melchizedek, which was after the order of Enoch, which was after the order of the Only Begotten Son. Wherefore, as it is written, **they are gods, even the sons of God** — Wherefore, all things are theirs, whether life or death, or things present, or things to come, all are theirs and they are Christ's, and Christ is God's.*
D&C 76: 51-59

388

To assist the Saints in receiving salvation, Joseph Smith was influenced to restore a church. But in reviewing all that the Prophet was trying to teach the Saints, it appears he also intended to restore the same ancient religion Adam and Eve taught to their posterity. Although information concerning this ancient gospel is scant, it seems a type of "Holy Order" was practiced by Father Adam and Mother Eve wherein those who received the fullness of the priesthood became kings and queens within their own sacred stewardship.

"The divine system of government in the heavens is patriarchal in nature…
This divine patriarchal system was given to Adam and Eve when they were placed upon the earth.
(see Abraham 1:26). They gave the spiritual and temporal guidance to their own children.
They did not attend church services because there was no church on the earth until the days of Moses,
when he organized an ecclesiastical structure to help in teaching and governing the children of Israel.
Adam and Eve were the ones who held all the authority necessary to initiate their children
into the ordinances of the gospel, from baptism on to the fullness of the priesthood.
It was Adam and Eve who were the first `temple president' and `matron' upon the earth.
They administered the same ordinances to their children which we receive today.
Many of their children must have received the fullness of the priesthood
which enabled them to come into the presence of the Lord."
Craig Mills, *Home Sanctuary* [692]

In the early days of the church those who had received the Second Anointing were empowered to organize independent family kingdoms within the church. In stark contrast with how we view "priesthood authority" today, those who had become "kings" and "queens" were allowed and expected to build up a self-governing kingdom unto the Lord.

"In a prayer meeting on 14 May 1844, Lyman Wight joined the Anointed Quorum,
a secret group of members and spouses who had received the Second Anointing, a mark of significance,
favor, and power within the elite ranks of the church's leading members. This gave Wight an almost-
independent authority as a "king" and "priest" in church and personal affairs. On 8 August 1844
Brigham Young spoke about the Second Anointing at a special general meeting in which
the Twelve were chosen to lead the church. Although Young insisted on the primacy of the Twelve
in church affairs, he certainly acknowledged the power of those endowed with the anointing,
stating that a specially anointed individual, 'if he is a king and priest, (then) let him go and build up
a kingdom unto himself; that is his right and it is the right of many here.' He reminded the audience,
however, that the Twelve-and not these "kings" and "priests"-
were the leading authority of the church."
Melvin C. Johnson, *Polygamy on the Pedernales* [693]

To work toward creating such independence, nobility, and personal stewardship, seems foreign today. And yet with God, life on earth was supposed to be a microcosm of eternity. "Family" was to be spiritual-not only biological. Heavenly-not just earthly, and spiritually expansive instead of religiously restrictive. Souls in the church were to be sealed unto Jesus Christ and adopted into the House of Israel. (see Truth #7). The intended result was that a united king and queen, who had been sealed by the Holy Spirit of Promise, would preside over a family kingdom. Their individual contribution to the kingdom of God would involve real power, abundant revelation, and angelic visitors. Could anything on earth be more beautiful, more noble, or more divine?

A Zion Family

This is the patriarchal order that governed the children of Adam & Eve for many generation.
But through wickedness, this order was finally lost among the people and there began
to be kings and rulers who would govern the people, and soon the earth was filled
with a diversity of types of governments."
Craig Mills, *Home Sanctuary* [694]

Ironically, it was one of these artificial governments that contributed to the death of Joseph Smith, but not before he explained to Apostle Orson Hyde the heavenly structure of "family."

"The eternal Father sits at the head, crowned King of kings and Lord of lords. Wherever the other
lines meet, there sits a king and a priest unto God, bearing rule, authority, and dominion under
the Father. He is one with the Father, because his kingdom is joined to his Father's and becomes part of it.
The most eminent and distinguished prophets who have laid down their lives for their testimony
(Jesus among the rest), will be crowned at the head of the largest kingdoms under the Father,
and will be one with Christ as Christ is one with his Father; for their kingdoms are all joined together,
and such as do the will of the Father, the same are his mothers, sisters, and brothers. He that has been
faithful over a few things, will be made ruler over many things; he that has been faithful over ten talents,
shall have dominion over ten cities, and he that has been faithful over five talents, shall have dominion
over five cities, and to every man will be given a kingdom and a dominion, according to his merit, powers,
and abilities to govern and control. It will be seen by the diagram that there are kingdoms of all sizes,
an infinite variety to suit all grades of merit and ability. The chosen vessels unto God are the kings and
priests that are placed at the head of these kingdoms. These have received their washings and anointings
in the temple of God on this earth; they have been chosen, ordained, and anointed kings and priests,
to reign as such in the resurrection of the just. Such as have not received the fulness of the priesthood,
(for the fulness of the priesthood includes the authority of both king and priest) and have not been anointed
and ordained in the temple of the Most High, may obtain salvation in the celestial kingdom,
but not a celestial crown. Many are called to enjoy a celestial glory, yet few are chosen
to wear a celestial crown, or rather, to be rulers in the celestial kingdom."[695]

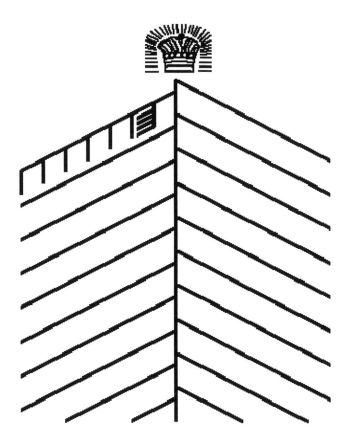

Reviewing this diagram gives greater meaning to the Lord's prayer, "*Thy Kingdom come. Thy will be done in Earth, as it is in heaven.*"(Matthew 6:10). Those who access the fullness of the priesthood are blessed with sealing power, and are then privileged to have their personal family kingdom embedded into the eternities. Referring to this process, Brigham Young stated, "*By this power men will be sealed to men back to Adam, completing and making perfect the priesthood from this day to the winding up scene.*"[696] Both men and women who desire to be bonded into God's family line are required to grow line upon line until the soul is prepared to be spiritually adopted to Joseph Smith and the Eternal Fathers. (see Truth #75).

The Lord's church as an institution will not survive beyond the telestial realm, but those family kingdoms sealed by the Holy Spirit of Promise will. In Christ, love is eternal, power will proclaim, and all that is ordained of God will endure!

Men and women, who obey God in all things great and small, will be made rulers over much in heaven. (Luke 12:42-44). To receive this glory requires a correct perspective concerning what it means to be a "ruler" in the spiritual mansions of the Father. Contrary to the politically corrupt examples we see today, to be a true "ruler" and "king" involves leading with love and being attentive each day to the needs of those in your kingdom. Nothing but humility, long-suffering, sincere condescension, pure virtue, and a deep desire to uplift others, can qualify the soul for eternal inheritance within the realm of heaven.

Meek and Lowly

Therefore when Jesus perceived that they were about to come and take Him by force to make Him king, He departed again to the mountain by Himself alone.

John 6:15

Jesus was not interested in worldly acclaim, but in *walking the way of The Christ*. The Lord's consistent rejection of false power is part of what makes Him our exemplar of majestic Godliness. Those serious about becoming "kings" and "queens" must be willing to overcome the temptation of "cultural power," while also considering their true spiritual standing in relation to "holding the priesthood."

The Prophet Joseph Smith declared, *"Those holding the fullness of the Melchizedek Priesthood are kings and priests of the Most High God, holding the keys of power and blessings."*[697]
In addition, the temple teaches us that becoming kings and queens is a future blessing conditional upon our faithfulness. Thus we must ask, is our initial ordination to the Melchizedek Priesthood preparatory? Have we as active members of the church really received the fullness of the priesthood, or is there an additional power and privilege yet to be realized for those who are chosen, called up and anointed kings and queens? **And what does it mean in Doctrine and Covenants 124:28 when the Lord confirms by revelation that the church had lost the fullness of the priesthood?** Was that fullness ever regained, and if so, where is the revelation saying it was returned? Those who believe in scripture should at least be willing to question: If the fullness of the Melchizedek Priesthood was pronounced lost in 1841, leaving the collective church to practice the lesser priesthood, is it still possible for an individual to regain all that God once offered?

"If a man gets a fullness of the priesthood of God he has to get it in the same way that Jesus Christ obtained it, and that was by keeping all the commandments and obeying all the ordinances of the house of the Lord."
Joseph Smith, *Teachings of the Prophet Joseph Smith* [698]

Obeying every commandment leads to receiving every blessing. Those who seek a true fullness of the gospel eventually receive the fullness of the priesthood. These are they, who having been true and faithful in all things, are prepared to be presented at the veil and received of the Lord. The climb is steep, but the view is glorious!

"I call your attention now to the washing and anointing that you received in the Temple.... When you went into the washing and anointing room, where you were washed and anointed with water and oil, you were given a new name, and you were promised that some day you would be called up to be a king and priest, or a queen and priestess."
Alvin R. Dyer, *For What Purpose* [699]

From this quote we can deduce it is the "second anointing" which correlates with celestial glory, fullness of the priesthood, sealing power, and being ordained a king or queen unto the Most High God. In relation to Elder Dyer's quote, we are the ones who determine when "someday" comes. The Lord is willing—heaven awaits.

"Sacred ordinances are performed in temples built for that very purpose. If we are faithful
to the covenants made there, we become inheritors not only of the Celestial Kingdom
but of exaltation, the highest glory within the heavenly kingdom,
and we obtain all the divine possibilities God can give."
D. Todd Christofferson, *The Power of Covenants* [700]

Most who marry in the temple "feel the Spirit" and assume they have been united to a sufficient degree to have a "celestial marriage." They do not yet understand that to be eternally secure in the heavens requires first, being personally sealed unto the Lord Jesus Christ, (Matthew 25:10), and second, having their marriage sealed by the Holy Spirit of Promise. (D&C 132:7).

To be sealed as a couple unto God requires deep personal repentance and intense marital harmony. As "one," both the husband and wife must act in unity with the Savior and the truth of all things.

Instead of waiting for death to become "kings and queens," some couples seek eternal union with the Bridegroom in this life. These are they who are sealed by the Holy Spirit of Promise and receive the "crowning" blessings of the patriarchal order for their family.

"The patriarchal order as far as we are concerned, centers in and revolves around celestial marriage
and when an individual progresses in the church to the point that he has the blessings
of that order of the priesthood, he has all the blessings of Abraham
and becomes a natural patriarch to his posterity."
Bruce R. McConkie, *BYU Lecture* [701]

As with Abraham and Sarah, there is no "king" without a "queen." In eternity, there is no exaltation without the oneness of the divine masculine and the divine feminine. Disciple Donna Nielsen explains, *"What we have in scripture is a patriarchal history replete with feminine imagery. Just as it took two--man and woman--to be called "Adam" (Genesis 5:2), the scriptures needed both elements to be complete. Their words show everyone how to become like Christ. Of course, this does not mean to assume a masculine role, but to imitate His good qualities. The traits and virtues that Christ exemplifies have both masculine and feminine associations. For example, justice is typically thought of as masculine, while mercy has a feminine correlation. Christ is perfect in both qualities. He is able to unify seemingly contradictory attributes and model the best of both in appropriate contexts."* [702]

With consistent effort men and women can become candidates for royal kingship and noble queenship. Those who actually receive the title do not live in the light of other humans, but worship and obey God as the head of their earthly family kingdom.

Standing in Power

"Now those men, or those women, who know no more about the power of God, and the influences of the Holy Spirit, than to be led entirely by another person, suspending their own understanding, and pinning their faith upon another's sleeve, will never be capable of entering into the Celestial glory, to be crowned as they anticipate, they will never be capable of becoming Gods. They cannot rule themselves, to say nothing of ruling others, but they must be dictated to in every trifle, like a child. They never can hold scepters of glory, majesty, and power in the celestial kingdom. Who will? Those who are valiant and inspired with the true independence of heaven, who will go forth boldly in the service of their God, leaving others to do as they please, determined to do right though all mankind besides should take the opposite course."
Brigham Young, *Journal of Discourses* [703]

Today, many appear to be choosing the "opposite course." References to Zion are sparse, and most active men in the church assume that the portion of priesthood they have received is sufficient. Occasionally, the brethren will suggest that the Saints represent a "royal priesthood," but in reality Joseph's vision of establishing a mighty nation of kings and queens is long forgotten.

God offered the Saints celestial glory, but the people wanted a telestial church. Joseph offered the Saints eternal nobility, but the members wanted religious security. After Joseph's death, the possibility of developing a massive army of righteous kings and queens was hindered for generations.

"Joseph's description of the restoration included a blueprint that was never followed. If followed, it would result in men and women becoming "kings and queens," priests and priestesses" with the ability to establish their own kingdoms. Joseph would preside as suzerain, others as vassals. But the "kings" would be responsible for going out into the world and establishing their own kingdoms. When they converted, taught, ordained, and endowed still other "kings" the "kingdom of God" would roll forth and fill the earth. All these various "kings" would be subject to Joseph as the head "king" or "vassal. The whole to be delivered to Christ, at His return."
Denver Snuffer, *Passing the Heavenly Gift* [704]

All who love God and His gospel can find hope in the reality that the Lord has not finished His work! Those privileged to greet the Savior at His return will include those who have reclaimed all that was once offered during the original Restoration, as well as greater light not yet revealed to mankind. Righteous family kingdoms will unify to create small communities that learn and practice the same ancient gospel Adam and Eve taught their posterity. This "re-restoration" will be provided for those who have escaped Babylon and stand in holy places. (D&C 87:8).

A Future Offering

"Whenever the gospel was restored to the earth after an apostasy, the patriarchal order was restored as well. This sacred system, however, was not given to the masses of people. It was given to the righteous who proved themselves worthy of such high blessings. The sacred ordinances which built the patriarchal order had to be restored only in sacred places, set apart from the world. In olden times such places were mountain tops, groves, wildernesses and caves-any place where the world was not."
Craig Mills, *Home Sanctuary* [705]

The spirituality of Zion will include what Adam and Eve, Lehi and Sariah, and Joseph, Emma, and Eliza worked to establish. What we currently term "the church," will involve those holy enough to merit the title of "king and queen," "priest and priestess." This was the title placed upon beloved Joseph, and this is the same glory and power that God invites us to receive.

And again, verily I say unto you, my servant Joseph...I am the Lord thy God, and will be with thee even unto the end of the world, and through all eternity; for verily I seal upon you your exaltation, and prepare a throne for you in the kingdom of my Father, with Abraham your father.
D&C 132:48-49

What matters today is that we realize the hope, purpose, and vision once provided by God through Joseph is now being offered again to those who are awake and hungry. This "Zion" includes a symphony of higher principles that currently remain hidden to the general population, but can be individually received from Christ through His higher ordinances. This process involves not just attending the temple, but becoming what the temple points us to. It requires more than just our preparatory ordination into the Melchizedek Priesthood, but an actual entrance into the Holy Order of the Fullness of the Priesthood.

To receive this glory does require a significant paradigm shift, but anyone willing to get honest about our current standing-can begin to grow into the king and queen Father intends us to be.

From being a good member of the church that does genealogy,
To being a king or queen sealed into the family of God.

From the structure of the priesthood being institutional,
To a personal ordination into the Holy Order.

From a Mormon who is content with a New Testament Church,
To a Saint who receives and practices the ancient gospel taught by Adam and Eve.

Latter Day Saints who hunger for all truth can still receive all truth! In Christ, they can then teach their children of their inherent potential and what Joseph originally taught the Saints. A true fullness is still available!

Culturally, most of us have been taught to look to the LDS church as *the kingdom of God on earth.* But in reality the *the kingdom of God is within you.* (Luke 17:21). When the internal kingdom is clean, an external kingdom can be manifested. All who are then "sealed as one" by the Holy Spirit of Promise will continue on into the eternities.

> *"...and I will bless him and multiply him and give unto him an hundred-fold in this world,*
> *of fathers and mothers, brothers and sisters, houses and lands, wives and children,*
> *and crowns of eternal lives in the eternal worlds.*
> D&C 132:55

The Lord's title of "King of Kings" is literal. (Revelations 19:16). During the millennial reign, He will personally be the King of many kings and the Lord of many lords. Just as Almighty Father is the Holy King of Jesus, the Messiah is the Holy King for those families who have been sealed unto Him in the flesh.

Today we determine: Who will have Jesus Christ to be their King?

The Lord wants all to receive it.

All arise.

CHAPTER SEVEN: LATTER-DAY ZION

Israel, Israel, God is calling.
Calling thee from lands of woe.

Babylon the great is falling;
God shall all her towers overthrow

Come to Zion, come to Zion
And within her walls rejoice…

Come to Zion, come to Zion
For your coming Lord is nigh.

Richard Smyth and Charles C. Converse, *Israel, Israel God is Calling* [706]

*"We have a great Work laid upon us, and we are responsible to God for the manner in which we make use of these blessings. **The Lord requires of us to build up Zion, to gather the honest-in-heart, restore Israel to their blessings**, redeem the earth from the power of the Devil, establish universal peace and **prepare a kingdom and a people for the coming and reign of the Messiah.**
When we do all we can to forward and accomplish this Work **then are we justified.**
This is the work of our lives, and it **makes life of some consequence to us.**"*
Wilford Woodruff, *Journal of Discourses* [707]

The word "Zion" is referred to in scripture and prophecy with multiple meanings. Disciple Joshua Mariano explains that Zion is a principle, place, and status of the heart.

1. The Pure in Heart (Doctrine and Covenants 97:21).
2. The City of Enoch (Moses 7:19).
3. The Ancient City of Jerusalem (2 Samuel 5:6–7).
4. The New Jerusalem (Doctrine and Covenants 45:66–67).
5. The Dwelling Place of those who are Exalted (Hebrews 12:22–23).
6. Location:
   a. Ward Building (Spencer W. Kimball, *Conference Report*).[708]
   b. Church (Doctrine and Covenants 82:14).
   c. Jackson County, Missouri (Doctrine and Covenants 57:1-2).
   d. America (Joseph Smith; *History of Church*).[709]
   e. Earth (Brigham Young; *Journal of Discourses*).[710]

Throughout the history of the church, there has always been a minority of Saints actively seeking Zion. Author John Pontius describes the progression frequently experienced by "the few."

The Hunger

*"In its infancy, the call of Zion is a quiet urging, a hunger of sorts that will not be filled by anything less than a glory your spirit knows awaits, but which you cannot yet name.
In its childhood, the call is a commitment to a belief that stretches the mortal mind;
to faith beyond the tensile strength of mortal logic. It is an emerging belief in things which eye hath not seen, nor ear heard, neither have entered into the heart of man. (1 Corinthians 2:9)
In its adulthood, the call is an invitation to obedience to covenants already made,
to finally understand glorious gifts promised in holy places; to approach the veil;
to knock, ask and receive; to at last enter into the divine presence.
This is the call of Zion, and it is being heard and heeded anew."*
John Pontius, *The Triumph of Zion* [711]

Because the Lord is in charge of when and how Zion will be organized, wisdom dictates leaving the details to Him and concentrating our personal efforts on becoming *pure in heart.* (D&C 97:21).

Opposite of the world's glitter, simple-humble-holiness is required to enter into His presence and fall at His feet in true worship. Surely nothing less than *Messiah* will do…No other name or glory can suffice…For in Him, we taste of His goodness and become more concerned about the welfare of another than ourselves. In Christ, the invitation to become *divine and holy* remains.

> *…Will ye not now return unto me, and repent of your sins, and be converted, that I may heal you?*
> *Yea, verily I say unto you, if ye will come unto me ye shall have eternal life. Behold, mine arm of mercy*
> *is extended towards you, and whosoever will come, him will I receive;*
> *and blessed are those who come unto me.*
> 3 Nephi 9:13-14

Despite our struggle to truly be a "Christ-centered" people, many refer to the Mormon culture as if it were already "Zion." In reality, monumental differences exist between the church as currently manifested and the Zion yet to be realized.

> ## Even if the establishment of Zion is not part of the four-fold mission of the Church,
> ## Is it part of your personal mission for Christ?

Perhaps the spiritual standard taught on Sunday is so low that focusing on Zion with the masses really would be inappropriate. Currently, *anyone* who is willing to make a few basic changes is invited to come out of the world and into the Lord's church. This is as it should be, but in the future only those in the church and throughout the earth *who have actually repented and become pure in heart will be comfortable dwelling in the peace, safety, and light of Zion.* Thus any member who desires to live into the Millennium must at this time, and in this order, grow from *world to church to Zion.*

> *"If we would establish Zion in our homes, branches, wards and stakes,*
> *we must rise to the standard. It will be necessary (1) to become unified in one heart and one mind;*
> *(2) to become, individually and collectively a holy people; and (3) to care for the poor and the*
> *needy with such effectiveness that we eliminate poverty among us. We cannot wait until Zion*
> *comes for these things to happen- Zion will come only as they happen."*
> D. Todd Chistofferson *Come to Zion* [712]

Today, the sacred invitation remains: Awake and arise! Cast off all sin into the Atonement of Jesus Christ, that through His merciful offering, we might be fully cleansed from the blood and sins of this generation. Now is the day: Come! Come to Zion!

> ## TRUTH #69 THE PURITY OF ZION MUST BE ACCOMPLISHED BY A SIGNIFICANT NUMBER OF SOULS INTERNALLY BEFORE AN EXTERNAL CITY CAN BE SUCCESSFULLY MANIFESTED.

Universal Power

*"**Universal family prayer could change the nations.** O my beloved hearers, what a world it would be if a **million families in this church** were to be on their knees like this every night and morning! And what a world it would be if nearly a hundred million families in this great land and other hundreds in other lands were praying for their sons and daughters twice daily! And what a world this would be if a **billion families through the world** were in home evenings and church activity and were on their physical knees pouring out their souls for their children, their families, their leaders, their governments! This kind of family life could bring us **back toward the translation experience of righteous Enoch. The millennium would be ushered in.**"*
Spencer W. Kimball, *The Teachings of Spencer W. Kimball* [713]

Every member contributes to the collective spirituality of the Church. To establish Zion externally, requires accumulative holiness internally. As discussed in Truth #35, Zion cannot be built using marketing models, surveys, and goal setting. The Zion of our Christ is rather the natural fruit of mass purity.

Do I Intend to Keep All of Fathers Commandments?

*And God spake unto Noah...I will establish my covenant with you, which I made unto your father Enoch, concerning your seed after you...And I will establish my covenant with you, which I made unto Enoch, concerning the remnants of your posterity...that I may remember the everlasting covenant... **that, when men should keep all my commandments, Zion should again come on the earth,** the city of Enoch which I have caught up unto myself...that when thy posterity shall embrace the truth, and look upward, then shall Zion look downward, and **all the heavens shall shake with gladness, and the earth shall tremble with joy...And the general assembly of the church of the firstborn shall come down out of heaven, and possess the earth,** and shall have place until the end come. And this is mine everlasting covenant, which I made with thy father Enoch.*
JST Genesis 9:15,17,21-23

The brilliance of *The Church of Jesus Christ of Latter Day Saints* centers on its continual invitation to come unto Christ. Those who accept the message partake of the simple and abundant compassion of Jesus. Overwhelmed by Him and His mercy, they are refined year after year until eventually they become *"pure in heart."* (3 Nephi 12:8).

An Individual Fulfillment of the Plan of Salvation

And it came to pass after they had fasted and prayed for the space of two days and two nights, the limbs of Alma received their strength, and he stood up and began to speak unto them, bidding them to be of good comfort: For, said he, I have repented of my sins, and have been redeemed of the Lord; behold I am born of the Spirit. And the Lord said unto me: Marvel not that all mankind, yea, men and women, all nations, kindreds, tongues and people, must be born again; yea, born of God, changed from their carnal and fallen state, to a state of righteousness, being redeemed of God, becoming his sons and daughters; And thus they become new creatures; and unless they do this, they can in nowise inherit the kingdom of God.

Mosiah 27:23-26

Soul by soul, God is sanctifying His children. When the mighty change of heart occurs within thousands, and even millions, then an Enoch type of society will again be born.

Until that time, "Zion" may initially be smaller, involving only a tender few. But what is consistent throughout the ages-is the presence of purity, holiness, and unity in Christ.

ONE

And Enoch continued his preaching in righteousness unto the people of God.
And it came to pass in his days, that he built a city that was called the City of Holiness, even ZION.
And the Lord called his people ZION, because they were of one heart and one mind,
and dwelt in righteousness; and there was no poor among them.

Moses 7: 19,18

When a man or woman is born again, the level of love and light within the body literally magnifies. The mind is "quickened" and the "vibration" of the soul intensifies. That individual no longer "resonates" with this fallen telestial realm, but can still choose to remain and minister to others in need.

When a number of these enlightened individuals are led to unify, spiritual power is exponentially increased. Whatever location they choose to reside in becomes sacred space. In simple terms: Holy people manifest holy cities.

A Collective Fulfillment of the Plan of Salvation

*And it came to pass that the Lord showed unto Enoch all the inhabitants of the earth; and he beheld, and lo, **Zion, in process of time, was taken up into heaven. And the Lord said unto Enoch: Behold mine abode forever.** And after that Zion was taken up into heaven, Enoch beheld, and lo, **all the nations of the earth were before him;** And there came generation upon generation; and **Enoch was high and lifted up, even in the bosom of the Father, and of the Son of Man...***

Moses 7:21-24

In the days of difficulty and destruction ahead, all will be invited to a greater repentance. Millions will grow from being converted to religion to being sanctified through the blood of the Lamb. This increase in personal righteousness will include growing in faith, knowledge, and power. Eventually, the overall righteousness of Latter Day Zion needs to be comparable to Enoch and his holy city. The question is, who will contribute?

It Can Be Done!

*"Even though it may seem impossible, or at the least improbable, that we could rise to such a lofty stratosphere as Enoch's Zion, **it is nonetheless entirely possible**. The Lord has placed within this very gospel we know and love, the way for us to accomplish this very thing. We need not look upward and fear that we are incapable of the climb. The height of the mountain is irrelevant. The only thing that matters is that **we keep climbing as the Lord directs**....God does not give us impossible tasks. Sometimes we fail because of weakness, but the commandment was not beyond us.*

*The invitation to become a Zion individual is played out before our eyes and ears each time we attend the temple. It is within those walls that we learn of the process that brings us unto the veil that separates us from Christ. And, it is at the veil that **we may request our place in Zion...The command to become pure, seek the face of God, and become Zion in our hearts still remains before us.***

*Many of us, perhaps most, covenant in the temples to sacrifice all to build up Zion with very little concept of what Zion is, or what we are promising to do. **A time of awakening seems to be upon us**, a time when the beauties of Zion are once again warming hearts and souls, and the pathway leading there is appearing beneath the snows of indifference. The sun of Zion appears to be rising in the east, lighting our minds and reawakening within us the promised glories awaiting us in Zion."*

John Pontius, *The Call to Zion* [714]

Some have criticized the institution for not teaching members what is required to live the Zion standard. Others who are starving within the church, and perhaps are over-zealous for an escape from Babylon, have ventured out into their own self-created communities. A few have temporarily succeeded, but on a massive scale, it appears we are not yet ready to maintain a true Zion society.

What must be understood is that only the Lord Himself can lead the gathering. He is the one qualified to judge the heart, and He is the one who can correctly determine the righteousness of His people. (Samuel 16:7). Waiting for Him and His timing is part of the Zion test.

Perhaps the day will come when the Lord will again command certain individuals to establish small gatherings, (see Truth #67), but for now it seems wise to repent within our own family kingdoms until the Lord determines to gather His final harvest.

Is It the Church or the People?

"Once again, let us carefully observe that the Church stands in its correct posture regarding Zion. Among many other things, in preparation for the future building of Zion, it perpetuates the priesthood, builds the temples and administers the holy ordinances specifically designed to bring us to Zion. All this is being done. As an organization, the church will not begin to build the actual cities of Zion until the Lord instructs His prophet to do so.

It is improbable that the Lord will instruct His Prophet to build a city that nobody is presently worthy to enter. *Thus, we are high centered upon our own worthiness, not upon some theological or ecclesiastical misstep of the church. In that light, it is quite astonishing but undeniably true, that the church has, for the moment, reached its full potential regarding Zion. **What remains to be done is for a million members to awaken and claim the blessings being offered.** That isn't something the church can control, or even influence more profoundly than it presently is. When we are ready and sanctified, then the church will have something more to do regarding Zion."*

John Pontius, *The Call to Zion* [715]

> **TRUTH #70** THE LORD JESUS CHRIST WILL RETURN IN FIRE AND GLORY
> TO DWELL AMONG HIS PEOPLE. WITHOUT A RIGHTEOUS REMNANT
> PREPARED TO RECEIVE THE SAVIOR,
> THE WHOLE EARTH WOULD BE UTTERLY WASTED AT HIS COMING.

"Zion and Jerusalem must both be built up before the coming of Christ."
Joseph Smith, *The Historian's Corner* [716]

Establishing a Holy City prior to the Second Coming is essential, for without a sacred place for pure souls to walk and talk with Jesus, the earth would be totally wasted at His coming.

*"It is also the concurrent testimony of all the Prophets, that **this gathering together of all the Saints, must take place before the Lord comes** to "take vengeance upon the ungodly," and to be glorified and admired by all those who obey the Gospel…Out of Zion, the perfection of beauty, God hath shined. Our God shall come and shall not keep silence; **a fire shall devour before Him, and it shall be very tempestuous round about Him**. He shall call to the heavens from above, and to the earth (that He may judge the people). **Gather my Saints together unto me;** those that have made covenant with me by sacrifice."*
Joseph and Hyrum Smith, *Proclamation of the First Presidency* [717]

According to Joseph Smith, this *"fire"* burns *"brighter than the noon day sun"* and is a literal power that, at the return of Jesus Christ, will consume the wicked.

***Listen to the voice of Jesus Christ**, your Redeemer, the Great I Am, whose arm of mercy hath atoned for your sins; Who will **gather his people** even as a hen gathereth her chickens under her wings, even as many as will hearken to my voice and humble themselves before me, and call upon me in mighty prayer. **Lift up your hearts and be glad, for I am in your midst**, and am your advocate with the Father; and it is his good will to **give you the kingdom**. And ye are called to bring to pass the **gathering of mine elect**; for mine elect hear my voice and harden not their hearts; Wherefore the decree hath gone forth from the Father that they shall be **gathered in unto one place** upon the face of this land, to **prepare their hearts** and be prepared in all things against the day when tribulation and desolation are sent forth upon the wicked. For the hour is nigh and the day soon at hand when the earth is ripe; and **all the proud and they that do wickedly shall be as stubble; and I will burn them up, saith the Lord of Hosts, that wickedness shall not be upon the earth;** For I will reveal myself from heaven with **power and great glory**, with all the hosts thereof, and dwell in righteousness with men on earth a thousand years, and the wicked shall not stand.*
D&C 29:1,2, 5,7-9,11

When Jesus came to fulfill His ministry in the meridian of time He came as a *Lamb.* (1 Nephi 14:2). Upon His global return He will come as the *Lion.* (Revelations 5:5). Only those who possess the energetic purity necessary to endure the light and glory of divinity will survive the day.

But behold, verily, verily, I say unto you that mine eyes are upon you. I am in your midst
and ye cannot see me; But the day soon cometh that ye shall see me, and know that I am;
for the veil of darkness shall soon be rent, and he that is not purified shall not abide the day.
Doctrine and Covenants 38:7-8

Zion will include those born of God, who have parted the veil and received their endowment directly from Him. These men and women will be similar to Lehi in that they have become fully sanctified, and are thus able to endure the glory of the Lord's presence.

Pillar of Fire

Wherefore it came to pass that my father, Lehi, as he went forth prayed unto the Lord, yea,
even with all his heart, in behalf of his people. And it came to pass as he prayed unto the Lord,
there came a pillar of fire and dwelt upon a rock before him; and he saw and heard much;
and because of the things which he saw and heard he did quake and tremble exceedingly.
1 Nephi 1:5-6

When Jesus Christ or any other God manifests in physical form, they can appear as a common mortal, or in the fire of their exalted glory. How the Lord and His angels choose to reveal themselves during visions or visitations is due in part to what the recipient can handle.

"Joseph sat firmly and calmly all the time in the midst of a magnificent glory,
but Sidney sat limp and pale, apparently as limber as a rag, observing which,
Joseph remarked, smilingly, 'Sidney is not used to it as I am.'"
Philo Dibble, *Juvenile Instructor* [718]

Many members look forward to the Second Coming of Jesus Christ, but in relation to the literal *"glory of the Lord,"* a premature appearance by the Savior to a fallen and unprepared people, would only result in their cellular destruction.

For the hour is nigh and the day soon at hand when the earth is ripe; and all the proud and they that
*do wickedly shall be as stubble; and **I will burn them up**, saith the Lord of Hosts…**For I will reveal***
myself from heaven with power and great glory, with all the hosts thereof,
*and dwell in righteousness with men on earth a thousand years, and **the wicked shall not stand.***
D&C 29:9-11

"Our leaders wear Babylonian business apparel, accept modest stipends with book deals and work
in offices, courthouses, on facebook, and in planes. Our people build the very walls of Babylon
daily and enthusiastically, all the while declaring Zion's mercies and praying in ignorance
for a Second Coming that will destroy the very world they are firmly rooted in."
Dan Mead, *Little Children in the Dust* [719]

Thankfully, it is the desire of our compassionate Redeemer to save us, not destroy us. Despite His patience and ongoing mercy, those who are in a state of rebellion at the time of His return, will not have a pleasant experience.

Who Can Withstand His Love?

For a desolating scourge shall go forth among the inhabitants of the earth, and shall continue to be poured out from time to time, if they repent not, until the earth is empty, and the inhabitants thereof are consumed away and utterly destroyed by the brightness of my coming.
Doctrine and Covenants 5:19

Saints who desire to survive the destruction and be received of the Lord in the flesh might ponder: Am I Holy? Do I have the pure love of Christ emanating from my soul? Can the cells of my body withstand the all-consuming presence of ALMIGHTY GOD? And to what degree must the natural man still be purged from my soul-that I might be able to dwell with Father in His realm of celestial light?

Walking with the Angels

"We have all been children, and are too much so at the present time; but we hope in the Lord that we may grow in grace and be prepared for all things which the bosom of futurity may disclose unto us. Time is rapidly rolling on, and the prophecies must be fulfilled. The days of tribulation are fast approaching, and the time to test the fidelity of the Saints has come…but in these times of sore trial, **let the Saints be patient and see the salvation of God. Those who cannot endure persecution, and stand in the day of affliction, cannot stand in the day when the Son of God shall burst the veil, and appear in all the glory of His Father, with all the holy angels."**
Joseph Smith, *History of the Church* [720]

Scripture teaches *"no unclean thing can dwell with God."*(1 Nephi 10:21). This standard is literal and assures us that those who participate in the Second Coming of Christ will have been purged to a sufficient and holy degree.

"All of them who are **pure in heart** *will* **behold the face of the Lord** *and that too* **before he comes** *in his glory in the clouds of heaven, for* **he will suddenly come to his Temple**, *and he will purify the sons of Moses and of Aaron, until they shall be prepared to offer in that Temple an offering that shall be acceptable in the sight of the Lord.* **In doing this, he will purify not only the minds of the Priesthood in that Temple, but he will purify their bodies until they shall be quickened, renewed and strengthened, and they will be partially changed, not to immortality, but changed in part that they can be filled with the power of God, and they can stand in the presence of Jesus, and behold his face in the midst of that Temple."**
Orson Pratt, *Journal of Discourses* [721]

To help us conceptualize the Lord's return, imagine Jesus Christ coming to the Salt Lake Temple clothed in a pillar of fire. When He arrives, the literal energy and light emanating from His soul slowly spreads out across the city. With power and glory of the Lion steadily encompasses the entire Wasatch Front. Saints who are as faithful as Shadrach, Meshach, and Abed-nego will survive the fire unharmed, (Daniel 3), while others who do not have the required oil in their lamps will not abide the day.

A Great and Dreadful Day
When the Son of man shall come in his glory, and all the holy angels with him,
*then shall he sit upon the throne of his glory: **And before him shall be gathered all nations**:*
and he shall separate them one from another, as a shepherd divideth his sheep from the goats:
***And he shall set the sheep on his right hand, but the goats on the left.** Then shall the King say*
*unto them on his right hand, **Come, ye blessed of my Father, inherit the kingdom prepared for you***
from the foundation of the world.
Matthew 25:31-34

Prior to the Son of Man coming in glory, 144,000 born-again high priests will be called to gather the elect and proclaim repentance to the kings of the earth. These "Modern-Day Moroni's" will face intense scenarios involving war, death, and destruction. Many of these missionary-prophets will require the gift of translation to accomplish their spiritual assignments.

Enoch and His city provide a model for understanding the gift of translation and how it relates to the last days. John Pontius in his book, *The Triumph of Zion*, explains *"translation is not a permanent state but an intermediate condition prior to resurrection. It has a specific purpose of giving individuals the power necessary to carry out express assignments that would otherwise not be possible for them to accomplish."*[722] In his book he also summarizes the powers and gifts of translation.

"Translated people will not endure the "pains" of death but will be changed in a twinkling of an eye.
(3 Nephi 28:8). Translated persons will not have pain or sorrow save it be for the sins of the world.
(3 Nephi 28:9). Translated beings enjoy a "fullness of joy" and will sit down in the kingdom of the Father.
(3 Nephi 28:10). Translated beings are changed into an immortal state and can behold the things of God.
(3 Nephi 28:15). Prisons cannot hold them, fire cannot harm them, wild beasts will not injure them.
(3 Nephi 28:19-22). Translated people can work among us and not be known. (3 Nephi 28:27-28).
They are "as the angels of God" and can show themselves to whomever it seems good to them.
(3 Nephi 28:30). They can work miracles and perform great and marvelous works. (3 Nephi 28:31-32).
They are changed. Satan cannot tempt them or have power over them. They are sanctified in the flesh
(D&C 84:33) and have power over the earth. (3 Nephi 28:39). This means they are not subject to the laws
of what we call nature. They can create objects they need and have mastery over all things mortal."
John Pontius, *The Triumph of Zion* [723]

Receiving the gift of translation is a priesthood ordinance that allows an individual to interact on both sides of the veil *while still in the flesh*. Initially, we may suppose that the gift of translation can not obtained in this life, but understanding the need for translation, as well as the real possibility of being translated, can be useful for increasing faith and spiritual motivation. In Christ, all things are possible!

Soul Mettle
"Within Zion there will be the divine presence, which will guarantee our peace, safety and joy…
In order for the latter-day Zion to fulfill its purpose, those who dwell within
must become of the same spiritual metal as Enoch's Zion."
John Pontius, *Call to Zion* [724]

There can be no Latter Day Zion without a righteous people worthy to welcome the Lord. If the masses never achieve the required standard, the Lord Jesus Christ will return to a very small and obscure Zion. This is a spiritual tragedy we cannot accept!

"...He will appear in the clouds of heaven with power and great glory...But before he appears in his glory he is going to build up Zion, that is, Zion must again be built up on the earth: and if there is not a Zion built up on the earth before he comes, or in other words, if there never is to be another Zion built up on the earth, then he never will come."
Orson Pratt, *Journal of Discourses* [725]

Enoch and his people progressed to the degree they could walk and talk with God. (Moses 7:69). Participants in Enoch's city were born again, glorified, and translated. They did it. So can we.

Prepared and Gathered

*And ye are called to bring to pass the **gathering of mine elect**; for mine elect hear my voice and harden not their hearts; Wherefore the decree hath gone forth from the Father that they shall be **gathered in unto one place** upon the face of this land, to **prepare their hearts** and be prepared in all things against the day when tribulation and desolation are sent forth upon the wicked.*
D&C 29:7-8

So, if we were invited to become a Zion people, what happened?

1830: The Church of Jesus Christ is organized.

The only true and living church upon the face of the whole earth,
with which I, the Lord, am well pleased, speaking unto the church collectively.
Doctrine and Covenants 1:30

1831: The Saints are given a five-year window from 1831-1836 to go to Zion.

*I the Lord will to retain a stronghold in Kirtland, for the space of **five years,** in the which I will*
*not overthrow the wicked, that thereby I might save some. And after that day, **I , the Lord,***
will not hold any guilty that shall go with an open heart up to the land of Zion;
for I, the Lord, require the hearts of the children of men.
Doctrine and Covenants 64:21-22

1832: Within two years, the membership had chosen vanity, unbelief, and condemnation.

And your minds in times past have been darkened because of unbelief, and because you
*have treated lightly the things you have received—**Which vanity and unbelief have brought***
the whole church under condemnation.
And this condemnation resteth upon the children of Zion, even all.
Doctrine and Covenants 84:54-56

1833: The church is again invited to become Zion internally and build Zion externally.

And, now, behold, if Zion do these things she shall prosper, and spread herself and become very
glorious, very great, and very terrible. And the nations of the earth shall honor her,
and shall say: Surely Zion is the city of our God, and surely Zion cannot fall, neither be moved
out of her place, for God is there, and the hand of the Lord is there; And he hath sworn
by the power of his might to be her salvation and her high tower.
Therefore, verily, thus saith the Lord, let Zion rejoice,
*for this is Zion—*THE PURE IN HEART…
Doctrine and Covenants 97:18-21

1834: Joseph promises that the scourge of condemnation will remain if Zion is not established.

"*Now my beloved brethren, you will learn by this **we have a great work to do**, and but little time to do it in; and if we do not exert ourselves to the utmost in gathering up the **strength of the Lord's house** that this thing may be accomplished, behold **there remaineth a scourge for the Church**, even that they shall be **driven from city to city**, and but **few shall remain to receive an inheritance**; if those things are not kept, there remaineth a scourge also; therefore, be wise this once, O ye children of Zion! And give heed to my counsel saith the Lord…use every effort to prevail on the churches to gather to those regions and locate themselves, to be in readiness to move into Jackson county in two years from the **eleventh of September next, which is the appointed time for the redemption of Zion.** If verily I say unto you –if the Church with one united effort perform their duties; **if they do this, the work shall be complete**—if they do not this in all humility, **making preparation** from this time forth, like Joseph in Egypt, laying up store against the time of Famine, every man having his tent, his horse, his chariots, his armory, his cattle, his family, and his whole substance in readiness against the time when it shall be said,*
"To your tents, O Israel…"
Joseph Smith, *History of the Church* [726]

1834: The love of money and property stalls the gathering.

*Behold, I say unto you, were it not for the transgressions of my people, speaking concerning the church and not individuals, they might have been **redeemed even now**. But behold, they have not learned to be obedient to the things which I required at their hands, but are full of all manner of evil, and do not impart of their substance, as becometh saints to the poor and afflicted among them; And they are not united according to the union required by the **law of the Celestial Kingdom**; And Zion cannot be built up unless it is by the principles of the law of the celestial kingdom; otherwise I cannot receive her unto myself. And my people must needs be chastened until they learn obedience, if it must needs be, **by the things which they suffer**… there are many who will say: **where is their God?** Behold, he will deliver them in times of trouble, otherwise **we will not go up to Zion, and will keep our moneys.** Therefore, in consequence of the transgressions of my people, it is expedient in me that mine elders should wait for a little season for the redemption of Zion-**That they themselves may be prepared, and that my people may be taught more perfectly**, and have experience, and know more perfectly concerning their duty, and the things which I require at their hands.*
Doctrine and Covenants 105:2-10

Zion Postponed

*"But they did not redeem Zion, because **the Saints were not prepared**.
Consequently, **the day for the redemption of Zion was postponed**, until the time should
come when the people, through the experiences they would be called to pass through,
should be prepared for the redemption of Zion and for the building of the House of God
at the center stake thereof. And the day was not yet come; and no man, so far as I know,
can foretell the day to the hour, the month or the year when the people of God are prepared to
go back, and not before. Whether it be in this generation or in the next generation, it matters not;
**it will only be when the people have prepared themselves to do it by their faithfulness
and obedience to the commands of God. I prophesy to you, in the name of the Lord,
that when the Latter-day Saints have prepared themselves through righteousness
to redeem Zion, they will accomplish that work, and God will go with them**.
No power will then be able to prevent them from accomplishing that work;
for the Lord has said it shall be done, and it will be done in the due time of the Lord,
when the people are prepared for it."*
Joseph F. Smith, *Latter-day Prophets and the Doctrine and Covenants* [727]

After a majority of the church rejected living the principles of Zion, great persecution and suffering afflicted the Saints.

Consequences Experienced

*Wherefore the land of Zion shall not be obtained but by purchase or by blood, otherwise there is
none inheritance for you…And if by blood, as you are forbidden to shed blood, lo your enemies
are upon you, and **ye shall be scourged from city to city**, and from synagogue to synagogue,
and few shall stand to receive an inheritance.*
Doctrine and Covenants 63:29-31

*And my people must needs be chastened until they learn obedience,
if it must needs be, by the things which they suffer.*
Doctrine and Covenants 105:6

Despite their struggle then, and our struggle now, a small portion of Latter Day Saints in each generation has *individually become Zion*. Many of these elect souls have *"died in faith, not having received the promises, but having seen them afar off…confessed that they were strangers and pilgrims on the earth."*(Hebrews 11:13).

Scripture assures the valiant that even though the journey is steep and often lonely, the Lord will never forget those who love to serve Him. For in the end, He will keep His promises and gather home His broken and bleeding disciples.

Required Affliction Assists the Sanctification Process

*Verily I say unto you, concerning your brethren who have been afflicted, and persecuted, and cast out from the land of their inheritance—I, the Lord, have suffered the affliction to come upon them, wherewith **they have been afflicted, in consequence of their transgressions;** Yet I will own them, and they shall be mine in that day when **I shall come to make up my jewels.** Therefore, they must needs be chastened and tried, even as Abraham, who was commanded to offer up his only son. For all those who will not endure chastening, but deny me, cannot be sanctified. Behold, I say unto you, there were jarrings, and contentions, and envyings, and strifes, and lustful and covetous desires among them; therefore by these things **they polluted their inheritances.** They were slow to hearken unto the voice of the Lord their God; therefore, the Lord their God is slow to hearken unto their prayers, to answer them in the day of their trouble. In the day of their peace they esteemed lightly my counsel; but, in the day of their trouble, of necessity they feel after me. Verily I say unto you, **notwithstanding their sins, my bowels are filled with compassion towards them. I will not utterly cast them off; and in the day of wrath I will remember mercy.***
Doctrine and Covenants 101:1-9

Today the Invitation Remains: Become Pure in Heart and Escape to Zion!

*Mine indignation is soon to be poured out without measure upon all nations; and this will I do when the cup of their iniquity is full. And in that day all who are found upon the watch-tower, or in other words, all mine Israel, shall be saved. **And they that have been scattered shall be gathered. And all they who have mourned shall be comforted. And all they who have given their lives for my name shall be crowned. Therefore, let your hearts be comforted concerning Zion; for all flesh is in mine hands; be still and know that I am God.** Zion shall not be moved out of her place, notwithstanding her children are scattered. **They that remain, and are pure in heart, shall return, and come to their inheritances, they and their children, with songs of everlasting joy, to build up the waste places of Zion.***
Doctrine and Covenants 101:11-18

> # Will history repeat?
> # Zion or Babylon?

Who will get in the ark?

"Now, if this exhortation does no one else any good, **I pray God it may do me good;** *that I may be strengthened and observe the things which God commands; that when the Elders preach unto me and my family friends that judgment is coming upon the earth, and they testify that* **this is the path of safety**, *we may heed their words. This is the way to sanctify the land unto the people who dwell upon it. It is the way which the Lord has signified.* **This ark of safety is offered to us. Shall we receive it?** *Or shall we go blindly forward, determined in our hearts to follow our own inclinations, and let the flood come, and say, "There is still a place of safety for me and mine;* **I can float with the current and be saved with the balance of the Saints of God?"** *I do not think I can do this. On the contrary, I think that the judgments of God are increasing, and that they are flooding the earth, and* **the Latter-day Saints must make this place of refuge a sanctified place for their salvation** *and the salvation of those who will listen to their testimonies."*
Brigham Young, Jr. *General Conference* [728]

With the world continuing its decent into moral decay and spiritual anarchy, we might expect more individuals would be interested in creating a Zion escape. Nevertheless, only a small number of souls seem interested in the victory Zion offers. Perhaps many assume that because they are in the Lord's church, *"it will all work out in the end,"* and that when the time comes, the Lord will just magically "poof" Zion into existence.

> *[The people] are not united according to the union required by the law of the celestial kingdom; And Zion cannot be built up unless it is by the principles of the law of the celestial kingdom; otherwise I cannot receive her unto myself.*
> D&C 105:4-5

Members who assume that God will always keep His church and its members on track do not understand eternal agency. Justice will not be minimized or negated to sooth the mainstream. We alone have the choice to rise or fall. It would therefore be wise to learn of Enoch's success, as well as from the failed Nephite and Jaredite societies.

Throughout history there have only been a few examples of Zion being successfully established. For those who ponder the significance of our Latter Day Zion being delayed, disciple John Pontius has listed the attempts to build Zion-while also reminding the impatient, *"it isn't God who succeeds or fails, it is His children."*[729]

Historical Efforts to Establish Zion

Adam	(Appears to have succeeded for a time, then failed)
Enoch	(Succeeded)
Noah	(Failed until Melchizedek)
Brother of Jared	(Failed)
Melchizedek	(Succeeded)
Abraham	(Unknown)
Jacob/Israel/Joseph	(Failed)
Moses & Israelites	(Failed)
Isaiah & Jeremiah	(Failed)
Lehi/Nephi/Jacob	(Failed)
Alma the Elder	(Succeeded very briefly)
Jesus Christ	(Succeeded briefly)
Nephi-after Christ	(Succeeded for 200 years)
Joseph Smith	(Failed initially)

The standard required for a Zion people to flourish will not be watered down to appease the masses. Our collective response to the fullness of the gospel will determine whether we as a people repeat the destiny of the destroyed Jaredites, or fulfill the glory of Enoch's Zion.

> *"The Lord has declared it to be His will that His people enter into a covenant,*
> *even as Enoch and his people did, which of necessity must be before*
> *we shall have the privilege of building up the Center Stake of Zion..."*
> Brigham Young, *Journal of Discourses* [730]

Both the City of Enoch and the Nephites who gathered at the temple in Bountiful offer us a prototype for unifying an entire civilization in Christ.

> *"Two separate groups of Saints have fully implemented this divine law. The first was the united order under Enoch, wherein the Lord designated this people Zion, "because they were of one heart and one mind, and dwelt in righteousness; and there was no poor among them" (Moses 7:18). A second instance was the Nephite civilization following the visit of the Savior to the Western Hemisphere after His resurrection (see 4 Nephi 3). The failure of the early Saints in this dispensation to live according to the Fullness of the law is explained by the Lord in revelations recorded in the Doctrine and Covenants. (see D&C 101;105)."*
> Ezra Taft Benson, *The Teachings of Ezra Taft Benson* [731]

From the Enoch example we learn that in relation to the *"power of the language which God had given him,"*(Moses 7:13), Enoch was able to gather the righteous **before the destruction** of the approaching Flood. The preventative repentance of the people, which admittedly took several generations, literally allowed them to by-pass the destruction and horror.

From this example, we might determine that repenting unto sanctification without having to be compelled is the preferable path.

In the Nephite model, the Lord appears to the surviving Saints at the Bountiful temple *after the destruction*. Previous to the Nephite cleansing, the people were lingering in apathy and apostasy. Only those *"more righteous than they"* were spared from physical death. (3 Nephi 9:13). It is grievous that only a righteous few survived, but after experiencing the overwhelming love of the Lord's presence, the remaining Nephites were able to establish a Zion society which lasted two hundred years.

Cultural indicators suggest that we in the LDS church are insisting our sanctification occur by the things in which we suffer. The lack of "Zion-hunger" in our midst requires the wheat to cling to the promise *"it is not the work of God, but the work of man that is frustrated."* (D&C 3:3). This reminds us that no matter what the Mormon mainstream does, we can individually choose to live our temple covenants, access a true fullness, and keep the fire of hope alive that Zion will yet be redeemed!

> *"**I do fear that we will defer the redemption of Zion indefinitely** through our unwillingness to do the things that God requires at our hands…**We need to be born again, and have new hearts put in us.** There is too much of the old leaven about us. We are not born again as we should be. Do you not believe that we ought to be born again? **Do you not believe that we should become new creatures in Christ Jesus, under the influence of the Gospel?** All will say, yes, who understand the Gospel. **You must be born again…** He wants us to have new hearts, new desires. He wants us to be a changed people when we embrace His Gospel, and to be animated by entirely new motives, and **have a faith that will lay hold of the promises of God."***
> George Q. Cannon, *Conference Report* [732]

Within each stage of the Lord's "one eternal round," there is usually just "a few" who truly come unto Christ and partake of His salvation. Jesus referred to this small group phenomenon when, at the end of His ministry among the surviving Nephites, He expressed great joy that none of those still living would be lost. (3 Nephi 27:30). The Lord then prophesied, *"But behold, it sorroweth me because of the fourth generation from this generation, for they are led away captive by him even as was the son of perdition; **for they will sell me for silver and for gold**, and for that which moth doth corrupt and which thieves can break through and steal."* (3 Nephi 27:32).

> *"Today the beautiful word Zion, with all its emotional and historical associations, is used as the name Christian was formerly used, to put the stamp of sanctity on whatever men chose to do. The Hebrew word for financial activity of any kind is mamonut, and the financier is a mamonai; that is, financing is, quite frankly, in that honest language, the business of Mammon. From the very first there were Latter-day Saints who thought to promote the cause of Zion by using the methods of Babylon. Indeed, once the Saints were told to make friends with the Mammon of unrighteousness (D&C 82:22), but that was only to save their lives in an emergency. We have the word of the Prophet Joseph that Zion is not to be built up by using the methods of Babylon. He says, "Here are those who begin to spread out buying up all the land they are able to do, to the exclusion of the poorer ones who are not so much blessed with this worlds goods, thinking to lay foundations for themselves only, looking to their own individual families and those who are to follow them…. Now I want to tell you that Zion cannot be built up in any such way."*
> Hugh Nibley, *Approaching Zion* [733]

Buying Zion Land

"The Church of Jesus Christ of Latter-day Saints confirmed Saturday that it purchased 6,000 acres
of Missouri farmland and three historical sites from the Community of Christ…
"The Church recently acquired operating farmland and several other non-farmland properties located
in Missouri and Ohio from the Community of Christ," LDS Church spokesperson Scott Trotter said.
"Non-farm sites include the Haun's Mill and the Far West Burying Ground in Missouri as well as the
Joseph Smith Sr. home in Kirtland, Ohio. "Trotter specified that no plans exist to develop the properties;
farm operations will continue and historic sites will be maintained."
Jamshid Ghazi Askar, *Deseret News* [734]

We need to understand that Zion cannot be planned, purchases, or managed into existence. When America is cleansed, the millions of dollars spent to buy up historical sites in Jackson County Missouri, as well as other areas around the country, will not secure a place for the church in Zion.

Sale of timberland to make the Mormon Church Florida's biggest private landowner

"The Mormon Church is poised to become the largest private landowner in the state…
The price tag of $565 million includes the bulk of St. Joe's timberland…The church already controls the
Deseret Ranches in Central Florida, which consists of about 290,000 acres spread over three counties.
The new deal would push its holdings above 650,000 acres….
A quote from former church president Gordon B. Hinckley explains the long-haul strategy:
'We have felt that good farms, over a long period, represent a safe investment where the assets of the
Church may be preserved and enhanced, while at the same time they are available as an agricultural
resource to feed people should there come a time of need.'" [735]

Preserving and enhancing church assets is a business strategy. The point here is not to question the decision making of the brethren, (or their good intentions to feed people), but to observe that the LDS Church has been fully integrated into the world's economic system. We as a people, and as an institution, have not "come out" from Babylon the Whore, but have instead partaken of her spoils.

This reality requires us to acknowledge the Book of Mormon was written for us, and about us. (2 Nephi 28, Ether 8, Helaman 5, Mormon 8, 3 Nephi 16, etc…). Those who believe in scripture are invited to do the necessary soul-searching and then ask: Is our common tendency to stay with the norms of the LDS mainstream really adequate? Like the fallen Nephites, will pride, apathy, and a love of money eventually bring destruction? And is there still time for us to awaken, repent, and become part of the humble few?

And it came to pass that when Jesus had ended these sayings he said unto his disciples:
Enter ye in at the strait gate; for strait is the gate, and narrow is the way that leads to life,
and few there be that find it; but wide is the gate, and broad the way which leads to death,
and many there be that travel therein, until the night cometh, wherein no man can work.
3 Nephi 27:33

Am I Zion Ready?

*"But when shall I be prepared to go there? **Not while I have in my heart the love of this world more than the love of God.** Not while I am possessed of that selfishness and greed that would induce me to cling to the world or my possessions in it, at the sacrifice of principle or truth. But when I am ready to say, "**Father all that I have, myself included, is Thine; my time, my substance, everything that I possess is on the altar, to be used freely, agreeable to Thy holy will, and not my will, but Thine, be done**," then perhaps I will be prepared to go and help to redeem Zion."*

Joseph F. Smith, *Millennial Star* [736]

To become Zion requires a willingness to sacrifice *all things* requested of the Lord. This does not necessarily mean that *all* will be taken, but that we must be willing to lay down *everything* the Lord requires. Similar to Abraham offering Isaac on the altar each of us has our own unique "Abrahamic trial." The Lord in His wisdom determines what, when, and how we will be invited to demonstrate our faith.

And he (God) said, Take now thy son, thine only son Isaac, whom thou lovest, and get thee into the land of Moriah; and offer him there for a burnt offering upon one of the mountains which I will tell thee of…And Abraham took the wood of the burnt offering, and laid it upon Isaac his son; and he took the fire in his hand, and a knife; and they went both of them together. And Isaac spake unto Abraham his father, and said, My father: and he said, Here am I, my son. And he said, Behold the fire and the wood: but where is the lamb for a burnt offering? And Abraham said, My son, God will provide himself a lamb for a burnt offering: so they went both of them together…

Genesis 22: 2,6-8

At the very moment God requires incredible faith, Satan will speak terrible fear. When Father requires the sacrifice of "all things," Satan will instead offer you the comforts of this world. One strategy he employs is to reassure the selfish that *"you can buy anything in this world with money."* Only those who define success as "being in God's will," are able to resist the fame, influence, and popularity Lucifer offers.

Working for Babylon or Zion?

*"If they enter upon their business without God in their thoughts, it is `How much can I get for this? and how much can I make on that? and how much will the people give for this and for that? and **how fast can I get rich?** and how long will it take me to be a millionaire?' **which thoughts should never come into the mind of a merchant who professes to be a Latter-day Saint.** But it should be `**What can I do to benefit this people**? And our mechanics, do they labor for the express purpose of building up Zion and the kingdom of God? I am sorry to say that I think*

416

there are very few into whose hearts it has entered or whose thoughts are occupied in the least with such a principle; but it is, 'how much can I make? Brother Joseph Smith gave us the word of the Lord; it was simply this: **'Never do another day's work to build up a Gentile city never lay out another dollar while you live, to advance the world in its present state; it is full of wickedness and violence;** *no regard is paid to the prophets, nor the prophecyings of the prophets, nor to Jesus nor his sayings, nor the word of the Lord that was given anciently, nor to that given in our day. They have gone astray, and they are building up themselves, and they are promoting sin and iniquity upon the earth; and,' said he, it is the word and commandment of the Lord to his servants that* **they shall never do another day's work, nor spend another dollar to build up a Gentile city."**
Brigham Young, *Journal of Discourses* [737]

The billions of dollars spent on the renovation of downtown Salt Lake would seem to suggest the church as an institution has not followed Brigham's council. In addition, many on a personal level have rationalized accumulating great wealth under the guise of "providing for their family."

"Every step in the direction of increasing one's personal holdings is a step away from Zion... one cannot serve two masters...so it is with God and business, for mammon is simply the standard Hebrew word for any kind of financial dealing."
Hugh Nibley, *Approaching Zion* [738]

The seduction of money, power, and fame has always been present in the Mormon culture, but never before has Satan been so successful with his subtle lies.

"So money is the name of the game by which the devil cleverly decoys the minds of the Saints from God's work to his. "Why does the Lord want us up here in the tops of these mountains?" Brigham asked twenty years after the first settling of the Valley. "He wishes us to build up Zion. What are the people doing? They are merchandizing, trafficking and trading."..."Instead of reflecting upon and searching for hidden things of the greatest value to them, [the Latter-day Saints] rather wish to learn how to secure their way through this world as easily and as comfortably as possible. The reflections, what they are here for, who produced them, and where they are from, far too seldom enter their minds."..."Are their eyes single to the building up of the Kingdom of God? No; they are single to the building up of themselves." "Does this congregation understand what idolatry is? The New Testament says that covetousness is idolatry; therefore, a covetous people is an idolatrous people." "Man is made in the image of God, but what do we know of him or of ourselves, when we suffer ourselves to love and worship the god of this world-riches?" Had the Latter-day Saints gone so far? They had, from the beginning; when the Church was only a year old, the Prophet Joseph observed that "God has often sealed up the heavens because of covetousness in the Church." Three years later, God revoked that "united order" by which Zion alone could exist on earth (D&C 104:52-53) – in their desire for wealth, the Saints had tried to embrace both Babylon and Zion by smooth double-talk..."
Hugh Nibley, *Approaching Zion* [739]

Instead of investing resources into a greedy and conniving marketplace and then simultaneously boasting of our charitable contributions, we should measure ourselves in comparison to Enoch and his holy city. Focusing on the Zion standard reveals that the praise of this twisted world is irrelevant and that only Christ and His gospel can provide the ultimate satisfaction for which our souls yearn.

"Saints must keep the covenant of consecration. The Lord has blessed us as a people with a prosperity unequaled in times past. The resources that have been placed in our power are good, and necessary to our work here on the earth. But I am afraid that many of us have been surfeited with flocks and herds and acres and barns and wealth and have begun to worship them as false gods, and they have power over us. Do we have more of these good things than our faith can stand? Many people spend most of their time working in the service of a self-image that includes sufficient money, stocks, bonds, investment portfolios, property, credit cards, furnishings, automobiles, and the like to guarantee carnal security throughout, it is hoped, a long and happy life. Forgotten is the fact that our assignment is to use these many resources in our families and quorums to build up the kingdom of God—to further the missionary effort and the genealogical and temple work; to raise our children up as fruitful servants unto the Lord; to bless others in every way, that they may also be fruitful. Instead, we expend these blessings on our own desires, and as Moroni said, "Ye adorn yourselves with that which hath no life, and yet suffer the hungry, and the needy, and the naked, and the sick and the afflicted to pass by you, and notice them not."
Spencer W. Kimball, *The Teachings of Spencer W. Kimball* [740]

Those who consecrate their daily performance unto God, experience a deep and abiding contentment in the Lord. By trusting Him to provide *"sufficient for their needs,"* they find the Lord to be most generous. For surely *"he that hath eternal life is rich."*(D&C 6:7).

"Like the people of Lehi and the primitive Christians, the Latter-day Saints were asked and forced to make a clean break with the world—"the world" meaning **explicitly the world's economy.** *The first commandment given to the Saints in this last dispensation, delivered at Harmony, Pennsylvania, in April of 1829, before the formal incorporation of the Church, was an ominous warning:* **"Seek not for riches but for wisdom"** *(D&C 6:7)—all in one brief mandate that does not allow compromise. Why start out on such a negative note? The Lord knew well that the great obstacle to the work would be what it always had been in the past. The warning is repeated throughout the Doctrine and Covenants and the Book of Mormon again and again. The positive and negative are here side by side and back to back, making it clear, as the scriptures often do, that the two quests are mutually exclusive—* **you cannot go after both, you cannot serve both God and Mammon,** *even if you should be foolish enough to try."*
Hugh Nibley, *Approaching Zion* [741]

If we believe we can't "serve two masters," why do we keep trying? Should financial affluence continue to be considered a sign of righteousness? And what does it mean when profits acquired from investing tithing funds are used to integrate the church ever deeper into the ways of the world? Does "the end" always justify "the means?"

Are You Ready?

"The time must come when there will be a separation between this kingdom and the kingdoms of the world, even in every point of view (D&C 63:53-54). The time must come when this kingdom must be free and independent from all other kingdoms.
Are you prepared to have the thread cut to-day?"
Brigham Young, *Journal of Discourses* [742]

In Mormonism today, there are those who love to see the Church display money, power, and flair. They want religion to be entertaining and appealing so they can be accepted by the media and the culture it serves.

In contrast, there are those who simply love God and His gospel. They don't need position, power, wealth, or acknowledgement to know that they are significant to Heavenly Father. Often, these are the simple and overlooked heroes for Christ.

Then shall the King say unto them on his right hand, Come, ye blessed of my Father, inherit the kingdom prepared for you from the foundation of the world: For I was an hungered, and ye gave me meat: I was thirsty, and ye gave me drink: I was a stranger, and ye took me in: Naked, and ye clothed me: I was sick, and ye visited me: I was in prison, and ye came unto me.
Then shall the righteous answer him, saying, Lord, when saw we thee an hungered, and fed thee? or thirsty, and gave thee drink? When saw we thee a stranger, and took thee in? or naked, and clothed thee? Or when saw we thee sick, or in prison, and came unto thee?
And the King shall answer and say unto them, Verily I say unto you, Inasmuch as ye have done it unto one of the least of these my brethren, ye have done it unto me.
Mathew 25:34-40

"Do you expect that every person will be destroyed from the face of the earth, but the Latter-day Saints? If you do, you will be mistaken... But the order of society will be as it is when Christ comes to reign a thousand years; there will be every sort of sect and party, and every individual following what he supposes to be the best in religion, and in everything else, similar to what it is now."
Brigham Young, *Journal of Discourses* [743]

Zion will be established before the Second Coming of Jesus Christ. The City of God will consist of a diverse population including souls from various spiritual backgrounds.

*"**If the Latter-day Saints think, when the kingdom of God is established on the earth, that all the inhabitants of the earth will join the Church called Latter-day Saints, they are egregiously mistaken**. I presume there will be as many sects and parties then as now. Still, when the kingdom of God triumphs, every knee shall bow and every tongue confess that Jesus is the Christ, to the glory of the Father. Even the Jews will do it then: but will the Jews and Gentiles be obliged to belong to the Church of Jesus Christ of Latter-day Saints? No; not by any means. Jesus said to his disciples, in my Father's house are many mansions; were it not so I would have told you; I go to prepare a place for you, that where I am, there ye may be also. There are mansions in sufficient numbers to suit the different classes of mankind, and a variety will always exist to all eternity, requiring a classification and an arrangement into societies and communities in the many mansions which are in the Lord's house, and this will be forever and ever."*
Brigham Young, *Journal of Discourses* [744]

The Church of Jesus Christ of Latter Day Saints is provided to invite the children of God to repent, come unto Christ, and be baptized. It is the only organization on earth that offers access to the power necessary to *"bind on earth"* what *"shall be bound in heaven."* (Matthew 16:19). It is an honor and privilege to participate in the ordinances which the church provides.

In addition to this religious reality, the light of Christ exists within every child of God. This life-sustaining force is *"in all and through all things."* (D&C 88:6). Whatever degree of "light" and "truth" exists within any particular individual, whether LDS or not, is the same degree of "gospel" present within that particular soul.

**Every Son and Daughter of GOD may Become ONE
with the Father, Mother, and the Truth of All Things.**

**Not because they are "Mormon,"
but because they align themselves with the Divinity of All Creation.**

---

*"We believe there is a spiritual influence that emanates from the presence of God to fill
the immensity of space. (See D&C 88:12). All human beings share an inheritance of divine light.
God operates among his children in all nations, and those who seek God are entitled to further
light and knowledge, regardless of their race, nationality, or cultural traditions."*
Howard W. Hunter, *That We Might Have Joy* [745]

To assume, believe, or act as if God doesn't work outside the realm of the LDS Church is to imagine a very puny and ineffectual God. This cultural attitude contributes to the unfortunate exclusion of many righteous men and women who are not LDS, but are still committed to Jesus Christ and His kingdom.

*"The truth is God is actively engaged with all who truly love and serve him, even if the doctrine
in their churches is incorrect, incomplete, or they lack priesthood authority. We know God's work
is to bring to pass the immortality and eternal life of man. His purpose is not limited to only
what occurs in our religion. When the Holy City of Zion is finally built it will involve the
"pure in heart" from various backgrounds. We should be open to non-members
who have a specific errand to accomplish."*
Anonymous Saint

In truth, many non-members possess the light of Christ and are abundantly happy. God answers their prayers and gives them assignments to fulfill just as He does with faithful Latter Day Saints. Wisdom would invite us to remember that life is not a "doctrine contest," and that even though our non-member friends do err in understanding, so do we.

Demonstrating pride and condescension toward others who are also seeking God is unacceptable to an Eternal Father who is *"no respecter of persons."* (Acts 10:34). Can we not learn from Protestants who praise, Buddhists who meditate, and the energy workers who use the light of Christ to heal? Perhaps the scope of God's work is more comprehensive, more universal, and more glorious than we previously imagined.

*"Elder Orson F. Whitney, in a conference address, explained that many great religious leaders
were inspired. He said: "[God] is using not only his covenant people, but other peoples as well,
to consummate a work, stupendous, magnificent, and altogether too arduous for this
little handful of Saints to accomplish by and of themselves..."*
Howard W. Hunter, *That We Might Have Joy* [746]

Mormons should not assume that all God's children desired a mortality where they would experience the "only true church." Each child has entered into this mortality to receive specific life lessons. God uses a variety of religious situations and life experiences to create that which is *appropriate and effective* for each soul. Understanding this will help us accept others as they fulfill their own personal covenants and sacred life purposes, even when they are significantly different than our own.

*"God has permitted His Spirit, which is the light of truth, and which manifests truth, **to be poured out upon all the inhabitants of the earth to some extent**; for in that they live and move and have their being, and **all people of any age, race or country who seek unto God with an honest heart in fervent prayer, desiring truth and to be taught of God, will be enlightened by Him.**"*
Charles W. Penrose, *Journal of Discourses* [747]

For Latter Day Saints, religious activity may be the primary method God uses to invite us to come unto Christ. However, the restoration of the LDS church is not His only *"marvelous work and a wonder."* For Endless are his ways, and Eternal are His purposes.

"The validity, the power, of our faith is not bound by history, nationality, or culture. It is not the peculiar property of any one people or any one age."
Howard W. Hunter, *That We Might Have Joy* [748]

God uses the gift of mortality to mold the soul in unique ways. There is a plan and a path for the Jew, Buddhist, Muslim, and non-believer. This ***does not*** mean, *"all roads lead to Rome,"* only that Father in Heaven does not give up on any of His children and that He will continue to provide them with the appropriate experiences they need to access Jesus Christ and the Truth of All Things, probation after probation…worlds without end. (see Truth #22).

Hope for the Lost

"There is never a time when the spirit is too old to approach God. All are within the reach of pardoning mercy, who have not committed the unpardonable sin, which hath no forgiveness, neither in this world, nor in the world to come. There is a way to release the spirits of the dead; that is by the power and authority of the Priesthood—by binding and loosing on earth. This doctrine appears glorious, inasmuch as it exhibits the greatness of divine compassion and benevolence in the extent of the plan of human salvation."
Joseph Smith, *History of the Church* [749]

Surely God Almighty, the Creator of all things, will guide us line upon line, life upon life, here a little and there a little, until we, visitors here in a telestial world, find the straight and narrow path to Jesus Christ!

"The great religious leaders of the world such as Mohammed, Confucius, and the Reformers, as well as philosophers including Socrates, Plato, and others, received a portion of God's light. Moral truths were given to them by God to enlighten whole nations and to bring a higher level of understanding to individuals. The Hebrew prophets prepared the way for the coming of Jesus Christ, the promised Messiah, who should provide salvation for all mankind who believe in the gospel. Consistent with these truths, we believe that God has given and will give to all peoples sufficient knowledge to help them on their way to eternal salvation, either in this life or in the life to come."
First Presidency, *God's Love For All Mankind* [750]

Sensing there is hope for all God's children does not negate eternal justice or the need for real priesthood ordinances. Rather, it is a reminder that God is fully committed to the exaltation of His diverse children, *"eternity to eternity."* (D&C 76:4).

For behold, this is my work and my glory to bring to pass
the immortality and eternal life of man.
Moses 1:39

Great is his wisdom, marvelous are his ways,
and the extent of his doings none can find out. His purposes fail not,
neither are there any who can stay his hand.
D&C 76:2-3

When we perceive the magnificence of God's work, daily life becomes more meaningful. With time and experience, we come to understand personally-and not just doctrinally, that on every level, and within every realm, *"all things work together for good to them that love God, to them who are the called according to his purpose."*(Romans 8:28). The practical reality of this principle, the fact that God is wise and in control, will be clearly demonstrated by the *unique diversity and oneness* present in Latter Day Zion.

Into the Unity of the Faith
"There will be a gigantic task to perform after America has been cleansed of her wickedness
but the wreckage and ruin of a whole civilization has been left behind. The first group will be the righteous
saints whom the Lord has preserved. All these will have been disciplined in Priesthood principles and will
have studied God's law so they will know what to do…the second group will be made up of the members
of God's kingdom from all over the world…and it shall come to pass that the righteous shall be gathered
out from among ALL NATIONS, and shall come to Zion, singing with songs of everlasting joy."
The third group to help reconstruct the western hemisphere will be the righteous gentiles who survive
the cleansing. This is an interesting group of people. They are of many faiths. They love the Lord,
they bow the knee in contemplation of his coming. They admire his Church and love the Saints,
But they don't join the Church…The amazing part is that God extends an invitation to the righteous
gentiles to be a part of the political kingdom of God. Brigham Young knew that a lot of the Saints
would expect the kingdom of God to be only members of the church, but President Young said that is
not the way the Lord planned it. Here are his words: The Kingdom of God consists in correct principles;
and it mattereth not what a man's religious faith is; whether he be a Presbyterian, or a Methodist,
or a Baptist, or a Latter-day Saint or "Mormon," or a Campbellite, or a Catholic, or an Episcopalian,
or Mohometan, or even pagan, or anything else, if he will bow the knee, and with his tongue confess
that Jesus is the Christ, and will support good and wholesome laws for the regulation of society,
we hail him as a brother, and will stand by him while he stands by us in these things;
for every man's religious faith is a matter between his own soul and his God alone.[751]
Finally, there is the fourth group…these are the peacemakers."
W. Cleon Skousen, *What We Might Expect in the Next Twenty-Five Years* [752]

When Zion is finally established it will be filled with deep and fascinating souls who are comfortable dwelling with their friend and Savior Jesus Christ. Intelligent and informed people from every background will teach one another the mysteries of God. Wisdom encourages us to seek out truth from every source. Although there are deceptions in the world, those who keep their core faith in Jesus Christ and follow the Holy Spirit need not fear. For those with inquisitive minds, the truth of all things awaits.

*"In regards to our religion, I will say that it embraces every principle of truth and intelligence pertaining to us as moral, intellectual, mortal and immortal beings, pertaining to this world and the world that is to come. **We are open to truth of every kind, no matter whence it comes, where it originates, or who believes in it**…it is the duty of all intelligent beings who are responsible and amenable to God for their acts, to search after truth, and to permit it to influence them and their acts and general course in life, independent of all bias or preconceived notions, however specious and plausible they may be. We, as Latter-day Saints, believe, first, in the gospel, and that is a great deal to say, for the gospel embraces principles that **dive deeper, spread wider, and extend further than anything else that we can conceive.**"*
John Taylor, *The Gospel Kingdom* [753]

TRUTH #75 THE LORD HAS CHOSEN JOSEPH SMITH TO BE THE PROPHET FOR THIS FINAL DISPENSATION. JOSEPH HAS NOT FINISHED HIS WORK AND WILL BE PERSONALLY INVOLVED IN THE ESTABLISHMENT OF MILLENNIAL ZION.

Note to Reader: There are many models of belief concerning what will occur just prior to the Second Coming of the Lord Jesus Christ. Possible scenarios include a "Davidic Servant," the yet future return of Elijah, and a special *"Elias"* who will come to *"gather together the tribes of Israel and restore all things."* (D&C 77: 9).

In relation to how this *"restoration of all things"* is to occur, scripture, and a variety of quotes, can be sited to support various possibilities. For years this author has believed that the fulfillment of prophecy would include the return of the Prophet Joseph Smith, and that he would be the *"one mighty and strong"* to complete the Restoration and *"set in order the house of God."* (D&C 85:7).

In addition to Joseph's future involvement, prophecy also confirms that John the Beloved will play an essential role in the restoration of all things.

Q. What are we to understand by the little book which was eaten by John,
As mentioned in the 10th chapter of Revelation?
A. We are to understand that it was a mission, and an ordinance, for him to gather the tribes
of Israel; behold, this is Elias, who, as it is written, must come and restore all things.
D&C 77:14

In relation to John being a future *"Elias,"* and how even now, several messengers of God are actively engaged in *"preparing the way,"* (D&C 34:6), it seems relevant to remember that the names of both "Joseph" and "John" are often used as sacred titles denoting a divine role.

This chapter has been organized to suggest that the Prophet Joseph Smith could literally return as a resurrected being to complete the Restoration and establish Latter Day Zion. In response to that hope, the Holy Spirit has suggested to this author that the return of Joseph Smith may be more symbolic than literal. And that what we can eagerly anticipate is not only the power and glory of the original Restoration, but also the return of an Ancient Gospel...even that which was once offered by the Elohim unto Father Adam and Mother Eve!

Thus, when pondering this chapter, the reader is encouraged to consider the information as being mostly symbolic of the greater light yet to be restored to the Earth. Regardless of whom the Lord uses to fulfill His prophecy, what matters most, is that a Restoration of All Things is completed-that our Lord may be received in Holiness by those who dwell in Millennial Zion. (D&C 105:4-5).

As we walk into the future, let us watch closely, listen deeply, and discern accurately, that we too might receive each of the true messengers that Father sends. Those who do so will be received of *The Christ*, and thus be blessed to once again partake of a true gospel fullness. The very same gospel of Jesus Christ...once taught and offered by Mighty Joseph.

There will be a New Way
To Restore the Old Way

Brigham's Expectation
"Joseph Smith Jr. will again be on this earth dictating plans...
and he will never cease his operations, under the directions of the Son of God,
until the last ones of the children of men are saved that can be, from Adam till now."[754]

Joseph Smith is the head of this final dispensation and remains the Lord's chosen prophet to preside over the gathering of Latter Day Zion. Even though priesthood keys have been technically passed down to each succeeding church president, those who know Joseph as prophet and friend realize he is the head of this final dispensation, and that his ministry to God's children continues today.

Thus saith the Lord, verily, verily I say unto you my son, thy sins are forgiven thee...
Therefore, thou art blessed from henceforth that bear the keys of the kingdom given unto you;
which kingdom is coming forth for the last time. Verily I say unto you,
the keys of this kingdom shall never be taken from you, while thou art in the world,
neither in the world to come; *Nevertheless, through you shall the oracles*
be given to another, yea, even unto the church.
D&C 90:1-4

Brigham Young believed, *"I will refer you to a discourse I delivered here last season upon the subject of the resurrection and the Millennium... Joseph, Hyrum, Father Smith and many others will be there to dictate and preside. Joseph will stand at the head of this dispensation and hold the keys of it, for they are not taken from him; they never were in time; they never will be in eternity. I shall be there if I live or if I die."*[755]

After Joseph's physical body was killed, Parley P. Pratt cried out to the Lord in anguish asking how he might comfort the grieving Saints. In response to his prayer, Parley was instructed, *"Lift up you head and rejoice. for behold, it is well with my servants Joseph and Hyrum.* ***My servant Joseph still holds the keys of my kingdom in this dispensation, and he shall stand in due time on the earth, in the flesh, and fulfill that to which he is appointed."***[756]

Eternal Keys
...Rebel not against my servant, Joseph; for verily I say unto you, I am with him
and my hand shall be over him; and the keys which I have given unto him...
shall not be taken from him till I come.
D&C 112:15

As a true prophet, seer, and revelator, Joseph knew his ministry would extend beyond the grave. On April 3, 1836, Joseph and Oliver received a visitation while in the Kirtland Temple. Joseph reported, *"The heavens were again opened unto us; and Moses appeared before us, and committed unto us the keys of the gathering of Israel from the four parts of the earth, and the leading of the ten tribes from the land of the north."*[757]

Whether those specific keys have been, or will be, passed to another is unclear. But regardless of how scripture is fulfilled, it has been prophesied that Joseph Smith will be instrumental in leading the ten tribes from the north and gathering Latter Day Israel to Zion. (D&C 110:11).

The Patriarchal Blessing of Joseph Smith

"Thou shalt stand upon the earth when it shall reel to and fro as a drunken man,
and be removed out of its place. Thou shalt stand upon Mount Zion
when the tribes of Jacob come shouting from the north."
Joseph Smith Sr., *Patriarchal Blessing Book* [758]

In addition to facilitating this righteous gathering, the Prophet will also be involved when the Restoration is completed. Members tend to conceptualize the Restoration as an "all or none event," but it is important to observe that after the death of the Prophet, revelation in the church decreased significantly. In addition to that which has not yet been restored, a considerable portion of what Joseph was able to provide is not even practiced or taught in the church today (United Order, law of consecration, plural marriage, full temple endowment, original garment, the greater nature of the Godhead, council of fifty, office of patriarch, fullness of the priesthood, etc…).

"What I have received from the Lord, I have received by Joseph Smith:
he was the instrument made use of. If I drop him, I must drop these principles:
they have not been revealed, declared, or explained by any other man
since the days of the Apostles."
Brigham Young, *Journal of Discourses* [759]

One of the key doctrines neglected over time is the principle of priesthood adoption. This little known aspect of the Restoration is no longer taught by the modern day church, but relates directly to being sealed to the Fathers and the Second Coming of Jesus Christ.

The law of adoption was a principle revealed to the Prophet Joseph that involved being personally sealed to him, and thus to the eternal Fathers. The principle was practiced in the church as a temple ordinance from 1846 to 1894.[760]

"If you have power to seal on earth and in heaven, then we should be wise. The first thing you do,
go and seal on earth your sons and your daughters unto yourself, and yourself unto the fathers
in eternal glory, and go ahead, and not go back, but use a little wisdom, and seal all you can,
and when you get to heaven tell your Father that what you seal on earth should be sealed
in heaven, according to his promise. I will walk through the gate of heaven and claim what I seal,
and those that follow me and my counsel."
Joseph Smith, *Teachings of the Prophet Joseph Smith* [761]

Joseph's encouragement to *"seal all you can"* to *"the fathers in eternal glory"* means much more than how we currently conceptualize temple marriage and geneology work. As practiced in the early church, spiritual adoption involved a man who held the priesthood, (but who was not necessarily related by blood), being sealed into a "father-son" relationship within the greater family kingdom.

The "fathers" Joseph is referring to includes Abraham, Isaac, and Jacob, who reign as righteous kings for the entire House of Israel. After Abraham was sealed unto Jesus Christ he was promised by God, *"I will multiply thy seed as the stars of the heaven, and as the sand which is upon the sea shore; and thy seed shall possess the gate of his enemies;"*(Genesis 22:17). As one who held patriarchal priesthood, Abraham was reassured that all who followed in his footsteps would also receive a fullness and become his descendants. Today being fully born again through the blood of Jesus Christ results in becoming a son or daughter of God within the Holy Order and receiving the same Fullness of the Priesthood the Fathers possess. *"For as many as receive this Gospel shall be called after thy name, and shall be accounted thy seed, and shall rise up and bless thee, as their father…and in thy seed after thee shall all the families of the Earth be blessed."*(Abraham 2:10-11).

As the head of this final dispensation, Joseph was the first Latter Day Saint to align himself with the Fathers of the House of Israel. (D&C 132:55-57). Upon receiving the promise that he would be exalted, Joseph was fully grafted into the eternal family of God. This achievement included being sealed unto all of the Fathers since the time of Adam-and resulted in Joseph becoming one with those gods who dwell among the Eloheim in glory.

Once Joseph had entered into this eternal union, the prophet could then offer that same spiritual link to others who were to be later sealed up unto eternal life through him. Theologian Jonathan Stapley summarizes the purpose of priesthood adoption:

> *"This system connected unmarried kin, created novel social units within Mormonism during the crucial exodus and Utah periods associated with Brigham Young's early leadership, and attempted, in essence, to tie all humanity to their first parents in a sacred network of belonging."*
> Jonathan A. Stapley, *Adoptive Sealing Ritual in Mormonism* [762]

Brigham Young explained, *"By this power men will be sealed to men back to Adam, completing and making perfect the priesthood from this day to the winding up scene."*[763]Being adopted to the "Fathers" was to occur through priesthood lineage, not earthly blood line. As a result, both men and women were sealed to the prophet Joseph in the early church, becoming his "sons" and "daughters" through priesthood ordinance.[764] In this sense, Joseph is our spiritual "Father" within the House of Israel. When Eliza R. Snow was asked about this practice, she responded, *"she didn't understand the law but had no objections to them being sealed to her husband."*[765]

This greater view of what constitutes "family" included a heavenly charity far beyond the social constructs of this world. Souls sealed unto Joseph would by association be sealed unto Abraham and the Fathers. Through Jesus Christ these righteous "family kingdoms" would then be grafted into the spiritual fabric of eternity. (see Truth #67). "Family" was to be spiritual, not only biological. Loving and holy relationships on earth were to mirror the structure of heaven. Those "children of God" willing to repent fully were to be adopted into "the family" and therefore spiritually aligned through Joseph Smith and Father Abraham into the House of Israel.

Jonathan Stapley summarizes, *"In a revelation to Newel K. Whitney in 1842, the Lord declared that, by entering into the new relationships formed through Joseph Smith's sealings, Whitney would attain "immortality and eternal life" for himself and for all his "house both old and young because of the lineage of my Priesthood saith the Lord. It shall be upon you and upon your children after you from generation to generation."*[766]Apparently when one member of a family is sealed unto Joseph, and thus the Fathers, they become a type of "savior" for other family members. (D&C 128:17).

> *"How are they to become saviors on Mount Zion? By building their temples, erecting their baptismal fonts, and going forth and receiving all the ordinances… in behalf of all their progenitors who are dead."*
> Joseph Smith, *Teachings of Presidents of the Church* [767]

The revelation to Brother Whitney also suggests that being sealed into the lineage of the priesthood would lead a man and his entire family into "immortality and eternal life." The principle of adoption provided a method and structure for God's will to be done here on earth...as it is in heaven. (Matthew 6:10). From God Almighty to Jesus Christ, and from Abraham to Joseph Smith, members who were sealed to the Prophet were grafted into the celestial family.

Welcome Home

"As the definition of salvation transformed to encompass the heavenly kinship network,
Kingship, priesthood, and salvation became synonymous."
Jonathan A. Stapley, *Adoptive Sealing Ritual* [768]

After Brigham Young was sealed to Joseph Smith, he was then sealed in the Nauvoo Temple to 38 other men.[769] This practice continued intermittently for several decades. President Wilford Woodruff reported that betwteen 1843 and 1894 he had personally been adopted to "45 persons."[770] He also stated that he had individually "officiated in adopting 96 men to men."[771]

Whether or not a soul has been fully adopted into the House of Israel not only influences eternity, but it also relates directly to the Second Coming of Jesus Christ.

"For behold, the day cometh that shall burn as an oven, and all the proud, yea, and all that
do wickedly shall burn as stubble; for they that come shall burn them, saith the Lord of Hosts,
that it shall leave them neither root nor branch...Behold, I will reveal unto you the Priesthood,
by the hand of Elijah the prophet, before the coming of the great and dreadful day of the Lord...
And he shall plant in the hearts of the children the promises made to the fathers,
and the hearts of the children shall turn to their fathers.
If it were not so, the whole earth would be utterly wasted at his coming."
Joseph Smith, *Joseph Smith History* [772]

To be one of those "children," whose hearts have been turned to the "fathers," involves much more than how we conceptualize genealogy and temple work for the dead. To join the "royal family" requires becoming clean from the blood and sins of this generation and being sealed by the Holy Spirit of Promise unto Jesus Christ. (D&C 132:7). Only those who obtain the purity, power, and title of "king" and "queen" can abide the day of the Savior's return. (see Truth #67 and #70).

"The whole earth is going to be smitten at His return, except only those who have had the
"hearts of the children" turn to them as "fathers." The original meaning meant connecting
living souls to Abraham, Isaac and Jacob through binding priesthood power and a living
covenant between God and man. Those souls who entered into that kind of covenant
would be able to stand in the presence of God. Because they could endure His glory
they would not be "cursed" at His return. They were adopted as children to those "fathers"
who now sit upon thrones..."
Denver Snuffer, *Passing the Heavenly Gift* [773]

Currently only a phantom form of being sealed unto the fathers exists in the LDS church. After Joseph was killed, church leaders were unsure how the ordinance should be taught and practiced. Brigham Young admitted, *"This principle [adoption] I am aware is not clearly understood by many of the Elders in this church at the present time as it will hereafter be: And I confess that I have had only a smattering of those things[;] but when it is necessary I will attain to more knowledge on the subject & consequently will be enabled to teach & practice more."*[774]

Over time the focus on being sealed to the fathers faded until Wilford Woodruff eventually announced in the 1894 General Conference, *"I have not felt satisfied, nor has any man since the Prophet Joseph Smith who has attended to the ordinance of adoption in the temples of our God. We have felt there was more to be revealed on this subject than we have received…and the duty that I want every man who presides over a Temple to see performed from this day henceforth, unless the Lord Almighty commands otherwise, is let every man be adopted to his father."*[775]

To facilite the new emphasis of being sealed only to direct anscestors, President Woodruff founded the *Genealogical Society of Utah.* [776]This new organization would lay the foundation for what we know today as the current geneology program of the church.

Currently, the ordinance of being sealed to Joseph and the Fathers is not acknowledged by the institution or offered to members of the church.

This doctrinal loss is another reason the faithful can expect a full Restoration of all that God once offered the Saints through Joseph Smith.

> *"After Joseph comes to us in his resurrected body He will more fully instruct us concerning*
> *Baptism for the dead and the sealing ordinances. He will say be baptized for this man*
> *and that man and that man be sealed to that man and such a man to such a man,*
> *and connect the priesthood together. I tell you there will not be much of this done until*
> *Joseph comes. He is our spiritual Father. Our hearts are already turned to him and his to us.*
> *This [is] the order of the Holy Priesthood and we shall continue to administer in the ordinances*
> *of the kingdom of God here on earth."*
> Brigham Young, *Complete Discourses of Brigham Young* [777]

In truth, all that has been lost or gone dormant, including the doctrine of priesthood adoption, will be re-instituted before the Second Coming of Jesus Christ. In preparation for that day, Joseph Smith is even now ministering in spirit to the remnant of Christ, that they might yet be sealed unto Him and the Holy Fathers.

Those who understand adoption, sealing power, and the process of becoming a king or queen, eagerly anticipate the day when Jesus Christ, either by His own hand or through the voice of His servant, will return to set the house of God in order.

> *And it shall come to pass that I, the Lord God, will send* **one mighty and strong**,
> *holding the scepter of power in his hand, clothed with light for a covering, whose mouth shall utter words,*
> *eternal words; while his bowels shall be a fountain of truth,* **to set in order the house of God**…
> Doctrine and Covenants 85:7

Over the years several disillusioned and egotistical men have claimed to be *"the one mighty and strong."* In response to the idea that the church needed to *"be set in order,"* church leaders made a statement in 1905 attempting to minimize and/or clarify the prophecy.

The First Presidency suggested that D&C 85:7 probably related to Bishop Edward Partridge struggling to fulfill his duties concerning the United Order. They suggested that the need to "set the house of God in order" related to Bishop Partridge and his need to repent. Their interpretation of who the *"one mighty and strong"* was, led them to pre-maturely consider *"the whole incident of the prophecy closed."*[778]

This religious explanation is spiritually unsatisfying to those who understand 3 Nephi 21:9 which states, *"for in that day, for my sake shall the Father work a work, which shall be a great and a marvelous work among them; and there shall be among them those who will not believe it, although a man shall declare it unto them. But behold, the life of my servant shall be in my hand; therefore they shall not hurt him, although he shall be marred because of them. Yet I will heal him, for I will show unto them that my wisdom is greater than the cunning of the devil."* In relation to this verse, many have wondered who will be the man like unto Moses? And could it be that the same servant who was once called to begin the work-will again be called to finish it? And if so, will we be able to recognize the servant when he arrives?

> *...The redemption of Zion must needs come by power; Therefore, **I will raise up unto my people a man,**
> **who shall lead them like as Moses led the children of Israel**.*
> *For ye are the children of Israel, and of the seed of Abraham, and ye must needs be led out of bondage*
> *by power, and with a stretched-out arm. And as your fathers were led at the first,*
> *even so shall the redemption of Zion.*
> D&C 103:15-18

> *Verily, verily I say unto you, that **my servant Joseph Smith, Jun. is the man** to whom I likened*
> *the servant to whom the Lord of the vineyard spake in the parable which I have given unto you.*
> D&C 103:21

In truth, Joseph Smith is *"mighty and strong."* He is a true messenger sent from Father. Similar to Moses leading the children of Israel out of Egypt, Joseph, or the one chosen to finish what Joseph started, will gather and guide the surviving Saints home to Zion.

> *And I will soften the hearts of the people, as I did the heart of Pharaoh, from time to time,*
> *until my servant Joseph Smith, Jun., and mine elders, whom I have appointed,*
> *shall have time to gather up the strength of my house.*
> Doctrine and Covenants 105:27

Perhaps in an general sense it would be wise to not get attached to "who," "when," and "how" the Lord will finish His work. As mentioned at the beginning of this chapter, the sacred role of John Beloved should not be overlooked. He also could be the sacred *"Elias"* that arrives on the scene to fulfill scripture and provide the gathering so desperately needed.

It is also interesting to consider that the Messiah Himself could come and fulfill prophecy. And yet, no matter how these great events leading up to the Second Coming are enacted, scripture assures us that Joseph Smith will continue to be actively engaged in strengthening those who really are in His church. (See Truth #12).

Behold I speak a few words unto you, Joseph; for thou also art under no condemnation
and thy calling also is to exhortation, and to strengthen the church;
and this is thy duty from henceforth and forever. Amen.
D&C 23:5

In truth, the Prophet Joseph Smith continues his ministry on both sides of the veil. Some have seen him in vision and others have been blessed by his healing touch. Whenever possible, he is among us, anxiously engaged in the Lord's work. Near the end of his life the Prophet confided, *"I could do so much more for my friends if I were on the other side of the veil."* He informed Benjamin Johnson, *"I would not be far from you, and if on the other side, I would still be working with you, and with a power greatly increased to roll on this kingdom."*[779]

Coming Back
"You will gather many people to the fastness of the Rocky Mountains, and many of those
who will come in under your ministry, because of their learning, will seek for position.
They will gain eminence over you, and you will walk in low places, unnoticed.
Yet you will know all that transpires in your midst. Those who are your friends are my friends,
and I promise you WHEN I COME AGAIN, I will lead you forth,
so that where I am you shall be with me."
Joseph Smith, *Personal Glimpses of the Prophet Joseph Smith* [780]

Those who love Jesus Christ and His gospel, as restored through the prophet Joseph Smith, are anxious for the Restoration to be completed. These are they who yearn to follow *Jesus and all of His true messengers* into Zion.

"Perhaps the most thrilling news of the latter-day dispensation is the prophecy that Joseph
will return as a resurrected being to complete his work here in mortality. Not only will he return,
but he will be resurrected many years before the Second Coming so that he can accomplish
the various tasks that were specifically assigned to him in the pre-mortal councils of God."
Richard Scousen, *His Return, Prophecy, Destiny and Hope* [781]

It is fascinating to ponder the manner in which prophecy will be fulfilled, as well as the possibilities surrounding Joseph's true identity. He told the early brethren, *"You do not know me, you do not know who I am"* [782] and *"if I was to reveal to this people what the Lord has revealed to me, there is not a man or a woman who would stay with me."* [783]

Regardless of the various roles each messenger will enact, it is believed by many that Joseph Smith could be the *"faithful and wise steward in the midst of mine house, a ruler in my kingdom."* (D&C 101:61). And that it may be noble Joseph who appears as a resurrected being to *"deal prudently"* with the nations of the earth. (Isaiah 52:13). His peculiar return may be the *"strange act"* of D&C 101:95, while also fulfilling Brigham Young's prophecy that *"Joseph will again be on this earth."*[784]

Almost two centuries ago the early Saints were struggling to build Zion. The Prophet offered them the encouragement they needed and then promised,

"Dear Brethren, and all others who are willing to lay down their lives for the cause
of our Lord Jesus Christ:…If I were with you I should take an active part in your sufferings,
and although nature shrinks, yet my spirit would not let me forsake you unto death,
God helping me. Oh be of good cheer, for our redemption draweth near. Oh, God save
my brethren in Zion. Oh brethren give up all to God, Forsake all for Christ's sake."
Joseph Smith, *The Personal Writings of Joseph Smith* [785]

What the Prophet taught then, is exactly what he proclaims to us now! How can we read these words and not feel his personal plea for us to push on in power! Just as John the Baptist prepared the way for Jesus Christ the first time, Joseph Smith, and several other messengers now called of God for that same purpose, are today inviting the wheat to prepare for the Bridegroom at His Second Coming.

Today's testimony meetings are often filled with casual references to Joseph Smith, but time and testing will reveal unto God who is really willing to stand with the Prophet and His teachings.

"Sadly we are more comfortable with prophets who tell us what we want to hear, who reinforce our
assumptions and assure us of our righteousness. Prophets that actually invite revolution and change
are just too uncomfortable and must be mentally stoned, rejected, avoided, or silenced."
And so it seems in harmony with "knowing God" and truly hearing his voice,
it appears that standard applies to Joseph as well. Will we be among the millions of valiant
who do know, and do see, and do believe Joseph when he comes again to finish the restoration,
re-institute that which has been lost, and usher in Zion with all of her doctrinal fullness?"
Anonymous Saint [786]

Those who *know God*, love *His Prophet*. These Saints yearn for the fullness of the gospel and are eager to make the journey to Zion. They know that those who are able to dwell in the Holy City, will in the end, be privileged to embrace both Jesus and Joseph with *"warm hearts and friendly hands."* (D&C 121:9).

"Praise to the man who communed with Jehovah…
millions shall know Brother Joseph again." [787]

TRUTH #76 THE KINGDOM OF GOD WILL BE FULLY ESTABLISHED UPON THE EARTH. JESUS CHRIST WILL REIGN AS KING OF KINGS AND LORD OF LORDS. THROUGHOUT THE EARTH EVERY KNEE SHALL BOW AND EVERY TONGUE CONFESS THAT "JESUS IS THE CHRIST!"

...Satan shall be bound, that he shall have no place in the hearts of the children of men...
and they shall multiply and wax strong, and their children shall grow up without sin unto
salvation. For the Lord shall be in their midst, and his glory shall be upon them,
and he will be their king and their lawgiver.
Doctrine and Covenants 45:55,58-59

The Lord Jesus Christ is the righteous heir of the entire earth. As King of Kings and Lord of Lords, He will reign among His people with compassion, honor, wisdom and power. During the Millennium, one key truth will supercede all others: **Jesus is The Christ!**

Wherefore God also hath highly exalted him, and given him a name which is above every name;
That at the name of Jesus every knee should bow, of things in heaven, and things in earth,
and things under the earth; And that every tongue should confess that Jesus Christ is Lord,
to the glory of God the Father.
JST Philippians 2:9-11

"When all nations are so subdued to Jesus that every knee shall bow and every tongue shall confess,
there will still be millions on the earth who will not believe in him;
but they will be obliged to acknowledge his kingly government."
Brigham Young, *Discourses of Brigham Young* [788]

Those who have survived the destructions will deserve a righteous kingdom. It will be unlike our current conceptualization of "government," but rather will exist as a righteous influence empowered through the holy priesthood of God.

Seeking True Government

"...There is no true government on earth but the government of God, or the holy Priesthood.
Shall I tell you what that is? In short, it is a perfect system of government—a kingdom of Gods
and angels and all beings who will submit themselves to that government.
There is no other true government in heaven or upon the earth."
Brigham Young, *Journal of Discourses* [789]

"Of necessity some form of government must be set up among them, as they will exist in a national
as well as an ecclesiastical capacity. This government will be a theocracy, or, in other words,
the kingdom of God. The laws, ordinances, regulations, etc., will be under the direction of
God's Priesthood, and the people will progress in arts, sciences, and everything that will produce
happiness, promote union, and establish them in strength, righteousness, and everlasting peace."
Charles W. Penrose, *Improvement Era* [790]

In Zion there will literally be no poor, no struggle, and no lack of physical, emotional, or spiritual prosperity. The Lord will dwell among His people. Angels will minister and spiritual gifts will abound. All participants will be united in the pure love of Christ. This newly established "kingdom of God on earth" will exist as a mortal microcosm of "heaven on earth."

King of the Earth

*"I have demonstrated . . . . that the **kingdom of God would be literally established on the earth**.
It will not be an aerial phantom, according to some visionaries, but a substantial reality.
It will be established, as before said, on a literal earth, and will be composed of literal men, women,
and children; of **living saints who keep the commandments of God**, and of **resurrected bodies who
shall actually come out of their graves, and live on the earth. The Lord will be king over all the
earth, and all mankind literally under his sovereignty, and every nation under the heavens will
have to acknowledge his authority, and bow to his sceptre.** Those who serve him in righteousness
will have communications with God, and with Jesus; will have the ministering of angels, and will know
the past, the present, and the future; and other people, who may not yield full obedience to his laws,
nor be fully instructed in his covenants, will, nevertheless, have to yield full obedience to his government.
For it will be the reign of God upon the earth, and he will enforce his laws, and command
that obedience from the nations of the world which is legitimately his right. Satan will not then be
permitted to control its inhabitants, for the **Lord God will be king over all the earth,**
and the kingdom and greatness of the kingdom under the whole heaven will be given to the saints..."*
John Taylor, *The Gospel Kingdom: Selections from the Writings and Discourses of John Taylor* [791]

In God's government there will be no hierarchies that manipulate with force and control. No crime to report, no unjust codes which oppress, and no taxes to claim. All who live within the walls of Zion will be "self-governing" and will naturally focus on the needs of their neighbors. (Moses 7:18). The same eternal truths that inspired the U.S. Constitution will be re-instituted within the greater paradigm of the United Order. Daily life will involve truth, justice, equality, and spiritual abundance. Instead of competing in a world of commerce and greed, citizens will live the law of consecration and share freely with all who dwell within the kingdom. For these souls, Jesus Christ and their love for Him will be the "law of the land." (3 Nephi 15:9).

*"...When the government of God shall be more extensively adopted, and when Jesus' prayer,
that he taught his disciples is answered, and God's kingdom comes on the earth, and his will is done here
as in heaven, then, and not till then, will universal love, peace, harmony, and union prevail."*
John Taylor, *Millennial Star* [792]

The false and temporary authority of man is self-serving, shallow, and ineffective. God's power is abundant, deep, and eternal. It will be this holy power that fuels God's government upon the earth.

What Is the Priesthood Really?

*"What is priesthood?...I shall briefly answer that it is the government of God, whether on the earth
or in the heavens, for it is by that power, agency, or principle that all things are upheld governed
on the earth and in the heavens, and by that power that all things are upheld and sustained.
It governs all things—it directs all things—it sustains all things—and has to do with all things
that God and truth are associated with. It is the power of God delegated to intelligences in the heavens*

and to men on the earth; and when we arrive in the celestial kingdom of God,
we shall find the most perfect order and harmony existing, because there is the perfect pattern,
the most perfect order of government carried out..."
John Taylor, *Millennial Star* [793]

Because the priesthood can be accessed through the LDS Church, many consider the organization itself to be *"the kingdom of God on earth."* The Lord however did not organize the LDS church as a final act, but rather as an introduction to a much greater ecclesiastical and political reality, THE KINDGOM OF GOD ON EARTH! (Daniel 2:44).

"It may be asked what I mean by the kingdom of God. The Church of Jesus Christ has been established
*now for many years, and **the kingdom of God has got to be established,***
even the kingdom which will circumscribe all the kingdoms of this world.
It will yet give laws to every nation that exists upon the earth.
This is the kingdom that Daniel, the prophet, saw should be set up in the last days..."
Brigham Young, *Journal of Discourses* [794]

If the Kingdom of God is to still arise from *The Church of Jesus Christ of Latter Day Saints*, it will not occur until after the Lord has cleansed His house.

"The Lord will be able to fulfill His purposes in the latter days, and bring about
the rise of the Kingdom of God. As the Church comes under attack by the wicked,
the Saints will be forced to withdraw from the influence and control of Babylon,
especially when the wicked halt all commerce with the righteous. (Revelations 13:16-17, 14:8-12).
Since the Saints will then be cut off from the government of the United States,
the political Kingdom of God will begin to be established among the members of the Church."
Richard Scousen, *His Return, Prophecy, Destiny and Hope* [795]

Duane Crowther, in his book *Prophecy, Key to the Future,* writes of one possible scenario. *"When law, order, and government collapse in the United States, the Church will be compelled to establish a government to preserve peace in the Western United States. This government will be known as the "Kingdom of God."*[796]

"When the Church was restored in 1830, it laid the foundation for the creation of the
*Kingdom of God. The Church of Jesus Christ of Latter Day Saints is the **kingdom of God**-*
the spiritual organization set up to preach the gospel, administer the saving ordinances
*and strengthen the faith of the Saints. But it is not the **Kingdom of God,***
which will be a non-denominational political organization that will protect the rights of all citizens
and religions. When Joseph is resurrected, he will help to complete the establishment of
the Kingdom of God, which will first grow from within the Church."
Richard Scousen, *His Return, Prophecy, Destiny and Hope* [797]

Before the greater kingdom can be established, all earthly governments will struggle and start to collapse. The presence of petty, superficial, and "deceptive politics," which have plagued the nations for centuries, will reach critical mass. Obscene political corruption will create massive global instability. The wicked will continue to destroy the wicked, until eventually there will be an *"end of all nations."* (D&C 87:6).

Despite wishful thinking, not even electing a Mormon president could have changed prophecy and eternal law. There is no political savior. The governments of men will fall. The government of God will prevail. With Jesus Christ as the captain of our soul, we need not despair, but can instead look forward to the day of His glorious return. This is the victory.

"The Church of Jesus Christ will produce this government, and cause it to grow and spread, and it will be a shield round about the Church. And under the influence and power of the Kingdom of God, the Church of God will rest secure and dwell in safety, without taking the trouble of governing and controlling the whole earth. The Kingdom of God will do this, it will control the kingdoms of the world... And you may pile on state after state, and kingdom after kingdom, and all hell on top, and we will roll on the Kingdom of our God, gather out the seed of Abraham, build the cities and temples of Zion, and establish the Kingdom of God to bear rule over all the earth, and let the oppressed of all nations go free."
Brigham Young, *Journal of Discourses* [798]

When sorrow, suffering, war, and poverty come upon the nations, and the precious lives of our children are hindered or lost...remember....oh remember... freedom and truth will win. Even when it appears pervasive darkness has overcome all that is good, let us stand in the hope that the *invincible Christ* will yet return and break down the shackles of tyranny! Let us maintain our peace by standing in the reality that nothing....absolutely nothing...can or will stop the victory of *"Messiah."*

He Comes!

*"The tongue of man falters, and the pen drops from the hand of the writer, as the mind is rapt in contemplation of the **sublime and awful majesty of his coming** to take vengeance on the ungodly and to reign as **King of the whole earth**. **He comes!** The earth shakes, and the tall mountains tremble; the mighty deep rolls back to the north as in fear, and the rent skies glow like molten brass. **He comes!** The dead Saints burst forth from their tombs, and "those who are alive and remain" are "caught up" with them to meet him. The ungodly rush to hide themselves from his presence, and call upon the quivering rocks to cover them. He comes! with all the hosts of the righteous glorified. The breath of his lips strikes death to the wicked. His glory is a consuming fire. The proud and rebellious are as stubble; they are burned and "left neither root nor branch." He sweeps the earth "as with the besom of destruction." He deluges the earth with the fiery floods of his wrath, and the filthiness and abominations of the world are consumed. Satan and his dark hosts are taken and bound — the prince of the power of the air has lost his dominion, for he **whose right it is to reign has come, and "the kingdoms of this world have become the kingdoms of our Lord and of his Christ."***
Charles W. Penrose, *Improvement Era* [799]

> **TRUTH #77** THE LORD JESUS CHRIST WILL RETURN IN VICTORY AND THE EARTH WILL RECEIVE HER PARADISIACAL GLORY. THE RIGHTEOUS WILL ENJOY A THOUSAND YEARS OF MILLENNIAL PEACE AND REST.

A Celestial Triumph!

Now, what do we hear in the gospel which we have received? A voice of gladness! A voice of mercy from heaven... **Brethren, shall we not go on in so great a cause? Go forward and not backward. Courage, brethren; and on, on to the victory!** *Let your hearts rejoice, and be exceedingly glad Let the earth break forth into singing... and let all the sons of God shout for joy!*
Doctrine and Covenants 128:19, 22-23

THE VICTORY over self and the world has always been, is now, and forever will be, in *THE CHRIST*. Jesus is our Savior in this life and in the worlds to come. No prophet will save us. No church can redeem us. No matter how deep the journey ahead, we know the Father's *"wisdom is greater than the cunning of the devil,"* and that in the end the Son of God will ultimately triumph! (3 Nephi 21:10).

"This Spirit of Christ fosters everything that is good, every virtue (see Moroni 7:16). It stands in brilliant, **indestructible opposition** *to anything that is coarse or ugly or profane or evil or wicked."*
Boyd K. Packer, *The Light of Christ* [800]

In truth, the moment of glory is fast approaching. The wheat of Christ acknowledges the daunting task ahead, but knows in whom they trust. As the world slowly implodes upon itself, many within the culture of Mormonism will continue their sleepy slide into apostasy and full fellowship with Babylon. All true Christians will be pushed to the brink of despair. Every soul who repents to the degree that they *"know the Lord"* can take comfort in the promise, *"He that seeketh me early shall find me, and shall not be forsaken."* (D&C 88:83).

The Promise of Zion

And they that have been scattered shall be gathered. And all they who have mourned shall be comforted. And all they who have given their lives for my name shall be crowned. Therefore, **let your hearts be comforted concerning Zion; for all flesh is in mine hands; be still and know that I am God. Zion shall not be moved out of her place, notwithstanding her children are scattered.** *They that remain, and are pure in heart, shall return, and come to their inheritances, they and their children, with songs of everlasting joy, to build up the waste places of Zion.*
Doctrine and Covenants 101:10-18

Even as disease, economic collapse, and death afflict family and friends, all who love God can look forward to the promised day when *"wickedness shall not be upon the earth...and the great and abominable church, which is the whore of all the earth, shall be cast down by devouring fire..."*(D&C 29:9,21). Yes, Babylon and all that is corrupt within her will fall, but those who are securely anchored in the Lord Jesus Christ can choose hope instead of despair.

Behold, God is my salvation; I will trust, and not be afraid:
for the LORD JEHOVAH is my strength and my song;
he also is become my salvation.
Isaiah 12:2

As prophecy unfolds, every willing soul can find peace, power, and protection in the Holy One of Israel. In Him, nothing real can be taken. In Him, nothing real can be lost. He is with us and He is our God!

I Am With You Always
Arise, shine; for thy light is come, and the glory of the LORD is risen upon thee.
For, behold, the darkness shall cover the earth, and gross darkness the people:
but the LORD shall arise upon thee, and his glory shall be seen upon thee.
Isaiah 60:1-2

Without Him, we cannot be saved. With Him, we cannot fail. Those willing to perfect their repentance in Christ discover they can do all things in Him. (Philippians 4:13). These are they who enter into the Kingdom of God on the earth-that when He returns they might sing songs of everlasting praise unto the Holy Father and Mother.

God Wins!
"Our course is onward; and are we going to stop? No. Zion must be built up, God has decreed it
and no power can stay its progress. Do you hear that? I prophecy that in the name of the Lord Jesus
Christ. For Zion must and will be built up despite all opposition,
the kingdom of God established upon the earth in accordance with the designs
and purposes of God. That is true, and you will find it to be true if you live long enough,
and if you die you will find it to be true; it will make no difference."
John Taylor, *Journal of Discourses* [801]

Empowered in His priesthood, protected by His angels, and guided by the Holy Spirit, the remnant of Christ will be triumphant! As the ongoing separation of the wheat and the tares comes to completion, the Lord will spare the righteous and protect those in Zion who are appointed to receive the City of Enoch. (Moses 7:63).

And righteousness and truth will I cause to sweep the earth as with a flood,
to gather out mine elect from the four quarters of the earth, unto a place which I shall prepare,
an Holy City, that my people may gird up their loins, and be looking forth for the time
of my coming; for there shall be my tabernacle, and it shall be called Zion, a New Jerusalem.
And the Lord said unto Enoch: Then shalt thou and all thy city meet them there,
and we will receive them into our bosom, and they shall see us; and we will fall
upon their necks, and they shall fall upon our necks, and we will kiss each other;
And there shall be mine abode, and it shall be Zion.
Moses 7:62-64

Those who have become clean from the blood and sins of this generation will dwell in the holy city of Zion. These are they who roar with the Lion of Judah, that even when faced with persecution and the possibility of death, they choose to make an irrefutable stand for truth. To make this holy offering, to take this essential stand, is to become a king or queen unto *THE CHRIST.*

Who Will Stand?

"May we declare ourselves to be more fully disciples of the Lord Jesus Christ, not in word only
and not only in the flush of comfortable times but in deed and in courage and in faith,
including when the path is lonely and when our cross is difficult to bear. This Easter week
and always, may we stand by Jesus Christ "at all times and in all things, and in all places
that [we] may be in, even until death," for surely that is how He stood by us
when it was unto death and when He had to stand entirely and utterly alone…"
Jeffrey R. Holland, *None Were With Him* [802]

Oh, that we might receive the Lord Jesus Christ and His true fullness! Now is the day to personally reclaim all that has been lost since the death of Joseph Smith. Even as the world falls, and the church falters, the remnant of God will not deny the Christ! For now is the time to stand for Him! Unafraid. Unashamed. Undaunted.

These are they who seek the last token of celestial glory, which is referred to in sacred circles as *"the nail in the sure place."* (Isaiah 22:23).

The Lord wants all to receive it.

All arise.

Acknowledgements

With adoration and gratitude forevermore: To my Savior and King, the Lord Jesus Christ.
For thou art the Holy One, the Alpha and the Omega of all that is.
O Mighty One, bear patiently with my weakness.
Have mercy on my soul when I fall before your feet.
For thou art the miracle and the greatest hope of my eternal soul.
Praise, Honor, and Glory, be unto thee and unto thy Holy Father and Holy Mother.
Now and Forever. So be it.

Hugh Nibley
Denver Snuffer
Bruce R. Mckonkie
Greg and Carleen Taylor
Henry B. Eyring
James and Jeanene Custer
Raven Corbridge
J. Reuben Clark Jr.
Orson Pratt
John Pontius
Gordon B. Hinkley
David and Kat Christenson
Joseph Fielding Smith
Dieter F. Uchtdorf
Paul R. Cheesman
Ken Bowers
W. Cleon Skousen
Daniel H. Wells
Joshua Mariano
Jim and Melanie Uhl
Marti Grobecker
Jeff Ostler
Wilford Woodruff
George Teasdale
Avraham Gileadi
Shane Clifford
Russell Fotheringham
Alan R. Cook
Natalie Smoot
David and Michelle Taylor
Margaret Barker
Steve Heinz
Larry and Jesses Winn

Joseph Smith Jr.
David A. Bednar
George Washington
Samantha W. Corbridge
M. Catherine Thomas
Neal A. Maxwell
Tiegan Corbridge
Rodney Turner
Oliver Cowdrey
Steven Co
David O. Mckay
Kent M. Keith
Jeanne Guyon
Dallin H. Oaks
Tim and Carol Malone
Gerald Lund
Choa Kok Sui
Heber C. Kimball
Duane S. Crowther
Jerel and Cara Clark
Mark Hudson
Tom Buchanan
David R. Stone
J. Golden Kimball
James E. Faust
Curtis R. Porritt
Dave Bingham
Rob Fotheringham
B.H. Roberts
Joseph McMurrin
Jeffrey R. Holland
Daniel Rogers
M. Russell Ballard

Ezra Taft Benson
Ron Paul
Alexis de Tocqueville
Melissa A. Chapple
H. Verlan Andersen
Howard W. Hunter
Vern Corbridge
Joseph F. Smith
Don B. Castleton
Kent M. Keith
Vaughn J. Featherstone
Eliza R. Snow
Todd D. Christofferson
Boyd K. Packer
Legrand Richards
Dan and Erin Mead
Marvin J. Ashton
Richard Skousen
Orson Spencer
Tom Smith
John Taylor
Emmett McKinney
Marion G. Romney
Spencer W. Kimball
George Q. Cannon
Kevin Kraut
Donna Nielsen
Brigham Young
Brian and Jennifer Bowler
Thomas Paine
Ian Clayton
Claude Wint
Paramahansa Yogananda

Bibliography

[1] Heber C. Kimball, as reported by Amanda Wilcox, Deseret News, May 23, 1931.

[2] Joseph Smith, *The King Follett Discourse,* Documentary of the History of the Church, Vol. VI, 302-317.

[3] Melvin J. Ballard, *Crusader for Righteousness*, p. 66; also, Marion G. Romney: *His Life and Faith*, p. 64.

[4] Bruce R. McConkie, *Mormon Doctrine*, 2d ed. Salt Lake City, Utah: Bookcraft, 1966, 237.

[5] Neal A. Maxwell, *Moving in his majesty and power*, [Salt Lake City, Utah: Deseret Book, 2004], 20.

[6] Bruce R. McConkie, *Mormon Doctrine*, 2d ed. Salt Lake City, Utah: Bookcraft, 1966, 333.

[7] Donald Hallstrom, *Converted to His Gospel through His Church*, General Conference April 2012.

[8] Dieter F. Uchdorf, *Come Join Us*, General Conference October 5, 2013.

[9] Lorenzo Snow, *The Teachings of Lorenzo Snow*, edited by Clyde J. Williams [Salt Lake City: Utah, BookCraft, 1984], 2.

[10] John Pontius, *The Triumph of Zion: Our Personal Quest for the New Jerusalem*, CFI, Springville, UT, pg 273.

[11] Neal A. Maxwell, *Meek and Lowly* [Salt Lake City: Deseret Book Co., 1987], 94.

[12] Brigham Young, *Journal of Discourses*, 26 vols. [London: Latter-day Saints' Book Depot, 1854-1886], 6: 194-195.

[13] Bruce C. Hafen, *The Broken Heart*: Applying the Atonement to Life's Experiences [Salt Lake City: Deseret Book Co., 1989].

[14] Spencer W. Kimball, *Conference Report*, October, 1977, pg 123.

[15] Neal A. Maxwell, Quoting William Law in *Smallest Part*, Salt Lake City: Deseret Book, Co., 1973], 16.

[16] Spencer W. Kimball, *The Teachings of Spencer W. Kimball*, edited by Edward L. Kimball [Salt Lake City: Bookcraft, 1982], 76.

[17] Joseph Smith, *Discourses of the Prophet Joseph Smith*, compiled by Alma P. Burton [Salt Lake City: Deseret Book Co., 1977], 272.

[18] Ezra Taft Benson, "*Jesus Christ-Gifts and Expectations*," New Era 5 [May 1975]: 17.

[19] Jeff Ostler, *My Choice, August 2010.*

[20] Jeff Ostler, *His Righteousness*, August 2010.

[21] Joseph Smith, meeting minutes of the female relief society at the grove, Nauvoo, IL, June 9, 1842 as reported by Eliza R. Snow.

[22] Jeff Ostler, *Saving ourselves*, August 2010.

[23] M. Catherine Thomas, *Shifting our Thinking and Bridging the Gap, Part 1:The First Shift.* Meridian Magazine March, 2010.

[24] John W. Taylor, *Conference Report, April 1899*, Second Day—Morning Session.

[25] Brigham Young, *Discourses of Brigham Young*, selected and arranged by John A. Widtsoe [Salt Lake City: Deseret Book Co., 1954], 3.

[26] Hugh Nibley, *Zeal without Knowledge*, Dialogue: A Journal of Mormon Thought, 1978, pg 6-7.

[27] Ezra Taft Benson, *Bonding Children To Scriptures*, Living Prophets essential, LDS Church News, 3/10/90.

[28] Joseph Smith, *Teachings of Prophet Joseph Smith*, pg. 364.

[29] Brigham Young, *Journal of Discourses*, 6:344.

[30] Heber J. Grant, Chapter 1: *Learning and Teaching the Gospel.*

[31] Bruce R. Mckonkie, *The Parable of the Unwise Builder*, Seminar for Regional Representatives, April 1981.

[32] Denver Snuffer, *Removing Condemnation*, Millcreek Press, 2010. pg 17.

[33] Ezra Taft Benson, *I Know That My Redeemer Lives: Latter-day Prophets Testify of the Savior* [Salt Lake City: Deseret Book Co., 1990], 210.

[34] John Pontius, *Call to Zion*, Daybreak Books.

[35] Neal A. Maxwell, *Men and Women of Christ* [Salt Lake City: Bookcraft, 1991], 41.

[36] Hugh Nibley, *Sophic and Mantic*, CWHN 10:332.

[37] John Pontius, *Call to Zion*, Daybreak Books, 110.

[38] Ezra Taft Benson, *Ensign*, May 1986, p. 78.

[39] Ezra Taft Benson, *News of the Church*, Ensign, Mar. 1987, 75.

[40] Ezra Taft Benson, *Cleansing the Inner Vessel*, Ensign, May 1986, 4.

[41] Ezra Taft Benson, *The Teachings of Ezra Taft Benson* [Salt Lake City: Bookcraft, 1988], 60.

[42] Joseph Smith, *Discourses of the Prophet Joseph Smith*, compiled by Alma P. Burton [Salt Lake City: Deseret Book Co., 1977], 69.

[43] Paul R. Cheesman, ed., *The Book of Mormon: The Keystone Scripture* [Provo: BYU Religious Studies Center, 1988], 116.

[44] Joseph Fielding Smith, *Answers to Gospel Questions,* 5 vols., SLC, Deseret Book Co., 1957- 1966, 1:137.

[45] H. Verlan Andersen, *The Great and Abominable Church of the Devil,* Orem UT, Sunrise Publishing, 1972, 164.

[46] H. Verlan Andersen, *The Great and Abominable Church of the Devil,* Orem UT, Sunrise Publishing, 1972, 163.

[47] Book of Mormon Title Page.

[48] Denver Snuffer, *Removing Condemnation,* Millcreek Press, 2010, pg. 45-46.

[49] Joseph Fielding Smith, *Doctrines of Salvation,* 3 vols., edited by Bruce R. McConkie [Salt Lake City: Bookcraft, 1954-1956], 2: 39.

[50] Joseph Fielding McConkie and Robert L. Millet, *Doctrinal Commentary on the Book of Mormon,* 4 vols. Salt Lake City: Bookcraft, 1987-1992, 2: 55.

[51] Hugh Nibley, *Promised Lands,* Maxwell Institute.

[52] Orson Pratt, *Journal of Discourses, 17:302.*

[53] Joseph Smith, *History of* the Church, *5:424.*

[54] Bruce R. McConkie, *The Ten Blessings of the Priesthood,* Ensign, Nov. 1977, 33.

[55] Boyd K. Packer, *The Power of the Priesthood,* April General Conference, 2010.

[56] Jeff Ostler, *Power in the Priesthood,* August 18, 2010.

[57] George Q. Cannon, *Truth.* Volume 6, pg 136-137.

[58] Brigham Young, *Journal of Discourses,* 10:273.

[59] Denver Snuffer, *Come Let Us Adore Him,* MillCreek Press, Salt Lake City, UT, pg 59-60.

[60] Mark Hudson, *Fullness of the Priesthood,* Fall 2010.

[61] Hugh Nibley, *Sunstone Magazine*: December 1990, 10-11.

[62] Jeanne Guyon, *Experiencing the depths of Jesus Christ,* SeedSowers Publishing, Jacksonville, FL, pg 38.

[63] Denver Snuffer, *a bit of a detour,* Blog, 6-28-2010.

[64] Dallin H. Oaks, *The Challenge to Become,* Ensign, November, 2000.

[65] Jeff Ostler, *True Obedience,* Sep 6, 2010.

[66] James Custer, *The Unspeakable Gift,* Keystone Publications, 1998, 49.

[67] Joseph Smith, *History of The Church of Jesus Christ of Latter-day Saints,* 7 Vols. 2:170).

[68] Neal A. Maxwell, *make Calling the Focus of Your Mission'* , LDS Church News, 1994, 09/17/94 .

[69] David A. Bednar, *Honorably Hold a name and Standing,* April General Conference 2009.

[70] James A. Custer, *The Unspeakable Gift,* Keystone Publications, 1998. pg. 101.

[71] Bruce R. McConkie, *A New Witness for the Articles of Faith* [SLC: Deseret Book Co., 1985], 51.

[72] Joseph Smith, *The King Follett Discourse,* Documentary of the History of the Church, Vol. VI, 302-317.

[73] Dallin H. Oaks, *His Holy Name,* [Salt Lake City: Utah, Bookcraft, 1998], 56.

[74] Jeanne Guyon, *Experiencing the Depths of Jesus Christ,* SeedSowers Publishing, Jacksonville, FL, pg 41.

[75] Brigham Young, *Discourses of Brigham Young,* selected and arranged by John A. Widtsoe [Salt Lake City: Deseret Book Co., 1954], 390.

[76] Brigham Young, *Discourses of Brigham Young,* selected and arranged by John A. Widtsoe [Salt Lake City: Deseret Book Co., 1954], 390.

[77] George Q. Cannon, *Journal of Discourses,*12:46 Salt Lake City, April 21st, 1867.

[78] Brigham Young, *Discourses of Brigham Young,* selected and arranged by John A. Widtsoe [Salt Lake City: Deseret Book Co., 1954], 390.

[79] J. Golden Kimball, *The Story of a Unique Personality,* Claude Richards. 1934.

[80] Brigham Young, *Journal of Discourses* 9:149-150.

[81] Ezra Taft Benson, *Conference Report, April 1965,* Afternoon Meeting 121.

[82] Joseph Smith, *Teachings of the Prophet Joseph Smith,* selected and arranged by Joseph Fielding Smith SLC, Deseret Book Co., 1976], 237.

[83] Howard W. Hunter, *The Teachings of Howard W. Hunter,* edited by Clyde J. Williams [Salt Lake City: Bookcraft, 1997], 42.)

[84] Dallin H. Oaks, Repentance and Change, Liahona November 2003.

[85] Ezra Taft Benson, *Ensign* Oct 1989, pg. 3.

[86] Heber J Grant, "*A Marvelous Growth,*" Juvenile Instructor, Dec. 1929, p. 697.

[87] James Custer, *The Church is not a Vehicle.* Year unknown.

[88] Bruce R. McConkie, *Mormon Doctrine*, 333.

[89] Denver Snuffer, *Weep for Zion, for Zion has fled*, From the desk of Denver Snuffer blog, June 5, 2010.

[90] Bruce R. McConkie, *Mormon Doctrine*, 2d ed. Salt Lake City: Bookcraft, 1966], 333.

[91] Neal A. Maxwell, *Meek and Lowly* [Salt Lake City: Deseret Book Co., 1987], 47.

[92] Hyrum L. Andrus, *Principles of Perfection [Salt Lake City: Bookcraft, 1970], 17.*

[93] John Pontius, *The Fullness of the Gospel*, Unblog my soul, January 3, 2012.

[94] David A. Bednar, *Lincoln Nebraska Stake Conference*, 2006.

[95] Joseph Fielding Smith, *Doctrines of Salvation* , 2:28.

[96] Joseph Smith, *Discourses of the Prophet Joseph Smith*, compiled by Alma P. Burton [Salt Lake City: Deseret Book Co., 1977], 72.

[97] Joseph Fielding Smith, *Church History and Modern Revelation*, 4 vols. [Salt Lake City: The Church of Jesus Christ of Latter-day Saints, 1946-1949], 1: 48 – 49.

[98] Dallin H. Oaks, *Sin and Suffering, Morality* [Salt Lake City: Bookcraft, 1992], 191 - 192.

[99] Joseph Smith, *Discourses of the Prophet Joseph Smith*, compiled by Alma P. Burton [Salt Lake City: Deseret Book Co., 1977], 204.

[100] Zebedee Coltrin as reported by Truman Coe, "Mormonism," *Cincinnati Journal and Western Luminary*, 25 August 1835. pg. 4.

[101] D. Todd Christofferson, *Come to Zion, General Conference*, October 2008.

[102] Wilford Woodruff, *Journal of Discourses*, 26 vols. [London: Latter-day Saints' Book Depot, 1854-1886], 17: 250.

[103] Brigham Young, *Journal of Discourses*, 15:220.

[104] Bruce R. McConkie, *A New Witness for the Articles of Faith* [SLC: Deseret Book Co., 1985], 616.

[105] David A. Bednar, *Clean Hands and a Pure Heart*, October 2007 General Conference, *Ensign*, November 2007, pp. 82.

[106] David R. Stone, *Zion in the Midst of Babylon*, General Conference, April 2006. 92.

[107] Joseph Smith, *Lectures on Faith*. Lecture Six.

[108] Ezra Taft Benson, *The Teachings of Ezra Taft Benson* [Salt Lake City: Bookcraft, 1988], 123.

[109] Ezra Taft Benson, "*Temple Blessings and Covenants*," Temple Presidents Seminar, Salt Lake City, Utah, 28 September 1982.

[110] Hugh Nibley, *Approaching Zion*, edited by Don E. Norton [Salt Lake City and Provo: Deseret Book Co., Foundation for Ancient Research and Mormon Studies, 1989], 342.

[111] Denver Snuffer Jr., *Beloved Enos*. Millcreek Press. Salt Lake City, 2009, 123-124.

[112] Brigham Young, *Journal of Discourses*, volume 5 pg. 98. August 2, 1857 Salt Lake City.

[113] Joseph Smith, *Teachings of the Prophet Joseph Smith*, pg 185.

[114] Hugh Nibley, *Approaching Zion* [Salt Lake City: DeseretBook, 1989], 37.

[115] David R. Stone, *Zion in the Midst of Babylon*, General Conference, April 2006.

[116] Joseph Smith, *Teachings of the Prophet Joseph Smith*, arranged by Joseph Fielding Smith [Salt Lake City: Deseret Book Co., 1976], 304.

[117] Denver Snuffer, *The Second Comforter-Conversing with the Lord through the Veil*, Salt Lake City Utah. Mill Creek Press, 2006. 274-285.

[118] Bruce R. McConkie, *The Mortal Messiah: From Bethlehem to Calvary*, 4 vols. [Salt Lake City: Deseret Book Co., 1979-1981], 1: 275.

[119] David Christenson, *Faith, Hope, and Charity*. Fall 2010.

[120] Brigham Young, *Discourses of Brigham Young*, selected and arranged by John A. Widtsoe [Salt Lake City: Deseret Book Co., 1954], 41.

[121] John A. Widtsoe, *Evidences and Reconciliations*, pg. 90.

[122] Denver Snuffer, *Eighteen Versus*, Millcreek Press, Salt Lake City, UT, 2007, 139.

[123] Denver Snuffer, *Eighteen Versus*, Salt Lake City, Ut. Millcreek Press, 133.

[124] Joseph Smith, *Teachings of the Prophet Joseph Smith*, pg 392.

[125] Boyd K. Packer, *The Twelve Apostles*, October General Conference, 1996.

[126] Jeanne Guyon, *Experiencing the Depths of Jesus Christ*, pg 61.

[127] Joseph Smith, *The King Follett Discourse*, Documentary of the History of the Church, Vol. VI, 302-317.

[128] George Q. Cannon, *Journal of Discourses*, 12:46.

[129] Wilford Woodruff, General Conference, April 4, 1890.

[130] Brigham Young, *Discourses of Brigham Young*, pp. 39-40.

[131] Bruce R. McConkie, The Ten Blessings of the Priesthood, Ensign, Nov. 1977, 33.

[132] Bruce R. McConkie, *A New Witness for the Articles of Faith* [Salt Lake City: Deseret Book, 1985], 373.

[133] Joseph Smith, Teachings of the Prophet Joseph Smith, pg. 119, 269.

[134] Wilford Woodruff, *Journal of Discourses* 13:165, December 12, 1869.

[135] Joseph Smith, Teachings of the Prophet Joseph Smith, pg. 206.

[136] Neal A. Maxwell, *Bonneville Communications,* General Conference April 1993. (Elder Maxwell's comments were not printed as stated, but instead were changed to imply that it was the church members who set themselves up as a light. Video of the talk provides his accurate teaching.)

[137] Jeff Ostler, True prophets, August 2010.

[138] Ezra Taft Benson. *Human Liberty is the Mainspring of Human Progress*, October General Conference, 1962.

[139] Spencer W. Kimball, *Instructor,* 95:527.

[140] Joseph Smith, Teachings of the Prophet Joseph Smith, pg. 21.

[141] Joseph Smith, *The Words of Joseph Smith.*

[142] Joseph Smith, *Teachings of Presidents of the Church,* chapter 33, p. 384.

[143] Denver Snuffer, *Passing the Heavenly Gift,* Millcreek Press, 2011, pg 292.

[144] Bruce R. McConkie, *A New Witness for the Articles of Faith* [Salt Lake City: Deseret Book, 1985], 489.

[145] Brigham Young, *Discourses of Brigham Young,* selected and arranged by John A. Widtsoe [Salt Lake City: Deseret Book Co., 1954], 41.

[146] Joseph Smith, *Teachings of the Prophet Joseph Smith*, p. 149.

[147] Joseph Smith, *Teachings of the Prophet Joseph Smith*, pg. 160.

[148] Joseph Smith, *Discourses of the Prophet Joseph Smith*, compiled by Alma P. Burton [Salt Lake City: Deseret Book Co., 1977], 150.) (HC 5:389.

[149] Bruce R. McConkie, *Doctrinal New Testament Commentary*, 3 vols. [Salt Lake City: Bookcraft, 1965-1973], 3: 331.

[150] Joseph Smith, *Discourses of the Prophet Joseph Smith*, compiled by Alma P. Burton [Salt Lake City: Deseret Book Co., 1977], 151.

[151] Marion G. Romney, Conference Report, October 1965, First Day—Morning Meeting 21.

[152] Daily Kos, *Marine jumps on grenade, saves squad*, by ECH. November 23, 2004.

[153] Hyrum L. Andrus and Helen Mae Andrus, comps., They Knew the Prophet [SLC: Bookcraft, 1974], 61.

[154] Joseph Smith, Discourses of the Prophet Joseph Smith, compiled by Alma P. Burton [Salt Lake City: Deseret Book Co., 1977], 41 - 42.

[155] Joseph Smith, *Teachings of the Prophet Joseph Smith,* 150.

[156] Marion G. Romney, Conference Report, April 1954, Afternoon Meeting 132.

[157] Joseph Smith, *Teachings of the Prophet Joseph Smith*, pg. 366.

[158] Joseph W. Mcmurrin, *Conference Report, April 1904*, Overflow Meeting 97.

[159] George Teasdale, *Conference Report, October 1901*, Afternoon Session 38 - 39.

[160] J. Golden Kimball, *Conference Report, October 1901*, Overflow Meeting 56.

[161] Bruce R. McConkie, *A New Witness for the Articles of Faith,* [Salt Lake City: Deseret Book Co., 1985], 490.

[162] Bruce R. McConkie, *The Promised Messiah: The First Coming of Christ* [Salt Lake City: Deseret Book Co., 1978], 583.

[163] John Pontius, *Call to Zion*, Daybreak Books, Wasilla, Alaska, 2008, pg 187.

[164] M. Catherine Thomas, *The Brother of Jared at the Veil* in Donald W. Parry, ed., *Temples of the Ancient World: Ritual and Symbolism* (Salt Lake City: Deseret Book and FARMS, 1994), 388–97.

[165] Denver Snuffer, Conversing with the Lord through the Veil, Millcreek Press, Salt Lake City, UT. 132.

[166] Unknown Author, *Experiencing the Mighty Change of Heart*, Chapter 27, toddjumper.com

[167] John Pontius, *The Triumph of Zion, our personal quest for the New Jerusalem,* CFI, Springville, UT, 2010, pg 332.

[168] Jeffrey R. Holland, *None were with Him*, April General Conference 2009.

[169] Brigham Young, *Discourses of Brigham Young,* selected and arranged by John A. Widtsoe Salt Lake City: Deseret Book Co., 1954], 114.

[170] Heber C. Kimball, *Journal of Discourses*, 1:357, November 14, 1852.

[171] Don Miguel Ruiz, *Beyond Fear*, Council Oaks Books, Tulsa, Ok, 1997, 51.

[172] David O. Mckay, *Conference Report, April 1958*, First Day—Morning Meeting 6 - 7.

[173] M. Catherine Thomas, *Christ-Stream-Why are We So Anxious?* Meridian Magazine, May 28, 2010.

[174] Brigham Young, *Teachings of Latter Day Prophets*, Tabernacle, May 1863.

[175] Spencer W. Kimball, *Conference Report*, 1977 Oct:123.

[176] Craig Mills, *Home Sanctuary*, pg 113.

[177] Brigham Young, *Journal of Discourses,* 26 vols. [London: Latter-day Saints Book Depot, 1854-1886], 17: 143.

[178] Joseph Smith, *The Personal Writings of Joseph Smith*, March 15, 1839, pg 386-387.

[179] B.H. Roberts, *New Witnesses for God.* Vol.1, pp. 391-392.

[180] Bruce R. McConkie, *"The Seven Deadly Heresies,"* Heresy number five, 1980.

[181] James E. Talmage, *The Articles of Faith*, 1899 Edition, pg, 420-421.

[182] Joseph F. Smith, *Gospel Doctrine. 442, and Teachings of Presidents of the Church: Joseph F. Smith*, (2011), 86–93.

[183] J. Reuben Clark, *Church News*, p. 3, 23 April 1960.

[184] Anonymous author, *Teachings of the Doctrine of Eternal Lives.*

[185] Heber C. Kimball, *Journal of Discourses* 1:161.

[186] Joseph Smith, *Teachings of The Prophet Joseph Smith*, 346-47.

[187] Brigham Young. *The Complete Discourses of Brigham Young*, Vol. 1, 1832 to 1852.

[188] Heber C. Kimball, *Journal of Discourses*, 6:63.

[189] Brigham Young, *Journal of Discourses* 2:124.

[190] Lorenzo Snow, MS 56:49-53; *Collected Discourses* 3:364-65.

[191] Heber C. Kimball, *Journal of Discourses*, 4:329.

[192] Joseph Smith, *History of the Church*, 4:425; from the minutes of a Church conference held on Oct. 3, 1841, Nauvoo, Illinois, published in *Times and Seasons,* Oct. 15, 1841, p. 577.

[193] Brigham Young, *Journal of Discourses* 6:344.

[194] Harold B. Lee, *Teachings of the Presidents of the Church: Harold B. Lee: Chapter 2.*

[195] Joan Rawlusyk, *Reach out and Touch Someone,* The PEO Record, Vol. 98, No. 5, May, 1985, as Printed in Speaker's Source Book Two, by Glenn van Ekeren, Paramus, NJ, Prentice Hall Press, 1994, 344.

[196] Joseph Fielding Smith, *Seek Ye Earnestly* [Salt Lake City: Deseret Book Co., 1970], 63 - 64.

[197] Joseph Fielding McConkie, *Joseph Smith: The Choice Seer* [Salt Lake City: Bookcraft, 1996].

[198] Paul R. Cheesman, *The Book of Mormon: The Keystone Scripture* [Provo: BYU Religious Studies Center, 1988], 116.

[199] Legrand Richards, *A Marvelous Work and a Wonder* [Salt Lake City: Deseret Book Co., 1950], 258.

[200] Ronald E. Poelman, *The Gospel and the Church,* October 1984 General Conference. Original version.

[201] Robert Young, *Analytical Concordance to the Bible,* WM. B. Eerdmans Publishing Company, Grand Rapids Michigan, 1964, 745.

[202] Paul R. Cheesman, ed., *The Book of Mormon: The Keystone Scripture* [Provo: BYU Religious Studies Center, 1988], 118.

[203] Brigham Young, *Contributor, vol. 10, 1889.*

[204] Ronald Poelman, *The Gospel and the Church*, October General Conference 1984. Original version.

[205] Parley P. Pratt, *Deseret News*, Apr. 30, 1853. Sermon April 7, 1853.

[206] Ezra Taft Benson, *BYU Speeches of the Year*, May 10, 1966.

[207] Joseph Smith, *Teachings of Presidents of the Church*: *"Gaining knowledge of Eternal Truths,"* 2007, 261–270.

[208] Joseph Smith, *Teachings of the Prophet Joseph Smith,* p. 158, pg 308.

[209] James E. Talmage, *The House of the Lord*, pg 84.

[210] The Prophets Message, Church News June 5, 1965.

[211] David B. Haight, *Joseph Smith the Prophet,* November Ensign 1979, pg 22.

[212] Ruth Todd, *LDS Church statement,* as reported by Joseph Walker, *LDS Church begins using new Temple Film,* Deseret News. August 4, 2013.

[213] Brigham Young, *Journal of Discourses,* 16:165.

[214] H. Verlan Andersen, *The Great and Abominable Church of the Devil,* Orem UT, Sunrise Publishing, 1972, 164.

[215] Denver Snuffer, Source Unknown.

[216] Mahatma Gandhi, Thinkexist.com

[217] Gospel of Thomas, 97, www.gnosis.org

[218] Brigham Young, *Journal of Discourses*, 18: 239.

[219] Orson Pratt, *Journal of Discourses*, 15:357.

[220] Joseph Fielding Smith, *Deseret News* Oct. 17, 1936.

[221] Joseph Fielding Smith, *The Life of Joseph Fielding Smith 212.* Deseret Book Co. Joseph Fielding Smith Journal, 28 December 1938.

[222] Ezra Taft Benson, "*A Divided Church? or the Destructive Precepts of Men*," General Conference April 1969.

[223] H. Verlan Andersen, *The Great and Abominable Church of the Devil,* Sunrise Publishing, Orem UT 1972, 168.

[224] Rodney Turner, Kent P. Jackson, ed., *Studies in Scripture,* Vol. 8: Alma 30 to Moroni [Salt Lake City: Deseret Book Co., 1988], 16.

[225] Ezra Taft Benson, *The Teachings of Ezra Taft Benson* [Salt Lake City: Bookcraft, 1988], 77.

[226] Joseph Fielding Smith, *Eternal Keys and the Right to Preside.* Pg 88.

[227] Howard W. Hunter, *The Teachings of Howard W. Hunter,* edited by Clyde J. Williams Salt Lake City: Bookcraft, 1997, 42.

[228] Ezra Taft Benson, A Sacred Responsibility, Ensign, May 1986, 77.

[229] Orson F. Whitney., *Conference Report, October 1912,* Third Day—Morning Session 71 - 72.

[230] Joseph Smith, *Discourses of the Prophet Joseph Smith,* compiled by Alma P. Burton [Salt Lake City: Deseret Book Co., 1977], 146.

[231] Joseph Smith, *Teachings of the Prophet Joseph Smith,* arranged by Joseph Fielding Smith [Salt Lake City: Deseret Book Co., 1976], 242.

[232] Joseph Smith, *The Personal Writings of Joseph Smith*, March 15, 1839, pg 386-387.

[233] Brigham Young, *Deseret News* 18 June 1872.

[234] Thomas Paine, *Common Sense,* 1776.

[235] Ezra Taft Benson, *Conference Report, April 1969*, First Day—Morning Meeting 11.

[236] Hugh Nibley, *Approaching Zion,* Deseret Book, Salt Lake City, UT, 1989, pg 45.

[237] Delbert L. Stapley, *BYU Speeches of the Year*, April 26, 1966, 9.

[238] Neal A. Maxwell, *Meek and Lowly* [Salt Lake City: Deseret Book Co., 1987], 47.

[239] Hugh Nibley, *Approaching Zion,* Provo: Deseret Book Co, *Teachings of the Prophet Joseph Smith,* pg 320.

[240] Dictionary.com

[241] Dictionary.com

[242] Joseph Smith, *History of the Church,* 5:554.

[243] Joseph Smith, *Times and Seasons* 5:490.

[244] Denver Snuffer, *Removing the Condemnation,* 2 Nephi 28:7-8, Mill Creek Press, Salt Lake City, UT, pg 160.

[245] Hugh Nibley, *Teachings of the Book of Mormon, Semester 4, F.A.R.M.S.,* 186.

[246] Joseph F. Smith, *Conference Report,* April, 1917.

[247] Brigham Young, *Salvation,* discourse delivered in the Tabernacle, Great Salt Lake City, January 16, 1853. As reported by G. D. Watt. Brigham Young, *Journal of Discourses* 1:2.

[248] Robert J. Woodford, "*The Historical Development of the Doctrine and Covenants*, Ph.D. dissertation, Brigham Young University, 1974, Volume two, pg 1175.

[249] Joseph Smith, *The Words of Joseph Smith,* pg. 378.

[250] Joseph Smith, *Teachings of the Prophet Joseph Smith,* pg. 370.

[251] Joseph Smith, *The King Follett Discourse,* Documentary of the History of the Church, Vol. VI, 302-317.

[252] Joseph Smith, *Doctrine and Covenants Preface,* by Joseph Smith, Oliver Cowdery, Sidney Rigdon and F. G. Williams. 1835.

[253] Bruce R. McConkie, *The Lord God of Joseph Smith,* Discourse delivered January 4, 1972.

[254] Boyd Kirkland, *Elohim and Jehovah in Mormonism and the Bible.* Dialogue: A Journal of Mormon Thought. SLC, Vol. 19, No.1, pg. 77.

[255] Joseph Smith, *Teachings of the Prophet Joseph Smith,* p. 158, pg 308.

[256] Margaret Barker, *Our Great High Priest. The Church as the New Temple,* Fr Alexander Schmemann Memorial Lecture, St. Vladimir's Orthodox Seminary, New York, January 28, 2012.

[257] David B. Haight, *Joseph Smith the Prophet,* November Ensign 1979, pg 22.

[258] Joseph Smith, *History of the Church* 5:423-24.

[259] Gospel Principles Manual, *The Church of Jesus Christ in Former Times,* Lesson 16, 2010. pg 91-92.

[260] James E. Talmage, *The House of the Lord,* pg 84.

[261] Dan Mead, *Zion,* Fall 2010.

[262] Denver Snuffer, Source Unknown.

[263] Brigham Young, The Essential Brigham Young, pg 196.

[264] The Prophets Message, *Church News*, June 5, 1965.

[265] Ldsendowment.org

[266] Denver Snuffer, *Come let us adore Him*, Mill Creek Press, pg. 50.

[267] Daniel H. Wells, *The saving ordinances of the gospel, Journal of Discourses*, 16:241.

[268] Brigham Young, *Journal of Discourses*, 12:96.

[269] Admiral Ben Moreel, *Prophet Principles and National Survival*, Jerreld L. Newquist, pg. 339.

[270] Ezra Taft Benson, *To the Humble Followers of Christ*, Conference Report, April 1969.

[271] H. Verlan Andersen, *The Great and Abominable Church of the Devil*, Orem UT, Sunrise Publishing, 1972, 166-168.

[272] Ezra Taft Benson, *To the Humble Followers of Christ*, Conference Report, April 1969.

[273] Ezra Taft Benson, *Beware of Pride*, Ensign, May 1989.

[274] Denver Snuffer, *Come let us adore Him*, Millcreek Press, Salt Lake City, UT. 2009. pg 35-36.

[275] Joseph Smith, *Mosiah Hancock Journal*, p.19.

[276] Spencer W. Kimball, *The Teachings of Spencer W. Kimball*, p.357.

[277] Spencer W. Kimball, *Ensign, June 1976.*

[278] Avrahma Gileadi, *Modern Idolatry: Twelve Diatribes.*

[279] Hugh Nibley, *Teachings of the Book of Mormon, Semester 4*, F.A.R.M.S., 186.

[280] Joseph F. Smith, Gospel Doctrine: *Selections from the Sermons and Writings of Joseph F. Smith*, 1914, pg 312-313.

[281] Samantha Corbridge, *Becoming a Sacrament*, Spring 2011.

[282] Orson Spencer, *History of the Church*, Vol. VI, p. 273) (Hyrum M. Smith and Janne M. Sjodahl, *Doctrine and Covenants Commentary* [Salt Lake City: Deseret Book Co., 1978],10.

[283] Joseph Fielding Smith, *The Progress of Man* [Salt Lake City: Deseret Book Co., 1964], 88 - 89.)

[284] Neal A. Maxwell, *All these things shall give thee experience*, Deseret Book, Salt Lake City, pg 104-105.

[285] Denver Snuffer, *The Second Comforter-Conversing with the Lord through the Veil*, Salt Lake City Utah. Mill Creek Press, 2006. 274-285.

[286] Denver Snuffer, *The Second Comforter-Conversing with the Lord through the Veil*, Salt Lake City Utah. Mill Creek Press, 2006. 274-285.

[287] Neal A. Maxwell, *All these things shall give thee experience*, Deseret Book, Salt Lake City, pg 101.

[288] Denver Snuffer, *Come Let us Adore Him*, Millcreek Press, 2009, pg. 70.

[289] Henry B. Eyring, *Our Hearts Knit as One*, Ensign, November 2008, 68.

[290] James Custer, *The Unspeakable Gift*, Keystone Publishing, 1998, 161.

[291] Neal A. Maxwell, *Behold the Enemy is Combined, General Conference*, April, 4 1993.

[292] H. Verlan Andersen, *The Great and Abominable Church of the Devil*, Orem UT, Sunrise Publishing, 1972, 161,163.

[293] Denver Snuffer Jr., *Beloved Enos*, Millcreek Press, Salt Lake City, UT. 2009, 168.

[294] Heber J Grant, Diary Excerpts 1887-1889.

[295] M. Russell Ballard, *Learning the Lessons of the Past*, General Conference April 2009.

[296] Brigham Young, *Journal of Discourses*, 4:297-298.

[297] Joseph F. Smith, *Gospel Doctrine: Selections from the Sermons and Writings of Joseph F. Smith*, 1914, pg 312-313.

[298] Todd Compton, *Apostasy, Encyclopedia of Mormonism*, 1992, pg 56.

[299] Church Handbook of Instructions, 2009. Pg 95.

[300] Church Handbook of Instructions, 2009. Pg 95.

[301] Dictionary.com

[302] Bret Corbridge, January 2012.

[303] Dieter F. Uchtdorf, *Developing Christlike Attributes*, Liahona, October 2008.

[304] Brigham Young, *Journal of Discourses* 18:72.

[305] Bruce R. Mckonkie, *The Parable of the Unwise Builder, Seminar for Regional Representatives*, April 1981.

[306] Joseph Smith, *Millennial Star*, Vol 14, Number 38, pages 593-595.

[307] David Christenson, *Building Babylon*, Summer 2011.

[308] Brigham Young, *Discourses of Brigham Young*, pg. 3.

[309] Ldsendowment.org

[310] Joseph Smith, *The Wentworth Letter*, Documented History of the Church, 4:535-541, March 1, 1842.

[311] Lorenzo Snow, *Journal of Discourses*, 26:368.

[312] James E Faust: *General Conference*, October 1994.

[313] Michael D. Quinn, *Mormon Hierarchy: Extensions of Power.*

[314] Oliver Cowdery, *History of the Church*, DHC 2:195-196. 1835.

[315] Brigham Young, *Journal of Discourses*, Volume 19, pg 117.

[316] Joseph Smith, *The Historical Record*, Andrew Jenson, Volumes 7&8, 1888, 1889.

[317] Orson Hyde, *Deseret News: Semi-Weekly,* June 21, 1870, p. 3.

[318] Hugh Nibley, *Beyond Politics, Nibley on the Timely and the Timeless: Classic Essays of Hugh W. Nibley*, 2nd ed. Provo, UT: Religious Studies Center, Brigham Young University, 2004, 301-328.

[319] Denver Snuffer, *The Prophetic and the Priestly*, Blog, June 19, 2012.

[320] Joseph Fielding Smith, *Eternal Keys and the Right to Preside*. Pg 88.

[321] Joseph Fielding Smith, *Teachings of the Presidents of the Church, The Church and Kingdom of God*. Pg 124.

[322] H. Verlan Andersen, *The Great and Abominable Church of the Devil,* Orem UT, Sunrise Publishing, 1972, 166-168.

[323] Joseph Smith, *Joseph Smith History,* 14, 15.

[324] Dieter F. Uchtdorf, *Christlike Attributes-The Wind beneath our Wings,* Ensign November 2005, 100.

[325] Frank O. May, Jr., "*General Handbook of Instructions,*", in Daniel H. Ludlow, (ed), *Encyclopedia of Mormonism*, New York: Macmillan Publishing, 1992) 2:541.

[326] Bruce R. McConkie, *The Mortal Messiah: From Bethlehem to Calvary,* 4 vols. [Salt Lake City: Deseret Book Co., 1979-1981], 1: 238.

[327] Avrahma Gileadi, *Modern Idolatry: Twelve Diatribes.*

[328] Religiousforums.com

[329] Religiousforums.com

[330] Religiousforums.com

[331] Boyd K. Packer, *The Twelve Apostles,* October General Conference, 1996.

[332] Brigham Young, *Journal of Discourses*, 11:294-295.

[333] Brigham Young, *Journal of Discourses* 17:38.

[334] Hugh Nibley, *Approaching Zion*, Deseret Book, pg 37-38.

[335] Hugh Nibley, *Approaching Zion* [Salt Lake City: DeseretBook, 1989], 37.

[336] David H. Burton, *Downtown Rising,* LDS church website: www.downtownrising.com

[337] Deseret News, *Salt Lake City high rise is ready for occupancy on Main*, November 4, 2009.

[338] Gordon B. Hinckley, "*A Prophet's Counsel and Prayer for Youth*," Ensign, Jan 2001, 2.

[339] David A. Edwards, "*Practically Out the Door,"* NewEra, Apr 2009, 42–43.

[340] Dan Mead, *Worshipping False Gods*, June 2011.

[341] Brigham Young, *Journal of Discourses,* 11:216.

[342] Spencer W. Kimball, *Teachings of Spencer W. Kimball*, pg 357.

[343] Gordon B. Hinckley, "*Questions and Answers*," Ensign, Nov 1985, pg. 49

[344] Dan Mead, *Apostasy, are you in it?* Weeping for Zion blog.

[345] D. Todd Christofferson, *Come to Zion, General Conference,* October 2008.

[346] Hugh Nibley, "*Leaders to Managers: The Fatal Shift,*" *Dialogue: A Journal of Mormon Thought* 16/4 Winter 1983: 12-21.

[347] Ezra Taft Benson, *The Teachings of Ezra Taft Benson* [Salt Lake City: Bookcraft, 1988], 385.

[348] Denver Snuffer Jr., *Beloved Enos,* Millcreek Press, Salt Lake City, UT. 2009, 157.

[349] David O. McKay, *David O. McKay and the Rise of Modern Mormonism,* SLC, University Press, 2005, pg. 150.

[350] Joseph Smith, *Discourses of the Prophet Joseph Smith,* compiled by Alma P. Burton [Salt Lake City: Deseret Book Co., 1977], 272.

[351] Spencer W. Kimball, *The Teachings of Spencer W. Kimball,* [Salt Lake City: Bookcraft, 1982], 76.

[352] Dictionary.com

[353] *Late Corporation of the Church of Jesus Christ of Latter-day Saints v. United States*, 136 U.S. 1 (1890).

[354] Brigham Young, *The Complete Discourses of Brigham Young,* Volume 4, pg 2357. JD 11:269.

[355] Wilford Woodruff, *Sixty-first Semiannual General Conference of the Church*, Monday, October 6, 1890, Salt Lake City, Utah.

[356] Cannon II, Kenneth (Jan–Mar 1983). "*After the Manifesto: Mormon Polygamy, 1890-1906* ". Sunstone: 27–35.

[357] Wilford Woodruff, *Excerpts from three addresses by President Wilford Woodruff regarding the Manifesto*, pg 292.

[358] Charles W. Penrose, *Bristol England Mission Conference*, May 25, 1908. As related by Thomas J. Rosser to Robert C. Newson, in a letter written 4 August 1956.

[359] Joseph F. Smith, *Official Statement, Improvement Era* 7:545–546 Apr. 1904.

[360] Joseph Smith, *Teachings of the Prophet Joseph Smith*, p. 136.

361 Joseph Smith, *Times & Seasons*, 5:490-491, April, 1, 1844.

362 LDS Newsroom, *Race and the Priesthood.* Included in the press release, *"Race and the Church: All are alike unto God."* The Church of Jesus Christ of Latter Day Saints. December 9, 2013.

363 LDS Newsroom, *Race and the Priesthood.* Included in the press release, *"Race and the Church: All are alike unto God."* The Church of Jesus Christ of Latter Day Saints. December 9, 2013.

364 George Q. Cannon, *Gospel Truth*, Vol. 1, p.319.

365 Joseph Smith, *Words of Joseph Smith*, Andrew Ehat. pg. 120. May 26, 1842.

366 Brigham Young, *Journal of Discourses* 18:248.

367 First Presidency Message, *Ensign,* August 1996)

368 Curtis Portitt, *Apostasy of the Church of Jesus Christ of Latter Day Saints*, pg 56.

369 Elaine Cannon, *Ensign*, Nov. 1978, p. 108.

370 Dan Mead, *The Kings of Babylon,* Fall 2010.

371 Joseph Smith, *Millennial Star,371.*

372 Brigham Young, *Journal of Discourses*, Vol. 12, pg 164.

373 Joseph Smith, *Teachings of the Prophet Joseph Smith*, pg. 278 DHC 5:265.

374 David Christenson, *Perplexed,* www.davidkat99.blogspot.com

375 George Q. Cannon, *Journal of Discourses*, 12:46.

376 Curtis Porritt, *The Apostasy of the Church of Jesus Christ of Latte Day Saints.* September 25, 1999,

377 Joseph Fielding Smith, *Answers to Gospel Questions,* 5 vols., SLC, Deseret Book Co., 1957-1966, 5: 89.

378 H. Verlan Andersen, *The Great and Abominable Church of the Devil,* Orem UT, Sunrise Publishing, 1972, 163.

379 John Pontius, *Call to Zion,* Daybreak Books,133-134.

380 Neal A. Maxwell, *Meek and Lowly* [Salt Lake City: Deseret Book Co., 1987], 53.

381 Spencer W. Kimball, *The Teachings of Spencer W. Kimball,* edited by Edward L. Kimball [Salt Lake City: Bookcraft, 1982], 76.

382 Denver Snuffer, *Removing Condemnation*, Millcreek Press, 2010, pg 46.

383 Curtis R. Porritt, *The Apostasy of the Church of Jesus Christ of Latter Day Saints*, September 25, 1999, pg. 16-17.

384 Joseph Smith, *"A Prophecy of Joseph the Seer,"* found in, *The Fate of the Persecutors of the Prophet Joseph Smith*, pg. 154, 156.

385 Wilford Woodruff, *Journal of Discourses,* 26 vols., LDS Book Depot, 1854-1886, 4: 233.

386 Joseph Smith, *Teachings of the Prophet Joseph Smith,* pg. 9.

387 Joseph Smith, *Teachings of the Prophet Joseph Smith,* selected and arranged by Joseph Fielding Smith Salt Lake City: Deseret Book Co., 1976], 309.

388 Eliza R. Snow, *Biography and Family Record of Lorenzo Snow*, SLC, Deseret News, 1884, 364-365.

389 Joseph Smith, *Teachings of the Prophet Joseph Smith,* arranged by Joseph Fielding Smith [Salt Lake City: Deseret Book Co.,1976], 331.

390 Ezra Taft Benson, *Conference Report, April 1969*, First Day—Morning Meeting 10.

391 Denver Snuffer, *Come let us adore Him*, Millcreek Press, pg 52-53.

392 Ezra Taft Benson, *Conference Report, April 1969*, First Day—Morning Meeting 11.

393 J. Reuben Clark, Jr., *Conference Report, April 1949*, Afternoon Meeting 163.

394 Dan Mead, *Authority*, Weeping for Zion Blog, February 23, 2012.

395 James Custer, *The Unspeakable Gift.*

396 Nathan Shackelford, *Soul Voice,* November 10, 2011.

397 Denver Snuffer, *Come, Let Us Adore Him*, Millcreek Press, pg 34.

398 Denver Snuffer, *Come let us adore Him*, Millcreek Press, pg 66.

399 Denver Snuffer, Source Unknown.

400 Dallin H. Oaks, *Unselfish Service,* April 2009 General Conference.

401 Anonymous Saint, from *The Apostasy of the Church of Jesus Christ of Latter Day Saints,* Curtis Portitt.

402 Kent M. Keith, *Anyway:The Paradoxical Commandments,* G.P. Putnam's Sons, 2001, 16-17.

403 Jeanne Guyon, *Experiencing The Depths of Jesus Christ*, pg. 77.

404 Dieter F. Uchtdorf, *Lift where you Stand,* October General Conference, 2008.

405 Richard Brady, *Orem Cascade Stake Conference*, Date unknown.

406 Jeff Ostler, *My Choice, August 2010.*

407 Henry B. Eyring, *Act in all diligence,* April 2010 General Conference.

[408] Joseph F. Smith, *Gospel Doctrine,* 5th ed. (Salt Lake City: Deseret Book, 1939), 442.

[409] Jeffrey R. Holland, *None were with Him,* General Conference April 2009.

[410] Dallin H. Oaks, *Unselfish Service,* April 2009 General Conference.

[411] Joseph Smith, *Teachings of the Prophet Joseph Smith,* pg 241.

[412] Denver Snuffer, *Removing the Condemnation,* Salt Lake City, Ut, Millcreek Press, 2010, pg 62.

[413] Troy Hallaway, *Judging* June 29, 2010.

[414] Denver Snuffer, *Be Firm and Steadfast,* May 24, 2010. Denversnuffer.blogspot.com

[415] Dali Lama, Source Unknown.

[416] Joseph Fielding Smith, *The Life of Joseph Fielding Smith* 212. Deseret Book Co. Joseph Fielding Smith Journal, 28 December 1938.

[417] Henry B. Eyring, Be One, Liahona, Sep 2008, 2-7.

[418] Ezra Taft Benson. *Our Immediate Responsibility.* BYU Devotional, October 25, 1966.

[419] Jeanene Custer, Stay with the Lord in His Church, March 2011.

[420] Ezra Taft Benson, Encyclopedia of Mormonism, 1-4 vols., edited by Daniel H. Ludlow (New York: Macmillan, 1992), 1732.

[421] Henry B. Eyring, "*Our Hearts Knit as One,*" Ensign, Nov 2008, 68–71.

[422] Bruce R. McConkie, *Mormon Doctrine,* 2d ed. Salt Lake City, Utah: Bookcraft, 1966, 333.

[423] Jeff Benedict, *Mormon faith more important to Jabari Parker than NBA stardom.* Sports Illustrated May 2012.

[424] Daniel Rogers, *The Second Comforter, My Testimony,* 11-1-2013.

[425] Joseph Smith, *History of the Church,* 6:478-479.

[426] Brigham Young, *The complete discourses of Brigham Young,* Volume 2, pg 1169-1170.

[427] Orson Pratt, *Journal of Discourses* 15:360.

[428] Ordinances and Covenants, *Church Ensign,* August 2001, page 23.

[429] Joseph Smith, Joseph Smith History, 1:19.

[430] Joseph Smith, Oct 25 1831 *Teachings of the Prophet Joseph Smith,* pg. 9.

[431] Joseph Fielding Smith, *The Progress of Man* [Salt Lake City: Deseret Book Co., 1964], 88 - 89.)

[432] Daniel Webster, Ken Bowers, *Hiding in Plain Site,* Springfield UT, Bonneville Books, 2000, Introduction, 1.

[433] Ron Paul, *The Proliferation of Federal Crimes,* Final Speech to Congress on November 14, 2012.

[434] The Church of Jesus Christ of Latter Day Saints Newsroom. *Political Neutrality.* February 2014.

[435] Ezra Taft Benson, *The Teachings of Ezra Taft Benson* [Salt Lake City: Bookcraft, 1988], 706.

[436] Myron Fagan, Craig Dunn, Tom Wood, *U.N. Blue Print for World Control,* Salt Lake City, UT, Laneshine House, 2005, 11.

[437] Myron Fagan, Craig Dunn, Tom Wood, *U.N. Blue Print for World Control,* Salt Lake City, UT, Laneshine House, 2005, 12.

[438] Ezra Taft Benson, Ensign, *May 1978, 33.*

[439] H Verlan Anderson, *The Great and Abominable Church of the Devil,* Sunshine Publishing, Orem, UT, 1972.

[440] Franklin Roosevelt, Myron Fagan, Craig Dunn, Tom Wood, *U.N. Blue Print for World Control,* Salt Lake City, UT, Laneshine House, 2005.

[441] Mark Hudson, *False Hope,* Fall 2010.

[442] Ezra Taft Benson, *BYU Speeches of the Year,* May 10, 1966, 10.

[443] James Custer, *The Law of the Land,* Keystone Publications.

[444] Revised Laws of Illinois, *Section 121,* 1833, p.198-99.

[445] Cannon II, Kenneth (Jan–Mar 1983). "After the Manifesto: Mormon Polygamy, 1890-1906". *Sunstone:* 27–35.

[446] Wikipedia.com

[447] Tom Hulet, *Taxes.* Fall 2009.

[448] J. Reuben Clark, Jr., Conference Report, April 1952, General Priesthood Meeting 80.

[449] R. Blair, Holmes, *When Truth was Treason* and Alan F. Keele *Inside Nazi Germany, Conformity, Opposition and Racism in Everyday Life* by Detlev J.K. Peukert. www.consciousangles.org

[450] Matt Whitaker. (2003). *Truth & Conviction.* [DVD]. Covenant Communications.

[451] "Film tells Anti-Nazi Mormon's Story," *Salt Lake Tribune.* 1-1-2003.

[452] Blair R. Holmes, ed (1995). *When Truth Was Treason.* Alan F. Keele. Urbana: University of Illinois Press. p. 291.

[453] Hübener at Dixie State College". 2005-03-14. Retrieved 2010-04-26.

[454] Helmuth Hubener, Wikipedia.com

[455] Matt Whitaker. (2003). *Truth & Conviction*. [DVD]. Covenant Communications.

[456] Hubener at Dixie State College. 2005-03-14. Retrieved 2010-04-26.

[457] Adolf Hitler, *speech at Koblenz, to the Germans of the Saar*, 26 Aug. 1934.

[458] Ezra Taft Benson, *The Crisis of our Constitution,* Valley central area special interest lecture serious, Harvard Ward, Salt Lake City, September 8, 1977.

[459] Ezra Taft Benson *Ensign*, November 1988, p. 87.

[460] Gordon B. Hinckley, "*A Testimony Vibrant and True,*" *Ensign*, Aug 2005, 2–6.

[461] Ezra Taft Benson, *God, Family, Country: Our Three Great Loyalties* [Salt Lake City: Deseret Book Co., 1974], 348.

[462] Spencer W. Kimball, *Biography of Spencer* by Edward J. Kimball, pp. 352-3.

[463] Mark Hudson, *Babylon and her Secret Combinations*, Fall 2010.

[464] Heber J. Grant, J. Ruben Clark, Jr., David O. McKay, *First Presidency Letter.*

[465] Heber J. Grant, J. Ruben Clark, Jr., David O. McKay, *First Presidency Letter.*

[466] James R. Clark, comp., Messages of the First Presidency of The Church of Jesus Christ of Latter-day Saints, 6 vols. (Salt Lake City: Bookcraft, 1965-75), 6: 107.

[467] Joseph Fielding Smith, *Doctrines of Salvation,* 3 vols., Bruce R. McConkie [Salt Lake City: Bookcraft, 1954-1956], 3: 326.

[468] Bruce R. Mckonkie, *Ensign,* May 1979, pp. 92-93.

[469] Gerald N. Lund*, The Coming of the Lord* [Salt Lake City: Bookcraft, 1971], 47.

[470] Bruce R. McConkie, *Ensign*, May 1980, pp. 71, 73.) (Blaine and Brenton Yorgason, *Spiritual Survival in the Last Days* [Salt Lake City: Deseret Book Co., 1990], 49.)

[471] Henry Kissenger, May 1992, Ken Bowers *Hiding in Plain Sight,* Springfield UT, Bonneville Books, 2000, 82.

[472] George H.W. Bush, September 11th, 1991, Myron Fagan, Craig Dunn, Tom Wood, *U.N. Blue Print for World Control*, Salt Lake City, UT, Laneshine House, 2005, 12.

[473] Thomas Jefferson, *Hiding in Plain Site,* Springfield UT, Bonneville Books, 2000, 24-25.

[474] Kurt Nimmo, *Infowars.com*, October 24, 2011.

[475] Abraham Lincoln, letter to Col. William F. Elkins on November 21, 1864.

[476] J. Rueben Clark, *Conference Report*, April 1944, 116.

[477] Pope Benedict, *Caritas in Veritate, or Charity in Truth*, July 7, 2009.

[478] Ken Bowers, *Hiding in Plain Site,* 96-97.

[479] Brigham Young, Deseret News, Vol. 9, p. 2, May 1, 1861. *Gerald N. Lund, The Coming of the Lord* Salt Lake City: Bookcraft, 1971, 68.

[480] Brigham Young, (Gerald N. Lund, The Coming of the Lord [Salt Lake City: Bookcraft, 1971]).

[481] Wilford Woodruff, Gerald N. Lund, *The Coming of the Lord* [Salt Lake City: Bookcraft, 1971], 47.

[482] Ron Paul, *Farewell Address to Congress*, November 14, 2012.

[483] Joseph Smith, *White Horse Prophecy*, May 6, 1843.

[484] Howard W. Hunter, The Teachings of Howard W. Hunter, edited by Clyde J. Williams [Salt Lake City: Bookcraft, 1997], 42.)

[485] George, Q. Cannon, Brian H. Stuy, ed., *Collected Discourses,* 5 vols. [Burbank, Calif., and Woodland Hills, Ut.: B.H.S. Publishing, 1987-1992], 2.

[486] Heber C. Kimball, *Life of Heber C Kimball* pp 449-450.

[487] J. Reuben Clark, Jr., Conference Report, April 1952, General Priesthood Meeting 80.

[488] J. Golden Kimball, *Conference Report*, October 1930, p.59.

[489] Boyd K. Packer, *BYU Devotional*, December 17, 2005.

[490] Dan Mead, *Real Apostasy,* Fall 2010.

[491] Paul R. Cheesman, ed., *The Book of Mormon: The Keystone Scripture* [Provo: BYU Religious Studies Center, 1988], 118.

[492] Brigham Young*, Journal of Discourses 10:32.*

[493] Ezra Taft Benson, *To The Humble Followers of Christ*, Improvement Era, June 1969 p. 42.

[494] Monte S. Nyman and Charles D. Tate, Jr., eds., *Alma, the Testimony of the Word* [Provo: BYU Religious Studies Center, 1992], 24.

[495] Ezra Taft Benson, *Conference Report, April 1965*, Afternoon Meeting 122.

[496] Vaughn J. Featherstone, *The Incomparable Christ: Our Master and Model* [Salt Lake City: Deseret Book Co.,1995], 3.

[497] Oliver Cowdrey, recorded in the *The Personal Writings of Joseph Smith,* compiled and edited by Dean C. Jessee [Salt Lake City: Deseret Book Co., 1984], 282.

[498] First Presidency and Quorum of the Twelve Apostles, *The Family, A Proclamation to the World.* General Relief Society Meeting, September 23, 1995. Salt Lake City, Utah.

[499] First Presidency, *Constitutional Amendment.* Pulpit Letter July 2004.

[500] John Taylor, *Journal of Discourses,* 26 vols. [London: LDS Book Depot, 1854-1886], 23:36.

[501] Carter Eskew, *"Mormon Church softening on gay marriage,"* Washington Post Opinion. May 11, 2012.

[502] Michael Otterson, *Mormons throw support behind gay-rights cause,* Eric Gorski (AP), November 11, 2009.

[503] Salt Lake Tribune, *Updated LDS handbook softens language on gays,* November 11, 2010.

[504] LDS Newsroom, *Church Responds to Boy Scouts Policy Vote,* May 23, 2013.

[505] Erik Eckholm, *Mormons Endorse Plan to Admit Gay Scouts,* New York Times, April 26, 2013.

[506] Michael Gryboski, *LDS Church Accepts New Boy Scout Policy on Gay Members,* Christian Post, May 24, 2013.

[507] Janet Boynes, *Called Out.* Janetboynesministries.com, July 2014.

[508] Church of Jesus Christ of Latter Day Saints, *Policy Manual,* 2006.

[509] P. Scott Richards, *Editorial for Understanding Homosexuality.* Association of Mormon Counselors and Psychotherapists, Volume 19, No 1. 1993. pg xi.

[510] Spencer W. Kimball, *The Miracle of Forgiveness.* Salt Lake City, UT. Bookcraft. pg 81-82.

[511] D.L. Foster, *Sex, Lies, and the Gay Debate,* Charisma Magazine Online. Revised Standard Version of the Bible possibly used when quoting 1 Corinthians 6:9-11.

[512] Yvette Schneider, *Ex-Lesbian Yvette Schneider Testifies to 'Complete' and Permanent Change.* Americans For Truth about Homosexuality, June 22, 2007.

[513] Rod Bastanmehr, *"Gay Marriage Approval Continues Sweep Across the Country."* Alternet.org. August 1, 2013.

[514] Dallin H. Oaks, *Religious Freedom,* BYU-Idaho University, Rexburg ID. October 13, 2009.

[515] Denver Snuffer, *Social and Cultural "Rights"* Denversnuffer.blogspot.com., Feb 21, 2010.

[516] Peggy Fletcher Stack, *Mormons join Hawaii's gay-marriage fight, but with a new approach,* The Salt Lake Tribune, September 18, 2013.

[517] Peggy Fletcher Stack, *Mormons join Hawaii's gay-marriage fight, but with a new approach,* The Salt Lake Tribune, September 18, 2013.

[518] Maurine Proctor, *"Same Sex Marriage Imposed on Utah,"* Meridian Magazine, December 23, 2013.

[519] LDS Newsroom, *Church Statement on Court Ruling Regarding Same-Sex Marriage in Utah* Dec 21, 2013.

[520] Hate Crimes Bill signed into Law. October 28, 2009.

[521] Salt Lake Tribune, January 30, 2010.

[522] Dan Mead, *Nothing less will do,* June 2010.

[523] Jim Uhl, *Political Apostasy,* June 2011.

[524] Brigham Young, *Journal of Discourses,* 12:83.

[525] Ezra Taft Benson, *Beware of Pride,* Ensign, May 1989, 4.

[526] David Christensen, *Ricks College,* 1993.

[527] Orson F. Whitney, *Life of Heber C. Kimball* [Salt Lake City, Bookcraft, 1945], 446. Gordon B. Hinckley, Teachings of Gordon B. Hinckley[Salt Lake City: Deseret Book Co., 1997], 611.

[528] Joseph F. Smith, *Journal of Discourses,* Vol.13, p.339 - p.340.

[529] Heber C. Kimball, as reported by Amanda Wilcox, Deseret News, May 23, 1931.

[530] Denver Snuffer, *Passing the Heavenly Gift,* Mill Creek Press, Salt Lake City, UT. 2011. Pg 408-409.

[531] National Weather Service, *A Scientific Report,* August 11, 1999.

[532] John Taylor, Blaine and Brenton Yorgason, *Spiritual Survival in the Last Days* [Salt Lake City: Deseret Book Co., 1990], 45.

[533] B. H. Roberts, *A Comprehensive History of The Church of Jesus Christ of Latter-day Saints,* 6 vols. Salt Lake City: Deseret News Press 1930, 5: 136.

[534] Bruce R. McConkie, *General Conference,* April 1980.

[535] George Q. Cannon, *Journal of Discourses,* 26 vols. [London: Latter-day Saints' Book Depot, 1854-1886], 24: 143 - 144.

[536] Orson Pratt, *Orson Pratt Works,* pg. 82-83.

[537] Brigham Young, *Journal of Discourses,* Vol. 19, p. 192, September 30, 1877.

[538] D. Todd Christofferson, *Come to Zion,* October 2008 General Conference.

[539] Dan Mead, *Cast out,* 10-23-2010.

[540] Heber C. Kimball, Discourse in the Tabernacle, Salt Lake City, Sunday, September 11, 1859.

[541] First Presidency, *Remain in Homelands*, Pulpit Letter, December 1999.

[542] Bruce R. McConkie, *Church News,* Sept. 2,1972.

[543] Brigham Young, *Journal of Discourses* 19:192.

[544] Jeanene Custer, *Seeking Zion,* Summer 2011.

[545] Joseph Smith*, History of the Church,* 2:52.

[546] Bruce R. McConkie, *Ensign,* May 1980, pp. 71, 73. Blaine and Brenton Yorgason,
Spiritual Survival in the Last Days [Salt Lake City: Deseret Book Co., 1990], 49.

[547] Eliza R. Snow, *Biography and Family Record of Lorenzo Snow* [SLC: Deseret News, 1884], 346.

[548] Orson Pratt, *Journal of Discourses,* 26 vols. [London: LDS Book Depot, 1854-1886], 7:188 - 189.

[549] Denver Snuffer, *Removing the Condemnation,* Millcreek Press, 2010. pg. 122-123.

[550] Vaughn J. Featherstone, *The Incomparable Christ: Our Master and Model* [Salt Lake
City: Deseret Book Co., 1995], 3.

[551] David A. Bednar, *Honorably Hold a name and Standing,* April General Conference 2009.

[552] Wilford Woodruff, *Journal,* spelling corrected, August 27, 1844.

[553] Heber C. Kimball, *Journal of Discourses*, Volume 8, pg 257.

[554] Vaughn J. Featherstone, *The Incomparable Christ: Our Master and Model* [Salt Lake
City: Deseret Book Co., 1995], 3.

[555] Joseph Smith, *Further Directions on Baptism of Dead*, Nauvoo, September 6, 1842. DHC 5:148-153.

[556] Church of Jesus Christ of Latter Day Saints*, Encyclopedia of Mormonism* p. 36-37.

[557] Craig Mills, *Home Sanctuary*, pg 83.

[558] Craig Mills, *Home Sanctuary*, pg 113.

[559] John Taylor, *Journal of Discourses* 25:355-356.

[560] Joseph Smith, *History of the Church,* 5:424.

[561] Joseph Fielding Smith, *Elijah the Prophet,* pp. 45–46.

[562] B. H. Roberts, *Comprehensive History of The Church of Jesus Christ of Latter-day Saints*, vol. 1.

[563] Alan Cook, *He Walks Among Us,* Summer 2009.

[564] Bruce R. Mckonkie, *The Coming Tests and Trials and Glory*, Ensign, May 1980.

[565] Joseph Smith, Kirtland, Ohio, December 1833, *History of the Church*, 1:46.

[566] Neal A. Maxwell, *Ensign,* November 1982, p. 67.

[567] Dali Lama, Source Unknown.

[568] Jeffrey R. Holland, *None were with Him*, April General Conference 2009.

[569] John A. Widtsoe, *Conference Report,* April 1942.

[570] Jeanne Guyon, *Experiencing the Depths of Jesus Christ*, SeedSowers Publishing, Jacksonville, FL, pg 46.

[571] Joseph Smith, *Teachings of Prophet Joseph Smith,* pg. 185

[572] Nelson Mandela, *Autobiography,* Nelsonmandelas.com

[573] Beth Velliquette, *"Carson ask Lovette to Pray with her,"* The Herald Sun*,* December 16, 2011.

[574] Dan Millman, *The Way of the Peaceful Warrior,* New World Library, Novato, CA,1980, 96.

[575] Tiegan Corbridge, *Winning the Heart,* Summer 2004.

[576] Boyd K. Packer, *The Light of Christ, Ensign* April 2005, 10.

[577] Carleen Taylor, *Call Me Dad,* [Salt Lake City: Utah, Exceptional Success Associates 1989], 31.

[578] Denver Snuffer, *Passing the Heavenly Gift,* Millcreek Press, Salt Lake City, 2011, pg 125.

[579] Gordon B. Hinkley, October 2005 General Conference, 2005 pg 4.

[580] Joseph Smith, *The Words of Joseph Smith, Wilford Woodruff Journal,* by Adrew Ehat
and Lyndon Cook, Brigham Young University Religious Studies Center, 1980. 8.

[581] Joseph Smith*, Teachings of the Prophet Joseph Smith,* pg 332.

[582] Joseph Smith, *The Wentworth Letter,* recorded in *Church History and Modern Revelation,* 4 vols. [Salt
Lake City: The Church of Jesus Christ of Latter-day Saints, 1946-1949], 4: 98.

[583] Joseph Smith, Hyrum Smith, *History of the Church,* 6:427.

[584] Bruce R. McConkie, *The Ten Blessings of the Priesthood.*

[585] Ezra Taft Benson, *Conference Report*, April 1989, 6.

[586] Brigham Young, *Contributor,* vol. 10 (Nov.1888-Oct. 1889), Vol. X. August, 1889. No. 10. 362.

[587] Daniel H. Wells, *Journal of Discourses,* 26 vols. London: LDS Book Depot, 1854-1886, 23:306 - 309.

[588] Brigham Young, *Journal of Discourses*, 26 vols. London: LDS Book Depot, 16:26.

[589] George Q. Cannon, *Journal of Discourses,* 26 vols. London: LDS Book Depot, 1854-1886, 24: 143 - 144.

454

[590] Daniel H. Wells, *Journal of Discourses,* 26 vols. London: LDS Book Depot, 1854-1886, 18:96.

[591] Heber C. Kimball, *Journal of Discourses,* 26 vols. London: LDS Book Depot, 1854-1886, 11:145-146.

[592] Brigham Young, *Journal of Discourses,* 26 vols. [London: Latter-day Saints' Book Depot, 1854-1886], 6: 194 - 195.

[593] Spencer W. Kimball, *Faith Precedes the Miracle* [Salt Lake City: Deseret Book Co., 1972], 253.

[594] Henry B. Eyring, *Our Hearts Knit as One*, General Conference October 2008.

[595] Lorenzo Snow, *Journal of Lorenzo Snow,* pg 181-182.

[596] Brigham Young, Jr., *General Conference*, October 5, 1894. Brian H. Stuy, ed., *Collected Discourses,* 5 vols. [Burbank, Calif., and Woodland Hills, Ut.: B.H.S. Publishing, 1987-1992], 4.

[597] ThinkExist.com Quotations. "Edward Everett Hale quotes". 1 Sep. 2012. 22 Oct. 2012.

[598] Jeanne Guyon, *Experiencing the Depths of Jesus Christ,* pg 81.

[599] Neal A. Maxwell from *Ensign, May 1988, p. 9, by Intellectual Reserve, Inc*

[600] Neal A. Maxwell, *Men and Women of Christ* [Salt Lake City: Bookcraft, 1991], 41.

[601] Denver Snuffer, *Jumping out a window,* Internet blog. Wed, February 24, 2010.

[602] Joseph Smith, *Autobiography of Parley P. Pratt,* Salt Lake City, Utah, Deseret Book, 1985, 254.

[603] John Pontius, *The Triumph of Zion, our personal quest for the New Jerusalem,* CFI, Springville, UT, 2010, pg 259.

[604] John Pontius, *Call to Zion,* Daybreak Books, Wasilla, Alaska, 2008, pg 192.

[605] Joseph Smith, reviewed by James R. Clark, comp., *Messages of the First Presidency of The Church of Jesus Christ of Latter-day Saints,* 6 vols. (Salt Lake City: Bookcraft, 1965-75), 4: 312.

[606] George Q. Cannon, *Journal of Discourses,* 12:45-46.

[607] Heber C. Kimball, *Heber C. Kimball Diary,* June 19, 1845.

[608] Joseph Fielding McConkie, *Answers: Straightforward Answers to Tough Gospel Questions.* Salt Lake City: Deseret Book Co., 1998, 150.

[609] Brigham Young, *Journal of Discourses,* 26 vols. [London: Latter-day Saints' Book Depot, 1854-1886], 13: 155.

[610] Jan Ostler, *Men and Women,* October 22, 2010.

[611] Joseph Smith, *Lectures on Faith.,* Latter-day Saints' Millennial Star, vol. 3, May 1842-April 1843, No. 10. February, 1843. Vol. III. 165.

[612] James Custer, *The Unspeakable Gift,* Keystone Publications, 1988.

[613] Leroi C. Snow, Devotion To a Divine Inspiration, *Improvement Era, 1919,* Vol. Xxii. June, 1919 No. 8.

[614] Brigham Young, *Discourses of Brigham Young,* selected and arranged by John A. Widtsoe, Salt Lake City: Deseret Book Co., 1954], 398.

[615] Alvin R. Dyer, *The Meaning of Truth,* rev. ed. [Salt Lake City: Deseret Book Co., 1973], 130.

[616] Brigham Young, *Discourses of Brigham Young,* selected and arranged by John A. Widtsoe [Salt Lake City: Deseret Book Co., 1954], 369.

[617] Gospel of Thomas, verse 77.

[618] Cleon Skousen, *A Personal Search for the Meaning of the Atonement,* 1980.

[619] Gordon B. Hinkley, *Personal worthiness to exercise the priesthood,* Ensign May 2002.

[620] Hugh Nibley, *Priesthood,* Sunstone Magazine, December 1990.

[621] Dallin H. Oaks, *Miracles,* CES Fireside Alberta, Canada. May 7, 2000.

[622] Marvin J. Ashton, *Faith* [Salt Lake City: Deseret Book Co., 1983], 45.

[623] M. Catherine Thomas, Meridian Magazine, *Shifting our Thinking: the Second Shift.* Feb 2010.

[624] Bruce R. McConkie, *The Ten Blessings of the Priesthood,* Ensign, Nov 1977, 33.

[625] Denver Snuffer, *Beloved Enos,* Salt Lake City, Millcreek Press, 17.

[626] Joseph Smith, *The King Follett Discourse,* Documentary of the History of the Church, Vol. VI, 302-317.

[627] Joseph Smith, *The King Follett Discourse,* Documentary of the History of the Church, Vol. VI, 302-317.

[628] LDS Endowment.

[629] John Taylor, *Journal of Discourses,* 26 vols. [London: Latter-day Saints' Book Depot, 1854-1886], 10: 148 - 149.

[630] David O. Mckay, *Conference Report, April 1958,* First Day—Morning Meeting 6 - 7.

[631] M. James Custer, *The Unspeakable gift,* Keystone Publications, 1998.

[632] Pierre Teilhard de Chardin, Philosopher, Priest, (1 May 1881 – 10 April 1955).

[633] Cleon Skousen, *A Personal Search for the Meaning of the Atonement,* 1980.

[634] John Taylor, *The Gospel Kingdom: Selections from the Writings and Discourses of John Taylor,* selected, arranged, and edited, with an introduction by G. Homer Durham. Salt Lake City: Improvement Era, 1941, 52.

[635] James Custer, *The Unspeakable Gift,* Keystone Publications, 1998.

[636] James Custer, *The Unspeakable Gift,* Camden Court Publishing, 1998, 117.

[637] LDS Endowment.

[638] Choa Kok Sui, *Achieving Oneness with the Higher Soul,* Institute for Inner Studies Publishing, Manila Philippines, 2005, 11.

[639] Boyd K. Packer, *The Light of Christ,* Ensign April 2005, 10.

[640] Joseph Smith, *The King Follett Discourse,* Documentary of the History of the Church, Vol. VI, 302-317.

[641] Hugh Nibley, *Nibley on the Timely and the Timeless: Classic Essays of Hugh W. Nibley,* Provo Ut. Brigham Young University Religious Studies Center, 1978, pg. 302.

[642] Bruce R. Mckonkie, Monte S. Nyman and Charles D. Tate, Jr., eds., *Joseph Smith Translation: The Restoration of Plain and Precious Things* [Provo: BYU Religious Studies Center, 1985], 20.

[643] Joseph Fielding Smith, *The Way to Perfection* [Salt Lake City: Genealogical Society of Utah, 1949, 291.

[644] Joseph Smith, *Article of Faith Ten,* 1842.

[645] Hugh Nibley, *Approaching Zion,* edited by Don E. Norton [Salt Lake City and Provo: Deseret Book Co., Foundation for Ancient Research and Mormon Studies, 1989], 1.

[646] Hugh Nibley, *Approaching Zion,* edited by Don E. Norton [Salt Lake City and Provo: Deseret Book Co., Foundation for Ancient Research and Mormon Studies, 1989], 1.

[647] John Pontius, *The Triumph of Zion, Our Personal Quest for the New Jerusalem,* CFI, Springville, UT. Pg 87-88.

[648] Brigham Young, *Discourses of Brigham Young,* selected and arranged by John A. Widtsoe [Salt Lake City: Deseret Book Co., 1954], 443.

[649] Joseph F. Smith, *Journal of Discourses,* Vol. 19, p. 192, September 30, 1877.

[650] Meli Cardullo, *Chicken Soup for the Latter Day Saint Soul,* Jack Canfield and Mark Victor Hansen, Health Communications Inc, Deerfield Beach, FL, 2005. pg 234-235.

[651] Howard W. Hunter, *The Teachings of Howard W. Hunter,* edited by Clyde J. Williams [Salt Lake City: Bookcraft, 1997], 201.

[652] Robert Young, *Analytical Concordance to the Bible,* William B. Eerdmans Publishing Company, Grand Rapids, Michigan, 1988.

[653] Robert D. Hales, *To Act for Ourselves: The Gift and Blessing of Agency,* April 2006.

[654] Brigham Young, *Journal of Discourses,* 19: 192.

[655] Joseph Smith, *Discourses of the Prophet Joseph Smith,* compiled by Alma P. Burton [Salt Lake City: Deseret Book Co., 1977], 234.

[656] Gerald N. Lund, *The Coming of the Lord* [Salt Lake City: Bookcraft, 1971], 85.

[657] Orson Pratt, *Journal of Discourses,* 15:361.

[658] Wilford Woodruff, *Prophetic Years,* by Anderson, p. 54.

[659] Wilford Woodruff, *Conference Report,* April 1898, pg 57.

[660] Joseph Smith, *Mosiah Hancock Autobiography,* BYU Special Collections, pg 28.

[661] Joseph Smith, *Article of Faith Ten,* Wentworth Letter, 1842.

[662] Joseph Smith as reported by Wilford Woodruff, *Conference Report,* Apr. 1898, 57.

[663] Joseph Smith; *History of the Church,* 6:318-19.

[664] Joseph Smith; *History of the Church,* 6:318-19.

[665] Orson Pratt, *Journal of Discourses,* 9:178.

[666] Launius, Roger D. (1997), *Alexander William Doniphan: Portrait of a Missouri Moderate,* Columbia, Missouri: University of Missouri Press. pg 13.

[667] Mormonwiki.com

[668] Oliver Cowdery, Kirtland Mills Ohio Aug 10th 1833.

[669] Joseph Smith at the end of Oliver Cowdery letter, Kirtland Mills Ohio Aug 10th 1833.

[670] Ye Elders of Israel, *Hymns of The Church of Jesus Christ of Latter-day Saints,* no. 319. *Text:* Cyrus H. Wheelock, 1813–1894. *Music:* Thomas H. Bayly, 1797–1839, adapted.

[671] Joseph Smith, *Millennial Star,* Vol. 54 (1852), p. 605.

[672] Joseph Smith, *Autobiography of Mosiah Hancock,* Compiled by Amy E. Baird, Victoria H. Jackson, and Laura L. Wassell (daughters of Mosiah Hancock).

[673] Marquardt, H. Michael (1999), *The Joseph Smith Revelations: Text and Commentary,* Signature Books.

[674] Arrington, Leonard J. (1992), *The Mormon Experience: A History of the Latter Day Saints,* University Illinois Press.

[675] Stephen Markham, *Letter to Wilford Woodruff* at Fort Supply, Wyoming, 20 June 1856, LDS Historical Department, Salt Lake City, p. 1.

[676] Richard Bushman, *Joseph Smith, Rough Stone Rolling,* 2005, pg 161.

[677] Author unknown.

[678] Stephen Markham, *Letter to Wilford Woodruff* at Fort Supply, Wyoming, 20 June 1856, LDS Historical Department, Salt Lake City, p. 1.

[679] Stephen Markham, *Letter to Wilford Woodruff* at Fort Supply, Wyoming, 20 June 1856, LDS Historical Department, Salt Lake City, p. 1.

[680] Joseph Smith, *Teachings of the Prophet Joseph Smith*, 376-377.

[681] Joseph Smith, *Teachings of the Prophet Joseph Smith, p. 377.*

[682] Joseph Smith, *Teachings of the Prophet Joseph Smith*, p. 377.

[683] Joseph Smith, *Mosiah Hancock Journal.* See also *"Autobiography of Mosiah Hancock,"* Compiled by Amy E. Baird, Victoria H. Jackson, and Laura L. Wassell. Typescript, BYU.

[684] Marion G. Romney - *"America's Fate and Ultimate Destiny,"* in Speeches of the Year, 1976 (Provo: Brigham Young University Press, 1977), p. 326.

[685] Joseph Smith, *Teachings of the Prophet Joseph Smith*, DHC 2:52. April 1834.

[686] Joseph Smith, *"A Prophecy of Joseph the Seer,"* found in, *The Fate of the Persecutors of the Prophet Joseph Smith*, pg. 154, 156.

[687] Denver Snuffer, *Removing the Condemnation,* 3 Nephi 21: 27-28, pg 136-138.

[688] Joseph Smith, July 17, 1831, west of Jackson County, Missouri, contained in a letter from W. W. Phelps to Brigham Young, dated August 12, 1861, Joseph Smith Collection, Church Historian's Office.

[689] Millennial Star, *Editorial*, 18:137.

[690] Joseph Smith, *History of the Church*, 8:224, 23 Feb 1844.

[691] Bruce R McConkie, *Doctrinal New Testament Commentary*, Vol 3, pg 295.

[692] Craig Mills, *Home Sanctuary*, pg 119.

[693] Melvin C. Johnson, *Polygamy on the Pedernales, Lyman Wight's Mormon Villages in Antebellum Texas 1845-1858.* Utah State University Press, Logan UT. 2006, pg 32.

[694] Craig Mills, *Home Sanctuary*, pg 120.

[695] Orson Hyde, "*A Diagram of the Kingdom of God*," Millennial Star 9 [15 January 1847]: 23-24.

[696] Brigham Young, *Journal of Discourses*, volume 9, pg. 269.

[697] Joseph Smith, *History of The Church of Jesus Christ of Latter-day Saints,* 7 Vols. 5:554, 555.

[698] Joseph Smith, *Teachings of the Prophet Joseph Smith,* Salt Lake City: Deseret Book Co., 1976, 308.

[699] Alvin R. Dyer, "*For What Propose*", March 18, 1961.

[700] D. Todd Christofferson, *The Power of Covenants*, April General Conference 2009.

[701] Bruce R. McConkie, *BYU Lecture to Seminary and Institute Teachers of the Church,* Summer 1967.

[702] Donna Nielsen, *Beloved Bridegroom, Finding Christ in Ancient Jewish Marriag and Family Customs,* Onyx Press, 1999, pg 159.

[703] Brigham Young, *Journal of Discourses* 1:312.

[704] Denver Snuffer, *Passing the Heavenly Gift*, MillCreek Press, Salt Lake City, UT, pg 394-395.

[705] Craig Mills, *Home Sanctuary*, pg 120.

[706] Richard Smyth and Charles C. Converse, The Church of Jesus Christ of Latter Day Saints, Hymn #7.

[707] Wilford Woodruff, *Journal of Discourses,* 26 vols., LDS, Book Depot, 1854-1886, 10: 218.

[708] Spencer W Kimball; *Conference Report*, 1976, page 3.

[709] Joseph Smith; *History of Church* 6:318-319.

[710] Brigham Young; *Journal of Discourses* 9:138.

[711] John Pontius, *The Triumph of Zion, our personal quest for the New Jerusalem,* CFI, Springville, UT. 2010, pg 85.

[712] D. Todd Christofferson, *Come to Zion, General Conference,* October 2008.

[713] Spencer W. Kimball, *The Teachings of Spencer W. Kimball,* edited by Edward L. Kimball [Salt Lake City: Bookcraft, 1982], 116.

[714] John Pontius, *The Call of Zion,* Daybreak Books, Wasilla, Alaska, 2008, pg 54-56.

[715] John Pontius, *The Call to Zion,* Daybreak Books, Wasilla, Alaska, 2008, pg 118.

[716] Joseph Smith, The Historians Corner, *BYU Studies, vol. 19 (1978-1979)*, Number 3 - Spring 1979 393.

[717] Joseph Smith, Hyrum Smith, Sydney Rigdon, A Proclamation of the First Presidency of the Church to the Saints Scattered Abroad, January 15, 1841, Nauvoo, Illinois.

[718] Philo Dibble, *Juvenile Instructor*, May 1892, pp. 303–4.

[719] Dan Mead, *Little Children in the Dust*, Weeping for Zion Blog, May 14, 2014.

[720] Joseph Smith, Kirtland, Ohio, December 1833, *History of the Church*, 1:468.

[721] Orson Pratt, *Journal of Discourses,* 26 vols. [London: Latter-day Saints' Book Depot, 1854-1886], 15: 366.

[722] John Pontius, *The Triumph of Zion,* Cedar Fort Inc. Springville, UT. 2010. 39.

[723] John Pontius, *The Triumph of Zion,* Cedar Fort Inc. Springville, UT. 2010. 40.

[724] John Pontius,*Call to Zion,* Daybreak Books, 21.

[725] Orson Pratt, *Journal of Discourses,* 26 vols. [London: Latter-day Saints' Book Depot, 1854-1886], 14: 348 - 349.)

[726] Joseph Smith, *History of the Church* Vol. 2, pg 145. August 16, 1834.

[727] Joseph F. Smith, Roy W. Doxey, comp., *Latter-day Prophets and the Doctrine and Covenants* [Salt Lake City: Deseret Book Co., 1978], 3: 458 - 459.

[728] Brigham Young, Jr., *General Conference,* October 5, 1894.

[729] John Pontius, *Call to Zion*, Daybreak Books, 41.

[730] Brigham Young, *Journal of Discourses,*18:263.

[731] Ezra Taft Benson, *The Teachings of Ezra Taft Benson* [Salt Lake City: Bookcraft, 1988], 122.

[732] President George Q. Cannon, *Conference Report, October 1899,* Afternoon Session.

[733] Hugh Nibley, "Our Glory or Our Condemnation," *Approaching Zion*, 20-21.

[734] Jamshid Ghazi Askar, *LDS Church buys farmland, Haun's Mill, Far West, Kirtland property from Community of Christ,* Deseret News, May 5, 2012.

[735] Jeff Harrington, *Sale of timberland to make the Mormon Church Florida's biggest private landowner,* Tampa Bay Times, Thursday November 7, 2013.

[736] Joseph F. Smith, *Millennial Star, June 18, 1894, 56:385-86.)* (Joseph F. Smith, Roy W. Doxey, comp., *Latter-day Prophets and the Doctrine and Covenants* [SLC: Deseret Book Co., 1978], 3: 458-459.

[737] Brigham Young, *Journal of Discourses*, 11:294-295.

[738] Hugh Nibley, *Approaching Zion* [Salt Lake City: DeseretBook, 1989], 37.

[739] Hugh Nibley, *Approaching Zion*, Deseret Book, pg 37-38.

[740] Spencer W. Kimball, *The Teachings of Spencer W. Kimball*, p.357.

[741] Hugh Nibley, *Approaching Zion,* edited by Don E. Norton [Salt Lake City and Provo: Deseret Book Co., Foundation for Ancient Research and Mormon Studies, 1989], 342.

[742] Brigham Young, *Journal of Discourses,* vol 5 pg 98. August 2, 1857 Salt Lake City.

[743] Brigham Young, *Journal of Discourses,* 26 vols. [London: LDS Book Depot, 1854-1886], 2: 316.)

[744] Brigham Young, *Journal of Discourses,* Vol. 11, page 275.

[745] Howard W. Hunter, *That We Might Have Joy* [Salt Lake City: Deseret Book Co., 1994], 60.

[746] Howard W. Hunter, *That We Might Have Joy* [Salt Lake City: Deseret Book Co., 1994], 60.

[747] Charles W. Penrose, *Journal of Discourses,* 26 vols. [London: Latter-day Saints' Book Depot, 1854-1886], 23: 347.

[748] Howard W. Hunter, *That We Might Have Joy* [Salt Lake City: Deseret Book Co., 1994], 62.

[749] Joseph Smith, *History of the Church,* 4:425; from the minutes of a Church conference held on Oct. 3, 1841, Nauvoo, Illinois, published in *Times and Seasons,* Oct. 15, 1841, p. 577.

[750] First Presidency statement, *God's Love for All Mankind,* 15 Feb, 1978.

[751] Brigham Young, *Millennial Star,* vol. 10, March 15, 1848, p. 87; Hyrum Andrus, *Doctrines of the Kingdom*, Salt Lake City Bookcraft, 1973, p. 396.

[752] W. Cleon Skousen, *What We Might Expect in the Next Twenty-Five Years*, ldsremnant.com

[753] John Taylor, *The Gospel Kingdom: Selections from the Writings and Discourses of John Taylor,* selected, arranged, and edited, with an introduction by G. Homer Durham [Salt Lake City: Improvement Era, 1941], 93.

[754] Brigham Young, October 9, 1859, *Journal of Discourses* 7:289.

[755] Brigham Young, *Journal of Discourses,* 6:308, April 8, 1953.

[756] Parley P. Pratt, *Autobiography of Parley P. Pratt,* (Salt Lake City: Deseret Book 1938, 1970), p. 333.

[757] Joseph Smith, April 3, 1836. *History of the Church* 2:435-36.

[758] Joseph Smith Sr. *Patriarchal Blessing Book,* Dec 9, 1834, Vol. 1, 3-4.

[759] Brigham Young, *Journal of Discourses, 6:279.*

[760] Wilford Woodruff, *Journal 1833-1898*, Edited by Scott G. Kenney, 1985, Volume 9, page 352.

[761] Joseph Smith, *Teachings of the Prophet Joseph Smith*, pg. 340.

[762] Jonathan A. Stapley, *Adoptive Sealing Ritual in Mormonism*, pg 55.

[763] Brigham Young, *Journal of Discourses*, volume 9, pg. 269.

[764] Juanita Brooks, (1992) [1961], *John Doyle Lee: Zealot, Pioneer Builder, Scapegoat*, Logan, UT: Utah State University Press, pg. 73.

[765] Jonathan Stapley, *Adoptive Sealing Ritual in Mormonism, The Journal of Mormon History*, pp 101-102.

[766] Joseph Smith, Revelation July 27, 1842. *Selected Collections from the Archives of the Church of Jesus Christ of Latter Day Saints*. 2 vol. As recorded in *Adoptive Sealing Ritual in Mormonism*, by Jonathan Stapley, pg. 57.

[767] Joseph Smith, *Becoming Saviors on Mount Zion*, Teachings of Presidents of the Church: Joseph Smith, 2007, Chapter 41, 468–478.

[768] Jonathan A. Stapley, *Adoptive Sealing Ritual*, pg 60.

[769] Juanita Brooks, (1992) [1961], *John Doyle Lee: Zealot, Pioneer Builder, Scapegoat*, Logan, UT: Utah State University Press, pg. 73.

[770] Wilford Woodruff, *Journal 1833-1898*, Edited by Scott G. Kenney, 1985, Volume 9, page 352.

[771] Wilford Woodruff, *Journal 1833-1898*, Edited by Scott G. Kenney, 1985, Volume 9, page 408.

[772] Joseph Smith, *Joseph Smith History*, 37-39.

[773] Denver Snuffer, *Passing the Heavenly Gift*, Millcreek Press, pg 388.

[774] Brigham Young, *Wilford Woodruff's Journal*, 3:134.

[775] Irving Gordon, *The Law of Adoption: One Phase of the Development of the Mormon Concept of Salvation,"* BYU Studies, 1974, pg. 312.

[776] Wilford Woodruff, *Law of Adoption*, wikipedia.

[777] Brigham Young, *Complete Discourses of Brigham Young*, Vol. 2, pg 1034.

[778] First Presidency Statement", *Deseret News*, 1905-11-11, reprinted as "One Mighty and Strong", *Improvement Era*, vol. 10, no. 12, pp. 929–943, Oct. 1907.

[779] Benjamin F. Johnson, Church Historian's Library, Salt Lake City, Utah; "An Interesting Letter," from Patriarch Benjamin F. Johnson to George S. Gibbs, 1903; Benjamin F. Johnson file, Church Historian's Library, Salt Lake City, and Hyrum L. Andrus and Helen Mae Andrus, comps., *They Knew the Prophet*, SLC, Bookcraft, 1974, 97.

[780] Joseph Smith, *Personal Glimpses of the Prophet Joseph Smith*, Hyrum L. and Helen Mae Andrus, Page 161; selected from the *Journal of Wandall Mace*, Pages 131-32, 155, BYU Library.

[781] Richard Scousen, *His Return, Prophecy, Destiny and Hope*, Verity Publishing, Orem UT, 2007,83.

[782] Hyrum L. Andrus, *Joseph Smith, the Man and the Seer* [Salt Lake City: Deseret Book Co. 1960], 136.

[783] Joseph Smith, *Journal of Discourses*, 26 vols. [London: Latter-day Saints' Book Depot, 1854-1886], 9: 298.

[784] Brigham Young, *Journal of Discourses*, Vol. 7, 89.

[785] Joseph Smith, *The Personal Writings of Joseph Smith*, compiled and edited by Dean C. Jessee [Salt Lake City: Deseret Book Co., 1984], 282.

[786] Source Unknown.

[787] William W. Phelps, *Praise to the Man*. August 1844.

[788] Brigham Young, *Discourses of Brigham Young*, selected and arranged by John A. Widtsoe [Salt Lake City: Deseret Book Co., 1954], 115.

[789] Brigham Young, *Journal of Discourses*, 26 vols. [London: LDS Book Depot, 1854-1886], 7: 142.

[790] Charles W. Penrose, *The Second Advent Improvement Era, 1924*, Vol. Xxvii. March, 1924. No. 5.

[791] John Taylor, *The Gospel Kingdom: Selections from the Writings and Discourses of John Taylor*, selected, arranged, and edited, with an introduction by G. Homer Durham, Salt Lake City: Improvement Era, 1941, 207 - 208.

[792] John Taylor, *Millennial Star*, 9:321, November 1, 1847.

[793] John Taylor, *Millennial Star*, 9:321, November 1, 1847.

[794] Brigham Young, *Journal of Discourses*, Vol. 11, page 275.

[795] Richard Scousen, *His Return, Prophecy, Destiny and Hope*, Verity Publishing, Orem UT, 2007,109.

[796] Duane S. Crowther, *Prophecy, Key to the Future*, Bookcraft, Salt Lake City, UT, 1962, 80.

[797] Richard Scousen, *His Return, Prophecy, Destiny and Hope*, Verity Publishing, Orem UT, 2007, 97.

[798] Brigham Young, *Journal of Discourses*, 26 vols. [London: Latter-day Saints' Book Depot, 1854-1886], 2: 317.

[799] Charles W. Penrose, *The Second Advent, Improvement Era, 1924*, Vol. Xxvii. March, 1924. No. 5.

[800] Boyd K. Packer, *The Light of Christ, Ensign* April 2005, 10.

[801] John Taylor, *Journal of Discourses,* 26 vols. [London: LDS Book Depot, 1854-1886], 23:36.

[802] Jeffrey R. Holland, *None were with Him*, April General Conference 2009.

Made in the USA
San Bernardino, CA
28 September 2014